NEW JERSEY RULES OF COURT

FEDERAL

2009

Mat #40578734

ISBN: 978–0–314–97395–5

PREFACE

This edition of the *New Jersey Rules of Court, Federal, 2009* replaces the 2008 edition. This volume provides in convenient form court rules governing federal practice in New Jersey and is current with amendments received through August 15, 2008.

THE PUBLISHER

September 2008

*

RELATED PRODUCTS FROM WEST

NEW JERSEY PRACTICE SERIES

Court Rules Annotated
John H. Klock

Evidence Rules Annotated...Evidence Rules
John H. Klock

Court Rules Annotated—Trial Lawyer's Manual
John H. Klock

Civil Practice Forms
James H. Walzer

Wills and Administration
Alfred C. Clapp and Dorothy G. Black

Family Law and Practice with Forms
Susan Reach Winters and Thomas D. Baldwin

Real Estate Law and Practice with Forms
John A. Celentano, Jr.

Legal Forms
James H. Walzer

Municipal Court Practice
Robert Ramsey

Employment Law
Marvin M. Goldstein and Stanley L. Goodman

Skills and Methods
John Lichtenberger, General Editor

Landlord and Tenant Law
Raymond I. Korona

Motor Vehicle Law and Practice
Robert Ramsey

Motor Vehicle Law and Practice Forms
James H. Walzer

Uniform Commercial Code Forms
Samuel N. Reiken

Law of Mortgages with Forms
Myron Weinstein

Criminal Practice and Procedure
Leonard N. Arnold

Criminal Law
Gerald D. Miller

RELATED PRODUCTS

Local Government Law
Michael A. Pane

Land Use Law
David J. Frizell

Administrative Law and Practice
Steven L. Lefelt, Anthony Miragliotta and Patricia Prunty

Workers' Compensation Law
Jon L. Gelman

Appellate Practice and Procedure
Edward A. Zunz, Jr. and Alan E. Kraus

Construction Law
Robert S. Peckar

Discovery
S. Robert Allcorn

State and Local Taxation
David E. Crabtree

Debtor–Creditor Law and Practice
Michael D. Sirota and Michael S. Meisel

Elder Law—Guardianships and Conservatorships
Sharon Rivenson Mark

Elder Law—New Jersey Medicaid Laws and Regulations
Sharon Rivenson Mark

New Jersey Attorney and Judicial Discipline
Robert Ramsey

New Jersey Administrative Code

New Jersey Digest

New Jersey Digest Law Finder

New Jersey Register

New Jersey Reports

New Jersey Rules of Court, State and Federal

New Jersey Statutes Annotated

New Jersey Statutes Compact Edition

New Jersey Tax Court Reports

New Jersey Business Organization Law

New Jersey Code of Criminal Justice and Motor Vehicle Laws

New Jersey Drunk Driving Law

RELATED PRODUCTS

New Jersey Estate and Probate Law

New Jersey Family Law

Guralnick's New Jersey Family Law Annotated

Westlaw®

WestCheck.com™

West CD–ROM Libraries™

To order any of these New Jersey practice tools, call your West Representative or **1–800–328–9352.**

NEED RESEARCH HELP?

You can get quality research results with free help—call the West Reference Attorneys when you have questions concerning Westlaw or West Publications at **1–800–REF–ATTY (1–800–733–2889)**.

INTERNET ACCESS

Contact the West Editorial Department directly with your questions and suggestions by e-mail at west.editor@thomson.com. Visit West's home page at west.thomson.com

*

WESTLAW ELECTRONIC RESEARCH GUIDE

Westlaw—Expanding the Reach of Your Library

Westlaw is West's online legal research service. With Westlaw, you experience the same quality and integrity that you have come to expect from West books, plus quick, easy access to West's vast collection of statutes, case law materials, public records, and other legal resources, in addition to current news articles and business information. For the most current and comprehensive legal research, combine the strengths of West books and Westlaw.

When you research with westlaw.com you get the convenience of the Internet combined with comprehensive and accurate Westlaw content, including exclusive editorial enhancements, plus features found only in westlaw.com such as ResultsPlus™ or StatutesPlus.™

Accessing Databases Using the Westlaw Directory

The Westlaw Directory lists all databases on Westlaw and contains links to detailed information relating to the content of each database. Click Directory on the westlaw.com toolbar. There are several ways to access a database even when you don't know the database identifier. Browse a directory view. Scan the directory. Type all or part of a database name in the Search these Databases box. The Find a Database Wizard can help you select relevant databases for your search. You can access up to ten databases at one time for user-defined multibase searching.

Retrieving a Specific Document

To retrieve a specific document by citation or title on westlaw.com click **Find&Print** on the toolbar to display the Find a Document page. If you are unsure of the correct citation format, type the publication abbreviation, e.g., **xx st** (where xx is a state's two-letter postal abbreviation), in the Find this document by citation box and click **Go** to display a fill-in-the-blank template. To retrieve a specific case when you know one or more parties' names, click **Find a Case by Party Name**.

KeyCite®

KeyCite, West's citation research service on Westlaw, makes it easy to trace the history of your case, statute, administrative decision or regulation to determine if there are recent updates, and to find other documents that cite your document. KeyCite will also find pending legislation relating to federal or state statutes. Access the powerful features of KeyCite from the westlaw.com toolbar, the **Links** tab, or KeyCite flags in a document display. KeyCite's red and yellow warning flags tell you at a glance whether your document has negative history. Depth-of-treatment stars help you focus on the most important citing references. KeyCite Alert allows you to monitor the status of your case, statute or rule, and automatically sends you updates at the frequency you specify.

ResultsPlus™

ResultsPlus is a Westlaw technology that automatically suggests additional information related to your search. The suggested materials are accessible by a set of links that appear to the right of your westlaw.com search results:

- Go directly to relevant ALR® articles and Am Jur® annotations.
- Find on-point resources by key number.
- See information from related treatises and law reviews.

StatutesPlus™

When you access a statutes database in westlaw.com you are brought to a powerful Search Center which collects, on one toolbar, the tools that are most useful for fast, efficient retrieval of statutes documents:

- Have a few key terms? Click **Statutes Index**.
- Know the common name? Click **Popular Name Table**.
- Familiar with the subject matter? Click **Table of Contents**.
- Have a citation or section number? Click **Find by Citation**.
- Interested in topical surveys providing citations across multiple state statutes? Click **50 State Surveys**.
- Or, simply search with **Natural Language** or **Terms and Connectors.**

When you access a statutes section, click on the **Links** tab for all relevant links for the current document that will also include a KeyCite section with a description of the KeyCite status flag. Depending on your document, links may also include administrative, bill text, and other sources that were previously only available by accessing and searching other databases.

Additional Information

Westlaw is available on the Web at www.westlaw.com.

For search assistance, call the West Reference Attorneys at:
1–800–REF–ATTY (1–800–733–2889).

For technical assistance, call West Customer Technical Support at:
1–800–WESTLAW (1–800–937–8529).

TABLE OF CONTENTS

*

FEDERAL RULES OF CIVIL PROCEDURE

Effective September 16, 1938

Including Amendments Effective December 1, 2008, Absent Contrary Congressional Action

Research Note

These rules may be searched electronically on Westlaw in the US–RULES database; updates to these rules may be found on Westlaw in US–RULES-UPDATES. For search tips, and a detailed summary of database content, consult the Westlaw Scope Screen of each database.

Table of Rules

SUPPLEMENTAL RULES FOR ADMIRALTY OR MARITIME CLAIMS AND ASSET FORFEITURE ACTIONS

TITLE I. SCOPE OF RULES; FORM OF ACTION

RULE 1. SCOPE AND PURPOSE

These rules govern the procedure in all civil actions and proceedings in the United States district courts, except as stated in Rule 81. They should be construed and administered to secure the just, speedy, and inexpensive determination of every action and proceeding.

[Amended December 29, 1948, effective October 20, 1949; February 28, 1966, effective July 1, 1966; April 22, 1993, effective December 1, 1993; April 30, 2007, effective December 1, 2007.]

RULE 2. ONE FORM OF ACTION

There is one form of action—the civil action.

[Amended April 30, 2007, effective December 1, 2007.]

TITLE II. COMMENCING AN ACTION; SERVICE OF PROCESS, PLEADINGS, MOTIONS, AND ORDERS

RULE 3. COMMENCING AN ACTION

A civil action is commenced by filing a complaint with the court.

[Amended April 30, 2007, effective December 1, 2007.]

RULE 4. SUMMONS

(a) Contents; Amendments.

(1) *Contents.* A summons must:

(A) name the court and the parties;

(B) be directed to the defendant;

(C) state the name and address of the plaintiff's attorney or—if unrepresented—of the plaintiff;

(D) state the time within which the defendant must appear and defend;

(E) notify the defendant that a failure to appear and defend will result in a default judgment against the defendant for the relief demanded in the complaint;

(F) be signed by the clerk; and

(G) bear the court's seal.

(2) *Amendments.* The court may permit a summons to be amended.

(b) Issuance. On or after filing the complaint, the plaintiff may present a summons to the clerk for signature and seal. If the summons is properly completed, the clerk must sign, seal, and issue it to the plaintiff for service on the defendant. A summons—or a copy of a summons that is addressed to multiple defendants—must be issued for each defendant to be served.

(c) Service.

(1) *In General.* A summons must be served with a copy of the complaint. The plaintiff is responsible for having the summons and complaint served within the time allowed by Rule 4(m) and must furnish the necessary copies to the person who makes service.

(2) *By Whom.* Any person who is at least 18 years old and not a party may serve a summons and complaint.

(3) *By a Marshal or Someone Specially Appointed.* At the plaintiff's request, the court may order that service be made by a United States marshal or deputy marshal or by a person specially appointed by the court. The court must so order if the plaintiff is authorized to proceed in forma pauperis under 28 U.S.C. § 1915 or as a seaman under 28 U.S.C. § 1916.

(d) Waiving Service.

(1) *Requesting a Waiver.* An individual, corporation, or association that is subject to service under Rule 4(e), (f), or (h) has a duty to avoid unnecessary expenses of serving the summons. The plaintiff may notify such a defendant that an action has been commenced and request that the defendant waive service of a summons. The notice and request must:

(A) be in writing and be addressed:

(i) to the individual defendant; or

(ii) for a defendant subject to service under Rule 4(h), to an officer, a managing or general agent, or any other agent authorized by appointment or by law to receive service of process;

(B) name the court where the complaint was filed;

(C) be accompanied by a copy of the complaint, two copies of a waiver form, and a prepaid means for returning the form;

(D) inform the defendant, using text prescribed in Form 5, of the consequences of waiving and not waiving service;

(E) state the date when the request is sent;

(F) give the defendant a reasonable time of at least 30 days after the request was sent—or at least 60 days if sent to the defendant outside any judicial district of the United States—to return the waiver; and

(G) be sent by first-class mail or other reliable means.

(2) *Failure to Waive.* If a defendant located within the United States fails, without good cause, to sign and return a waiver requested by a plaintiff located within the United States, the court must impose on the defendant:

(A) the expenses later incurred in making service; and

(B) the reasonable expenses, including attorney's fees, of any motion required to collect those service expenses.

(3) *Time to Answer After a Waiver.* A defendant who, before being served with process, timely returns a waiver need not serve an answer to the complaint until 60 days after the request was sent—or until 90 days after it was sent to the defendant outside any judicial district of the United States.

(4) *Results of Filing a Waiver.* When the plaintiff files a waiver, proof of service is not required and these rules apply as if a summons and complaint had been served at the time of filing the waiver.

(5) *Jurisdiction and Venue Not Waived.* Waiving service of a summons does not waive any objection to personal jurisdiction or to venue.

(e) Serving an Individual Within a Judicial District of the United States. Unless federal law provides otherwise, an individual—other than a minor, an incompetent person, or a person whose waiver has been filed—may be served in a judicial district of the United States by:

(1) following state law for serving a summons in an action brought in courts of general jurisdiction in the state where the district court is located or where service is made; or

(2) doing any of the following:

(A) delivering a copy of the summons and of the complaint to the individual personally;

(B) leaving a copy of each at the individual's dwelling or usual place of abode with someone of suitable age and discretion who resides there; or

(C) delivering a copy of each to an agent authorized by appointment or by law to receive service of process.

(f) Serving an Individual in a Foreign Country. Unless federal law provides otherwise, an individual—other than a minor, an incompetent person, or a person whose waiver has been filed—may be served at a place not within any judicial district of the United States:

(1) by any internationally agreed means of service that is reasonably calculated to give notice, such as those authorized by the Hague Convention on the Service Abroad of Judicial and Extrajudicial Documents;

(2) if there is no internationally agreed means, or if an international agreement allows but does not specify other means, by a method that is reasonably calculated to give notice:

(A) as prescribed by the foreign country's law for service in that country in an action in its courts of general jurisdiction;

(B) as the foreign authority directs in response to a letter rogatory or letter of request; or

(C) unless prohibited by the foreign country's law, by:

(i) delivering a copy of the summons and of the complaint to the individual personally; or

(ii) using any form of mail that the clerk addresses and sends to the individual and that requires a signed receipt; or

(3) by other means not prohibited by international agreement, as the court orders.

(g) Serving a Minor or an Incompetent Person. A minor or an incompetent person in a judicial district of the United States must be served by following state law for serving a summons or like process on such a defendant in an action brought in the courts of general jurisdiction of the state where service is made. A minor or an incompetent person who is not within any judicial district of the United States must be served in the manner prescribed by Rule 4(f)(2)(A), (f)(2)(B), or (f)(3).

(h) Serving a Corporation, Partnership, or Association. Unless federal law provides otherwise or the defendant's waiver has been filed, a domestic or foreign corporation, or a partnership or other unincorporated association that is subject to suit under a common name, must be served:

(1) in a judicial district of the United States:

(A) in the manner prescribed by Rule 4(e)(1) for serving an individual; or

(B) by delivering a copy of the summons and of the complaint to an officer, a managing or general agent, or any other agent authorized by appointment or by law to receive service of process and—if the agent is one authorized by statute and the statute so requires—by also mailing a copy of each to the defendant; or

(2) at a place not within any judicial district of the United States, in any manner prescribed by Rule 4(f) for serving an individual, except personal delivery under (f)(2)(C)(i).

(i) Serving the United States and Its Agencies, Corporations, Officers, or Employees.

(1) *United States.* To serve the United States, a party must:

(A)(i) deliver a copy of the summons and of the complaint to the United States attorney for the district where the action is brought—or to an assistant United States attorney or clerical employee whom the United States attorney designates in a writing filed with the court clerk—or

(ii) send a copy of each by registered or certified mail to the civil-process clerk at the United States attorney's office;

(B) send a copy of each by registered or certified mail to the Attorney General of the United States at Washington, D.C.; and

(C) if the action challenges an order of a nonparty agency or officer of the United States, send a copy of each by registered or certified mail to the agency or officer.

(2) *Agency; Corporation; Officer or Employee Sued in an Official Capacity.* To serve a United States agency or corporation, or a United States officer or employee sued only in an official capacity, a party must serve the United States and also send a copy of the summons and of the complaint by registered or certified mail to the agency, corporation, officer, or employee.

(3) *Officer or Employee Sued Individually.* To serve a United States officer or employee sued in an individual capacity for an act or omission occurring in connection with duties performed on the United States' behalf (whether or not the officer or employee is also sued in an official capacity), a party must serve the United States and also serve the officer or employee under Rule 4(e), (f), or (g).

(4) *Extending Time.* The court must allow a party a reasonable time to cure its failure to:

(A) serve a person required to be served under Rule 4(i)(2), if the party has served either the United States attorney or the Attorney General of the United States; or

(B) serve the United States under Rule 4(i)(3), if the party has served the United States officer or employee.

(j) Serving a Foreign, State, or Local Government.

(1) *Foreign State.* A foreign state or its political subdivision, agency, or instrumentality must be served in accordance with 28 U.S.C. § 1608.

(2) *State or Local Government.* A state, a municipal corporation, or any other state-created governmental organization that is subject to suit must be served by:

(A) delivering a copy of the summons and of the complaint to its chief executive officer; or

(B) serving a copy of each in the manner prescribed by that state's law for serving a summons or like process on such a defendant.

(k) Territorial Limits of Effective Service.

(1) *In General.* Serving a summons or filing a waiver of service establishes personal jurisdiction over a defendant:

(A) who is subject to the jurisdiction of a court of general jurisdiction in the state where the district court is located;

(B) who is a party joined under Rule 14 or 19 and is served within a judicial district of the United States and not more than 100 miles from where the summons was issued; or

(C) when authorized by a federal statute.

(2) *Federal Claim Outside State-Court Jurisdiction.* For a claim that arises under federal law, serving a summons or filing a waiver of service establishes personal jurisdiction over a defendant if:

(A) the defendant is not subject to jurisdiction in any state's courts of general jurisdiction; and

(B) exercising jurisdiction is consistent with the United States Constitution and laws.

(*l*) Proving Service.

(1) *Affidavit Required.* Unless service is waived, proof of service must be made to the court. Except for service by a United States marshal or deputy marshal, proof must be by the server's affidavit.

(2) *Service Outside the United States.* Service not within any judicial district of the United States must be proved as follows:

(A) if made under Rule 4(f)(1), as provided in the applicable treaty or convention; or

(B) if made under Rule 4(f)(2) or (f)(3), by a receipt signed by the addressee, or by other evidence satisfying the court that the summons and complaint were delivered to the addressee.

(3) *Validity of Service; Amending Proof.* Failure to prove service does not affect the validity of service. The court may permit proof of service to be amended.

(m) Time Limit for Service. If a defendant is not served within 120 days after the complaint is filed, the court—on motion or on its own after notice to the plaintiff—must dismiss the action without prejudice against that defendant or order that service be made within a specified time. But if the plaintiff shows good cause for the failure, the court must extend the time for service for an appropriate period. This subdivision (m) does not apply to service in a foreign country under Rule 4(f) or 4(j)(1).

(n) Asserting Jurisdiction over Property or Assets.

(1) *Federal Law.* The court may assert jurisdiction over property if authorized by a federal statute. Notice to claimants of the property must be given as provided in the statute or by serving a summons under this rule.

(2) *State Law.* On a showing that personal jurisdiction over a defendant cannot be obtained in the district where the action is brought by reasonable efforts to serve a summons under this rule, the court may assert jurisdiction over the defendant's assets found in the district. Jurisdiction is acquired by seizing the assets under the circumstances and in the manner provided by state law in that district.

[Amended January 21, 1963, effective July 1, 1963; February 28, 1966, effective July 1, 1966; April 29, 1980, effective August 1, 1980; amended by Pub.L. 97-462, § 2, January 12, 1983, 96 Stat. 2527, effective 45 days after January 12, 1983; amended March 2, 1987, effective August 1, 1987; April 22, 1993, effective December 1, 1993; April 17, 2000, effective December 1, 2000; April 30, 2007, effective December 1, 2007.]

RULE 4.1 SERVING OTHER PROCESS

(a) In General. Process—other than a summons under Rule 4 or a subpoena under Rule 45—must be served by a United States marshal or deputy marshal or by a person specially appointed for that purpose. It may be served anywhere within the territorial limits of the state where the district court is located and, if authorized by a federal statute, beyond those limits. Proof of service must be made under Rule 4(*l*).

(b) Enforcing Orders: Committing for Civil Contempt. An order committing a person for civil contempt of a decree or injunction issued to enforce federal law may be served and enforced in any district. Any other order in a civil-contempt proceeding may be served only in the state where the issuing court is located or elsewhere in the United States within 100 miles from where the order was issued.

[Adopted April 22, 1993, effective December 1, 1993; amended April 30, 2007, effective December 1, 2007.]

RULE 5. SERVING AND FILING PLEADINGS AND OTHER PAPERS

(a) Service: When Required.

(1) *In General.* Unless these rules provide otherwise, each of the following papers must be served on every party:

(A) an order stating that service is required;

(B) a pleading filed after the original complaint, unless the court orders otherwise under Rule 5(c) because there are numerous defendants;

(C) a discovery paper required to be served on a party, unless the court orders otherwise;

(D) a written motion, except one that may be heard ex parte; and

(E) a written notice, appearance, demand, or offer of judgment, or any similar paper.

(2) *If a Party Fails to Appear.* No service is required on a party who is in default for failing to appear. But a pleading that asserts a new claim for relief against such a party must be served on that party under Rule 4.

(3) *Seizing Property.* If an action is begun by seizing property and no person is or need be named as a defendant, any service required before the filing of an appearance, answer, or claim must be made on the person who had custody or possession of the property when it was seized.

(b) Service: How Made.

(1) *Serving an Attorney.* If a party is represented by an attorney, service under this rule must be made on the attorney unless the court orders service on the party.

(2) *Service in General.* A paper is served under this rule by:

(A) handing it to the person;

(B) leaving it:

(i) at the person's office with a clerk or other person in charge or, if no one is in charge, in a conspicuous place in the office; or

(ii) if the person has no office or the office is closed, at the person's dwelling or usual place of abode with someone of suitable age and discretion who resides there;

(C) mailing it to the person's last known address—in which event service is complete upon mailing;

(D) leaving it with the court clerk if the person has no known address;

(E) sending it by electronic means if the person consented in writing—in which event service is complete upon transmission, but is not effective if the serving party learns that it did not reach the person to be served; or

(F) delivering it by any other means that the person consented to in writing—in which event service is complete when the person making service delivers it to the agency designated to make delivery.

(3) *Using Court Facilities.* If a local rule so authorizes, a party may use the court's transmission facilities to make service under Rule 5(b)(2)(E).

(c) Serving Numerous Defendants.

(1) *In General.* If an action involves an unusually large number of defendants, the court may, on motion or on its own, order that:

(A) defendants' pleadings and replies to them need not be served on other defendants;

(B) any crossclaim, counterclaim, avoidance, or affirmative defense in those pleadings and replies to them will be treated as denied or avoided by all other parties; and

(C) filing any such pleading and serving it on the plaintiff constitutes notice of the pleading to all parties.

(2) *Notifying Parties.* A copy of every such order must be served on the parties as the court directs.

(d) Filing.

(1) *Required Filings; Certificate of Service.* Any paper after the complaint that is required to be served—together with a certificate of service—must be filed within a reasonable time after service. But disclosures under Rule 26(a)(1) or (2) and the following discovery requests and responses must not be filed until they are used in the proceeding or the court orders filing: depositions, interrogatories, requests for documents or tangible things or to permit entry onto land, and requests for admission.

(2) *How Filing Is Made—In General.* A paper is filed by delivering it:

(A) to the clerk; or

(B) to a judge who agrees to accept it for filing, and who must then note the filing date on the paper and promptly send it to the clerk.

(3) *Electronic Filing, Signing, or Verification.* A court may, by local rule, allow papers to be filed, signed, or verified by electronic means that are consistent with any technical standards established by the Judicial Conference of the United States. A local rule may require electronic filing only if reasonable exceptions are allowed. A paper filed electronically in compliance with a local rule is a written paper for purposes of these rules.

(4) *Acceptance by the Clerk.* The clerk must not refuse to file a paper solely because it is not in the form prescribed by these rules or by a local rule or practice.

[Amended January 21, 1963, effective July 1, 1963; March 30, 1970, effective July 1, 1970; April 29, 1980, effective August 1, 1980; March 2, 1987, effective August 1, 1987; April 30, 1991, effective December 1, 1991; April 22, 1993, effective December 1, 1993; April 23, 1996, effective December 1, 1996; April 17, 2000, effective December 1, 2000; April 23, 2001, effective December 1, 2001; April 12, 2006, effective December 1, 2006; April 30, 2007, effective December 1, 2007.]

RULE 5.1 CONSTITUTIONAL CHALLENGE TO A STATUTE—NOTICE, CERTIFICATION, AND INTERVENTION

(a) Notice by a Party. A party that files a pleading, written motion, or other paper drawing into question the constitutionality of a federal or state statute must promptly:

(1) file a notice of constitutional question stating the question and identifying the paper that raises it, if:

(A) a federal statute is questioned and the parties do not include the United States, one of its agencies, or one of its officers or employees in an official capacity; or

(B) a state statute is questioned and the parties do not include the state, one of its agencies, or one of its officers or employees in an official capacity; and

(2) serve the notice and paper on the Attorney General of the United States if a federal statute is questioned—or on the state attorney general if a state statute is questioned—either by certified or registered mail or by sending it to an electronic address designated by the attorney general for this purpose.

(b) Certification by the Court. The court must, under 28 U.S.C. § 2403, certify to the appropriate attorney general that a statute has been questioned.

(c) Intervention; Final Decision on the Merits. Unless the court sets a later time, the attorney general may intervene within 60 days after the notice is filed or after the court certifies the challenge, whichever is earlier. Before the time to intervene expires, the court may reject the constitutional challenge, but may not enter a final judgment holding the statute unconstitutional.

(d) No Forfeiture. A party's failure to file and serve the notice, or the court's failure to certify, does not forfeit a constitutional claim or defense that is otherwise timely asserted.

[Effective December 1, 2006; amended April 30, 2007, effective December 1, 2007.]

RULE 5.2 PRIVACY PROTECTION FOR FILINGS MADE WITH THE COURT

(a) Redacted Filings. Unless the court orders otherwise, in an electronic or paper filing with the court that contains an individual's social-security number, taxpayer-identification number, or birth date, the name of an individual known to be a minor, or a financial-account number, a party or nonparty making the filing may include only:

(1) the last four digits of the social-security number and taxpayer-identification number;

(2) the year of the individual's birth;

(3) the minor's initials; and

(4) the last four digits of the financial-account number.

(b) Exemptions from the Redaction Requirement. The redaction requirement does not apply to the following:

(1) a financial-account number that identifies the property allegedly subject to forfeiture in a forfeiture proceeding;

(2) the record of an administrative or agency proceeding;

(3) the official record of a state-court proceeding;

(4) the record of a court or tribunal, if that record was not subject to the redaction requirement when originally filed;

(5) a filing covered by Rule 5.2(c) or (d); and

(6) a pro se filing in an action brought under 28 U.S.C. §§ 2241, 2254, or 2255.

(c) Limitations on Remote Access to Electronic Files; Social-Security Appeals and Immigration Cases. Unless the court orders otherwise, in an action for benefits under the Social Security Act, and in an action or proceeding relating to an order of removal, to relief from removal, or to immigration benefits or detention, access to an electronic file is authorized as follows:

(1) the parties and their attorneys may have remote electronic access to any part of the case file, including the administrative record;

(2) any other person may have electronic access to the full record at the courthouse, but may have remote electronic access only to:

(A) the docket maintained by the court; and

(B) an opinion, order, judgment, or other disposition of the court, but not any other part of the case file or the administrative record.

(d) Filings Made Under Seal. The court may order that a filing be made under seal without redaction. The court may later unseal the filing or order the person who made the filing to file a redacted version for the public record.

(e) Protective Orders. For good cause, the court may by order in a case:

(1) require redaction of additional information; or

(2) limit or prohibit a nonparty's remote electronic access to a document filed with the court.

(f) Option for Additional Unredacted Filing Under Seal. A person making a redacted filing may also file an unredacted copy under seal. The court must retain the unredacted copy as part of the record.

(g) Option for Filing a Reference List. A filing that contains redacted information may be filed together with a reference list that identifies each item of redacted information and specifies an appropriate identifier that uniquely corresponds to each item listed. The list must be filed under seal and may be amended as of right. Any reference in the case to a listed identifier will be construed to refer to the corresponding item of information.

(h) Waiver of Protection of Identifiers. A person waives the protection of Rule 5.2(a) as to the person's own information by filing it without redaction and not under seal.

[Adopted April 30, 2007, effective December 1, 2007.]

RULE 6. COMPUTING AND EXTENDING TIME; TIME FOR MOTION PAPERS

(a) Computing Time. The following rules apply in computing any time period specified in these rules or in any local rule, court order, or statute:

(1) *Day of the Event Excluded.* Exclude the day of the act, event, or default that begins the period.

(2) *Exclusions from Brief Periods.* Exclude intermediate Saturdays, Sundays, and legal holidays when the period is less than 11 days.

(3) *Last Day.* Include the last day of the period unless it is a Saturday, Sunday, legal holiday, or—if the act to be done is filing a paper in court—a day on which weather or other conditions make the clerk's office inaccessible. When the last day is excluded, the period runs until the end of the next day that is not a Saturday, Sunday, legal holiday, or day when the clerk's office is inaccessible.

(4) *"Legal Holiday" Defined.* As used in these rules, "legal holiday" means:

(A) the day set aside by statute for observing New Year's Day, Martin Luther King Jr.'s Birthday, Washington's Birthday, Memorial Day, Independence Day, Labor Day, Columbus Day, Veterans' Day, Thanksgiving Day, or Christmas Day; and

(B) any other day declared a holiday by the President, Congress, or the state where the district court is located.

(b) Extending Time.

(1) *In General.* When an act may or must be done within a specified time, the court may, for good cause, extend the time:

(A) with or without motion or notice if the court acts, or if a request is made, before the original time or its extension expires; or

(B) on motion made after the time has expired if the party failed to act because of excusable neglect.

(2) *Exceptions.* A court must not extend the time to act under Rules 50(b) and (d), 52(b), 59(b), (d), and (e), and 60(b), except as those rules allow.

(c) Motions, Notices of Hearing, and Affidavits.

(1) *In General.* A written motion and notice of the hearing must be served at least 5 days before the time specified for the hearing, with the following exceptions:

(A) when the motion may be heard ex parte;

(B) when these rules set a different time; or

(C) when a court order—which a party may, for good cause, apply for ex parte—sets a different time.

(2) *Supporting Affidavit.* Any affidavit supporting a motion must be served with the motion. Except as Rule 59(c) provides otherwise, any opposing affidavit must be served at least 1 day before the hearing, unless the court permits service at another time.

(d) Additional Time After Certain Kinds of Service. When a party may or must act within a specified time after service and service is made under Rule 5(b)(2)(C), (D), (E), or (F), 3 days are added after the period would otherwise expire under Rule 6(a).

[Amended December 27, 1946, effective March 19, 1948; January 21, 1963, effective July 1, 1963; February 28, 1966, effective July 1, 1966; December 4, 1967, effective July 1, 1968; March 1, 1971, effective July 1, 1971; April 28, 1983, effective August 1, 1983; April 29, 1985, effective August 1, 1985; March 2, 1987, effective August 1, 1987; April 29, 1999, effective December 1, 1999; April 23, 2001, effective December 1, 2001; April 25, 2005, effective December 1, 2005; April 30, 2007, effective December 1, 2007.]

TITLE III. PLEADINGS AND MOTIONS

RULE 7. PLEADINGS ALLOWED; FORM OF MOTIONS AND OTHER PAPERS

(a) Pleadings. Only these pleadings are allowed:

(1) a complaint;

(2) an answer to a complaint;

(3) an answer to a counterclaim designated as a counterclaim;

(4) an answer to a crossclaim;

(5) a third-party complaint;

(6) an answer to a third-party complaint; and

(7) if the court orders one, a reply to an answer.

(b) Motions and Other Papers.

(1) *In General.* A request for a court order must be made by motion. The motion must:

(A) be in writing unless made during a hearing or trial;

(B) state with particularity the grounds for seeking the order; and

(C) state the relief sought.

(2) *Form.* The rules governing captions and other matters of form in pleadings apply to motions and other papers.

[Amended December 27, 1946, effective March 19, 1948; January 21, 1963, effective July 1, 1963; April 28, 1983, effective August 1, 1983; April 30, 2007, effective December 1, 2007.]

RULE 7.1 DISCLOSURE STATEMENT

(a) Who Must File; Contents. A nongovernmental corporate party must file two copies of a disclosure statement that:

(1) identifies any parent corporation and any publicly held corporation owning 10% or more of its stock; or

(2) states that there is no such corporation.

(b) Time to File; Supplemental Filing. A party must:

(1) file the disclosure statement with its first appearance, pleading, petition, motion, response, or other request addressed to the court; and

(2) promptly file a supplemental statement if any required information changes.

[Adopted April 29, 2002, effective December 1, 2002; April 30, 2007, effective December 1, 2007.]

RULE 8. GENERAL RULES OF PLEADING

(a) Claim for Relief. A pleading that states a claim for relief must contain:

(1) a short and plain statement of the grounds for the court's jurisdiction, unless the court already has jurisdiction and the claim needs no new jurisdictional support;

(2) a short and plain statement of the claim showing that the pleader is entitled to relief; and

(3) a demand for the relief sought, which may include relief in the alternative or different types of relief.

(b) Defenses; Admissions and Denials.

(1) *In General.* In responding to a pleading, a party must:

(A) state in short and plain terms its defenses to each claim asserted against it; and

(B) admit or deny the allegations asserted against it by an opposing party.

(2) *Denials—Responding to the Substance.* A denial must fairly respond to the substance of the allegation.

(3) *General and Specific Denials.* A party that intends in good faith to deny all the allegations of a

pleading—including the jurisdictional grounds—may do so by a general denial. A party that does not intend to deny all the allegations must either specifically deny designated allegations or generally deny all except those specifically admitted.

(4) *Denying Part of an Allegation.* A party that intends in good faith to deny only part of an allegation must admit the part that is true and deny the rest.

(5) *Lacking Knowledge or Information.* A party that lacks knowledge or information sufficient to form a belief about the truth of an allegation must so state, and the statement has the effect of a denial.

(6) *Effect of Failing to Deny.* An allegation—other than one relating to the amount of damages—is admitted if a responsive pleading is required and the allegation is not denied. If a responsive pleading is not required, an allegation is considered denied or avoided.

(c) Affirmative Defenses.

(1) *In General.* In responding to a pleading, a party must affirmatively state any avoidance or affirmative defense, including:

- accord and satisfaction;
- arbitration and award;
- assumption of risk;
- contributory negligence;
- discharge in bankruptcy;
- duress;
- estoppel;
- failure of consideration;
- fraud;
- illegality;
- injury by fellow servant;
- laches;
- license;
- payment;
- release;
- res judicata;
- statute of frauds;
- statute of limitations; and
- waiver.

(2) *Mistaken Designation.* If a party mistakenly designates a defense as a counterclaim, or a counterclaim as a defense, the court must, if justice requires, treat the pleading as though it were correctly designated, and may impose terms for doing so.

(d) Pleading to Be Concise and Direct; Alternative Statements; Inconsistency.

(1) *In General.* Each allegation must be simple, concise, and direct. No technical form is required.

(2) *Alternative Statements of a Claim or Defense.* A party may set out 2 or more statements of a claim or defense alternatively or hypothetically, either in a single count or defense or in separate ones. If a party makes alternative statements, the pleading is sufficient if any one of them is sufficient.

(3) *Inconsistent Claims or Defenses.* A party may state as many separate claims or defenses as it has, regardless of consistency.

(e) Construing Pleadings. Pleadings must be construed so as to do justice.

[Amended February 28, 1966, effective July 1, 1966; March 2, 1987, effective August 1, 1987; April 30, 2007, effective December 1, 2007.]

RULE 9. PLEADING SPECIAL MATTERS

(a) Capacity or Authority to Sue; Legal Existence.

(1) *In General.* Except when required to show that the court has jurisdiction, a pleading need not allege:

(A) a party's capacity to sue or be sued;

(B) a party's authority to sue or be sued in a representative capacity; or

(C) the legal existence of an organized association of persons that is made a party.

(2) *Raising Those Issues.* To raise any of those issues, a party must do so by a specific denial, which must state any supporting facts that are peculiarly within the party's knowledge.

(b) Fraud or Mistake; Conditions of Mind. In alleging fraud or mistake, a party must state with particularity the circumstances constituting fraud or mistake. Malice, intent, knowledge, and other conditions of a person's mind may be alleged generally.

(c) Conditions Precedent. In pleading conditions precedent, it suffices to allege generally that all conditions precedent have occurred or been performed. But when denying that a condition precedent has occurred or been performed, a party must do so with particularity.

(d) Official Document or Act. In pleading an official document or official act, it suffices to allege that the document was legally issued or the act legally done.

(e) Judgment. In pleading a judgment or decision of a domestic or foreign court, a judicial or quasi-judicial tribunal, or a board or officer, it suffices to plead the judgment or decision without showing jurisdiction to render it.

(f) Time and Place. An allegation of time or place is material when testing the sufficiency of a pleading.

(g) Special Damages. If an item of special damage is claimed, it must be specifically stated.

(h) Admiralty or Maritime Claim.

(1) *How Designated.* If a claim for relief is within the admiralty or maritime jurisdiction and also within the court's subject-matter jurisdiction on some other ground, the pleading may designate the claim as an admiralty or maritime claim for purposes of Rules 14(c), 38(e), and 82 and the Supplemental Rules for Admiralty or Maritime Claims and Asset Forfeiture Actions. A claim cognizable only in the admiralty or maritime jurisdiction is an admiralty or maritime claim for those purposes, whether or not so designated.

(2) *Designation for Appeal.* A case that includes an admiralty or maritime claim within this subdivision (h) is an admiralty case within 28 U.S.C. § 1292(a)(3).

[Amended February 28, 1966, effective July 1, 1966; December 4, 1967, effective July 1, 1968; March 30, 1970, effective July 1, 1970; March 2, 1987, effective August 1, 1987; April 11, 1997, effective December 1, 1997; April 12, 2006, effective December 1, 2006; April 30, 2007, effective December 1, 2007.]

RULE 10. FORM OF PLEADINGS

(a) Caption; Names of Parties. Every pleading must have a caption with the court's name, a title, a file number, and a Rule 7(a) designation. The title of the complaint must name all the parties; the title of other pleadings, after naming the first party on each side, may refer generally to other parties.

(b) Paragraphs; Separate Statements. A party must state its claims or defenses in numbered paragraphs, each limited as far as practicable to a single set of circumstances. A later pleading may refer by number to a paragraph in an earlier pleading. If doing so would promote clarity, each claim founded on a separate transaction or occurrence—and each defense other than a denial—must be stated in a separate count or defense.

(c) Adoption by Reference; Exhibits. A statement in a pleading may be adopted by reference elsewhere in the same pleading or in any other pleading or motion. A copy of a written instrument that is an exhibit to a pleading is a part of the pleading for all purposes.

[Amended April 30, 2007, effective December 1, 2007.]

RULE 11. SIGNING PLEADINGS, MOTIONS, AND OTHER PAPERS; REPRESENTATIONS TO THE COURT; SANCTIONS

(a) Signature. Every pleading, written motion, and other paper must be signed by at least one attorney of record in the attorney's name—or by a party personally if the party is unrepresented. The paper must state the signer's address, e-mail address, and telephone number. Unless a rule or statute specifically states otherwise, a pleading need not be verified or accompanied by an affidavit. The court must strike an unsigned paper unless the omission is promptly corrected after being called to the attorney's or party's attention.

(b) Representations to the Court. By presenting to the court a pleading, written motion, or other paper—whether by signing, filing, submitting, or later advocating it—an attorney or unrepresented party certifies that to the best of the person's knowledge, information, and belief, formed after an inquiry reasonable under the circumstances:

(1) it is not being presented for any improper purpose, such as to harass, cause unnecessary delay, or needlessly increase the cost of litigation;

(2) the claims, defenses, and other legal contentions are warranted by existing law or by a nonfrivolous argument for extending, modifying, or reversing existing law or for establishing new law;

(3) the factual contentions have evidentiary support or, if specifically so identified, will likely have evidentiary support after a reasonable opportunity for further investigation or discovery; and

(4) the denials of factual contentions are warranted on the evidence or, if specifically so identified, are reasonably based on belief or a lack of information.

(c) Sanctions.

(1) *In General.* If, after notice and a reasonable opportunity to respond, the court determines that Rule 11(b) has been violated, the court may impose an appropriate sanction on any attorney, law firm, or party that violated the rule or is responsible for the violation. Absent exceptional circumstances, a law firm must be held jointly responsible for a violation committed by its partner, associate, or employee.

(2) *Motion for Sanctions.* A motion for sanctions must be made separately from any other motion and must describe the specific conduct that allegedly violates Rule 11(b). The motion must be served under Rule 5, but it must not be filed or be presented to the court if the challenged paper, claim, defense, contention, or denial is withdrawn or appropriately corrected within 21 days after service or within another time the court sets. If warranted, the court may award to the prevailing party the reasonable expenses, including attorney's fees, incurred for the motion.

(3) *On the Court's Initiative.* On its own, the court may order an attorney, law firm, or party to show cause why conduct specifically described in the order has not violated Rule 11(b).

(4) *Nature of a Sanction.* A sanction imposed under this rule must be limited to what suffices to deter repetition of the conduct or comparable conduct by others similarly situated. The sanction may include nonmonetary directives; an order to pay a penalty into court; or, if imposed on motion and warranted for

effective deterrence, an order directing payment to the movant of part or all of the reasonable attorney's fees and other expenses directly resulting from the violation.

(5) *Limitations on Monetary Sanctions.* The court must not impose a monetary sanction:

(A) against a represented party for violating Rule 11(b)(2); or

(B) on its own, unless it issued the show-cause order under Rule 11(c)(3) before voluntary dismissal or settlement of the claims made by or against the party that is, or whose attorneys are, to be sanctioned.

(6) *Requirements for an Order.* An order imposing a sanction must describe the sanctioned conduct and explain the basis for the sanction.

(d) Inapplicability to Discovery. This rule does not apply to disclosures and discovery requests, responses, objections, and motions under Rules 26 through 37.

[Amended April 28, 1983, effective August 1, 1983; March 2, 1987, effective August 1, 1987; April 22, 1993, effective December 1, 1993; April 30, 2007, effective December 1, 2007.]

RULE 12. DEFENSES AND OBJECTIONS: WHEN AND HOW PRESENTED; MOTION FOR JUDGMENT ON THE PLEADINGS; CONSOLIDATING MOTIONS; WAIVING DEFENSES; PRETRIAL HEARING

(a) Time to Serve a Responsive Pleading.

(1) *In General.* Unless another time is specified by this rule or a federal statute, the time for serving a responsive pleading is as follows:

(A) A defendant must serve an answer:

(i) within 20 days after being served with the summons and complaint; or

(ii) if it has timely waived service under Rule 4(d), within 60 days after the request for a waiver was sent, or within 90 days after it was sent to the defendant outside any judicial district of the United States.

(B) A party must serve an answer to a counterclaim or crossclaim within 20 days after being served with the pleading that states the counterclaim or crossclaim.

(C) A party must serve a reply to an answer within 20 days after being served with an order to reply, unless the order specifies a different time.

(2) *United States and Its Agencies, Officers, or Employees Sued in an Official Capacity.* The United States, a United States agency, or a United States officer or employee sued only in an official capacity must serve an answer to a complaint, counterclaim, or crossclaim within 60 days after service on the United States attorney.

(3) *United States Officers or Employees Sued in an Individual Capacity.* A United States officer or employee sued in an individual capacity for an act or omission occurring in connection with duties performed on the United States' behalf must serve an answer to a complaint, counterclaim, or crossclaim within 60 days after service on the officer or employee or service on the United States attorney, whichever is later.

(4) *Effect of a Motion.* Unless the court sets a different time, serving a motion under this rule alters these periods as follows:

(A) if the court denies the motion or postpones its disposition until trial, the responsive pleading must be served within 10 days after notice of the court's action; or

(B) if the court grants a motion for a more definite statement, the responsive pleading must be served within 10 days after the more definite statement is served.

(b) How to Present Defenses. Every defense to a claim for relief in any pleading must be asserted in the responsive pleading if one is required. But a party may assert the following defenses by motion:

(1) lack of subject-matter jurisdiction;

(2) lack of personal jurisdiction;

(3) improper venue;

(4) insufficient process;

(5) insufficient service of process;

(6) failure to state a claim upon which relief can be granted; and

(7) failure to join a party under Rule 19.

A motion asserting any of these defenses must be made before pleading if a responsive pleading is allowed. If a pleading sets out a claim for relief that does not require a responsive pleading, an opposing party may assert at trial any defense to that claim. No defense or objection is waived by joining it with one or more other defenses or objections in a responsive pleading or in a motion.

(c) Motion for Judgment on the Pleadings. After the pleadings are closed—but early enough not to delay trial—a party may move for judgment on the pleadings.

(d) Result of Presenting Matters Outside the Pleadings. If, on a motion under Rule 12(b)(6) or 12(c), matters outside the pleadings are presented to and not excluded by the court, the motion must be treated as one for summary judgment under Rule 56. All parties must be given a reasonable opportunity to present all the material that is pertinent to the motion.

(e) Motion for a More Definite Statement. A party may move for a more definite statement of a pleading to which a responsive pleading is allowed but which is so vague or ambiguous that the party cannot reasonably prepare a response. The motion must be made before filing a responsive pleading and must point out the defects complained of and the details desired. If the court orders a more definite statement and the order is not obeyed within 10 days after notice of the order or within the time the court sets, the court may strike the pleading or issue any other appropriate order.

(f) Motion to Strike. The court may strike from a pleading an insufficient defense or any redundant, immaterial, impertinent, or scandalous matter. The court may act:

(1) on its own; or

(2) on motion made by a party either before responding to the pleading or, if a response is not allowed, within 20 days after being served with the pleading.

(g) Joining Motions.

(1) *Right to Join.* A motion under this rule may be joined with any other motion allowed by this rule.

(2) *Limitation on Further Motions.* Except as provided in Rule 12(h)(2) or (3), a party that makes a motion under this rule must not make another motion under this rule raising a defense or objection that was available to the party but omitted from its earlier motion.

(h) Waiving and Preserving Certain Defenses.

(1) *When Some Are Waived.* A party waives any defense listed in Rule 12(b)(2)-(5) by:

(A) omitting it from a motion in the circumstances described in Rule 12(g)(2); or

(B) failing to either:

(i) make it by motion under this rule; or

(ii) include it in a responsive pleading or in an amendment allowed by Rule 15(a)(1) as a matter of course.

(2) *When to Raise Others.* Failure to state a claim upon which relief can be granted, to join a person required by Rule 19(b), or to state a legal defense to a claim may be raised:

(A) in any pleading allowed or ordered under Rule 7(a);

(B) by a motion under Rule 12(c); or

(C) at trial.

(3) *Lack of Subject-Matter Jurisdiction.* If the court determines at any time that it lacks subject-matter jurisdiction, the court must dismiss the action.

(i) Hearing Before Trial. If a party so moves, any defense listed in Rule 12(b)(1)-(7)—whether made in a pleading or by motion—and a motion under Rule 12(c) must be heard and decided before trial unless the court orders a deferral until trial.

[Amended December 27, 1946, effective March 19, 1948; January 21, 1963, effective July 1, 1963; February 28, 1966, effective July 1, 1966; March 2, 1987, effective August 1, 1987; April 22, 1993, effective December 1, 1993; April 17, 2000, effective December 1, 2000; April 30, 2007, effective December 1, 2007.]

RULE 13. COUNTERCLAIM AND CROSSCLAIM

(a) Compulsory Counterclaim.

(1) *In General.* A pleading must state as a counterclaim any claim that—at the time of its service—the pleader has against an opposing party if the claim:

(A) arises out of the transaction or occurrence that is the subject matter of the opposing party's claim; and

(B) does not require adding another party over whom the court cannot acquire jurisdiction.

(2) *Exceptions.* The pleader need not state the claim if:

(A) when the action was commenced, the claim was the subject of another pending action; or

(B) the opposing party sued on its claim by attachment or other process that did not establish personal jurisdiction over the pleader on that claim, and the pleader does not assert any counterclaim under this rule.

(b) Permissive Counterclaim. A pleading may state as a counterclaim against an opposing party any claim that is not compulsory.

(c) Relief Sought in a Counterclaim. A counterclaim need not diminish or defeat the recovery sought by the opposing party. It may request relief that exceeds in amount or differs in kind from the relief sought by the opposing party.

(d) Counterclaim Against the United States. These rules do not expand the right to assert a counterclaim—or to claim a credit—against the United States or a United States officer or agency.

(e) Counterclaim Maturing or Acquired After Pleading. The court may permit a party to file a supplemental pleading asserting a counterclaim that matured or was acquired by the party after serving an earlier pleading.

(f) Omitted Counterclaim. The court may permit a party to amend a pleading to add a counterclaim if it was omitted through oversight, inadvertence, or excusable neglect or if justice so requires.

(g) Crossclaim Against a Coparty. A pleading may state as a crossclaim any claim by one party against a coparty if the claim arises out of the transaction or occurrence that is the subject matter of the original action or of a counterclaim, or if the claim relates to any property that is the subject matter of the original action. The crossclaim may include a claim that the coparty is or may be liable to the cross-claimant for all or part of a claim asserted in the action against the cross-claimant.

(h) Joining Additional Parties. Rules 19 and 20 govern the addition of a person as a party to a counterclaim or crossclaim.

(i) Separate Trials; Separate Judgments. If the court orders separate trials under Rule 42(b), it may enter judgment on a counterclaim or crossclaim under Rule 54(b) when it has jurisdiction to do so, even if the opposing party's claims have been dismissed or otherwise resolved.

[Amended December 27, 1946, effective March 19, 1948; January 21, 1963, effective July 1, 1963; February 28, 1966, effective July 1, 1966; March 2, 1987, effective August 1, 1987; April 30, 2007, effective December 1, 2007.]

RULE 14. THIRD–PARTY PRACTICE

(a) When a Defending Party May Bring in a Third Party.

(1) *Timing of the Summons and Complaint.* A defending party may, as third-party plaintiff, serve a summons and complaint on a nonparty who is or may be liable to it for all or part of the claim against it. But the third-party plaintiff must, by motion, obtain the court's leave if it files the third-party complaint more than 10 days after serving its original answer.

(2) *Third–Party Defendant's Claims and Defenses.* The person served with the summons and third-party complaint—the "third-party defendant":

(A) must assert any defense against the third-party plaintiff's claim under Rule 12;

(B) must assert any counterclaim against the third-party plaintiff under Rule 13(a), and may assert any counterclaim against the third-party plaintiff under Rule 13(b) or any crossclaim against another third-party defendant under Rule 13(g);

(C) may assert against the plaintiff any defense that the third-party plaintiff has to the plaintiff's claim; and

(D) may also assert against the plaintiff any claim arising out of the transaction or occurrence that is the subject matter of the plaintiff's claim against the third-party plaintiff.

(3) *Plaintiff's Claims Against a Third–Party Defendant.* The plaintiff may assert against the third-party defendant any claim arising out of the transaction or occurrence that is the subject matter of the plaintiff's claim against the third-party plaintiff. The third-party defendant must then assert any defense under Rule 12 and any counterclaim under Rule 13(a), and may assert any counterclaim under Rule 13(b) or any crossclaim under Rule 13(g).

(4) *Motion to Strike, Sever, or Try Separately.* Any party may move to strike the third-party claim, to sever it, or to try it separately.

(5) *Third–Party Defendant's Claim Against a Nonparty.* A third-party defendant may proceed under this rule against a nonparty who is or may be liable to the third-party defendant for all or part of any claim against it.

(6) *Third–Party Complaint In Rem.* If it is within the admiralty or maritime jurisdiction, a third-party complaint may be in rem. In that event, a reference in this rule to the "summons" includes the warrant of arrest, and a reference to the defendant or third-party plaintiff includes, when appropriate, a person who asserts a right under Supplemental Rule C(6)(a)(i) in the property arrested.

(b) When a Plaintiff May Bring in a Third Party. When a claim is asserted against a plaintiff, the plaintiff may bring in a third party if this rule would allow a defendant to do so.

(c) Admiralty or Maritime Claim.

(1) *Scope of Impleader.* If a plaintiff asserts an admiralty or maritime claim under Rule 9(h), the defendant or a person who asserts a right under Supplemental Rule C(6)(a)(i) may, as a third-party plaintiff, bring in a third-party defendant who may be wholly or partly liable—either to the plaintiff or to the third-party plaintiff—for remedy over, contribution, or otherwise on account of the same transaction, occurrence, or series of transactions or occurrences.

(2) *Defending Against a Demand for Judgment for the Plaintiff.* The third-party plaintiff may demand judgment in the plaintiff's favor against the third-party defendant. In that event, the third-party defendant must defend under Rule 12 against the plaintiff's claim as well as the third-party plaintiff's claim; and the action proceeds as if the plaintiff had sued both the third-party defendant and the third-party plaintiff.

[Amended December 27, 1946, effective March 19, 1948; January 21, 1963, effective July 1, 1963; February 28, 1966, effective July 1, 1966; March 2, 1987, effective August 1, 1987; April 17, 2000, effective December 1, 2000; April 12, 2006, effective December 1, 2006; April 30, 2007, effective December 1, 2007.]

RULE 15. AMENDED AND SUPPLEMENTAL PLEADINGS

(a) Amendments Before Trial.

(1) *Amending as a Matter of Course.* A party may amend its pleading once as a matter of course:

(A) before being served with a responsive pleading; or

(B) within 20 days after serving the pleading if a responsive pleading is not allowed and the action is not yet on the trial calendar.

(2) *Other Amendments.* In all other cases, a party may amend its pleading only with the opposing party's written consent or the court's leave. The court should freely give leave when justice so requires.

(3) *Time to Respond.* Unless the court orders otherwise, any required response to an amended pleading must be made within the time remaining to respond to the original pleading or within 10 days after service of the amended pleading, whichever is later.

(b) Amendments During and After Trial.

(1) *Based on an Objection at Trial.* If, at trial, a party objects that evidence is not within the issues raised in the pleadings, the court may permit the pleadings to be amended. The court should freely permit an amendment when doing so will aid in presenting the merits and the objecting party fails to satisfy the court that the evidence would prejudice that party's action or defense on the merits. The court may grant a continuance to enable the objecting party to meet the evidence.

(2) *For Issues Tried by Consent.* When an issue not raised by the pleadings is tried by the parties' express or implied consent, it must be treated in all respects as if raised in the pleadings. A party may move—at any time, even after judgment—to amend the pleadings to conform them to the evidence and to raise an unpleaded issue. But failure to amend does not affect the result of the trial of that issue.

(c) Relation Back of Amendments.

(1) *When an Amendment Relates Back.* An amendment to a pleading relates back to the date of the original pleading when:

(A) the law that provides the applicable statute of limitations allows relation back;

(B) the amendment asserts a claim or defense that arose out of the conduct, transaction, or occurrence set out—or attempted to be set out—in the original pleading; or

(C) the amendment changes the party or the naming of the party against whom a claim is asserted, if Rule 15(c)(1)(B) is satisfied and if, within the period provided by Rule 4(m) for serving the summons and complaint, the party to be brought in by amendment:

(i) received such notice of the action that it will not be prejudiced in defending on the merits; and

(ii) knew or should have known that the action would have been brought against it, but for a mistake concerning the proper party's identity.

(2) *Notice to the United States.* When the United States or a United States officer or agency is added as a defendant by amendment, the notice requirements of Rule 15(c)(1)(C)(i) and (ii) are satisfied if, during the stated period, process was delivered or mailed to the United States attorney or the United States attorney's designee, to the Attorney General of the United States, or to the officer or agency.

(d) Supplemental Pleadings. On motion and reasonable notice, the court may, on just terms, permit a party to serve a supplemental pleading setting out any transaction, occurrence, or event that happened after the date of the pleading to be supplemented. The court may permit supplementation even though the original pleading is defective in stating a claim or defense. The court may order that the opposing party plead to the supplemental pleading within a specified time.

[Amended January 21, 1963, effective July 1, 1963; February 28, 1966, effective July 1, 1966; March 2, 1987, effective August 1, 1987; April 30, 1991, effective December 1, 1991; amended by Pub.L. 102–198, § 11, December 9, 1991, 105 Stat. 1626; amended April 22, 1993, effective December 1, 1993; April 30, 2007, effective December 1, 2007.]

RULE 16. PRETRIAL CONFERENCES; SCHEDULING; MANAGEMENT

(a) Purposes of a Pretrial Conference. In any action, the court may order the attorneys and any unrepresented parties to appear for one or more pretrial conferences for such purposes as:

(1) expediting disposition of the action;

(2) establishing early and continuing control so that the case will not be protracted because of lack of management;

(3) discouraging wasteful pretrial activities;

(4) improving the quality of the trial through more thorough preparation; and

(5) facilitating settlement.

(b) Scheduling.

(1) *Scheduling Order.* Except in categories of actions exempted by local rule, the district judge—or a magistrate judge when authorized by local rule—must issue a scheduling order:

(A) after receiving the parties' report under Rule 26(f); or

(B) after consulting with the parties' attorneys and any unrepresented parties at a scheduling conference or by telephone, mail, or other means.

(2) *Time to Issue.* The judge must issue the scheduling order as soon as practicable, but in any event within the earlier of 120 days after any defendant has been served with the complaint or 90 days after any defendant has appeared.

(3) *Contents of the Order.*

(A) Required Contents. The scheduling order must limit the time to join other parties, amend the pleadings, complete discovery, and file motions.

(B) Permitted Contents. The scheduling order may:

(i) modify the timing of disclosures under Rules 26(a) and 26(e)(1);

(ii) modify the extent of discovery;

(iii) provide for disclosure or discovery of electronically stored information;

(iv) include any agreements the parties reach for asserting claims of privilege or of protection as trial-preparation material after information is produced;

(v) set dates for pretrial conferences and for trial; and

(vi) include other appropriate matters.

(4) *Modifying a Schedule.* A schedule may be modified only for good cause and with the judge's consent.

(c) Attendance and Matters for Consideration at a Pretrial Conference.

(1) *Attendance.* A represented party must authorize at least one of its attorneys to make stipulations and admissions about all matters that can reasonably be anticipated for discussion at a pretrial conference. If appropriate, the court may require that a party or its representative be present or reasonably available by other means to consider possible settlement.

(2) *Matters for Consideration.* At any pretrial conference, the court may consider and take appropriate action on the following matters:

(A) formulating and simplifying the issues, and eliminating frivolous claims or defenses;

(B) amending the pleadings if necessary or desirable;

(C) obtaining admissions and stipulations about facts and documents to avoid unnecessary proof, and ruling in advance on the admissibility of evidence;

(D) avoiding unnecessary proof and cumulative evidence, and limiting the use of testimony under Federal Rule of Evidence 702;

(E) determining the appropriateness and timing of summary adjudication under Rule 56;

(F) controlling and scheduling discovery, including orders affecting disclosures and discovery under Rule 26 and Rules 29 through 37;

(G) identifying witnesses and documents, scheduling the filing and exchange of any pretrial briefs, and setting dates for further conferences and for trial;

(H) referring matters to a magistrate judge or a master;

(I) settling the case and using special procedures to assist in resolving the dispute when authorized by statute or local rule;

(J) determining the form and content of the pretrial order;

(K) disposing of pending motions;

(L) adopting special procedures for managing potentially difficult or protracted actions that may involve complex issues, multiple parties, difficult legal questions, or unusual proof problems;

(M) ordering a separate trial under Rule 42(b) of a claim, counterclaim, crossclaim, third-party claim, or particular issue;

(N) ordering the presentation of evidence early in the trial on a manageable issue that might, on the evidence, be the basis for a judgment as a matter of law under Rule 50(a) or a judgment on partial findings under Rule 52(c);

(O) establishing a reasonable limit on the time allowed to present evidence; and

(P) facilitating in other ways the just, speedy, and inexpensive disposition of the action.

(d) Pretrial Orders. After any conference under this rule, the court should issue an order reciting the action taken. This order controls the course of the action unless the court modifies it.

(e) Final Pretrial Conference and Orders. The court may hold a final pretrial conference to formulate a trial plan, including a plan to facilitate the admission of evidence. The conference must be held as close to the start of trial as is reasonable, and must be attended by at least one attorney who will conduct the trial for each party and by any unrepresented party. The court may modify the order issued after a final pretrial conference only to prevent manifest injustice.

(f) Sanctions.

(1) *In General.* On motion or on its own, the court may issue any just orders, including those authorized by Rule 37(b)(2)(A)(ii)-(vii), if a party or its attorney:

(A) fails to appear at a scheduling or other pretrial conference;

(B) is substantially unprepared to participate—or does not participate in good faith—in the conference; or

(C) fails to obey a scheduling or other pretrial order.

(2) *Imposing Fees and Costs.* Instead of or in addition to any other sanction, the court must order the party, its attorney, or both to pay the reasonable expenses—including attorney's fees—incurred because of any noncompliance with this rule, unless the noncompliance was substantially justified or other circumstances make an award of expenses unjust.

[Amended April 28, 1983, effective August 1, 1983; March 2, 1987, effective August 1, 1987; April 22, 1993, effective December 1, 1993; April 12, 2006, effective December 1, 2006; April 30, 2007, effective December 1, 2007.]

TITLE IV. PARTIES

RULE 17. PLAINTIFF AND DEFENDANT; CAPACITY; PUBLIC OFFICERS

(a) Real Party in Interest.

(1) *Designation in General.* An action must be prosecuted in the name of the real party in interest. The following may sue in their own names without joining the person for whose benefit the action is brought:

(A) an executor;

(B) an administrator;

(C) a guardian;

(D) a bailee;

(E) a trustee of an express trust;

(F) a party with whom or in whose name a contract has been made for another's benefit; and

(G) a party authorized by statute.

(2) *Action in the Name of the United States for Another's Use or Benefit.* When a federal statute so provides, an action for another's use or benefit must be brought in the name of the United States.

(3) *Joinder of the Real Party in Interest.* The court may not dismiss an action for failure to prosecute in the name of the real party in interest until, after an objection, a reasonable time has been allowed for the real party in interest to ratify, join, or be substituted into the action. After ratification, joinder, or substitution, the action proceeds as if it had been originally commenced by the real party in interest.

(b) Capacity to Sue or Be Sued. Capacity to sue or be sued is determined as follows:

(1) for an individual who is not acting in a representative capacity, by the law of the individual's domicile;

(2) for a corporation, by the law under which it was organized; and

(3) for all other parties, by the law of the state where the court is located, except that:

(A) a partnership or other unincorporated association with no such capacity under that state's law may sue or be sued in its common name to enforce a substantive right existing under the United States Constitution or laws; and

(B) 28 U.S.C. §§ 754 and 959(a) govern the capacity of a receiver appointed by a United States court to sue or be sued in a United States court.

(c) Minor or Incompetent Person.

(1) *With a Representative.* The following representatives may sue or defend on behalf of a minor or an incompetent person:

(A) a general guardian;

(B) a committee;

(C) a conservator; or

(D) a like fiduciary.

(2) *Without a Representative.* A minor or an incompetent person who does not have a duly appointed representative may sue by a next friend or by a guardian ad litem. The court must appoint a guardian ad litem—or issue another appropriate order—to protect a minor or incompetent person who is unrepresented in an action.

(d) Public Officer's Title and Name. A public officer who sues or is sued in an official capacity may be designated by official title rather than by name, but the court may order that the officer's name be added.

[Amended December 27, 1946, effective March 19, 1948; December 29, 1948, effective October 20, 1949; February 28, 1966, effective July 1, 1966; March 2, 1987, effective August 1, 1987; April 25, 1988, effective August 1, 1988; amended by Pub.L. 100–690, Title VII, § 7049, November 18, 1988, 102 Stat. 4401 (although amendment by Pub.L. 100–690 could not be executed due to prior amendment by Court order which made the same change effective August 1, 1988); April 30, 2007, effective December 1, 2007.]

RULE 18. JOINDER OF CLAIMS

(a) In General. A party asserting a claim, counterclaim, crossclaim, or third-party claim may join, as independent or alternative claims, as many claims as it has against an opposing party.

(b) Joinder of Contingent Claims. A party may join two claims even though one of them is contingent on the disposition of the other; but the court may grant relief only in accordance with the parties' relative substantive rights. In particular, a plaintiff may state a claim for money and a claim to set aside a conveyance that is fraudulent as to that plaintiff, without first obtaining a judgment for the money.

[Amended February 28, 1966, effective July 1, 1966; March 2, 1987, effective August 1, 1987; April 30, 2007, effective December 1, 2007.]

RULE 19. REQUIRED JOINDER OF PARTIES

(a) Persons Required to Be Joined if Feasible.

(1) *Required Party.* A person who is subject to service of process and whose joinder will not deprive the court of subject-matter jurisdiction must be joined as a party if:

(A) in that person's absence, the court cannot accord complete relief among existing parties; or

(B) that person claims an interest relating to the subject of the action and is so situated that disposing of the action in the person's absence may:

(i) as a practical matter impair or impede the person's ability to protect the interest; or

(ii) leave an existing party subject to a substantial risk of incurring double, multiple, or otherwise inconsistent obligations because of the interest.

(2) *Joinder by Court Order.* If a person has not been joined as required, the court must order that the person be made a party. A person who refuses to join as a plaintiff may be made either a defendant or, in a proper case, an involuntary plaintiff.

(3) *Venue.* If a joined party objects to venue and the joinder would make venue improper, the court must dismiss that party.

(b) When Joinder Is Not Feasible. If a person who is required to be joined if feasible cannot be joined, the court must determine whether, in equity and good conscience, the action should proceed among the existing parties or should be dismissed. The factors for the court to consider include:

(1) the extent to which a judgment rendered in the person's absence might prejudice that person or the existing parties;

(2) the extent to which any prejudice could be lessened or avoided by:

(A) protective provisions in the judgment;

(B) shaping the relief; or

(C) other measures;

(3) whether a judgment rendered in the person's absence would be adequate; and

(4) whether the plaintiff would have an adequate remedy if the action were dismissed for nonjoinder.

(c) Pleading the Reasons for Nonjoinder. When asserting a claim for relief, a party must state:

(1) the name, if known, of any person who is required to be joined if feasible but is not joined; and

(2) the reasons for not joining that person.

(d) Exception for Class Actions. This rule is subject to Rule 23.

[Amended February 28, 1966, effective July 1, 1966; March 2, 1987, effective August 1, 1987; April 30, 2007, effective December 1, 2007.]

RULE 20. PERMISSIVE JOINDER OF PARTIES

(a) Persons Who May Join or Be Joined.

(1) *Plaintiffs.* Persons may join in one action as plaintiffs if:

(A) they assert any right to relief jointly, severally, or in the alternative with respect to or arising out of the same transaction, occurrence, or series of transactions or occurrences; and

(B) any question of law or fact common to all plaintiffs will arise in the action.

(2) *Defendants.* Persons—as well as a vessel, cargo, or other property subject to admiralty process in rem—may be joined in one action as defendants if:

(A) any right to relief is asserted against them jointly, severally, or in the alternative with respect to or arising out of the same transaction, occurrence, or series of transactions or occurrences; and

(B) any question of law or fact common to all defendants will arise in the action.

(3) *Extent of Relief.* Neither a plaintiff nor a defendant need be interested in obtaining or defending against all the relief demanded. The court may grant judgment to one or more plaintiffs according to their rights, and against one or more defendants according to their liabilities.

(b) Protective Measures. The court may issue orders—including an order for separate trials—to protect a party against embarrassment, delay, expense, or other prejudice that arises from including a person against whom the party asserts no claim and who asserts no claim against the party.

[Amended February 28, 1966, effective July 1, 1966; March 2, 1987, effective August 1, 1987; April 30, 2007, effective December 1, 2007.]

RULE 21. MISJOINDER AND NONJOINDER OF PARTIES

Misjoinder of parties is not a ground for dismissing an action. On motion or on its own, the court may at any time, on just terms, add or drop a party. The court may also sever any claim against a party.

[Amended April 30, 2007, effective December 1, 2007.]

RULE 22. INTERPLEADER

(a) Grounds.

(1) *By a Plaintiff.* Persons with claims that may expose a plaintiff to double or multiple liability may be joined as defendants and required to interplead. Joinder for interpleader is proper even though:

(A) the claims of the several claimants, or the titles on which their claims depend, lack a common origin or are adverse and independent rather than identical; or

(B) the plaintiff denies liability in whole or in part to any or all of the claimants.

(2) *By a Defendant.* A defendant exposed to similar liability may seek interpleader through a crossclaim or counterclaim.

(b) Relation to Other Rules and Statutes. This rule supplements—and does not limit—the joinder of parties allowed by Rule 20. The remedy this rule provides is in addition to—and does not supersede or limit—the remedy provided by 28 U.S.C. §§ 1335, 1397, and 2361. An action under those statutes must be conducted under these rules.

[Amended December 29, 1948, effective October 20, 1949; March 2, 1987, effective August 1, 1987; April 30, 2007, effective December 1, 2007.]

RULE 23. CLASS ACTIONS

(a) Prerequisites. One or more members of a class may sue or be sued as representative parties on behalf of all members only if:

(1) the class is so numerous that joinder of all members is impracticable;

(2) there are questions of law or fact common to the class;

(3) the claims or defenses of the representative parties are typical of the claims or defenses of the class; and

(4) the representative parties will fairly and adequately protect the interests of the class.

(b) Types of Class Actions. A class action may be maintained if Rule 23(a) is satisfied and if:

(1) prosecuting separate actions by or against individual class members would create a risk of:

(A) inconsistent or varying adjudications with respect to individual class members that would establish incompatible standards of conduct for the party opposing the class; or

(B) adjudications with respect to individual class members that, as a practical matter, would be dispositive of the interests of the other members not parties to the individual adjudications or would substantially impair or impede their ability to protect their interests;

(2) the party opposing the class has acted or refused to act on grounds that apply generally to the class, so that final injunctive relief or corresponding declaratory relief is appropriate respecting the class as a whole; or

(3) the court finds that the questions of law or fact common to class members predominate over any questions affecting only individual members, and that a class action is superior to other available methods for fairly and efficiently adjudicating the controversy. The matters pertinent to these findings include:

(A) the class members' interests in individually controlling the prosecution or defense of separate actions;

(B) the extent and nature of any litigation concerning the controversy already begun by or against class members;

(C) the desirability or undesirability of concentrating the litigation of the claims in the particular forum; and

(D) the likely difficulties in managing a class action.

(c) Certification Order; Notice to Class Members; Judgment; Issues Classes; Subclasses.

(1) *Certification Order.*

(A) Time to Issue. At an early practicable time after a person sues or is sued as a class representative, the court must determine by order whether to certify the action as a class action.

(B) Defining the Class; Appointing Class Counsel. An order that certifies a class action must define the class and the class claims, issues, or defenses, and must appoint class counsel under Rule 23(g).

(C) Altering or Amending the Order. An order that grants or denies class certification may be altered or amended before final judgment.

(2) *Notice.*

(A) For (b)(1) or (b)(2) Classes. For any class certified under Rule 23(b)(1) or (b)(2), the court may direct appropriate notice to the class.

(B) For (b)(3) Classes. For any class certified under Rule 23(b)(3), the court must direct to class members the best notice that is practicable under the circumstances, including individual notice to all members who can be identified through reasonable effort. The notice must clearly and concisely state in plain, easily understood language:

(i) the nature of the action;

(ii) the definition of the class certified;

(iii) the class claims, issues, or defenses;

(iv) that a class member may enter an appearance through an attorney if the member so desires;

(v) that the court will exclude from the class any member who requests exclusion;

(vi) the time and manner for requesting exclusion; and

(vii) the binding effect of a class judgment on members under Rule 23(c)(3).

(3) *Judgment.* Whether or not favorable to the class, the judgment in a class action must:

(A) for any class certified under Rule 23(b)(1) or (b)(2), include and describe those whom the court finds to be class members; and

(B) for any class certified under Rule 23(b)(3), include and specify or describe those to whom the Rule 23(c)(2) notice was directed, who have not requested exclusion, and whom the court finds to be class members.

(4) *Particular Issues.* When appropriate, an action may be brought or maintained as a class action with respect to particular issues.

(5) *Subclasses.* When appropriate, a class may be divided into subclasses that are each treated as a class under this rule.

(d) Conducting the Action.

(1) *In General.* In conducting an action under this rule, the court may issue orders that:

(A) determine the course of proceedings or prescribe measures to prevent undue repetition or complication in presenting evidence or argument;

(B) require—to protect class members and fairly conduct the action—giving appropriate notice to some or all class members of:

(i) any step in the action;

(ii) the proposed extent of the judgment; or

(iii) the members' opportunity to signify whether they consider the representation fair and adequate, to intervene and present claims or defenses, or to otherwise come into the action;

(C) impose conditions on the representative parties or on intervenors;

(D) require that the pleadings be amended to eliminate allegations about representation of absent persons and that the action proceed accordingly; or

(E) deal with similar procedural matters.

(2) *Combining and Amending Orders.* An order under Rule 23(d)(1) may be altered or amended from time to time and may be combined with an order under Rule 16.

(e) Settlement, Voluntary Dismissal, or Compromise. The claims, issues, or defenses of a certified class may be settled, voluntarily dismissed, or compromised only with the court's approval. The following procedures apply to a proposed settlement, voluntary dismissal, or compromise:

(1) The court must direct notice in a reasonable manner to all class members who would be bound by the proposal.

(2) If the proposal would bind class members, the court may approve it only after a hearing and on finding that it is fair, reasonable, and adequate.

(3) The parties seeking approval must file a statement identifying any agreement made in connection with the proposal.

(4) If the class action was previously certified under Rule 23(b)(3), the court may refuse to approve a settlement unless it affords a new opportunity to request exclusion to individual class members who had an earlier opportunity to request exclusion but did not do so.

(5) Any class member may object to the proposal if it requires court approval under this subdivision (e); the objection may be withdrawn only with the court's approval.

(f) Appeals. A court of appeals may permit an appeal from an order granting or denying class-action certification under this rule if a petition for permission to appeal is filed with the circuit clerk within 10 days after the order is entered. An appeal does not stay proceedings in the district court unless the district judge or the court of appeals so orders.

(g) Class Counsel.

(1) *Appointing Class Counsel.* Unless a statute provides otherwise, a court that certifies a class must appoint class counsel. In appointing class counsel, the court:

(A) must consider:

(i) the work counsel has done in identifying or investigating potential claims in the action;

(ii) counsel's experience in handling class actions, other complex litigation, and the types of claims asserted in the action;

(iii) counsel's knowledge of the applicable law; and

(iv) the resources that counsel will commit to representing the class;

(B) may consider any other matter pertinent to counsel's ability to fairly and adequately represent the interests of the class;

(C) may order potential class counsel to provide information on any subject pertinent to the appointment and to propose terms for attorney's fees and nontaxable costs;

(D) may include in the appointing order provisions about the award of attorney's fees or nontaxable costs under Rule 23(h); and

(E) may make further orders in connection with the appointment.

(2) *Standard for Appointing Class Counsel.* When one applicant seeks appointment as class counsel, the court may appoint that applicant only if the applicant is adequate under Rule 23(g)(1) and (4). If more than one adequate applicant seeks appointment, the court must appoint the applicant best able to represent the interests of the class.

(3) *Interim Counsel.* The court may designate interim counsel to act on behalf of a putative class before determining whether to certify the action as a class action.

(4) *Duty of Class Counsel.* Class counsel must fairly and adequately represent the interests of the class.

(h) Attorney's Fees and Nontaxable Costs. In a certified class action, the court may award reasonable attorney's fees and nontaxable costs that are authorized by law or by the parties' agreement. The following procedures apply:

(1) A claim for an award must be made by motion under Rule 54(d)(2), subject to the provisions of this subdivision (h), at a time the court sets. Notice of the motion must be served on all parties and, for motions by class counsel, directed to class members in a reasonable manner.

(2) A class member, or a party from whom payment is sought, may object to the motion.

(3) The court may hold a hearing and must find the facts and state its legal conclusions under Rule 52(a).

(4) The court may refer issues related to the amount of the award to a special master or a magistrate judge, as provided in Rule 54(d)(2)(D).

[Amended February 28, 1966, effective July 1, 1966; March 2, 1987, effective August 1, 1987; April 24, 1998, effective December 1, 1998; March 27, 2003, effective December 1, 2003; April 30, 2007, effective December 1, 2007.]

RULE 23.1 DERIVATIVE ACTIONS

(a) Prerequisites. This rule applies when one or more shareholders or members of a corporation or an unincorporated association bring a derivative action to enforce a right that the corporation or association may properly assert but has failed to enforce. The derivative action may not be maintained if it appears that the plaintiff does not fairly and adequately represent the interests of shareholders or members who are similarly situated in enforcing the right of the corporation or association.

(b) Pleading Requirements. The complaint must be verified and must:

(1) allege that the plaintiff was a shareholder or member at the time of the transaction complained of, or that the plaintiff's share or membership later devolved on it by operation of law;

(2) allege that the action is not a collusive one to confer jurisdiction that the court would otherwise lack; and

(3) state with particularity:

(A) any effort by the plaintiff to obtain the desired action from the directors or comparable authority and, if necessary, from the shareholders or members; and

(B) the reasons for not obtaining the action or not making the effort.

(c) Settlement, Dismissal, and Compromise. A derivative action may be settled, voluntarily dismissed, or compromised only with the court's approval. Notice of a proposed settlement, voluntary dismissal, or compromise must be given to shareholders or members in the manner that the court orders.

[Adopted February 28, 1966, effective July 1, 1966; amended March 2, 1987, effective August 1, 1987; April 30, 2007, effective December 1, 2007.]

RULE 23.2 ACTIONS RELATING TO UNINCORPORATED ASSOCIATIONS

This rule applies to an action brought by or against the members of an unincorporated association as a class by naming certain members as representative parties. The action may be maintained only if it appears that those parties will fairly and adequately protect the interests of the association and its members. In conducting the action, the court may issue any appropriate orders corresponding with those in Rule 23(d), and the procedure for settlement, voluntary dismissal, or compromise must correspond with the procedure in Rule 23(e).

[Adopted February 28, 1966, effective July 1, 1966; amended April 30, 2007, effective December 1, 2007.]

RULE 24. INTERVENTION

(a) Intervention of Right. On timely motion, the court must permit anyone to intervene who:

(1) is given an unconditional right to intervene by a federal statute; or

(2) claims an interest relating to the property or transaction that is the subject of the action, and is so situated that disposing of the action may as a practical matter impair or impede the movant's ability to protect its interest, unless existing parties adequately represent that interest.

(b) Permissive Intervention.

(1) *In General.* On timely motion, the court may permit anyone to intervene who:

(A) is given a conditional right to intervene by a federal statute; or

(B) has a claim or defense that shares with the main action a common question of law or fact.

(2) *By a Government Officer or Agency.* On timely motion, the court may permit a federal or state governmental officer or agency to intervene if a party's claim or defense is based on:

(A) a statute or executive order administered by the officer or agency; or

(B) any regulation, order, requirement, or agreement issued or made under the statute or executive order.

(3) *Delay or Prejudice.* In exercising its discretion, the court must consider whether the intervention will unduly delay or prejudice the adjudication of the original parties' rights.

(c) Notice and Pleading Required. A motion to intervene must be served on the parties as provided in Rule 5. The motion must state the grounds for intervention and be accompanied by a pleading that sets out the claim or defense for which intervention is sought.

[Amended December 27, 1946, effective March 19, 1948; December 29, 1948, effective October 20, 1949; January 21, 1963, effective July 1, 1963; February 28, 1966, effective July 1, 1966; March 2, 1987, effective August 1, 1987; April 30, 1991, effective December 1, 1991; April 12, 2006, effective December 1, 2006; April 30, 2007, effective December 1, 2007.]

RULE 25. SUBSTITUTION OF PARTIES

(a) Death.

(1) *Substitution if the Claim Is Not Extinguished.* If a party dies and the claim is not extinguished, the court may order substitution of the proper party. A motion for substitution may be made by any party or by the decedent's successor or representative. If the motion is not made within 90 days after service of a statement noting the death, the action by or against the decedent must be dismissed.

(2) *Continuation Among the Remaining Parties.* After a party's death, if the right sought to be enforced survives only to or against the remaining parties, the action does not abate, but proceeds in favor of or against the remaining parties. The death should be noted on the record.

(3) *Service.* A motion to substitute, together with a notice of hearing, must be served on the parties as provided in Rule 5 and on nonparties as provided in Rule 4. A statement noting death must be served in the same manner. Service may be made in any judicial district.

(b) Incompetency. If a party becomes incompetent, the court may, on motion, permit the action to be continued by or against the party's representative. The motion must be served as provided in Rule 25(a)(3).

(c) Transfer of Interest. If an interest is transferred, the action may be continued by or against the original party unless the court, on motion, orders the transferee to be substituted in the action or joined with the original party. The motion must be served as provided in Rule 25(a)(3).

(d) Public Officers; Death or Separation from Office. An action does not abate when a public officer who is a party in an official capacity dies, resigns, or otherwise ceases to hold office while the action is pending. The officer's successor is automatically substituted as a party. Later proceedings should be in the substituted party's name, but any misnomer not affecting the parties' substantial rights must be disregarded. The court may order substitution at any time, but the absence of such an order does not affect the substitution.

[Amended December 29, 1948, effective October 20, 1949; April 17, 1961, effective July 19, 1961; January 21, 1963, effective July 1, 1963; March 2, 1987, effective August 1, 1987; April 30, 2007, effective December 1, 2007.]

TITLE V. DISCLOSURES AND DISCOVERY

RULE 26. DUTY TO DISCLOSE; GENERAL PROVISIONS GOVERNING DISCOVERY

(a) Required Disclosures.

(1) *Initial Disclosure.*

(A) In General. Except as exempted by Rule 26(a)(1)(B) or as otherwise stipulated or ordered by the court, a party must, without awaiting a discovery request, provide to the other parties:

(i) the name and, if known, the address and telephone number of each individual likely to have discoverable information—along with the subjects of that information—that the disclosing party may use to support its claims or defenses, unless the use would be solely for impeachment;

(ii) a copy—or a description by category and location—of all documents, electronically stored information, and tangible things that the disclosing party has in its possession, custody, or control and may use to support its claims or defenses, unless the use would be solely for impeachment;

(iii) a computation of each category of damages claimed by the disclosing party—who must also make available for inspection and copying as under Rule 34 the documents or other evidentiary material, unless privileged or protected from disclosure, on which each computation is based, including materials bearing on the nature and extent of injuries suffered; and

(iv) for inspection and copying as under Rule 34, any insurance agreement under which an insurance business may be liable to satisfy all or part of a possible judgment in the action or to indemnify or reimburse for payments made to satisfy the judgment.

(B) Proceedings Exempt from Initial Disclosure. The following proceedings are exempt from initial disclosure:

(i) an action for review on an administrative record;

(ii) a forfeiture action in rem arising from a federal statute;

(iii) a petition for habeas corpus or any other proceeding to challenge a criminal conviction or sentence;

(iv) an action brought without an attorney by a person in the custody of the United States, a state, or a state subdivision;

(v) an action to enforce or quash an administrative summons or subpoena;

(vi) an action by the United States to recover benefit payments;

(vii) an action by the United States to collect on a student loan guaranteed by the United States;

(viii) a proceeding ancillary to a proceeding in another court; and

(ix) an action to enforce an arbitration award.

(C) Time for Initial Disclosures—In General. A party must make the initial disclosures at or within 14 days after the parties' Rule 26(f) conference unless a different time is set by stipulation or court order, or unless a party objects during the conference that initial disclosures are not appropriate in this action and states the objection in the proposed discovery plan. In ruling on the objection, the court must determine what disclosures, if any, are to be made and must set the time for disclosure.

(D) Time for Initial Disclosures—For Parties Served or Joined Later. A party that is first served or otherwise joined after the Rule 26(f) conference must make the initial disclosures within 30 days after being served or joined, unless a different time is set by stipulation or court order.

(E) Basis for Initial Disclosure; Unacceptable Excuses. A party must make its initial disclosures based on the information then reasonably available to it. A party is not excused from making its disclosures because it has not fully investigated the case or because it challenges the sufficiency of another party's disclosures or because another party has not made its disclosures.

(2) *Disclosure of Expert Testimony.*

(A) In General. In addition to the disclosures required by Rule 26(a)(1), a party must disclose to the other parties the identity of any witness it may use at trial to present evidence under Federal Rule of Evidence 702, 703, or 705.

(B) Written Report. Unless otherwise stipulated or ordered by the court, this disclosure must be accompanied by a written report—prepared and signed by the witness—if the witness is one retained or specially employed to provide expert testimony in the case or one whose duties as the party's employee regularly involve giving expert testimony. The report must contain:

(i) a complete statement of all opinions the witness will express and the basis and reasons for them;

(ii) the data or other information considered by the witness in forming them;

(iii) any exhibits that will be used to summarize or support them;

(iv) the witness's qualifications, including a list of all publications authored in the previous 10 years;

(v) a list of all other cases in which, during the previous four years, the witness testified as an expert at trial or by deposition; and

(vi) a statement of the compensation to be paid for the study and testimony in the case.

(C) Time to Disclose Expert Testimony. A party must make these disclosures at the times and in the sequence that the court orders. Absent a stipulation or a court order, the disclosures must be made:

(i) at least 90 days before the date set for trial or for the case to be ready for trial; or

(ii) if the evidence is intended solely to contradict or rebut evidence on the same subject matter identified by another party under Rule 26(a)(2)(B), within 30 days after the other party's disclosure.

(D) Supplementing the Disclosure. The parties must supplement these disclosures when required under Rule 26(e).

(3) *Pretrial Disclosures.*

(A) In General. In addition to the disclosures required by Rule 26(a)(1) and (2), a party must provide to the other parties and promptly file the following information about the evidence that it may present at trial other than solely for impeachment:

(i) the name and, if not previously provided, the address and telephone number of each witness—separately identifying those the party expects to present and those it may call if the need arises;

(ii) the designation of those witnesses whose testimony the party expects to present by deposition and, if not taken stenographically, a transcript of the pertinent parts of the deposition; and

(iii) an identification of each document or other exhibit, including summaries of other evidence—separately identifying those items the party expects to offer and those it may offer if the need arises.

(B) Time for Pretrial Disclosures; Objections. Unless the court orders otherwise, these disclosures must be made at least 30 days before trial. Within 14 days after they are made, unless the court sets a different time, a party may serve and promptly file a list of the following objections: any objections to the use under Rule 32(a) of a deposition designated by another party under Rule 26(a)(3)(A)(ii); and any objection, together with the grounds for it, that may be made to the admissibility of materials identified under Rule 26(a)(3)(A)(iii). An objection not so made—except for one under Federal Rule of Evidence 402 or 403—is waived unless excused by the court for good cause.

(4) *Form of Disclosures.* Unless the court orders otherwise, all disclosures under Rule 26(a) must be in writing, signed, and served.

(b) Discovery Scope and Limits.

(1) *Scope in General.* Unless otherwise limited by court order, the scope of discovery is as follows:

Parties may obtain discovery regarding any nonprivileged matter that is relevant to any party's claim or defense—including the existence, description, nature, custody, condition, and location of any documents or other tangible things and the identity and location of persons who know of any discoverable matter. For good cause, the court may order discovery of any matter relevant to the subject matter involved in the action. Relevant information need not be admissible at the trial if the discovery appears reasonably calculated to lead to the discovery of admissible evidence. All discovery is subject to the limitations imposed by Rule 26(b)(2)(C).

(2) *Limitations on Frequency and Extent.*

(A) When Permitted. By order, the court may alter the limits in these rules on the number of depositions and interrogatories or on the length of depositions under Rule 30. By order or local rule, the court may also limit the number of requests under Rule 36.

(B) Specific Limitations on Electronically Stored Information. A party need not provide discovery of electronically stored information from sources that the party identifies as not reasonably accessible because of undue burden or cost. On motion to compel discovery or for a protective order, the party from whom discovery is sought must show that the information is not reasonably accessible because of undue burden or cost. If that showing is made, the court may nonetheless order discovery from such sources if the requesting party shows good cause, considering the limitations of Rule 26(b)(2)(C). The court may specify conditions for the discovery.

(C) When Required. On motion or on its own, the court must limit the frequency or extent of discovery otherwise allowed by these rules or by local rule if it determines that:

(i) the discovery sought is unreasonably cumulative or duplicative, or can be obtained from some other source that is more convenient, less burdensome, or less expensive;

(ii) the party seeking discovery has had ample opportunity to obtain the information by discovery in the action; or

(iii) the burden or expense of the proposed discovery outweighs its likely benefit, considering the needs of the case, the amount in controversy, the parties' resources, the importance of the issues at stake in the action, and the importance of the discovery in resolving the issues.

(3) *Trial Preparation: Materials.*

(A) Documents and Tangible Things. Ordinarily, a party may not discover documents and tangible things that are prepared in anticipation of litigation or for trial by or for another party or its representative (including the other party's attorney, consultant, surety, indemnitor, insurer, or agent). But, subject to Rule 26(b)(4), those materials may be discovered if:

(i) they are otherwise discoverable under Rule 26(b)(1); and

(ii) the party shows that it has substantial need for the materials to prepare its case and cannot, without undue hardship, obtain their substantial equivalent by other means.

(B) Protection Against Disclosure. If the court orders discovery of those materials, it must protect against disclosure of the mental impressions, conclusions, opinions, or legal theories of a party's attorney or other representative concerning the litigation.

(C) Previous Statement. Any party or other person may, on request and without the required showing, obtain the person's own previous statement about the action or its subject matter. If the request is refused, the person may move for a court order, and Rule 37(a)(5) applies to the award of expenses. A previous statement is either:

(i) a written statement that the person has signed or otherwise adopted or approved; or

(ii) a contemporaneous stenographic, mechanical, electrical, or other recording—or a transcription of it—that recites substantially verbatim the person's oral statement.

(4) *Trial Preparation: Experts.*

(A) Expert Who May Testify. A party may depose any person who has been identified as an expert whose opinions may be presented at trial. If Rule 26(a)(2)(B) requires a report from the expert, the deposition may be conducted only after the report is provided.

(B) Expert Employed Only for Trial Preparation. Ordinarily, a party may not, by interrogatories or deposition, discover facts known or opinions held by an expert who has been retained or specially employed by another party in anticipation of litigation or to prepare for trial and who is not expected to be called as a witness at trial. But a party may do so only:

(i) as provided in Rule 35(b); or

(ii) on showing exceptional circumstances under which it is impracticable for the party to obtain facts or opinions on the same subject by other means.

(C) Payment. Unless manifest injustice would result, the court must require that the party seeking discovery:

(i) pay the expert a reasonable fee for time spent in responding to discovery under Rule 26(b)(4)(A) or (B); and

(ii) for discovery under (B), also pay the other party a fair portion of the fees and expenses it reasonably incurred in obtaining the expert's facts and opinions.

(5) *Claiming Privilege or Protecting Trial-Preparation Materials.*

(A) Information Withheld. When a party withholds information otherwise discoverable by claiming that the information is privileged or subject to protection as trial-preparation material, the party must:

(i) expressly make the claim; and

(ii) describe the nature of the documents, communications, or tangible things not produced or disclosed—and do so in a manner that, without revealing information itself privileged or protected, will enable other parties to assess the claim.

(B) Information Produced. If information produced in discovery is subject to a claim of privilege or of protection as trial-preparation material, the party making the claim may notify any party that received the information of the claim and the basis for it. After being notified, a party must promptly return, sequester, or destroy the specified information and any copies it has; must not use or disclose the information until the claim is resolved; must take reasonable steps to retrieve the information if the party disclosed it before being notified; and may promptly present the information to the court under seal for a determination of the claim. The producing party must preserve the information until the claim is resolved.

(c) Protective Orders.

(1) *In General.* A party or any person from whom discovery is sought may move for a protective order in the court where the action is pending—or as an alternative on matters relating to a deposition, in the court for the district where the deposition will be taken. The motion must include a certification that the movant has in good faith conferred or attempted to confer with other affected parties in an effort to resolve the dispute without court action. The court may, for good cause, issue an order to protect a party or person from annoyance, embarrassment, oppression, or undue burden or expense, including one or more of the following:

(A) forbidding the disclosure or discovery;

(B) specifying terms, including time and place, for the disclosure or discovery;

(C) prescribing a discovery method other than the one selected by the party seeking discovery;

(D) forbidding inquiry into certain matters, or limiting the scope of disclosure or discovery to certain matters;

(E) designating the persons who may be present while the discovery is conducted;

(F) requiring that a deposition be sealed and opened only on court order;

(G) requiring that a trade secret or other confidential research, development, or commercial information not be revealed or be revealed only in a specified way; and

(H) requiring that the parties simultaneously file specified documents or information in sealed envelopes, to be opened as the court directs.

(2) *Ordering Discovery.* If a motion for a protective order is wholly or partly denied, the court may, on just terms, order that any party or person provide or permit discovery.

(3) *Awarding Expenses.* Rule 37(a)(5) applies to the award of expenses.

(d) Timing and Sequence of Discovery.

(1) *Timing.* A party may not seek discovery from any source before the parties have conferred as required by Rule 26(f), except in a proceeding exempted from initial disclosure under Rule 26(a)(1)(B), or when authorized by these rules, by stipulation, or by court order.

(2) *Sequence.* Unless, on motion, the court orders otherwise for the parties' and witnesses' convenience and in the interests of justice:

(A) methods of discovery may be used in any sequence; and

(B) discovery by one party does not require any other party to delay its discovery.

(e) Supplementing Disclosures and Responses.

(1) *In General.* A party who has made a disclosure under Rule 26(a)—or who has responded to an interrogatory, request for production, or request for admission—must supplement or correct its disclosure or response:

(A) in a timely manner if the party learns that in some material respect the disclosure or response is incomplete or incorrect, and if the additional or corrective information has not otherwise been made known to the other parties during the discovery process or in writing; or

(B) as ordered by the court.

(2) *Expert Witness.* For an expert whose report must be disclosed under Rule 26(a)(2)(B), the party's duty to supplement extends both to information in-

cluded in the report and to information given during the expert's deposition. Any additions or changes to this information must be disclosed by the time the party's pretrial disclosures under Rule 26(a)(3) are due.

(f) Conference of the Parties; Planning for Discovery.

(1) *Conference Timing.* Except in a proceeding exempted from initial disclosure under Rule 26(a)(1)(B) or when the court orders otherwise, the parties must confer as soon as practicable—and in any event at least 21 days before a scheduling conference is to be held or a scheduling order is due under Rule 16(b).

(2) *Conference Content; Parties' Responsibilities.* In conferring, the parties must consider the nature and basis of their claims and defenses and the possibilities for promptly settling or resolving the case; make or arrange for the disclosures required by Rule 26(a)(1); discuss any issues about preserving discoverable information; and develop a proposed discovery plan. The attorneys of record and all unrepresented parties that have appeared in the case are jointly responsible for arranging the conference, for attempting in good faith to agree on the proposed discovery plan, and for submitting to the court within 14 days after the conference a written report outlining the plan. The court may order the parties or attorneys to attend the conference in person.

(3) *Discovery Plan.* A discovery plan must state the parties' views and proposals on:

(A) what changes should be made in the timing, form, or requirement for disclosures under Rule 26(a), including a statement of when initial disclosures were made or will be made;

(B) the subjects on which discovery may be needed, when discovery should be completed, and whether discovery should be conducted in phases or be limited to or focused on particular issues;

(C) any issues about disclosure or discovery of electronically stored information, including the form or forms in which it should be produced;

(D) any issues about claims of privilege or of protection as trial-preparation materials, including—if the parties agree on a procedure to assert these claims after production—whether to ask the court to include their agreement in an order;

(E) what changes should be made in the limitations on discovery imposed under these rules or by local rule, and what other limitations should be imposed; and

(F) any other orders that the court should issue under Rule 26(c) or under Rule 16(b) and (c).

(4) *Expedited Schedule.* If necessary to comply with its expedited schedule for Rule 16(b) conferences, a court may by local rule:

(A) require the parties' conference to occur less than 21 days before the scheduling conference is held or a scheduling order is due under Rule 16(b); and

(B) require the written report outlining the discovery plan to be filed less than 14 days after the parties' conference, or excuse the parties from submitting a written report and permit them to report orally on their discovery plan at the Rule 16(b) conference.

(g) Signing Disclosures and Discovery Requests, Responses, and Objections.

(1) *Signature Required; Effect of Signature.* Every disclosure under Rule 26(a)(1) or (a)(3) and every discovery request, response, or objection must be signed by at least one attorney of record in the attorney's own name—or by the party personally, if unrepresented—and must state the signer's address, e-mail address, and telephone number. By signing, an attorney or party certifies that to the best of the person's knowledge, information, and belief formed after a reasonable inquiry:

(A) with respect to a disclosure, it is complete and correct as of the time it is made; and

(B) with respect to a discovery request, response, or objection, it is:

(i) consistent with these rules and warranted by existing law or by a nonfrivolous argument for extending, modifying, or reversing existing law, or for establishing new law;

(ii) not interposed for any improper purpose, such as to harass, cause unnecessary delay, or needlessly increase the cost of litigation; and

(iii) neither unreasonable nor unduly burdensome or expensive, considering the needs of the case, prior discovery in the case, the amount in controversy, and the importance of the issues at stake in the action.

(2) *Failure to Sign.* Other parties have no duty to act on an unsigned disclosure, request, response, or objection until it is signed, and the court must strike it unless a signature is promptly supplied after the omission is called to the attorney's or party's attention.

(3) *Sanction for Improper Certification.* If a certification violates this rule without substantial justification, the court, on motion or on its own, must impose an appropriate sanction on the signer, the party on whose behalf the signer was acting, or both. The sanction may include an order to pay the reasonable expenses, including attorney's fees, caused by the violation.

[Amended December 27, 1946, effective March 19, 1948; January 21, 1963, effective July 1, 1963; February 28, 1966, effective July 1, 1966; March 30, 1970, effective July 1, 1970; April 29, 1980, effective August 1, 1980; April 28, 1983, effective August 1, 1983; March 2, 1987, effective August 1,

1987; April 22, 1993, effective December 1, 1993; April 17, 2000, effective December 1, 2000; April 12, 2006, effective December 1, 2006; April 30, 2007, effective December 1, 2007.]

RULE 27. DEPOSITIONS TO PERPETUATE TESTIMONY

(a) Before an Action Is Filed.

(1) *Petition.* A person who wants to perpetuate testimony about any matter cognizable in a United States court may file a verified petition in the district court for the district where any expected adverse party resides. The petition must ask for an order authorizing the petitioner to depose the named persons in order to perpetuate their testimony. The petition must be titled in the petitioner's name and must show:

(A) that the petitioner expects to be a party to an action cognizable in a United States court but cannot presently bring it or cause it to be brought;

(B) the subject matter of the expected action and the petitioner's interest;

(C) the facts that the petitioner wants to establish by the proposed testimony and the reasons to perpetuate it;

(D) the names or a description of the persons whom the petitioner expects to be adverse parties and their addresses, so far as known; and

(E) the name, address, and expected substance of the testimony of each deponent.

(2) *Notice and Service.* At least 20 days before the hearing date, the petitioner must serve each expected adverse party with a copy of the petition and a notice stating the time and place of the hearing. The notice may be served either inside or outside the district or state in the manner provided in Rule 4. If that service cannot be made with reasonable diligence on an expected adverse party, the court may order service by publication or otherwise. The court must appoint an attorney to represent persons not served in the manner provided in Rule 4 and to cross-examine the deponent if an unserved person is not otherwise represented. If any expected adverse party is a minor or is incompetent, Rule 17(c) applies.

(3) *Order and Examination.* If satisfied that perpetuating the testimony may prevent a failure or delay of justice, the court must issue an order that designates or describes the persons whose depositions may be taken, specifies the subject matter of the examinations, and states whether the depositions will be taken orally or by written interrogatories. The depositions may then be taken under these rules, and the court may issue orders like those authorized by Rules 34 and 35. A reference in these rules to the court where an action is pending means, for purposes of this rule, the court where the petition for the deposition was filed.

(4) *Using the Deposition.* A deposition to perpetuate testimony may be used under Rule 32(a) in any later-filed district-court action involving the same subject matter if the deposition either was taken under these rules or, although not so taken, would be admissible in evidence in the courts of the state where it was taken.

(b) Pending Appeal.

(1) *In General.* The court where a judgment has been rendered may, if an appeal has been taken or may still be taken, permit a party to depose witnesses to perpetuate their testimony for use in the event of further proceedings in that court.

(2) *Motion.* The party who wants to perpetuate testimony may move for leave to take the depositions, on the same notice and service as if the action were pending in the district court. The motion must show:

(A) the name, address, and expected substance of the testimony of each deponent; and

(B) the reasons for perpetuating the testimony.

(3) *Court Order.* If the court finds that perpetuating the testimony may prevent a failure or delay of justice, the court may permit the depositions to be taken and may issue orders like those authorized by Rules 34 and 35. The depositions may be taken and used as any other deposition taken in a pending district-court action.

(c) Perpetuation by an Action. This rule does not limit a court's power to entertain an action to perpetuate testimony.

[Amended December 27, 1946, effective March 19, 1948; December 29, 1948, effective October 20, 1949; March 1, 1971, effective July 1, 1971; March 2, 1987, effective August 1, 1987; April 25, 2005, effective December 1, 2005; April 30, 2007, effective December 1, 2007.]

RULE 28. PERSONS BEFORE WHOM DEPOSITIONS MAY BE TAKEN

(a) Within the United States.

(1) *In General.* Within the United States or a territory or insular possession subject to United States jurisdiction, a deposition must be taken before:

(A) an officer authorized to administer oaths either by federal law or by the law in the place of examination; or

(B) a person appointed by the court where the action is pending to administer oaths and take testimony.

(2) *Definition of "Officer".* The term "officer" in Rules 30, 31, and 32 includes a person appointed by the court under this rule or designated by the parties under Rule 29(a).

(b) In a Foreign Country.

(1) *In General.* A deposition may be taken in a foreign country:

(A) under an applicable treaty or convention;

(B) under a letter of request, whether or not captioned a "letter rogatory";

(C) on notice, before a person authorized to administer oaths either by federal law or by the law in the place of examination; or

(D) before a person commissioned by the court to administer any necessary oath and take testimony.

(2) *Issuing a Letter of Request or a Commission.* A letter of request, a commission, or both may be issued:

(A) on appropriate terms after an application and notice of it; and

(B) without a showing that taking the deposition in another manner is impracticable or inconvenient.

(3) *Form of a Request, Notice, or Commission.* When a letter of request or any other device is used according to a treaty or convention, it must be captioned in the form prescribed by that treaty or convention. A letter of request may be addressed "To the Appropriate Authority in [name of country]." A deposition notice or a commission must designate by name or descriptive title the person before whom the deposition is to be taken.

(4) *Letter of Request—Admitting Evidence.* Evidence obtained in response to a letter of request need not be excluded merely because it is not a verbatim transcript, because the testimony was not taken under oath, or because of any similar departure from the requirements for depositions taken within the United States.

(c) Disqualification. A deposition must not be taken before a person who is any party's relative, employee, or attorney; who is related to or employed by any party's attorney; or who is financially interested in the action.

[Amended December 27, 1946, effective March 19, 1948; January 21, 1963, effective July 1, 1963; April 29, 1980, effective August 1, 1980; March 2, 1987, effective August 1, 1987; April 22, 1993, effective December 1, 1993; April 30, 2007, effective December 1, 2007.]

RULE 29. STIPULATIONS ABOUT DISCOVERY PROCEDURE

Unless the court orders otherwise, the parties may stipulate that:

(a) a deposition may be taken before any person, at any time or place, on any notice, and in the manner specified—in which event it may be used in the same way as any other deposition; and

(b) other procedures governing or limiting discovery be modified—but a stipulation extending the time for any form of discovery must have court approval if it would interfere with the time set for completing discovery, for hearing a motion, or for trial.

[Amended March 30, 1970, effective July 1, 1970; April 22, 1993, effective December 1, 1993; April 30, 2007, effective December 1, 2007.]

RULE 30. DEPOSITIONS BY ORAL EXAMINATION

(a) When a Deposition May Be Taken.

(1) *Without Leave.* A party may, by oral questions, depose any person, including a party, without leave of court except as provided in Rule 30(a)(2). The deponent's attendance may be compelled by subpoena under Rule 45.

(2) *With Leave.* A party must obtain leave of court, and the court must grant leave to the extent consistent with Rule 26(b)(2):

(A) if the parties have not stipulated to the deposition and:

(i) the deposition would result in more than 10 depositions being taken under this rule or Rule 31 by the plaintiffs, or by the defendants, or by the third-party defendants;

(ii) the deponent has already been deposed in the case; or

(iii) the party seeks to take the deposition before the time specified in Rule 26(d), unless the party certifies in the notice, with supporting facts, that the deponent is expected to leave the United States and be unavailable for examination in this country after that time; or

(B) if the deponent is confined in prison.

(b) Notice of the Deposition; Other Formal Requirements.

(1) *Notice in General.* A party who wants to depose a person by oral questions must give reasonable written notice to every other party. The notice must state the time and place of the deposition and, if known, the deponent's name and address. If the name is unknown, the notice must provide a general description sufficient to identify the person or the particular class or group to which the person belongs.

(2) *Producing Documents.* If a subpoena duces tecum is to be served on the deponent, the materials designated for production, as set out in the subpoena, must be listed in the notice or in an attachment. The notice to a party deponent may be accompanied by a request under Rule 34 to produce documents and tangible things at the deposition.

(3) *Method of Recording.*

(A) Method Stated in the Notice. The party who notices the deposition must state in the notice the method for recording the testimony. Unless the court orders otherwise, testimony may be recorded by audio, audiovisual, or stenographic means. The noticing party bears the recording costs. Any party may arrange to transcribe a deposition.

(B) Additional Method. With prior notice to the deponent and other parties, any party may designate another method for recording the testimony in addition to that specified in the original notice. That party bears the expense of the additional record or transcript unless the court orders otherwise.

(4) *By Remote Means.* The parties may stipulate—or the court may on motion order—that a deposition be taken by telephone or other remote means. For the purpose of this rule and Rules 28(a), 37(a)(2), and 37(b)(1), the deposition takes place where the deponent answers the questions.

(5) *Officer's Duties.*

(A) Before the Deposition. Unless the parties stipulate otherwise, a deposition must be conducted before an officer appointed or designated under Rule 28. The officer must begin the deposition with an on-the-record statement that includes:

(i) the officer's name and business address;

(ii) the date, time, and place of the deposition;

(iii) the deponent's name;

(iv) the officer's administration of the oath or affirmation to the deponent; and

(v) the identity of all persons present.

(B) Conducting the Deposition; Avoiding Distortion. If the deposition is recorded non-stenographically, the officer must repeat the items in Rule 30(b)(5)(A)(i)-(iii) at the beginning of each unit of the recording medium. The deponent's and attorneys' appearance or demeanor must not be distorted through recording techniques.

(C) After the Deposition. At the end of a deposition, the officer must state on the record that the deposition is complete and must set out any stipulations made by the attorneys about custody of the transcript or recording and of the exhibits, or about any other pertinent matters.

(6) *Notice or Subpoena Directed to an Organization.* In its notice or subpoena, a party may name as the deponent a public or private corporation, a partnership, an association, a governmental agency, or other entity and must describe with reasonable particularity the matters for examination. The named organization must then designate one or more officers, directors, or managing agents, or designate other persons who consent to testify on its behalf; and it may set out the matters on which each person designated will testify. A subpoena must advise a nonparty organization of its duty to make this designation. The persons designated must testify about information known or reasonably available to the organization. This paragraph (6) does not preclude a deposition by any other procedure allowed by these rules.

(c) Examination and Cross-Examination; Record of the Examination; Objections; Written Questions.

(1) *Examination and Cross-Examination.* The examination and cross-examination of a deponent proceed as they would at trial under the Federal Rules of Evidence, except Rules 103 and 615. After putting the deponent under oath or affirmation, the officer must record the testimony by the method designated under Rule 30(b)(3)(A). The testimony must be recorded by the officer personally or by a person acting in the presence and under the direction of the officer.

(2) *Objections.* An objection at the time of the examination—whether to evidence, to a party's conduct, to the officer's qualifications, to the manner of taking the deposition, or to any other aspect of the deposition—must be noted on the record, but the examination still proceeds; the testimony is taken subject to any objection. An objection must be stated concisely in a nonargumentative and nonsuggestive manner. A person may instruct a deponent not to answer only when necessary to preserve a privilege, to enforce a limitation ordered by the court, or to present a motion under Rule 30(d)(3).

(3) *Participating Through Written Questions.* Instead of participating in the oral examination, a party may serve written questions in a sealed envelope on the party noticing the deposition, who must deliver them to the officer. The officer must ask the deponent those questions and record the answers verbatim.

(d) Duration; Sanction; Motion to Terminate or Limit.

(1) *Duration.* Unless otherwise stipulated or ordered by the court, a deposition is limited to 1 day of 7 hours. The court must allow additional time consistent with Rule 26(b)(2) if needed to fairly examine the deponent or if the deponent, another person, or any other circumstance impedes or delays the examination.

(2) *Sanction.* The court may impose an appropriate sanction—including the reasonable expenses and attorney's fees incurred by any party—on a person who impedes, delays, or frustrates the fair examination of the deponent.

(3) *Motion to Terminate or Limit.*

(A) Grounds. At any time during a deposition, the deponent or a party may move to terminate or limit it on the ground that it is being conducted in bad faith or in a manner that unreasonably annoys, embarrasses, or oppresses the deponent or party. The motion may be filed in the court where the action is pending or the deposition is being taken. If the objecting deponent or party so demands, the deposition must be suspended for the time necessary to obtain an order.

(B) Order. The court may order that the deposition be terminated or may limit its scope and manner as provided in Rule 26(c). If terminated, the deposition may be resumed only by order of the court where the action is pending.

(C) Award of Expenses. Rule 37(a)(5) applies to the award of expenses.

(e) Review by the Witness; Changes.

(1) *Review; Statement of Changes.* On request by the deponent or a party before the deposition is completed, the deponent must be allowed 30 days after being notified by the officer that the transcript or recording is available in which:

(A) to review the transcript or recording; and

(B) if there are changes in form or substance, to sign a statement listing the changes and the reasons for making them.

(2) *Changes Indicated in the Officer's Certificate.* The officer must note in the certificate prescribed by Rule 30(f)(1) whether a review was requested and, if so, must attach any changes the deponent makes during the 30–day period.

(f) Certification and Delivery; Exhibits; Copies of the Transcript or Recording; Filing.

(1) *Certification and Delivery.* The officer must certify in writing that the witness was duly sworn and that the deposition accurately records the witness's testimony. The certificate must accompany the record of the deposition. Unless the court orders otherwise, the officer must seal the deposition in an envelope or package bearing the title of the action and marked "Deposition of [witness's name]" and must promptly send it to the attorney who arranged for the transcript or recording. The attorney must store it under conditions that will protect it against loss, destruction, tampering, or deterioration.

(2) *Documents and Tangible Things.*

(A) Originals and Copies. Documents and tangible things produced for inspection during a deposition must, on a party's request, be marked for identification and attached to the deposition. Any party may inspect and copy them. But if the person who produced them wants to keep the originals, the person may:

(i) offer copies to be marked, attached to the deposition, and then used as originals—after giving all parties a fair opportunity to verify the copies by comparing them with the originals; or

(ii) give all parties a fair opportunity to inspect and copy the originals after they are marked—in which event the originals may be used as if attached to the deposition.

(B) Order Regarding the Originals. Any party may move for an order that the originals be attached to the deposition pending final disposition of the case.

(3) *Copies of the Transcript or Recording.* Unless otherwise stipulated or ordered by the court, the officer must retain the stenographic notes of a deposition taken stenographically or a copy of the recording of a deposition taken by another method. When paid reasonable charges, the officer must furnish a copy of the transcript or recording to any party or the deponent.

(4) *Notice of Filing.* A party who files the deposition must promptly notify all other parties of the filing.

(g) Failure to Attend a Deposition or Serve a Subpoena; Expenses. A party who, expecting a deposition to be taken, attends in person or by an attorney may recover reasonable expenses for attending, including attorney's fees, if the noticing party failed to:

(1) attend and proceed with the deposition; or

(2) serve a subpoena on a nonparty deponent, who consequently did not attend.

[Amended January 21, 1963, effective July 1, 1963; March 30, 1970, effective July 1, 1970; March 1, 1971, effective July 1, 1971; November 20, 1972, effective July 1, 1975; April 29, 1980, effective August 1, 1980; March 2, 1987, effective August 1, 1987; April 22, 1993, effective December 1, 1993; April 17, 2000, effective December 1, 2000; April 30, 2007, effective December 1, 2007.]

RULE 31. DEPOSITIONS BY WRITTEN QUESTIONS

(a) When a Deposition May Be Taken.

(1) *Without Leave.* A party may, by written questions, depose any person, including a party, without leave of court except as provided in Rule 31(a)(2). The deponent's attendance may be compelled by subpoena under Rule 45.

(2) *With Leave.* A party must obtain leave of court, and the court must grant leave to the extent consistent with Rule 26(b)(2):

(A) if the parties have not stipulated to the deposition and:

(i) the deposition would result in more than 10 depositions being taken under this rule or Rule 30 by the plaintiffs, or by the defendants, or by the third-party defendants;

(ii) the deponent has already been deposed in the case; or

(iii) the party seeks to take a deposition before the time specified in Rule 26(d); or

(B) if the deponent is confined in prison.

(3) *Service; Required Notice.* A party who wants to depose a person by written questions must serve them on every other party, with a notice stating, if known, the deponent's name and address. If the name is unknown, the notice must provide a general description sufficient to identify the person or the particular

class or group to which the person belongs. The notice must also state the name or descriptive title and the address of the officer before whom the deposition will be taken.

(4) *Questions Directed to an Organization.* A public or private corporation, a partnership, an association, or a governmental agency may be deposed by written questions in accordance with Rule 30(b)(6).

(5) *Questions from Other Parties.* Any questions to the deponent from other parties must be served on all parties as follows: cross-questions, within 14 days after being served with the notice and direct questions; redirect questions, within 7 days after being served with cross-questions; and recross-questions, within 7 days after being served with redirect questions. The court may, for good cause, extend or shorten these times.

(b) Delivery to the Officer; Officer's Duties. The party who noticed the deposition must deliver to the officer a copy of all the questions served and of the notice. The officer must promptly proceed in the manner provided in Rule 30(c), (e), and (f) to:

(1) take the deponent's testimony in response to the questions;

(2) prepare and certify the deposition; and

(3) send it to the party, attaching a copy of the questions and of the notice.

(c) Notice of Completion or Filing.

(1) *Completion.* The party who noticed the deposition must notify all other parties when it is completed.

(2) *Filing.* A party who files the deposition must promptly notify all other parties of the filing.

[Amended March 30, 1970, effective July 1, 1970; March 2, 1987, effective August 1, 1987; April 22, 1993, effective December 1, 1993; April 30, 2007, effective December 1, 2007.]

RULE 32. USING DEPOSITIONS IN COURT PROCEEDINGS

(a) Using Depositions.

(1) *In General.* At a hearing or trial, all or part of a deposition may be used against a party on these conditions:

(A) the party was present or represented at the taking of the deposition or had reasonable notice of it;

(B) it is used to the extent it would be admissible under the Federal Rules of Evidence if the deponent were present and testifying; and

(C) the use is allowed by Rule 32(a)(2) through (8).

(2) *Impeachment and Other Uses.* Any party may use a deposition to contradict or impeach the testimony given by the deponent as a witness, or for any other purpose allowed by the Federal Rules of Evidence.

(3) *Deposition of Party, Agent, or Designee.* An adverse party may use for any purpose the deposition of a party or anyone who, when deposed, was the party's officer, director, managing agent, or designee under Rule 30(b)(6) or 31(a)(4).

(4) *Unavailable Witness.* A party may use for any purpose the deposition of a witness, whether or not a party, if the court finds:

(A) that the witness is dead;

(B) that the witness is more than 100 miles from the place of hearing or trial or is outside the United States, unless it appears that the witness's absence was procured by the party offering the deposition;

(C) that the witness cannot attend or testify because of age, illness, infirmity, or imprisonment;

(D) that the party offering the deposition could not procure the witness's attendance by subpoena; or

(E) on motion and notice, that exceptional circumstances make it desirable—in the interest of justice and with due regard to the importance of live testimony in open court—to permit the deposition to be used.

(5) *Limitations on Use.*

(A) Deposition Taken on Short Notice. A deposition must not be used against a party who, having received less than 11 days' notice of the deposition, promptly moved for a protective order under Rule 26(c)(1)(B) requesting that it not be taken or be taken at a different time or place—and this motion was still pending when the deposition was taken.

(B) Unavailable Deponent; Party Could Not Obtain an Attorney. A deposition taken without leave of court under the unavailability provision of Rule 30(a)(2)(A)(iii) must not be used against a party who shows that, when served with the notice, it could not, despite diligent efforts, obtain an attorney to represent it at the deposition.

(6) *Using Part of a Deposition.* If a party offers in evidence only part of a deposition, an adverse party may require the offeror to introduce other parts that in fairness should be considered with the part introduced, and any party may itself introduce any other parts.

(7) *Substituting a Party.* Substituting a party under Rule 25 does not affect the right to use a deposition previously taken.

(8) *Deposition Taken in an Earlier Action.* A deposition lawfully taken and, if required, filed in any federal- or state-court action may be used in a later action involving the same subject matter between the same parties, or their representatives or successors in interest, to the same extent as if taken in the later

action. A deposition previously taken may also be used as allowed by the Federal Rules of Evidence.

(b) Objections to Admissibility. Subject to Rules 28(b) and 32(d)(3), an objection may be made at a hearing or trial to the admission of any deposition testimony that would be inadmissible if the witness were present and testifying.

(c) Form of Presentation. Unless the court orders otherwise, a party must provide a transcript of any deposition testimony the party offers, but may provide the court with the testimony in nontranscript form as well. On any party's request, deposition testimony offered in a jury trial for any purpose other than impeachment must be presented in nontranscript form, if available, unless the court for good cause orders otherwise.

(d) Waiver of Objections.

(1) *To the Notice.* An objection to an error or irregularity in a deposition notice is waived unless promptly served in writing on the party giving the notice.

(2) *To the Officer's Qualification.* An objection based on disqualification of the officer before whom a deposition is to be taken is waived if not made:

(A) before the deposition begins; or

(B) promptly after the basis for disqualification becomes known or, with reasonable diligence, could have been known.

(3) *To the Taking of the Deposition.*

(A) Objection to Competence, Relevance, or Materiality. An objection to a deponent's competence—or to the competence, relevance, or materiality of testimony—is not waived by a failure to make the objection before or during the deposition, unless the ground for it might have been corrected at that time.

(B) Objection to an Error or Irregularity. An objection to an error or irregularity at an oral examination is waived if:

(i) it relates to the manner of taking the deposition, the form of a question or answer, the oath or affirmation, a party's conduct, or other matters that might have been corrected at that time; and

(ii) it is not timely made during the deposition.

(C) Objection to a Written Question. An objection to the form of a written question under Rule 31 is waived if not served in writing on the party submitting the question within the time for serving responsive questions or, if the question is a recross-question, within 5 days after being served with it.

(4) *To Completing and Returning the Deposition.* An objection to how the officer transcribed the testimony—or prepared, signed, certified, sealed, endorsed, sent, or otherwise dealt with the deposition—is waived unless a motion to suppress is made promptly after the error or irregularity becomes known or, with reasonable diligence, could have been known.

[Amended March 30, 1970, effective July 1, 1970; November 20, 1972, effective July 1, 1975; April 29, 1980, effective August 1, 1980; March 2, 1987, effective August 1, 1987; April 22, 1993, effective December 1, 1993; April 30, 2007, effective December 1, 2007.]

RULE 33. INTERROGATORIES TO PARTIES

(a) In General.

(1) *Number.* Unless otherwise stipulated or ordered by the court, a party may serve on any other party no more than 25 written interrogatories, including all discrete subparts. Leave to serve additional interrogatories may be granted to the extent consistent with Rule 26(b)(2).

(2) *Scope.* An interrogatory may relate to any matter that may be inquired into under Rule 26(b). An interrogatory is not objectionable merely because it asks for an opinion or contention that relates to fact or the application of law to fact, but the court may order that the interrogatory need not be answered until designated discovery is complete, or until a pretrial conference or some other time.

(b) Answers and Objections.

(1) *Responding Party.* The interrogatories must be answered:

(A) by the party to whom they are directed; or

(B) if that party is a public or private corporation, a partnership, an association, or a governmental agency, by any officer or agent, who must furnish the information available to the party.

(2) *Time to Respond.* The responding party must serve its answers and any objections within 30 days after being served with the interrogatories. A shorter or longer time may be stipulated to under Rule 29 or be ordered by the court.

(3) *Answering Each Interrogatory.* Each interrogatory must, to the extent it is not objected to, be answered separately and fully in writing under oath.

(4) *Objections.* The grounds for objecting to an interrogatory must be stated with specificity. Any ground not stated in a timely objection is waived unless the court, for good cause, excuses the failure.

(5) *Signature.* The person who makes the answers must sign them, and the attorney who objects must sign any objections.

(c) Use. An answer to an interrogatory may be used to the extent allowed by the Federal Rules of Evidence.

(d) Option to Produce Business Records. If the answer to an interrogatory may be determined by examining, auditing, compiling, abstracting, or summarizing a party's business records (including electronically stored information), and if the burden of deriving or ascertaining the answer will be substantially the same for either party, the responding party may answer by:

(1) specifying the records that must be reviewed, in sufficient detail to enable the interrogating party to locate and identify them as readily as the responding party could; and

(2) giving the interrogating party a reasonable opportunity to examine and audit the records and to make copies, compilations, abstracts, or summaries.

[Amended December 27, 1946, effective March 19, 1948; March 30, 1970, effective July 1, 1970; April 29, 1980, effective August 1, 1980; April 22, 1993, effective December 1, 1993; April 12, 2006, effective December 1, 2006; April 30, 2007, effective December 1, 2007.]

RULE 34. PRODUCING DOCUMENTS, ELECTRONICALLY STORED INFORMATION, AND TANGIBLE THINGS, OR ENTERING ONTO LAND, FOR INSPECTION AND OTHER PURPOSES

(a) In General. A party may serve on any other party a request within the scope of Rule 26(b):

(1) to produce and permit the requesting party or its representative to inspect, copy, test, or sample the following items in the responding party's possession, custody, or control:

(A) any designated documents or electronically stored information—including writings, drawings, graphs, charts, photographs, sound recordings, images, and other data or data compilations—stored in any medium from which information can be obtained either directly or, if necessary, after translation by the responding party into a reasonably usable form; or

(B) any designated tangible things; or

(2) to permit entry onto designated land or other property possessed or controlled by the responding party, so that the requesting party may inspect, measure, survey, photograph, test, or sample the property or any designated object or operation on it.

(b) Procedure.

(1) *Contents of the Request.* The request:

(A) must describe with reasonable particularity each item or category of items to be inspected;

(B) must specify a reasonable time, place, and manner for the inspection and for performing the related acts; and

(C) may specify the form or forms in which electronically stored information is to be produced.

(2) *Responses and Objections.*

(A) Time to Respond. The party to whom the request is directed must respond in writing within 30 days after being served. A shorter or longer time may be stipulated to under Rule 29 or be ordered by the court.

(B) Responding to Each Item. For each item or category, the response must either state that inspection and related activities will be permitted as requested or state an objection to the request, including the reasons.

(C) Objections. An objection to part of a request must specify the part and permit inspection of the rest.

(D) Responding to a Request for Production of Electronically Stored Information. The response may state an objection to a requested form for producing electronically stored information. If the responding party objects to a requested form—or if no form was specified in the request—the party must state the form or forms it intends to use.

(E) Producing the Documents or Electronically Stored Information. Unless otherwise stipulated or ordered by the court, these procedures apply to producing documents or electronically stored information:

(i) A party must produce documents as they are kept in the usual course of business or must organize and label them to correspond to the categories in the request;

(ii) If a request does not specify a form for producing electronically stored information, a party must produce it in a form or forms in which it is ordinarily maintained or in a reasonably usable form or forms; and

(iii) A party need not produce the same electronically stored information in more than one form.

(c) Nonparties. As provided in Rule 45, a nonparty may be compelled to produce documents and tangible things or to permit an inspection.

[Amended December 27, 1946, effective March 19, 1948; March 30, 1970, effective July 1, 1970; April 29, 1980, effective August 1, 1980; March 2, 1987, effective August 1, 1987; April 30, 1991, effective December 1, 1991; April 22, 1993, effective December 1, 1993; April 12, 2006, effective December 1, 2006; April 30, 2007, effective December 1, 2007.]

RULE 35. PHYSICAL AND MENTAL EXAMINATIONS

(a) Order for an Examination.

(1) *In General.* The court where the action is pending may order a party whose mental or physical condition—including blood group—is in controversy to submit to a physical or mental examination by a suitably licensed or certified examiner. The court has the same authority to order a party to produce for examination a person who is in its custody or under its legal control.

(2) *Motion and Notice; Contents of the Order.* The order:

(A) may be made only on motion for good cause and on notice to all parties and the person to be examined; and

(B) must specify the time, place, manner, conditions, and scope of the examination, as well as the person or persons who will perform it.

(b) Examiner's Report.

(1) *Request by the Party or Person Examined.* The party who moved for the examination must, on request, deliver to the requester a copy of the examiner's report, together with like reports of all earlier examinations of the same condition. The request may be made by the party against whom the examination order was issued or by the person examined.

(2) *Contents.* The examiner's report must be in writing and must set out in detail the examiner's findings, including diagnoses, conclusions, and the results of any tests.

(3) *Request by the Moving Party.* After delivering the reports, the party who moved for the examination may request—and is entitled to receive—from the party against whom the examination order was issued like reports of all earlier or later examinations of the same condition. But those reports need not be delivered by the party with custody or control of the person examined if the party shows that it could not obtain them.

(4) *Waiver of Privilege.* By requesting and obtaining the examiner's report, or by deposing the examiner, the party examined waives any privilege it may have—in that action or any other action involving the same controversy—concerning testimony about all examinations of the same condition.

(5) *Failure to Deliver a Report.* The court on motion may order—on just terms—that a party deliver the report of an examination. If the report is not provided, the court may exclude the examiner's testimony at trial.

(6) *Scope.* This subdivision (b) applies also to an examination made by the parties' agreement, unless the agreement states otherwise. This subdivision does not preclude obtaining an examiner's report or deposing an examiner under other rules.

[Amended March 30, 1970, effective July 1, 1970; March 2, 1987, effective August 1, 1987; amended by Pub.L. 100–690, Title VII, § 7047(b), November 18, 1988, 102 Stat. 4401; amended April 30, 1991, effective December 1, 1991; April 30, 2007, effective December 1, 2007.]

RULE 36. REQUESTS FOR ADMISSION

(a) Scope and Procedure.

(1) *Scope.* A party may serve on any other party a written request to admit, for purposes of the pending action only, the truth of any matters within the scope of Rule 26(b)(1) relating to:

(A) facts, the application of law to fact, or opinions about either; and

(B) the genuineness of any described documents.

(2) *Form; Copy of a Document.* Each matter must be separately stated. A request to admit the genuineness of a document must be accompanied by a copy of the document unless it is, or has been, otherwise furnished or made available for inspection and copying.

(3) *Time to Respond; Effect of Not Responding.* A matter is admitted unless, within 30 days after being served, the party to whom the request is directed serves on the requesting party a written answer or objection addressed to the matter and signed by the party or its attorney. A shorter or longer time for responding may be stipulated to under Rule 29 or be ordered by the court.

(4) *Answer.* If a matter is not admitted, the answer must specifically deny it or state in detail why the answering party cannot truthfully admit or deny it. A denial must fairly respond to the substance of the matter; and when good faith requires that a party qualify an answer or deny only a part of a matter, the answer must specify the part admitted and qualify or deny the rest. The answering party may assert lack of knowledge or information as a reason for failing to admit or deny only if the party states that it has made reasonable inquiry and that the information it knows or can readily obtain is insufficient to enable it to admit or deny.

(5) *Objections.* The grounds for objecting to a request must be stated. A party must not object solely on the ground that the request presents a genuine issue for trial.

(6) *Motion Regarding the Sufficiency of an Answer or Objection.* The requesting party may move to determine the sufficiency of an answer or objection. Unless the court finds an objection justified, it must order that an answer be served. On finding that an answer does not comply with this rule, the court may order either that the matter is admitted or that an amended answer be served. The court may defer its final decision until a pretrial conference or a specified time before trial. Rule 37(a)(5) applies to an award of expenses.

(b) Effect of an Admission; Withdrawing or Amending It. A matter admitted under this rule is conclusively established unless the court, on motion, permits the admission to be withdrawn or amended. Subject to Rule 16(e), the court may permit withdrawal or amendment if it would promote the presentation of the merits of the action and if the court is not persuaded that it would prejudice the requesting party in maintaining or defending the action on the merits. An admission under this rule is not an admission for any other purpose and cannot be used against the party in any other proceeding.

[Amended December 27, 1946, effective March 19, 1948; March 30, 1970, effective July 1, 1970; March 2, 1987, effective August 1, 1987; April 22, 1993, effective December 1, 1993; April 30, 2007, effective December 1, 2007.]

RULE 37. FAILURE TO MAKE DISCLOSURES OR TO COOPERATE IN DISCOVERY; SANCTIONS

(a) Motion for an Order Compelling Disclosure or Discovery.

(1) *In General.* On notice to other parties and all affected persons, a party may move for an order compelling disclosure or discovery. The motion must include a certification that the movant has in good faith conferred or attempted to confer with the person or party failing to make disclosure or discovery in an effort to obtain it without court action.

(2) *Appropriate Court.* A motion for an order to a party must be made in the court where the action is pending. A motion for an order to a nonparty must be made in the court where the discovery is or will be taken.

(3) *Specific Motions.*

(A) To Compel Disclosure. If a party fails to make a disclosure required by Rule 26(a), any other party may move to compel disclosure and for appropriate sanctions.

(B) To Compel a Discovery Response. A party seeking discovery may move for an order compelling an answer, designation, production, or inspection. This motion may be made if:

(i) a deponent fails to answer a question asked under Rule 30 or 31;

(ii) a corporation or other entity fails to make a designation under Rule 30(b)(6) or 31(a)(4);

(iii) a party fails to answer an interrogatory submitted under Rule 33; or

(iv) a party fails to respond that inspection will be permitted—or fails to permit inspection—as requested under Rule 34.

(C) Related to a Deposition. When taking an oral deposition, the party asking a question may complete or adjourn the examination before moving for an order.

(4) *Evasive or Incomplete Disclosure, Answer, or Response.* For purposes of this subdivision (a), an evasive or incomplete disclosure, answer, or response must be treated as a failure to disclose, answer, or respond.

(5) *Payment of Expenses; Protective Orders.*

(A) If the Motion Is Granted (or Disclosure or Discovery Is Provided After Filing). If the motion is granted—or if the disclosure or requested discovery is provided after the motion was filed—the court must, after giving an opportunity to be heard, require the party or deponent whose conduct necessitated the motion, the party or attorney advising that conduct, or both to pay the movant's reasonable expenses incurred in making the motion, including attorney's fees. But the court must not order this payment if:

(i) the movant filed the motion before attempting in good faith to obtain the disclosure or discovery without court action;

(ii) the opposing party's nondisclosure, response, or objection was substantially justified; or

(iii) other circumstances make an award of expenses unjust.

(B) If the Motion Is Denied. If the motion is denied, the court may issue any protective order authorized under Rule 26(c) and must, after giving an opportunity to be heard, require the movant, the attorney filing the motion, or both to pay the party or deponent who opposed the motion its reasonable expenses incurred in opposing the motion, including attorney's fees. But the court must not order this payment if the motion was substantially justified or other circumstances make an award of expenses unjust.

(C) If the Motion Is Granted in Part and Denied in Part. If the motion is granted in part and denied in part, the court may issue any protective order authorized under Rule 26(c) and may, after giving an opportunity to be heard, apportion the reasonable expenses for the motion.

(b) Failure to Comply with a Court Order.

(1) *Sanctions in the District Where the Deposition Is Taken.* If the court where the discovery is taken orders a deponent to be sworn or to answer a question and the deponent fails to obey, the failure may be treated as contempt of court.

(2) *Sanctions in the District Where the Action Is Pending.*

(A) For Not Obeying a Discovery Order. If a party or a party's officer, director, or managing agent—or a witness designated under Rule 30(b)(6) or 31(a)(4)—fails to obey an order to provide or permit discovery, including an order under Rule 26(f), 35, or 37(a), the court where the action is pending may issue further just orders. They may include the following:

(i) directing that the matters embraced in the order or other designated facts be taken as established for purposes of the action, as the prevailing party claims;

(ii) prohibiting the disobedient party from supporting or opposing designated claims or defenses, or from introducing designated matters in evidence;

(iii) striking pleadings in whole or in part;

(iv) staying further proceedings until the order is obeyed;

(v) dismissing the action or proceeding in whole or in part;

(vi) rendering a default judgment against the disobedient party; or

(vii) treating as contempt of court the failure to obey any order except an order to submit to a physical or mental examination.

(B) For Not Producing a Person for Examination. If a party fails to comply with an order under Rule 35(a) requiring it to produce another person for examination, the court may issue any of the orders listed in Rule 37(b)(2)(A)(i)-(vi), unless the disobedient party shows that it cannot produce the other person.

(C) Payment of Expenses. Instead of or in addition to the orders above, the court must order the disobedient party, the attorney advising that party, or both to pay the reasonable expenses, including attorney's fees, caused by the failure, unless the failure was substantially justified or other circumstances make an award of expenses unjust.

(c) Failure to Disclose, to Supplement an Earlier Response, or to Admit.

(1) *Failure to Disclose or Supplement.* If a party fails to provide information or identify a witness as required by Rule 26(a) or (e), the party is not allowed to use that information or witness to supply evidence on a motion, at a hearing, or at a trial, unless the failure was substantially justified or is harmless. In addition to or instead of this sanction, the court, on motion and after giving an opportunity to be heard:

(A) may order payment of the reasonable expenses, including attorney's fees, caused by the failure;

(B) may inform the jury of the party's failure; and

(C) may impose other appropriate sanctions, including any of the orders listed in Rule 37(b)(2)(A)(i)-(vi).

(2) *Failure to Admit.* If a party fails to admit what is requested under Rule 36 and if the requesting party later proves a document to be genuine or the matter true, the requesting party may move that the party who failed to admit pay the reasonable expenses, including attorney's fees, incurred in making that proof. The court must so order unless:

(A) the request was held objectionable under Rule 36(a);

(B) the admission sought was of no substantial importance;

(C) the party failing to admit had a reasonable ground to believe that it might prevail on the matter; or

(D) there was other good reason for the failure to admit.

(d) Party's Failure to Attend Its Own Deposition, Serve Answers to Interrogatories, or Respond to a Request for Inspection.

(1) *In General.*

(A) Motion; Grounds for Sanctions. The court where the action is pending may, on motion, order sanctions if:

(i) a party or a party's officer, director, or managing agent—or a person designated under Rule 30(b)(6) or 31(a)(4)—fails, after being served with proper notice, to appear for that person's deposition; or

(ii) a party, after being properly served with interrogatories under Rule 33 or a request for inspection under Rule 34, fails to serve its answers, objections, or written response.

(B) Certification. A motion for sanctions for failing to answer or respond must include a certification that the movant has in good faith conferred or attempted to confer with the party failing to act in an effort to obtain the answer or response without court action.

(2) *Unacceptable Excuse for Failing to Act.* A failure described in Rule 37(d)(1)(A) is not excused on the ground that the discovery sought was objectionable, unless the party failing to act has a pending motion for a protective order under Rule 26(c).

(3) *Types of Sanctions.* Sanctions may include any of the orders listed in Rule 37(b)(2)(A)(i)-(vi). Instead of or in addition to these sanctions, the court must require the party failing to act, the attorney advising that party, or both to pay the reasonable expenses, including attorney's fees, caused by the failure, unless the failure was substantially justified or other circumstances make an award of expenses unjust.

(e) Failure to Provide Electronically Stored Information. Absent exceptional circumstances, a court may not impose sanctions under these rules on a party for failing to provide electronically stored information lost as a result of the routine, good-faith operation of an electronic information system.

(f) Failure to Participate in Framing a Discovery Plan. If a party or its attorney fails to participate in good faith in developing and submitting a proposed discovery plan as required by Rule 26(f), the court may, after giving an opportunity to be heard, require that party or attorney to pay to any other party the reasonable expenses, including attorney's fees, caused by the failure.

[Amended December 29, 1948, effective October 20, 1949; March 30, 1970, effective July 1, 1970; April 29, 1980, effective August 1, 1980; amended by Pub.L. 96–481, Title II, § 205(a), October 21, 1980, 94 Stat. 2330, effective October 1, 1981; amended March 2, 1987, effective August 1, 1987; April 22, 1993, effective December 1, 1993; April 17, 2000, effective December 1, 2000; April 12, 2006, effective December 1, 2006; April 30, 2007, effective December 1, 2007.]

TITLE VI. TRIALS

RULE 38. RIGHT TO A JURY TRIAL; DEMAND

(a) Right Preserved. The right of trial by jury as declared by the Seventh Amendment to the Constitution—or as provided by a federal statute—is preserved to the parties inviolate.

(b) Demand. On any issue triable of right by a jury, a party may demand a jury trial by:

(1) serving the other parties with a written demand—which may be included in a pleading—no later than 10 days after the last pleading directed to the issue is served; and

(2) filing the demand in accordance with Rule 5(d).

(c) Specifying Issues. In its demand, a party may specify the issues that it wishes to have tried by a jury; otherwise, it is considered to have demanded a jury trial on all the issues so triable. If the party has demanded a jury trial on only some issues, any other party may—within 10 days after being served with the demand or within a shorter time ordered by the court—serve a demand for a jury trial on any other or all factual issues triable by jury.

(d) Waiver; Withdrawal. A party waives a jury trial unless its demand is properly served and filed. A proper demand may be withdrawn only if the parties consent.

(e) Admiralty and Maritime Claims. These rules do not create a right to a jury trial on issues in a claim that is an admiralty or maritime claim under Rule 9(h).

[Amended February 28, 1966, effective July 1, 1966; March 2, 1987, effective August 1, 1987; April 22, 1993, effective December 1, 1993; April 30, 2007, effective December 1, 2007.]

RULE 39. TRIAL BY JURY OR BY THE COURT

(a) When a Demand Is Made. When a jury trial has been demanded under Rule 38, the action must be designated on the docket as a jury action. The trial on all issues so demanded must be by jury unless:

(1) the parties or their attorneys file a stipulation to a nonjury trial or so stipulate on the record; or

(2) the court, on motion or on its own, finds that on some or all of those issues there is no federal right to a jury trial.

(b) When No Demand Is Made. Issues on which a jury trial is not properly demanded are to be tried by the court. But the court may, on motion, order a jury trial on any issue for which a jury might have been demanded.

(c) Advisory Jury; Jury Trial by Consent. In an action not triable of right by a jury, the court, on motion or on its own:

(1) may try any issue with an advisory jury; or

(2) may, with the parties' consent, try any issue by a jury whose verdict has the same effect as if a jury trial had been a matter of right, unless the action is against the United States and a federal statute provides for a nonjury trial.

[Amended April 30, 2007, effective December 1, 2007.]

RULE 40. SCHEDULING CASES FOR TRIAL

Each court must provide by rule for scheduling trials. The court must give priority to actions entitled to priority by a federal statute.

[Amended April 30, 2007, effective December 1, 2007.]

RULE 41. DISMISSAL OF ACTIONS

(a) Voluntary Dismissal.

(1) *By the Plaintiff.*

(A) Without a Court Order. Subject to Rules 23(e), 23.1(c), 23.2, and 66 and any applicable federal statute, the plaintiff may dismiss an action without a court order by filing:

(i) a notice of dismissal before the opposing party serves either an answer or a motion for summary judgment; or

(ii) a stipulation of dismissal signed by all parties who have appeared.

(B) Effect. Unless the notice or stipulation states otherwise, the dismissal is without prejudice. But if the plaintiff previously dismissed any federal-or state-court action based on or including the same claim, a notice of dismissal operates as an adjudication on the merits.

(2) *By Court Order; Effect.* Except as provided in Rule 41(a)(1), an action may be dismissed at the plaintiff's request only by court order, on terms that the court considers proper. If a defendant has pleaded a counterclaim before being served with the plaintiff's motion to dismiss, the action may be dismissed over

the defendant's objection only if the counterclaim can remain pending for independent adjudication. Unless the order states otherwise, a dismissal under this paragraph (2) is without prejudice.

(b) Involuntary Dismissal; Effect. If the plaintiff fails to prosecute or to comply with these rules or a court order, a defendant may move to dismiss the action or any claim against it. Unless the dismissal order states otherwise, a dismissal under this subdivision (b) and any dismissal not under this rule—except one for lack of jurisdiction, improper venue, or failure to join a party under Rule 19—operates as an adjudication on the merits.

(c) Dismissing a Counterclaim, Crossclaim, or Third–Party Claim. This rule applies to a dismissal of any counterclaim, crossclaim, or third-party claim. A claimant's voluntary dismissal under Rule 41(a)(1)(A)(i) must be made:

(1) before a responsive pleading is served; or

(2) if there is no responsive pleading, before evidence is introduced at a hearing or trial.

(d) Costs of a Previously Dismissed Action. If a plaintiff who previously dismissed an action in any court files an action based on or including the same claim against the same defendant, the court:

(1) may order the plaintiff to pay all or part of the costs of that previous action; and

(2) may stay the proceedings until the plaintiff has complied.

[Amended December 27, 1946, effective March 19, 1948; January 21, 1963, effective July 1, 1963; February 28, 1966, effective July 1, 1966; December 4, 1967, effective July 1, 1968; March 2, 1987, effective August 1, 1987; April 30, 1991, effective December 1, 1991; April 30, 2007, effective December 1, 2007.]

RULE 42. CONSOLIDATION; SEPARATE TRIALS

(a) Consolidation. If actions before the court involve a common question of law or fact, the court may:

(1) join for hearing or trial any or all matters at issue in the actions;

(2) consolidate the actions; or

(3) issue any other orders to avoid unnecessary cost or delay.

(b) Separate Trials. For convenience, to avoid prejudice, or to expedite and economize, the court may order a separate trial of one or more separate issues, claims, crossclaims, counterclaims, or third-party claims. When ordering a separate trial, the court must preserve any federal right to a jury trial.

[Amended February 28, 1966, effective July 1, 1966; April 30, 2007, effective December 1, 2007.]

RULE 43. TAKING TESTIMONY

(a) In Open Court. At trial, the witnesses' testimony must be taken in open court unless a federal statute, the Federal Rules of Evidence, these rules, or other rules adopted by the Supreme Court provide otherwise. For good cause in compelling circumstances and with appropriate safeguards, the court may permit testimony in open court by contemporaneous transmission from a different location.

(b) Affirmation Instead of an Oath. When these rules require an oath, a solemn affirmation suffices.

(c) Evidence on a Motion. When a motion relies on facts outside the record, the court may hear the matter on affidavits or may hear it wholly or partly on oral testimony or on depositions.

(d) Interpreter. The court may appoint an interpreter of its choosing; fix reasonable compensation to be paid from funds provided by law or by one or more parties; and tax the compensation as costs.

[Amended February 28, 1966, effective July 1, 1966; November 20, 1972, and December 18, 1972, effective July 1, 1975; March 2, 1987, effective August 1, 1987; April 23, 1996, effective December 1, 1996; April 30, 2007, effective December 1, 2007.]

RULE 44. PROVING AN OFFICIAL RECORD

(a) Means of Proving.

(1) *Domestic Record.* Each of the following evidences an official record—or an entry in it—that is otherwise admissible and is kept within the United States, any state, district, or commonwealth, or any territory subject to the administrative or judicial jurisdiction of the United States:

(A) an official publication of the record; or

(B) a copy attested by the officer with legal custody of the record—or by the officer's deputy—and accompanied by a certificate that the officer has custody. The certificate must be made under seal:

(i) by a judge of a court of record in the district or political subdivision where the record is kept; or

(ii) by any public officer with a seal of office and with official duties in the district or political subdivision where the record is kept.

(2) *Foreign Record.*

(A) In General. Each of the following evidences a foreign official record—or an entry in it—that is otherwise admissible:

(i) an official publication of the record; or

(ii) the record—or a copy—that is attested by an authorized person and is accompanied either by a final certification of genuineness or by a certification under a treaty or convention to which the United States and the country where the record is located are parties.

(B) Final Certification of Genuineness. A final certification must certify the genuineness of the signature and official position of the attester or of any foreign official whose certificate of genuineness relates to the attestation or is in a chain of certificates of genuineness relating to the attestation. A final certification may be made by a secretary of a United States embassy or legation; by a consul general, vice consul, or consular agent of the United States; or by a diplomatic or consular official of the foreign country assigned or accredited to the United States.

(C) Other Means of Proof. If all parties have had a reasonable opportunity to investigate a foreign record's authenticity and accuracy, the court may, for good cause, either:

(i) admit an attested copy without final certification; or

(ii) permit the record to be evidenced by an attested summary with or without a final certification.

(b) Lack of a Record. A written statement that a diligent search of designated records revealed no record or entry of a specified tenor is admissible as evidence that the records contain no such record or entry. For domestic records, the statement must be authenticated under Rule 44(a)(1). For foreign records, the statement must comply with (a)(2)(C)(ii).

(c) Other Proof. A party may prove an official record—or an entry or lack of an entry in it—by any other method authorized by law.

[Amended February 28, 1966, effective July 1, 1966; March 2, 1987, effective August 1, 1987; April 30, 1991, effective December 1, 1991; April 30, 2007, effective December 1, 2007.]

RULE 44.1 DETERMINING FOREIGN LAW

A party who intends to raise an issue about a foreign country's law must give notice by a pleading or other writing. In determining foreign law, the court may consider any relevant material or source, including testimony, whether or not submitted by a party or admissible under the Federal Rules of Evidence. The court's determination must be treated as a ruling on a question of law.

[Adopted February 28, 1966, effective July 1, 1966; amended November 20, 1972, effective July 1, 1975; March 2, 1987, effective August 1, 1987; April 30, 2007, effective December 1, 2007.]

RULE 45. SUBPOENA

(a) In General.

(1) *Form and Contents.*

(A) Requirements—In General. Every subpoena must:

(i) state the court from which it issued;

(ii) state the title of the action, the court in which it is pending, and its civil-action number;

(iii) command each person to whom it is directed to do the following at a specified time and place: attend and testify; produce designated documents, electronically stored information, or tangible things in that person's possession, custody, or control; or permit the inspection of premises; and

(iv) set out the text of Rule 45(c) and (d).

(B) Command to Attend a Deposition—Notice of the Recording Method. A subpoena commanding attendance at a deposition must state the method for recording the testimony.

(C) Combining or Separating a Command to Produce or to Permit Inspection; Specifying the Form for Electronically Stored Information. A command to produce documents, electronically stored information, or tangible things or to permit the inspection of premises may be included in a subpoena commanding attendance at a deposition, hearing, or trial, or may be set out in a separate subpoena. A subpoena may specify the form or forms in which electronically stored information is to be produced.

(D) Command to Produce; Included Obligations. A command in a subpoena to produce documents, electronically stored information, or tangible things requires the responding party to permit inspection, copying, testing, or sampling of the materials.

(2) *Issued from Which Court.* A subpoena must issue as follows:

(A) for attendance at a hearing or trial, from the court for the district where the hearing or trial is to be held;

(B) for attendance at a deposition, from the court for the district where the deposition is to be taken; and

(C) for production or inspection, if separate from a subpoena commanding a person's attendance, from the court for the district where the production or inspection is to be made.

(3) *Issued by Whom.* The clerk must issue a subpoena, signed but otherwise in blank, to a party who requests it. That party must complete it before service. An attorney also may issue and sign a subpoena as an officer of:

(A) a court in which the attorney is authorized to practice; or

(B) a court for a district where a deposition is to be taken or production is to be made, if the attorney is authorized to practice in the court where the action is pending.

(b) Service.

(1) *By Whom; Tendering Fees; Serving a Copy of Certain Subpoenas.* Any person who is at least 18 years old and not a party may serve a subpoena. Serving a subpoena requires delivering a copy to the named person and, if the subpoena requires that person's attendance, tendering the fees for 1 day's attendance and the mileage allowed by law. Fees and mileage need not be tendered when the subpoena issues on behalf of the United States or any of its officers or agencies. If the subpoena commands the production of documents, electronically stored information, or tangible things or the inspection of premises before trial, then before it is served, a notice must be served on each party.

(2) *Service in the United States.* Subject to Rule 45(c)(3)(A)(ii), a subpoena may be served at any place:

(A) within the district of the issuing court;

(B) outside that district but within 100 miles of the place specified for the deposition, hearing, trial, production, or inspection;

(C) within the state of the issuing court if a state statute or court rule allows service at that place of a subpoena issued by a state court of general jurisdiction sitting in the place specified for the deposition, hearing, trial, production, or inspection; or

(D) that the court authorizes on motion and for good cause, if a federal statute so provides.

(3) *Service in a Foreign Country.* 28 U.S.C. § 1783 governs issuing and serving a subpoena directed to a United States national or resident who is in a foreign country.

(4) *Proof of Service.* Proving service, when necessary, requires filing with the issuing court a statement showing the date and manner of service and the names of the persons served. The statement must be certified by the server.

(c) Protecting a Person Subject to a Subpoena.

(1) *Avoiding Undue Burden or Expense; Sanctions.* A party or attorney responsible for issuing and serving a subpoena must take reasonable steps to avoid imposing undue burden or expense on a person subject to the subpoena. The issuing court must enforce this duty and impose an appropriate sanction—which may include lost earnings and reasonable attorney's fees—on a party or attorney who fails to comply.

(2) *Command to Produce Materials or Permit Inspection.*

(A) Appearance Not Required. A person commanded to produce documents, electronically stored information, or tangible things, or to permit the inspection of premises, need not appear in person at the place of production or inspection unless also commanded to appear for a deposition, hearing, or trial.

(B) Objections. A person commanded to produce documents or tangible things or to permit inspection may serve on the party or attorney designated in the subpoena a written objection to inspecting, copying, testing or sampling any or all of the materials or to inspecting the premises—or to producing electronically stored information in the form or forms requested. The objection must be served before the earlier of the time specified for compliance or 14 days after the subpoena is served. If an objection is made, the following rules apply:

(i) At any time, on notice to the commanded person, the serving party may move the issuing court for an order compelling production or inspection.

(ii) These acts may be required only as directed in the order, and the order must protect a person who is neither a party nor a party's officer from significant expense resulting from compliance.

(3) *Quashing or Modifying a Subpoena.*

(A) When Required. On timely motion, the issuing court must quash or modify a subpoena that:

(i) fails to allow a reasonable time to comply;

(ii) requires a person who is neither a party nor a party's officer to travel more than 100 miles from where that person resides, is employed, or regularly transacts business in person—except that, subject to Rule 45(c)(3)(B)(iii), the person may be commanded to attend a trial by traveling from any such place within the state where the trial is held;

(iii) requires disclosure of privileged or other protected matter, if no exception or waiver applies; or

(iv) subjects a person to undue burden.

(B) When Permitted. To protect a person subject to or affected by a subpoena, the issuing court may, on motion, quash or modify the subpoena if it requires:

(i) disclosing a trade secret or other confidential research, development, or commercial information;

(ii) disclosing an unretained expert's opinion or information that does not describe specific occurrences in dispute and results from the expert's study that was not requested by a party; or

(iii) a person who is neither a party nor a party's officer to incur substantial expense to travel more than 100 miles to attend trial.

(C) Specifying Conditions as an Alternative. In the circumstances described in Rule 45(c)(3)(B), the court may, instead of quashing or modifying a subpoena, order appearance or production under specified conditions if the serving party:

(i) shows a substantial need for the testimony or material that cannot be otherwise met without undue hardship; and

(ii) ensures that the subpoenaed person will be reasonably compensated.

(d) Duties in Responding to a Subpoena.

(1) *Producing Documents or Electronically Stored Information.* These procedures apply to producing documents or electronically stored information:

(A) Documents. A person responding to a subpoena to produce documents must produce them as they are kept in the ordinary course of business or must organize and label them to correspond to the categories in the demand.

(B) Form for Producing Electronically Stored Information Not Specified. If a subpoena does not specify a form for producing electronically stored information, the person responding must produce it in a form or forms in which it is ordinarily maintained or in a reasonably usable form or forms.

(C) Electronically Stored Information Produced in Only One Form. The person responding need not produce the same electronically stored information in more than one form.

(D) Inaccessible Electronically Stored Information. The person responding need not provide discovery of electronically stored information from sources that the person identifies as not reasonably accessible because of undue burden or cost. On motion to compel discovery or for a protective order, the person responding must show that the information is not reasonably accessible because of undue burden or cost. If that showing is made, the court may nonetheless order discovery from such sources if the requesting party shows good cause, considering the limitations of Rule 26(b)(2)(C). The court may specify conditions for the discovery.

(2) *Claiming Privilege or Protection.*

(A) Information Withheld. A person withholding subpoenaed information under a claim that it is privileged or subject to protection as trial-preparation material must:

(i) expressly make the claim; and

(ii) describe the nature of the withheld documents, communications, or tangible things in a manner that, without revealing information itself privileged or protected, will enable the parties to assess the claim.

(B) Information Produced. If information produced in response to a subpoena is subject to a claim of privilege or of protection as trial-preparation material, the person making the claim may notify any party that received the information of the claim and the basis for it. After being notified, a party must promptly return, sequester, or destroy the specified information and any copies it has; must not use or disclose the information until the claim is resolved; must take reasonable steps to retrieve the information if the party disclosed it before being notified; and may promptly present the information to the court under seal for a determination of the claim. The person who produced the information must preserve the information until the claim is resolved.

(e) Contempt. The issuing court may hold in contempt a person who, having been served, fails without adequate excuse to obey the subpoena. A nonparty's failure to obey must be excused if the subpoena purports to require the nonparty to attend or produce at a place outside the limits of Rule 45(c)(3)(A)(ii).

[Amended December 27, 1946, effective March 19, 1948; December 29, 1948, effective October 20, 1949; March 30, 1970, effective July 1, 1970; April 29, 1980, effective August 1, 1980; April 29, 1985, effective August 1, 1985; March 2, 1987, effective August 1, 1987; April 30, 1991, effective December 1, 1991; April 25, 2005, effective December 1, 2005; April 12, 2006, effective December 1, 2006; April 30, 2007, effective December 1, 2007.]

RULE 46. OBJECTING TO A RULING OR ORDER

A formal exception to a ruling or order is unnecessary. When the ruling or order is requested or made, a party need only state the action that it wants the court to take or objects to, along with the grounds for the request or objection. Failing to object does not prejudice a party who had no opportunity to do so when the ruling or order was made.

[Amended March 2, 1987, effective August 1, 1987; April 30, 2007, effective December 1, 2007.]

RULE 47. SELECTING JURORS

(a) Examining Jurors. The court may permit the parties or their attorneys to examine prospective jurors or may itself do so. If the court examines the jurors, it must permit the parties or their attorneys to make any further inquiry it considers proper, or must itself ask any of their additional questions it considers proper.

(b) Peremptory Challenges. The court must allow the number of peremptory challenges provided by 28 U.S.C. § 1870.

(c) Excusing a Juror. During trial or deliberation, the court may excuse a juror for good cause.

[Amended February 28, 1966, effective July 1, 1966; April 30, 1991, effective December 1, 1991; April 30, 2007, effective December 1, 2007.]

RULE 48. NUMBER OF JURORS; VERDICT

A jury must initially have at least 6 and no more than 12 members, and each juror must participate in the verdict unless excused under Rule 47(c). Unless the parties stipulate otherwise, the verdict must be unanimous and be returned by a jury of at least 6 members.

[Amended April 30, 1991, effective December 1, 1991; April 30, 2007, effective December 1, 2007.]

RULE 49. SPECIAL VERDICT; GENERAL VERDICT AND QUESTIONS

(a) Special Verdict.

(1) *In General.* The court may require a jury to return only a special verdict in the form of a special written finding on each issue of fact. The court may do so by:

(A) submitting written questions susceptible of a categorical or other brief answer;

(B) submitting written forms of the special findings that might properly be made under the pleadings and evidence; or

(C) using any other method that the court considers appropriate.

(2) *Instructions.* The court must give the instructions and explanations necessary to enable the jury to make its findings on each submitted issue.

(3) *Issues Not Submitted.* A party waives the right to a jury trial on any issue of fact raised by the pleadings or evidence but not submitted to the jury unless, before the jury retires, the party demands its submission to the jury. If the party does not demand submission, the court may make a finding on the issue. If the court makes no finding, it is considered to have made a finding consistent with its judgment on the special verdict.

(b) General Verdict with Answers to Written Questions.

(1) *In General.* The court may submit to the jury forms for a general verdict, together with written questions on one or more issues of fact that the jury must decide. The court must give the instructions and explanations necessary to enable the jury to render a general verdict and answer the questions in writing, and must direct the jury to do both.

(2) *Verdict and Answers Consistent.* When the general verdict and the answers are consistent, the court must approve, for entry under Rule 58, an appropriate judgment on the verdict and answers.

(3) *Answers Inconsistent with the Verdict.* When the answers are consistent with each other but one or more is inconsistent with the general verdict, the court may:

(A) approve, for entry under Rule 58, an appropriate judgment according to the answers, notwithstanding the general verdict;

(B) direct the jury to further consider its answers and verdict; or

(C) order a new trial.

(4) *Answers Inconsistent with Each Other and the Verdict.* When the answers are inconsistent with each other and one or more is also inconsistent with the general verdict, judgment must not be entered; instead, the court must direct the jury to further consider its answers and verdict, or must order a new trial.

[Amended January 21, 1963, effective July 1, 1963; March 2, 1987, effective August 1, 1987; April 30, 2007, effective December 1, 2007.]

RULE 50. JUDGMENT AS A MATTER OF LAW IN A JURY TRIAL; RELATED MOTION FOR A NEW TRIAL; CONDITIONAL RULING

(a) Judgment as a Matter of Law.

(1) *In General.* If a party has been fully heard on an issue during a jury trial and the court finds that a reasonable jury would not have a legally sufficient evidentiary basis to find for the party on that issue, the court may:

(A) resolve the issue against the party; and

(B) grant a motion for judgment as a matter of law against the party on a claim or defense that, under the controlling law, can be maintained or defeated only with a favorable finding on that issue.

(2) *Motion.* A motion for judgment as a matter of law may be made at any time before the case is submitted to the jury. The motion must specify the judgment sought and the law and facts that entitle the movant to the judgment.

(b) Renewing the Motion After Trial; Alternative Motion for a New Trial. If the court does not grant a motion for judgment as a matter of law made under Rule 50(a), the court is considered to have submitted the action to the jury subject to the court's later deciding the legal questions raised by the motion. No later than 10 days after the entry of judgment—or if the motion addresses a jury issue not decided by a verdict, no later than 10 days after the jury was discharged—the movant may file a renewed motion for judgment as a matter of law and may include an alternative or joint request for a new trial under Rule 59. In ruling on the renewed motion, the court may:

(1) allow judgment on the verdict, if the jury returned a verdict;

(2) order a new trial; or

(3) direct the entry of judgment as a matter of law.

(c) Granting the Renewed Motion; Conditional Ruling on a Motion for a New Trial.

(1) *In General.* If the court grants a renewed motion for judgment as a matter of law, it must also conditionally rule on any motion for a new trial by determining whether a new trial should be granted if the judgment is later vacated or reversed. The court

must state the grounds for conditionally granting or denying the motion for a new trial.

(2) *Effect of a Conditional Ruling.* Conditionally granting the motion for a new trial does not affect the judgment's finality; if the judgment is reversed, the new trial must proceed unless the appellate court orders otherwise. If the motion for a new trial is conditionally denied, the appellee may assert error in that denial; if the judgment is reversed, the case must proceed as the appellate court orders.

(d) Time for a Losing Party's New-Trial Motion. Any motion for a new trial under Rule 59 by a party against whom judgment as a matter of law is rendered must be filed no later than 10 days after the entry of the judgment.

(e) Denying the Motion for Judgment as a Matter of Law; Reversal on Appeal. If the court denies the motion for judgment as a matter of law, the prevailing party may, as appellee, assert grounds entitling it to a new trial should the appellate court conclude that the trial court erred in denying the motion. If the appellate court reverses the judgment, it may order a new trial, direct the trial court to determine whether a new trial should be granted, or direct the entry of judgment.

[Amended January 21, 1963, effective July 1, 1963; March 2, 1987, effective August 1, 1987; April 30, 1991, effective December 1, 1991; April 22, 1993, effective December 1, 1993; April 27, 1995, effective December 1, 1995; April 12, 2006, effective December 1, 2006; April 30, 2007, effective December 1, 2007.]

RULE 51. INSTRUCTIONS TO THE JURY; OBJECTIONS; PRESERVING A CLAIM OF ERROR

(a) Requests.

(1) *Before or at the Close of the Evidence.* At the close of the evidence or at any earlier reasonable time that the court orders, a party may file and furnish to every other party written requests for the jury instructions it wants the court to give.

(2) *After the Close of the Evidence.* After the close of the evidence, a party may:

(A) file requests for instructions on issues that could not reasonably have been anticipated by an earlier time that the court set for requests; and

(B) with the court's permission, file untimely requests for instructions on any issue.

(b) Instructions. The court:

(1) must inform the parties of its proposed instructions and proposed action on the requests before instructing the jury and before final jury arguments;

(2) must give the parties an opportunity to object on the record and out of the jury's hearing before the instructions and arguments are delivered; and

(3) may instruct the jury at any time before the jury is discharged.

(c) Objections.

(1) *How to Make.* A party who objects to an instruction or the failure to give an instruction must do so on the record, stating distinctly the matter objected to and the grounds for the objection.

(2) *When to Make.* An objection is timely if:

(A) a party objects at the opportunity provided under Rule 51(b)(2); or

(B) a party was not informed of an instruction or action on a request before that opportunity to object, and the party objects promptly after learning that the instruction or request will be, or has been, given or refused.

(d) Assigning Error; Plain Error.

(1) *Assigning Error.* A party may assign as error:

(A) an error in an instruction actually given, if that party properly objected; or

(B) a failure to give an instruction, if that party properly requested it and—unless the court rejected the request in a definitive ruling on the record—also properly objected.

(2) *Plain Error.* A court may consider a plain error in the instructions that has not been preserved as required by Rule 51(d)(1) if the error affects substantial rights.

[Amended March 2, 1987, effective August 1, 1987; March 27, 2003, effective December 1, 2003; April 30, 2007, effective December 1, 2007.]

RULE 52. FINDINGS AND CONCLUSIONS BY THE COURT; JUDGMENT ON PARTIAL FINDINGS

(a) Findings and Conclusions.

(1) *In General.* In an action tried on the facts without a jury or with an advisory jury, the court must find the facts specially and state its conclusions of law separately. The findings and conclusions may be stated on the record after the close of the evidence or may appear in an opinion or a memorandum of decision filed by the court. Judgment must be entered under Rule 58.

(2) *For an Interlocutory Injunction.* In granting or refusing an interlocutory injunction, the court must similarly state the findings and conclusions that support its action.

(3) *For a Motion.* The court is not required to state findings or conclusions when ruling on a motion under Rule 12 or 56 or, unless these rules provide otherwise, on any other motion.

(4) *Effect of a Master's Findings.* A master's findings, to the extent adopted by the court, must be considered the court's findings.

(5) *Questioning the Evidentiary Support.* A party may later question the sufficiency of the evidence supporting the findings, whether or not the party requested findings, objected to them, moved to amend them, or moved for partial findings.

(6) *Setting Aside the Findings.* Findings of fact, whether based on oral or other evidence, must not be set aside unless clearly erroneous, and the reviewing court must give due regard to the trial court's opportunity to judge the witnesses' credibility.

(b) Amended or Additional Findings. On a party's motion filed no later than 10 days after the entry of judgment, the court may amend its findings—or make additional findings—and may amend the judgment accordingly. The motion may accompany a motion for a new trial under Rule 59.

(c) Judgment on Partial Findings. If a party has been fully heard on an issue during a nonjury trial and the court finds against the party on that issue, the court may enter judgment against the party on a claim or defense that, under the controlling law, can be maintained or defeated only with a favorable finding on that issue. The court may, however, decline to render any judgment until the close of the evidence. A judgment on partial findings must be supported by findings of fact and conclusions of law as required by Rule 52(a).

[Amended December 27, 1946, effective March 19, 1948; January 21, 1963, effective July 1, 1963; April 28, 1983, effective August 1, 1983; April 29, 1985, effective August 1, 1985; April 30, 1991, effective December 1, 1991; April 22, 1993, effective December 1, 1993; April 27, 1995, effective December 1, 1995; April 30, 2007, effective December 1, 2007.]

RULE 53. MASTERS

(a) Appointment.

(1) *Scope.* Unless a statute provides otherwise, a court may appoint a master only to:

(A) perform duties consented to by the parties;

(B) hold trial proceedings and make or recommend findings of fact on issues to be decided without a jury if appointment is warranted by:

(i) some exceptional condition; or

(ii) the need to perform an accounting or resolve a difficult computation of damages; or

(C) address pretrial and posttrial matters that cannot be effectively and timely addressed by an available district judge or magistrate judge of the district.

(2) *Disqualification.* A master must not have a relationship to the parties, attorneys, action, or court that would require disqualification of a judge under 28 U.S.C. § 455, unless the parties, with the court's approval, consent to the appointment after the master discloses any potential grounds for disqualification.

(3) *Possible Expense or Delay.* In appointing a master, the court must consider the fairness of imposing the likely expenses on the parties and must protect against unreasonable expense or delay.

(b) Order Appointing a Master.

(1) *Notice.* Before appointing a master, the court must give the parties notice and an opportunity to be heard. Any party may suggest candidates for appointment.

(2) *Contents.* The appointing order must direct the master to proceed with all reasonable diligence and must state:

(A) the master's duties, including any investigation or enforcement duties, and any limits on the master's authority under Rule 53(c);

(B) the circumstances, if any, in which the master may communicate ex parte with the court or a party;

(C) the nature of the materials to be preserved and filed as the record of the master's activities;

(D) the time limits, method of filing the record, other procedures, and standards for reviewing the master's orders, findings, and recommendations; and

(E) the basis, terms, and procedure for fixing the master's compensation under Rule 53(g).

(3) *Issuing.* The court may issue the order only after:

(A) the master files an affidavit disclosing whether there is any ground for disqualification under 28 U.S.C. § 455; and

(B) if a ground is disclosed, the parties, with the court's approval, waive the disqualification.

(4) *Amending.* The order may be amended at any time after notice to the parties and an opportunity to be heard.

(c) Master's Authority.

(1) *In General.* Unless the appointing order directs otherwise, a master may:

(A) regulate all proceedings;

(B) take all appropriate measures to perform the assigned duties fairly and efficiently; and

(C) if conducting an evidentiary hearing, exercise the appointing court's power to compel, take, and record evidence.

(2) *Sanctions.* The master may by order impose on a party any noncontempt sanction provided by Rule 37 or 45, and may recommend a contempt sanction against a party and sanctions against a nonparty.

(d) Master's Orders. A master who issues an order must file it and promptly serve a copy on each party. The clerk must enter the order on the docket.

(e) Master's Reports. A master must report to the court as required by the appointing order. The master must file the report and promptly serve a copy on each party, unless the court orders otherwise.

(f) Action on the Master's Order, Report, or Recommendations.

(1) *Opportunity for a Hearing; Action in General.* In acting on a master's order, report, or recommendations, the court must give the parties notice and an opportunity to be heard; may receive evidence; and may adopt or affirm, modify, wholly or partly reject or reverse, or resubmit to the master with instructions.

(2) *Time to Object or Move to Adopt or Modify.* A party may file objections to—or a motion to adopt or modify—the master's order, report, or recommendations no later than 20 days after a copy is served, unless the court sets a different time.

(3) *Reviewing Factual Findings.* The court must decide de novo all objections to findings of fact made or recommended by a master, unless the parties, with the court's approval, stipulate that:

(A) the findings will be reviewed for clear error; or

(B) the findings of a master appointed under Rule 53(a)(1)(A) or (C) will be final.

(4) *Reviewing Legal Conclusions.* The court must decide de novo all objections to conclusions of law made or recommended by a master.

(5) *Reviewing Procedural Matters.* Unless the appointing order establishes a different standard of review, the court may set aside a master's ruling on a procedural matter only for an abuse of discretion.

(g) Compensation.

(1) *Fixing Compensation.* Before or after judgment, the court must fix the master's compensation on the basis and terms stated in the appointing order, but the court may set a new basis and terms after giving notice and an opportunity to be heard.

(2) *Payment.* The compensation must be paid either:

(A) by a party or parties; or

(B) from a fund or subject matter of the action within the court's control.

(3) *Allocating Payment.* The court must allocate payment among the parties after considering the nature and amount of the controversy, the parties' means, and the extent to which any party is more responsible than other parties for the reference to a master. An interim allocation may be amended to reflect a decision on the merits.

(h) Appointing a Magistrate Judge. A magistrate judge is subject to this rule only when the order referring a matter to the magistrate judge states that the reference is made under this rule.

[Amended February 28, 1966, effective July 1, 1966; April 28, 1983, effective August 1, 1983; March 2, 1987, effective August 1, 1987; April 30, 1991, effective December 1, 1991; April 22, 1993, effective December 1, 1993; March 27, 2003, effective December 1, 2003; April 30, 2007, effective December 1, 2007.]

TITLE VII. JUDGMENT

RULE 54. JUDGMENT; COSTS

(a) Definition; Form. "Judgment" as used in these rules includes a decree and any order from which an appeal lies. A judgment should not include recitals of pleadings, a master's report, or a record of prior proceedings.

(b) Judgment on Multiple Claims or Involving Multiple Parties. When an action presents more than one claim for relief—whether as a claim, counterclaim, crossclaim, or third-party claim—or when multiple parties are involved, the court may direct entry of a final judgment as to one or more, but fewer than all, claims or parties only if the court expressly determines that there is no just reason for delay. Otherwise, any order or other decision, however designated, that adjudicates fewer than all the claims or the rights and liabilities of fewer than all the parties does not end the action as to any of the claims or parties and may be revised at any time before the entry of a judgment adjudicating all the claims and all the parties' rights and liabilities.

(c) Demand for Judgment; Relief to Be Granted. A default judgment must not differ in kind from, or exceed in amount, what is demanded in the pleadings. Every other final judgment should grant the relief to which each party is entitled, even if the party has not demanded that relief in its pleadings.

(d) Costs; Attorney's Fees.

(1) *Costs Other Than Attorney's Fees.* Unless a federal statute, these rules, or a court order provides otherwise, costs—other than attorney's fees—should be allowed to the prevailing party. But costs against the United States, its officers, and its agencies may be imposed only to the extent allowed by law. The clerk may tax costs on 1 day's notice. On motion served within the next 5 days, the court may review the clerk's action.

(2) *Attorney's Fees.*

(A) Claim to Be by Motion. A claim for attorney's fees and related nontaxable expenses must be made by motion unless the substantive law requires those fees to be proved at trial as an element of damages.

(B) Timing and Contents of the Motion. Unless a statute or a court order provides otherwise, the motion must:

(i) be filed no later than 14 days after the entry of judgment;

(ii) specify the judgment and the statute, rule, or other grounds entitling the movant to the award;

(iii) state the amount sought or provide a fair estimate of it; and

(iv) disclose, if the court so orders, the terms of any agreement about fees for the services for which the claim is made.

(C) Proceedings. Subject to Rule 23(h), the court must, on a party's request, give an opportunity for adversary submissions on the motion in accordance with Rule 43(c) or 78. The court may decide issues of liability for fees before receiving submissions on the value of services. The court must find the facts and state its conclusions of law as provided in Rule 52(a).

(D) Special Procedures by Local Rule; Reference to a Master or a Magistrate Judge. By local rule, the court may establish special procedures to resolve fee-related issues without extensive evidentiary hearings. Also, the court may refer issues concerning the value of services to a special master under Rule 53 without regard to the limitations of Rule 53(a)(1), and may refer a motion for attorney's fees to a magistrate judge under Rule 72(b) as if it were a dispositive pretrial matter.

(E) Exceptions. Subparagraphs (A)-(D) do not apply to claims for fees and expenses as sanctions for violating these rules or as sanctions under 28 U.S.C. § 1927.

[Amended December 27, 1946, effective March 19, 1948; April 17, 1961, effective July 19, 1961; March 2, 1987, effective August 1, 1987; April 22, 1993, effective December 1, 1993; April 29, 2002, effective December 1, 2002; March 27, 2003, effective December 1, 2003; April 30, 2007, effective December 1, 2007.]

RULE 55. DEFAULT; DEFAULT JUDGMENT

(a) Entering a Default. When a party against whom a judgment for affirmative relief is sought has failed to plead or otherwise defend, and that failure is shown by affidavit or otherwise, the clerk must enter the party's default.

(b) Entering a Default Judgment.

(1) *By the Clerk.* If the plaintiff's claim is for a sum certain or a sum that can be made certain by computation, the clerk—on the plaintiff's request, with an affidavit showing the amount due—must enter judgment for that amount and costs against a defendant who has been defaulted for not appearing and who is neither a minor nor an incompetent person.

(2) *By the Court.* In all other cases, the party must apply to the court for a default judgment. A default judgment may be entered against a minor or incompetent person only if represented by a general guardian, conservator, or other like fiduciary who has appeared. If the party against whom a default judgment is sought has appeared personally or by a representative, that party or its representative must be served with written notice of the application at least 3 days before the hearing. The court may conduct hearings or make referrals—preserving any federal statutory right to a jury trial—when, to enter or effectuate judgment, it needs to:

(A) conduct an accounting;

(B) determine the amount of damages;

(C) establish the truth of any allegation by evidence; or

(D) investigate any other matter.

(c) Setting Aside a Default or a Default Judgment. The court may set aside an entry of default for good cause, and it may set aside a default judgment under Rule 60(b).

(d) Judgment Against the United States. A default judgment may be entered against the United States, its officers, or its agencies only if the claimant establishes a claim or right to relief by evidence that satisfies the court.

[Amended March 2, 1987, effective August 1, 1987; April 30, 2007, effective December 1, 2007.]

RULE 56. SUMMARY JUDGMENT

(a) By a Claiming Party. A party claiming relief may move, with or without supporting affidavits, for summary judgment on all or part of the claim. The motion may be filed at any time after:

(1) 20 days have passed from commencement of the action; or

(2) the opposing party serves a motion for summary judgment.

(b) By a Defending Party. A party against whom relief is sought may move at any time, with or without supporting affidavits, for summary judgment on all or part of the claim.

(c) Serving the Motion; Proceedings. The motion must be served at least 10 days before the day set for the hearing. An opposing party may serve opposing affidavits before the hearing day. The judgment sought should be rendered if the pleadings, the discovery and disclosure materials on file, and any affidavits show that there is no genuine issue as to any material fact and that the movant is entitled to judgment as a matter of law.

(d) Case Not Fully Adjudicated on the Motion.

(1) *Establishing Facts.* If summary judgment is not rendered on the whole action, the court should, to the extent practicable, determine what material facts are not genuinely at issue. The court should so determine by examining the pleadings and evidence before it and by interrogating the attorneys. It should then issue an order specifying what facts—including items of damages or other relief—are not genuinely at issue. The facts so specified must be treated as established in the action.

(2) *Establishing Liability.* An interlocutory summary judgment may be rendered on liability alone, even if there is a genuine issue on the amount of damages.

(e) Affidavits; Further Testimony.

(1) *In General.* A supporting or opposing affidavit must be made on personal knowledge, set out facts that would be admissible in evidence, and show that the affiant is competent to testify on the matters stated. If a paper or part of a paper is referred to in an affidavit, a sworn or certified copy must be attached to or served with the affidavit. The court may permit an affidavit to be supplemented or opposed by depositions, answers to interrogatories, or additional affidavits.

(2) *Opposing Party's Obligation to Respond.* When a motion for summary judgment is properly made and supported, an opposing party may not rely merely on allegations or denials in its own pleading; rather, its response must—by affidavits or as otherwise provided in this rule—set out specific facts showing a genuine issue for trial. If the opposing party does not so respond, summary judgment should, if appropriate, be entered against that party.

(f) When Affidavits Are Unavailable. If a party opposing the motion shows by affidavit that, for specified reasons, it cannot present facts essential to justify its opposition, the court may:

(1) deny the motion;

(2) order a continuance to enable affidavits to be obtained, depositions to be taken, or other discovery to be undertaken; or

(3) issue any other just order.

(g) Affidavit Submitted in Bad Faith. If satisfied that an affidavit under this rule is submitted in bad faith or solely for delay, the court must order the submitting party to pay the other party the reasonable expenses, including attorney's fees, it incurred as a result. An offending party or attorney may also be held in contempt.

[Amended December 27, 1946, effective March 19, 1948; January 21, 1963, effective July 1, 1963; March 2, 1987, effective August 1, 1987; April 30, 2007, effective December 1, 2007.]

RULE 57. DECLARATORY JUDGMENT

These rules govern the procedure for obtaining a declaratory judgment under 28 U.S.C. § 2201. Rules 38 and 39 govern a demand for a jury trial. The existence of another adequate remedy does not preclude a declaratory judgment that is otherwise appropriate. The court may order a speedy hearing of a declaratory-judgment action.

[Amended December 29, 1948, effective October 20, 1949; April 30, 2007, effective December 1, 2007.]

RULE 58. ENTERING JUDGMENT

(a) Separate Document. Every judgment and amended judgment must be set out in a separate document, but a separate document is not required for an order disposing of a motion:

(1) for judgment under Rule 50(b);

(2) to amend or make additional findings under Rule 52(b);

(3) for attorney's fees under Rule 54;

(4) for a new trial, or to alter or amend the judgment, under Rule 59; or

(5) for relief under Rule 60.

(b) Entering Judgment.

(1) *Without the Court's Direction.* Subject to Rule 54(b) and unless the court orders otherwise, the clerk must, without awaiting the court's direction, promptly prepare, sign, and enter the judgment when:

(A) the jury returns a general verdict;

(B) the court awards only costs or a sum certain; or

(C) the court denies all relief.

(2) *Court's Approval Required.* Subject to Rule 54(b), the court must promptly approve the form of the judgment, which the clerk must promptly enter, when:

(A) the jury returns a special verdict or a general verdict with answers to written questions; or

(B) the court grants other relief not described in this subdivision (b).

(c) Time of Entry. For purposes of these rules, judgment is entered at the following times:

(1) if a separate document is not required, when the judgment is entered in the civil docket under Rule 79(a); or

(2) if a separate document is required, when the judgment is entered in the civil docket under Rule 79(a) and the earlier of these events occurs:

(A) it is set out in a separate document; or

(B) 150 days have run from the entry in the civil docket.

(d) Request for Entry. A party may request that judgment be set out in a separate document as required by Rule 58(a).

(e) Cost or Fee Awards. Ordinarily, the entry of judgment may not be delayed, nor the time for appeal extended, in order to tax costs or award fees. But if a timely motion for attorney's fees is made under Rule 54(d)(2), the court may act before a notice of appeal has been filed and become effective to order that the motion have the same effect under Federal Rule of Appellate Procedure 4(a)(4) as a timely motion under Rule 59.

[Amended December 27, 1946, effective March 19, 1948; January 21, 1963, effective July 1, 1963; April 22, 1993, effective December 1, 1993; April 29, 2002, effective December 1, 2002; April 30, 2007, effective December 1, 2007.]

RULE 59. NEW TRIAL; ALTERING OR AMENDING A JUDGMENT

(a) In General.

(1) *Grounds for New Trial.* The court may, on motion, grant a new trial on all or some of the issues—and to any party—as follows:

(A) after a jury trial, for any reason for which a new trial has heretofore been granted in an action at law in federal court; or

(B) after a nonjury trial, for any reason for which a rehearing has heretofore been granted in a suit in equity in federal court.

(2) *Further Action After a Nonjury Trial.* After a nonjury trial, the court may, on motion for a new trial, open the judgment if one has been entered, take additional testimony, amend findings of fact and conclusions of law or make new ones, and direct the entry of a new judgment.

(b) Time to File a Motion for a New Trial. A motion for a new trial must be filed no later than 10 days after the entry of judgment.

(c) Time to Serve Affidavits. When a motion for a new trial is based on affidavits, they must be filed with the motion. The opposing party has 10 days after being served to file opposing affidavits; but that period may be extended for up to 20 days, either by the court for good cause or by the parties' stipulation. The court may permit reply affidavits.

(d) New Trial on the Court's Initiative or for Reasons Not in the Motion. No later than 10 days after the entry of judgment, the court, on its own, may order a new trial for any reason that would justify granting one on a party's motion. After giving the parties notice and an opportunity to be heard, the court may grant a timely motion for a new trial for a reason not stated in the motion. In either event, the court must specify the reasons in its order.

(e) Motion to Alter or Amend a Judgment. A motion to alter or amend a judgment must be filed no later than 10 days after the entry of the judgment.

[Amended December 27, 1946, effective March 19, 1948; February 28, 1966, effective July 1, 1966; April 27, 1995, effective December 1, 1995; April 30, 2007, effective December 1, 2007.]

RULE 60. RELIEF FROM A JUDGMENT OR ORDER

(a) Corrections Based on Clerical Mistakes; Oversights and Omissions. The court may correct a clerical mistake or a mistake arising from oversight or omission whenever one is found in a judgment, order, or other part of the record. The court may do so on motion or on its own, with or without notice. But after an appeal has been docketed in the appellate court and while it is pending, such a mistake may be corrected only with the appellate court's leave.

(b) Grounds for Relief from a Final Judgment, Order, or Proceeding. On motion and just terms, the court may relieve a party or its legal representative from a final judgment, order, or proceeding for the following reasons:

(1) mistake, inadvertence, surprise, or excusable neglect;

(2) newly discovered evidence that, with reasonable diligence, could not have been discovered in time to move for a new trial under Rule 59(b);

(3) fraud (whether previously called intrinsic or extrinsic), misrepresentation, or misconduct by an opposing party;

(4) the judgment is void;

(5) the judgment has been satisfied, released or discharged; it is based on an earlier judgment that has been reversed or vacated; or applying it prospectively is no longer equitable; or

(6) any other reason that justifies relief.

(c) Timing and Effect of the Motion.

(1) *Timing.* A motion under Rule 60(b) must be made within a reasonable time—and for reasons (1), (2), and (3) no more than a year after the entry of the judgment or order or the date of the proceeding.

(2) *Effect on Finality.* The motion does not affect the judgment's finality or suspend its operation.

(d) Other Powers to Grant Relief. This rule does not limit a court's power to:

(1) entertain an independent action to relieve a party from a judgment, order, or proceeding;

(2) grant relief under 28 U.S.C. § 1655 to a defendant who was not personally notified of the action; or

(3) set aside a judgment for fraud on the court.

(e) Bills and Writs Abolished. The following are abolished: bills of review, bills in the nature of bills of review, and writs of coram nobis, coram vobis, and audita querela.

[Amended December 27, 1946, effective March 19, 1948; December 29, 1948, effective October 20, 1949; March 2, 1987, effective August 1, 1987; April 30, 2007, effective December 1, 2007.]

RULE 61. HARMLESS ERROR

Unless justice requires otherwise, no error in admitting or excluding evidence—or any other error by the court or a party—is ground for granting a new trial, for setting aside a verdict, or for vacating, modifying, or otherwise disturbing a judgment or order. At every stage of the proceeding, the court must disregard all errors and defects that do not affect any party's substantial rights.

[Amended April 30, 2007, effective December 1, 2007.]

RULE 62. STAY OF PROCEEDINGS TO ENFORCE A JUDGMENT

(a) Automatic Stay; Exceptions for Injunctions, Receiverships, and Patent Accountings. Except as stated in this rule, no execution may issue on a judgment, nor may proceedings be taken to enforce it, until 10 days have passed after its entry. But unless the court orders otherwise, the following are not stayed after being entered, even if an appeal is taken:

(1) an interlocutory or final judgment in an action for an injunction or a receivership; or

(2) a judgment or order that directs an accounting in an action for patent infringement.

(b) Stay Pending the Disposition of a Motion. On appropriate terms for the opposing party's security, the court may stay the execution of a judgment—or any proceedings to enforce it—pending disposition of any of the following motions:

(1) under Rule 50, for judgment as a matter of law;

(2) under Rule 52(b), to amend the findings or for additional findings;

(3) under Rule 59, for a new trial or to alter or amend a judgment; or

(4) under Rule 60, for relief from a judgment or order.

(c) Injunction Pending an Appeal. While an appeal is pending from an interlocutory order or final judgment that grants, dissolves, or denies an injunction, the court may suspend, modify, restore, or grant an injunction on terms for bond or other terms that secure the opposing party's rights. If the judgment appealed from is rendered by a statutory three-judge district court, the order must be made either:

(1) by that court sitting in open session; or

(2) by the assent of all its judges, as evidenced by their signatures.

(d) Stay with Bond on Appeal. If an appeal is taken, the appellant may obtain a stay by supersedeas bond, except in an action described in Rule 62(a)(1) or (2). The bond may be given upon or after filing the notice of appeal or after obtaining the order allowing the appeal. The stay takes effect when the court approves the bond.

(e) Stay Without Bond on an Appeal by the United States, Its Officers, or Its Agencies. The court must not require a bond, obligation, or other security from the appellant when granting a stay on an appeal by the United States, its officers, or its agencies or on an appeal directed by a department of the federal government.

(f) Stay in Favor of a Judgment Debtor Under State Law. If a judgment is a lien on the judgment debtor's property under the law of the state where the court is located, the judgment debtor is entitled to the same stay of execution the state court would give.

(g) Appellate Court's Power Not Limited. This rule does not limit the power of the appellate court or one of its judges or justices:

(1) to stay proceedings—or suspend, modify, restore, or grant an injunction—while an appeal is pending; or

(2) to issue an order to preserve the status quo or the effectiveness of the judgment to be entered.

(h) Stay with Multiple Claims or Parties. A court may stay the enforcement of a final judgment entered under Rule 54(b) until it enters a later judgment or judgments, and may prescribe terms necessary to secure the benefit of the stayed judgment for the party in whose favor it was entered.

[Amended December 27, 1946, effective March 19, 1948; December 29, 1948, effective October 20, 1949; April 17, 1961, effective July 19, 1961; March 2, 1987, effective August 1, 1987; April 30, 2007, effective December 1, 2007.]

RULE 63. JUDGE'S INABILITY TO PROCEED

If a judge conducting a hearing or trial is unable to proceed, any other judge may proceed upon certifying familiarity with the record and determining that the case may be completed without prejudice to the parties. In a hearing or a nonjury trial, the successor judge must, at a party's request, recall any witness whose testimony is material and disputed and who is available to testify again without undue burden. The successor judge may also recall any other witness.

[Amended March 2, 1987, effective August 1, 1987; April 30, 1991, effective December 1, 1991; April 30, 2007, effective December 1, 2007.]

TITLE VIII. PROVISIONAL AND FINAL REMEDIES

RULE 64. SEIZING A PERSON OR PROPERTY

(a) Remedies Under State Law—In General. At the commencement of and throughout an action, every remedy is available that, under the law of the state where the court is located, provides for seizing a person or property to secure satisfaction of the potential judgment. But a federal statute governs to the extent it applies.

(b) Specific Kinds of Remedies. The remedies available under this rule include the following—however designated and regardless of whether state procedure requires an independent action:

- arrest;
- attachment;
- garnishment;
- replevin;
- sequestration; and
- other corresponding or equivalent remedies.

[Amended April 30, 2007, effective December 1, 2007.]

RULE 65. INJUNCTIONS AND RESTRAINING ORDERS

(a) Preliminary Injunction.

(1) *Notice.* The court may issue a preliminary injunction only on notice to the adverse party.

(2) *Consolidating the Hearing with the Trial on the Merits.* Before or after beginning the hearing on a motion for a preliminary injunction, the court may advance the trial on the merits and consolidate it with the hearing. Even when consolidation is not ordered, evidence that is received on the motion and that would be admissible at trial becomes part of the trial record and need not be repeated at trial. But the court must preserve any party's right to a jury trial.

(b) Temporary Restraining Order.

(1) *Issuing Without Notice.* The court may issue a temporary restraining order without written or oral notice to the adverse party or its attorney only if:

(A) specific facts in an affidavit or a verified complaint clearly show that immediate and irreparable injury, loss, or damage will result to the movant before the adverse party can be heard in opposition; and

(B) the movant's attorney certifies in writing any efforts made to give notice and the reasons why it should not be required.

(2) *Contents; Expiration.* Every temporary restraining order issued without notice must state the date and hour it was issued; describe the injury and state why it is irreparable; state why the order was issued without notice; and be promptly filed in the clerk's office and entered in the record. The order expires at the time after entry—not to exceed 10 days—that the court sets, unless before that time the court, for good cause, extends it for a like period or the adverse party consents to a longer extension. The reasons for an extension must be entered in the record.

(3) *Expediting the Preliminary-Injunction Hearing.* If the order is issued without notice, the motion for a preliminary injunction must be set for hearing at the earliest possible time, taking precedence over all other matters except hearings on older matters of the same character. At the hearing, the party who obtained the order must proceed with the motion; if the party does not, the court must dissolve the order.

(4) *Motion to Dissolve.* On 2 days' notice to the party who obtained the order without notice—or on shorter notice set by the court—the adverse party may appear and move to dissolve or modify the order. The court must then hear and decide the motion as promptly as justice requires.

(c) Security. The court may issue a preliminary injunction or a temporary restraining order only if the movant gives security in an amount that the court considers proper to pay the costs and damages sustained by any party found to have been wrongfully enjoined or restrained. The United States, its officers, and its agencies are not required to give security.

(d) Contents and Scope of Every Injunction and Restraining Order.

(1) *Contents.* Every order granting an injunction and every restraining order must:

(A) state the reasons why it issued;

(B) state its terms specifically; and

(C) describe in reasonable detail—and not by referring to the complaint or other document—the act or acts restrained or required.

(2) *Persons Bound.* The order binds only the following who receive actual notice of it by personal service or otherwise:

(A) the parties;

(B) the parties' officers, agents, servants, employees, and attorneys; and

(C) other persons who are in active concert or participation with anyone described in Rule 65(d)(2)(A) or (B).

(e) Other Laws Not Modified. These rules do not modify the following:

(1) any federal statute relating to temporary restraining orders or preliminary injunctions in actions affecting employer and employee;

(2) 28 U.S.C. § 2361, which relates to preliminary injunctions in actions of interpleader or in the nature of interpleader; or

(3) 28 U.S.C. § 2284, which relates to actions that must be heard and decided by a three-judge district court.

(f) Copyright Impoundment. This rule applies to copyright-impoundment proceedings.

[Amended December 27, 1946, effective March 19, 1948; December 29, 1948, effective October 20, 1949; February 28, 1966, effective July 1, 1966; March 2, 1987, effective August 1, 1987; April 23, 2001, effective December 1, 2001; April 30, 2007, effective December 1, 2007.]

RULE 65.1 PROCEEDINGS AGAINST A SURETY

Whenever these rules (including the Supplemental Rules for Admiralty or Maritime Claims and Asset Forfeiture Actions) require or allow a party to give security, and security is given through a bond or other undertaking with one or more sureties, each surety submits to the court's jurisdiction and irrevocably appoints the court clerk as its agent for receiving service of any papers that affect its liability on the bond or undertaking. The surety's liability may be enforced on motion without an independent action. The motion and any notice that the court orders may be served on the court clerk, who must promptly mail a copy of each to every surety whose address is known.

[Adopted February 28, 1966, effective July 1, 1966; amended March 2, 1987, effective August 1, 1987; April 12, 2006, effective December 1, 2006; April 30, 2007, effective December 1, 2007.]

RULE 66. RECEIVERS

These rules govern an action in which the appointment of a receiver is sought or a receiver sues or is sued. But the practice in administering an estate by a receiver or a similar court-appointed officer must accord with the historical practice in federal courts or with a local rule. An action in which a receiver has been appointed may be dismissed only by court order.

[Amended December 27, 1946, effective March 19, 1948; December 29, 1948, effective October 20, 1949; April 30, 2007, effective December 1, 2007.]

RULE 67. DEPOSIT INTO COURT

(a) Depositing Property. If any part of the relief sought is a money judgment or the disposition of a sum of money or some other deliverable thing, a party—on notice to every other party and by leave of court—may deposit with the court all or part of the money or thing, whether or not that party claims any of it. The depositing party must deliver to the clerk a copy of the order permitting deposit.

(b) Investing and Withdrawing Funds. Money paid into court under this rule must be deposited and withdrawn in accordance with 28 U.S.C. §§ 2041 and 2042 and any like statute. The money must be deposited in an interest-bearing account or invested in a court-approved, interest-bearing instrument.

[Amended December 29, 1948, effective October 20, 1949; April 28, 1983, effective August 1, 1983; April 30, 2007, effective December 1, 2007.]

RULE 68. OFFER OF JUDGMENT

(a) Making an Offer; Judgment on an Accepted Offer. More than 10 days before the trial begins, a party defending against a claim may serve on an opposing party an offer to allow judgment on specified terms, with the costs then accrued. If, within 10 days after being served, the opposing party serves written notice accepting the offer, either party may then file the offer and notice of acceptance, plus proof of service. The clerk must then enter judgment.

(b) Unaccepted Offer. An unaccepted offer is considered withdrawn, but it does not preclude a later offer. Evidence of an unaccepted offer is not admissible except in a proceeding to determine costs.

(c) Offer After Liability Is Determined. When one party's liability to another has been determined but the extent of liability remains to be determined by further proceedings, the party held liable may make an offer of judgment. It must be served within a reasonable time—but at least 10 days—before a hearing to determine the extent of liability.

(d) Paying Costs After an Unaccepted Offer. If the judgment that the offeree finally obtains is not more favorable than the unaccepted offer, the offeree must pay the costs incurred after the offer was made.

[Amended December 27, 1946, effective March 19, 1948; February 28, 1966, effective July 1, 1966; March 2, 1987, effective August 1, 1987; April 30, 2007, effective December 1, 2007.]

RULE 69. EXECUTION

(a) In General.

(1) *Money Judgment; Applicable Procedure.* A money judgment is enforced by a writ of execution, unless the court directs otherwise. The procedure on execution—and in proceedings supplementary to and in aid of judgment or execution—must accord with the procedure of the state where the court is located, but a federal statute governs to the extent it applies.

(2) *Obtaining Discovery.* In aid of the judgment or execution, the judgment creditor or a successor in interest whose interest appears of record may obtain discovery from any person—including the judgment debtor—as provided in these rules or by the procedure of the state where the court is located.

(b) Against Certain Public Officers. When a judgment has been entered against a revenue officer in the circumstances stated in 28 U.S.C. § 2006, or against an officer of Congress in the circumstances stated in 2 U.S.C. § 118, the judgment must be satisfied as those statutes provide.

[Amended December 29, 1948, effective October 20, 1949; March 30, 1970, effective July 1, 1970; March 2, 1987 effective August 1, 1987; April 30, 2007, effective December 1, 2007.]

RULE 70. ENFORCING A JUDGMENT FOR A SPECIFIC ACT

(a) Party's Failure to Act; Ordering Another to Act. If a judgment requires a party to convey land, to deliver a deed or other document, or to perform any other specific act and the party fails to comply within the time specified, the court may order the act to be done—at the disobedient party's expense—by another person appointed by the court. When done, the act has the same effect as if done by the party.

(b) Vesting Title. If the real or personal property is within the district, the court—instead of ordering a conveyance—may enter a judgment divesting any party's title and vesting it in others. That judgment has the effect of a legally executed conveyance.

(c) Obtaining a Writ of Attachment or Sequestration. On application by a party entitled to performance of an act, the clerk must issue a writ of attachment or sequestration against the disobedient party's property to compel obedience.

(d) Obtaining a Writ of Execution or Assistance. On application by a party who obtains a judgment or order for possession, the clerk must issue a writ of execution or assistance.

(e) Holding in Contempt. The court may also hold the disobedient party in contempt.

[Amended April 30, 2007, effective December 1, 2007.]

RULE 71. ENFORCING RELIEF FOR OR AGAINST A NONPARTY

When an order grants relief for a nonparty or may be enforced against a nonparty, the procedure for enforcing the order is the same as for a party.

[Amended March 2, 1987, effective August 1, 1987; April 30, 2007, effective December 1, 2007.]

TITLE IX. SPECIAL PROCEEDINGS

RULE 71.1 CONDEMNING REAL OR PERSONAL PROPERTY

(a) Applicability of Other Rules. These rules govern proceedings to condemn real and personal property by eminent domain, except as this rule provides otherwise.

(b) Joinder of Properties. The plaintiff may join separate pieces of property in a single action, no matter whether they are owned by the same persons or sought for the same use.

(c) Complaint.

(1) *Caption.* The complaint must contain a caption as provided in Rule 10(a). The plaintiff must, however, name as defendants both the property—designated generally by kind, quantity, and location—and at least one owner of some part of or interest in the property.

(2) *Contents.* The complaint must contain a short and plain statement of the following:

(A) the authority for the taking;

(B) the uses for which the property is to be taken;

(C) a description sufficient to identify the property;

(D) the interests to be acquired; and

(E) for each piece of property, a designation of each defendant who has been joined as an owner or owner of an interest in it.

(3) *Parties.* When the action commences, the plaintiff need join as defendants only those persons who have or claim an interest in the property and whose names are then known. But before any hearing on compensation, the plaintiff must add as defendants all those persons who have or claim an interest and whose names have become known or can be found by a reasonably diligent search of the records, considering both the property's character and value and the interests to be acquired. All others may be made defendants under the designation "Unknown Owners."

(4) *Procedure.* Notice must be served on all defendants as provided in Rule 71.1(d), whether they were named as defendants when the action commenced or were added later. A defendant may answer as provided in Rule 71.1(e). The court, meanwhile, may order any distribution of a deposit that the facts warrant.

(5) *Filing; Additional Copies.* In addition to filing the complaint, the plaintiff must give the clerk at least one copy for the defendants' use and additional copies at the request of the clerk or a defendant.

(d) Process.

(1) *Delivering Notice to the Clerk.* On filing a complaint, the plaintiff must promptly deliver to the clerk joint or several notices directed to the named defendants. When adding defendants, the plaintiff must deliver to the clerk additional notices directed to the new defendants.

(2) *Contents of the Notice.*

(A) Main Contents. Each notice must name the court, the title of the action, and the defendant to whom it is directed. It must describe the property sufficiently to identify it, but need not describe any property other than that to be taken from the named defendant. The notice must also state:

(i) that the action is to condemn property;

(ii) the interest to be taken;

(iii) the authority for the taking;

(iv) the uses for which the property is to be taken;

(v) that the defendant may serve an answer on the plaintiff's attorney within 20 days after being served with the notice;

(vi) that the failure to so serve an answer constitutes consent to the taking and to the court's authority to proceed with the action and fix the compensation; and

(vii) that a defendant who does not serve an answer may file a notice of appearance.

(B) Conclusion. The notice must conclude with the name, telephone number, and e-mail address of the plaintiff's attorney and an address within the district in which the action is brought where the attorney may be served.

(3) *Serving the Notice.*

(A) Personal Service. When a defendant whose address is known resides within the United States or a territory subject to the administrative or judicial jurisdiction of the United States, personal service of the notice (without a copy of the complaint) must be made in accordance with Rule 4.

(B) Service by Publication.

(i) A defendant may be served by publication only when the plaintiff's attorney files a certificate stating that the attorney believes the defendant cannot be personally served, because after diligent inquiry within the state where the complaint is filed, the defendant's place of residence is still unknown or, if known, that it is beyond the territorial limits of personal service. Service is then made by publishing the notice—once a week for at least three successive weeks—in a newspaper published in the county where the property is located or, if there is no such newspaper, in a newspaper with general circulation where the property is located. Before the last publication, a copy of the notice must also be mailed to every defendant who cannot be personally served but whose place of residence is then known. Unknown owners may be served by publication in the same manner by a notice addressed to "Unknown Owners."

(ii) Service by publication is complete on the date of the last publication. The plaintiff's attorney must prove publication and mailing by a certificate, attach a printed copy of the published notice, and mark on the copy the newspaper's name and the dates of publication.

(4) *Effect of Delivery and Service.* Delivering the notice to the clerk and serving it have the same effect as serving a summons under Rule 4.

(5) *Amending the Notice; Proof of Service and Amending the Proof.* Rule 4(a)(2) governs amending the notice. Rule 4(*l*) governs proof of service and amending it.

(e) Appearance or Answer.

(1) *Notice of Appearance.* A defendant that has no objection or defense to the taking of its property may serve a notice of appearance designating the property in which it claims an interest. The defendant must then be given notice of all later proceedings affecting the defendant.

(2) *Answer.* A defendant that has an objection or defense to the taking must serve an answer within 20 days after being served with the notice. The answer must:

(A) identify the property in which the defendant claims an interest;

(B) state the nature and extent of the interest; and

(C) state all the defendant's objections and defenses to the taking.

(3) *Waiver of Other Objections and Defenses; Evidence on Compensation.* A defendant waives all objections and defenses not stated in its answer. No other pleading or motion asserting an additional objection or defense is allowed. But at the trial on compensation, a defendant—whether or not it has previously appeared or answered—may present evidence on the amount of compensation to be paid and may share in the award.

(f) Amending Pleadings. Without leave of court, the plaintiff may—as often as it wants—amend the complaint at any time before the trial on compensation. But no amendment may be made if it would result in a dismissal inconsistent with Rule 71.1(i)(1) or (2). The plaintiff need not serve a copy of an amendment, but must serve notice of the filing, as provided in Rule 5(b), on every affected party who has appeared and, as provided in Rule 71.1(d), on every affected party who has not appeared. In addition, the plaintiff must give the clerk at least one copy of each amendment for the defendants' use, and additional copies at the request of the clerk or a defendant. A defendant may appear or answer in the time and manner and with the same effect as provided in Rule 71.1(e).

(g) Substituting Parties. If a defendant dies, becomes incompetent, or transfers an interest after being joined, the court may, on motion and notice of hearing, order that the proper party be substituted.

Service of the motion and notice on a nonparty must be made as provided in Rule 71.1(d)(3).

(h) Trial of the Issues.

(1) *Issues Other Than Compensation; Compensation.* In an action involving eminent domain under federal law, the court tries all issues, including compensation, except when compensation must be determined:

(A) by any tribunal specially constituted by a federal statute to determine compensation; or

(B) if there is no such tribunal, by a jury when a party demands one within the time to answer or within any additional time the court sets, unless the court appoints a commission.

(2) *Appointing a Commission; Commission's Powers and Report.*

(A) Reasons for Appointing. If a party has demanded a jury, the court may instead appoint a three-person commission to determine compensation because of the character, location, or quantity of the property to be condemned or for other just reasons.

(B) Alternate Commissioners. The court may appoint up to two additional persons to serve as alternate commissioners to hear the case and replace commissioners who, before a decision is filed, the court finds unable or disqualified to perform their duties. Once the commission renders its final decision, the court must discharge any alternate who has not replaced a commissioner.

(C) Examining the Prospective Commissioners. Before making its appointments, the court must advise the parties of the identity and qualifications of each prospective commissioner and alternate, and may permit the parties to examine them. The parties may not suggest appointees, but for good cause may object to a prospective commissioner or alternate.

(D) Commission's Powers and Report. A commission has the powers of a master under Rule 53(c). Its action and report are determined by a majority. Rule 53(d), (e), and (f) apply to its action and report.

(i) Dismissal of the Action or a Defendant.

(1) *Dismissing the Action.*

(A) By the Plaintiff. If no compensation hearing on a piece of property has begun, and if the plaintiff has not acquired title or a lesser interest or taken possession, the plaintiff may, without a court order, dismiss the action as to that property by filing a notice of dismissal briefly describing the property.

(B) By Stipulation. Before a judgment is entered vesting the plaintiff with title or a lesser interest in or possession of property, the plaintiff and affected defendants may, without a court order, dismiss the action in whole or in part by filing a stipulation of dismissal. And if the parties so stipulate, the court may vacate a judgment already entered.

(C) By Court Order. At any time before compensation has been determined and paid, the court may, after a motion and hearing, dismiss the action as to a piece of property. But if the plaintiff has already taken title, a lesser interest, or possession as to any part of it, the court must award compensation for the title, lesser interest, or possession taken.

(2) *Dismissing a Defendant.* The court may at any time dismiss a defendant who was unnecessarily or improperly joined.

(3) *Effect.* A dismissal is without prejudice unless otherwise stated in the notice, stipulation, or court order.

(j) Deposit and Its Distribution.

(1) *Deposit.* The plaintiff must deposit with the court any money required by law as a condition to the exercise of eminent domain and may make a deposit when allowed by statute.

(2) *Distribution; Adjusting Distribution.* After a deposit, the court and attorneys must expedite the proceedings so as to distribute the deposit and to determine and pay compensation. If the compensation finally awarded to a defendant exceeds the amount distributed to that defendant, the court must enter judgment against the plaintiff for the deficiency. If the compensation awarded to a defendant is less than the amount distributed to that defendant, the court must enter judgment against that defendant for the overpayment.

(k) Condemnation Under a State's Power of Eminent Domain. This rule governs an action involving eminent domain under state law. But if state law provides for trying an issue by jury—or for trying the issue of compensation by jury or commission or both—that law governs.

(*l*) Costs. Costs are not subject to Rule 54(d).

[Adopted April 30, 1951, effective August 1, 1951; amended January 21, 1963, effective July 1, 1963; April 29, 1985, effective August 1, 1985; March 2, 1987, effective August 1, 1987; April 25, 1988, effective August 1, 1988; amended by Pub.L. 100–690, Title VII, § 7050, November 18, 1988, 102 Stat. 4401 (although amendment by Pub.L. 100–690 could not be executed due to prior amendment by Court order which made the same change effective August 1, 1988); amended April 22, 1993, effective December 1, 1993; March 27, 2003, effective December 1, 2003; April 30, 2007, effective December 1, 2007.]

RULE 72. MAGISTRATE JUDGES: PRETRIAL ORDER

(a) Nondispositive Matters. When a pretrial matter not dispositive of a party's claim or defense is referred to a magistrate judge to hear and decide, the magistrate judge must promptly conduct the required proceedings and, when appropriate, issue a written order stating the decision. A party may serve and file objections to the order within 10 days after being served with a copy. A party may not assign as error a defect in the order not timely objected to. The district judge in the case must consider timely objections and modify or set aside any part of the order that is clearly erroneous or is contrary to law.

(b) Dispositive Motions and Prisoner Petitions.

(1) *Findings and Recommendations.* A magistrate judge must promptly conduct the required proceedings when assigned, without the parties' consent, to hear a pretrial matter dispositive of a claim or defense or a prisoner petition challenging the conditions of confinement. A record must be made of all evidentiary proceedings and may, at the magistrate judge's discretion, be made of any other proceedings. The magistrate judge must enter a recommended disposition, including, if appropriate, proposed findings of fact. The clerk must promptly mail a copy to each party.

(2) *Objections.* Within 10 days after being served with a copy of the recommended disposition, a party may serve and file specific written objections to the proposed findings and recommendations. A party may respond to another party's objections within 10 days after being served with a copy. Unless the district judge orders otherwise, the objecting party must promptly arrange for transcribing the record, or whatever portions of it the parties agree to or the magistrate judge considers sufficient.

(3) *Resolving Objections.* The district judge must determine de novo any part of the magistrate judge's disposition that has been properly objected to. The district judge may accept, reject, or modify the recommended disposition; receive further evidence; or return the matter to the magistrate judge with instructions.

[Former Rule 72 abrogated December 4, 1967, effective July 1, 1968; new Rule 72 adopted April 28, 1983, effective August 1, 1983; amended April 30, 1991, effective December 1, 1991; April 22, 1993, effective December 1, 1993; April 30, 2007, effective December 1, 2007.]

RULE 73. MAGISTRATE JUDGES: TRIAL BY CONSENT; APPEAL

(a) Trial by Consent. When authorized under 28 U.S.C. § 636(c), a magistrate judge may, if all parties consent, conduct a civil action or proceeding, including a jury or nonjury trial. A record must be made in accordance with 28 U.S.C. § 636(c)(5).

(b) Consent Procedure.

(1) *In General.* When a magistrate judge has been designated to conduct civil actions or proceedings, the clerk must give the parties written notice of their opportunity to consent under 28 U.S.C. § 636(c). To signify their consent, the parties must jointly or separately file a statement consenting to the referral. A district judge or magistrate judge may be informed of a party's response to the clerk's notice only if all parties have consented to the referral.

(2) *Reminding the Parties About Consenting.* A district judge, magistrate judge, or other court official may remind the parties of the magistrate judge's availability, but must also advise them that they are free to withhold consent without adverse substantive consequences.

(3) *Vacating a Referral.* On its own for good cause—or when a party shows extraordinary circumstances—the district judge may vacate a referral to a magistrate judge under this rule.

(c) Appealing a Judgment. In accordance with 28 U.S.C. § 636(c)(3), an appeal from a judgment entered at a magistrate judge's direction may be taken to the court of appeals as would any other appeal from a district-court judgment.

[Former Rule 73 abrogated December 4, 1967, effective July 1, 1968; new Rule 73 adopted April 28, 1983, effective August 1, 1983; amended March 2, 1987, effective August 1, 1987; April 22, 1993, effective December 1, 1993; April 11, 1997, effective December 1, 1997; April 30, 2007, effective December 1, 2007.]

RULE 74. METHOD OF APPEAL FROM MAGISTRATE JUDGE TO DISTRICT JUDGE UNDER TITLE 28, U.S.C. § 636(c)(4) AND RULE 73(d) [ABROGATED]

[Former Rule 74 abrogated December 4, 1967, effective July 1, 1968; new Rule 74 adopted April 28, 1983, effective August 1, 1983; amended April 22, 1993, effective December 1, 1993; abrogated April 11, 1997, effective December 1, 1997; April 30, 2007, effective December 1, 2007.]

RULE 75. PROCEEDINGS ON APPEAL FROM MAGISTRATE JUDGE TO DISTRICT JUDGE UNDER RULE 73(d) [ABROGATED]

[Former Rule 75 abrogated December 4, 1967, effective July 1, 1968; new Rule 75 adopted April 28, 1983, effective August 1, 1983; amended March 2, 1987, effective August 1, 1987; April 22, 1993, effective December 1, 1993; abrogated April 11, 1997, effective December 1, 1997; April 30, 2007, effective December 1, 2007.]

RULE 76. JUDGMENT OF THE DISTRICT JUDGE ON THE APPEAL UNDER RULE 73(d) AND COSTS [ABROGATED]

[Former Rule 76 abrogated December 4, 1967, effective July 1, 1968; new Rule 76 adopted April 28, 1983, effective August 1, 1983; amended April 22, 1993, effective December 1, 1993; abrogated April 11, 1997, effective December 1, 1997; April 30, 2007, effective December 1, 2007.]

TITLE X. DISTRICT COURTS AND CLERKS: CONDUCTING BUSINESS; ISSUING ORDERS

RULE 77. CONDUCTING BUSINESS; CLERK'S AUTHORITY; NOTICE OF AN ORDER OR JUDGMENT

(a) When Court Is Open. Every district court is considered always open for filing any paper, issuing and returning process, making a motion, or entering an order.

(b) Place for Trial and Other Proceedings. Every trial on the merits must be conducted in open court and, so far as convenient, in a regular courtroom. Any other act or proceeding may be done or conducted by a judge in chambers, without the attendance of the clerk or other court official, and anywhere inside or outside the district. But no hearing—other than one ex parte—may be conducted outside the district unless all the affected parties consent.

(c) Clerk's Office Hours; Clerk's Orders.

(1) *Hours.* The clerk's office—with a clerk or deputy on duty—must be open during business hours every day except Saturdays, Sundays, and legal holidays. But a court may, by local rule or order, require that the office be open for specified hours on Saturday or a particular legal holiday other than one listed in Rule 6(a)(4)(A).

(2) *Orders.* Subject to the court's power to suspend, alter, or rescind the clerk's action for good cause, the clerk may:

(A) issue process;

(B) enter a default;

(C) enter a default judgment under Rule 55(b)(1); and

(D) act on any other matter that does not require the court's action.

(d) Serving Notice of an Order or Judgment.

(1) *Service.* Immediately after entering an order or judgment, the clerk must serve notice of the entry, as provided in Rule 5(b), on each party who is not in default for failing to appear. The clerk must record the service on the docket. A party also may serve notice of the entry as provided in Rule 5(b).

(2) *Time to Appeal Not Affected by Lack of Notice.* Lack of notice of the entry does not affect the time for appeal or relieve—or authorize the court to relieve—a party for failing to appeal within the time allowed, except as allowed by Federal Rule of Appellate Procedure (4)(a).

[Amended December 27, 1946, effective March 19, 1948; January 21, 1963, effective July 1, 1963; December 4, 1967, effective July 1, 1968; March 1, 1971, effective July 1, 1971; March 2, 1987, effective August 1, 1987; April 30, 1991, effective December 1, 1991; April 23, 2001, effective December 1, 2001; April 30, 2007, effective December 1, 2007.]

RULE 78. HEARING MOTIONS; SUBMISSION ON BRIEFS

(a) Providing a Regular Schedule for Oral Hearings. A court may establish regular times and places for oral hearings on motions.

(b) Providing for Submission on Briefs. By rule or order, the court may provide for submitting and determining motions on briefs, without oral hearings.

[Amended March 2, 1987, effective August 1, 1987; April 30, 2007, effective December 1, 2007.]

RULE 79. RECORDS KEPT BY THE CLERK

(a) Civil Docket.

(1) *In General.* The clerk must keep a record known as the "civil docket" in the form and manner prescribed by the Director of the Administrative Office of the United States Courts with the approval of the Judicial Conference of the United States. The clerk must enter each civil action in the docket. Actions must be assigned consecutive file numbers, which must be noted in the docket where the first entry of the action is made.

(2) *Items to be Entered.* The following items must be marked with the file number and entered chronologically in the docket:

(A) papers filed with the clerk;

(B) process issued, and proofs of service or other returns showing execution; and

(C) appearances, orders, verdicts, and judgments.

(3) *Contents of Entries; Jury Trial Demanded.* Each entry must briefly show the nature of the paper filed or writ issued, the substance of each proof of service or other return, and the substance and date of entry of each order and judgment. When a jury trial has been properly demanded or ordered, the clerk must enter the word "jury" in the docket.

(b) Civil Judgments and Orders. The clerk must keep a copy of every final judgment and appealable order; of every order affecting title to or a lien on real or personal property; and of any other order that the court directs to be kept. The clerk must keep these in the form and manner prescribed by the Director of the Administrative Office of the United States Courts with the approval of the Judicial Conference of the United States.

(c) Indexes; Calendars. Under the court's direction, the clerk must:

(1) keep indexes of the docket and of the judgments and orders described in Rule 79(b); and

(2) prepare calendars of all actions ready for trial, distinguishing jury trials from nonjury trials.

(d) Other Records. The clerk must keep any other records required by the Director of the Administrative Office of the United States Courts with the approval of the Judicial Conference of the United States.

[Amended December 27, 1946, effective March 19, 1948; December 29, 1948, effective October 20, 1949; January 21, 1963, effective July 1, 1963; April 30, 2007, effective December 1, 2007.]

RULE 80. STENOGRAPHIC TRANSCRIPT AS EVIDENCE

If stenographically reported testimony at a hearing or trial is admissible in evidence at a later trial, the testimony may be proved by a transcript certified by the person who reported it.

[Amended December 27, 1946, effective March 19, 1948; April 30, 2007, effective December 1, 2007.]

TITLE XI. GENERAL PROVISIONS

RULE 81. APPLICABILITY OF THE RULES IN GENERAL; REMOVED ACTIONS

(a) Applicability to Particular Proceedings.

(1) *Prize Proceedings.* These rules do not apply to prize proceedings in admiralty governed by 10 U.S.C. §§ 7651–7681.

(2) *Bankruptcy.* These rules apply to bankruptcy proceedings to the extent provided by the Federal Rules of Bankruptcy Procedure.

(3) *Citizenship.* These rules apply to proceedings for admission to citizenship to the extent that the practice in those proceedings is not specified in federal statutes and has previously conformed to the practice in civil actions. The provisions of 8 U.S.C. § 1451 for service by publication and for answer apply in proceedings to cancel citizenship certificates.

(4) *Special Writs.* These rules apply to proceedings for habeas corpus and for quo warranto to the extent that the practice in those proceedings:

(A) is not specified in a federal statute, the Rules Governing Section 2254 Cases, or the Rules Governing Section 2255 Cases; and

(B) has previously conformed to the practice in civil actions.

(5) *Proceedings Involving a Subpoena.* These rules apply to proceedings to compel testimony or the production of documents through a subpoena issued by a United States officer or agency under a federal statute, except as otherwise provided by statute, by local rule, or by court order in the proceedings.

(6) *Other Proceedings.* These rules, to the extent applicable, govern proceedings under the following laws, except as these laws provide other procedures:

(A) 7 U.S.C. §§ 292, 499g(c), for reviewing an order of the Secretary of Agriculture;

(B) 9 U.S.C., relating to arbitration;

(C) 15 U.S.C. § 522, for reviewing an order of the Secretary of the Interior;

(D) 15 U.S.C. § 715d(c), for reviewing an order denying a certificate of clearance;

(E) 29 U.S.C. §§ 159, 160, for enforcing an order of the National Labor Relations Board;

(F) 33 U.S.C. §§ 918, 921, for enforcing or reviewing a compensation order under the Longshore and Harbor Workers' Compensation Act; and

(G) 45 U.S.C. § 159, for reviewing an arbitration award in a railway-labor dispute.

(b) Scire Facias and Mandamus. The writs of scire facias and mandamus are abolished. Relief previously available through them may be obtained by appropriate action or motion under these rules.

(c) Removed Actions.

(1) *Applicability.* These rules apply to a civil action after it is removed from a state court.

(2) *Further Pleading.* After removal, repleading is unnecessary unless the court orders it. A defendant who did not answer before removal must answer or present other defenses or objections under these rules within the longest of these periods:

(A) 20 days after receiving—through service or otherwise—a copy of the initial pleading stating the claim for relief;

(B) 20 days after being served with the summons for an initial pleading on file at the time of service; or

(C) 5 days after the notice of removal is filed.

(3) *Demand for a Jury Trial.*

(A) As Affected by State Law. A party who, before removal, expressly demanded a jury trial in accordance with state law need not renew the demand after removal. If the state law did not require an express demand for a jury trial, a party need not make one after removal unless the court orders the parties to do so within a specified time. The court must so order at a party's request and may so order on its own. A party who fails to make a demand when so ordered waives a jury trial.

(B) Under Rule 38. If all necessary pleadings have been served at the time of removal, a party entitled to a jury trial under Rule 38 must be given one if the party serves a demand within 10 days after:

(i) it files a notice of removal; or

(ii) it is served with a notice of removal filed by another party.

(d) Law Applicable.

(1) *State Law.* When these rules refer to state law, the term "law" includes the state's statutes and the state's judicial decisions.

(2) *District of Columbia.* The term "state" includes, where appropriate, the District of Columbia. When these rules provide for state law to apply, in the District Court for the District of Columbia:

(A) the law applied in the District governs; and

(B) the term "federal statute" includes any Act of Congress that applies locally to the District.

[Amended December 28, 1939, effective April 3, 1941; December 27, 1946, effective March 19, 1948; December 29, 1948, effective October 20, 1949; April 30, 1951, effective August 1, 1951; January 21, 1963, effective July 1, 1963; February 28, 1966, effective July 1, 1966; December 4, 1967, effective July 1, 1968; March 1, 1971, effective July 1, 1971; March 2, 1987, effective August 1, 1987; April 23, 2001, effective December 1, 2001; April 29, 2002, effective December 1, 2002; April 30, 2007, effective December 1, 2007.]

RULE 82. JURISDICTION AND VENUE UNAFFECTED

These rules do not extend or limit the jurisdiction of the district courts or the venue of actions in those courts. An admiralty or maritime claim under Rule 9(h) is not a civil action for purposes of 28 U.S.C. §§ 1391–1392.

[Amended December 29, 1948, effective October 20, 1949; February 28, 1966, effective July 1, 1966; April 23, 2001, effective December 1, 2001; April 30, 2007, effective December 1, 2007.]

RULE 83. RULES BY DISTRICT COURTS; JUDGE'S DIRECTIVES

(a) Local Rules.

(1) *In General.* After giving public notice and an opportunity for comment, a district court, acting by a majority of its district judges, may adopt and amend rules governing its practice. A local rule must be consistent with—but not duplicate—federal statutes and rules adopted under 28 U.S.C. §§ 2072 and 2075, and must conform to any uniform numbering system prescribed by the Judicial Conference of the United States. A local rule takes effect on the date specified by the district court and remains in effect unless amended by the court or abrogated by the judicial council of the circuit. Copies of rules and amendments must, on their adoption, be furnished to the judicial council and the Administrative Office of the United States Courts and be made available to the public.

(2) *Requirement of Form.* A local rule imposing a requirement of form must not be enforced in a way that causes a party to lose any right because of a nonwillful failure to comply.

(b) Procedure When There Is No Controlling Law. A judge may regulate practice in any manner consistent with federal law, rules adopted under 28 U.S.C. §§ 2072 and 2075, and the district's local rules. No sanction or other disadvantage may be imposed for noncompliance with any requirement not in federal law, federal rules, or the local rules unless the alleged violator has been furnished in the particular case with actual notice of the requirement.

[Amended April 29, 1985, effective August 1, 1985; April 27, 1995, effective December 1, 1995; April 30, 2007, effective December 1, 2007.]

RULE 84. FORMS

The forms in the Appendix suffice under these rules and illustrate the simplicity and brevity that these rules contemplate.

[Amended December 27, 1946, effective March 19, 1948; April 30, 2007, effective December 1, 2007.]

RULE 85. TITLE

These rules may be cited as the Federal Rules of Civil Procedure.

[Amended April 30, 2007, effective December 1, 2007.]

RULE 86. EFFECTIVE DATES

(a) In General. These rules and any amendments take effect at the time specified by the Supreme Court, subject to 28 U.S.C. § 2074. They govern:

(1) proceedings in an action commenced after their effective date; and

(2) proceedings after that date in an action then pending unless:

(A) the Supreme Court specifies otherwise; or

(B) the court determines that applying them in a particular action would be infeasible or work an injustice.

(b) December 1, 2007 Amendments. If any provision in Rules 1–5.1, 6–73, or 77–86 conflicts with another law, priority in time for the purpose of 28 U.S.C. § 2072(b) is not affected by the amendments taking effect on December 1, 2007.

[Amended December 27, 1946, effective March 19, 1948; December 29, 1948, effective October 20, 1949; April 17, 1961, effective July 19, 1961; January 21, 1963, and March 18, 1963, effective July 1, 1963; April 30, 2007, effective December 1, 2007.]

APPENDIX OF FORMS

FORM 1. CAPTION

(Use on every summons, complaint, answer, motion, or other document.)

United States District Court
for the
_____ District of _____

A B, Plaintiff	)	
	)	
v.	)	
	)	Civil Action No. _____
C D, Defendant	)	
	)	
v.	)	
	)	
E F, Third–Party Defendant	)	
(Use if needed.)	)	

(Name of Document)

[Effective December 1, 2007.]

FORM 2. DATE, SIGNATURE, ADDRESS, E–MAIL ADDRESS, AND TELEPHONE NUMBER

(Use at the conclusion of pleadings and other papers that require a signature.)

Date _____ _____

____
(Signature of the attorney or unrepresented party)

____
(Printed name)

____
(Address)

____
(E-mail address)

____
(Telephone number)

[Effective December 1, 2007.]

FORM 3. SUMMONS

(Caption—See Form 1.)

To *name the defendant*:

A lawsuit has been filed against you.

Within 20 days after service of this summons on you (not counting the day you received it), you must serve on the plaintiff an answer to the attached complaint or a motion under Rule 12 of the Federal Rules of Civil Procedure. The answer or motion must be served on the plaintiff's attorney, ______, whose address is ______. If you fail to do so, judgment by default will be entered against you for the relief demanded in the complaint. You also must file your answer or motion with the court.

Date ________

____
Clerk of Court

(Court Seal)

(*Use 60 days if the defendant is the United States or a United States agency, or is an officer or employee of the United States allowed 60 days by Rule 12(a)(3).*)

[Effective December 1, 2007.]

FORM 4. SUMMONS ON A THIRD-PARTY COMPLAINT

(Caption—See Form 1.)

To *name the third-party defendant*:

A lawsuit has been filed against defendant ______, who as third-party plaintiff is making this claim against you to pay part or all of what [he] may owe to the plaintiff ______.

Within 20 days after service of this summons on you (not counting the day you received it), you must serve on the plaintiff and on the defendant an answer to the attached third-party complaint or a motion under Rule 12 of the Federal Rules of Civil Procedure. The answer or motion must be served on the defendant's attorney, ________, whose address is, ________, and also on the plaintiff's attorney, ________, whose address is, ________. If you fail to do so, judgment by default will be entered against you for the relief demanded in the third-party complaint. You also must file the answer or motion with the court and serve it on any other parties.

A copy of the plaintiff's complaint is also attached. You may—but are not required to—respond to it.

Date ______

____
Clerk of Court

(Court Seal)

[Effective December 1, 2007.]

FORM 5. NOTICE OF A LAWSUIT AND REQUEST TO WAIVE SERVICE OF A SUMMONS

(Caption—See Form 1.)

To (*name the defendant—or if the defendant is a corporation, partnership, or association name an officer or agent authorized to receive service*):

Why are you getting this?

A lawsuit has been filed against you, or the entity you represent, in this court under the number shown above. A copy of the complaint is attached.

This is not a summons, or an official notice from the court. It is a request that, to avoid expenses, you waive formal service of a summons by signing and returning the enclosed waiver. To avoid these expenses, you must return the signed waiver within (*give at least 30 days or at least 60 days if the defendant is outside any judicial district of the United States*) from the date shown below, which is the date this notice was sent. Two copies of the waiver form are enclosed, along with a stamped, self-addressed envelope or other prepaid means for returning one copy. You may keep the other copy.

What happens next?

If you return the signed waiver, I will file it with the court. The action will then proceed as if you had been served on the date the waiver is filed, but no summons will be served on you and you will have 60 days from the date this notice is sent (see the date below) to answer the complaint (or 90 days if this notice is sent to you outside any judicial district of the United States).

If you do not return the signed waiver within the time indicated, I will arrange to have the summons and complaint served on you. And I will ask the court to require you, or the entity you represent, to pay the expenses of making service.

Please read the enclosed statement about the duty to avoid unnecessary expenses.

I certify that this request is being sent to you on the date below.

(Date and sign—See Form 2.)

[Effective December 1, 2007.]

FORM 6. WAIVER OF THE SERVICE OF SUMMONS

(Caption—See Form 1.)

To *name the plaintiff's attorney or the unrepresented plaintiff*:

I have received your request to waive service of a summons in this action along with a copy of the complaint, two copies of this waiver form, and a prepaid means of returning one signed copy of the form to you.

I, or the entity I represent, agree to save the expense of serving a summons and complaint in this case.

I understand that I, or the entity I represent, will keep all defenses or objections to the lawsuit, the court's jurisdiction, and the venue of the action, but that I waive any objections to the absence of a summons or of service.

I also understand that I, or the entity I represent, must file and serve an answer or a motion under Rule 12 within 60 days from ______, the date when this request was sent (or 90 days if it was sent outside the United States). If I fail to do so, a default judgment will be entered against me or the entity I represent.

(Date and sign—See Form 2.)

(Attach the following to Form 6.)

Duty to Avoid Unnecessary Expenses of Serving a Summons

Rule 4 of the Federal Rules of Civil Procedure requires certain defendants to cooperate in saving unnecessary expenses of serving a summons and complaint. A defendant who is located in the United States and who fails to return a signed waiver of service requested by a plaintiff located in the United States will be required to pay the expenses of service, unless the defendant shows good cause for the failure.

"Good cause" does *not* include a belief that the lawsuit is groundless, or that it has been brought in an improper venue, or that the court has no jurisdiction over this matter or over the defendant or the defendant's property.

If the waiver is signed and returned, you can still make these and all other defenses and objections, but you cannot object to the absence of a summons or of service.

If you waive service, then you must, within the time specified on the waiver form, serve an answer or a motion under Rule 12 on the plaintiff and file a copy with the court. By signing and returning the waiver form, you are allowed more time to respond than if a summons had been served.

[Effective December 1, 2007.]

FORM 7. STATEMENT OF JURISDICTION

a. (*For diversity-of-citizenship jurisdiction.*) The plaintiff is [a citizen of *Michigan*] [a corporation incorporated under the laws of *Michigan* with its principal place of business in *Michigan*]. The defendant is [a citizen of *New York*] [a corporation incorporated under the laws of *New York* with its principal place of business in *New York*]. The amount in controversy, without interest and costs, exceeds the sum or value specified by 28 U.S.C. § 1332.

b. (*For federal-question jurisdiction.*) This action arises under [the United States Constitution, *specify the article or amendment and the section*] [a United States treaty *specify*] [a federal statute, ___U.S.C. § __].

c. (*For a claim in the admiralty or maritime jurisdiction.*) This is a case of admiralty or maritime jurisdiction. *(To invoke admiralty status under Rule 9(h) use the following:* This is an admiralty or maritime claim within the meaning of Rule 9(h).)

[Effective December 1, 2007.]

FORM 8. STATEMENT OF REASONS FOR OMITTING A PARTY

(*If a person who ought to be made a party under Rule 19(a) is not named, include this statement in accordance with Rule 19(c).*)

This complaint does not join as a party *name* who [is not subject to this court's personal jurisdiction] [cannot be made a party without depriving this court of subject-matter jurisdiction] because *state the reason.*

[Effective December 1, 2007.]

FORM 9. STATEMENT NOTING A PARTY'S DEATH

(Caption—See Form 1.)

In accordance with Rule 25(a) *name the person,* who is [a party to this action] [a representative of or successor to the deceased party] notes the death during the pendency of this action of *name*, [*describe as party* in this action].

(Date and sign—See Form 2.)

[Effective December 1, 2007.]

FORM 10. COMPLAINT TO RECOVER A SUM CERTAIN

(Caption—See Form 1.)

1. (Statement of Jurisdiction–See Form 7.)

(Use one or more of the following as appropriate and include a demand for judgment.)

(a) On a Promissory Note

2. On date, the defendant executed and delivered a note promising to pay the plaintiff on date the sum of $______ with interest at the rate of __ percent. A copy of the note [is attached as Exhibit A] [is summarized as follows: ______.]

3. The defendant has not paid the amount owed.

(b) On an Account

2. The defendant owes the plaintiff $______ according to the account set out in Exhibit A.

(c) For Goods Sold and Delivered

2. The defendant owes the plaintiff $______ for goods sold and delivered by the plaintiff to the defendant from date to date.

(d) For Money Lent

2. The defendant owes the plaintiff $______ for money lent by the plaintiff to the defendant on date.

(e) For Money Paid by Mistake

2. The defendant owes the plaintiff $______ for money paid by mistake to the defendant on date under these circumstances: *describe with particularity in accordance with Rule 9(b).*

(f) For Money Had and Received

2. The defendant owes the plaintiff $______ for money that was received from name on date to be paid by the defendant to the plaintiff.

Demand for Judgment

Therefore, the plaintiff demands judgment against the defendant for $______, plus interest and costs.

(Date and sign—See Form 2.)

[Effective December 1, 2007.]

FORM 11. COMPLAINT FOR NEGLIGENCE

(Caption—See Form 1.)

1. (Statement of Jurisdiction–See Form 7.)

2. On _date_, at _place_, the defendant negligently drove a motor vehicle against the plaintiff.

3. As a result, the plaintiff was physically injured, lost wages or income, suffered physical and mental pain, and incurred medical expenses of $ ______.

Therefore, the plaintiff demands judgment against the defendant for $ ______, plus costs.

(Date and sign—See Form 2).

[Effective December 1, 2007.]

FORM 12. COMPLAINT FOR NEGLIGENCE WHEN THE PLAINTIFF DOES NOT KNOW WHO IS RESPONSIBLE

(Caption—See Form 1.)

1. (Statement of Jurisdiction–See Form 7.)

2. On _date_, at _place_, defendant _name_ or defendant _name_ or both of them willfully or recklessly or negligently drove, or caused to be driven, a motor vehicle against the plaintiff.

3. As a result, the plaintiff was physically injured, lost wages or income, suffered mental and physical pain, and incurred medical expenses of $ ______.

Therefore, the plaintiff demands judgment against one or both defendants for $ ______, plus costs.

(Date and sign—See Form 2.)

[Effective December 1, 2007.]

FORM 13. COMPLAINT FOR NEGLIGENCE UNDER THE FEDERAL EMPLOYERS' LIABILITY ACT

(Caption—See Form 1.)

1. (Statement of Jurisdiction—See Form 7.)

2. At the times below, the defendant owned and operated in interstate commerce a railroad line that passed through a tunnel located at ______.

3. On _date_, the plaintiff was working to repair and enlarge the tunnel to make it convenient and safe for use in interstate commerce.

4. During this work, the defendant, as the employer, negligently put the plaintiff to work in a section of the tunnel that the defendant had left unprotected and unsupported.

5. The defendant's negligence caused the plaintiff to be injured by a rock that fell from an unsupported portion of the tunnel.

6. As a result, the plaintiff was physically injured, lost wages or income, suffered mental and physical pain, and incurred medical expenses of $______.

Therefore, the plaintiff demands judgment against the defendant for $______, and costs.

(Date and sign—See Form 2.)

[Effective December 1, 2007.]

FORM 14. COMPLAINT FOR DAMAGES UNDER THE MERCHANT MARINE ACT

(Caption—See Form 1.)

1. (Statement of Jurisdiction—See Form 7.)

2. At the times below, the defendant owned and operated the vessel _name_ and used it to transport cargo for hire by water in interstate and foreign commerce.

3. On _date_, at _place_, the defendant hired the plaintiff under seamen's articles of customary form for a voyage from ______ to ______ and return at a wage of $______ a month and found, which is equal to a shore worker's wage of $______ a month.

4. On _date_, the vessel was at sea on the return voyage. (*Describe the weather and the condition of the vessel.*)

5. (*Describe as in Form 11 the defendant's negligent conduct.*)

6. As a result of the defendant's negligent conduct and the unseaworthiness of the vessel, the plaintiff was physically injured, has been incapable of any gainful activity, suffered mental and physical pain, and has incurred medical expenses of $______.

Therefore, the plaintiff demands judgment against the defendant for $, plus costs.

(Date and sign—See Form 2.)

[Effective December 1, 2007.]

FORM 15. COMPLAINT FOR THE CONVERSION OF PROPERTY

(Caption—See Form 1.)

1. (Statement of Jurisdiction—See Form 7.)

2. On date, at place, the defendant converted to the defendant's own use property owned by the plaintiff. The property converted consists of *describe*.

3. The property is worth $ _______.

Therefore, the plaintiff demands judgment against the defendant for $ _______, plus costs.

(Date and sign—See Form 2.)

[Effective December 1, 2007.]

FORM 16. THIRD–PARTY COMPLAINT

(Caption—See Form 1.)

1. Plaintiff *name* has filed against defendant *name* a complaint, a copy of which is attached.

2. (*State grounds entitling defendant's name to recover from third-party defendant's name for (all or an identified share) of any judgment for plaintiff's name against defendant's name.*)

Therefore, the defendant demands judgment against *third-party defendant's name* for *all or an identified share* of sums that may be adjudged against the defendant in the plaintiff's favor.

(Date and sign—See Form 2.)

[Effective December 1, 2007.]

FORM 17. COMPLAINT FOR SPECIFIC PERFORMANCE OF A CONTRACT TO CONVEY LAND

(Caption—See Form 1.)

1. (Statement of Jurisdiction–See Form 7.)

2. On *date*, the parties agreed to the contract [attached as Exhibit A][summarize the contract].

3. As agreed, the plaintiff tendered the purchase price and requested a conveyance of the land, but the defendant refused to accept the money or make a conveyance.

4. The plaintiff now offers to pay the purchase price.

Therefore, the plaintiff demands that:

(a) the defendant be required to specifically perform the agreement and pay damages of $ ______, plus interest and costs, or

(b) if specific performance is not ordered, the defendant be required to pay damages of $ ______, plus interest and costs.

(Date and sign—See Form 2.)

[Effective December 1, 2007.]

FORM 18. COMPLAINT FOR PATENT INFRINGEMENT

(Caption—See Form 1.)

1. (Statement of Jurisdiction—See Form 7.)

2. On *date*, United States Letters Patent No. ______ were issued to the plaintiff for an invention in an *electric motor*. The plaintiff owned the patent throughout the period of the defendant's infringing acts and still owns the patent.

3. The defendant has infringed and is still infringing the Letters Patent by making, selling, and using *electric motors* that embody the patented invention, and the defendant will continue to do so unless enjoined by this court.

4. The plaintiff has complied with the statutory requirement of placing a notice of the Letters Patent on all *electric motors* it manufactures and sells and has given the defendant written notice of the infringement.

Therefore, the plaintiff demands:

(a) a preliminary and final injunction against the continuing infringement;

(b) an accounting for damages; and

(c) interest and costs.

(Date and sign—See Form 2.)

[Effective December 1, 2007.]

FORM 19. COMPLAINT FOR COPYRIGHT INFRINGEMENT AND UNFAIR COMPETITION

(Caption—See Form 1.)

1. (Statement of Jurisdiction–See Form 7.)

2. Before *date*, the plaintiff, a United States citizen, wrote a book entitled ________.

3. The book is an original work that may be copyrighted under United States law. A copy of the book is attached as Exhibit A.

4. Between *date* and *date*, the plaintiff applied to the copyright office and received a certificate of registration dated ________ and identified as *date, class, number*.

5. Since *date*, the plaintiff has either published or licensed for publication all copies of the book in compliance with the copyright laws and has remained the sole owner of the copyright.

6. After the copyright was issued, the defendant infringed the copyright by publishing and selling a book entitled ________, which was copied largely from the plaintiff's book. A copy of the defendant's book is attached as Exhibit B.

7. The plaintiff has notified the defendant in writing of the infringement.

8. The defendant continues to infringe the copyright by continuing to publish and sell the infringing book in violation of the copyright, and further has engaged in unfair trade practices and unfair competition in connection with its publication and sale of the infringing book, thus causing irreparable damage.

Therefore, the plaintiff demands that:

(a) until this case is decided the defendant and the defendant's agents be enjoined from disposing of any copies of the defendant's book by sale or otherwise;

(b) the defendant account for and pay as damages to the plaintiff all profits and advantages gained from unfair trade practices and unfair competition in selling the defendant's book, and all profits and advantages gained from infringing the plaintiff's copyright (but no less than the statutory minimum);

(c) the defendant deliver for impoundment all copies of the book in the defendant's possession or control and deliver for destruction all infringing copies and all plates, molds, and other materials for making infringing copies;

(d) the defendant pay the plaintiff interest, costs, and reasonable attorney's fees; and

(e) the plaintiff be awarded any other just relief.

(Date and sign—See Form 2.)

[Effective December 1, 2007.]

FORM 20. COMPLAINT FOR INTERPLEADER AND DECLARATORY RELIEF

(Caption—See Form 1.)

1. (Statement of Jurisdiction–See Form 7.)

2. On *date*, the plaintiff issued a life insurance policy on the life of *name* with *name* as the named beneficiary.

3. As a condition for keeping the policy in force, the policy required payment of a premium during the first year and then annually.

4. The premium due on *date* was never paid, and the policy lapsed after that date.

5. On *date*, after the policy had lapsed, both the insured and the named beneficiary died in an automobile collision.

6. Defendant *name* claims to be the beneficiary in place of *name* and has filed a claim to be paid the policy's full amount.

7. The other two defendants are representatives of the deceased persons' estates. Each defendant has filed a claim on behalf of each estate to receive payment of the policy's full amount.

8. If the policy was in force at the time of death, the plaintiff is in doubt about who should be paid.

Therefore, the plaintiff demands that:

(a) each defendant be restrained from commencing any action against the plaintiff on the policy;

(b) a judgment be entered that no defendant is entitled to the proceeds of the policy or any part of it, but if the court determines that the policy was in effect at the time of the insured's death, that the defendants be required to interplead and settle among themselves their rights to the proceeds, and that the plaintiff be discharged from all liability except to the defendant determined to be entitled to the proceeds; and

(c) the plaintiff recover its costs.

(Date and sign—See Form 2.)

[Effective December 1, 2007.]

FORM 21. COMPLAINT ON A CLAIM FOR A DEBT AND TO SET ASIDE A FRAUDULENT CONVEYANCE UNDER RULE 18(B)

(Caption—See Form 1.)

1. (Statement of Jurisdiction—See Form 7.)

2. On date, defendant name signed a note promising to pay to the plaintiff on date the sum of $ _____ with interest at the rate of ___ percent. [The pleader may, but need not, attach a copy or plead the note verbatim.]

3. Defendant name owes the plaintiff the amount of the note and interest.

4. On date, defendant name conveyed all defendant's real and personal property *if less than all, describe it fully* to defendant name for the purpose of defrauding the plaintiff and hindering or delaying the collection of the debt.

Therefore, the plaintiff demands that:

(a) judgment for $ _____, plus costs, be entered against defendant(s) *name(s)*; and

(b) the conveyance to defendant name be declared void and any judgment granted be made a lien on the property.

(Date and sign—See Form 2.)

[Effective December 1, 2007.]

FORM 30. ANSWER PRESENTING DEFENSES UNDER RULE 12(B)

(Caption—See Form 1.)

Responding to Allegations in the Complaint

1. Defendant admits the allegations in paragraphs _______.

2. Defendant lacks knowledge or information sufficient to form a belief about the truth of the allegations in paragraphs _______.

3. Defendant admits *identify part of the allegation* in paragraph _______ and denies or lacks knowledge or information sufficient to form a belief about the truth of the rest of the paragraph.

Failure to State a Claim

4. The complaint fails to state a claim upon which relief can be granted.

Failure to Join a Required Party

5. If there is a debt, it is owed jointly by the defendant and *name* who is a citizen of _______. This person can be made a party without depriving this court of jurisdiction over the existing parties.

Affirmative Defense—Statute of Limitations

6. The plaintiff's claim is barred by the statute of limitations because it arose more than _______ years before this action was commenced.

Counterclaim

7. (*Set forth any counterclaim in the same way a claim is pleaded in a complaint. Include a further statement of jurisdiction if needed.*)

Crossclaim

8. (*Set forth a crossclaim against a coparty in the same way a claim is pleaded in a complaint. Include a further statement of jurisdiction if needed.*)

(Date and sign—See Form 2.)

[Effective December 1, 2007.]

FORM 31. ANSWER TO A COMPLAINT FOR MONEY HAD AND RECEIVED WITH A COUNTERCLAIM FOR INTERPLEADER

(Caption—See Form 1.)

Response to the Allegations in the Complaint

(See Form 30)

Counterclaim for Interpleader

1. The defendant received from name a deposit of $ ______.

2. The plaintiff demands payment of the deposit because of a purported assignment from name, who has notified the defendant that the assignment is not valid and who continues to hold the defendant responsible for the deposit.

Therefore, the defendant demands that:

(a) name be made a party to this action;

(b) the plaintiff and name be required to interplead their respective claims;

(c) the court decide whether the plaintiff or name or either of them is entitled to the deposit and discharge the defendant of any liability except to the person entitled to the deposit; and

(d) the defendant recover costs and attorney's fees.

(Date and sign—See Form 2.)

[Effective December 1, 2007.]

FORM 40. MOTION TO DISMISS UNDER RULE 12(B) FOR LACK OF JURISDICTION, IMPROPER VENUE, INSUFFICIENT SERVICE OF PROCESS, OR FAILURE TO STATE A CLAIM

(Caption—See Form 1.)

The defendant moves to dismiss the action because:

1. the amount in controversy is less than the sum or value specified by 28 U.S.C. § 1332;

2. the defendant is not subject to the personal jurisdiction of this court;

3. venue is improper (this defendant does not reside in this district and no part of the events or omissions giving rise to the claim occurred in the district);

4. the defendant has not been properly served, as shown by the attached affidavits of ______; or

5. the complaint fails to state a claim upon which relief can be granted.

(Date and sign—See Form 2.)

[Effective December 1, 2007.]

FORM 41. MOTION TO BRING IN A THIRD–PARTY DEFENDANT

(Caption—See Form 1.)

The defendant, as third-party plaintiff, moves for leave to serve on _name_ a summons and third-party complaint, copies of which are attached.

(Date and sign—See Form 2.)

[Effective December 1, 2007.]

FORM 42. MOTION TO INTERVENE AS A DEFENDANT UNDER RULE 24

(Caption—See Form 1.)

1. _Name_ moves for leave to intervene as a defendant in this action and to file the attached answer.

(_State grounds under Rule 24(a) or (b)._)

2. The plaintiff alleges patent infringement. We manufacture and sell to the defendant the articles involved, and we have a defense to the plaintiff's claim.
3. Our defense presents questions of law and fact that are common to this action.

(Date and sign—See Form 2.)

[An Intervener's Answer must be attached. See Form 30.]

[Effective December 1, 2007.]

FORM 50. REQUEST TO PRODUCE DOCUMENTS AND TANGIBLE THINGS, OR TO ENTER ONTO LAND UNDER RULE 34

(Caption—See Form 1.)

The plaintiff <u>name</u> requests that the defendant <u>name</u> respond within ____ days to the following requests:

1. To produce and permit the plaintiff to inspect and copy and to test or sample the following documents, including electronically stored information:

(Describe each document and the electronically stored information, either individually or by category.)

(State the time, place, and manner of the inspection and any related acts.)

2. To produce and permit the plaintiff to inspect and copy—and to test or sample—the following tangible things:

(Describe each thing, either individually or by category.)

(State the time, place, and manner of the inspection and any related acts.)

3. To permit the plaintiff to enter onto the following land to inspect, photograph, test, or sample the property or an object or operation on the property.

(Describe the property and each object or operation.)

(State the time and manner of the inspection and any related acts.)

(Date and sign—See Form 2.)

[Effective December 1, 2007.]

FORM 51. REQUEST FOR ADMISSIONS UNDER RULE 36

(Caption—See Form 1.)

The plaintiff <u>name</u> asks the defendant <u>name</u> to respond within 30 days to these requests by admitting, for purposes of this action only and subject to objections to admissibility at trial:

1. The genuineness of the following documents, copies of which [are attached] [are or have been furnished or made available for inspection and copying].

(List each document.)

2. The truth of each of the following statements:

(List each statement.)

(Date and sign—See Form 2.)

[Effective December 1, 2007.]

FORM 52. REPORT OF THE PARTIES' PLANNING MEETING

(Caption—See Form 1.)

1. The following persons participated in a Rule 26(f) conference on date by *state the method of conferring*:

(*e.g.*, *name* representing the plaintiff.)

2. Initial Disclosures. The parties [have completed] [will complete by date] the initial disclosures required by Rule 26(a)(1).

3. Discovery Plan. The parties propose this discovery plan:

(*Use separate paragraphs or subparagraphs if the parties disagree.*)

(a) Discovery will be needed on these subjects: (*describe.*)

(b) (Dates for commencing and completing discovery, including discovery to be commenced or completed before other discovery.)

(c) (Maximum number of interrogatories by each party to another party, along with the dates the answers are due.)

(d) (Maximum number of requests for admission, along with the dates responses are due.)

(e) (Maximum number of depositions by each party.)

(f) (Limits on the length of depositions, in hours.)

(g) (Dates for exchanging reports of expert witnesses.)

(h) (Dates for supplementations under Rule 26(e).)

4. Other Items:

(a) (A date if the parties ask to meet with the court before a scheduling order.)

(b) (Requested dates for pretrial conferences.)

(c) (Final dates for the plaintiff to amend pleadings or to join parties.)

(d) (Final dates for the defendant to amend pleadings or to join parties.)

(e) (Final dates to file dispositive motions.)

(f) (State the prospects for settlement.)

(g) (Identify any alternative dispute resolution procedure that may enhance settlement prospects.)

(h) (Final dates for submitting Rule 26(a)(3) witness lists, designations of witnesses whose testimony will be presented by deposition, and exhibit lists.)

(i) (Final dates to file objections under Rule 26(a)(3).)

(j) (Suggested trial date and estimate of trial length.)

(k) (Other matters.)

(Date and sign—see Form 2.)

[Effective December 1, 2007.]

FORM 60. NOTICE OF CONDEMNATION

(Caption—See Form 1.)

To *name the defendant*.

1. A complaint in condemnation has been filed in the United States District Court for the ______ District of ______, to take property to use for *purpose*. The interest to be taken is *describe*. The court is located in the United States courthouse at this address: ______.

2. The property to be taken is described below. You have or claim an interest in it.

(*Describe the property.*)

3. The authority for taking this property is *cite*.

4. If you want to object or present any defense to the taking you must serve an answer on the plaintiff's attorney within 20 days [after being served with this notice][from (insert the date of the last publication of notice)]. Send your answer to this address: ______.

5. Your answer must identify the property in which you claim an interest, state the nature and extent of that interest, and state all your objections and defenses to the taking. Objections and defenses not presented are waived.

6. If you fail to answer you consent to the taking and the court will enter a judgment that takes your described property interest.

7. Instead of answering, you may serve on the plaintiff's attorney a notice of appearance that designates the property in which you claim an interest. After you do that, you will receive a notice of any proceedings that affect you. Whether or not you have previously appeared or answered, you may present evidence at a trial to determine compensation for the property and share in the overall award.

(Date and sign—See Form 2.)

[Effective December 1, 2007.]

FORM 61. COMPLAINT FOR CONDEMNATION

(Caption—See Form 1; name as defendants the property and at least one owner.)

1. (Statement of Jurisdiction—See Form 7.)

2. This is an action to take property under the power of eminent domain and to determine just compensation to be paid to the owners and parties in interest.

3. The authority for the taking is ______.

4. The property is to be used for ______.

5. The property to be taken is (*describe in enough detail for identification—or attach the description and state "is described in Exhibit A, attached."*)

6. The interest to be acquired is ______.

7. The persons known to the plaintiff to have or claim an interest in the property are: ______. (*For each person include the interest claimed.*)

8. There may be other persons who have or claim an interest in the property and whose names could not be found after a reasonably diligent search. They are made parties under the designation "Unknown Owners."

Therefore, the plaintiff demands judgment:

(a) condemning the property;

(b) determining and awarding just compensation; and

(c) granting any other lawful and proper relief.

(Date and sign—See Form 2.)

[Effective December 1, 2007.]

FORM 70. JUDGMENT ON A JURY VERDICT

(Caption—See Form 1.)

This action was tried by a jury with Judge ______ presiding, and the jury has rendered a verdict.

It is ordered that:

[the plaintiff *name* recover from the defendant *name* the amount of $______ with interest at the rate of __%, along with costs.]

[the plaintiff recover nothing, the action be dismissed on the merits, and the defendant *name* recover costs from the plaintiff *name*.]

Date ______ ______

____
Clerk of Court

[Effective December 1, 2007.]

FORM 71. JUDGMENT BY THE COURT WITHOUT A JURY

(Caption—See Form 1.)

This action was tried by Judge _______ without a jury and the following decision was reached:

It is ordered that [the plaintiff name recover from the defendant name the amount of $ _______, with prejudgment interest at the rate of _____%, postjudgment interest at the rate of _____%, along with costs.] [the plaintiff recover nothing, the action be dismissed on the merits, and the defendant name recover costs from the plaintiff name.]

Date _______________

____
Clerk of Court

[Effective December 1, 2007.]

FORM 80. NOTICE OF A MAGISTRATE JUDGE'S AVAILABILITY

1. A magistrate judge is available under title 28 U.S.C. § 636(c) to conduct the proceedings in this case, including a jury or nonjury trial and the entry of final judgment. But a magistrate judge can be assigned only if all parties voluntarily consent.

2. You may withhold your consent without adverse substantive consequences. The identity of any party consenting or withholding consent will not be disclosed to the judge to whom the case is assigned or to any magistrate judge.

3. If a magistrate judge does hear your case, you may appeal directly to a United States court of appeals as you would if a district judge heard it.

A form called *Consent to an Assignment to a United States Magistrate Judge* is available from the court clerk's office.

[Effective December 1, 2007.]

FORM 81. CONSENT TO AN ASSIGNMENT TO A MAGISTRATE JUDGE

(Caption—See Form 1.)

I voluntarily consent to have a United States magistrate judge conduct all further proceedings in this case, including a trial, and order the entry of final judgment. (Return this form to the court clerk—not to a judge or magistrate judge.)

Date ______________

____
Signature of the Party

[Effective December 1, 2007.]

FORM 82. ORDER OF ASSIGNMENT TO A MAGISTRATE JUDGE

(Caption—See Form 1.)

With the parties' consent it is ordered that this case be assigned to United States Magistrate Judge _______ of this district to conduct all proceedings and enter final judgment in accordance with 28 U.S.C. § 636(c).

Date ______________

____
United States District Judge

[Effective December 1, 2007.]

SUPPLEMENTAL RULES FOR ADMIRALTY OR MARITIME CLAIMS AND ASSET FORFEITURE ACTIONS

Effective July 1, 1966

Including Amendments Effective December 1, 2008, Absent Contrary Congressional Action

RULE A. SCOPE OF RULES

(1) These Supplemental Rules apply to:

(A) the procedure in admiralty and maritime claims within the meaning of Rule 9(h) with respect to the following remedies:

(i) maritime attachment and garnishment,

(ii) actions in rem,

(iii) possessory, petitory, and partition actions, and

(iv) actions for exoneration from or limitation of liability;

(B) forfeiture actions in rem arising from a federal statute; and

(C) the procedure in statutory condemnation proceedings analogous to maritime actions in rem, whether within the admiralty and maritime jurisdiction or not. Except as otherwise provided, references in these Supplemental Rules to actions in rem include such analogous statutory condemnation proceedings.

(2) The Federal Rules of Civil Procedure also apply to the foregoing proceedings except to the extent that they are inconsistent with these Supplemental Rules.

[Amended effective December 1, 2006.]

RULE B. IN PERSONAM ACTIONS; ATTACHMENT AND GARNISHMENT

(1) When Available; Complaint, Affidavit, Judicial Authorization, and Process. In an in personam action:

(a) If a defendant is not found within the district when a verified complaint praying for attachment and the affidavit required by Rule B(1)(b) are filed, a verified complaint may contain a prayer for process to attach the defendant's tangible or intangible personal property—up to the amount sued for—in the hands of garnishees named in the process.

(b) The plaintiff or the plaintiff's attorney must sign and file with the complaint an affidavit stating that, to the affiant's knowledge, or on information and belief, the defendant cannot be found within the district. The court must review the complaint and affidavit and, if the conditions of this Rule B appear to exist, enter an order so stating and authorizing process of attachment and garnishment. The clerk may issue supplemental process enforcing the court's order upon application without further court order.

(c) If the plaintiff or the plaintiff's attorney certifies that exigent circumstances make court review impracticable, the clerk must issue the summons and process of attachment and garnishment. The plaintiff has the burden in any post-attachment hearing under Rule E(4)(f) to show that exigent circumstances existed.

(d)(i) If the property is a vessel or tangible property on board a vessel, the summons, process, and any supplemental process must be delivered to the marshal for service.

(ii) If the property is other tangible or intangible property, the summons, process, and any supplemental process must be delivered to a person or organization authorized to serve it, who may be (A) a marshal; (B) someone under contract with the United States; (C) someone specially appointed by the court for that purpose; or, (D) in an action brought by the United States, any officer or employee of the United States.

(e) The plaintiff may invoke state-law remedies under Rule 64 for seizure of person or property for the purpose of securing satisfaction of the judgment.

(2) Notice to Defendant. No default judgment may be entered except upon proof—which may be by affidavit—that:

(a) the complaint, summons, and process of attachment or garnishment have been served on the defendant in a manner authorized by Rule 4;

(b) the plaintiff or the garnishee has mailed to the defendant the complaint, summons, and process of attachment or garnishment, using any form of mail requiring a return receipt; or

(c) the plaintiff or the garnishee has tried diligently to give notice of the action to the defendant but could not do so.

(3) Answer.

(a) *By Garnishee.* The garnishee shall serve an answer, together with answers to any interrogatories served with the complaint, within 20 days after service of process upon the garnishee. Interrogatories to the garnishee may be served with the complaint without leave of court. If the garnishee refuses or neglects to answer on oath as to the debts, credits, or effects of the defendant in the garnishee's hands, or any interrogatories concerning such debts, credits, and effects that may be propounded by the plaintiff, the court may award compulsory process against the garnishee. If the garnishee admits any debts, credits, or effects, they shall be held in the garnishee's hands or paid into the registry of the court, and shall be held in either case subject to the further order of the court.

(b) *By Defendant.* The defendant shall serve an answer within 30 days after process has been executed, whether by attachment of property or service on the garnishee.

[Amended April 29, 1985, effective August 1, 1985; March 2, 1987, effective August 1, 1987; April 17, 2000, effective December 1, 2000; April 25, 2005, effective December 1, 2005.]

RULE C. IN REM ACTIONS: SPECIAL PROVISIONS

(1) When Available. An action in rem may be brought:

(a) To enforce any maritime lien;

(b) Whenever a statute of the United States provides for a maritime action in rem or a proceeding analogous thereto.

Except as otherwise provided by law a party who may proceed in rem may also, or in the alternative, proceed in personam against any person who may be liable.

Statutory provisions exempting vessels or other property owned or possessed by or operated by or for the United States from arrest or seizure are not affected by this rule. When a statute so provides, an action against the United States or an instrumentality thereof may proceed on in rem principles.

(2) Complaint. In an action in rem the complaint must:

(a) be verified;

(b) describe with reasonable particularity the property that is the subject of the action; and

(c) state that the property is within the district or will be within the district while the action is pending.

(3) Judicial Authorization and Process.

(a) *Arrest Warrant.*

(i) The court must review the complaint and any supporting papers. If the conditions for an in rem action appear to exist, the court must issue an order directing the clerk to issue a warrant for the arrest of the vessel or other property that is the subject of the action.

(ii) If the plaintiff or the plaintiff's attorney certifies that exigent circumstances make court review impracticable, the clerk must promptly issue a summons and a warrant for the arrest of the vessel or other property that is the subject of the action. The plaintiff has the burden in any post-arrest hearing under Rule E(4)(f) to show that exigent circumstances existed.

(b) *Service.*

(i) If the property that is the subject of the action is a vessel or tangible property on board a vessel, the warrant and any supplemental process must be delivered to the marshal for service.

(ii) If the property that is the subject of the action is other property, tangible or intangible, the warrant and any supplemental process must be delivered to a person or organization authorized to enforce it, who may be: (A) a marshal; (B) someone under contract with the United States; (C) someone specially appointed by the court for that purpose; or, (D) in an action brought by the United States, any officer or employee of the United States.

(c) *Deposit in Court.* If the property that is the subject of the action consists in whole or in part of freight, the proceeds of property sold, or other intangible property, the clerk must issue—in addition to the warrant—a summons directing any person controlling the property to show cause why it should not be deposited in court to abide the judgment.

(d) *Supplemental Process.* The clerk may upon application issue supplemental process to enforce the court's order without further court order.

(4) Notice. No notice other than execution of process is required when the property that is the subject of the action has been released under Rule E(5). If the property is not released within 10 days after execution, the plaintiff must promptly—or within the time that the court allows—give public notice of the action and arrest in a newspaper designated by court order and having general circulation in the district, but publication may be terminated if the property is released before publication is completed. The notice must specify the time under Rule C(6) to file a statement of interest in or right against the seized property and to answer. This rule does not affect the notice requirements in an action to foreclose a preferred ship mortgage under 46 U.S.C. §§ 31301 et seq., as amended.

(5) Ancillary Process. In any action in rem in which process has been served as provided by this rule, if any part of the property that is the subject of the action has not been brought within the control of the court because it has been removed or sold, or because it is intangible property in the hands of a person who has not been served with process, the court may, on motion, order any person having possession or control of such property or its proceeds to show cause why it should not be delivered into the custody of the marshal or other person or organization having a warrant for the arrest of the property, or paid into court to abide the judgment; and, after hearing, the court may enter such judgment as law and justice may require.

(6) Responsive Pleading; Interrogatories.

[Text of paragraph (6)(a) effective until December 1, 2008. For text of paragraph (6)(a) effective December 1, 2008, absent contrary Congressional action, see, post.]

(a) *Maritime Arrests and Other Proceedings.*

(i) a person who asserts a right of possession or any ownership interest in the property that is the subject of the action must file a verified statement of right or interest:

(A) within 10 days after the execution of process, or

(B) within the time that the court allows;

(ii) the statement of right or interest must describe the interest in the property that supports the person's demand for its restitution or right to defend the action;

(iii) an agent, bailee, or attorney must state the authority to file a statement of right or interest on behalf of another; and

(iv) a person who asserts a right of possession or any ownership interest must serve an answer within 20 days after filing the statement of interest or right.

[Text of paragraph (6)(a) effective December 1, 2008, absent contrary Congressional action. For text of paragraph (6)(a) effective until December 1, 2008, see, ante.]

(a) *Statement of Interest; Answer.* In an action in rem:

(i) a person who asserts a right of possession or any ownership interest in the property that is the subject of the action must file a verified statement of right or interest:

(A) within 10 days after the execution of process, or

(B) within the time that the court allows;

(ii) the statement of right or interest must describe the interest in the property that supports the person's demand for its restitution or right to defend the action;

(iii) an agent, bailee, or attorney must state the authority to file a statement of right or interest on behalf of another; and

(iv) a person who asserts a right of possession or any ownership interest must serve an answer within 20 days after filing the statement of interest or right.

(b) *Interrogatories.* Interrogatories may be served with the complaint in an in rem action without leave of court. Answers to the interrogatories must be served with the answer to the complaint.

[Amended April 29, 1985, effective August 1, 1985; March 2, 1987, effective August 1, 1987; April 30, 1991, effective December 1, 1991; April 17, 2000, effective December 1, 2000; April 29, 2002, effective December 1, 2002; April 25, 2005, effective December 1, 2005; April 12, 2006, effective December 1, 2006; April 23, 2008, effective December 1, 2008, absent contrary Congressional action.]

RULE D. POSSESSORY, PETITORY, AND PARTITION ACTIONS

In all actions for possession, partition, and to try title maintainable according to the course of the admiralty practice with respect to a vessel, in all actions so maintainable with respect to the possession of cargo or other maritime property, and in all actions by one or more part owners against the others to obtain security for the return of the vessel from any voyage undertaken without their consent, or by one or more part owners against the others to obtain possession of the vessel for any voyage on giving security for its safe return, the process shall be by a warrant of arrest of the vessel, cargo, or other property, and by notice in the manner provided by Rule B(2) to the adverse party or parties.

RULE E. ACTIONS IN REM AND QUASI IN REM: GENERAL PROVISIONS

(1) Applicability. Except as otherwise provided, this rule applies to actions in personam with process of maritime attachment and garnishment, actions in rem, and petitory, possessory, and partition actions, supplementing Rules B, C, and D.

(2) Complaint; Security.

(a) *Complaint.* In actions to which this rule is applicable the complaint shall state the circumstances from which the claim arises with such particularity that the defendant or claimant will be able, without moving for a more definite statement, to commence an investigation of the facts and to frame a responsive pleading.

(b) *Security for Costs.* Subject to the provisions of Rule 54(d) and of relevant statutes, the court may, on the filing of the complaint or on the appearance of any defendant, claimant, or any other party, or at any later time, require the plaintiff, defendant, claimant, or other party to give security, or additional security, in such sum as the court shall direct to pay all costs and expenses that shall be awarded against the party by any interlocutory order or by the final judgment, or on appeal by any appellate court.

(3) Process.

(a) In admiralty and maritime proceedings process in rem or of maritime attachment and garnishment may be served only within the district.

(b) *Issuance and Delivery.* Issuance and delivery of process in rem, or of maritime attachment and garnishment, shall be held in abeyance if the plaintiff so requests.

(4) Execution of Process; Marshal's Return; Custody of Property; Procedures for Release.

(a) *In General.* Upon issuance and delivery of the process, or, in the case of summons with process of attachment and garnishment, when it appears that the defendant cannot be found within the district, the marshal or other person or organization having a warrant shall forthwith execute the process in accordance with this subdivision (4), making due and prompt return.

(b) *Tangible Property.* If tangible property is to be attached or arrested, the marshal or other person or organization having the warrant shall take it into the marshal's possession for safe custody. If the character or situation of the property is such that the taking of actual possession is impracticable, the marshal or other person executing the process shall affix a copy thereof to the property in a conspicuous place and leave a copy of the complaint and process with the person having possession or the person's agent. In furtherance of the marshal's custody of any vessel the marshal is authorized to make a written request to the collector of customs not to grant clearance to such vessel until notified by the marshal or deputy marshal or by the clerk that the vessel has been released in accordance with these rules.

(c) *Intangible Property.* If intangible property is to be attached or arrested the marshal or other person or organization having the warrant shall execute the process by leaving with the garnishee or other obligor a copy of the complaint and process requiring the garnishee or other obligor to answer as provided in Rules B(3)(a) and C(6); or the marshal may accept for payment into the registry of the court the amount owed to the extent of the amount claimed by the plaintiff with interest and costs, in which event the garnishee or other obligor shall not be required to answer unless alias process shall be served.

(d) *Directions With Respect to Property in Custody.* The marshal or other person or organization having the warrant may at any time apply to the court for directions with respect to property that has been attached or arrested, and shall give notice of such application to any or all of the parties as the court may direct.

(e) *Expenses of Seizing and Keeping Property; Deposit.* These rules do not alter the provisions of Title 28, U.S.C., § 1921, as amended, relative to the expenses of seizing and keeping property attached or arrested and to the requirement of deposits to cover such expenses.

(f) *Procedure for Release From Arrest or Attachment.* Whenever property is arrested or attached, any person claiming an interest in it shall be entitled to a prompt hearing at which the plaintiff shall be required to show why the arrest or attachment should not be vacated or other relief granted consistent with these rules. This subdivision shall have no application to suits for seamen's wages when process is issued upon a certification of sufficient cause filed pursuant to Title 46, U.S.C. §§ 603 and 604* or to actions by the United States for forfeitures for violation of any statute of the United States.

(5) Release of Property.

(a) *Special Bond.* Whenever process of maritime attachment and garnishment or process in rem is issued the execution of such process shall be stayed, or the property released, on the giving of security, to be approved by the court or clerk, or by stipulation of the parties, conditioned to answer the judgment of the court or of any appellate court. The parties may stipulate the amount and nature of such security. In the event of the inability or refusal of the parties so to stipulate the court shall fix the principal sum of the bond or stipulation at an amount sufficient to cover the amount of the plaintiff's claim fairly stated with accrued interest and costs; but the principal sum shall in no event exceed (i) twice the amount of the plaintiff's claim or (ii) the value of the property on due appraisement, whichever is smaller. The bond or stipulation shall be conditioned for the payment of the principal sum and interest thereon at 6 per cent per annum.

(b) *General Bond.* The owner of any vessel may file a general bond or stipulation, with sufficient surety, to be approved by the court, conditioned to answer the judgment of such court in all or any actions that may be brought thereafter in such court in which the vessel is attached or arrested. Thereupon the execution of all such process against such vessel shall be stayed so long as the amount secured by such bond or stipulation is at least double the aggregate amount claimed by plaintiffs in all actions begun and pending in which such vessel has been attached or arrested. Judgments and remedies may be had on such bond or stipulation as if a special bond or stipulation had been filed in each of such actions. The district court may make necessary orders to carry this rule into effect, particularly as to the giving of proper notice of any action against or attachment of a vessel for which a general bond has been filed. Such bond or stipulation shall be indorsed by the clerk with a minute of the actions wherein process is so stayed. Further security may be required by the court at any time.

If a special bond or stipulation is given in a particular case, the liability on the general bond or stipulation shall cease as to that case.

(c) *Release by Consent or Stipulation; Order of Court or Clerk; Costs.* Any vessel, cargo, or other property in the custody of the marshal or other person or organization having the warrant may be released forthwith upon the marshal's acceptance and approval of a stipulation, bond, or other security, signed by the party on whose behalf the property is detained or the party's attorney and expressly authorizing such release, if all costs and charges of the court and its officers shall have first been paid. Otherwise no property in the custody of the marshal, other person or organization having the warrant, or other officer of the court shall be released without an order of the court; but such order may be entered as of course by the clerk, upon the giving of approved security as provided by law and these rules, or upon the dismissal or discontinuance of the action; but the marshal or other person or organization having the warrant shall not deliver any property so released until the costs and charges of the officers of the court shall first have been paid.

(d) *Possessory, Petitory, and Partition Actions.* The foregoing provisions of this subdivision (5) do not apply to petitory, possessory, and partition actions. In such cases the property arrested shall be released only by order of the court, on such terms and conditions and on the giving of such security as the court may require.

(6) Reduction or Impairment of Security. Whenever security is taken the court may, on motion and hearing, for good cause shown, reduce the amount of security given; and if the surety shall be or become insufficient, new or additional sureties may be required on motion and hearing.

(7) Security on Counterclaim.

(a) When a person who has given security for damages in the original action asserts a counterclaim that arises from the transaction or occurrence that is the subject of the original action, a plaintiff for whose benefit the security has been given must give security for damages demanded in the counterclaim unless the court, for cause shown, directs otherwise. Proceedings on the original claim must be stayed until this security is given, unless the court directs otherwise.

(b) The plaintiff is required to give security under Rule E(7)(a) when the United States or its corporate instrumentality counterclaims and would have been required to give security to respond in damages if a private party but is relieved by law from giving security.

(8) Restricted Appearance. An appearance to defend against an admiralty and maritime claim with respect to which there has issued process in rem, or process of attachment and garnishment, may be expressly restricted to the defense of such claim, and in that event is not an appearance for the purposes of any other claim with respect to which such process is not available or has not been served.

(9) Disposition of Property; Sales.

(a) *Interlocutory Sales; Delivery.*

(i) On application of a party, the marshal, or other person having custody of the property, the court may order all or part of the property sold—with the sales proceeds, or as much of them as will satisfy the judgment, paid into court to await further orders of the court—if:

(A) the attached or arrested property is perishable, or liable to deterioration, decay, or injury by being detained in custody pending the action;

(B) the expense of keeping the property is excessive or disproportionate; or

(C) there is an unreasonable delay in securing release of the property.

(ii) In the circumstances described in Rule E(9)(a)(i), the court, on motion by a defendant or a person filing a statement of interest or right under Rule C(6), may order that the property, rather than being sold, be delivered to the movant upon giving security under these rules.

(b) *Sales, Proceeds.* All sales of property shall be made by the marshal or a deputy marshal, or by other person or organization having the warrant, or by any other person assigned by the court where the marshal or other person or organization having the warrant is a party in interest; and the proceeds of sale shall be forthwith paid into the registry of the court to be disposed of according to law.

(10) Preservation of Property. When the owner or another person remains in possession of property attached or arrested under the provisions of Rule E(4)(b) that permit execution of process without taking actual possession, the court, on a party's motion or on its own, may enter any order necessary to preserve the property and to prevent its removal.

* Law Revision Counsel Note: Repealed by Pub.L. 98–89, § 4(b), August 26, 1983, 97 Stat. 600, section 1 of which enacted Title 46, Shipping.

[Amended April 29, 1985, effective August 1, 1985; March 2, 1987, effective August 1, 1987; April 30, 1991, effective December 1, 1991; April 17, 2000, effective December 1, 2000; April 12, 2006, effective December 1, 2006.]

RULE F. LIMITATION OF LIABILITY

(1) Time for Filing Complaint; Security. Not later than six months after receipt of a claim in writing, any vessel owner may file a complaint in the appropriate district court, as provided in subdivision (9) of this rule, for limitation of liability pursuant to statute. The owner (a) shall deposit with the court, for the benefit of claimants, a sum equal to the amount or value of the owner's interest in the vessel and pending freight, or approved security therefor, and in addition such sums, or approved security therefor, as the court may from time to time fix as necessary to carry out the provisions of the statutes as amended; or (b) at the owner's option shall transfer to a trustee to be appointed by the court, for the benefit of claimants, the owner's interest in the vessel and pending freight, together with such sums, or approved security therefor, as the court may from time to time fix as necessary to carry out the provisions of the statutes as amended. The plaintiff shall also give security for costs and, if the plaintiff elects to give security, for interest at the rate of 6 percent per annum from the date of the security.

(2) Complaint. The complaint shall set forth the facts on the basis of which the right to limit liability is asserted and all facts necessary to enable the court to determine the amount to which the owner's liability shall be limited. The complaint may demand exoneration from as well as limitation of liability. It shall state the voyage if any, on which the demands sought to be limited arose, with the date and place of its termination; the amount of all demands including all unsatisfied liens or claims of lien, in contract or in tort or otherwise, arising on that voyage, so far as known to the plaintiff, and what actions and proceedings, if any, are pending thereon; whether the vessel was damaged, lost, or abandoned, and, if so, when and where; the value of the vessel at the close of the voyage or, in case of wreck, the value of her wreckage, strippings, or proceeds, if any, and where and in whose possession they are; and the amount of any pending freight recovered or recoverable. If the plaintiff elects to transfer the plaintiff's interest in the vessel to a trustee, the complaint must further show any prior paramount liens thereon, and what voyages or trips, if any, she has made since the voyage or trip on which the claims sought to be limited arose, and any existing liens arising upon any such subsequent voyage or trip, with the amounts and causes thereof, and the names and addresses of the lienors, so far as known; and whether the vessel sustained any injury upon or by reason of such subsequent voyage or trip.

(3) Claims Against Owner; Injunction. Upon compliance by the owner with the requirements of subdivision (1) of this rule all claims and proceedings against the owner or the owner's property with respect to the matter in question shall cease. On application of the plaintiff the court shall enjoin the further prosecution of any action or proceeding against the plaintiff or the plaintiff's property with respect to any claim subject to limitation in the action.

(4) Notice to Claimants. Upon the owner's compliance with subdivision (1) of this rule the court shall issue a notice to all persons asserting claims with respect to which the complaint seeks limitation, admonishing them to file their respective claims with the clerk of the court and to serve on the attorneys for the plaintiff a copy thereof on or before a date to be named in the notice. The date so fixed shall not be less than 30 days after issuance of the notice. For cause shown, the court may enlarge the time within which claims may be filed. The notice shall be published in such newspaper or newspapers as the court may direct once a week for four successive weeks prior to the date fixed for the filing of claims. The plaintiff not later than the day of second publication shall also mail a copy of the notice to every person known to have made any claim against the vessel or the plaintiff arising out of the voyage or trip on which the claims sought to be limited arose. In cases involving death a copy of such notice shall be mailed to the decedent at the decedent's last known address, and also to any person who shall be known to have made any claim on account of such death.

(5) Claims and Answer. Claims shall be filed and served on or before the date specified in the notice provided for in subdivision (4) of this rule. Each claim shall specify the facts upon which the claimant relies in support of the claim, the items thereof, and the dates on which the same accrued. If a claimant desires to contest either the right to exoneration from or the right to limitation of liability the claimant shall file and serve an answer to the complaint unless the claim has included an answer.

(6) Information to Be Given Claimants. Within 30 days after the date specified in the notice for filing claims, or within such time as the court thereafter may allow, the plaintiff shall mail to the attorney for each claimant (or if the claimant has no attorney to the claimant) a list setting forth (a) the name of each claimant, (b) the name and address of the claimant's attorney (if the claimant is known to have one), (c) the nature of the claim, i.e., whether property loss, property damage, death, personal injury etc., and (d) the amount thereof.

(7) Insufficiency of Fund or Security. Any claimant may by motion demand that the funds deposited in court or the security given by the plaintiff be increased on the ground that they are less than the value of the plaintiff's interest in the vessel and pending freight. Thereupon the court shall cause due appraisement to be made of the value of the plaintiff's interest in the vessel and pending freight; and if the court finds that the deposit or security is either insufficient or excessive it shall order its increase or reduction. In like manner any claimant may demand that the deposit or security be increased on the ground that it is insufficient to carry out the provisions of the statutes relating to claims in respect of loss of life or bodily injury; and, after notice and hearing, the court may similarly order that the deposit or security be increased or reduced.

(8) Objections to Claims: Distribution of Fund. Any interested party may question or controvert any claim without filing an objection thereto. Upon determination of liability the fund deposited or secured, or the proceeds of the vessel and pending freight, shall be divided pro rata, subject to all relevant provisions of law, among the several claimants in proportion to the amounts of their respective claims, duly proved, saving, however, to all parties any priority to which they may be legally entitled.

(9) Venue; Transfer. The complaint shall be filed in any district in which the vessel has been attached or arrested to answer for any claim with respect to which the plaintiff seeks to limit liability; or, if the vessel has not been attached or arrested, then in any district in which the owner has been sued with respect to any such claim. When the vessel has not been attached or arrested to answer the matters aforesaid, and suit has not been commenced against the owner, the proceedings may be had in the district in which the vessel may be, but if the vessel is not within any district and no suit has been commenced in any district, then the complaint may be filed in any district. For the convenience of parties and witnesses, in the interest of justice, the court may transfer the action to any district; if venue is wrongly laid the court shall dismiss or, if it be in the interest of justice, transfer the action to any district in which it could have been brought. If the vessel shall have been sold, the proceeds shall represent the vessel for the purposes of these rules.

[Amended March 2, 1987, effective August 1, 1987.]

RULE G. FORFEITURE ACTIONS IN REM

(1) Scope. This rule governs a forfeiture action in rem arising from a federal statute. To the extent that this rule does not address an issue, Supplemental Rules C and E and the Federal Rules of Civil Procedure also apply.

(2) Complaint. The complaint must:

(a) be verified;

(b) state the grounds for subject-matter jurisdiction, in rem jurisdiction over the defendant property, and venue;

(c) describe the property with reasonable particularity;

(d) if the property is tangible, state its location when any seizure occurred and—if different—its location when the action is filed;

(e) identify the statute under which the forfeiture action is brought; and

(f) state sufficiently detailed facts to support a reasonable belief that the government will be able to meet its burden of proof at trial.

(3) Judicial Authorization and Process.

(a) *Real Property.* If the defendant is real property, the government must proceed under 18 U.S.C. § 985.

(b) *Other Property; Arrest Warrant.* If the defendant is not real property:

(i) the clerk must issue a warrant to arrest the property if it is in the government's possession, custody, or control;

(ii) the court—on finding probable cause—must issue a warrant to arrest the property if it is not in the government's possession, custody, or control and is not subject to a judicial restraining order; and

(iii) a warrant is not necessary if the property is subject to a judicial restraining order.

(c) *Execution of Process.*

(i) The warrant and any supplemental process must be delivered to a person or organization authorized to execute it, who may be: (A) a marshal or any other United States officer or employee; (B) someone under contract with the United States; or (C) someone specially appointed by the court for that purpose.

(ii) The authorized person or organization must execute the warrant and any supplemental process on property in the United States as soon as practicable unless:

(A) the property is in the government's possession, custody, or control; or

(B) the court orders a different time when the complaint is under seal, the action is stayed before the warrant and supplemental process are executed, or the court finds other good cause.

(iii) The warrant and any supplemental process may be executed within the district or, when authorized by statute, outside the district.

(iv) If executing a warrant on property outside the United States is required, the warrant may be transmitted to an appropriate authority for serving process where the property is located.

(4) Notice.

(a) *Notice by Publication.*

(i) When Publication Is Required. A judgment of forfeiture may be entered only if the government has published notice of the action within a reasonable time after filing the complaint or at a time the court orders. But notice need not be published if:

(A) the defendant property is worth less than $1,000 and direct notice is sent under Rule G(4)(b) to every person the government can reasonably identify as a potential claimant; or

(B) the court finds that the cost of publication exceeds the property's value and that other means of notice would satisfy due process.

(ii) Content of the Notice. Unless the court orders otherwise, the notice must:

(A) describe the property with reasonable particularity;

(B) state the times under Rule G(5) to file a claim and to answer; and

(C) name the government attorney to be served with the claim and answer.

(iii) Frequency of Publication. Published notice must appear:

(A) once a week for three consecutive weeks; or

(B) only once if, before the action was filed, notice of nonjudicial forfeiture of the same property was published on an official internet government forfeiture site for at least 30 consecutive days, or in a newspaper of general circulation for three consecutive weeks in a district where publication is authorized under Rule G(4)(a)(iv).

(iv) Means of Publication. The government should select from the following options a means of publication reasonably calculated to notify potential claimants of the action:

(A) if the property is in the United States, publication in a newspaper generally circulated in the district where the action is filed, where the property was seized, or where property that was not seized is located;

(B) if the property is outside the United States, publication in a newspaper generally circulated in a district where the action is filed, in a newspaper generally circulated in the country where the property is located, or in legal notices published and generally circulated in the country where the property is located; or

(C) instead of (A) or (B), posting a notice on an official internet government forfeiture site for at least 30 consecutive days.

(b) *Notice to Known Potential Claimants.*

(i) Direct Notice Required. The government must send notice of the action and a copy of the complaint to any person who reasonably appears to be a potential claimant on the facts known to the government before the end of the time for filing a claim under Rule G(5)(a)(ii)(B).

(ii) Content of the Notice. The notice must state:

(A) the date when the notice is sent;

(B) a deadline for filing a claim, at least 35 days after the notice is sent;

(C) that an answer or a motion under Rule 12 must be filed no later than 20 days after filing the claim; and

(D) the name of the government attorney to be served with the claim and answer.

(iii) Sending Notice.

(A) The notice must be sent by means reasonably calculated to reach the potential claimant.

(B) Notice may be sent to the potential claimant or to the attorney representing the potential claimant with respect to the seizure of the property or in a related investigation, administrative forfeiture proceeding, or criminal case.

(C) Notice sent to a potential claimant who is incarcerated must be sent to the place of incarceration.

(D) Notice to a person arrested in connection with an offense giving rise to the forfeiture who is not incarcerated when notice is sent may be sent to the address that person last gave to the agency that arrested or released the person.

(E) Notice to a person from whom the property was seized who is not incarcerated when notice is sent may be sent to the last address that person gave to the agency that seized the property.

(iv) When Notice Is Sent. Notice by the following means is sent on the date when it is placed in the mail, delivered to a commercial carrier, or sent by electronic mail.

(v) Actual Notice. A potential claimant who had actual notice of a forfeiture action may not oppose or seek relief from forfeiture because of the government's failure to send the required notice.

(5) Responsive Pleadings.

(a) *Filing a Claim.*

(i) A person who asserts an interest in the defendant property may contest the forfeiture by filing a claim in the court where the action is pending. The claim must:

(A) identify the specific property claimed;

(B) identify the claimant and state the claimant's interest in the property;

(C) be signed by the claimant under penalty of perjury; and

(D) be served on the government attorney designated under Rule G(4)(a)(ii)(C) or (b)(ii)(D).

(ii) Unless the court for good cause sets a different time, the claim must be filed:

(A) by the time stated in a direct notice sent under Rule G(4)(b);

(B) if notice was published but direct notice was not sent to the claimant or the claimant's attorney, no later than 30 days after final publication of newspaper notice or legal notice under Rule G(4)(a) or no later than 60 days after the first day of publication on an official internet government forfeiture site; or

(C) if notice was not published and direct notice was not sent to the claimant or the claimant's attorney:

(1) if the property was in the government's possession, custody, or control when the complaint was filed, no later than 60 days after the filing, not counting any time when the complaint was under seal or when the action was stayed before execution of a warrant issued under Rule G(3)(b); or

(2) if the property was not in the government's possession, custody, or control when the complaint was filed, no later than 60 days after the government complied with 18 U.S.C. § 985(c) as to real property, or 60 days after process was executed on the property under Rule G(3).

(iii) A claim filed by a person asserting an interest as a bailee must identify the bailor, and if filed on the bailor's behalf must state the authority to do so.

(b) *Answer.* A claimant must serve and file an answer to the complaint or a motion under Rule 12 within 20 days after filing the claim. A claimant waives an objection to in rem jurisdiction or to venue if the objection is not made by motion or stated in the answer.

(6) Special Interrogatories.

(a) *Time and Scope.* The government may serve special interrogatories limited to the claimant's identity and relationship to the defendant property without the court's leave at any time after the claim is filed and before discovery is closed. But if the claimant serves a motion to dismiss the action, the government must serve the interrogatories within 20 days after the motion is served.

(b) *Answers or Objections.* Answers or objections to these interrogatories must be served within 20 days after the interrogatories are served.

(c) *Government's Response Deferred.* The government need not respond to a claimant's motion to dismiss the action under Rule G(8)(b) until 20 days after the claimant has answered these interrogatories.

(7) Preserving, Preventing Criminal Use, and Disposing of Property; Sales.

(a) *Preserving and Preventing Criminal Use of Property.* When the government does not have actual possession of the defendant property the court, on motion or on its own, may enter any order necessary to preserve the property, to prevent its removal or encumbrance, or to prevent its use in a criminal offense.

(b) *Interlocutory Sale or Delivery.*

(i) Order to Sell. On motion by a party or a person having custody of the property, the court may order all or part of the property sold if:

(A) the property is perishable or at risk of deterioration, decay, or injury by being detained in custody pending the action;

(B) the expense of keeping the property is excessive or is disproportionate to its fair market value;

(C) the property is subject to a mortgage or to taxes on which the owner is in default; or

(D) the court finds other good cause.

(ii) Who Makes the Sale. A sale must be made by a United States agency that has authority to sell the property, by the agency's contractor, or by any person the court designates.

(iii) Sale Procedures. The sale is governed by 28 U.S.C. §§ 2001, 2002, and 2004, unless all parties, with the court's approval, agree to the sale, aspects of the sale, or different procedures.

(iv) Sale Proceeds. Sale proceeds are a substitute res subject to forfeiture in place of the property that was sold. The proceeds must be held in an interest-bearing account maintained by the United States pending the conclusion of the forfeiture action.

(v) Delivery on a Claimant's Motion. The court may order that the property be delivered to the claimant pending the conclusion of the action if the claimant shows circumstances that would permit sale under Rule G(7)(b)(i) and gives security under these rules.

(c) *Disposing of Forfeited Property.* Upon entry of a forfeiture judgment, the property or proceeds from selling the property must be disposed of as provided by law.

(8) Motions.

(a) *Motion To Suppress Use of the Property as Evidence.* If the defendant property was seized, a party with standing to contest the lawfulness of the seizure may move to suppress use of the property as evidence. Suppression does not affect forfeiture of the property based on independently derived evidence.

(b) *Motion To Dismiss the Action.*

(i) A claimant who establishes standing to contest forfeiture may move to dismiss the action under Rule 12(b).

(ii) In an action governed by 18 U.S.C. § 983(a)(3)(D) the complaint may not be dismissed on the ground that the government did not have adequate evidence at the time the complaint was filed to establish the forfeitability of the property. The sufficiency of the complaint is governed by Rule G(2).

(c) *Motion To Strike a Claim or Answer.*

(i) At any time before trial, the government may move to strike a claim or answer:

(A) for failing to comply with Rule G(5) or (6), or

(B) because the claimant lacks standing.

(ii) The motion:

(A) must be decided before any motion by the claimant to dismiss the action; and

(B) may be presented as a motion for judgment on the pleadings or as a motion to determine after a hearing or by summary judgment whether the claimant can carry the burden of establishing standing by a preponderance of the evidence.

(d) *Petition To Release Property.*

(i) If a United States agency or an agency's contractor holds property for judicial or nonjudicial forfeiture under a statute governed by 18 U.S.C. § 983(f), a person who has filed a claim to the property may petition for its release under § 983(f).

(ii) If a petition for release is filed before a judicial forfeiture action is filed against the property, the petition may be filed either in the district where the property was seized or in the district where a warrant to seize the property issued. If a judicial forfeiture action against the property is later filed in another district—or if the government shows that the action will be filed in another district—the petition may be transferred to that district under 28 U.S.C. § 1404.

(e) *Excessive Fines.* A claimant may seek to mitigate a forfeiture under the Excessive Fines Clause of the Eighth Amendment by motion for summary judgment or by motion made after entry of a forfeiture judgment if:

(i) the claimant has pleaded the defense under Rule 8; and

(ii) the parties have had the opportunity to conduct civil discovery on the defense.

(9) Trial. Trial is to the court unless any party demands trial by jury under Rule 38.

[Effective December 1, 2006.]

INDEX TO FEDERAL RULES OF CIVIL PROCEDURE

*

FEDERAL RULES OF EVIDENCE

Effective July 1, 1975

Including Amendments Effective December 1, 2006

Research Note

These rules may be searched electronically on Westlaw in the US–RULES database; updates to these rules may be found on Westlaw in US–RULES-UPDATES. For search tips, and a detailed summary of database content, consult the Westlaw Scope Screen of each database.

Table of Rules

ARTICLE I. GENERAL PROVISIONS

RULE 101. SCOPE

These rules govern proceedings in the courts of the United States and before the United States bankruptcy judges and United States magistrate judges, to the extent and with the exceptions stated in rule 1101.

[Amended March 2, 1987, effective October 1, 1987; April 25, 1988, effective November 1, 1988; April 22, 1993, effective December 1, 1993.]

RULE 102. PURPOSE AND CONSTRUCTION

These rules shall be construed to secure fairness in administration, elimination of unjustifiable expense and delay, and promotion of growth and development of the law of evidence to the end that the truth may be ascertained and proceedings justly determined.

RULE 103. RULINGS ON EVIDENCE

(a) Effect of Erroneous Ruling. Error may not be predicated upon a ruling which admits or excludes evidence unless a substantial right of the party is affected, and

(1) *Objection.* In case the ruling is one admitting evidence, a timely objection or motion to strike appears of record, stating the specific ground of objection, if the specific ground was not apparent from the context; or

(2) *Offer of Proof.* In case the ruling is one excluding evidence, the substance of the evidence was made known to the court by offer or was apparent from the context within which questions were asked.

Once the court makes a definitive ruling on the record admitting or excluding evidence, either at or before trial, a party need not renew an objection or offer of proof to preserve a claim of error for appeal.

(b) Record of Offer and Ruling. The court may add any other or further statement which shows the character of the evidence, the form in which it was offered, the objection made, and the ruling thereon. It may direct the making of an offer in question and answer form.

(c) Hearing of Jury. In jury cases, proceedings shall be conducted, to the extent practicable, so as to prevent inadmissible evidence from being suggested to the jury by any means, such as making statements or offers of proof or asking questions in the hearing of the jury.

(d) Plain Error. Nothing in this rule precludes taking notice of plain errors affecting substantial rights although they were not brought to the attention of the court.

[Amended April 17, 2000, effective December 1, 2000.]

RULE 104. PRELIMINARY QUESTIONS

(a) Questions of Admissibility Generally. Preliminary questions concerning the qualification of a person to be a witness, the existence of a privilege, or the admissibility of evidence shall be determined by the court, subject to the provisions of subdivision (b). In making its determination it is not bound by the rules of evidence except those with respect to privileges.

(b) Relevancy Conditioned on Fact. When the relevancy of evidence depends upon the fulfillment of a condition of fact, the court shall admit it upon, or subject to, the introduction of evidence sufficient to support a finding of the fulfillment of the condition.

(c) Hearing of Jury. Hearings on the admissibility of confessions shall in all cases be conducted out of the hearing of the jury. Hearings on other preliminary matters shall be so conducted when the interests of justice require, or when an accused is a witness and so requests.

(d) Testimony by Accused. The accused does not, by testifying upon a preliminary matter, become subject to cross-examination as to other issues in the case.

(e) Weight and Credibility. This rule does not limit the right of a party to introduce before the jury evidence relevant to weight or credibility.

[Amended March 2, 1987, effective October 1, 1987.]

RULE 105. LIMITED ADMISSIBILITY

When evidence which is admissible as to one party or for one purpose but not admissible as to another party or for another purpose is admitted, the court, upon request, shall restrict the evidence to its proper scope and instruct the jury accordingly.

RULE 106. REMAINDER OF OR RELATED WRITINGS OR RECORDED STATEMENTS

When a writing or recorded statement or part thereof is introduced by a party, an adverse party may require the introduction at that time of any other part or any other writing or recorded statement which ought in fairness to be considered contemporaneously with it.

[Amended March 2, 1987, effective October 1, 1987.]

ARTICLE II. JUDICIAL NOTICE

RULE 201. JUDICIAL NOTICE OF ADJUDICATIVE FACTS

(a) Scope of Rule. This rule governs only judicial notice of adjudicative facts.

(b) Kinds of Facts. A judicially noticed fact must be one not subject to reasonable dispute in that it is either (1) generally known within the territorial jurisdiction of the trial court or (2) capable of accurate and ready determination by resort to sources whose accuracy cannot reasonably be questioned.

(c) When Discretionary. A court may take judicial notice, whether requested or not.

(d) When Mandatory. A court shall take judicial notice if requested by a party and supplied with the necessary information.

(e) Opportunity to Be Heard. A party is entitled upon timely request to an opportunity to be heard as to the propriety of taking judicial notice and the tenor of the matter noticed. In the absence of prior notification, the request may be made after judicial notice has been taken.

(f) Time of Taking Notice. Judicial notice may be taken at any stage of the proceeding.

(g) Instructing Jury. In a civil action or proceeding, the court shall instruct the jury to accept as conclusive any fact judicially noticed. In a criminal case, the court shall instruct the jury that it may, but is not required to, accept as conclusive any fact judicially noticed.

ARTICLE III. PRESUMPTIONS IN CIVIL ACTIONS AND PROCEEDINGS

RULE 301. PRESUMPTIONS IN GENERAL IN CIVIL ACTIONS AND PROCEEDINGS

In all civil actions and proceedings not otherwise provided for by Act of Congress or by these rules, a presumption imposes on the party against whom it is directed the burden of going forward with evidence to rebut or meet the presumption, but does not shift to such party the burden of proof in the sense of the risk of nonpersuasion, which remains throughout the trial upon the party on whom it was originally cast.

RULE 302. APPLICABILITY OF STATE LAW IN CIVIL ACTIONS AND PROCEEDINGS

In civil actions and proceedings, the effect of a presumption respecting a fact which is an element of a claim or defense as to which State law supplies the rule of decision is determined in accordance with State law.

ARTICLE IV. RELEVANCY AND ITS LIMITS

RULE 401. DEFINITION OF "RELEVANT EVIDENCE"

"Relevant evidence" means evidence having any tendency to make the existence of any fact that is of consequence to the determination of the action more probable or less probable than it would be without the evidence.

RULE 402. RELEVANT EVIDENCE GENERALLY ADMISSIBLE; IRRELEVANT EVIDENCE INADMISSIBLE

All relevant evidence is admissible, except as otherwise provided by the Constitution of the United States, by Act of Congress, by these rules, or by other rules prescribed by the Supreme Court pursuant to statutory authority. Evidence which is not relevant is not admissible.

RULE 403. EXCLUSION OF RELEVANT EVIDENCE ON GROUNDS OF PREJUDICE, CONFUSION, OR WASTE OF TIME

Although relevant, evidence may be excluded if its probative value is substantially outweighed by the danger of unfair prejudice, confusion of the issues, or misleading the jury, or by considerations of undue delay, waste of time, or needless presentation of cumulative evidence.

RULE 404. CHARACTER EVIDENCE NOT ADMISSIBLE TO PROVE CONDUCT; EXCEPTIONS; OTHER CRIMES

(a) Character Evidence Generally. Evidence of a person's character or a trait of character is not admissible for the purpose of proving action in conformity therewith on a particular occasion, except:

(1) *Character of Accused.* In a criminal case, evidence of a pertinent trait of character offered by an accused, or by the prosecution to rebut the same, or if evidence of a trait of character of the alleged victim of the crime is offered by an accused and admitted under Rule 404(a)(2), evidence of the same trait of character of the accused offered by the prosecution;

(2) *Character of Alleged Victim.* In a criminal case, and subject to the limitations imposed by Rule 412, evidence of a pertinent trait of character of the alleged victim of the crime offered by an accused, or by the prosecution to rebut the same, or evidence of a character trait of peacefulness of the alleged victim offered by the prosecution in a homicide case to rebut evidence that the alleged victim was the first aggressor;

(3) *Character of Witness.* Evidence of the character of a witness, as provided in Rules 607, 608, and 609.

(b) Other Crimes, Wrongs, or Acts. Evidence of other crimes, wrongs, or acts is not admissible to prove the character of a person in order to show action in conformity therewith. It may, however, be admissible for other purposes, such as proof of motive, opportunity, intent, preparation, plan, knowledge, identity, or absence of mistake or accident, provided that upon request by the accused, the prosecution in a criminal case shall provide reasonable notice in advance of trial, or during trial if the court excuses pretrial notice on good cause shown, of the general nature of any such evidence it intends to introduce at trial.

[Amended March 2, 1987, effective October 1, 1987; April 30, 1991, effective December 1, 1991; April 17, 2000, effective December 1, 2000; April 12, 2006, effective December 1, 2006.]

RULE 405. METHODS OF PROVING CHARACTER

(a) Reputation or Opinion. In all cases in which evidence of character or a trait of character of a person is admissible, proof may be made by testimony as to reputation or by testimony in the form of an opinion. On cross-examination, inquiry is allowable into relevant specific instances of conduct.

(b) Specific Instances of Conduct. In cases in which character or a trait of character of a person is an essential element of a charge, claim, or defense, proof may also be made of specific instances of that person's conduct.

[Amended March 2, 1987, effective October 1, 1987.]

RULE 406. HABIT; ROUTINE PRACTICE

Evidence of the habit of a person or of the routine practice of an organization, whether corroborated or not and regardless of the presence of eyewitnesses, is relevant to prove that the conduct of the person or organization on a particular occasion was in conformity with the habit or routine practice.

RULE 407. SUBSEQUENT REMEDIAL MEASURES

When, after an injury or harm allegedly caused by an event, measures are taken that, if taken previously, would have made the injury or harm less likely to occur, evidence of the subsequent measures is not admissible to prove negligence, culpable conduct, a defect in a product, a defect in a product's design, or a need for a warning or instruction. This rule does not require the exclusion of evidence of subsequent measures when offered for another purpose, such as proving ownership, control, or feasibility of precautionary measures, if controverted, or impeachment.

[Amended April 11, 1997, effective December 1, 1997.]

RULE 408. COMPROMISE AND OFFERS TO COMPROMISE

(a) Prohibited Uses. Evidence of the following is not admissible on behalf of any party, when offered to prove liability for, invalidity of, or amount of a claim that was disputed as to validity or amount, or to impeach through a prior inconsistent statement or contradiction:

(1) furnishing or offering or promising to furnish—or accepting or offering or promising to accept—a valuable consideration in compromising or attempting to compromise the claim; and

(2) conduct or statements made in compromise negotiations regarding the claim, except when offered in a criminal case and the negotiations related to a claim by a public office or agency in the exercise of regulatory, investigative, or enforcement authority.

(b) Permitted Uses. This rule does not require exclusion if the evidence is offered for purposes not prohibited by subdivision (a). Examples of permissible purposes include proving a witness's bias or prejudice; negating a contention of undue delay; and proving an effort to obstruct a criminal investigation or prosecution.

[Amended effective December 1, 2006.]

RULE 409. PAYMENT OF MEDICAL AND SIMILAR EXPENSES

Evidence of furnishing or offering or promising to pay medical, hospital, or similar expenses occasioned by an injury is not admissible to prove liability for the injury.

RULE 410. INADMISSIBILITY OF PLEAS, PLEA DISCUSSIONS, AND RELATED STATEMENTS

Except as otherwise provided in this rule, evidence of the following is not, in any civil or criminal proceeding, admissible against the defendant who made the plea or was a participant in the plea discussions:

(1) a plea of guilty which was later withdrawn;

(2) a plea of nolo contendere;

(3) any statement made in the course of any proceedings under Rule 11 of the Federal Rules of Criminal Procedure or comparable state procedure regarding either of the foregoing pleas; or

(4) any statement made in the course of plea discussions with an attorney for the prosecuting authority which do not result in a plea of guilty or which result in a plea of guilty later withdrawn.

However, such a statement is admissible (i) in any proceeding wherein another statement made in the course of the same plea or plea discussions has been introduced and the statement ought in fairness be considered contemporaneously with it, or (ii) in a criminal proceeding for perjury or false statement if the statement was made by the defendant under oath, on the record and in the presence of counsel.

[Amended by Pub.L. 94–149, § 1(9), December 12, 1975, 89 Stat. 805; amended April 30, 1979, effective December 1, 1980 (effective date pursuant to Pub.L. 96–42, July 31, 1979, 93 Stat. 326).]

RULE 411. LIABILITY INSURANCE

Evidence that a person was or was not insured against liability is not admissible upon the issue whether the person acted negligently or otherwise wrongfully. This rule does not require the exclusion of evidence of insurance against liability when offered for another purpose, such as proof of agency, ownership, or control, or bias or prejudice of a witness.

[Amended March 2, 1987, effective October 1, 1987.]

RULE 412. SEX OFFENSE CASES; RELEVANCE OF ALLEGED VICTIM'S PAST SEXUAL BEHAVIOR OR ALLEGED SEXUAL PREDISPOSITION

(a) Evidence Generally Inadmissible. The following evidence is not admissible in any civil or criminal proceeding involving alleged sexual misconduct except as provided in subdivisions (b) and (c):

(1) Evidence offered to prove that any alleged victim engaged in other sexual behavior.

(2) Evidence offered to prove any alleged victim's sexual predisposition.

(b) Exceptions.

(1) In a criminal case, the following evidence is admissible, if otherwise admissible under these rules:

(A) evidence of specific instances of sexual behavior by the alleged victim offered to prove that a person other than the accused was the source of semen, injury or other physical evidence;

(B) evidence of specific instances of sexual behavior by the alleged victim with respect to the person accused of the sexual misconduct offered by the accused to prove consent or by the prosecution; and

(C) evidence the exclusion of which would violate the constitutional rights of the defendant.

(2) In a civil case, evidence offered to prove the sexual behavior or sexual predisposition of any alleged victim is admissible if it is otherwise admissible under these rules and its probative value substantially outweighs the danger of harm to any victim and of unfair prejudice to any party. Evidence of an alleged vic-

tim's reputation is admissible only if it has been placed in controversy by the alleged victim.

(c) Procedure to Determine Admissibility.

(1) A party intending to offer evidence under subdivision (b) must—

(A) file a written motion at least 14 days before trial specifically describing the evidence and stating the purpose for which it is offered unless the court, for good cause, requires a different time for filing or permits filing during trial; and

(B) serve the motion on all parties and notify the alleged victim or, when appropriate, the alleged victim's guardian or representative.

(2) Before admitting evidence under this rule the court must conduct a hearing in camera and afford the victim and parties a right to attend and be heard. The motion, related papers, and the record of the hearing must be sealed and remain under seal unless the court orders otherwise.

[Adopted by Pub.L. 95–540, § 2(a), October 28, 1978, 92 Stat. 2046, applicable to trials that begin more than 30 days after October 28, 1978; amended by Pub.L. 100–690, Title VII, § 7046(a), November 18, 1988, 102 Stat. 4400; amended April 29, 1994, effective December 1, 1994; amended by Pub.L. 103–322, Title IV, § 40141(b), September 13, 1994, 108 Stat. 1919, effective December 1, 1994.]

RULE 413. EVIDENCE OF SIMILAR CRIMES IN SEXUAL ASSAULT CASES

(a) In a criminal case in which the defendant is accused of an offense of sexual assault, evidence of the defendant's commission of another offense or offenses of sexual assault is admissible, and may be considered for its bearing on any matter to which it is relevant.

(b) In a case in which the Government intends to offer evidence under this rule, the attorney for the Government shall disclose the evidence to the defendant, including statements of witnesses or a summary of the substance of any testimony that is expected to be offered, at least fifteen days before the scheduled date of trial or at such later time as the court may allow for good cause.

(c) This rule shall not be construed to limit the admission or consideration of evidence under any other rule.

(d) For purposes of this rule and Rule 415, "offense of sexual assault" means a crime under Federal law or the law of a State (as defined in section 513 of title 18, United States Code) that involved—

(1) any conduct proscribed by chapter 109A of title 18, United States Code;

(2) contact, without consent, between any part of the defendant's body or an object and the genitals or anus of another person;

(3) contact, without consent, between the genitals or anus of the defendant and any part of another person's body;

(4) deriving sexual pleasure or gratification from the infliction of death, bodily injury, or physical pain on another person; or

(5) an attempt or conspiracy to engage in conduct described in paragraphs (1)–(4).

[Adopted by Pub.L. 103–322, Title XXXII, § 320935(a), September 13, 1994, 108 Stat. 2135, applicable to proceedings commenced on or after July 9, 1995, including all trials commenced on or after July 9, 1995 (Pub.L. 103–322, Title XXXII, § 320935(e), September 13, 1994, 108 Stat. 2137, as amended by Pub.L. 104–208, Div. A, Title I, § 101(a) [Title I, § 120], September 30, 1996, 110 Stat. 3009–25).]

RULE 414. EVIDENCE OF SIMILAR CRIMES IN CHILD MOLESTATION CASES

(a) In a criminal case in which the defendant is accused of an offense of child molestation, evidence of the defendant's commission of another offense or offenses of child molestation is admissible, and may be considered for its bearing on any matter to which it is relevant.

(b) In a case in which the Government intends to offer evidence under this rule, the attorney for the Government shall disclose the evidence to the defendant, including statements of witnesses or a summary of the substance of any testimony that is expected to be offered, at least fifteen days before the scheduled date of trial or at such later time as the court may allow for good cause.

(c) This rule shall not be construed to limit the admission or consideration of evidence under any other rule.

(d) For purposes of this rule and Rule 415, "child" means a person below the age of fourteen, and "offense of child molestation" means a crime under Federal law or the law of a State (as defined in section 513 of title 18, United States Code) that involved—

(1) any conduct proscribed by chapter 109A of title 18, United States Code, that was committed in relation to a child;

(2) any conduct proscribed by chapter 110 of title 18, United States Code;

(3) contact between any part of the defendant's body or an object and the genitals or anus of a child;

(4) contact between the genitals or anus of the defendant and any part of the body of a child;

(5) deriving sexual pleasure or gratification from the infliction of death, bodily injury, or physical pain on a child; or

(6) an attempt or conspiracy to engage in conduct described in paragraphs (1)–(5).

[Adopted by Pub.L. 103–322, Title XXXII, § 320935(a), September 13, 1994, 108 Stat. 2135, applicable to proceedings commenced on or after July 9, 1995, including all trials commenced on or after July 9, 1995 (Pub.L. 103–322, Title XXXII, § 320935(e), September 13, 1994, 108 Stat. 2137, as amended by Pub.L. 104–208, Div. A, Title I, § 101(a) [Title I, § 120], September 30, 1996, 110 Stat. 3009–25).]

RULE 415. EVIDENCE OF SIMILAR ACTS IN CIVIL CASES CONCERNING SEXUAL ASSAULT OR CHILD MOLESTATION

(a) In a civil case in which a claim for damages or other relief is predicated on a party's alleged commission of conduct constituting an offense of sexual assault or child molestation, evidence of that party's commission of another offense or offenses of sexual assault or child molestation is admissible and may be considered as provided in Rule 413 and Rule 414 of these rules.

(b) A party who intends to offer evidence under this Rule shall disclose the evidence to the party against whom it will be offered, including statements of witnesses or a summary of the substance of any testimony that is expected to be offered, at least fifteen days before the scheduled date of trial or at such later time as the court may allow for good cause.

(c) This rule shall not be construed to limit the admission or consideration of evidence under any other rule.

[Adopted by Pub.L. 103–322, Title XXXII, § 320935(a), September 13, 1994, 108 Stat. 2135, applicable to proceedings commenced on or after July 9, 1995, including all trials commenced on or after July 9, 1995 (Pub.L. 103–322, Title XXXII, § 320935(e), September 13, 1994, 108 Stat. 2137, as amended by Pub.L. 104–208, Div. A, Title I, § 101(a) [Title I, § 120], September 30, 1996, 110 Stat. 3009–25).]

ARTICLE V. PRIVILEGES

RULE 501. GENERAL RULE

Except as otherwise required by the Constitution of the United States or provided by Act of Congress or in rules prescribed by the Supreme Court pursuant to statutory authority, the privilege of a witness, person, government, State, or political subdivision thereof shall be governed by the principles of the common law as they may be interpreted by the courts of the United States in the light of reason and experience. However, in civil actions and proceedings, with respect to an element of a claim or defense as to which State law supplies the rule of decision, the privilege of a witness, person, government, State, or political subdivision thereof shall be determined in accordance with State law.

ARTICLE VI. WITNESSES

RULE 601. GENERAL RULE OF COMPETENCY

Every person is competent to be a witness except as otherwise provided in these rules. However, in civil actions and proceedings, with respect to an element of a claim or defense as to which State law supplies the rule of decision, the competency of a witness shall be determined in accordance with State law.

RULE 602. LACK OF PERSONAL KNOWLEDGE

A witness may not testify to a matter unless evidence is introduced sufficient to support a finding that the witness has personal knowledge of the matter. Evidence to prove personal knowledge may, but need not, consist of the witness' own testimony. This rule is subject to the provisions of rule 703, relating to opinion testimony by expert witnesses.

[Amended March 2, 1987, effective October 1, 1987; April 25, 1988, effective November 1, 1988.]

RULE 603. OATH OR AFFIRMATION

Before testifying, every witness shall be required to declare that the witness will testify truthfully, by oath or affirmation administered in a form calculated to awaken the witness' conscience and impress the witness' mind with the duty to do so.

[Amended March 2, 1987, effective October 1, 1987.]

RULE 604. INTERPRETERS

An interpreter is subject to the provisions of these rules relating to qualification as an expert and the administration of an oath or affirmation to make a true translation.

[Amended March 2, 1987, effective October 1, 1987.]

RULE 605. COMPETENCY OF JUDGE AS WITNESS

The judge presiding at the trial may not testify in that trial as a witness. No objection need be made in order to preserve the point.

RULE 606. COMPETENCY OF JUROR AS WITNESS

(a) At the Trial. A member of the jury may not testify as a witness before that jury in the trial of the case in which the juror is sitting. If the juror is called so to testify, the opposing party shall be afforded an opportunity to object out of the presence of the jury.

(b) Inquiry Into Validity of Verdict or Indictment. Upon an inquiry into the validity of a verdict or indictment, a juror may not testify as to any matter or statement occurring during the course of the jury's deliberations or to the effect of anything upon that or any other juror's mind or emotions as influencing the juror to assent to or dissent from the verdict or indictment or concerning the juror's mental processes in connection therewith. But a juror may testify about (1) whether extraneous prejudicial information was improperly brought to the jury's attention, (2) whether any outside influence was improperly brought to bear upon any juror, or (3) whether there was a mistake in entering the verdict onto the verdict form. A juror's affidavit or evidence of any statement by the juror may not be received on a matter about which the juror would be precluded from testifying.

[Amended by Pub.L. 94–149, § 1(10), December 12, 1975, 89 Stat. 805; amended March 2, 1987, effective October 1, 1987; April 12, 2006, effective December 1, 2006.]

RULE 607. WHO MAY IMPEACH

The credibility of a witness may be attacked by any party, including the party calling the witness.

[Amended March 2, 1987, effective October 1, 1987.]

RULE 608. EVIDENCE OF CHARACTER AND CONDUCT OF WITNESS

(a) Opinion and Reputation Evidence of Character. The credibility of a witness may be attacked or supported by evidence in the form of opinion or reputation, but subject to these limitations: (1) the evidence may refer only to character for truthfulness or untruthfulness, and (2) evidence of truthful character is admissible only after the character of the witness for truthfulness has been attacked by opinion or reputation evidence or otherwise.

(b) Specific Instances of Conduct. Specific instances of the conduct of a witness, for the purpose of attacking or supporting the witness' character for truthfulness, other than conviction of crime as provided in rule 609, may not be proved by extrinsic evidence. They may, however, in the discretion of the court, if probative of truthfulness or untruthfulness, be inquired into on cross-examination of the witness (1) concerning the witness' character for truthfulness or untruthfulness, or (2) concerning the character for truthfulness or untruthfulness of another witness as to which character the witness being cross-examined has testified.

The giving of testimony, whether by an accused or by any other witness, does not operate as a waiver of the accused's or the witness' privilege against self-incrimination when examined with respect to matters that relate only to character for truthfulness.

[Amended March 2, 1987, effective October 1, 1987; April 25, 1988, effective November 1, 1988; March 27, 2003, effective December 1, 2003.]

RULE 609. IMPEACHMENT BY EVIDENCE OF CONVICTION OF CRIME

(a) General Rule. For the purpose of attacking the character for truthfulness of a witness,

(1) evidence that a witness other than an accused has been convicted of a crime shall be admitted, subject to Rule 403, if the crime was punishable by death or imprisonment in excess of one year under the law under which the witness was convicted, and evidence that an accused has been convicted of such a crime shall be admitted if the court determines that the probative value of admitting this evidence outweighs its prejudicial effect to the accused; and

(2) evidence that any witness has been convicted of a crime shall be admitted regardless of the punishment, if it readily can be determined that establishing the elements of the crime required proof or admission of an act of dishonesty or false statement by the witness.

(b) Time Limit. Evidence of a conviction under this rule is not admissible if a period of more than ten years has elapsed since the date of the conviction or of the release of the witness from the confinement imposed for that conviction, whichever is the later date, unless the court determines, in the interests of justice, that the probative value of the conviction supported by specific facts and circumstances substantially outweighs its prejudicial effect. However, evidence of a conviction more than 10 years old as calculated herein, is not admissible unless the proponent gives to the adverse party sufficient advance written notice of intent to use such evidence to provide the adverse party with a fair opportunity to contest the use of such evidence.

(c) Effect of Pardon, Annulment, or Certificate of Rehabilitation. Evidence of a conviction is not admissible under this rule if (1) the conviction has been the subject of a pardon, annulment, certificate of rehabilitation, or other equivalent procedure based on a finding of the rehabilitation of the person convicted, and that person has not been convicted of a subsequent crime that was punishable by death or imprisonment in excess of one year, or (2) the conviction has been the subject of a pardon, annulment, or other equivalent procedure based on a finding of innocence.

(d) Juvenile Adjudications. Evidence of juvenile adjudications is generally not admissible under this rule. The court may, however, in a criminal case allow evidence of a juvenile adjudication of a witness other than the accused if conviction of the offense would be admissible to attack the credibility of an adult and the court is satisfied that admission in evidence is necessary for a fair determination of the issue of guilt or innocence.

(e) Pendency of Appeal. The pendency of an appeal therefrom does not render evidence of a conviction inadmissible. Evidence of the pendency of an appeal is admissible.

[Amended March 2, 1987, effective October 1, 1987; January 26, 1990, effective December 1, 1990; April 12, 2006, effective December 1, 2006.]

RULE 610. RELIGIOUS BELIEFS OR OPINIONS

Evidence of the beliefs or opinions of a witness on matters of religion is not admissible for the purpose of showing that by reason of their nature the witness' credibility is impaired or enhanced.

[Amended March 2, 1987, effective October 1, 1987.]

RULE 611. MODE AND ORDER OF INTERROGATION AND PRESENTATION

(a) Control by Court. The court shall exercise reasonable control over the mode and order of interrogating witnesses and presenting evidence so as to (1) make the interrogation and presentation effective for the ascertainment of the truth, (2) avoid needless consumption of time, and (3) protect witnesses from harassment or undue embarrassment.

(b) Scope of Cross-Examination. Cross-examination should be limited to the subject matter of the direct examination and matters affecting the credibility of the witness. The court may, in the exercise of discretion, permit inquiry into additional matters as if on direct examination.

(c) Leading Questions. Leading questions should not be used on the direct examination of a witness except as may be necessary to develop the witness' testimony. Ordinarily leading questions should be permitted on cross-examination. When a party calls a hostile witness, an adverse party, or a witness identified with an adverse party, interrogation may be by leading questions.

[Amended March 2, 1987, effective October 1, 1987.]

RULE 612. WRITING USED TO REFRESH MEMORY

Except as otherwise provided in criminal proceedings by section 3500 of title 18, United States Code, if a witness uses a writing to refresh memory for the purpose of testifying, either—

(1) while testifying, or

(2) before testifying, if the court in its discretion determines it is necessary in the interests of justice,

an adverse party is entitled to have the writing produced at the hearing, to inspect it, to cross-examine the witness thereon, and to introduce in evidence those portions which relate to the testimony of the witness. If it is claimed that the writing contains matters not related to the subject matter of the testimony the court shall examine the writing in camera, excise any portions not so related, and order delivery of the remainder to the party entitled thereto. Any portion withheld over objections shall be preserved and made available to the appellate court in the event of an appeal. If a writing is not produced or delivered pursuant to order under this rule, the court shall make any order justice requires, except that in criminal cases when the prosecution elects not to comply, the order shall be one striking the testimony or, if the court in its discretion determines that the interests of justice so require, declaring a mistrial.

[Amended March 2, 1987, effective October 1, 1987.]

RULE 613. PRIOR STATEMENTS OF WITNESSES

(a) Examining Witness Concerning Prior Statement. In examining a witness concerning a prior statement made by the witness, whether written or not, the statement need not be shown nor its contents disclosed to the witness at that time, but on request the same shall be shown or disclosed to opposing counsel.

(b) Extrinsic Evidence of Prior Inconsistent Statement of Witness. Extrinsic evidence of a prior inconsistent statement by a witness is not admissible unless the witness is afforded an opportunity to explain or deny the same and the opposite party is afforded an opportunity to interrogate the witness thereon, or the interests of justice otherwise require. This provision does not apply to admissions of a party-opponent as defined in rule 801(d)(2).

[Amended March 2, 1987, effective October 1, 1987; April 25, 1988, effective November 1, 1988.]

RULE 614. CALLING AND INTERROGATION OF WITNESSES BY COURT

(a) Calling by Court. The court may, on its own motion or at the suggestion of a party, call witnesses, and all parties are entitled to cross-examine witnesses thus called.

(b) Interrogation by Court. The court may interrogate witnesses, whether called by itself or by a party.

(c) Objections. Objections to the calling of witnesses by the court or to interrogation by it may be made at the time or at the next available opportunity when the jury is not present.

RULE 615. EXCLUSION OF WITNESSES

At the request of a party the court shall order witnesses excluded so that they cannot hear the testimony of other witnesses, and it may make the order of its own motion. This rule does not authorize exclusion of (1) a party who is a natural person, or (2) an officer or employee of a party which is not a natural person designated as its representative by its attorney, or (3) a person whose presence is shown by a party to be essential to the presentation of the party's cause, or (4) a person authorized by statute to be present.

[Amended March 2, 1987, effective October 1, 1987; April 25, 1988, effective November 1, 1988; amended by Pub.L. 100–690, Title VII, § 7075(a), November 18, 1988, 102 Stat. 4405 (although amendment by Pub.L. 100–690 could not be executed due to prior amendment by Court order which made the same change effective November 1, 1988); amended April 24, 1998, effective December 1, 1998.]

ARTICLE VII. OPINIONS AND EXPERT TESTIMONY

RULE 701. OPINION TESTIMONY BY LAY WITNESSES

If the witness is not testifying as an expert, the witness' testimony in the form of opinions or inferences is limited to those opinions or inferences which are (a) rationally based on the perception of the witness, (b) helpful to a clear understanding of the witness' testimony or the determination of a fact in issue, and (c) not based on scientific, technical, or other specialized knowledge within the scope of Rule 702.

[Amended March 2, 1987, effective October 1, 1987; April 17, 2000, effective December 1, 2000.]

RULE 702. TESTIMONY BY EXPERTS

If scientific, technical, or other specialized knowledge will assist the trier of fact to understand the evidence or to determine a fact in issue, a witness qualified as an expert by knowledge, skill, experience, training, or education, may testify thereto in the form of an opinion or otherwise, if (1) the testimony is based upon sufficient facts or data, (2) the testimony is the product of reliable principles and methods, and (3) the witness has applied the principles and methods reliably to the facts of the case.

[Amended April 17, 2000, effective December 1, 2000.]

RULE 703. BASES OF OPINION TESTIMONY BY EXPERTS

The facts or data in the particular case upon which an expert bases an opinion or inference may be those perceived by or made known to the expert at or before the hearing. If of a type reasonably relied upon by experts in the particular field in forming opinions or inferences upon the subject, the facts or data need not be admissible in evidence in order for the opinion or inference to be admitted. Facts or data that are otherwise inadmissible shall not be disclosed to the jury by the proponent of the opinion or inference unless the court determines that their probative value in assisting the jury to evaluate the expert's opinion substantially outweighs their prejudicial effect.

[Amended March 2, 1987, effective October 1, 1987; April 17, 2000, effective December 1, 2000.]

RULE 704. OPINION ON ULTIMATE ISSUE

(a) Except as provided in subdivision (b), testimony in the form of an opinion or inference otherwise admissible is not objectionable because it embraces an ultimate issue to be decided by the trier of fact.

(b) No expert witness testifying with respect to the mental state or condition of a defendant in a criminal case may state an opinion or inference as to whether the defendant did or did not have the mental state or condition constituting an element of the crime charged or of a defense thereto. Such ultimate issues are matters for the trier of fact alone.

[Amended by Pub.L. 98–473, Title II, § 406, October 12, 1984, 98 Stat. 2067.]

RULE 705. DISCLOSURE OF FACTS OR DATA UNDERLYING EXPERT OPINION

The expert may testify in terms of opinion or inference and give reasons therefor without first testifying to the underlying facts or data, unless the court requires otherwise. The expert may in any event be required to disclose the underlying facts or data on cross-examination.

[Amended March 2, 1987, effective October 1, 1987; April 22, 1993, effective December 1, 1993.]

RULE 706. COURT APPOINTED EXPERTS

(a) Appointment. The court may on its own motion or on the motion of any party enter an order to show cause why expert witnesses should not be appointed, and may request the parties to submit nominations. The court may appoint any expert witnesses agreed upon by the parties, and may appoint expert witnesses of its own selection. An expert witness shall not be appointed by the court unless the witness consents to act. A witness so appointed shall be informed of the witness' duties by the court in writing, a copy of which shall be filed with the clerk, or at a conference in which the parties shall have opportunity to participate. A witness so appointed shall advise the parties of the witness' findings, if any; the witness' deposition may be taken by any party; and the witness may be called to testify by the court or any party. The witness shall be subject to cross-examination by each party, including a party calling the witness.

(b) Compensation. Expert witnesses so appointed are entitled to reasonable compensation in whatever sum the court may allow. The compensation thus fixed is payable from funds which may be provided by law in criminal cases and civil actions and proceedings involving just compensation under the fifth amendment. In other civil actions and proceedings the compensation shall be paid by the parties in such proportion and at such time as the court directs, and thereafter charged in like manner as other costs.

(c) Disclosure of Appointment. In the exercise of its discretion, the court may authorize disclosure to the jury of the fact that the court appointed the expert witness.

(d) Parties' Experts of Own Selection. Nothing in this rule limits the parties in calling expert witnesses of their own selection.

[Amended March 2, 1987, effective October 1, 1987.]

ARTICLE VIII. HEARSAY

RULE 801. DEFINITIONS

The following definitions apply under this article:

(a) Statement. A "statement" is (1) an oral or written assertion or (2) nonverbal conduct of a person, if it is intended by the person as an assertion.

(b) Declarant. A "declarant" is a person who makes a statement.

(c) Hearsay. "Hearsay" is a statement, other than one made by the declarant while testifying at the trial or hearing, offered in evidence to prove the truth of the matter asserted.

(d) Statements Which Are Not Hearsay. A statement is not hearsay if—

(1) *Prior Statement by Witness.* The declarant testifies at the trial or hearing and is subject to cross-examination concerning the statement, and the statement is (A) inconsistent with the declarant's testimony, and was given under oath subject to the penalty of perjury at a trial, hearing, or other proceeding, or in a deposition, or (B) consistent with the declarant's testimony and is offered to rebut an express or implied charge against the declarant of recent fabrication or improper influence or motive, or (C) one of identification of a person made after perceiving the person; or

(2) *Admission by Party-Opponent.* The statement is offered against a party and is (A) the party's own statement, in either an individual or a representative capacity or (B) a statement of which the party has manifested an adoption or belief in its truth, or (C) a statement by a person authorized by the party to make a statement concerning the subject, or (D) a statement by the party's agent or servant concerning a matter within the scope of the agency or employment, made during the existence of the relationship, or (E) a statement by a coconspirator of a party during the course and in furtherance of the conspiracy. The contents of the statement shall be considered but are not alone sufficient to establish the declarant's authority under subdivision (C), the agency or employment relationship and scope thereof under subdivision (D), or the existence of the conspiracy and the participation therein of the declarant and the party against whom the statement is offered under subdivision (E).

[Amended by Pub.L. 94–113, § 1, October 16, 1975, 89 Stat. 576; amended March 2, 1987, effective October 1, 1987; April 11, 1997, effective December 1, 1997.]

RULE 802. HEARSAY RULE

Hearsay is not admissible except as provided by these rules or by other rules prescribed by the Supreme Court pursuant to statutory authority or by Act of Congress.

RULE 803. HEARSAY EXCEPTIONS; AVAILABILITY OF DECLARANT IMMATERIAL

The following are not excluded by the hearsay rule, even though the declarant is available as a witness:

(1) Present Sense Impression. A statement describing or explaining an event or condition made while the declarant was perceiving the event or condition, or immediately thereafter.

(2) Excited Utterance. A statement relating to a startling event or condition made while the declarant was under the stress of excitement caused by the event or condition.

(3) Then Existing Mental, Emotional, or Physical Condition. A statement of the declarant's then existing state of mind, emotion, sensation, or physical condition (such as intent, plan, motive, design, mental feeling, pain, and bodily health), but not including a statement of memory or belief to prove the fact remembered or believed unless it relates to the execution, revocation, identification, or terms of declarant's will.

(4) Statements for Purposes of Medical Diagnosis or Treatment. Statements made for purposes of medical diagnosis or treatment and describing medical history, or past or present symptoms, pain, or sensations, or the inception or general character of the cause or external source thereof insofar as reasonably pertinent to diagnosis or treatment.

(5) Recorded Recollection. A memorandum or record concerning a matter about which a witness once had knowledge but now has insufficient recollection to enable the witness to testify fully and accurately, shown to have been made or adopted by the witness when the matter was fresh in the witness' memory and to reflect that knowledge correctly. If admitted, the memorandum or record may be read into evidence but may not itself be received as an exhibit unless offered by an adverse party.

(6) Records of Regularly Conducted Activity. A memorandum, report, record, or data compilation, in any form, of acts, events, conditions, opinions, or diagnoses, made at or near the time by, or from information transmitted by, a person with knowledge, if kept in the course of a regularly conducted business activity, and if it was the regular practice of that business activity to make the memorandum, report, record, or data compilation, all as shown by the testimony of the custodian or other qualified witness, or by certification that complies with Rule 902(11), Rule 902(12), or a statute permitting certification, unless the source of information or the method or circumstances of preparation indicate lack of trustworthiness. The term "business" as used in this paragraph includes business, institution, association, profession, occupation, and calling of every kind, whether or not conducted for profit.

(7) Absence of Entry in Records Kept in Accordance With the Provisions of Paragraph (6). Evidence that a matter is not included in the memoranda reports, records, or data compilations, in any form, kept in accordance with the provisions of paragraph (6), to prove the nonoccurrence or nonexistence of the matter, if the matter was of a kind of which a memorandum, report, record, or data compilation was regularly made and preserved, unless the sources of information or other circumstances indicate lack of trustworthiness.

(8) Public Records and Reports. Records, reports, statements, or data compilations, in any form, of public offices or agencies, setting forth (A) the activities of the office or agency, or (B) matters observed pursuant to duty imposed by law as to which matters there was a duty to report, excluding, however, in criminal cases matters observed by police officers and other law enforcement personnel, or (C) in civil actions and proceedings and against the Government in criminal cases, factual findings resulting from an investigation made pursuant to authority granted by law, unless the sources of information or other circumstances indicate lack of trustworthiness.

(9) Records of Vital Statistics. Records or data compilations, in any form, of births, fetal deaths, deaths, or marriages, if the report thereof was made to a public office pursuant to requirements of law.

(10) Absence of Public Record or Entry. To prove the absence of a record, report, statement, or data compilation, in any form, or the nonoccurrence or nonexistence of a matter of which a record, report, statement, or data compilation, in any form, was regularly made and preserved by a public office or agency, evidence in the form of a certification in accordance with rule 902, or testimony, that diligent search failed to disclose the record, report, statement, or data compilation, or entry.

(11) Records of Religious Organizations. Statements of births, marriages, divorces, deaths, legitimacy, ancestry, relationship by blood or marriage, or other similar facts of personal or family history, contained in a regularly kept record of a religious organization.

(12) Marriage, Baptismal, and Similar Certificates. Statements of fact contained in a certificate that the maker performed a marriage or other ceremony or administered a sacrament, made by a clergyman, public official, or other person authorized by the rules or practices of a religious organization or by law to perform the act certified, and purporting to have been issued at the time of the act or within a reasonable time thereafter.

(13) Family Records. Statements of fact concerning personal or family history contained in family Bibles, genealogies, charts, engravings on rings, inscriptions on family portraits, engravings on urns, crypts, or tombstones, or the like.

(14) Records of Documents Affecting an Interest in Property. The record of a document purporting to establish or affect an interest in property, as proof of the content of the original recorded document and its execution and delivery by each person by whom it purports to have been executed, if the record is a record of a public office and an applicable statute authorizes the recording of documents of that kind in that office.

(15) Statements in Documents Affecting an Interest in Property. A statement contained in a document purporting to establish or affect an interest in property if the matter stated was relevant to the purpose of the document, unless dealings with the property since the document was made have been inconsistent with the truth of the statement or the purport of the document.

(16) Statements in Ancient Documents. Statements in a document in existence twenty years or more the authenticity of which is established.

(17) Market Reports, Commercial Publications. Market quotations, tabulations, lists, directories, or other published compilations, generally used and relied upon by the public or by persons in particular occupations.

(18) Learned Treatises. To the extent called to the attention of an expert witness upon cross-examination or relied upon by the expert witness in direct examination, statements contained in published treatises, periodicals, or pamphlets on a subject of history, medicine, or other science or art, established as a reliable authority by the testimony or admission of the witness or by other expert testimony or by judicial notice. If admitted, the statements may be read into evidence but may not be received as exhibits.

(19) Reputation Concerning Personal or Family History. Reputation among members of a person's family by blood, adoption, or marriage, or among a person's associates, or in the community, concerning a person's birth, adoption, marriage, divorce, death, legitimacy, relationship by blood, adoption, or marriage, ancestry, or other similar fact of personal or family history.

(20) Reputation Concerning Boundaries or General History. Reputation in a community, arising before the controversy, as to boundaries of or customs affecting lands in the community, and reputation as to events of general history important to the community or State or nation in which located.

(21) Reputation as to Character. Reputation of a person's character among associates or in the community.

(22) Judgment of Previous Conviction. Evidence of a final judgment, entered after a trial or upon a plea of guilty (but not upon a plea of nolo contendere), adjudging a person guilty of a crime punishable by death or imprisonment in excess of one year, to prove any fact essential to sustain the judgment, but not including, when offered by the Government in a criminal prosecution for purposes other than impeachment, judgments against persons other than the accused. The pendency of an appeal may be shown but does not affect admissibility.

(23) Judgment as to Personal, Family, or General History, or Boundaries. Judgments as proof of matters of personal, family or general history, or boundaries, essential to the judgment, if the same would be provable by evidence of reputation.

(24) [Transferred to Rule 807.]

[Amended by Pub.L. 94–149, § 1(11), December 12, 1975, 89 Stat. 805; amended March 2, 1987, effective October 1, 1987; April 11, 1997, effective December 1, 1997; April 17, 2000, effective December 1, 2000.]

RULE 804. HEARSAY EXCEPTIONS; DECLARANT UNAVAILABLE

(a) Definition of Unavailability. "Unavailability as a witness" includes situations in which the declarant—

(1) is exempted by ruling of the court on the ground of privilege from testifying concerning the subject matter of the declarant's statement; or

(2) persists in refusing to testify concerning the subject matter of the declarant's statement despite an order of the court to do so; or

(3) testifies to a lack of memory of the subject matter of the declarant's statement; or

(4) is unable to be present or to testify at the hearing because of death or then existing physical or mental illness or infirmity; or

(5) is absent from the hearing and the proponent of a statement has been unable to procure the declarant's attendance (or in the case of a hearsay exception under subdivision (b)(2), (3), or (4), the declarant's attendance or testimony) by process or other reasonable means.

A declarant is not unavailable as a witness if exemption, refusal, claim of lack of memory, inability, or absence is due to the procurement or wrongdoing of the proponent of a statement for the purpose of preventing the witness from attending or testifying.

(b) Hearsay Exceptions. The following are not excluded by the hearsay rule if the declarant is unavailable as a witness:

(1) *Former Testimony.* Testimony given as a witness at another hearing of the same or a different proceeding, or in a deposition taken in compliance with law in the course of the same or another proceeding, if the party against whom the testimony is now offered, or, in a civil action or proceeding, a predecessor in interest, had an opportunity and similar motive to develop the testimony by direct, cross, or redirect examination.

(2) *Statement Under Belief of Impending Death.* In a prosecution for homicide or in a civil action or proceeding, a statement made by a declarant while believing that the declarant's death was imminent, concerning the cause or circumstances of what the declarant believed to be impending death.

(3) *Statement Against Interest.* A statement which was at the time of its making so far contrary to the declarant's pecuniary or proprietary interest, or so far tended to subject the declarant to civil or criminal liability, or to render invalid a claim by the declarant against another, that a reasonable person in the declarant's position would not have made the statement unless believing it to be true. A statement tending to expose the declarant to criminal liability and offered to exculpate the accused is not admissible unless

corroborating circumstances clearly indicate the trustworthiness of the statement.

(4) *Statement of Personal or Family History.*

(A) A statement concerning the declarant's own birth, adoption, marriage, divorce, legitimacy, relationship by blood, adoption, or marriage, ancestry, or other similar fact of personal or family history, even though declarant had no means of acquiring personal knowledge of the matter stated; or

(B) a statement concerning the foregoing matters, and death also, of another person, if the declarant was related to the other by blood, adoption, or marriage or was so intimately associated with the other's family as to be likely to have accurate information concerning the matter declared.

(5) *[Transferred to Rule 807.]*

(6) *Forfeiture by Wrongdoing.* A statement offered against a party that has engaged or acquiesced in wrongdoing that was intended to, and did, procure the unavailability of the declarant as a witness.

[Amended by Pub.L. 94–149, § 1(12) and (13), December 12, 1975, 89 Stat. 806; amended March 2, 1987, effective October 1, 1987; amended by Pub.L. 100–690, Title VII, § 7075(b), November 18, 1988, 102 Stat. 4405; amended April 11, 1997, effective December 1, 1997.]

RULE 805. HEARSAY WITHIN HEARSAY

Hearsay included within hearsay is not excluded under the hearsay rule if each part of the combined statements conforms with an exception to the hearsay rule provided in these rules.

RULE 806. ATTACKING AND SUPPORTING CREDIBILITY OF DECLARANT

When a hearsay statement, or a statement defined in Rule 801(d)(2)(C), (D), or (E), has been admitted in evidence, the credibility of the declarant may be attacked, and if attacked may be supported, by any evidence which would be admissible for those purposes if declarant had testified as a witness. Evidence of a statement or conduct by the declarant at any time, inconsistent with the declarant's hearsay statement, is not subject to any requirement that the declarant may have been afforded an opportunity to deny or explain. If the party against whom a hearsay statement has been admitted calls the declarant as a witness, the party is entitled to examine the declarant on the statement as if under cross-examination.

[Amended March 2, 1987, effective October 1, 1987; April 11, 1997, effective December 1, 1997.]

RULE 807. RESIDUAL EXCEPTION

A statement not specifically covered by Rule 803 or 804 but having equivalent circumstantial guarantees of trustworthiness, is not excluded by the hearsay rule, if the court determines that (A) the statement is offered as evidence of a material fact; (B) the statement is more probative on the point for which it is offered than any other evidence which the proponent can procure through reasonable efforts; and (C) the general purposes of these rules and the interests of justice will best be served by admission of the statement into evidence. However, a statement may not be admitted under this exception unless the proponent of it makes known to the adverse party sufficiently in advance of the trial or hearing to provide the adverse party with a fair opportunity to prepare to meet it, the proponent's intention to offer the statement and the particulars of it, including the name and address of the declarant.

[Adopted April 11, 1997, effective December 1, 1997.]

ARTICLE IX. AUTHENTICATION AND IDENTIFICATION

RULE 901. REQUIREMENT OF AUTHENTICATION OR IDENTIFICATION

(a) General Provision. The requirement of authentication or identification as a condition precedent to admissibility is satisfied by evidence sufficient to support a finding that the matter in question is what its proponent claims.

(b) Illustrations. By way of illustration only, and not by way of limitation, the following are examples of authentication or identification conforming with the requirements of this rule:

(1) *Testimony of Witness With Knowledge.* Testimony that a matter is what it is claimed to be.

(2) *Nonexpert Opinion on Handwriting.* Nonexpert opinion as to the genuineness of handwriting, based upon familiarity not acquired for purposes of the litigation.

(3) *Comparison by Trier or Expert Witness.* Comparison by the trier of fact or by expert witnesses with specimens which have been authenticated.

(4) *Distinctive Characteristics and the Like.* Appearance, contents, substance, internal patterns, or other distinctive characteristics, taken in conjunction with circumstances.

(5) *Voice Identification.* Identification of a voice, whether heard firsthand or through mechanical or electronic transmission or recording, by opinion based upon hearing the voice at any time under circumstances connecting it with the alleged speaker.

(6) *Telephone Conversations.* Telephone conversations, by evidence that a call was made to the number assigned at the time by the telephone company to a

particular person or business, if (A) in the case of a person, circumstances, including self-identification, show the person answering to be the one called, or (B) in the case of a business, the call was made to a place of business and the conversation related to business reasonably transacted over the telephone.

(7) *Public Records or Reports.* Evidence that a writing authorized by law to be recorded or filed and in fact recorded or filed in a public office, or a purported public record, report, statement, or data compilation, in any form, is from the public office where items of this nature are kept.

(8) *Ancient Documents or Data Compilation.* Evidence that a document or data compilation, in any form, (A) is in such condition as to create no suspicion concerning its authenticity, (B) was in a place where it, if authentic, would likely be, and (C) has been in existence 20 years or more at the time it is offered.

(9) *Process or System.* Evidence describing a process or system used to produce a result and showing that the process or system produces an accurate result.

(10) *Methods Provided by Statute or Rule.* Any method of authentication or identification provided by Act of Congress or by other rules prescribed by the Supreme Court pursuant to statutory authority.

RULE 902. SELF-AUTHENTICATION

Extrinsic evidence of authenticity as a condition precedent to admissibility is not required with respect to the following:

(1) Domestic Public Documents Under Seal. A document bearing a seal purporting to be that of the United States, or of any State, district, Commonwealth, territory, or insular possession thereof, or the Panama Canal Zone, or the Trust Territory of the Pacific Islands, or of a political subdivision, department, officer, or agency thereof, and a signature purporting to be an attestation or execution.

(2) Domestic Public Documents Not Under Seal. A document purporting to bear the signature in the official capacity of an officer or employee of any entity included in paragraph (1) hereof, having no seal, if a public officer having a seal and having official duties in the district or political subdivision of the officer or employee certifies under seal that the signer has the official capacity and that the signature is genuine.

(3) Foreign Public Documents. A document purporting to be executed or attested in an official capacity by a person authorized by the laws of a foreign country to make the execution or attestation, and accompanied by a final certification as to the genuineness of the signature and official position (A) of the executing or attesting person, or (B) of any foreign official whose certificate of genuineness of signature and official position relates to the execution or attestation or is in a chain of certificates of genuineness of signature and official position relating to the execution or attestation. A final certification may be made by a secretary of an embassy or legation, consul general, consul, vice consul, or consular agent of the United States, or a diplomatic or consular official of the foreign country assigned or accredited to the United States. If reasonable opportunity has been given to all parties to investigate the authenticity and accuracy of official documents, the court may, for good cause shown, order that they be treated as presumptively authentic without final certification or permit them to be evidenced by an attested summary with or without final certification.

(4) Certified Copies of Public Records. A copy of an official record or report or entry therein, or of a document authorized by law to be recorded or filed and actually recorded or filed in a public office, including data compilations in any form, certified as correct by the custodian or other person authorized to make the certification, by certificate complying with paragraph (1), (2), or (3) of this rule or complying with any Act of Congress or rule prescribed by the Supreme Court pursuant to statutory authority.

(5) Official Publications. Books, pamphlets, or other publications purporting to be issued by public authority.

(6) Newspapers and Periodicals. Printed materials purporting to be newspapers or periodicals.

(7) Trade Inscriptions and the Like. Inscriptions, signs, tags, or labels purporting to have been affixed in the course of business and indicating ownership, control, or origin.

(8) Acknowledged Documents. Documents accompanied by a certificate of acknowledgment executed in the manner provided by law by a notary public or other officer authorized by law to take acknowledgments.

(9) Commercial Paper and Related Documents. Commercial paper, signatures thereon, and documents relating thereto to the extent provided by general commercial law.

(10) Presumptions Under Acts of Congress. Any signature, document, or other matter declared by Act of Congress to be presumptively or prima facie genuine or authentic.

(11) Certified Domestic Records of Regularly Conducted Activity. The original or a duplicate of a domestic record of regularly conducted activity that would be admissible under Rule 803(6) if accompanied by a written declaration of its custodian or other qualified person, in a manner complying with any Act of Congress or rule prescribed by the Supreme Court pursuant to statutory authority, certifying that the record—

(A) was made at or near the time of the occurrence of the matters set forth by, or from information transmitted by, a person with knowledge of those matters;

(B) was kept in the course of the regularly conducted activity; and

(C) was made by the regularly conducted activity as a regular practice.

A party intending to offer a record into evidence under this paragraph must provide written notice of that intention to all adverse parties, and must make the record and declaration available for inspection sufficiently in advance of their offer into evidence to provide an adverse party with a fair opportunity to challenge them.

(12) Certified Foreign Records of Regularly Conducted Activity. In a civil case, the original or a duplicate of a foreign record of regularly conducted activity that would be admissible under Rule 803(6) if accompanied by a written declaration by its custodian or other qualified person certifying that the record—

(A) was made at or near the time of the occurrence of the matters set forth by, or from information transmitted by, a person with knowledge of those matters;

(B) was kept in the course of the regularly conducted activity; and

(C) was made by the regularly conducted activity as a regular practice.

The declaration must be signed in a manner that, if falsely made, would subject the maker to criminal penalty under the laws of the country where the declaration is signed. A party intending to offer a record into evidence under this paragraph must provide written notice of that intention to all adverse parties, and must make the record and declaration available for inspection sufficiently in advance of their offer into evidence to provide an adverse party with a fair opportunity to challenge them.

[Amended March 2, 1987, effective October 1, 1987; April 25, 1988, effective November 1, 1988; April 17, 2000, effective December 1, 2000.]

RULE 903. SUBSCRIBING WITNESS' TESTIMONY UNNECESSARY

The testimony of a subscribing witness is not necessary to authenticate a writing unless required by the laws of the jurisdiction whose laws govern the validity of the writing.

ARTICLE X. CONTENTS OF WRITINGS, RECORDINGS, AND PHOTOGRAPHS

RULE 1001. DEFINITIONS

For purposes of this article the following definitions are applicable:

(1) Writings and Recordings. "Writings" and "recordings" consist of letters, words, or numbers, or their equivalent, set down by handwriting, typewriting, printing, photostating, photographing, magnetic impulse, mechanical or electronic recording, or other form of data compilation.

(2) Photographs. "Photographs" include still photographs, X-ray films, video tapes, and motion pictures.

(3) Original. An "original" of a writing or recording is the writing or recording itself or any counterpart intended to have the same effect by a person executing or issuing it. An "original" of a photograph includes the negative or any print therefrom. If data are stored in a computer or similar device, any printout or other output readable by sight, shown to reflect the data accurately, is an "original".

(4) Duplicate. A "duplicate" is a counterpart produced by the same impression as the original, or from the same matrix, or by means of photography, including enlargements and miniatures, or by mechanical or electronic re-recording, or by chemical reproduction, or by other equivalent techniques which accurately reproduces the original.

RULE 1002. REQUIREMENT OF ORIGINAL

To prove the content of a writing, recording, or photograph, the original writing, recording, or photograph is required, except as otherwise provided in these rules or by Act of Congress.

RULE 1003. ADMISSIBILITY OF DUPLICATES

A duplicate is admissible to the same extent as an original unless (1) a genuine question is raised as to the authenticity of the original or (2) in the circumstances it would be unfair to admit the duplicate in lieu of the original.

RULE 1004. ADMISSIBILITY OF OTHER EVIDENCE OF CONTENTS

The original is not required, and other evidence of the contents of a writing, recording, or photograph is admissible if—

(1) Originals Lost or Destroyed. All originals are lost or have been destroyed, unless the proponent lost or destroyed them in bad faith; or

(2) Original Not Obtainable. No original can be obtained by any available judicial process or procedure; or

(3) Original in Possession of Opponent. At a time when an original was under the control of the party against whom offered, that party was put on notice, by the pleadings or otherwise, that the contents would be a subject of proof at the hearing, and that party does not produce the original at the hearing; or

(4) Collateral Matters. The writing, recording, or photograph is not closely related to a controlling issue.

[Amended March 2, 1987, effective October 1, 1987.]

RULE 1005. PUBLIC RECORDS

The contents of an official record, or of a document authorized to be recorded or filed and actually recorded or filed, including data compilations in any form, if otherwise admissible, may be proved by copy, certified as correct in accordance with rule 902 or testified to be correct by a witness who has compared it with the original. If a copy which complies with the foregoing cannot be obtained by the exercise of reasonable diligence, then other evidence of the contents may be given.

RULE 1006. SUMMARIES

The contents of voluminous writings, recordings, or photographs which cannot conveniently be examined in court may be presented in the form of a chart, summary, or calculation. The originals, or duplicates, shall be made available for examination or copying, or both, by other parties at reasonable time and place. The court may order that they be produced in court.

RULE 1007. TESTIMONY OR WRITTEN ADMISSION OF PARTY

Contents of writings, recordings, or photographs may be proved by the testimony or deposition of the party against whom offered or by that party's written admission, without accounting for the nonproduction of the original.

[Amended March 2, 1987, effective October 1, 1987.]

RULE 1008. FUNCTIONS OF COURT AND JURY

When the admissibility of other evidence of contents of writings, recordings, or photographs under these rules depends upon the fulfillment of a condition of fact, the question whether the condition has been fulfilled is ordinarily for the court to determine in accordance with the provisions of rule 104. However, when an issue is raised (a) whether the asserted writing ever existed, or (b) whether another writing, recording, or photograph produced at the trial is the original, or (c) whether other evidence of contents correctly reflects the contents, the issue is for the trier of fact to determine as in the case of other issues of fact.

ARTICLE XI. MISCELLANEOUS RULES

RULE 1101. APPLICABILITY OF RULES

(a) Courts and Judges. These rules apply to the United States district courts, the District Court of Guam, the District Court of the Virgin Islands, the District Court for the Northern Mariana Islands, the United States courts of appeals, the United States Claims Court, and to United States bankruptcy judges and United States magistrate judges, in the actions, cases, and proceedings and to the extent hereinafter set forth. The terms "judge" and "court" in these rules include United States bankruptcy judges and United States magistrate judges.

(b) Proceedings Generally. These rules apply generally to civil actions and proceedings, including admiralty and maritime cases, to criminal cases and proceedings, to contempt proceedings except those in which the court may act summarily, and to proceedings and cases under title 11, United States Code.

(c) Rule of Privilege. The rule with respect to privileges applies at all stages of all actions, cases, and proceedings.

(d) Rules Inapplicable. The rules (other than with respect to privileges) do not apply in the following situations:

(1) *Preliminary Questions of Fact.* The determination of questions of fact preliminary to admissibility of evidence when the issue is to be determined by the court under rule 104.

(2) *Grand Jury.* Proceedings before grand juries.

(3) *Miscellaneous Proceedings.* Proceedings for extradition or rendition; preliminary examinations in criminal cases; sentencing, or granting or revoking probation; issuance of warrants for arrest, criminal summonses, and search warrants; and proceedings with respect to release on bail or otherwise.

(e) Rules Applicable in Part. In the following proceedings these rules apply to the extent that matters of evidence are not provided for in the statutes which govern procedure therein or in other rules prescribed by the Supreme Court pursuant to statutory authority: the trial of misdemeanors and other petty offenses before United States magistrate judges; review of agency actions when the facts are subject to trial de novo under section 706(2)(F) of title 5, United States Code; review of orders of the Secretary of Agriculture under section 2 of the Act entitled "An Act to authorize association of producers of agricultural products" approved February 18, 1922 (7 U.S.C.

292), and under sections 6 and 7(c) of the Perishable Agricultural Commodities Act, 1930 (7 U.S.C. 499f, 499g(c)); naturalization and revocation of naturalization under sections 310–318 of the Immigration and Nationality Act (8 U.S.C. 1421–1429); prize proceedings in admiralty under sections 7651–7681 of title 10, United States Code; review of orders of the Secretary of the Interior under section 2 of the Act entitled "An Act authorizing associations of producers of aquatic products" approved June 25, 1934 (15 U.S.C. 522); review of orders of petroleum control boards under section 5 of the Act entitled "An Act to regulate interstate and foreign commerce in petroleum and its products by prohibiting the shipment in such commerce of petroleum and its products produced in violation of State law, and for other purposes", approved February 22, 1935 (15 U.S.C. 715d); actions for fines, penalties, or forfeitures under part V of title IV of the Tariff Act of 1930 (19 U.S.C. 1581–1624), or under the Anti-Smuggling Act (19 U.S.C. 1701–1711); criminal libel for condemnation, exclusion of imports, or other proceedings under the Federal Food, Drug, and Cosmetic Act (21 U.S.C. 301–392); disputes between seamen under sections 4079, 4080, and 4081 of the Revised Statutes (22 U.S.C. 256–258); habeas corpus under sections 2241–2254 of title 28, United States Code; motions to vacate, set aside or correct sentence under section 2255 of title 28, United States Code; actions for penalties for refusal to transport destitute seamen under section 4578 of the Revised Statutes (46 U.S.C. 679);* actions against the United States under the Act entitled "An Act authorizing suits against the United States in admiralty for damage caused by and salvage service rendered to public vessels belonging to the United States, and for other purposes", approved March 3, 1925 (46 U.S.C. 781–790), as implemented by section 7730 of title 10, United States Code.

* Law Revision Counsel Note: Repealed and reenacted as 46 U.S.C. 11104(b)-(d) by Pub.L. 98–89, §§ 1, 2(a), 4(b), August 26, 1983, 97 Stat. 500.

[Amended by Pub.L. 94–149, § 1(14), December 12, 1975, 89 Stat. 806; Pub.L. 95–598, Title II, § 251, November 6, 1978, 92 Stat. 2673, effective October 1, 1979; Pub.L. 97–164, Title I, § 142, April 2, 1982, 96 Stat. 45, effective October 1, 1982; amended March 2, 1987, effective October 1, 1987; April 25, 1988, effective November 1, 1988; amended by Pub.L. 100–690, Title VII, § 7075(c)(1), November 18, 1988, 102 Stat. 4405 (although amendment by Pub.L. 100-690 could not be executed due to prior amendment by Court order which made the same change effective November 1, 1988); amended April 22, 1993, effective December 1, 1993.]

RULE 1102. AMENDMENTS

Amendments to the Federal Rules of Evidence may be made as provided in section 2072 of title 28 of the United States Code.

[Amended April 30, 1991, effective December 1, 1991.]

RULE 1103. TITLE

These rules may be known and cited as the Federal Rules of Evidence.

INDEX TO FEDERAL RULES OF EVIDENCE

*

FEDERAL RULES OF APPELLATE PROCEDURE

Adopted Effective July 1, 1968

Including Amendments Effective December 1, 2007

Research Note

These rules may be searched electronically on Westlaw in the US–RULES database; updates to these rules may be found on Westlaw in US–RULES-UPDATES. For search tips, and a detailed summary of database content, consult the Westlaw Scope Screen of each database.

Table of Rules

TITLE I. APPLICABILITY OF RULES

FRAP 1. SCOPE OF RULES; TITLE

(a) Scope of Rules.

(1) These rules govern procedure in the United States courts of appeals.

(2) When these rules provide for filing a motion or other document in the district court, the procedure must comply with the practice of the district court.

(b) [Abrogated].

(c) Title. These rules are to be known as the Federal Rules of Appellate Procedure.

[Amended April 30, 1979, effective August 1, 1979; April 25, 1989, effective December 1, 1989; former Rule 48 renumbered as Rule 1(c) April 29, 1994, effective December 1, 1994; April 24, 1998, effective December 1, 1998; April 29, 2002, effective December 1, 2002.]

FRAP 2. SUSPENSION OF RULES

On its own or a party's motion, a court of appeals may—to expedite its decision or for other good cause—suspend any provision of these rules in a particular case and order proceedings as it directs, except as otherwise provided in Rule 26(b).

[Amended April 24, 1998, effective December 1, 1998.]

TITLE II. APPEAL FROM A JUDGMENT OR ORDER OF A DISTRICT COURT

FRAP 3. APPEAL AS OF RIGHT—HOW TAKEN

(a) Filing the Notice of Appeal.

(1) An appeal permitted by law as of right from a district court to a court of appeals may be taken only by filing a notice of appeal with the district clerk within the time allowed by Rule 4. At the time of filing, the appellant must furnish the clerk with enough copies of the notice to enable the clerk to comply with Rule 3(d).

(2) An appellant's failure to take any step other than the timely filing of a notice of appeal does not affect the validity of the appeal, but is ground only for the court of appeals to act as it considers appropriate, including dismissing the appeal.

(3) An appeal from a judgment by a magistrate judge in a civil case is taken in the same way as an appeal from any other district court judgment.

(4) An appeal by permission under 28 U.S.C. § 1292(b) or an appeal in a bankruptcy case may be taken only in the manner prescribed by Rules 5 and 6, respectively.

(b) Joint or Consolidated Appeals.

(1) When two or more parties are entitled to appeal from a district-court judgment or order, and their interests make joinder practicable, they may file a joint notice of appeal. They may then proceed on appeal as a single appellant.

(2) When the parties have filed separate timely notices of appeal, the appeals may be joined or consolidated by the court of appeals.

(c) Contents of the Notice of Appeal.

(1) The notice of appeal must:

(A) specify the party or parties taking the appeal by naming each one in the caption or body of the notice, but an attorney representing more than one party may describe those parties with such terms as "all plaintiffs," "the defendants," "the plaintiffs A, B, et al.," or "all defendants except X";

(B) designate the judgment, order, or part thereof being appealed; and

(C) name the court to which the appeal is taken.

(2) A pro se notice of appeal is considered filed on behalf of the signer and the signer's spouse and minor children (if they are parties), unless the notice clearly indicates otherwise.

(3) In a class action, whether or not the class has been certified, the notice of appeal is sufficient if it names one person qualified to bring the appeal as representative of the class.

(4) An appeal must not be dismissed for informality of form or title of the notice of appeal, or for failure to name a party whose intent to appeal is otherwise clear from the notice.

(5) Form 1 in the Appendix of Forms is a suggested form of a notice of appeal.

(d) Serving the Notice of Appeal.

(1) The district clerk must serve notice of the filing of a notice of appeal by mailing a copy to each party's counsel of record—excluding the appellant's—or, if a party is proceeding pro se, to the party's last known address. When a defendant in a criminal case appeals, the clerk must also serve a copy of the notice of appeal on the defendant, either by personal service or by mail addressed to the defendant. The clerk must promptly send a copy of the notice of appeal and of the docket entries—and any later docket entries—to the clerk of the court of appeals named in the notice. The district clerk must note, on each copy, the date when the notice of appeal was filed.

(2) If an inmate confined in an institution files a notice of appeal in the manner provided by Rule 4(c), the district clerk must also note the date when the clerk docketed the notice.

(3) The district clerk's failure to serve notice does not affect the validity of the appeal. The clerk must note on the docket the names of the parties to whom the clerk mails copies, with the date of mailing. Service is sufficient despite the death of a party or the party's counsel.

(e) Payment of Fees. Upon filing a notice of appeal, the appellant must pay the district clerk all required fees. The district clerk receives the appellate docket fee on behalf of the court of appeals.

[Amended April 30, 1979, effective August 1, 1979; March 10, 1986, effective July 1, 1986; April 25, 1989, effective December 1, 1989; April 22, 1993, effective December 1, 1993; April 29, 1994, effective December 1, 1994; April 24, 1998, effective December 1, 1998.]

FRAP 3.1 APPEAL FROM A JUDGMENT OF A MAGISTRATE JUDGE IN A CIVIL CASE [ABROGATED]

[Adopted March 10, 1986, effective July 1, 1986; amended April 22, 1993, effective December 1, 1993; abrogated effective December 1, 1998.]

FRAP 4. APPEAL AS OF RIGHT—WHEN TAKEN

(a) Appeal in a Civil Case.

(1) *Time for Filing a Notice of Appeal.*

(A) In a civil case, except as provided in Rules 4(a)(1)(B), 4(a)(4), and 4(c), the notice of appeal required by Rule 3 must be filed with the district clerk within 30 days after the judgment or order appealed from is entered.

(B) When the United States or its officer or agency is a party, the notice of appeal may be filed by any party within 60 days after the judgment or order appealed from is entered.

(C) An appeal from an order granting or denying an application for a writ of error coram nobis is an appeal in a civil case for purposes of Rule 4(a).

(2) *Filing Before Entry of Judgment.* A notice of appeal filed after the court announces a decision or order—but before the entry of the judgment or order—is treated as filed on the date of and after the entry.

(3) *Multiple Appeals.* If one party timely files a notice of appeal, any other party may file a notice of appeal within 14 days after the date when the first notice was filed, or within the time otherwise prescribed by this Rule 4(a), whichever period ends later.

(4) *Effect of a Motion on a Notice of Appeal.*

(A) If a party timely files in the district court any of the following motions under the Federal Rules of Civil Procedure, the time to file an appeal runs for all parties from the entry of the order disposing of the last such remaining motion:

(i) for judgment under Rule 50(b);

(ii) to amend or make additional factual findings under Rule 52(b), whether or not granting the motion would alter the judgment;

(iii) for attorney's fees under Rule 54 if the district court extends the time to appeal under Rule 58;

(iv) to alter or amend the judgment under Rule 59;

(v) for a new trial under Rule 59; or

(vi) for relief under Rule 60 if the motion is filed no later than 10 days after the judgment is entered.

(B)(i) If a party files a notice of appeal after the court announces or enters a judgment—but before it disposes of any motion listed in Rule 4(a)(4)(A)—the notice becomes effective to appeal a judgment or order, in whole or in part, when the order disposing of the last such remaining motion is entered.

(ii) A party intending to challenge an order disposing of any motion listed in Rule 4(a)(4)(A), or a judgment altered or amended upon such a motion, must file a notice of appeal, or an amended notice of appeal—in compliance with Rule 3(c)—within the time prescribed by this Rule measured from the entry of the order disposing of the last such remaining motion.

(iii) No additional fee is required to file an amended notice.

(5) *Motion for Extension of Time.*

(A) The district court may extend the time to file a notice of appeal if:

(i) a party so moves no later than 30 days after the time prescribed by this Rule 4(a) expires; and

(ii) regardless of whether its motion is filed before or during the 30 days after the time prescribed by this Rule 4(a) expires, that party shows excusable neglect or good cause.

(B) A motion filed before the expiration of the time prescribed in Rule 4(a)(1) or (3) may be ex parte unless the court requires otherwise. If the motion is filed after the expiration of the prescribed time, notice must be given to the other parties in accordance with local rules.

(C) No extension under this Rule 4(a)(5) may exceed 30 days after the prescribed time or 10 days after the date when the order granting the motion is entered, whichever is later.

(6) *Reopening the Time to File an Appeal.* The district court may reopen the time to file an appeal for a period of 14 days after the date when its order to reopen is entered, but only if all the following conditions are satisfied:

(A) the court finds that the moving party did not receive notice under Federal Rule of Civil Procedure 77(d) of the entry of the judgment or order sought to be appealed within 21 days after entry;

(B) the motion is filed within 180 days after the judgment or order is entered or within 7 days after the moving party receives notice under Federal Rule of Civil Procedure 77(d) of the entry, whichever is earlier; and

(C) the court finds that no party would be prejudiced.

(7) *Entry Defined.*

(A) A judgment or order is entered for purposes of this Rule 4(a):

(i) if Federal Rule of Civil Procedure 58(a)(1) does not require a separate document, when the judgment or order is entered in the civil docket under Federal Rule of Civil Procedure 79(a); or

(ii) if Federal Rule of Civil Procedure 58(a)(1) requires a separate document, when the judgment or order is entered in the civil docket under Federal Rule of Civil Procedure 79(a) and when the earlier of these events occurs:

- the judgment or order is set forth on a separate document, or
- 150 days have run from entry of the judgment or order in the civil docket under Federal Rule of Civil Procedure 79(a).

(B) A failure to set forth a judgment or order on a separate document when required by Federal Rule of Civil Procedure 58(a)(1) does not affect the validity of an appeal from that judgment or order.

(b) Appeal in a Criminal Case.

(1) *Time for Filing a Notice of Appeal.*

(A) In a criminal case, a defendant's notice of appeal must be filed in the district court within 10 days after the later of:

(i) the entry of either the judgment or the order being appealed; or

(ii) the filing of the government's notice of appeal.

(B) When the government is entitled to appeal, its notice of appeal must be filed in the district court within 30 days after the later of:

(i) the entry of the judgment or order being appealed; or

(ii) the filing of a notice of appeal by any defendant.

(2) *Filing Before Entry of Judgment.* A notice of appeal filed after the court announces a decision, sentence, or order—but before the entry of the judgment or order—is treated as filed on the date of and after the entry.

(3) *Effect of a Motion on a Notice of Appeal.*

(A) If a defendant timely makes any of the following motions under the Federal Rules of Criminal Procedure, the notice of appeal from a judgment of conviction must be filed within 10 days after the entry of the order disposing of the last such remaining motion, or within 10 days after the entry of the judgment of conviction, whichever period ends later. This provision applies to a timely motion:

(i) for judgment of acquittal under Rule 29;

(ii) for a new trial under Rule 33, but if based on newly discovered evidence, only if the motion is made no later than 10 days after the entry of the judgment; or

(iii) for arrest of judgment under Rule 34.

(B) A notice of appeal filed after the court announces a decision, sentence, or order—but before it disposes of any of the motions referred to in Rule 4(b)(3)(A)—becomes effective upon the later of the following:

(i) the entry of the order disposing of the last such remaining motion; or

(ii) the entry of the judgment of conviction.

(C) A valid notice of appeal is effective—without amendment—to appeal from an order disposing of any of the motions referred to in Rule 4(b)(3)(A).

(4) *Motion for Extension of Time.* Upon a finding of excusable neglect or good cause, the district court may—before or after the time has expired, with or without motion and notice—extend the time to file a notice of appeal for a period not to exceed 30 days from the expiration of the time otherwise prescribed by this Rule 4(b).

(5) *Jurisdiction.* The filing of a notice of appeal under this Rule 4(b) does not divest a district court of jurisdiction to correct a sentence under Federal Rule of Criminal Procedure 35(a), nor does the filing of a motion under 35(a) affect the validity of a notice of appeal filed before entry of the order disposing of the motion. The filing of a motion under Federal Rule of Criminal Procedure 35(a) does not suspend the time for filing a notice of appeal from a judgment of conviction.

(6) *Entry Defined.* A judgment or order is entered for purposes of this Rule 4(b) when it is entered on the criminal docket.

(c) Appeal by an Inmate Confined in an Institution.

(1) If an inmate confined in an institution files a notice of appeal in either a civil or a criminal case, the notice is timely if it is deposited in the institution's internal mail system on or before the last day for filing. If an institution has a system designed for legal mail, the inmate must use that system to receive the benefit of this rule. Timely filing may be shown by a declaration in compliance with 28 U.S.C. § 1746 or by a notarized statement, either of which must set forth the date of deposit and state that first-class postage has been prepaid.

(2) If an inmate files the first notice of appeal in a civil case under this Rule 4(c), the 14-day period provided in Rule 4(a)(3) for another party to file a notice of appeal runs from the date when the district court dockets the first notice.

(3) When a defendant in a criminal case files a notice of appeal under this Rule 4(c), the 30-day period for the government to file its notice of appeal runs from the entry of the judgment or order appealed from or from the district court's docketing of the defendant's notice of appeal, whichever is later.

(d) Mistaken Filing in the Court of Appeals. If a notice of appeal in either a civil or a criminal case is mistakenly filed in the court of appeals, the clerk of that court must note on the notice the date when it was received and send it to the district clerk. The notice is then considered filed in the district court on the date so noted.

[Amended April 30, 1979, effective August 1, 1979; amended by Pub.L. 100–690, Title VII, § 7111, November 18, 1988, 102 Stat. 4419; amended April 30, 1991, effective December 1, 1991; April 22, 1993, effective December 1, 1993; April 27, 1995, effective December 1, 1995; April 24, 1998, effective December 1, 1998; April 29, 2002, effective December 1, 2002; April 25, 2005, effective December 1, 2005.]

FRAP 5. APPEAL BY PERMISSION

(a) Petition for Permission to Appeal.

(1) To request permission to appeal when an appeal is within the court of appeals' discretion, a party must file a petition for permission to appeal. The petition must be filed with the circuit clerk with proof of service on all other parties to the district-court action.

(2) The petition must be filed within the time specified by the statute or rule authorizing the appeal or, if no such time is specified, within the time provided by Rule 4(a) for filing a notice of appeal.

(3) If a party cannot petition for appeal unless the district court first enters an order granting permission to do so or stating that the necessary conditions are met, the district court may amend its order, either on its own or in response to a party's motion, to include the required permission or statement. In that event, the time to petition runs from entry of the amended order.

(b) Contents of the Petition; Answer or Cross–Petition; Oral Argument.

(1) The petition must include the following:

(A) the facts necessary to understand the question presented;

(B) the question itself;

(C) the relief sought;

(D) the reasons why the appeal should be allowed and is authorized by a statute or rule; and

(E) an attached copy of:

(i) the order, decree, or judgment complained of and any related opinion or memorandum, and

(ii) any order stating the district court's permission to appeal or finding that the necessary conditions are met.

(2) A party may file an answer in opposition or a cross-petition within 7 days after the petition is served.

(3) The petition and answer will be submitted without oral argument unless the court of appeals orders otherwise.

(c) Form of Papers; Number of Copies. All papers must conform to Rule 32(c)(2). Except by the court's permission, a paper must not exceed 20 pages, exclusive of the disclosure statement, the proof of service, and the accompanying documents required by Rule 5(b)(1)(E). An original and 3 copies must be filed unless the court requires a different number by local rule or by order in a particular case.

(d) Grant of Permission; Fees; Cost Bond; Filing the Record.

(1) Within 10 days after the entry of the order granting permission to appeal, the appellant must:

(A) pay the district clerk all required fees; and

(B) file a cost bond if required under Rule 7.

(2) A notice of appeal need not be filed. The date when the order granting permission to appeal is entered serves as the date of the notice of appeal for calculating time under these rules.

(3) The district clerk must notify the circuit clerk once the petitioner has paid the fees. Upon receiving this notice, the circuit clerk must enter the appeal on the docket. The record must be forwarded and filed in accordance with Rules 11 and 12(c).

[Amended April 30, 1979, effective August 1, 1979; April 29, 1994, effective December 1, 1994; April 24, 1998, effective December 1, 1998; April 29, 2002, effective December 1, 2002.]

FRAP 5.1 APPEAL BY PERMISSION UNDER 28 U.S.C. § 636(c)(5) [ABROGATED]

[Adopted March 10, 1986, effective July 1, 1986; amended April 22, 1993, effective December 1, 1993; April 29, 1994, effective December 1, 1994; abrogated effective December 1, 1998.]

FRAP 6. APPEAL IN A BANKRUPTCY CASE FROM A FINAL JUDGMENT, ORDER, OR DECREE OF A DISTRICT COURT OR BANKRUPTCY APPELLATE PANEL

(a) Appeal From a Judgment, Order, or Decree of a District Court Exercising Original Jurisdiction in a Bankruptcy Case. An appeal to a court of appeals from a final judgment, order, or decree of a district court exercising jurisdiction under 28 U.S.C. § 1334 is taken as any other civil appeal under these rules.

(b) Appeal From a Judgment, Order, or Decree of a District Court or Bankruptcy Appellate Panel Exercising Appellate Jurisdiction in a Bankruptcy Case.

(1) *Applicability of Other Rules.* These rules apply to an appeal to a court of appeals under 28 U.S.C. § 158(d) from a final judgment, order, or decree of a district court or bankruptcy appellate panel exercising appellate jurisdiction under 28 U.S.C. § 158(a) or (b). But there are 3 exceptions:

(A) Rules 4(a)(4), 4(b), 9, 10, 11, 12(b), 13–20, 22–23, and 24(b) do not apply;

(B) the reference in Rule 3(c) to "Form 1 in the Appendix of Forms" must be read as a reference to Form 5; and

(C) when the appeal is from a bankruptcy appellate panel, the term "district court," as used in any applicable rule, means "appellate panel."

(2) *Additional Rules.* In addition to the rules made applicable by Rule 6(b)(1), the following rules apply:

(A) Motion for rehearing.

(i) If a timely motion for rehearing under Bankruptcy Rule 8015 is filed, the time to appeal for all parties runs from the entry of the order disposing of the motion. A notice of appeal filed after the district court or bankruptcy appellate panel announces or enters a judgment, order, or decree—but before disposition of the motion for rehearing—becomes effective when the order disposing of the motion for rehearing is entered.

(ii) Appellate review of the order disposing of the motion requires the party, in compliance with Rules 3(c) and 6(b)(1)(B), to amend a previously filed notice of appeal. A party intending to challenge an altered or amended judgment, order, or decree must file a notice of appeal or amended notice of appeal within the time prescribed by Rule 4—excluding Rules 4(a)(4) and 4(b)—measured from the entry of the order disposing of the motion.

(iii) No additional fee is required to file an amended notice.

(B) The record on appeal.

(i) Within 10 days after filing the notice of appeal, the appellant must file with the clerk possessing the record assembled in accordance with Bankruptcy Rule 8006—and serve on the appellee—a statement of the issues to be presented on appeal and a designation of the record to be certified and sent to the circuit clerk.

(ii) An appellee who believes that other parts of the record are necessary must, within 10 days after being served with the appellant's designation, file with the clerk and serve on the appellant a designation of additional parts to be included.

(iii) The record on appeal consists of:

- the redesignated record as provided above;
- the proceedings in the district court or bankruptcy appellate panel; and

- a certified copy of the docket entries prepared by the clerk under Rule 3(d).

(C) Forwarding the record.

(i) When the record is complete, the district clerk or bankruptcy appellate panel clerk must number the documents constituting the record and send them promptly to the circuit clerk together with a list of the documents correspondingly numbered and reasonably identified. Unless directed to do so by a party or the circuit clerk, the clerk will not send to the court of appeals documents of unusual bulk or weight, physical exhibits other than documents, or other parts of the record designated for omission by local rule of the court of appeals. If the exhibits are unusually bulky or heavy, a party must arrange with the clerks in advance for their transportation and receipt.

(ii) All parties must do whatever else is necessary to enable the clerk to assemble and forward the record. The court of appeals may provide by rule or order that a certified copy of the docket entries be sent in place of the redesignated record, but any party may request at any time during the pendency of the appeal that the redesignated record be sent.

(D) Filing the record. Upon receiving the record—or a certified copy of the docket entries sent in place of the redesignated record—the circuit clerk must file it and immediately notify all parties of the filing date.

[Former Rule 6 amended April 30, 1979, effective August 1, 1979; repealed and new Rule 6 adopted April 25, 1989, effective December 1, 1989; caption amended April 30, 1991, effective December 1, 1991; caption and text amended April 22, 1993, effective December 1, 1993; April 24, 1998, effective December 1, 1998.]

FRAP 7. BOND FOR COSTS ON APPEAL IN A CIVIL CASE

In a civil case, the district court may require an appellant to file a bond or provide other security in any form and amount necessary to ensure payment of costs on appeal. Rule 8(b) applies to a surety on a bond given under this rule.

[Amended April 30, 1979, effective August 1, 1979; April 24, 1998, effective December 1, 1998.]

FRAP 8. STAY OR INJUNCTION PENDING APPEAL

(a) Motion for Stay.

(1) *Initial Motion in the District Court.* A party must ordinarily move first in the district court for the following relief:

(A) a stay of the judgment or order of a district court pending appeal;

(B) approval of a supersedeas bond; or

(C) an order suspending, modifying, restoring, or granting an injunction while an appeal is pending.

(2) *Motion in the Court of Appeals; Conditions on Relief.* A motion for the relief mentioned in Rule 8(a)(1) may be made to the court of appeals or to one of its judges.

(A) The motion must:

(i) show that moving first in the district court would be impracticable; or

(ii) state that, a motion having been made, the district court denied the motion or failed to afford the relief requested and state any reasons given by the district court for its action.

(B) The motion must also include:

(i) the reasons for granting the relief requested and the facts relied on;

(ii) originals or copies of affidavits or other sworn statements supporting facts subject to dispute; and

(iii) relevant parts of the record.

(C) The moving party must give reasonable notice of the motion to all parties.

(D) A motion under this Rule 8(a)(2) must be filed with the circuit clerk and normally will be considered by a panel of the court. But in an exceptional case in which time requirements make that procedure impracticable, the motion may be made to and considered by a single judge.

(E) The court may condition relief on a party's filing a bond or other appropriate security in the district court.

(b) Proceeding Against a Surety. If a party gives security in the form of a bond or stipulation or other undertaking with one or more sureties, each surety submits to the jurisdiction of the district court and irrevocably appoints the district clerk as the surety's agent on whom any papers affecting the surety's liability on the bond or undertaking may be served. On motion, a surety's liability may be enforced in the district court without the necessity of an independent action. The motion and any notice that the district court prescribes may be served on the district clerk, who must promptly mail a copy to each surety whose address is known.

(c) Stay in a Criminal Case. Rule 38 of the Federal Rules of Criminal Procedure governs a stay in a criminal case.

[Amended March 10, 1986, effective July 1, 1986; April 27, 1995, effective December 1, 1995; April 24, 1998, effective December 1, 1998.]

FRAP 9. RELEASE IN A CRIMINAL CASE

(a) Release Before Judgment of Conviction.

(1) The district court must state in writing, or orally on the record, the reasons for an order regarding the release or detention of a defendant in a criminal case. A party appealing from the order must file with the court of appeals a copy of the district court's order and the court's statement of reasons as soon as practicable after filing the notice of appeal. An appellant who questions the factual basis for the district court's order must file a transcript of the release proceedings or an explanation of why a transcript was not obtained.

(2) After reasonable notice to the appellee, the court of appeals must promptly determine the appeal on the basis of the papers, affidavits, and parts of the record that the parties present or the court requires. Unless the court so orders, briefs need not be filed.

(3) The court of appeals or one of its judges may order the defendant's release pending the disposition of the appeal.

(b) Release After Judgment of Conviction. A party entitled to do so may obtain review of a district-court order regarding release after a judgment of conviction by filing a notice of appeal from that order in the district court, or by filing a motion in the court of appeals if the party has already filed a notice of appeal from the judgment of conviction. Both the order and the review are subject to Rule 9(a). The papers filed by the party seeking review must include a copy of the judgment of conviction.

(c) Criteria for Release. The court must make its decision regarding release in accordance with the applicable provisions of 18 U.S.C. §§ 3142, 3143, and 3145(c).

[Amended April 24, 1972, effective October 1, 1972; amended by Pub.L. 98–473, Title II, § 210, October 12, 1984, 98 Stat. 1987; April 29, 1994, effective December 1, 1994; April 24, 1998, effective December 1, 1998.]

FRAP 10. THE RECORD ON APPEAL

(a) Composition of the Record on Appeal. The following items constitute the record on appeal:

(1) the original papers and exhibits filed in the district court;

(2) the transcript of proceedings, if any; and

(3) a certified copy of the docket entries prepared by the district clerk.

(b) The Transcript of Proceedings.

(1) *Appellant's Duty to Order.* Within 10 days after filing the notice of appeal or entry of an order disposing of the last timely remaining motion of a type specified in Rule 4(a)(4)(A), whichever is later, the appellant must do either of the following:

(A) order from the reporter a transcript of such parts of the proceedings not already on file as the appellant considers necessary, subject to a local rule of the court of appeals and with the following qualifications:

(i) the order must be in writing;

(ii) if the cost of the transcript is to be paid by the United States under the Criminal Justice Act, the order must so state; and

(iii) the appellant must, within the same period, file a copy of the order with the district clerk; or

(B) file a certificate stating that no transcript will be ordered.

(2) *Unsupported Finding or Conclusion.* If the appellant intends to urge on appeal that a finding or conclusion is unsupported by the evidence or is contrary to the evidence, the appellant must include in the record a transcript of all evidence relevant to that finding or conclusion.

(3) *Partial Transcript.* Unless the entire transcript is ordered:

(A) the appellant must—within the 10 days provided in Rule 10(b)(1)—file a statement of the issues that the appellant intends to present on the appeal and must serve on the appellee a copy of both the order or certificate and the statement;

(B) if the appellee considers it necessary to have a transcript of other parts of the proceedings, the appellee must, within 10 days after the service of the order or certificate and the statement of the issues, file and serve on the appellant a designation of additional parts to be ordered; and

(C) unless within 10 days after service of that designation the appellant has ordered all such parts, and has so notified the appellee, the appellee may within the following 10 days either order the parts or move in the district court for an order requiring the appellant to do so.

(4) *Payment.* At the time of ordering, a party must make satisfactory arrangements with the reporter for paying the cost of the transcript.

(c) Statement of the Evidence When the Proceedings Were Not Recorded or When a Transcript Is Unavailable. If the transcript of a hearing or trial is unavailable, the appellant may prepare a statement of the evidence or proceedings from the best available means, including the appellant's recollection. The statement must be served on the appellee, who may serve objections or proposed amendments within 10 days after being served. The statement and any objections or proposed amendments must then be submitted to the district court for settlement and approval. As settled and approved, the statement must be included by the district clerk in the record on appeal.

(d) Agreed Statement as the Record on Appeal. In place of the record on appeal as defined in Rule 10(a), the parties may prepare, sign, and submit to the district court a statement of the case showing how the issues presented by the appeal arose and were decided in the district court. The statement must set forth only those facts averred and proved or sought to be proved that are essential to the court's resolution of the issues. If the statement is truthful, it—together with any additions that the district court may consider necessary to a full presentation of the issues on appeal—must be approved by the district court and must then be certified to the court of appeals as the record on appeal. The district clerk must then send it to the circuit clerk within the time provided by Rule 11. A copy of the agreed statement may be filed in place of the appendix required by Rule 30.

(e) Correction or Modification of the Record.

(1) If any difference arises about whether the record truly discloses what occurred in the district court, the difference must be submitted to and settled by that court and the record conformed accordingly.

(2) If anything material to either party is omitted from or misstated in the record by error or accident, the omission or misstatement may be corrected and a supplemental record may be certified and forwarded:

(A) on stipulation of the parties;

(B) by the district court before or after the record has been forwarded; or

(C) by the court of appeals.

(3) All other questions as to the form and content of the record must be presented to the court of appeals.

[Amended April 30, 1979, effective August 1, 1979; March 10, 1986, effective July 1, 1986; April 30, 1991, effective December 1, 1991; April 22, 1993, effective December 1, 1993; April 27, 1995, effective December 1, 1995; April 24, 1998, effective December 1, 1998.]

FRAP 11. FORWARDING THE RECORD

(a) Appellant's Duty. An appellant filing a notice of appeal must comply with Rule 10(b) and must do whatever else is necessary to enable the clerk to assemble and forward the record. If there are multiple appeals from a judgment or order, the clerk must forward a single record.

(b) Duties of Reporter and District Clerk.

(1) *Reporter's Duty to Prepare and File a Transcript.* The reporter must prepare and file a transcript as follows:

(A) Upon receiving an order for a transcript, the reporter must enter at the foot of the order the date of its receipt and the expected completion date and send a copy, so endorsed, to the circuit clerk.

(B) If the transcript cannot be completed within 30 days of the reporter's receipt of the order, the reporter may request the circuit clerk to grant additional time to complete it. The clerk must note on the docket the action taken and notify the parties.

(C) When a transcript is complete, the reporter must file it with the district clerk and notify the circuit clerk of the filing.

(D) If the reporter fails to file the transcript on time, the circuit clerk must notify the district judge and do whatever else the court of appeals directs.

(2) *District Clerk's Duty to Forward.* When the record is complete, the district clerk must number the documents constituting the record and send them promptly to the circuit clerk together with a list of the documents correspondingly numbered and reasonably identified. Unless directed to do so by a party or the circuit clerk, the district clerk will not send to the court of appeals documents of unusual bulk or weight, physical exhibits other than documents, or other parts of the record designated for omission by local rule of the court of appeals. If the exhibits are unusually bulky or heavy, a party must arrange with the clerks in advance for their transportation and receipt.

(c) Retaining the Record Temporarily in the District Court for Use in Preparing the Appeal. The parties may stipulate, or the district court on motion may order, that the district clerk retain the record temporarily for the parties to use in preparing the papers on appeal. In that event the district clerk must certify to the circuit clerk that the record on appeal is complete. Upon receipt of the appellee's brief, or earlier if the court orders or the parties agree, the appellant must request the district clerk to forward the record.

(d) [Abrogated.]

(e) Retaining the Record by Court Order.

(1) The court of appeals may, by order or local rule, provide that a certified copy of the docket entries be forwarded instead of the entire record. But a party may at any time during the appeal request that designated parts of the record be forwarded.

(2) The district court may order the record or some part of it retained if the court needs it while the appeal is pending, subject, however, to call by the court of appeals.

(3) If part or all of the record is ordered retained, the district clerk must send to the court of appeals a copy of the order and the docket entries together with the parts of the original record allowed by the district court and copies of any parts of the record designated by the parties.

(f) Retaining Parts of the Record in the District Court by Stipulation of the Parties. The parties may agree by written stipulation filed in the district court that designated parts of the record be retained in the district court subject to call by the court of appeals or request by a party. The parts of the record so designated remain a part of the record on appeal.

(g) Record for a Preliminary Motion in the Court of Appeals. If, before the record is forwarded, a party makes any of the following motions in the court of appeals:

- for dismissal;
- for release;
- for a stay pending appeal;
- for additional security on the bond on appeal or on a supersedeas bond; or
- for any other intermediate order—

the district clerk must send the court of appeals any parts of the record designated by any party.

[Amended April 30, 1979, effective August 1, 1979; March 10, 1986, effective July 1, 1986; April 24, 1998, effective December 1, 1998.]

FRAP 12. DOCKETING THE APPEAL; FILING A REPRESENTATION STATEMENT; FILING THE RECORD

(a) Docketing the Appeal. Upon receiving the copy of the notice of appeal and the docket entries from the district clerk under Rule 3(d), the circuit clerk must docket the appeal under the title of the district-court action and must identify the appellant, adding the appellant's name if necessary.

(b) Filing a Representation Statement. Unless the court of appeals designates another time, the attorney who filed the notice of appeal must, within 10 days after filing the notice, file a statement with the circuit clerk naming the parties that the attorney represents on appeal.

(c) Filing the Record, Partial Record, or Certificate. Upon receiving the record, partial record, or district clerk's certificate as provided in Rule 11, the circuit clerk must file it and immediately notify all parties of the filing date.

[Amended April 30, 1979, effective August 1, 1979; March 10, 1986, effective July 1, 1986; April 22, 1993, effective December 1, 1993; April 24, 1998, effective December 1, 1998.]

TITLE III. REVIEW OF A DECISION OF THE UNITED STATES TAX COURT

FRAP 13. REVIEW OF A DECISION OF THE TAX COURT

(a) How Obtained; Time for Filing Notice of Appeal.

(1) Review of a decision of the United States Tax Court is commenced by filing a notice of appeal with the Tax Court clerk within 90 days after the entry of the Tax Court's decision. At the time of filing, the appellant must furnish the clerk with enough copies of the notice to enable the clerk to comply with Rule 3(d). If one party files a timely notice of appeal, any other party may file a notice of appeal within 120 days after the Tax Court's decision is entered.

(2) If, under Tax Court rules, a party makes a timely motion to vacate or revise the Tax Court's decision, the time to file a notice of appeal runs from the entry of the order disposing of the motion or from the entry of a new decision, whichever is later.

(b) Notice of Appeal; How Filed. The notice of appeal may be filed either at the Tax Court clerk's office in the District of Columbia or by mail addressed to the clerk. If sent by mail the notice is considered filed on the postmark date, subject to § 7502 of the Internal Revenue Code, as amended, and the applicable regulations.

(c) Contents of the Notice of Appeal; Service; Effect of Filing and Service. Rule 3 prescribes the contents of a notice of appeal, the manner of service, and the effect of its filing and service. Form 2 in the Appendix of Forms is a suggested form of a notice of appeal.

(d) The Record on Appeal; Forwarding; Filing.

(1) An appeal from the Tax Court is governed by the parts of Rules 10, 11, and 12 regarding the record on appeal from a district court, the time and manner of forwarding and filing, and the docketing in the court of appeals. References in those rules and in Rule 3 to the district court and district clerk are to be read as referring to the Tax Court and its clerk.

(2) If an appeal from a Tax Court decision is taken to more than one court of appeals, the original record must be sent to the court named in the first notice of appeal filed. In an appeal to any other court of appeals, the appellant must apply to that other court to make provision for the record.

[Amended April 30, 1979, effective August 1, 1979; April 29, 1994, effective December 1, 1994; April 24, 1998, effective December 1, 1998.]

FRAP 14. APPLICABILITY OF OTHER RULES TO THE REVIEW OF A TAX COURT DECISION

All provisions of these rules, except Rules 4–9, 15–20, and 22–23, apply to the review of a Tax Court decision.

[Amended April 24, 1998, effective December 1, 1998.]

TITLE IV. REVIEW OR ENFORCEMENT OF AN ORDER OF AN ADMINISTRATIVE AGENCY, BOARD, COMMISSION, OR OFFICER

FRAP 15. REVIEW OR ENFORCEMENT OF AN AGENCY ORDER—HOW OBTAINED; INTERVENTION

(a) Petition for Review; Joint Petition.

(1) Review of an agency order is commenced by filing, within the time prescribed by law, a petition for review with the clerk of a court of appeals authorized to review the agency order. If their interests make joinder practicable, two or more persons may join in a petition to the same court to review the same order.

(2) The petition must:

(A) name each party seeking review either in the caption or the body of the petition—using such terms as "et al.," "petitioners," or "respondents" does not effectively name the parties;

(B) name the agency as a respondent (even though not named in the petition, the United States is a respondent if required by statute); and

(C) specify the order or part thereof to be reviewed.

(3) Form 3 in the Appendix of Forms is a suggested form of a petition for review.

(4) In this rule "agency" includes an agency, board, commission, or officer; "petition for review" includes a petition to enjoin, suspend, modify, or otherwise review, or a notice of appeal, whichever form is indicated by the applicable statute.

(b) Application or Cross–Application to Enforce an Order; Answer; Default.

(1) An application to enforce an agency order must be filed with the clerk of a court of appeals authorized to enforce the order. If a petition is filed to review an agency order that the court may enforce, a party opposing the petition may file a cross-application for enforcement.

(2) Within 20 days after the application for enforcement is filed, the respondent must serve on the applicant an answer to the application and file it with the clerk. If the respondent fails to answer in time, the court will enter judgment for the relief requested.

(3) The application must contain a concise statement of the proceedings in which the order was entered, the facts upon which venue is based, and the relief requested.

(c) Service of the Petition or Application. The circuit clerk must serve a copy of the petition for review, or an application or cross-application to enforce an agency order, on each respondent as prescribed by Rule 3(d), unless a different manner of service is prescribed by statute. At the time of filing, the petitioner must:

(1) serve, or have served, a copy on each party admitted to participate in the agency proceedings, except for the respondents;

(2) file with the clerk a list of those so served; and

(3) give the clerk enough copies of the petition or application to serve each respondent.

(d) Intervention. Unless a statute provides another method, a person who wants to intervene in a proceeding under this rule must file a motion for leave to intervene with the circuit clerk and serve a copy on all parties. The motion—or other notice of intervention authorized by statute—must be filed within 30 days after the petition for review is filed and must contain a concise statement of the interest of the moving party and the grounds for intervention.

(e) Payment of Fees. When filing any separate or joint petition for review in a court of appeals, the petitioner must pay the circuit clerk all required fees.

[Amended April 22, 1993, effective December 1, 1993; April 24, 1998, effective December 1, 1998.]

FRAP 15.1 BRIEFS AND ORAL ARGUMENT IN A NATIONAL LABOR RELATIONS BOARD PROCEEDING

In either an enforcement or a review proceeding, a party adverse to the National Labor Relations Board proceeds first on briefing and at oral argument, unless the court orders otherwise.

[Adopted March 10, 1986, effective July 1, 1986; April 24, 1998, effective December 1, 1998.]

FRAP 16. THE RECORD ON REVIEW OR ENFORCEMENT

(a) Composition of the Record. The record on review or enforcement of an agency order consists of:

(1) the order involved;

(2) any findings or report on which it is based; and

(3) the pleadings, evidence, and other parts of the proceedings before the agency.

(b) Omissions From or Misstatements in the Record. The parties may at any time, by stipulation, supply any omission from the record or correct a misstatement, or the court may so direct. If necessary, the court may direct that a supplemental record be prepared and filed.

[Amended April 24, 1998, effective December 1, 1998.]

FRAP 17. FILING THE RECORD

(a) Agency to File; Time for Filing; Notice of Filing. The agency must file the record with the circuit clerk within 40 days after being served with a petition for review, unless the statute authorizing review provides otherwise, or within 40 days after it files an application for enforcement unless the respondent fails to answer or the court orders otherwise. The court may shorten or extend the time to file the record. The clerk must notify all parties of the date when the record is filed.

(b) Filing—What Constitutes.

(1) The agency must file:

(A) the original or a certified copy of the entire record or parts designated by the parties; or

(B) a certified list adequately describing all documents, transcripts of testimony, exhibits, and other material constituting the record, or describing those parts designated by the parties.

(2) The parties may stipulate in writing that no record or certified list be filed. The date when the stipulation is filed with the circuit clerk is treated as the date when the record is filed.

(3) The agency must retain any portion of the record not filed with the clerk. All parts of the record retained by the agency are a part of the record on review for all purposes and, if the court or a party so requests, must be sent to the court regardless of any prior stipulation.

[Amended April 24, 1998, effective December 1, 1998.]

FRAP 18. STAY PENDING REVIEW

(a) Motion for a Stay.

(1) *Initial Motion Before the Agency.* A petitioner must ordinarily move first before the agency for a stay pending review of its decision or order.

(2) *Motion in the Court of Appeals.* A motion for a stay may be made to the court of appeals or one of its judges.

(A) The motion must:

(i) show that moving first before the agency would be impracticable; or

(ii) state that, a motion having been made, the agency denied the motion or failed to afford the relief requested and state any reasons given by the agency for its action.

(B) The motion must also include:

(i) the reasons for granting the relief requested and the facts relied on;

(ii) originals or copies of affidavits or other sworn statements supporting facts subject to dispute; and

(iii) relevant parts of the record.

(C) The moving party must give reasonable notice of the motion to all parties.

(D) The motion must be filed with the circuit clerk and normally will be considered by a panel of the court. But in an exceptional case in which time requirements make that procedure impracticable, the motion may be made to and considered by a single judge.

(b) Bond. The court may condition relief on the filing of a bond or other appropriate security.

[Amended April 24, 1998, effective December 1, 1998.]

FRAP 19. SETTLEMENT OF A JUDGMENT ENFORCING AN AGENCY ORDER IN PART

When the court files an opinion directing entry of judgment enforcing the agency's order in part, the agency must within 14 days file with the clerk and serve on each other party a proposed judgment conforming to the opinion. A party who disagrees with the agency's proposed judgment must within 7 days file with the clerk and serve the agency with a proposed judgment that the party believes conforms to the opinion. The court will settle the judgment and direct entry without further hearing or argument.

[Amended March 10, 1986, effective July 1, 1986; April 24, 1998, effective December 1, 1998.]

FRAP 20. APPLICABILITY OF RULES TO THE REVIEW OR ENFORCEMENT OF AN AGENCY ORDER

All provisions of these rules, except Rules 3–14 and 22–23, apply to the review or enforcement of an agency order. In these rules, "appellant" includes a petitioner or applicant, and "appellee" includes a respondent.

[Amended April 24, 1998, effective December 1, 1998.]

TITLE V. EXTRAORDINARY WRITS

FRAP 21. WRITS OF MANDAMUS AND PROHIBITION, AND OTHER EXTRAORDINARY WRITS

(a) Mandamus or Prohibition to a Court: Petition, Filing, Service, and Docketing.

(1) A party petitioning for a writ of mandamus or prohibition directed to a court must file a petition with the circuit clerk with proof of service on all parties to the proceeding in the trial court. The party must also provide a copy to the trial-court judge. All parties to the proceeding in the trial court other than the petitioner are respondents for all purposes.

(2)(A) The petition must be titled "In re [name of petitioner]."

(B) The petition must state:

(i) the relief sought;

(ii) the issues presented;

(iii) the facts necessary to understand the issue presented by the petition; and

(iv) the reasons why the writ should issue.

(C) The petition must include a copy of any order or opinion or parts of the record that may be essential to understand the matters set forth in the petition.

(3) Upon receiving the prescribed docket fee, the clerk must docket the petition and submit it to the court.

(b) Denial; Order Directing Answer; Briefs; Precedence.

(1) The court may deny the petition without an answer. Otherwise, it must order the respondent, if any, to answer within a fixed time.

(2) The clerk must serve the order to respond on all persons directed to respond.

(3) Two or more respondents may answer jointly.

(4) The court of appeals may invite or order the trial-court judge to address the petition or may invite an amicus curiae to do so. The trial-court judge may request permission to address the petition but may not do so unless invited or ordered to do so by the court of appeals.

(5) If briefing or oral argument is required, the clerk must advise the parties, and when appropriate, the trial-court judge or amicus curiae.

(6) The proceeding must be given preference over ordinary civil cases.

(7) The circuit clerk must send a copy of the final disposition to the trial-court judge.

(c) Other Extraordinary Writs. An application for an extraordinary writ other than one provided for in Rule 21(a) must be made by filing a petition with the circuit clerk with proof of service on the respondents. Proceedings on the application must conform, so far as is practicable, to the procedures prescribed in Rule 21(a) and (b).

(d) Form of Papers; Number of Copies. All papers must conform to Rule 32(c)(2). Except by the court's permission, a paper must not exceed 30 pages, exclusive of the disclosure statement, the proof of service, and the accompanying documents required by Rule 21(a)(2)(C). An original and 3 copies must be filed unless the court requires the filing of a different number by local rule or by order in a particular case.

[Amended April 29, 1994, effective December 1, 1994; April 23, 1996, effective December 1, 1996; April 24, 1998, effective December 1, 1998; April 29, 2002, effective December 1, 2002.]

TITLE VI. HABEAS CORPUS; PROCEEDINGS IN FORMA PAUPERIS

FRAP 22. HABEAS CORPUS AND SECTION 2255 PROCEEDINGS

(a) Application for the Original Writ. An application for a writ of habeas corpus must be made to the appropriate district court. If made to a circuit judge, the application must be transferred to the appropriate district court. If a district court denies an application made or transferred to it, renewal of the application before a circuit judge is not permitted. The applicant may, under 28 U.S.C. § 2253, appeal to the court of appeals from the district court's order denying the application.

(b) Certificate of Appealability.

(1) In a habeas corpus proceeding in which the detention complained of arises from process issued by a state court, or in a 28 U.S.C. § 2255 proceeding, the applicant cannot take an appeal unless a circuit justice or a circuit or district judge issues a certificate of appealability under 28 U.S.C. § 2253(c). If an applicant files a notice of appeal, the district judge who rendered the judgment must either issue a certificate of appealability or state why a certificate should not issue. The district clerk must send the certificate or statement to the court of appeals with the notice of appeal and the file of the district-court proceedings. If the district judge has denied the certificate, the

applicant may request a circuit judge to issue the certificate.

(2) A request addressed to the court of appeals may be considered by a circuit judge or judges, as the court prescribes. If no express request for a certificate is filed, the notice of appeal constitutes a request addressed to the judges of the court of appeals.

(3) A certificate of appealability is not required when a state or its representative or the United States or its representative appeals.

[Amended by Pub.L. 104–32, § 103, April 24, 1996, 110 Stat. 1218; amended April 24, 1998, effective December 1, 1998.]

FRAP 23. CUSTODY OR RELEASE OF A PRISONER IN A HABEAS CORPUS PROCEEDING

(a) Transfer of Custody Pending Review. Pending review of a decision in a habeas corpus proceeding commenced before a court, justice, or judge of the United States for the release of a prisoner, the person having custody of the prisoner must not transfer custody to another unless a transfer is directed in accordance with this rule. When, upon application, a custodian shows the need for a transfer, the court, justice, or judge rendering the decision under review may authorize the transfer and substitute the successor custodian as a party.

(b) Detention or Release Pending Review of Decision Not to Release. While a decision not to release a prisoner is under review, the court or judge rendering the decision, or the court of appeals, or the Supreme Court, or a judge or justice of either court, may order that the prisoner be:

(1) detained in the custody from which release is sought;

(2) detained in other appropriate custody; or

(3) released on personal recognizance, with or without surety.

(c) Release Pending Review of Decision Ordering Release. While a decision ordering the release of a prisoner is under review, the prisoner must—unless the court or judge rendering the decision, or the court of appeals, or the Supreme Court, or a judge or justice of either court orders otherwise—be released on personal recognizance, with or without surety.

(d) Modification of the Initial Order on Custody. An initial order governing the prisoner's custody or release, including any recognizance or surety, continues in effect pending review unless for special reasons shown to the court of appeals or the Supreme Court, or to a judge or justice of either court, the order is modified or an independent order regarding custody, release, or surety is issued.

[Amended March 10, 1986, effective July 1, 1986; April 24, 1998, effective December 1, 1998.]

FRAP 24. PROCEEDING IN FORMA PAUPERIS

(a) Leave to Proceed In Forma Pauperis.

(1) *Motion in the District Court.* Except as stated in Rule 24(a)(3), a party to a district-court action who desires to appeal in forma pauperis must file a motion in the district court. The party must attach an affidavit that:

(A) shows in the detail prescribed by Form 4 of the Appendix of Forms the party's inability to pay or to give security for fees and costs;

(B) claims an entitlement to redress; and

(C) states the issues that the party intends to present on appeal.

(2) *Action on the Motion.* If the district court grants the motion, the party may proceed on appeal without prepaying or giving security for fees and costs, unless a statute provides otherwise. If the district court denies the motion, it must state its reasons in writing.

(3) *Prior Approval.* A party who was permitted to proceed in forma pauperis in the district-court action, or who was determined to be financially unable to obtain an adequate defense in a criminal case, may proceed on appeal in forma pauperis without further authorization, unless:

(A) the district court—before or after the notice of appeal is filed—certifies that the appeal is not taken in good faith or finds that the party is not otherwise entitled to proceed in forma pauperis and states in writing its reasons for the certification or finding; or

(B) a statute provides otherwise.

(4) *Notice of District Court's Denial.* The district clerk must immediately notify the parties and the court of appeals when the district court does any of the following:

(A) denies a motion to proceed on appeal in forma pauperis;

(B) certifies that the appeal is not taken in good faith; or

(C) finds that the party is not otherwise entitled to proceed in forma pauperis.

(5) *Motion in the Court of Appeals.* A party may file a motion to proceed on appeal in forma pauperis in the court of appeals within 30 days after service of the notice prescribed in Rule 24(a)(4). The motion must include a copy of the affidavit filed in the district court and the district court's statement of reasons for its action. If no affidavit was filed in the district court, the party must include the affidavit prescribed by Rule 24(a)(1).

(b) Leave to Proceed In Forma Pauperis on Appeal or Review of an Administrative Agency Pro-

ceeding. When an appeal or review of a proceeding before an administrative agency, board, commission, or officer (including for the purpose of this rule the United States Tax Court) proceeds directly in a court of appeals, a party may file in the court of appeals a motion for leave to proceed on appeal in forma pauperis with an affidavit prescribed by Rule 24(a)(1).

(c) Leave to Use Original Record. A party allowed to proceed on appeal in forma pauperis may request that the appeal be heard on the original record without reproducing any part.

[Amended April 30, 1979, effective August 1, 1979; March 10, 1986, effective July 1, 1986; April 24, 1998, effective December 1, 1998; April 29, 2002, effective December 1, 2002.]

TITLE VII. GENERAL PROVISIONS

FRAP 25. FILING AND SERVICE

(a) Filing.

(1) *Filing With the Clerk.* A paper required or permitted to be filed in a court of appeals must be filed with the clerk.

(2) *Filing: Method and Timeliness.*

(A) In General. Filing may be accomplished by mail addressed to the clerk, but filing is not timely unless the clerk receives the papers within the time fixed for filing.

(B) A Brief or Appendix. A brief or appendix is timely filed, however, if on or before the last day for filing, it is:

(i) mailed to the clerk by First–Class Mail, or other class of mail that is at least as expeditious, postage prepaid; or

(ii) dispatched to a third-party commercial carrier for delivery to the clerk within 3 calendar days.

(C) Inmate Filing. A paper filed by an inmate confined in an institution is timely if deposited in the institution's internal mailing system on or before the last day for filing. If an institution has a system designed for legal mail, the inmate must use that system to receive the benefit of this rule. Timely filing may be shown by a declaration in compliance with 28 U.S.C. § 1746 or by a notarized statement, either of which must set forth the date of deposit and state that first-class postage has been prepaid.

(D) Electronic Filing. A court of appeals may by local rule permit or require papers to be filed, signed, or verified by electronic means that are consistent with technical standards, if any, that the Judicial Conference of the United States establishes. A local rule may require filing by electronic means only if reasonable exceptions are allowed. A paper filed by electronic means in compliance with a local rule constitutes a written paper for the purpose of applying these rules.

(3) *Filing a Motion With a Judge.* If a motion requests relief that may be granted by a single judge, the judge may permit the motion to be filed with the judge; the judge must note the filing date on the motion and give it to the clerk.

(4) *Clerk's Refusal of Documents.* The clerk must not refuse to accept for filing any paper presented for that purpose solely because it is not presented in proper form as required by these rules or by any local rule or practice.

(5) *Privacy Protection.* An appeal in a case whose privacy protection was governed by Federal Rule of Bankruptcy Procedure 9037, Federal Rule of Civil Procedure 5.2, or Federal Rule of Criminal Procedure 49.1 is governed by the same rule on appeal. In all other proceedings, privacy protection is governed by Federal Rule of Civil Procedure 5.2, except that Federal Rule of Criminal Procedure 49.1 governs when an extraordinary writ is sought in a criminal case.

(b) Service of All Papers Required. Unless a rule requires service by the clerk, a party must, at or before the time of filing a paper, serve a copy on the other parties to the appeal or review. Service on a party represented by counsel must be made on the party's counsel.

(c) Manner of Service.

(1) Service may be any of the following:

(A) personal, including delivery to a responsible person at the office of counsel;

(B) by mail;

(C) by third-party commercial carrier for delivery within 3 calendar days; or

(D) by electronic means, if the party being served consents in writing.

(2) If authorized by local rule, a party may use the court's transmission equipment to make electronic service under Rule 25(c)(1)(D).

(3) When reasonable considering such factors as the immediacy of the relief sought, distance, and cost, service on a party must be by a manner at least as expeditious as the manner used to file the paper with the court.

(4) Service by mail or by commercial carrier is complete on mailing or delivery to the carrier. Service by electronic means is complete on transmission, unless the party making service is notified that the paper was not received by the party served.

(d) Proof of Service.

(1) A paper presented for filing must contain either of the following:

(A) an acknowledgment of service by the person served; or

(B) proof of service consisting of a statement by the person who made service certifying:

(i) the date and manner of service;

(ii) the names of the persons served; and

(iii) their mail or electronic addresses, facsimile numbers, or the addresses of the places of delivery, as appropriate for the manner of service.

(2) When a brief or appendix is filed by mailing or dispatch in accordance with Rule 25(a)(2)(B), the proof of service must also state the date and manner by which the document was mailed or dispatched to the clerk.

(3) Proof of service may appear on or be affixed to the papers filed.

(e) Number of Copies. When these rules require the filing or furnishing of a number of copies, a court may require a different number by local rule or by order in a particular case.

[Amended March 10, 1986, effective July 1, 1986; April 30, 1991, effective December 1, 1991; April 22, 1993, effective December 1, 1993; April 29, 1994, effective December 1, 1994; April 23, 1996, effective December 1, 1996; April 24, 1998, effective December 1, 1998; April 29, 2002, effective December 1, 2002; April 12, 2006, effective December 1, 2006; April 30, 2007, effective December 1, 2007.]

FRAP 26. COMPUTING AND EXTENDING TIME

(a) Computing Time. The following rules apply in computing any period of time specified in these rules or in any local rule, court order, or applicable statute:

(1) Exclude the day of the act, event, or default that begins the period.

(2) Exclude intermediate Saturdays, Sundays, and legal holidays when the period is less than 11 days, unless stated in calendar days.

(3) Include the last day of the period unless it is a Saturday, Sunday, legal holiday, or—if the act to be done is filing a paper in court—a day on which the weather or other conditions make the clerk's office inaccessible.

(4) As used in this rule, "legal holiday" means New Year's Day, Martin Luther King, Jr.'s Birthday, Washington's Birthday, Memorial Day, Independence Day, Labor Day, Columbus Day, Veterans' Day, Thanksgiving Day, Christmas Day, and any other day declared a holiday by the President, Congress, or the state in which is located either the district court that rendered the challenged judgment or order, or the circuit clerk's principal office.

(b) Extending Time. For good cause, the court may extend the time prescribed by these rules or by its order to perform any act, or may permit an act to be done after that time expires. But the court may not extend the time to file:

(1) a notice of appeal (except as authorized in Rule 4) or a petition for permission to appeal; or

(2) a notice of appeal from or a petition to enjoin, set aside, suspend, modify, enforce, or otherwise review an order of an administrative agency, board, commission, or officer of the United States, unless specifically authorized by law.

(c) Additional Time After Service. When a party is required or permitted to act within a prescribed period after a paper is served on that party, 3 calendar days are added to the prescribed period unless the paper is delivered on the date of service stated in the proof of service. For purposes of this Rule 26(c), a paper that is served electronically is not treated as delivered on the date of service stated in the proof of service.

[Amended March 1, 1971, effective July 1, 1971; March 10, 1986, effective July 1, 1986; April 25, 1989, effective December 1, 1989; April 30, 1991, effective December 1, 1991; April 23, 1996, effective December 1, 1996; April 24, 1998, effective December 1, 1998; April 29, 2002, effective December 1, 2002; April 25, 2005, effective December 1, 2005.]

FRAP 26.1 CORPORATE DISCLOSURE STATEMENT

(a) Who Must File. Any nongovernmental corporate party to a proceeding in a court of appeals must file a statement that identifies any parent corporation and any publicly held corporation that owns 10% or more of its stock or states that there is no such corporation.

(b) Time for Filing; Supplemental Filing. A party must file the Rule 26.1(a) statement with the principal brief or upon filing a motion, response, petition, or answer in the court of appeals, whichever occurs first, unless a local rule requires earlier filing. Even if the statement has already been filed, the party's principal brief must include the statement before the table of contents. A party must supplement its statement whenever the information that must be disclosed under Rule 26.1(a) changes.

(c) Number of Copies. If the Rule 26.1(a) statement is filed before the principal brief, or if a supplemental statement is filed, the party must file an original and 3 copies unless the court requires a different number by local rule or by order in a particular case.

[Adopted April 25, 1989, effective December 1, 1989; amended April 30, 1991, effective December 1, 1991; April 29, 1994, effective December 1, 1994; April 24, 1998, effective December 1, 1998; April 29, 2002, effective December 1, 2002.]

FRAP 27. MOTIONS

(a) In General.

(1) *Application for Relief.* An application for an order or other relief is made by motion unless these rules prescribe another form. A motion must be in writing unless the court permits otherwise.

(2) *Contents of a Motion.*

(A) Grounds and relief sought. A motion must state with particularity the grounds for the motion, the relief sought, and the legal argument necessary to support it.

(B) Accompanying documents.

(i) Any affidavit or other paper necessary to support a motion must be served and filed with the motion.

(ii) An affidavit must contain only factual information, not legal argument.

(iii) A motion seeking substantive relief must include a copy of the trial court's opinion or agency's decision as a separate exhibit.

(C) Documents barred or not required.

(i) A separate brief supporting or responding to a motion must not be filed.

(ii) A notice of motion is not required.

(iii) A proposed order is not required.

(3) *Response.*

(A) Time to file. Any party may file a response to a motion; Rule 27(a)(2) governs its contents. The response must be filed within 8 days after service of the motion unless the court shortens or extends the time. A motion authorized by Rules 8, 9, 18, or 41 may be granted before the 8–day period runs only if the court gives reasonable notice to the parties that it intends to act sooner.

(B) Request for affirmative relief. A response may include a motion for affirmative relief. The time to respond to the new motion, and to reply to that response, are governed by Rule 27(a)(3)(A) and (a)(4). The title of the response must alert the court to the request for relief.

(4) *Reply to Response.* Any reply to a response must be filed within 5 days after service of the response. A reply must not present matters that do not relate to the response.

(b) Disposition of a Motion for a Procedural Order. The court may act on a motion for a procedural order—including a motion under Rule 26(b)—at any time without awaiting a response, and may, by rule or by order in a particular case, authorize its clerk to act on specified types of procedural motions. A party adversely affected by the court's, or the clerk's, action may file a motion to reconsider, vacate, or modify that action. Timely opposition filed after the motion is granted in whole or in part does not constitute a request to reconsider, vacate, or modify the disposition; a motion requesting that relief must be filed.

(c) Power of a Single Judge to Entertain a Motion. A circuit judge may act alone on any motion, but may not dismiss or otherwise determine an appeal or other proceeding. A court of appeals may provide by rule or by order in a particular case that only the court may act on any motion or class of motions. The court may review the action of a single judge.

(d) Form of Papers; Page Limits; and Number of Copies.

(1) *Format.*

(A) Reproduction. A motion, response, or reply may be reproduced by any process that yields a clear black image on light paper. The paper must be opaque and unglazed. Only one side of the paper may be used.

(B) Cover. A cover is not required, but there must be a caption that includes the case number, the name of the court, the title of the case, and a brief descriptive title indicating the purpose of the motion and identifying the party or parties for whom it is filed. If a cover is used, it must be white.

(C) Binding. The document must be bound in any manner that is secure, does not obscure the text, and permits the document to lie reasonably flat when open.

(D) Paper Size, Line Spacing, and Margins. The document must be on 8½ by 11 inch paper. The text must be double-spaced, but quotations more than two lines long may be indented and single-spaced. Headings and footnotes may be single-spaced. Margins must be at least one inch on all four sides. Page numbers may be placed in the margins, but no text may appear there.

(E) Typeface and Type Styles. The document must comply with the typeface requirements of Rule 32(a)(5) and the type-style requirements of Rule 32(a)(6).

(2) *Page Limits.* A motion or a response to a motion must not exceed 20 pages, exclusive of the corporate disclosure statement and accompanying documents authorized by Rule 27(a)(2)(B), unless the court permits or directs otherwise. A reply to a response must not exceed 10 pages.

(3) *Number of Copies.* An original and 3 copies must be filed unless the court requires a different number by local rule or by order in a particular case.

(e) Oral Argument. A motion will be decided without oral argument unless the court orders otherwise.

[Amended April 30, 1979, effective August 1, 1979; April 25, 1989, effective December 1, 1989; April 29, 1994, effective December 1, 1994; April 24, 1998, effective December 1,

1998; April 29, 2002, effective December 1, 2002; April 25, 2005, effective December 1, 2005.]

FRAP 28. BRIEFS

(a) Appellant's Brief. The appellant's brief must contain, under appropriate headings and in the order indicated:

(1) a corporate disclosure statement if required by Rule 26.1;

(2) a table of contents, with page references;

(3) a table of authorities—cases (alphabetically arranged), statutes, and other authorities—with references to the pages of the brief where they are cited;

(4) a jurisdictional statement, including:

(A) the basis for the district court's or agency's subject-matter jurisdiction, with citations to applicable statutory provisions and stating relevant facts establishing jurisdiction;

(B) the basis for the court of appeals' jurisdiction, with citations to applicable statutory provisions and stating relevant facts establishing jurisdiction;

(C) the filing dates establishing the timeliness of the appeal or petition for review; and

(D) an assertion that the appeal is from a final order or judgment that disposes of all parties' claims, or information establishing the court of appeals' jurisdiction on some other basis;

(5) a statement of the issues presented for review;

(6) a statement of the case briefly indicating the nature of the case, the course of proceedings, and the disposition below;

(7) a statement of facts relevant to the issues submitted for review with appropriate references to the record (see Rule 28(e));

(8) a summary of the argument, which must contain a succinct, clear, and accurate statement of the arguments made in the body of the brief, and which must not merely repeat the argument headings;

(9) the argument, which must contain:

(A) appellant's contentions and the reasons for them, with citations to the authorities and parts of the record on which the appellant relies; and

(B) for each issue, a concise statement of the applicable standard of review (which may appear in the discussion of the issue or under a separate heading placed before the discussion of the issues);

(10) a short conclusion stating the precise relief sought; and

(11) the certificate of compliance, if required by Rule 32(a)(7).

(b) Appellee's Brief. The appellee's brief must conform to the requirements of Rule 28(a)(1)–(9) and (11), except that none of the following need appear unless the appellee is dissatisfied with the appellant's statement:

(1) the jurisdictional statement;

(2) the statement of the issues;

(3) the statement of the case;

(4) the statement of the facts; and

(5) the statement of the standard of review.

(c) Reply Brief. The appellant may file a brief in reply to the appellee's brief. Unless the court permits, no further briefs may be filed. A reply brief must contain a table of contents, with page references, and a table of authorities—cases (alphabetically arranged), statutes, and other authorities—with references to the pages of the reply brief where they are cited.

(d) References to Parties. In briefs and at oral argument, counsel should minimize use of the terms "appellant" and "appellee." To make briefs clear, counsel should use the parties' actual names or the designations used in the lower court or agency proceeding, or such descriptive terms as "the employee," "the injured person," "the taxpayer," "the ship," "the stevedore."

(e) References to the Record. References to the parts of the record contained in the appendix filed with the appellant's brief must be to the pages of the appendix. If the appendix is prepared after the briefs are filed, a party referring to the record must follow one of the methods detailed in Rule 30(c). If the original record is used under Rule 30(f) and is not consecutively paginated, or if the brief refers to an unreproduced part of the record, any reference must be to the page of the original document. For example:

- Answer p. 7;
- Motion for Judgment p. 2;
- Transcript p. 231.

Only clear abbreviations may be used. A party referring to evidence whose admissibility is in controversy must cite the pages of the appendix or of the transcript at which the evidence was identified, offered, and received or rejected.

(f) Reproduction of Statutes, Rules, Regulations, etc. If the court's determination of the issues presented requires the study of statutes, rules, regulations, etc., the relevant parts must be set out in the brief or in an addendum at the end, or may be supplied to the court in pamphlet form.

(g) [Reserved].

(h) [Reserved].

(i) Briefs in a Case Involving Multiple Appellants or Appellees. In a case involving more than one appellant or appellee, including consolidated cases, any number of appellants or appellees may join in a brief, and any party may adopt by reference a part of another's brief. Parties may also join in reply briefs.

(j) Citation of Supplemental Authorities. If pertinent and significant authorities come to a party's attention after the party's brief has been filed—or after oral argument but before decision—a party may promptly advise the circuit clerk by letter, with a copy to all other parties, setting forth the citations. The letter must state the reasons for the supplemental citations, referring either to the page of the brief or to a point argued orally. The body of the letter must not exceed 350 words. Any response must be made promptly and must be similarly limited.

[Amended April 30, 1979, effective August 1, 1979; March 10, 1986, effective July 1, 1986; April 25, 1989, effective December 1, 1989; April 30, 1991, effective December 1, 1991; April 22, 1993, effective December 1, 1993; April 29, 1994, effective December 1, 1994; April 24, 1998, effective December 1, 1998; April 29, 2002, effective December 1, 2002; April 1, 2005, effective December 1, 2005.]

FRAP 28.1 CROSS–APPEALS

(a) Applicability. This rule applies to a case in which a cross-appeal is filed. Rules 28(a)–(c), 31(a)(1), 32(a)(2), and 32(a)(7)(A)–(B) do not apply to such a case, except as otherwise provided in this rule.

(b) Designation of Appellant. The party who files a notice of appeal first is the appellant for the purposes of this rule and Rules 30 and 34. If notices are filed on the same day, the plaintiff in the proceeding below is the appellant. These designations may be modified by the parties' agreement or by court order.

(c) Briefs. In a case involving a cross-appeal:

(1) *Appellant's Principal Brief.* The appellant must file a principal brief in the appeal. That brief must comply with Rule 28(a).

(2) *Appellee's Principal and Response Brief.* The appellee must file a principal brief in the cross-appeal and must, in the same brief, respond to the principal brief in the appeal. That appellee's brief must comply with Rule 28(a), except that the brief need not include a statement of the case or a statement of the facts unless the appellee is dissatisfied with the appellant's statement.

(3) *Appellant's Response and Reply Brief.* The appellant must file a brief that responds to the principal brief in the cross-appeal and may, in the same brief, reply to the response in the appeal. That brief must comply with Rule 28(a)(2)–(9) and (11), except that none of the following need appear unless the appellant is dissatisfied with the appellee's statement in the cross-appeal:

(A) the jurisdictional statement;

(B) the statement of the issues;

(C) the statement of the case;

(D) the statement of the facts; and

(E) the statement of the standard of review.

(4) *Appellee's Reply Brief.* The appellee may file a brief in reply to the response in the cross-appeal. That brief must comply with Rule 28(a)(2)–(3) and (11) and must be limited to the issues presented by the cross-appeal.

(5) *No Further Briefs.* Unless the court permits, no further briefs may be filed in a case involving a cross-appeal.

(d) Cover. Except for filings by unrepresented parties, the cover of the appellant's principal brief must be blue; the appellee's principal and response brief, red; the appellant's response and reply brief, yellow; the appellee's reply brief, gray; an intervenor's or amicus curiae's brief, green; and any supplemental brief, tan. The front cover of a brief must contain the information required by Rule 32(a)(2).

(e) Length.

(1) *Page Limitation.* Unless it complies with Rule 28.1(e)(2) and (3), the appellant's principal brief must not exceed 30 pages; the appellee's principal and response brief, 35 pages; the appellant's response and reply brief, 30 pages; and the appellee's reply brief, 15 pages.

(2) *Type-Volume Limitation.*

(A) The appellant's principal brief or the appellant's response and reply brief is acceptable if:

(i) it contains no more than 14,000 words; or

(ii) it uses a monospaced face and contains no more than 1,300 lines of text.

(B) The appellee's principal and response brief is acceptable if:

(i) it contains no more than 16,500 words; or

(ii) it uses a monospaced face and contains no more than 1,500 lines of text.

(C) The appellee's reply brief is acceptable if it contains no more than half of the type volume specified in Rule 28.1(e)(2)(A).

(3) *Certificate of Compliance.* A brief submitted under Rule 28.1(e)(2) must comply with Rule 32(a)(7)(C).

(f) Time to Serve and File a Brief. Briefs must be served and filed as follows:

(1) the appellant's principal brief, within 40 days after the record is filed;

(2) the appellee's principal and response brief, within 30 days after the appellant's principal brief is served;

(3) the appellant's response and reply brief, within 30 days after the appellee's principal and response brief is served; and

(4) the appellee's reply brief, within 14 days after the appellant's response and reply brief is served, but at least 3 days before argument unless the court, for good cause, allows a later filing.

[Amended April 25, 2005, effective December 1, 2005.]

FRAP 29. BRIEF OF AN AMICUS CURIAE

(a) When Permitted. The United States or its officer or agency, or a State, Territory, Commonwealth, or the District of Columbia may file an amicus-curiae brief without the consent of the parties or leave of court. Any other amicus curiae may file a brief only by leave of court or if the brief states that all parties have consented to its filing.

(b) Motion for Leave to File. The motion must be accompanied by the proposed brief and state:

(1) the movant's interest; and

(2) the reason why an amicus brief is desirable and why the matters asserted are relevant to the disposition of the case.

(c) Contents and Form. An amicus brief must comply with Rule 32. In addition to the requirements of Rule 32, the cover must identify the party or parties supported and indicate whether the brief supports affirmance or reversal. If an amicus curiae is a corporation, the brief must include a disclosure statement like that required of parties by Rule 26.1. An amicus brief need not comply with Rule 28, but must include the following:

(1) a table of contents, with page references;

(2) a table of authorities—cases (alphabetically arranged), statutes and other authorities—with references to the pages of the brief where they are cited;

(3) a concise statement of the identity of the amicus curiae, its interest in the case, and the source of its authority to file;

(4) an argument, which may be preceded by a summary and which need not include a statement of the applicable standard of review; and

(5) a certificate of compliance, if required by Rule 32(a)(7).

(d) Length. Except by the court's permission, an amicus brief may be no more than one-half the maximum length authorized by these rules for a party's principal brief. If the court grants a party permission to file a longer brief, that extension does not affect the length of an amicus brief.

(e) Time for Filing. An amicus curiae must file its brief, accompanied by a motion for filing when necessary, no later than 7 days after the principal brief of the party being supported is filed. An amicus curiae that does not support either party must file its brief no later than 7 days after the appellant's or petitioner's principal brief is filed. A court may grant leave for later filing, specifying the time within which an opposing party may answer.

(f) Reply Brief. Except by the court's permission, an amicus curiae may not file a reply brief.

(g) Oral Argument. An amicus curiae may participate in oral argument only with the court's permission.

[Amended April 24, 1998, effective December 1, 1998.]

FRAP 30. APPENDIX TO THE BRIEFS

(a) Appellant's Responsibility.

(1) *Contents of the Appendix.* The appellant must prepare and file an appendix to the briefs containing:

(A) the relevant docket entries in the proceeding below;

(B) the relevant portions of the pleadings, charge, findings, or opinion;

(C) the judgment, order, or decision in question; and

(D) other parts of the record to which the parties wish to direct the court's attention.

(2) *Excluded Material.* Memoranda of law in the district court should not be included in the appendix unless they have independent relevance. Parts of the record may be relied on by the court or the parties even though not included in the appendix.

(3) *Time to File; Number of Copies.* Unless filing is deferred under Rule 30(c), the appellant must file 10 copies of the appendix with the brief and must serve one copy on counsel for each party separately represented. An unrepresented party proceeding in forma pauperis must file 4 legible copies with the clerk, and one copy must be served on counsel for each separately represented party. The court may by local rule or by order in a particular case require the filing or service of a different number.

(b) All Parties' Responsibilities.

(1) *Determining the Contents of the Appendix.* The parties are encouraged to agree on the contents of the appendix. In the absence of an agreement, the appellant must, within 10 days after the record is filed, serve on the appellee a designation of the parts of the record the appellant intends to include in the appendix and a statement of the issues the appellant intends to present for review. The appellee may, within 10 days after receiving the designation, serve on the appellant a designation of additional parts to which it wishes to direct the court's attention. The appellant must include the designated parts in the appendix. The parties must not engage in unnecessary designation of parts of the record, because the entire record is available to the court. This paragraph applies also to a cross-appellant and a cross-appellee.

(2) *Costs of Appendix.* Unless the parties agree otherwise, the appellant must pay the cost of the appendix. If the appellant considers parts of the record designated by the appellee to be unnecessary, the appellant may advise the appellee, who must then advance the cost of including those parts. The cost of the appendix is a taxable cost. But if any party causes unnecessary parts of the record to be included in the appendix, the court may impose the cost of those parts on that party. Each circuit must, by local rule, provide for sanctions against attorneys who unreasonably and vexatiously increase litigation costs by including unnecessary material in the appendix.

(c) Deferred Appendix.

(1) *Deferral Until After Briefs Are Filed.* The court may provide by rule for classes of cases or by order in a particular case that preparation of the appendix may be deferred until after the briefs have been filed and that the appendix may be filed 21 days after the appellee's brief is served. Even though the filing of the appendix may be deferred, Rule 30(b) applies; except that a party must designate the parts of the record it wants included in the appendix when it serves its brief, and need not include a statement of the issues presented.

(2) *References to the Record.*

(A) If the deferred appendix is used, the parties may cite in their briefs the pertinent pages of the record. When the appendix is prepared, the record pages cited in the briefs must be indicated by inserting record page numbers, in brackets, at places in the appendix where those pages of the record appear.

(B) A party who wants to refer directly to pages of the appendix may serve and file copies of the brief within the time required by Rule 31(a), containing appropriate references to pertinent pages of the record. In that event, within 14 days after the appendix is filed, the party must serve and file copies of the brief, containing references to the pages of the appendix in place of or in addition to the references to the pertinent pages of the record. Except for the correction of typographical errors, no other changes may be made to the brief.

(d) Format of the Appendix. The appendix must begin with a table of contents identifying the page at which each part begins. The relevant docket entries must follow the table of contents. Other parts of the record must follow chronologically. When pages from the transcript of proceedings are placed in the appendix, the transcript page numbers must be shown in brackets immediately before the included pages. Omissions in the text of papers or of the transcript must be indicated by asterisks. Immaterial formal matters (captions, subscriptions, acknowledgments, etc.) should be omitted.

(e) Reproduction of Exhibits. Exhibits designated for inclusion in the appendix may be reproduced in a separate volume, or volumes, suitably indexed. Four copies must be filed with the appendix, and one copy must be served on counsel for each separately represented party. If a transcript of a proceeding before an administrative agency, board, commission, or officer was used in a district-court action and has been designated for inclusion in the appendix, the transcript must be placed in the appendix as an exhibit.

(f) Appeal on the Original Record Without an Appendix. The court may, either by rule for all cases or classes of cases or by order in a particular case, dispense with the appendix and permit an appeal to proceed on the original record with any copies of the record, or relevant parts, that the court may order the parties to file.

[Amended March 30, 1970, effective July 1, 1970; March 10, 1986, effective July 1, 1986; April 30, 1991, effective December 1, 1991; April 29, 1994, effective December 1, 1994; April 24, 1998, effective December 1, 1998.]

FRAP 31. SERVING AND FILING BRIEFS

(a) Time to Serve and File a Brief.

(1) The appellant must serve and file a brief within 40 days after the record is filed. The appellee must serve and file a brief within 30 days after the appellant's brief is served. The appellant may serve and file a reply brief within 14 days after service of the appellee's brief but a reply brief must be filed at least 3 days before argument, unless the court, for good cause, allows a later filing.

(2) A court of appeals that routinely considers cases on the merits promptly after the briefs are filed may shorten the time to serve and file briefs, either by local rule or by order in a particular case.

(b) Number of Copies. Twenty-five copies of each brief must be filed with the clerk and 2 copies must be served on each unrepresented party and on counsel for each separately represented party. An unrepresented party proceeding in forma pauperis must file 4 legible copies with the clerk, and one copy must be served on each unrepresented party and on counsel for each separately represented party. The court may by local rule or by order in a particular case require the filing or service of a different number.

(c) Consequence of Failure to File. If an appellant fails to file a brief within the time provided by this rule, or within an extended time, an appellee may move to dismiss the appeal. An appellee who fails to file a brief will not be heard at oral argument unless the court grants permission.

[Amended March 30, 1970, effective July 1, 1970; March 10, 1986, effective July 1, 1986; April 29, 1994, effective December 1, 1994; April 24, 1998, effective December 1, 1998; April 29, 2002, effective December 1, 2002.]

FRAP 32. FORM OF BRIEFS, APPENDICES, AND OTHER PAPERS

(a) Form of a Brief.

(1) *Reproduction.*

(A) A brief may be reproduced by any process that yields a clear black image on light paper. The paper must be opaque and unglazed. Only one side of the paper may be used.

(B) Text must be reproduced with a clarity that equals or exceeds the output of a laser printer.

(C) Photographs, illustrations, and tables may be reproduced by any method that results in a good copy of the original; a glossy finish is acceptable if the original is glossy.

(2) *Cover.* Except for filings by unrepresented parties, the cover of the appellant's brief must be blue; the appellee's, red; an intervenor's or amicus curiae's, green; any reply brief, gray; and any supplemental brief, tan. The front cover of a brief must contain:

(A) the number of the case centered at the top;

(B) the name of the court;

(C) the title of the case (see Rule 12(a));

(D) the nature of the proceeding (e.g., Appeal, Petition for Review) and the name of the court, agency, or board below;

(E) the title of the brief, identifying the party or parties for whom the brief is filed; and

(F) the name, office address, and telephone number of counsel representing the party for whom the brief is filed.

(3) *Binding.* The brief must be bound in any manner that is secure, does not obscure the text, and permits the brief to lie reasonably flat when open.

(4) *Paper Size, Line Spacing, and Margins.* The brief must be on 8½ by 11 inch paper. The text must be double-spaced, but quotations more than two lines long may be indented and single-spaced. Headings and footnotes may be single-spaced. Margins must be at least one inch on all four sides. Page numbers may be placed in the margins, but no text may appear there.

(5) *Typeface.* Either a proportionally spaced or a monospaced face may be used.

(A) A proportionally spaced face must include serifs, but sans-serif type may be used in headings and captions. A proportionally spaced face must be 14-point or larger.

(B) A monospaced face may not contain more than 10½ characters per inch.

(6) *Type Styles.* A brief must be set in a plain, roman style, although italics or boldface may be used for emphasis. Case names must be italicized or underlined.

(7) *Length.*

(A) Page limitation. A principal brief may not exceed 30 pages, or a reply brief 15 pages, unless it complies with Rule 32(a)(7)(B) and (C).

(B) Type-volume limitation.

(i) A principal brief is acceptable if:

- it contains no more than 14,000 words; or
- it uses a monospaced face and contains no more than 1,300 lines of text.

(ii) A reply brief is acceptable if it contains no more than half of the type volume specified in Rule 32(a)(7)(B)(i).

(iii) Headings, footnotes, and quotations count toward the word and line limitations. The corporate disclosure statement, table of contents, table of citations, statement with respect to oral argument, any addendum containing statutes, rules or regulations, and any certificates of counsel do not count toward the limitation.

(C) Certificate of Compliance.

(i) A brief submitted under Rules 28.1(e)(2) or 32(a)(7)(B) must include a certificate by the attorney, or an unrepresented party, that the brief complies with the type-volume limitation. The person preparing the certificate may rely on the word or line count of the word-processing system used to prepare the brief. The certificate must state either:

- the number of words in the brief; or
- the number of lines of monospaced type in the brief.

(ii) Form 6 in the Appendix of Forms is a suggested form of a certificate of compliance. Use of Form 6 must be regarded as sufficient to meet the requirements of Rules 28.1(e)(3) and 32(a)(7)(C)(i).

(b) Form of an Appendix. An appendix must comply with Rule 32(a)(1), (2), (3), and (4), with the following exceptions:

(1) The cover of a separately bound appendix must be white.

(2) An appendix may include a legible photocopy of any document found in the record or of a printed judicial or agency decision.

(3) When necessary to facilitate inclusion of odd-sized documents such as technical drawings, an appendix may be a size other than 8½ by 11 inches, and need not lie reasonably flat when opened.

(c) Form of Other Papers.

(1) *Motion.* The form of a motion is governed by Rule 27(d).

(2) *Other Papers.* Any other paper, including a petition for panel rehearing and a petition for hearing or rehearing en banc, and any response to such a petition, must be reproduced in the manner prescribed by Rule 32(a), with the following exceptions:

(A) A cover is not necessary if the caption and signature page of the paper together contain the information required by Rule 32(a)(2). If a cover is used, it must be white.

(B) Rule 32(a)(7) does not apply.

(d) Signature. Every brief, motion, or other paper filed with the court must be signed by the party filing the paper or, if the party is represented, by one of the party's attorneys.

(e) Local Variation. Every court of appeals must accept documents that comply with the form requirements of this rule. By local rule or order in a particular case a court of appeals may accept documents that do not meet all of the form requirements of this rule.

[Amended April 24, 1998, effective December 1, 1998; April 29, 2002, effective December 1, 2002; April 25, 2005, effective December 1, 2005.]

FRAP 32.1 CITING JUDICIAL DISPOSITIONS

(a) Citation Permitted. A court may not prohibit or restrict the citation of federal judicial opinions, orders, judgments, or other written dispositions that have been:

(i) designated as "unpublished," "not for publication," "non-precedential," "not precedent," or the like; and

(ii) issued on or after January 1, 2007.

(b) Copies Required. If a party cites a federal judicial opinion, order, judgment, or other written disposition that is not available in a publicly accessible electronic database, the party must file and serve a copy of that opinion, order, judgment, or disposition with the brief or other paper in which it is cited.

Effective December 1, 2006.

FRAP 33. APPEAL CONFERENCES

The court may direct the attorneys—and, when appropriate, the parties to participate in one or more conferences to address any matter that may aid in disposing of the proceedings, including simplifying the issues and discussing settlement. A judge or other person designated by the court may preside over the conference, which may be conducted in person or by telephone. Before a settlement conference, the attorneys must consult with their clients and obtain as much authority as feasible to settle the case. The court may, as a result of the conference, enter an order controlling the course of the proceedings or implementing any settlement agreement.

[Amended April 29, 1994, effective December 1, 1994; April 24, 1998, effective December 1, 1998.]

FRAP 34. ORAL ARGUMENT

(a) In General.

(1) *Party's Statement.* Any party may file, or a court may require by local rule, a statement explaining why oral argument should, or need not, be permitted.

(2) *Standards.* Oral argument must be allowed in every case unless a panel of three judges who have examined the briefs and record unanimously agrees that oral argument is unnecessary for any of the following reasons:

(A) the appeal is frivolous;

(B) the dispositive issue or issues have been authoritatively decided; or

(C) the facts and legal arguments are adequately presented in the briefs and record, and the decisional process would not be significantly aided by oral argument.

(b) Notice of Argument; Postponement. The clerk must advise all parties whether oral argument will be scheduled, and, if so, the date, time, and place for it, and the time allowed for each side. A motion to postpone the argument or to allow longer argument must be filed reasonably in advance of the hearing date.

(c) Order and Contents of Argument. The appellant opens and concludes the argument. Counsel must not read at length from briefs, records, or authorities.

(d) Cross-Appeals and Separate Appeals. If there is a cross-appeal, Rule 28.1(b) determines which party is the appellant and which is the appellee for purposes of oral argument. Unless the court directs otherwise, a cross-appeal or separate appeal must be argued when the initial appeal is argued. Separate parties should avoid duplicative argument.

(e) Non-Appearance of a Party. If the appellee fails to appear for argument, the court must hear appellant's argument. If the appellant fails to appear for argument, the court may hear the appellee's argument. If neither party appears, the case will be decided on the briefs, unless the court orders otherwise.

(f) Submission on Briefs. The parties may agree to submit a case for decision on the briefs, but the court may direct that the case be argued.

(g) Use of Physical Exhibits at Argument; Removal. Counsel intending to use physical exhibits other than documents at the argument must arrange to place them in the courtroom on the day of the argument before the court convenes. After the argument, counsel must remove the exhibits from the courtroom, unless the court directs otherwise. The clerk may destroy or dispose of the exhibits if counsel does not reclaim them within a reasonable time after the clerk gives notice to remove them.

[Amended April 30, 1979, effective August 1, 1979; March 10, 1986, effective July 1, 1986; April 30, 1991, effective December 1, 1991; April 22, 1993, effective December 1, 1993; April 24, 1998, effective December 1, 1998; April 25, 2005, effective December 1, 2005.]

FRAP 35. EN BANC DETERMINATION

(a) When Hearing or Rehearing En Banc May Be Ordered. A majority of the circuit judges who are in regular active service and who are not disqualified may order that an appeal or other proceeding be heard or reheard by the court of appeals en banc. An en banc hearing or rehearing is not favored and ordinarily will not be ordered unless:

(1) en banc consideration is necessary to secure or maintain uniformity of the court's decisions; or

(2) the proceeding involves a question of exceptional importance.

(b) Petition for Hearing or Rehearing En Banc. A party may petition for a hearing or rehearing en banc.

(1) The petition must begin with a statement that either:

(A) the panel decision conflicts with a decision of the United States Supreme Court or of the court to which the petition is addressed (with citation to the conflicting case or cases) and consideration by the full court is therefore necessary to secure and maintain uniformity of the court's decisions; or

(B) the proceeding involves one or more questions of exceptional importance, each of which must be concisely stated; for example, a petition may assert that a proceeding presents a question of exceptional importance if it involves an issue on which the panel decision conflicts with the authoritative decisions of other United States Courts of Appeals that have addressed the issue.

(2) Except by the court's permission, a petition for an en banc hearing or rehearing must not exceed 15 pages, excluding material not counted under Rule 32.

(3) For purposes of the page limit in Rule 35(b)(2), if a party files both a petition for panel rehearing and a petition for rehearing en banc, they are considered a single document even if they are filed separately, unless separate filing is required by local rule.

(c) Time for Petition for Hearing or Rehearing En Banc. A petition that an appeal be heard initially en banc must be filed by the date when the appellee's brief is due. A petition for a rehearing en banc must be filed within the time prescribed by Rule 40 for filing a petition for rehearing.

(d) Number of Copies. The number of copies to be filed must be prescribed by local rule and may be altered by order in a particular case.

(e) Response. No response may be filed to a petition for an en banc consideration unless the court orders a response.

(f) Call for a Vote. A vote need not be taken to determine whether the case will be heard or reheard en banc unless a judge calls for a vote.

[Amended April 30, 1979, effective August 1, 1979; April 29, 1994, effective December 1, 1994; April 24, 1998, effective December 1, 1998; April 1, 2005, effective December 1, 2005.]

FRAP 36. ENTRY OF JUDGMENT; NOTICE

(a) Entry. A judgment is entered when it is noted on the docket. The clerk must prepare, sign, and enter the judgment:

(1) after receiving the court's opinion—but if settlement of the judgment's form is required, after final settlement; or

(2) if a judgment is rendered without an opinion, as the court instructs.

(b) Notice. On the date when judgment is entered, the clerk must serve on all parties a copy of the opinion—or the judgment, if no opinion was written—and a notice of the date when the judgment was entered.

[Amended April 24, 1998, effective December 1, 1998; April 29, 2002, effective December 1, 2002.]

FRAP 37. INTEREST ON JUDGMENT

(a) When the Court Affirms. Unless the law provides otherwise, if a money judgment in a civil case is affirmed, whatever interest is allowed by law is payable from the date when the district court's judgment was entered.

(b) When the Court Reverses. If the court modifies or reverses a judgment with a direction that a money judgment be entered in the district court, the mandate must contain instructions about the allowance of interest.

[Amended April 24, 1998, effective December 1, 1998.]

FRAP 38. FRIVOLOUS APPEAL—DAMAGES AND COSTS

If a court of appeals determines that an appeal is frivolous, it may, after a separately filed motion or notice from the court and reasonable opportunity to respond, award just damages and single or double costs to the appellee.

[Amended April 29, 1994, effective December 1, 1994; April 24, 1998, effective December 1, 1998.]

FRAP 39. COSTS

(a) Against Whom Assessed. The following rules apply unless the law provides or the court orders otherwise:

(1) if an appeal is dismissed, costs are taxed against the appellant, unless the parties agree otherwise;

(2) if a judgment is affirmed, costs are taxed against the appellant;

(3) if a judgment is reversed, costs are taxed against the appellee;

(4) if a judgment is affirmed in part, reversed in part, modified, or vacated, costs are taxed only as the court orders.

(b) Costs For and Against the United States. Costs for or against the United States, its agency, or officer will be assessed under Rule 39(a) only if authorized by law.

(c) Costs of Copies. Each court of appeals must, by local rule, fix the maximum rate for taxing the cost of producing necessary copies of a brief or appendix, or copies of records authorized by Rule 30(f). The rate must not exceed that generally charged for such work in the area where the clerk's office is located and should encourage economical methods of copying.

(d) Bill of Costs: Objections; Insertion in Mandate.

(1) A party who wants costs taxed must—within 14 days after entry of judgment—file with the circuit clerk, with proof of service, an itemized and verified bill of costs.

(2) Objections must be filed within 10 days after service of the bill of costs, unless the court extends the time.

(3) The clerk must prepare and certify an itemized statement of costs for insertion in the mandate, but issuance of the mandate must not be delayed for taxing costs. If the mandate issues before costs are finally determined, the district clerk must—upon the circuit clerk's request—add the statement of costs, or any amendment of it, to the mandate.

(e) Costs on Appeal Taxable in the District Court. The following costs on appeal are taxable in the district court for the benefit of the party entitled to costs under this rule:

(1) the preparation and transmission of the record;

(2) the reporter's transcript, if needed to determine the appeal;

(3) premiums paid for a supersedeas bond or other bond to preserve rights pending appeal; and

(4) the fee for filing the notice of appeal.

[Amended April 30, 1979, effective August 1, 1979; March 10, 1986, effective July 1, 1986; April 24, 1998, effective December 1, 1998.]

FRAP 40. PETITION FOR PANEL REHEARING

(a) Time to File; Contents; Answer; Action by the Court if Granted.

(1) *Time.* Unless the time is shortened or extended by order or local rule, a petition for panel rehearing may be filed within 14 days after entry of judgment. But in a civil case, if the United States or its officer or agency is a party, the time within which any party may seek rehearing is 45 days after entry of judgment, unless an order shortens or extends the time.

(2) *Contents.* The petition must state with particularity each point of law or fact that the petitioner believes the court has overlooked or misapprehended and must argue in support of the petition. Oral argument is not permitted.

(3) *Answer.* Unless the court requests, no answer to a petition for panel rehearing is permitted. But ordinarily rehearing will not be granted in the absence of such a request.

(4) *Action by the Court.* If a petition for panel rehearing is granted, the court may do any of the following:

(A) make a final disposition of the case without reargument;

(B) restore the case to the calendar for reargument or resubmission; or

(C) issue any other appropriate order.

(b) Form of Petition; Length. The petition must comply in form with Rule 32. Copies must be served and filed as Rule 31 prescribes. Unless the court permits or a local rule provides otherwise, a petition for panel rehearing must not exceed 15 pages.

[Amended April 30, 1979, effective August 1, 1979; April 29, 1994, effective December 1, 1994; April 24, 1998, effective December 1, 1998.]

FRAP 41. MANDATE: CONTENTS; ISSUANCE AND EFFECTIVE DATE; STAY

(a) Contents. Unless the court directs that a formal mandate issue, the mandate consists of a certified copy of the judgment, a copy of the court's opinion, if any, and any direction about costs.

(b) When Issued. The court's mandate must issue 7 calendar days after the time to file a petition for rehearing expires, or 7 calendar days after entry of an order denying a timely petition for panel rehearing, petition for rehearing en banc, or motion for stay of mandate, whichever is later. The court may shorten or extend the time.

(c) Effective Date. The mandate is effective when issued.

(d) Staying the Mandate.

(1) *On Petition for Rehearing or Motion.* The timely filing of a petition for panel rehearing, petition for rehearing en banc, or motion for stay of mandate, stays the mandate until disposition of the petition or motion, unless the court orders otherwise.

(2) *Pending Petition for Certiorari.*

(A) A party may move to stay the mandate pending the filing of a petition for a writ of certiorari in the Supreme Court. The motion must be served on all parties and must show that the certiorari petition would present a substantial question and that there is good cause for a stay.

(B) The stay must not exceed 90 days, unless the period is extended for good cause or unless the party who obtained the stay files a petition for the writ and so notifies the circuit clerk in writing within the period of the stay. In that case, the stay continues until the Supreme Court's final disposition.

(C) The court may require a bond or other security as a condition to granting or continuing a stay of the mandate.

(D) The court of appeals must issue the mandate immediately when a copy of a Supreme Court order denying the petition for writ of certiorari is filed.

[Amended April 29, 1994, effective December 1, 1994; April 24, 1998, effective December 1, 1998; April 29, 2002, effective December 1, 2002.]

FRAP 42. VOLUNTARY DISMISSAL

(a) Dismissal in the District Court. Before an appeal has been docketed by the circuit clerk, the district court may dismiss the appeal on the filing of a stipulation signed by all parties or on the appellant's motion with notice to all parties.

(b) Dismissal in the Court of Appeals. The circuit clerk may dismiss a docketed appeal if the parties file a signed dismissal agreement specifying how costs are to be paid and pay any fees that are due. But no mandate or other process may issue without a court order. An appeal may be dismissed on the appellant's motion on terms agreed to by the parties or fixed by the court.

[Amended April 24, 1998, effective December 1, 1998.]

FRAP 43. SUBSTITUTION OF PARTIES

(a) Death of a Party.

(1) *After Notice of Appeal Is Filed.* If a party dies after a notice of appeal has been filed or while a proceeding is pending in the court of appeals, the decedent's personal representative may be substituted as a party on motion filed with the circuit clerk by the representative or by any party. A party's motion must be served on the representative in accordance with Rule 25. If the decedent has no representative, any party may suggest the death on the record, and the court of appeals may then direct appropriate proceedings.

(2) *Before Notice of Appeal Is Filed—Potential Appellant.* If a party entitled to appeal dies before filing a notice of appeal, the decedent's personal representative—or, if there is no personal representative, the decedent's attorney of record—may file a notice of appeal within the time prescribed by these rules. After the notice of appeal is filed, substitution must be in accordance with Rule 43(a)(1).

(3) *Before Notice of Appeal Is Filed—Potential Appellee.* If a party against whom an appeal may be taken dies after entry of a judgment or order in the district court, but before a notice of appeal is filed, an appellant may proceed as if the death had not occurred. After the notice of appeal is filed, substitution must be in accordance with Rule 43(a)(1).

(b) Substitution for a Reason Other Than Death. If a party needs to be substituted for any reason other than death, the procedure prescribed in Rule 43(a) applies.

(c) Public Officer: Identification; Substitution.

(1) *Identification of Party.* A public officer who is a party to an appeal or other proceeding in an official capacity may be described as a party by the public officer's official title rather than by name. But the court may require the public officer's name to be added.

(2) *Automatic Substitution of Officeholder.* When a public officer who is a party to an appeal or other proceeding in an official capacity dies, resigns, or otherwise ceases to hold office, the action does not abate. The public officer's successor is automatically substituted as a party. Proceedings following the substitution are to be in the name of the substituted party, but any misnomer that does not affect the substantial rights of the parties may be disregarded. An order of substitution may be entered at any time, but failure to enter an order does not affect the substitution.

[Amended March 10, 1986, effective July 1, 1986; April 24, 1998, effective December 1, 1998.]

FRAP 44. CASE INVOLVING A CONSTITUTIONAL QUESTION WHEN THE UNITED STATES OR THE RELEVANT STATE IS NOT A PARTY

(a) Constitutional Challenge to Federal Statute. If a party questions the constitutionality of an Act of

Congress in a proceeding in which the United States or its agency, officer, or employee is not a party in an official capacity, the questioning party must give written notice to the circuit clerk immediately upon the filing of the record or as soon as the question is raised in the court of appeals. The clerk must then certify that fact to the Attorney General.

(b) Constitutional Challenge to State Statute. If a party questions the constitutionality of a statute of a State in a proceeding in which that State or its agency, officer, or employee is not a party in an official capacity, the questioning party must give written notice to the circuit clerk immediately upon the filing of the record or as soon as the question is raised in the court of appeals. The clerk must then certify that fact to the attorney general of the State.

[Amended April 24, 1998, effective December 1, 1998; April 29, 2002, effective December 1, 2002.]

FRAP 45. CLERK'S DUTIES

(a) General Provisions.

(1) *Qualifications.* The circuit clerk must take the oath and post any bond required by law. Neither the clerk nor any deputy clerk may practice as an attorney or counselor in any court while in office.

(2) *When Court Is Open.* The court of appeals is always open for filing any paper, issuing and returning process, making a motion, and entering an order. The clerk's office with the clerk or a deputy in attendance must be open during business hours on all days except Saturdays, Sundays, and legal holidays. A court may provide by local rule or by order that the clerk's office be open for specified hours on Saturdays or on legal holidays other than New Year's Day, Martin Luther King, Jr.'s Birthday, Washington's Birthday, Memorial Day, Independence Day, Labor Day, Columbus Day, Veterans' Day, Thanksgiving Day, and Christmas Day.

(b) Records.

(1) *The Docket.* The circuit clerk must maintain a docket and an index of all docketed cases in the manner prescribed by the Director of the Administrative Office of the United States Courts. The clerk must record all papers filed with the clerk and all process, orders, and judgments.

(2) *Calendar.* Under the court's direction, the clerk must prepare a calendar of cases awaiting argument. In placing cases on the calendar for argument, the clerk must give preference to appeals in criminal cases and to other proceedings and appeals entitled to preference by law.

(3) *Other Records.* The clerk must keep other books and records required by the Director of the Administrative Office of the United States Courts, with the approval of the Judicial Conference of the United States, or by the court.

(c) Notice of an Order or Judgment. Upon the entry of an order or judgment, the circuit clerk must immediately serve a notice of entry on each party, with a copy of any opinion, and must note the date of service on the docket. Service on a party represented by counsel must be made on counsel.

(d) Custody of Records and Papers. The circuit clerk has custody of the court's records and papers. Unless the court orders or instructs otherwise, the clerk must not permit an original record or paper to be taken from the clerk's office. Upon disposition of the case, original papers constituting the record on appeal or review must be returned to the court or agency from which they were received. The clerk must preserve a copy of any brief, appendix, or other paper that has been filed.

[Amended March 1, 1971, effective July 1, 1971; March 10, 1986, effective July 1, 1986; April 24, 1998, effective December 1, 1998; April 29, 2002, effective December 1, 2002; April 25, 2005, effective December 1, 2005.]

FRAP 46. ATTORNEYS

(a) Admission to the Bar.

(1) *Eligibility.* An attorney is eligible for admission to the bar of a court of appeals if that attorney is of good moral and professional character and is admitted to practice before the Supreme Court of the United States, the highest court of a state, another United States court of appeals, or a United States district court (including the district courts for Guam, the Northern Mariana Islands, and the Virgin Islands).

(2) *Application.* An applicant must file an application for admission, on a form approved by the court that contains the applicant's personal statement showing eligibility for membership. The applicant must subscribe to the following oath or affirmation:

> "I, _______________, do solemnly swear [or affirm] that I will conduct myself as an attorney and counselor of this court, uprightly and according to law; and that I will support the Constitution of the United States."

(3) *Admission Procedures.* On written or oral motion of a member of the court's bar, the court will act on the application. An applicant may be admitted by oral motion in open court. But, unless the court orders otherwise, an applicant need not appear before the court to be admitted. Upon admission, an applicant must pay the clerk the fee prescribed by local rule or court order.

(b) Suspension or Disbarment.

(1) *Standard.* A member of the court's bar is subject to suspension or disbarment by the court if the member:

(A) has been suspended or disbarred from practice in any other court; or

(B) is guilty of conduct unbecoming a member of the court's bar.

(2) *Procedure.* The member must be given an opportunity to show good cause, within the time prescribed by the court, why the member should not be suspended or disbarred.

(3) *Order.* The court must enter an appropriate order after the member responds and a hearing is held, if requested, or after the time prescribed for a response expires, if no response is made.

(c) Discipline. A court of appeals may discipline an attorney who practices before it for conduct unbecoming a member of the bar or for failure to comply with any court rule. First, however, the court must afford the attorney reasonable notice, an opportunity to show cause to the contrary, and, if requested, a hearing.

[Amended March 10, 1986, effective July 1, 1986; April 24, 1998, effective December 1, 1998.]

FRAP 47. LOCAL RULES BY COURTS OF APPEALS

(a) Local Rules.

(1) Each court of appeals acting by a majority of its judges in regular active service may, after giving appropriate public notice and opportunity for comment, make and amend rules governing its practice. A generally applicable direction to parties or lawyers regarding practice before a court must be in a local rule rather than an internal operating procedure or standing order. A local rule must be consistent with—but not duplicative of—Acts of Congress and rules adopted under 28 U.S.C. § 2072 and must conform to any uniform numbering system prescribed by the Judicial Conference of the United States. Each circuit clerk must send the Administrative Office of the United States Courts a copy of each local rule and internal operating procedure when it is promulgated or amended.

(2) A local rule imposing a requirement of form must not be enforced in a manner that causes a party to lose rights because of a nonwillful failure to comply with the requirement.

(b) Procedure When There Is No Controlling Law. A court of appeals may regulate practice in a particular case in any manner consistent with federal law, these rules, and local rules of the circuit. No sanction or other disadvantage may be imposed for noncompliance with any requirement not in federal law, federal rules, or the local circuit rules unless the alleged violator has been furnished in the particular case with actual notice of the requirement.

[Amended April 27, 1995, effective December 1, 1995; April 24, 1998, effective December 1, 1998.]

FRAP 48. MASTERS

(a) Appointment; Powers. A court of appeals may appoint a special master to hold hearings, if necessary, and to recommend factual findings and disposition in matters ancillary to proceedings in the court. Unless the order referring a matter to a master specifies or limits the master's powers, those powers include, but are not limited to, the following:

(1) regulating all aspects of a hearing;

(2) taking all appropriate action for the efficient performance of the master's duties under the order;

(3) requiring the production of evidence on all matters embraced in the reference; and

(4) administering oaths and examining witnesses and parties.

(b) Compensation. If the master is not a judge or court employee, the court must determine the master's compensation and whether the cost is to be charged to any party.

[Former Rule 48 renumbered as Rule 1(c) and new Rule 48 adopted April 29, 1994, effective December 1, 1994; April 24, 1998, effective December 1, 1998.]

APPENDIX OF FORMS

FRAP FORM 1. NOTICE OF APPEAL TO A COURT OF APPEALS FROM A JUDGMENT OR ORDER OF A DISTRICT COURT

United States District Court for the
______ District of ______

File Number ______

A. B., Plaintiff)
v.) Notice of Appeal
C. D., Defendant)

Notice is hereby given that (here name all parties taking the appeal), (plaintiffs) (defendants) in the above named case,* hereby appeal to the United States Court of Appeals for the ________ Circuit (from the final judgment) (from an order (describing it)) entered in this action on the ___ day of ________, ______.

(s)____________________
Attorney for ____________
Address:________________

* See Rule 3(c) for permissible ways of identifying appellants.

[Amended April 22, 1993, effective December 1, 1993; amended March 27, 2003, effective December 1, 2003.]

FRAP FORM 2. NOTICE OF APPEAL TO A COURT OF APPEALS FROM A DECISION OF THE UNITED STATES TAX COURT

UNITED STATES TAX COURT
Washington, D.C.

A.B., Petitioner)
)
v.) Docket No. ______
)
Commissioner of Internal)
Revenue, Respondent)

Notice of Appeal

Notice is hereby given that (here name all parties taking the appeal) * hereby appeal to the United States Court of Appeals for the ________ Circuit from (that part of) the decision of this court entered in the above captioned proceeding on the ___ day of ________, ______ (relating to ________).

(s)____________________
Counsel for ____________
Address:________________

* See Rule 3(c) for permissible ways of identifying appellants.

[Amended April 22, 1993, effective December 1, 1993; amended March 27, 2003, effective December 1, 2003.]

FRAP FORM 3. PETITION FOR REVIEW OF ORDER OF AN AGENCY, BOARD, COMMISSION OR OFFICER

United States Court of Appeals
for the ________ Circuit

A.B., Petitioner)
)
v.) Petition for Review
XYZ Commission,)
Respondent)

(here name all parties bringing the petition)* hereby petition the court for review of the Order of the XYZ Commission (describe the order) entered on ________, 20___.

(s)________________
Attorney for Petitioners
Address:________________

* See Rule 15.

[Amended April 22, 1993, effective December 1, 1993; amended March 27, 2003, effective December 1, 2003.]

FRAP FORM 4. AFFIDAVIT ACCOMPANYING MOTION FOR PERMISSION TO APPEAL IN FORMA PAUPERIS

United States District Court for the ____ District of ____

A.B., Plaintiff
v.
C.D., Defendant

Case No. ______

Affidavit in Support of Motion

I swear or affirm under penalty of perjury that, because of my poverty, I cannot prepay the docket fees of my appeal or post a bond for them. I believe I am entitled to redress. I swear or affirm under penalty of perjury under United States laws that my answers on this form are true and correct. (28 U.S.C. § 1746; 18 U.S.C. § 1621.)

Signed: ________________

Instructions

Complete all questions in this application and then sign it. Do not leave any blanks: if the answer to a question is "0," "none," or "not applicable (N/A)," write in that response. If you need more space to answer a question or to explain your answer, attach a separate sheet of paper identified with your name, your case's docket number, and the question number.

Date: ________________

My issues on appeal are:

1. *For both you and your spouse estimate the average amount of money received from each of the following sources during the past 12 months. Adjust any amount that was received weekly, biweekly, quarterly, semiannually, or annually to show the monthly rate. Use gross amounts, that is, amounts before any deductions for taxes or otherwise.*

Income source	**Average monthly amount during the past 12 months**		**Amount expected next month**	
	You	**Spouse**	**You**	**Spouse**
Employment	$_____	$_____	$_____	$_____
Self-employment	$_____	$_____	$_____	$_____
Income from real property (such as rental income)	$_____	$_____	$_____	$_____
Interest and dividends	$_____	$_____	$_____	$_____

Gifts	$_____	$_____	$_____	$_____
Alimony	$_____	$_____	$_____	$_____
Child support	$_____	$_____	$_____	$_____
Retirement (such as Social Security, pensions, annuities, insurance)	$_____	$_____	$_____	$_____
Disability (such as Social Security, insurance payments)	$_____	$_____	$_____	$_____
Unemployment payments	$_____	$_____	$_____	$_____
Public-assistance (such as welfare)	$_____	$_____	$_____	$_____
Other (specify): _____	$_____	$_____	$_____	$_____
Total monthly income:	$_____	$_____	$_____	$_____

2. *List your employment history, most recent employer first. (Gross monthly pay is before taxes or other deductions.)*

Employer	**Address**	**Dates of employment**	**Gross monthly pay**

3. *List your spouse's employment history, most recent employer first. (Gross monthly pay is before taxes or other deductions.)*

Employer	**Address**	**Dates of employment**	**Gross monthly pay**

4. *How much cash do you and your spouse have?* $_____

Below, state any money you or your spouse have in bank accounts or in any other financial institution.

Financial institution	**Type of account**	**Amount you have**	**Amount your spouse has**
		$_____	$_____
		$_____	$_____
		$_____	$_____

If you are a prisoner, seeking to appeal a judgment in a civil action or proceeding, you must attach a statement certified by the appropriate institutional officer showing all receipts, expenditures, and balances during the last six months in your institutional accounts. If you have multiple accounts, perhaps because you have been in multiple institutions, attach one certified statement of each account.

5. *List the assets, and their values, which you own or your spouse owns. Do not list clothing and ordinary household furnishings.*

Home (Value)	**Other real estate** (Value)	**Motor vehicle # 1** (Value)
		Make & year: _____
		Model: _____
		Registration # : _____

Other Assets (Value)	**Other assets** (Value)	**Motor vehicle # 2** (Value)
		Make & year: _____
		Model: _____
		Registration # : _____

6. *State every person, business, or organization owing you or your spouse money, and the amount owed.*

Person owing you or your spouse money	**Amount owed to you**	**Amount owed to your spouse**

7. *State the persons who rely on you or your spouse for support.*

Name	**Relationship**	**Age**

8. *Estimate the average monthly expenses of you and your family. Show separately the amounts paid by your spouse. Adjust any payments that are made weekly, biweekly, quarterly, semiannually, or annually to show the monthly rate.*

	You	**Your Spouse**
Rent or home-mortgage payment (include lot rented for mobile home)	$_____	$_____
Are real-estate taxes included? ☐ Yes ☐ No		
Is property insurance included? ☐ Yes ☐ No		
Utilities (electricity, heating fuel, water, sewer, and Telephone)	$_____	$_____
Home maintenance (repairs and upkeep)	$_____	$_____
Food	$_____	$_____
Clothing	$_____	$_____
Laundry and dry-cleaning	$_____	$_____
Medical and dental expenses	$_____	$_____
Transportation (not including motor vehicle payments)	$_____	$_____
Recreation, entertainment, newspapers, magazines, etc.	$_____	$_____
Insurance (not deducted from wages or included in Mortgage payments)	$_____	$_____
Homeowner's or renter's	$_____	$_____
Life	$_____	$_____
Health	$_____	$_____
Motor Vehicle	$_____	$_____
Other: _______________________	$_____	$_____
Taxes (not deducted from wages or included in Mortgage payments) (specify): __________	$_____	$_____
Installment payments	$_____	$_____
Motor Vehicle	$_____	$_____
Credit card (name): ____________________	$_____	$_____
Department store (name): ______________	$_____	$_____
Other: _______________________	$_____	$_____
Alimony, maintenance, and support paid to others	$_____	$_____
Regular expenses for operation of business, profession, or farm (attach detailed statement)	$_____	$_____
Other (specify): _________________________	$_____	$_____
Total monthly expenses:	$_____	$_____

9. *Do you expect any major changes to your monthly income or expenses or in your assets or liabilities during the next 12 months?*

☐ Yes ☐ No If yes, describe on an attached sheet.

10. *Have you paid—or will you be paying—an attorney any money for services in connection with this case, including the completion of this form?* Yes No

If yes, how much? $__________

If yes, state the attorney's name, address, and telephone number:

____

____

____

11. *Have you paid—or will you be paying—anyone other than an attorney (such as a paralegal or a typist) any money for services in connection with this case, including the completion of this form?*

☐ Yes ☐ No

If yes, how much? $__________

If yes, state the person's name, address, and telephone number:

____

____

____

12. *Provide any other information that will help explain why you cannot pay the docket fees for your appeal.*

13. *State the address of your legal residence.*

____

____

Your daytime phone number: (___) __________
Your age: ______ Your years of schooling: ______
Your social-security number: __________

[Amended April 24, 1998, effective December 1, 1998; December 1, 2007.]

FRAP FORM 5. NOTICE OF APPEAL TO A COURT OF APPEALS FROM A JUDGMENT OR ORDER OF A DISTRICT COURT OR A BANKRUPTCY APPELLATE PANEL

United States District Court for the
______ District of ______

In re)
________________________)
Debtor)
________________________) File No. ________
A.B., Plaintiff)
v.)
________________________)
C.D., Defendant)

Notice of Appeal to
United States Court of Appeals
for the ______ Circuit

__________, the plaintiff [or defendant or other party] appeals to the United States Court of Appeals for the ______ Circuit from the final judgment [or order or decree] of the district court for the district of ______ [or bankruptcy appellate panel of the ______ circuit], entered in this case on ______, __ [here describe the judgment, order, or decree] __________.

The parties to the judgment [or order or decree] appealed from and the names and addresses of their respective attorneys are as follows:

Dated ____________________

Signed ____________________
Attorney for Appellant

Address: ____________________
____

[Adopted April 25, 1989, effective December 1, 1989; amended March 27, 2003, effective December 1, 2003.]

FRAP FORM 6. CERTIFICATE OF COMPLIANCE WITH RULE 32(a)

Certificate of Compliance With Type–Volume Limitation,
Typeface Requirements, and Type Style Requirements

1. This brief complies with the type-volume limitation of Fed. R. App. P. 32(a)(7)(B) because:

☐ this brief contains [*state the number of*] words, excluding the parts of the brief exempted by Fed. R. App. P. 32(a)(7)(B)(iii), *or*

☐ this brief uses a monospaced typeface and contains [*state the number of*] lines of text, excluding the parts of the brief exempted by Fed. R. App. P. 32(a)(7)(B)(iii).

2. This brief complies with the typeface requirements of Fed. R. App. P. 32(a)(5) and the type style requirements of Fed. R. App. P. 32(a)(6) because:

☐ this brief has been prepared in a proportionally spaced typeface using [*state name and version of word processing program*] in [*state font size and name of type style*], *or*

☐ this brief has been prepared in a monospaced typeface using [*state name and version of word processing program*] with [*state number of characters per inch and name of type style*].

(s)__________________________

Attorney for _____________________

Dated: _______

[Adopted April 29, 2002, effective December 1, 2002.]

INDEX TO FEDERAL RULES OF APPELLATE PROCEDURE

UNITED STATES COURT OF APPEALS FOR THE THIRD CIRCUIT LOCAL APPELLATE RULES AND PROCEDURES

Research Note

These rules may be searched electronically on WESTLAW *in the* US–RULES *database; updates to these rules may be found on* WESTLAW *in* US–RULESUPDATES. *For search tips, and a detailed summary of database content, consult the* WESTLAW *Scope Screen of each database.*

Summary of Contents

THIRD CIRCUIT LOCAL APPELLATE RULES

Effective July 1, 1995

Current with Amendments Received Through August 15, 2008

MISCELLANEOUS LOCAL APPELLATE RULES

THIRD CIRCUIT LOCAL APPELLATE RULES

LAR 1.0. SCOPE AND TITLE OF RULES

1.1 Scope and Organization of Rules.

The following Local Appellate Rules (LAR) are adopted by the United States Court of Appeals for the Third Circuit as supplementary to the Federal Rules of Appellate Procedure (FRAP) and apply to procedure in this court. The numbering of the Local Appellate Rules has been organized to follow the numbering system of the Federal Rules of Appellate Procedure in order to increase public accessibility to the Rules. Where a local rule has no counterpart in the Federal Rules of Appellate Procedure it is classified as a Miscellaneous Rule. The Miscellaneous Local Appellate Rules begin with Rule 101.0.

Source: 1988 Court Rule 1.1

Cross-references: 28 U.S.C. § 2072; FRAP 1, 47

Committee Comments:

The Local Appellate Rules bind all litigants in this court. Each Local Appellate Rule is numbered to correspond to its counterpart in the Federal Rules, e.g., Local Appellate Rule 1.0 corresponds to Federal Rule of Appellate Procedure 1. Cross-references are provided for convenience and are not intended to be exhaustive. Committee Comments are provided by the court's Rules Committee and are intended to guide, but not bind, litigants in this court.

1.2 Title; Citation Form

These rules may be known as the Third Circuit Local Appellate Rules, and cited as 3rd Cir. LAR ___ (1997).

Source: None

Cross-references: FRAP 1

Committee Comments:

The Local Rules Project of the Judicial Conference Committee on Rules and Practice recommends that all courts of appeals follow a uniform numbering and citation system, for ease of reference and indexing of local rules. This court follows the recommendation of the Local Rules Project. (As amended Nov. 1997.)

LAR 3.0. APPEAL AS OF RIGHT—HOW TAKEN

3.1 Notice To Trial Judge; Opinion In Support Of Order

At the time of the filing of the notice of appeal, the appellant shall mail a copy thereof by ordinary mail to the trial judge. Within 15 days thereafter, the trial judge may file and mail to the parties a written opinion or a written amplification of a prior written or oral recorded ruling or opinion. Failure to give notice of the appeal to the trial judge shall not affect the jurisdiction of this court.

Source: 1988 Court Rules 8.4

Cross–References: FRAP 3, 24, Form 1, Form 3

Committee Comments:

A district court may properly prepare an opinion or memorandum explaining a decision after an appeal is taken. The rule is not intended to inhibit or discourage district courts from preparing opinions as they presently do. To the contrary, the rule was designed to provide more flexibility. Prior Court Rule 8.4 has been amended to apply to all appellants, not simply *pro se* habeas corpus petitioners. Otherwise, no substantive change from prior Court Rule 8.4 is intended. This rule does not authorize a trial judge to change a prior ruling except as provided by rule 5.9.

3.2 Joint Notice of Appeal

When parties have filed a joint notice of appeal, only one appeal will be docketed and only one docketing fee paid. Parties filing a joint notice of appeal shall file a single consolidated brief and appendix.

Source: None

Cross-references: FRAP 3(b), 28(i), 31

Committee Comments:

New provision.

3.3 Payment of Fees

(a) If a proceeding is docketed without prepayment of the applicable docketing fee, the appellant shall pay the fee within fourteen (14) days after docketing. If the appellant fails to do so, the clerk is authorized to dismiss the appeal.

(b) If an action has been dismissed pursuant to 28 U.S.C. § 1915 as frivolous or malicious, or if the district court certifies pursuant to § 1915(a) and FRAP 24(a) that an appeal is not taken in good faith, the appellant may either pay the applicable docketing fee or file a motion to proceed *in forma pauperis* within 14 days after docketing. If appellant fails to either pay the applicable docketing fee or file the motion to proceed *in forma pauperis*, the clerk is authorized to dismiss the appeal 30 days after docketing of the appeal.

Source: 1988 Court Rule 28.1

Cross–References: 28 U.S.C. § 1915; FRAP 3(a), 24(a); 3rd Cir. LAR 39.2, Misc. 107.2(a)

Committee Comments:

Subsection (b) is a new provision which codifies existing practice. Subsection (b) is not intended to preclude a litigant who did not seek leave to proceed in forma pauperis in the district court from requesting leave to proceed in forma pauperis in the court of appeals.

3.4 Notice of Appeal in Pro Se Cases

The court shall deem a paper filed by a pro se litigant after the decision of the district court in a civil, criminal, or habeas corpus case to be a notice of appeal despite informality in its form or title, if it evidences an intention to appeal. The court shall deem an application for leave to appeal in forma pauperis or an application to this court for a certificate of appealability to be a notice of appeal if no formal notice has been filed. The grant or denial of a certificate of appealability by the district court shall not be treated as a notice of appeal.

Source: 1988 Court Rules 8.1, 8.3

Cross–References: 28 U.S.C. § 2253; FRAP 3, 22(b), 24, Form 1, Form 3

Committee Comments:

This rule is designed to emphasize that the jurisdictional requirement of a notice of appeal is met in a *pro se* case by the filing of either an informal document or a request for certificate of appealability or a motion for *in forma pauperis* status in this court, but not by the mere granting or denial by the district court of a certificate of appealability. The portions of prior Court Rule 8 that were repetitive of FRAP 3 and 4 have been deleted; otherwise no substantive change from prior Court Rule 8 is intended. Technical changes were made to conform to the Antiterrorism and Effective Death Penalty Act. This rule takes no position on the question of whether a district court can grant or deny a certificate of appealability.

(As amended Nov. 1997.)

LAR 4.0. APPEAL AS OF RIGHT—WHEN TAKEN

4.1 Expedited Appeals

A party who seeks an expedited appeal shall file a motion within fourteen (14) days of the notice of appeal setting forth the exceptional reason that warrants expedition. If a reason for expedition arises thereafter, the moving party shall file a motion within fourteen (14) days of the date the reason occurred. Motions seeking an expedited appeal shall include a proposed briefing schedule that has been agreed upon by the parties, if possible, but if they cannot agree, they should submit their own proposal with reasons in the motion or response. The non-moving party may agree to a proposed briefing schedule without conceding that expedition is necessary. A response to the motion, if any, shall be filed within seven (7) days after service of the motion and any reply within three (3) days after service of the response unless otherwise directed by the court or clerk. The court or clerk may direct that service be made in the manner provided by L.A.R. 27.7.

Source: None

Cross-references: FRAP 4

Committee Comments:

New provision. This rule has been added to emphasize that a request for an expedited appeal should be made promptly.

(As amended Nov. 1997; Nov. 1999, eff. Jan. 1, 2000; eff. Jan. 1, 2002.)

LAR 8.0. STAY OR INJUNCTION PENDING APPEAL

8.1 Motion for Stay in Court of Appeals

A motion for a stay of the judgment or order of a district court or the decision of the United States Tax Court pending appeal, or for an order suspending, modifying, restoring or granting an injunction during the pendency of an appeal shall include a copy of any relevant judgment, decision, or order of the district court or the decision of the United States Tax Court and any accompanying opinion. Failure to do so shall be grounds for dismissal of the motion.

Source: 1988 Court Rules 11.2, 11.4

Cross-references: FRAP 8, 18, 27; 3rd Cir. LAR 18.0, 27.0

Committee Comments:

This rule has been revised to apply to decisions of the United States Tax Court as well as the judgments and orders of the United States district court. Otherwise, no substantive change from prior Court Rules 11.2 or 11.4 is intended. The rule was amended to delete references to a supersedeas bond, because approval of a supersedeas bond must be sought in the district court under Fed. R. App. Pro. 8.1(C).

8.2 Expedited Consideration

If the court or clerk determines that a motion under L.A.R. 8.1 requires expedited treatment, proceedings in regard to the motion will be in accordance with L.A.R. 27.7.

Source: New provision

Cross-references: None

Committee Comments:

Section 8.2 was added to clarify procedures in expedited cases.

8.3 Death Penalty Cases

Except as provided in 28 U.S.C. § 2262, the provisions of 3rd Cir. LAR Misc. 111.0 shall govern all stay proceedings in death penalty cases, including appeals from the grant or denial of a petition under 28 U.S.C. §§ 2254 or 2255, applications to file a second or successive petition under 28 U.S.C. § 2244 and/or § 2255, and in original habeas corpus actions challenging a conviction in which a sentence of death has been imposed. In a direct appeal of conviction or sentence in a criminal case in which the district court has imposed a sentence of death, an order shall be entered staying the sentence.

Source: None

Cross-references: FRAP 8, 22; Fed.R.Crim.Pro. 38(a); 3rd Cir. LAR Misc. 111.0

Committee Comments:

New provision. To the extent consistent with F.R.A.P. and applicable statutes, all local procedure in death penalty proceedings will be governed by 3rd Cir. LAR Misc. 111.0. Technical changes were made to conform to the Antiterrorism and Effective Death Penalty Act.

(As amended Nov. 1997; eff. Jan. 1, 2002.)

LAR 9.0. RELEASE IN CRIMINAL CASES

9.1 Appeals of Orders Relating to Release or Detention; Release Before Judgment of Conviction

(a) *Appeals of Orders Relating to Release or Detention Before Judgment of Conviction.* An appeal from an order granting or denying release from custody with or without bail or for detention of a defendant prior to judgment of conviction shall be by motion filed either concurrently with or promptly after filing a notice of appeal. The movant shall set forth in the body of the motion the applicable facts and law and attach a copy of the reasons given by the district court for its order. The opposing party may file a response within three (3) days after service of the motion, unless the court directs that the time shall be shortened or extended.

(b) *Release After Judgment of Conviction.* Requests for release from custody or for detention of a defendant after judgment of conviction shall be by motion filed expeditiously. The time periods and form requirements set forth in 3rd Cir. LAR 9.1(a) are applicable to such motions.

Source: 1988 Court Rules 11.3, 11.4

Cross-references: FRAP 9, 27; 3rd Cir. LAR 27.0

Committee Comments:

No substantive change is intended from prior Court Rule 11.3.

(As amended Nov. 1997; Nov. 1999, eff. Jan. 1, 2000.)

LAR 11.0. TRANSMISSION OF THE RECORD

11.1 Duty of Appellant

Within ten (10) days after filing a notice of appeal, the appellant shall deposit with the court reporter the estimated cost of the transcript of all or the necessary part of the notes of testimony taken at trial. Where an appellant cannot afford the cost of transcripts, counsel for appellant, or the appellant *pro se*, shall make application to the district court within 10 days of the notice of appeal for the provision of such transcript pursuant to 28 U.S.C. § 753(f). If the district court denies the application, appellant shall, within 10 days of the order denying the application, either deposit with the court reporter the fees for such transcript or apply to the court of appeals for the transcript at government expense. Failure to comply with this rule shall be grounds for dismissal of the appeal.

Source: 1988 Court Rule 15.1

Cross-references: 28 U.S.C. § 753(f); FRAP 10(b), 11(a); 3rd Cir. LAR 10.1(b), Misc. 107.1(b)

Committee Comments:

No substantive change from prior Court Rule 15.1 is intended. The rule codifies current practice.

11.2 Retention of the Record in the District Court

A certified copy of the docket entries in the district court shall be transmitted to the clerk of this court in lieu of the entire record in all counseled appeals. In all *pro se* cases, the entire record, including briefs filed in support of dispositive motions, shall be certified and transmitted to the clerk of this court. The clerk of the district court shall transmit the entire district court record in any state habeas case or habeas case emanating from any territorial courts, whether counseled or *pro se.* In such cases, the clerk of the district court shall transmit to the court of appeals any state or territorial records lodged with the district court during its determination of the habeas case.

Source: 1988 Court Rule 14.1

Cross-references: FRAP 11(e); 22(b)

Committee Comments:

No substantive change from current practice or prior Court Rule 14.1 is intended. The granting of a motion to proceed on the original record exempt a litigant from filing an appendix. Transmission of the record by the district court to the court of appeals is not a prerequisite to the granting of such motion. The fact that the district court clerk has transmitted the record to the court of appeals does not dictate the granting of the motion.

(As amended Nov. 1997.)

LAR 15.0. REVIEW OR ENFORCEMENT OF AGENCY ORDERS—HOW OBTAINED; INTERVENTION

15.1 Brief and Argument in Enforcement and Review Proceedings

In any enforcement or review proceeding with respect to an order or action of a federal agency or board, each party adverse to the agency or board shall be considered to be the petitioner(s) and the federal agency or board to be the respondent, solely for the procedural purposes of briefing and oral argument, unless the court orders otherwise. Nothing in this rule shall have the effect of changing or modifying the burden of the agency or board of establishing its right to enforcement.

Source: 1988 Court Rule 26.1

Cross-references: FRAP 15

Committee Comments:

The portions of prior Court Rule 26.1 that were repetitive of FRAP 15 have been deleted. This rule has been designed to expand the procedure which FRAP 15.1 limits to a single agency, the National Labor Relations Board, to encompass all federal administrative agencies.

(As amended Nov. 1997.)

LAR 18.0. STAY PENDING REVIEW

18.1 Stay of an Order or Decision of an Agency

An application to this court for stay of the judgment or order of an agency pending review, for approval of a supersedeas bond, or for an order suspending, modifying, restoring, or granting an injunction during the pendency of an appeal shall include a copy of the relevant judgment, decision, or order of the agency and any accompanying opinion. Failure to do so shall be grounds for dismissal of the motion.

Source: 1988 Court Rules 11.2, 11.4

Cross-references: FRAP 8, 18, 27; 3rd Cir. LAR 27.0

Committee Comments:

No substantive change from prior Court Rules 1.2 or 11.4 is intended.

(As amended Nov. 1997.)

LAR 22.0. HABEAS CORPUS PROCEEDINGS

22.1 Necessity of Certificate of Appealability

(a) When a certificate of appealability is required, a formal application should be filed with the court of appeals, but the court may deem a paper filed by a habeas corpus petitioner that discloses the intent to obtain appellate review to be an application for a certificate of appealability, regardless of its title or form. If an application is not filed with the notice of appeal, the appellant may file and serve an application within 21 days of either the docketing of the appeal in the court of appeals or of the entry of the order of the district court denying a certificate, whichever is later. The respondents may, but need not unless directed by the court, file a memorandum in opposition to the granting of a certificate, within 14 days of service of the application. The appellant may, but need not, file a reply within 10 days of service of the response. The length and form of any application, response, or reply must conform to the requirements of Fed. R. App. P. 27 governing motions.

(b) If the district court grants a certificate of appealability as to only some issues, the court of appeals will not consider uncertified issues unless petitioner first seeks, and the court of appeals grants, certification of additional issues. Petitioners desiring certification of additional issues must file, in the court of appeals, a separate motion for additional certification, along with a statement of the reasons why a certificate should be granted as to any issue(s) within 21 days of the docketing of the appeal in the court of appeals. Respondents may file a memorandum in opposition within 14 days of service of the application. Petitioner's reply, if any, must be filed within 10 days of the service of the response. The length and form of any application, response, or reply, must conform to the requirements of Rule 27, Fed. R. App. Pro. governing motions. If granted, the order must be attached to the petitioner's brief included in volume one of the appendix, which may be attached to the petitioner's brief. If the motions panel denies the motion to certify additional issues, the parties should brief only the issues certified unless the merits panel directs briefing of any additional issues.

(c) In a multi-issue case if the district court grants a certificate of appealability, but does not specify on which issues the certificate is granted as required by 28 U.S.C. § 2253(c)(3), the clerk shall remand the case for specification of the issues.

(d) A certificate of appealability is required if a petitioner files a cross-appeal. The petitioner should apply to the district court for a certificate in the first instance.

Source: 1988 Court Rule 13.1

Cross-references: 28 U.S.C. § 2253; F.R.A.P. 3, 22; 3rd Cir. L.A.R. 3.4

Committee Comments:

The portions of prior Court Rule 13 that were repetitive of F.R.A.P. 22 have been deleted; otherwise no substantive change from prior Court Rule 13.1 is intended. Technical changes were made to conform to Fed. R. App. P. 27. The response time was lengthened to permit litigants sufficient time to file an application or response.

22.2 Statement of Reasons for Certificate of Appealability

At the time a final order denying a petition under 28 U.S.C. § 2254 or § 2255 is issued, the district judge shall make a determination as to whether a certificate of appealability should issue. If the district judge issues a certificate, the judge shall state the specific issue or issues that satisfy the criteria of 28 U.S.C. § 2253. If an order denying a petition under § 2254 or § 2255 is accompanied by an opinion or a magistrate judge's report, it is sufficient if the order denying the certificate references the opinion or report. If the district judge has not made a determination as to whether to issue a certificate of appealability by the time of the docketing of the appeal, the clerk shall enter an order remanding the case to the district court for a prompt determination as to whether a certificate should issue.

Source: F.R.A.P. 22

Cross-references: 28 U.S.C. §§ 2253, 2254, 2255; F.R.A.P. 22

Committee Comments:

Technical changes were made to conform to the Antiterrorism and Effective Death Penalty Act. This rule takes no position on the question of whether a district court can grant or deny a certificate of appealability.

22.3 Review of Application for Certificate of Appealability

An application for a certificate of appealability will be referred to a panel of three judges. If all the judges on the panel conclude that the certificate should not issue, the certificate will be denied, but if any judge of the panel is of the opinion that the applicant has made the showing required by 28 U.S.C. § 2253, the certificate will issue.

Source: FRAP 22

Cross-references: 28 U.S.C. § 2253; FRAP 22

Committee Comments:

Technical changes were made to conform to the Antiterrorism and Effective Death Penalty Act.

22.4 Death Penalty Cases

The provisions of 3rd Cir. LAR Misc. 111.0 shall govern all appeals from the grant or denial of a petition for writ of habeas corpus or original habeas corpus proceedings challenging a conviction in which a sentence of death has been imposed.

Source: None

Cross-references: FRAP 8, 22; 3rd Cir. LAR 8.0, Misc. 111.0

Committee Comments:

New provision. To the extent consistent with FRAP and applicable, local procedure in all death penalty proceedings will be governed by 3rd Cir. LAR Misc. 111.0.

22.5 Application for Authorization to File a Second or Successive Petition Under 28 U.S.C. § 2254 or § 2255

(a) Forms for filing an application to file a second or successive petition under 28 U.S.C. § 2254 or § 2255 are available from the clerk. If the form application is not used, the application must contain the information requested in the form. The application must be accompanied by:

(1) the proposed new § 2254 or § 2255 petition;

(2) copies of all prior § 2254 or § 2255 petitions;

(3) copies of the docket entries in all prior § 2254 or § 2255 proceedings;

(4) copies of all magistrate judge's reports, district court opinions and orders disposing of the prior petitions; and

(5) any other relevant documents.

(b) The application may be accompanied by a memorandum, not exceeding 20 pages, clearly stating how the standards of § 2244(b) and/or § 2255 are satisfied.

(c) The movant shall serve a copy of the application for authorization to file a second or successive petition and all accompanying attachments on the appropriate respondent.

(d) Any response to the application must be filed within 7 days of the filing of the application with the clerk.

(e) If the court determines that the motion and accompanying materials are not sufficiently complete to assess the motion, the court may deny the motion with or without prejudice to refiling or may in its discretion treat the motion as lodged, the filing being deemed complete when the deficiency is remedied.

(f) The clerk shall transmit a copy of any order granting authorization to file a second or successive petition to the appropriate district court together with a copy of the petition.

(g) No filing fee is required for an application to file a second or successive petition. If the application is granted, the filing of the petition in the district court will be subject to the requirements of 28 U.S.C. § 1915(a).

(h) If the district court enters an order transferring to the court of appeals an application to file a second or successive petition or a § 2254 or § 2255 petition that the district court deems to be a second or successive petition requiring authorization, the clerk of the district court shall promptly transmit the record to the court of appeals. The record shall include the documents listed in part (a)(1) through (5) of this rule. The clerk of the district court shall transmit copies of its order of transfer and any necessary documents to the appropriate respondent.

(i) If a case transferred by the district court does not contain a statement by the applicant as to how the standards of § 2244(b) or § 2255 are satisfied, the clerk may direct the applicant to file a memorandum clearly stating how the statutory standards are met. Failure to file a memorandum as directed will result in the dismissal of the case by the clerk without further notice. If the applicant files a memorandum as directed, the time prescribed in § 2244(b)(3)(D) for deciding the application will run from the date the memorandum is filed.

(j) If an appeal is taken in a case in which the district court issued an order denying a petition under § 2254 or § 2255 on the grounds that it is a second or successive petition that requires authorization under § 2244, the record on appeal transmitted to this court shall include the documents listed in part (a)(1) through (5) of this rule.

Source: F.R.A.P. 22

Cross-references: 28 U.S.C. §§ 2244, 2253, 2254, 2255; F.R.A.P. 22

Committee Comments:

Technical changes were made to conform to the Antiterrorism and Effective Death Penalty Act.

The portions of prior Court Rule 13 that were repetitive of F.R.A.P. 22 have been deleted; otherwise no substantive change from prior Court Rule 13.1 is intended. Technical changes were made to conform to Fed. R. App. P. 27. The response time was lengthened to permit litigants sufficient time to file an application or response.

(As amended Nov. 1997; Nov. 1999, eff. Jan. 1, 2000; eff. Jan. 1, 2002.)

LAR 24.0. PROCEEDINGS IN FORMA PAUPERIS

24.1 Documents Required with Application

(a) In civil cases in which 28 U.S.C. § 1915(b) applies, prisoners seeking to proceed on appeal in forma pauperis shall file the following documents in the court of appeals:

(1) an affidavit of poverty that includes the amount in the prisoner's prison account;

(2) a certified copy of the prison account statement(s) (or institutional equivalent) for the 6 month period immediately preceding the filing of the notice of appeal; and

(3) a signed form authorizing prison officials to assess and deduct the filing fees in accordance with 28 U.S.C. § 1915(b).

(b) After the filing of the documents required in subsection (a) in civil cases in which 28 U.S.C. § 1915(b) applies, the clerk will issue an order directing the warden of the prison to assess and deduct the filing fees in accordance with 28 U.S.C. § 1915(b).

(c) In cases filed in which 28 U.S.C. § 1915(b) does not apply, prisoners seeking to proceed on appeal in forma pauperis shall file an affidavit of poverty in the form prescribed by the Federal Rules of Appellate Procedure accompanied by a certified statement of the prison account statement(s) (or institutional equivalent) for the 6 month period preceding the filing of the notice of appeal or petition for extraordinary writ. No assessment order will be entered unless the court determines that the case is subject to the requirements of § 1915(b) and directs that assessments be made.

Source: None

Cross-references: 28 U.S.C. § 1915

Committee Comments:

Technical changes were made to conform to the Prison Litigation Reform Act.

24.2 Failure to File

Failure to file any of the documents specified in Rule 24.1 will result in the dismissal of the appeal by the clerk under LAR Misc. 107.1(a).

Source: None

Cross-references: LAR Misc. 107.1(a)

Committee Comments:

None

24.3 Issuance of Order

If the affidavit in support of a motion to proceed in forma pauperis demonstrates that the appellant qualifies for in forma pauperis status and the appellant is not precluded from proceeding in forma pauperis under 28 U.S.C. § 1915(g), the clerk will issue an order granting in forma pauperis status. If 28 U.S.C. § 1915(b) applies, the order shall direct prison officials to assess and deduct the filing fees in accordance with the statute and transmit such fees to the appropriate district court. The clerk shall send a copy of the order to the prisoner, the warden of the prison where appellant is incarcerated, and the appropriate district court.

Source: None

Cross-references: 28 U.S.C. § 1915

Committee Comments:

Technical changes were made to conform to the Prison Litigation Reform Act.

(Added Nov. 1997, as amended eff. Jan. 1, 2002.)

LAR 25.0. FILING AND SERVICE

25.1 Facsimile Filing

Papers may not be filed by facsimile without prior authorization by the clerk. Authorization may be secured only in situations determined by the clerk to be of an emergency nature or other compelling circumstance. In such cases, the original signed document must be filed promptly thereafter.

Source: None

Cross-references: None

Committee Comments:

This rule deals solely with filing by fax. The filing of briefs by e-mail or other electronic means (not including fax) is governed by LAR 31.1.

(As amended Nov. 1997.)

LAR 26.1.0. CORPORATE DISCLOSURE STATEMENT

26.1.1 Disclosure of Corporate Affiliations and Financial Interest

(a) Promptly after the notice of appeal is filed, each corporation that is a party to an appeal, whether in a civil, bankruptcy, or criminal case, shall file a corporate affiliate/financial interest disclosure statement on a form provided by the clerk that identifies every publicly owned corporation not named in the appeal with which it is affiliated. The form shall be completed whether or not the corporation has anything to report.

(b) Every party to an appeal shall identify on the disclosure statement required by FRAP 26.1 every publicly owned corporation not a party to the appeal, if any, that has a financial interest in the outcome of the litigation and the nature of that interest. The form shall be completed only if a party has something to report under this section.

(c) In all bankruptcy appeals, counsel for the debtor or trustee of the bankruptcy estate shall promptly provide to the clerk in writing a list identifying (1) the debtor, if not named in the caption, (2) the members of the creditors' committees or the top 20 unsecured creditors, and (3) any entity not named in the caption which is an active participant in the proceeding. If the debtor or trustee of the bankruptcy estate is not a party, the appellant shall file this list with the clerk.

Source: 1988 Court Rule 25

Cross-references: 28 U.S.C. § 455; FRAP 26.1

Committee Comments:

Subsection (c) is new. Prior Court Rule 25 imposed an obligation upon all parties to civil or bankruptcy cases and all corporate defendants in criminal cases to file a corporate affiliate/financial interest disclosure statement. 3rd Cir. LAR 26.1.1(a) limits that obligation to corporate parties only. The rule also provides that the statement shall be filed promptly after the notice of appeal is filed, and shall be made on a form provided by the clerk. 3rd Cir. LAR 26.1.1(b) retains the requirement that every party to an appeal disclose the identity of every publicly owned corporation, not a party to an appeal, that has a financial interest in the outcome of the litigation. The revised rule specifies that, under these circumstances, a negative report need not be filed.

26.1.2 Notice of Possible Judicial Disqualification

If any judge of this court participated at any stage of the case, in the trial court or in related state court proceedings, appellant, promptly after filing the notice of appeal, shall separately notify the clerk in writing of the judge and the other action, and shall send a copy of such notice to appellee's counsel. Appellee has a corresponding responsibility to so notify the clerk if, for any reason, appellant fails to comply with this rule fully and accurately.

Source: 1988 Court Rule 19.1

Cross-references: 28 U.S.C. §§ 144, 455; FRAP 26.1

Committee Comments:

Prior Court Rule 19.1 required appellant to notify the clerk of a possible judicial disqualification when filing the opening brief. 3rd Cir. LAR 26.1.2 now requires appellant to notify the clerk of such disqualification promptly after filing the notice of appeal. 3rd Cir. LAR 26.1.2 adds a new requirement that appellee notify the clerk of any possible disqualification if appellant fails to do so.

(As amended Nov. 1997.)

LAR 27.0. MOTIONS

27.1 No Oral Argument Except When Ordered

Motions are considered and decided by the court upon the motion papers and briefs without oral argument unless ordered by the court or a judge thereof. Counsel may assume there will not be oral argument unless advised by the clerk to appear at a time and place fixed by the court.

Source: 1988 Court Rule 11.1

Cross-references: FRAP 8, 9, 18, 21, 27, 34, 40; 3rd Cir. LAR 8.1, 9.0, 18.0

Committee Comments:

No substantive change from prior Court Rule 11.1 is intended.

27.2 Service

Motions shall ordinarily be served on other parties by means equally expeditious to those used to file the motion with the court. When time does not permit actual service on other parties, or the moving party has reason to believe that another party may not receive the motion in sufficient time to respond before the court acts (as in certain emergency motions), the moving party should notify such other parties by telephone or facsimile of the filing of the motion.

Source: None

Cross-references: FRAP 8, 9, 18, 25, 27, 41; 3rd Cir. LAR 8.1, 9.0, 18.0

Committee Comments:

New provision. The seven-day period for filing a response provided by FRAP 27(a) runs from the time of service. If service is not effectuated promptly, the disposition of the motion may be delayed or parties opposing the motion may not have an opportunity to respond before the court rules on the motion.

27.3 Uncontested Motions

Each uncontested motion shall be certified as uncontested by counsel. In the absence of a timely response, the court may treat a motion without such certification as uncontested.

Source: None

Cross-references: FRAP 8, 9, 18, 27, 41; 3rd Cir. LAR 8.1, 9.0, 18.0

Committee Comments:

New provision. The seven-day period for filing a response provided by FRAP 27(a) is unnecessary where a motion is uncontested. A certification to that effect will aid in the speedy disposition of the motion.

27.4 Motions for Summary Action

A party may move for summary action affirming, enforcing, vacating, remanding, modifying, setting aside or reversing a judgment, decree or order, alleging that no substantial question is presented or that subsequent precedent or a change in circumstances warrants such action. In addition, the court may *sua sponte* list a case for summary action.

Source: Third Circuit Internal Operating Procedures 10.6 (1990)

Cross-references: 28 U.S.C. § 2106; FRAP 27; Third Circuit Internal Operating Procedure 10.6 (1994)

Committee Comments:

No substantive change from current practice or IOP 10.6 is intended. The filing of a motion for summary action does not stay the regular briefing schedule set forth in FRAP 31(a).

27.5 Powers Of Single Judge

A single judge of the court may not grant or deny a motion that the court has ordered to be acted on by the court or a panel thereof, and ordinarily a single judge will not entertain and grant or deny a motion for release or for modification of the conditions of release pending review in a criminal case, a motion for leave to intervene, or a motion to postpone the oral argument in a case which has been included by the clerk in the argument list for a particular weekly session of the court. The action of a single judge may be reviewed by a panel of the court.

Source: 1988 Court Rule 2.4

Cross-references: FRAP 27(c); Third Circuit Internal Operating Procedure 10.5 (1994)

Committee Comments:

Prior Court Rule 2.4 provided that a single judge could not entertain a motion for leave to file a brief as amicus curiae or a motion that a party requests be heard orally by the Court. 3rd Cir. LAR 27.5 removes these restrictions and permits a single judge to entertain such motions.

27.6 Motions Decided By The Clerk

If the court so orders, the clerk may entertain and dispose of any motion that can ordinarily be disposed of by a single judge of this court under the provisions of FRAP 27(c) and 3rd Cir. LAR 27.5, provided the subject of the motion is ministerial, relates to the preparation or printing of the appendix and briefs on appeal, or relates to calendar control. If application is promptly made, the action of the clerk may be reviewed in the first instance by a single judge or by a panel of the court.

Source: 1988 Court Rule 11.5

Cross-references: FRAP 27

Committee Comments:

No substantive change from prior Court Rule 11.5 is intended.

27.7 Motions in Which Expedited Consideration Is Requested

If the court or clerk determines that a motion requires expedited consideration, the court or the clerk shall direct that a response in opposition, if any, must be filed within seven (7) days after service of the motion and any reply within three (3) days after service of the response unless a shorter time is directed by the court or clerk. Service of documents filed under this rule, including the initial motion shall be in accordance with L.A.R. 27.2 unless the court or clerk directs that a more expeditious method of service be used. To the fullest extent possible, the clerk should be given advance notice that a motion requiring expedited consideration may be filed.

Source: New Provision

Cross-references: LAR 8.0

Committee Comments:

Section 27.7 was added to clarify procedures for expedited motions.

27.8 Electronic Transmission of Emergency Motions. A party may file an emergency motion by electronic transmission only with prior approval of the Clerk. Approval of the Clerk may be obtained by telephone. Any emergency motion or any other document submitted electronically without first receiving prior permission from the Clerk will not be filed and no action will be taken on the motion or document.

Motions which are submitted electronically must be in either PDF, Word Perfect 8 or higher version, or Microsoft Word 2000 or higher version. The page limitations set forth in FRAP 27(d)(2) will be strictly enforced. Any exhibits in support of the motion must be submitted as a separate file.

Service of any emergency motion submitted electronically must be by electronic transmission, fax, or hand delivery. The certificate of service shall specify the manner of service. A hard copy of the motion and its exhibits must be forwarded to the Clerk by overnight mail.

The requirements for motions set forth in this rule shall apply to any responses or replies which may be submitted electronically. A party filing a response or reply electronically shall alert the Clerk by telephone prior to the transmission of the document.

(As amended Nov. 1997; eff. Jan. 1, 2002; Sept. 11, 2002.)

LAR 28.0. BRIEFS

28.1 Brief of the Appellant

(a) The brief of appellant/petitioner shall include, in addition to the sections enumerated in F.R.A.P. 28, the following:

(1) in the statement of the issues presented for review required by F.R.A.P. 28(a)(5), a designation by reference to specific pages of the appendix or place in the proceedings at which each issue on appeal was raised, objected to, and ruled upon;

(2) a statement of related cases and proceedings, stating whether this case or proceeding has been before this court previously, and whether the party is aware of any other case or proceeding that is in any way related, completed, pending or about to be presented before this court or any other court or agency, state or federal. If the party is aware of any previous or pending appeals before this court arising out of the same case or proceeding, the statement should identify each such case; and

(3) See LAR 32.2(c) for other attachments to the brief.

(b) The statement of the standard or scope of review for each issue on appeal, i.e., whether the trial court abused its discretion; whether its fact findings are clearly erroneous; whether it erred in formulating or applying a legal precept, in which case review is plenary; whether, on appeal or petition for review of an agency action, there is substantial evidence in the record as a whole to support the order or decision, or whether the agency's action, findings and conclusions should be held unlawful and set aside for the reasons set forth in 5 U.S.C. § 706(2), should appear under a separate heading placed before the discussion of the issue in the argument section.

(c) The court expects counsel to exercise appropriate professional behavior in all briefs and to refrain from making ad hominem attacks on opposing counsel or parties.

Source: 1988 Court Rule 21.1

Cross-references: F.R.A.P. 28–32, 39; 3rd Cir. L.A.R. 29–32, 39

Committee Comments:

3rd Cir. L.A.R. 28.1 contains a new requirement that the appellant must designate where in the proceedings each issue was preserved for appeal. Appellant should cite to the appendix, but if the germane portion of the record is not included in the appendix, the appellant shall cite to the original record. If the matter has not been filed of record in the district court, appellant may cite to the original document. 3rd Cir. L.A.R. 28.1 no longer requires parties to file a separate statement with the Clerk's Office identifying any previous or pending appeals because such matters must be identified in the briefs. 3rd Cir. L.A.R. 28.1 also makes explicit for the first time the court's expectation that counsel will write briefs in a professional manner and refrain from making ad hominem attacks on the opposing side. The portions of prior Court Rule 21.1 that were repetitive of F.R.A.P. 28 have been deleted. See L.A.R. 32.2(c) for permissible attachments to the brief.

28.2 Brief of the Appellee

The brief of the appellee or respondent shall conform to the requirements of FRAP 28(b) and 3rd Cir. LAR 28.1(a)(ii), (b) and (c). If the appellee is also a cross-appellant, the appellee's brief shall also comply with rules 28.1(a)(i) and (a)(iii). The brief of an appellee who has been permitted to file one brief in consolidated appeals shall contain an appropriate cross reference index which clearly identifies and relates appellee's answering contentions to the specific contentions of the various appellants. The index shall contain an appropriate reference by appellee to the question raised and the page in the brief of each appellant.

Source: 1988 Court Rule 21.1

Cross-references: FRAP 28–32; 3rd Cir. LAR 29–32

Committee Comments:

The portions of prior Court Rule 21.1 that were repetitive of FRAP 28 have been deleted. Otherwise no substantive change from prior Court Rule 21.1 is intended.

28.3 Citation Form; Certification

(a) In the argument section of the brief required by F.R.A.P. 28(a)(9), citations to federal opinions that have been reported shall be to the United States Reports, the Federal Reporter, the Federal Supplement or the Federal Rules Decisions, and shall identify the judicial circuit or district, and year of decision. Citations to the United States Supreme Court opinions that have not yet appeared in the official reports may be to the Supreme Court Reporter, the Lawyer's Edition or United States Law Week in that order of preference. Citations to United States Law Week shall include the month, day and year of the decision. Citations to federal decisions that have not been formally reported shall identify the court, docket number and date, and refer to the electronically transmitted decision. Citations to services and topical reports, whether permanent or looseleaf, and to electronic citation systems, shall not be used if the text of the case cited has been reported in the United States Reports, the Federal Reporter, the Federal Supplement, or the Federal Rules Decisions. Citations to state court decisions should include the West Reporter system whenever possible, with an identification of the state court.

(b) For each legal proposition supported by citations in the argument, counsel shall cite to any opposing authority if such authority is binding on this court, e.g., U.S. Supreme Court decisions, published decisions of this court, or, in diversity cases, decisions of the applicable state supreme court.

(c) All assertions of fact in briefs shall be supported by a specific reference to the record. All references to portions of the record contained in the appendix shall be supported by a citation to the appendix, followed by a parenthetical description of the document referred to, unless otherwise apparent from context.

(d) Except as otherwise authorized by law, each party shall include a certification in the initial brief filed by that party with the court that at least one of the attorneys whose names appear on the brief is a member of the bar of this court, or has filed an application for admission pursuant to 3rd Cir. LAR 46.1.

Source: 1988 Court Rule 21.1

Cross-references: 28 U.S.C. §§ 515, 517, 518; Third Circuit Internal Operating Procedure 9.1 (1994)

Committee Comments:

Subsection (b) is new. It imposes upon each party the obligation to cite to authority that is binding on this court, whether that authority supports or opposes the party's propositions. Otherwise, no substantive change from prior Court Rule 21.1 is intended, including the court's longstanding practice of not requiring attorneys representing the United States, or any agency thereof, to be a member of the bar of this court.

28.4 Signing the Brief

All briefs must be signed in accordance with the provision of LAR 46.4. Electronic briefs may be signed with either an electronically generated signature or "/s typed name" in the signature location. Counsel's Bar number and address and phone number shall be included with the signature.

Source: Fed.R.Civ.P. 11

Cross-references: LAR 46.4

Committee Comments:

This rule is derived from Fed.R.Civ.P. 11 which requires signatures on all papers. The signing of documents is important because it constitutes a certificate by the attorney or party that he or she has read the pleading or brief to ensure that it complies with all federal and local rules. The requirement is interpreted broadly and the attorney of record may designate another person to sign the brief. If a party is represented by multiple counsel, the signature from only one attorney of record is required.

28.5 Page Limitations in Cross Appeals

The briefs in a cross appeal shall have the following page limitations:

1st brief (appellant's principal brief)	30 pages or compliance with F.R.A.P. 32(a)(7)(B) and (C).
2nd brief (appellee's answering brief in direct appeal, cross appellant's principal brief)	30 pages or compliance with F.R.A.P. 32(a)(7)(B) and (C).
3rd brief (appellant's reply brief in direct appeal, cross appellee's answering brief)	30 pages or compliance with F.R.A.P. 32(a)(7)(B) and (C).
4th brief (cross appellant's reply)	15 pages or compliance with Rule 32(a)(7)(B)(ii) and (C).

"Appellant" and "appellee" in cross appeals are defined in F.R.A.P. 28(h).

Source: None.

Cross-references: Fed.R.App.P. 28(h)

Committee Comments:

New provision. This rule has been added for clarification of the page limitations.

(As amended Nov. 1997; Nov. 1999, eff. Jan. 1, 2000; eff. Jan. 1, 2002.)

LAR 29.0. AMICI CURIAE BRIEFS

29.1 Time for Filing Amici Curiae Briefs on Rehearing

In a case ordered for rehearing before the court en banc or before the original panel, if the court permits the parties to file additional briefs, any amicus curiae shall file its brief in accordance with Rule 29(e) of the Federal Rules of Appellate Procedure. In a case ordered for rehearing in which no additional briefing is directed, unless the court directs otherwise any amicus brief must be filed within 28 days after the date of the order granting rehearing, and any party may file a response to such an amicus brief within 21 days after the amicus brief is served. Before completing the preparation of an amicus brief, counsel for an amicus curiae shall attempt to ascertain the arguments that will be made in the brief of any party whose position the amicus is supporting, with a view to avoiding any unnecessary repetition or restatement of those arguments in the amicus brief.

Source: None.

Cross-references: Fed. R. App. P. 29(e).

Committee Comments:

New provision.

(Added Nov. 1999, eff. Jan. 1, 2000.)

LAR 30.0. APPENDIX TO THE BRIEFS

30.1 Number To Be Filed

Four copies of the appendix shall be filed, unless otherwise ordered. In Virgin Island cases only, one additional copy of the appendix shall be filed with the clerk of the district court in the location from which the appeal is taken (St. Thomas or St. Croix). When hearing or rehearing by the court en banc is ordered, the parties will be directed to file additional copies for the court's use.

Source: 1988 Court Rule 10.1

Cross-references: FRAP 30(a); 3rd Cir. LAR 31.1

Committee Comments:

The portions of prior Court Rule 10.1 that were repetitive of FRAP 30(a) have been deleted. The rule now clarifies that upon the grant of a petition for rehearing, additional copies of the appendix as well as the briefs will be ordered. Otherwise no substantive change from prior Court Rule 10.1 is intended.

30.2 Hearing On Original Papers

In cases involving applications for a writ of habeas corpus under 28 U.S.C. §§ 2241, 2254 or 2255, or when permission has been granted for the appellant to proceed *in forma pauperis*, the appeal will be heard on the original record. Appellants in such cases must strictly comply with the requirements of 3rd Cir. LAR 32.2(c) with respect to inclusion of the trial court's opinion or order in the brief, and shall also include copies of the docket entries in the proceedings below and the notice of appeal. In any other case, this court, upon motion, may dispense with the requirement of an appendix and permit an appeal or petition to be heard on the original record, with such copies of the record, or relevant parts thereof, as the court may require.

Source: 1988 Court Rule 10.2

Cross-references: FRAP 30(f)

Committee Comments:

The requirement of prior Court Rule 10.2 that habeas corpus petitioners or appellants proceeding *in forma pauperis* attach to their briefs copies of the district court opinion or order appealed from has been deleted as repetitious of 3rd Cir. LAR 32.2(c). 3rd Cir. LAR 30.2 cautions such appellants of the importance of complying with 3rd Cir. LAR 32.2(c), and further requires them to attach copies of the docket entries below and notice of appeal to the opening brief.

30.3 Contents of Appendix

(a) Relevant portions of a trial transcript, exhibit, or other parts of the record referred to in the briefs shall be included in the appendix at such length as may be necessary to preserve context. Relevant portions of the district court briefs may be included in the appendix only if necessary to show whether an issue was raised or an argument was made in the district court or in the proceeding being reviewed. Transcript portions are not considered relevant under this rule merely because they are referred to in the Statement of the Case or Statement of Facts, if they are not otherwise necessary for an understanding of the issues presented for decision. Whenever an appeal challenges the sufficiency of the evidence to support a verdict or other determination (including an argument that a finding is clearly erroneous), the appendix shall reprint all the evidence of record which supports the challenged determination. In all appeals in this court, the appendix shall contain, in addition to the requirements of F.R.A.P. 30(a), a table of contents with page references, a copy of the notice of appeal, the relevant opinions of the trial court or bankruptcy court, or the opinion or report and recommendation of the magistrate judge, or the decision of the administrative agency, and a copy of any order granting a certificate of appealability.

(b) Records sealed in the district court and not unsealed by order of the court shall not be included in the appendix, but may be submitted in a separate, sealed volume of appendix.

(c) In an appeal challenging a criminal sentence, the appellant shall file, at the time of filing the appendix, four copies of the Presentence Investigation Report, in a sealed envelope appropriately labeled.

Source: 1988 Court Rule 10.3

Cross-references: FRAP 30(a), (b) and (f); 3rd Cir. LAR 32.0, Misc. 106.1(c)

Committee Comments:

The portions of prior Court Rule 10.3 that were repetitive of FRAP 30 have been deleted. The portion of prior Court Rule 10.3 addressed to those cases in which the court by order has dispensed with the requirement of an appendix has also been deleted from this rule. Such cases are now addressed by 3rd Cir. LAR 30.2. Briefs submitted to the trial court or agency should not be included in the appendix unless the brief serves as evidence that an issue has been preserved or specifically waived. Trial exhibits which are important to the court's understanding of the issues should be reproduced either in the appendix or as exhibits to the brief.

30.4 Deferred Appendix

The use of a deferred appendix pursuant to FRAP 30(c) is not favored.

Source: 1988 Court Rule 10.4

Cross-references: FRAP 30, 32; 3rd Cir. LAR 32.0

Committee Comments:

No substantive change from prior Court Rule 10.4 is intended.

30.5 Sanctions Pursuant to F.R.A.P. 30(b)(2)

(a) The court, sua sponte by Rule to Show Cause or on the motion of any party, may impose sanctions in the form of denial of all or some of the costs of the appeal upon finding that any party has unreasonably and vexatiously caused the inclusion of materials in an appendix that are unnecessary for the determination of the issues presented on appeal.

(b) A party filing such a motion shall do so not later than ten (10) days after a bill of costs has been served. The movant shall submit with the motion an itemized statement specifically setting forth, by name and appendix page number, the item or items that the movant asserts were unnecessarily included in the appendix.

(c) Any party against whom sanctions are requested may file an answer to the motion or Rule to Show Cause, which shall be filed within ten (10) days after service of the motion or Rule to Show Cause.

Source: 1988 Court Rule 20.4

Cross-references: FRAP 30(b), 39; 3rd Cir. LAR Misc. 107.4

Committee Comments:

No substantive change from prior Court Rule 20.4 is intended.

(As amended Nov. 1997; Nov. 1999, eff. Jan. 1, 2000; eff. Jan. 1, 2002.)

LAR 31.0. FILING AND SERVICE OF BRIEFS

31.1 Number of Copies to be Filed and Served

(a) Unless otherwise required by this court, each party shall file ten (10) paper copies of each brief with the clerk and, unless counsel has consented to electronic service, serve two (2) paper copies on counsel for each party separately represented. In Virgin Islands cases only, one additional paper copy of the briefs shall be filed with the clerk of the district court in the location from which the appeal is taken (St. Thomas or St. Croix). When hearing or rehearing by the court en banc is ordered, the parties will be directed to file additional paper copies for the court's use.

(b) In addition to the paper briefs, counsel for any party or amicus curiae must file with the court the same brief in electronic form.

(1) Filing must be by e-mail or such other method as the court specifies.

(2) The brief must be in PDF format. The Clerk may prescribe additional requirements to aid in transmission.

(3) The date of filing the brief is the date the electronic version of the brief is received by the Clerk, provided that ten paper copies are mailed as provided in Rule 25(a)(2)(B), Fed. R. App. Pro. on the same day as electronic transmission.

(4) The electronic version of the brief is the official record copy of the brief; if corrections are required to be made to the paper brief, a corrected copy of the electronic brief must be provided.

(5) Litigants proceeding pro se need not file an electronic brief.

(c) In addition to the certification of type-volume limitations required by Rule 32(a)(7)(C), and in the same document, counsel must certify that the text of the electronic brief is identical to the text in the paper copies. Counsel must also certify that a virus detection program has been run on the file and that no virus was detected. The certification must specify the version of the virus detection program used. Sanctions may be imposed if a filing contains a computer virus or worm.

(d) A party may serve the opposing party electronically only with the prior consent of the opposing party. If electronic service is used, the filing party must note in the certificate of service that the opposing party consented to electronic service. If parties consent to electronic service, paper copies need not be served.

Source: 1988 Court Rule 21.2

Cross-references: FRAP 28–32; 3rd Cir. LAR 28–32

Committee Comments:

This rule was amended to require electronic filing of briefs. Instructions on electronic filing can be found on the court's web site at *www.ca3.uscourts.gov.* A party proceeding pro se need not file electronically, but if the party wishes to file electronically, this rule must be followed. PDF format makes a document more stable when electronically transmitted. This format also insures that pagination remains the same regardless of what printer is used to print the document.

31.2 Appellee's Brief

A local, state or federal entity or agency, which was served in the district court and which is the appellee, must file a brief in all cases in which a briefing schedule is issued unless the court has granted a motion seeking permission to be excused from filing a brief. This rule does not apply to entities or agencies that are respondents to a petition for review unless the entity or agency is the sole respondent or to entities or agencies which acted solely as an adjudicatory tribunal.

Source: None

Cross-references: F.R.A.P. 28–32; 3rd Cir. L.A.R. 28–32

Committee Comments:

New Rule 31.2 is intended to change the practice of some agencies who choose not to file briefs when they are named as appellee.

31.3 Supplemental Pro Se Briefs Prohibited

Except in cases in which counsel has filed a motion to withdraw under Anders v. California, 386 U.S. 738 (1967), parties represented by counsel may not file a brief pro se. If a party sends a pro se brief to the court, the clerk shall forward the brief to the party's attorney of record. Counsel may choose to include the arguments in his or her brief or may in the unusual case file a motion to file a supplemental brief, if appropriate.

Source: None

Cross-references: None

Committee Comments:

New Rule 31.3 is intended to establish a uniform policy of dealing with pro se briefs from parties who are represented by counsel.

31.4 Motions for Extension of Time to File a Brief

A party's first request for an extension of time to file a brief must set forth good cause. Generalities, such as that the purpose of the motion is not for delay or that counsel is too busy, are not sufficient. A first request for an extension of fourteen (14) calendar days or less may be made by telephone or in writing. Counsel should endeavor to notify opposing counsel in advance that such a request is being made. The grant or denial by the clerk of the extension shall be entered on the court docket. If a request for extension of time is made and granted orally, counsel must send a confirming letter to the clerk and to opposing counsel within seven (7) calendar days. A first request for an extension of time should be made at least three (3) calendar days in advance of the due date for filing the brief. A motion filed less than three (3) calendar days in advance of the due date must be in writing and must demonstrate that the good cause on which the motion is based did not exist earlier or could not with due diligence have been known or communicated to the court earlier. Subsequent requests for an extension of time must be made in writing and will be granted only upon a showing of good cause that was not foreseeable at the time the first request was made. Only one motion for extension of time to file a reply brief may be granted.

Source: None

Cross-references: None

Committee Comments:

The rule was adopted to permit the oral granting of a short extension of time.

(As amended Nov. 1997; Nov. 1999, eff. Jan. 1, 2000; eff. Jan. 1, 2002.)

LAR 32.0. FORM OF BRIEFS, THE APPENDIX AND OTHER PAPERS

32.1 Forms of Briefs, Appendices, Motions, and Other Papers

All briefs, appendices, motions and other papers (collectively "papers") shall conform to the following requirements, unless otherwise provided by the FRAP:

(a) All papers shall be firmly bound at the left margin, and any metal fasteners or staples must be covered. All fasteners must have smooth edges. Use of backbones or spines without stapling is prohibited. Forms of binding such as velo binding and spiral binding are acceptable forms of binding.

(b) All papers shall have margins on both sides of each page that are no less than one (1) inch wide, and margins on the top and bottom of each page that are no less than three-quarters (3/4) of an inch wide.

(c) Typeface. Briefs shall comply with the provisions of F.R.A.P. 32(a)(5) and (6).

(d) Electronic briefs must be in PDF format; the entire brief must be contained in one electronic file. Only paper copies of the appendix are required.

Source: 1988 Court Rules 21.2(B), 22 and 22.1

Cross-references: F.R.A.P. 27, 32, 40; 3rd Cir. L.A.R. 27.0, 35.1 and 35.2

Committee Comments:

The portions of prior Court Rules 21.2(B) and 22.1 that were repetitive of F.R.A.P. 32 have been deleted. The rule was amended to require electronic filing of the brief. Binding volume one of the appendix into the paper brief only, which is preferred, does not prevent counsel from certifying as required in L.A.R. 31.1(c) that the text of the paper brief and the electronic brief are identical.

32.2 Form of Briefs and Appendices

(a) Excessive footnotes in briefs are discouraged. Footnotes shall be printed in the same size type utilized in the text.

(b) Where a transparent cover is utilized, the underlying cover sheet of the brief or appendix must nevertheless conform to the color requirements of F.R.A.P. 32(a)(2) and 32(b)(1).

(c) Volume one of the appendix must consist only of (1) a copy of the notice of appeal, (2) the order or judgment from which the appeal is taken, and any other order or orders of the trial court which pertain to the issues raised on appeal (3) the relevant opinions of the district court or bankruptcy court, or the opinion or report and recommendation of the magistrate judge, or the decision of the administrative agency, if any and (4) any order granting a certificate of appealability, and (5) no more than 25 additional pages. Volume one of the appendix may be bound in the brief and shall not be counted toward the page or type volume limitations on the brief. All other volumes of the appendix must be separately bound. Where there is a multi-volume appendix, counsel should specify on the cover of each volume the pages contained therein, e.g., Vol. 2, pp. 358–722. Costs to the party entitled to them will be allowed for documents appended to the brief.

Source: 1988 Court Rule 21.2

Cross-references: Fed. R. App. P. 28–32; 3rd Cir. LAR 28–32

Committee Comments:

The portions of prior Court Rule 21.2A that were repetitive of FRAP 32(a) have been deleted. Subsection (a) has been added to curtail the use of footnotes as a means to circumvent the page limitations set forth in FRAP. The Rule has been amended to require that additional relevant opinions be bound in the brief.

32.3 Form of Motions and Other Papers Only

(a) Briefs and memoranda in support of or in opposition to motions need not comply with the color requirements of FRAP 32(a).

(b) Suggestions for rehearing en banc in which petitioner is represented by counsel shall contain the "Statement of Counsel" required by 3rd Cir. LAR 35.1. All petitions or suggestions seeking either panel rehearing or rehearing en banc shall include as an exhibit a copy of the panel's judgment, order, and opinion, if any, as to which rehearing is sought.

Source: 1988 Court Rules 21.2(B), 22 and 22.1

Cross-references: FRAP 27, 32, 40; 3rd Cir. LAR 27.0, 35.1 and 35.2

Committee Comments:

The portions of prior Court Rules 21.2(B) and 22.1 that were repetitive of FRAP 32 have been deleted. Otherwise no substantive change from prior Court Rules 21.2(B) and 22.1 is intended.

(As amended Nov. 1997; Nov. 1999, eff. Jan. 1, 2000; eff. Jan. 1, 2002.)

LAR 33.0. APPELLATE MEDIATION PROGRAM

33.1 Appellate Mediation Program

Appeals in civil cases and petitions for review or for enforcement of administrative action are referred to the Appellate Mediation Program to facilitate settlement or otherwise to assist in the expeditious handling of the appeal or petition. A special master shall serve as the program director and, in cooperation with the clerk, shall manage the Appellate Mediation Program. Mediations will be conducted by a senior judge of the court of appeals, a senior judge of a district court, the special master, or other person designated pursuant to Rule 48, F.R.A.P. Parties may confidentially request mediation by telephone or by letter directed to the special master. In all cases, however, the special master will determine which cases are appropriate for mediation and will assign the matter to a mediator.

33.2 Eligibility for Appellate Mediation Program

All civil appeals and petitions for review or for enforcement of agency action shall be eligible for referral to the Appellate Mediation Program except: (1) original proceedings (such as petitions for writ of mandamus); (2) appeals or petitions in social security, immigration or deportation, or black lung cases; (3) prisoner petitions; (4) habeas corpus petitions or motions filed pursuant to 28 U.S.C. Sec. 2255; (5) petitions for leave to file second or successive habeas petitions; and (6) pro se cases. In all cases eligible for appellate mediation, the appellant or petitioner shall file with the clerk, within ten (10) days of the docketing of the appeal with service on all parties, an original and two (2) copies of a Civil Appeals Information Statement and a Concise Summary of the Case, on forms to be supplied by the clerk. Appellant shall attach to the Concise Summary of the Case copies of the order(s) being appealed and any accompanying opinion or memorandum of the district court or agency. In the event the order(s) being appealed or any accompanying opinion or memorandum adopt, affirm, or otherwise refer to the report and recommendation of a magistrate judge or the decision of a bankruptcy judge, the report and recommendation or decision shall also be attached. In addition, any judge or panel of the court may refer to the special master any appeal, petition, motion or other procedural matter for review and possible amicable resolution.

33.3. Initial Screening and Deferral of Briefing for Cases Selected for Mediation

The Clerk will provide the special master with a copy of the judgment or order on appeal, any opinion or memorandum issued by the district court or agency, appellant's Civil Appeal Information Statement and Concise Summary of the Case and any relevant motions. Following review of these materials, the special master may refer an appeal or petition to a senior judge, himself or herself, or such other person designated pursuant to Rule 48, F.R.A.P. for mediation. The special master shall advise the parties, the chosen mediator, and the clerk of the referral.

If a case is referred to mediation, a briefing schedule shall be deferred during the pendency of mediation unless the court or special master determines otherwise. A referral to mediation shall not, however, defer or extend the time for ordering any necessary transcripts.

If a case is not accepted for mediation, or if accepted but is not resolved through mediation, it will proceed in the appellate process as if mediation had not been considered or initiated.

33.4 Referral of Matters to Mediation by a Judge or Panel of the Court

At any time during the pendency of an appeal or petition, any judge or panel of the court may refer the appeal or petition to the special master for mediation or any other purpose consistent with this rule. In addition, any judge or panel of the court may refer any appeal, petition, motion or other procedural matters for review and possible amicable resolution. The procedures set forth in LAR 33.5 are applicable to matters referred for mediation pursuant to LAR 33.4 unless otherwise directed by the special master. Documents, including but not limited to, those specified in LAR 33.5(a) may be required.

33.5 Proceedings After Selection for the Program

(a) Submission of Position Papers and Documents

Within fifteen (15) days of the case's selection for mediation by the special master, each counsel shall prepare and submit to the mediator a confidential position paper of no more than ten (10) pages, stating counsel's views on the key facts and legal issues in the case, as well as on key factors relating to settlement. The position paper will include a statement of motions filed in the court of appeals and their status. Copies of position papers submitted by the parties directly to the mediator should not be served upon opposing counsel. Documents prepared for mediation sessions are not to be filed with the Clerk's Office and are not to be of record in the case.

(b) Mediation Sessions

The mediator will notify the parties of the time, date, and place of the mediation session and whether it will be conducted in person or telephonically. Unless the mediator directs otherwise, mediation sessions must be attended by the senior lawyer for each party responsible for the appeal and by the person or persons with actual authority to negotiate a settlement of the case. If settlement is not reached at the initial mediation session, but the mediator believes further mediation sessions or discussions would be productive, the mediator may conduct additional mediation sessions in person or telephonically.

(c) Confidentiality of Mediation Proceedings

The mediator shall not disclose to anyone statements made or information developed during the mediation process. The attorneys and other persons attending the mediation are likewise prohibited from disclosing statements made or information developed during the mediation process to anyone other than clients, principals or co-counsel, and then, only upon receiving due assurances that the recipients will honor the confidentiality of the information. Similarly, the parties are prohibited from using any information obtained as a result of the mediation process as a basis for any motion or argument to any court. The mediation proceedings shall be considered compromise negotiations under Rule 408 of the Federal Rules of Evidence. Notwithstanding the foregoing, the bare fact that a settlement has been reached as a result of mediation shall not be considered confidential.

(d) Settlement

No party shall be bound by statements or actions at a mediation session unless a settlement is reached. If a settlement is reached, the agreement shall be reduced to writing and shall be binding upon all parties to the agreement, and counsel shall file a stipulation of dismissal of the appeal pursuant to Rule 42(b), F.R.A.P. Such a stipulation must be filed within thirty (30) days after settlement is reached unless an extension thereof is granted by the special master.

Source: New rule

Cross-references: None

Committee Comments:

None

33.6 Mediation in Pro Se Cases

In appropriate cases, the Director of the Mediation Program may request counsel to represent pro se litigants for purposes of mediation only. Counsel must agree to take the case on a pro bono basis, except that if an applicable statute authorizes the award of attorneys' fees, counsel may enter into a written agreement with the client assigning to the attorney any amounts designated as attorneys' fees. The case will be treated as any other case subject to mediation and all provisions of L.A.R. 33 will apply. If mediation is unsuccessful, counsel may discontinue his or her representation; however, counsel may continue to represent the litigant through the rest of the appeal if counsel wishes and the party agrees. The Director of the

Mediation Program may adopt and implement specific procedures in furtherance of this rule.

Source: New rule

Cross-references: None

Committee Comments:

None

(Added Nov. 1999, eff. Jan. 1, 2000; eff. Jan. 1, 2002.)

LAR 34.0. ORAL ARGUMENT

34.1 In General

(a) The court shall allow oral argument in all cases unless the panel, after examination of the briefs and records or appendices, is unanimously of the opinion that oral argument is not needed.

(b) Any party to the appeal shall have the right to file a statement with the court setting forth the reasons why, in the party's opinion, oral argument should be heard. Such statement shall be filed with the clerk within seven (7) days after the filing of appellee's or respondent's brief. The request shall set forth the amount of argument time sought.

(c) In certain appeals, the clerk will inform the parties by letter of a particular issue(s) that the panel wishes the parties to address.

(d) The court shall grant a motion requesting rescheduling of the argument only where the moving party shows extraordinary circumstances.

(e) If parties request oral argument by video-conference, a joint statement of all parties to that effect shall be filed with the clerk fourteen (14) days after the filing of the appellee's or respondent's brief. Granting of the request shall be at the Court's discretion.

Source: 1988 Court Rule 12.6

Cross-references: FRAP 21(b), 34; 3rd Cir. LAR 27.1; Third Circuit Internal Operating Procedures, Chapter 2 (1994)

Committee Comments:

Because the panels are constituted in advance for a specific sitting, rescheduling of an argument may result in a second panel being assigned an appeal when one panel has already performed the necessary study of the briefs and appendix. Alternatively, it may result in members of the panel having to travel to Philadelphia at additional government expense, disrupting previously established schedules. Such needless waste of judicial resources underlies this court's precedent of declining to reschedule except upon a showing of extraordinary circumstances. Subsection (c) contains a new provision that counsel in certain cases will be notified prior to the oral argument of a particular issue, if any, that is of concern to the court. The portions of prior Court Rule 12.6 that were repetitive of FRAP have been deleted. Otherwise no substantive change from prior Court Rule 12.6 is intended.

34.2 Continuance

For good cause the court may pass a case listed for oral argument or order its continuance. No stipulation to pass or continue a case will be recognized as binding upon the court.

Source: 1988 Court Rule 12.5

Cross-references: FRAP 34; 3rd Cir. LAR 34.1

Committee Comments:

No substantive change from prior Court Rule 12.5 is intended.

34.3 No Oral Argument on Motions Except When Ordered

The court shall consider and decide motions upon the motion papers and briefs, and shall not hear oral argument unless ordered by the court or a judge thereof. Counsel may assume there will not be oral argument unless advised by the clerk to appear at a time and place fixed by the court.

Source: 1988 Court Rule 11.1

Cross-references: FRAP 8, 9, 18, 27, 34, 40, 41; 3rd Cir. LAR 27.1

Committee Comments:

This rule is identical to 3rd Cir. LAR 27.1. No substantive change from prior Court Rule 11.1 is intended.

(As amended Nov. 1997; eff. Jan. 1, 2002.)

LAR 35.0. DETERMINATION OF CAUSES BY THE COURT EN BANC

35.1 Required Statement for Rehearing En Banc

Where the party suggesting rehearing en banc is represented by counsel, the suggestion shall contain, so far as is pertinent, the following statement of counsel:

> "I express a belief, based on a reasoned and studied professional judgment, that the panel decision is contrary to decisions of the United States Court of Appeals for the Third Circuit or the Supreme Court of the United States, and that consideration by the full court is necessary to secure and maintain uniformity of decisions in this court, *i.e.*, the panel's decision is contrary to the decision of this court or the Supreme Court in [citing specifically the case or cases], OR, that this appeal involves a question of exceptional importance, *i.e.* [set forth in one sentence]."

Source: 1988 Court Rule 22

Cross-references: FRAP 32(b), 35, 40; 3rd Cir. LAR 32.3; Third Circuit Internal Operating Procedures, Chapter 9 (1994)

Committee Comments:

No substantive change from prior Court Rule 22 is intended.

35.2 Required Attachments to Petition for Rehearing

(a) A petition seeking rehearing en banc shall include as an exhibit a copy of the panel's judgment, order, and opinion, if any, as to which rehearing is sought.

(b) An original and fourteen (14) copies of a petition for rehearing en banc shall be filed unless otherwise directed by the court.

Source: 1988 Court Rule 22.1

Cross-references: F.R.A.P. 32(b), (c), 35, 40; 3rd Cir. L.A.R. 32.3

Committee Comments:

No substantive change from prior Court Rule 22.1 is intended.

The addition of subsection (b) is not intended to alter the provisions of IOP 9.5.1 which provide that an unlabeled petition will be construed as requesting both panel rehearing and rehearing en banc.

35.3 Composition of En Banc Quorum

For purposes of determining the majority number necessary to grant a petition for rehearing, all circuit judges currently in regular active service who are not disqualified will be counted. However, a petition for rehearing shall not be granted unless a majority of the judges in regular active service are not disqualified from voting on the petition.

Source: 1988 Court Rule 2.3

Cross-references: FRAP 35; 3rd Cir. LAR Misc. 101.0

Committee Comments:

Changes were made to conform the rule to Internal Operating Procedure Chapter 9.

35.4 Caution

As noted in FRAP 35, en banc hearing or rehearing of appeals is not favored. Counsel have a duty to the court commensurate with that owed their clients to read with attention and observe with restraint the required statement for rehearing en banc set forth in 3rd Cir. LAR 35.1. Counsel are reminded that in every case the duty of counsel is fully discharged without filing a suggestion for rehearing en banc unless the case meets the rigorous requirements of FRAP 35 and 3rd Cir. LAR 35.1.

Source: None

Cross-references: 28 U.S.C. § 1927; FRAP 35, 38; 3rd Cir. LAR 35.1; Third Circuit Internal Operating Procedures, Chapter 9 (1994)

Committee Comments:

New provision. This rule is modeled after U.S.Ct. of App. 5th Cir. Rule 35 (1991). The purpose of the rule is to emphasize that the court does not favor requests for hearing or rehearing en banc, and to discourage inappropriate requests from being made.

35.5 Death Penalty Cases

The provisions of 3rd Cir. LAR Misc. 111.7 shall govern all petitions seeking hearing or rehearing by the court en banc in all actions challenging a conviction in which a sentence of death has been imposed.

Source: 3rd Cir. LAR 8.2, 22.2

Cross-references: FRAP 35, 3rd Cir. LAR Misc. 111.7

Committee Comments:

New provision. To the extent consistent with FRAP and applicable, local procedure in all death penalty proceedings will be governed by 3rd Cir. LAR Misc. 111.0.

(As amended Nov. 1997; Nov. 1999, eff. Jan. 1, 2000; eff. Jan. 1, 2002.)

LAR 36.0. ENTRY OF JUDGMENT

36.1 Opinions

All written opinions of the court and of the panels thereof shall be filed with and preserved by the clerk. All opinions shall be printed under the supervision of the clerk. Printed opinions need not be copied into the minutes but shall be bound and kept in the Clerk's Office, and when bound shall be deemed to have been recorded.

Source: 1988 Court Rule 16

Cross-references: FRAP 36

Committee Comments:

No substantive change from prior Court Rule 16 is intended.

36.2 Copies of Printed Opinions

(a) Parties. Each party to an appeal shall receive one copy of the court's printed opinion free of charge.

(b) Subscriptions. Subscriptions for the printed opinions of this court may be received by the clerk at a fee to be set by order of the court from time to time, which may set a lesser fee for non-profit institutions.

(c) "Public Interest List." Copies of printed opinions will be furnished free of charge to those appearing on a "Public Interest List" established by order of the court in the interest of providing proper and adequate dissemination to the general public.

(d) Other. All other persons desiring a copy of a printed opinion of this court may receive one from the clerk at a fee to be set by order of the court from time to time.

Source: 1988 Court Rules 17.2 and 17.3

Cross-references: FRAP 36

Committee Comments:

No substantive change from prior Court Rules 17.2 and 17.3 is intended.

(As amended Nov. 1997.)

LAR 39.0. COSTS

39.1 Certification or Certiorari to Supreme Court

In all cases certified to the Supreme Court or removed thereto by certiorari, the fees of the clerk of this court shall be paid before a transcript of the record shall be transmitted to the Supreme Court.

Source: 1988 Court Rule 17.1

Cross-references: 28 U.S.C. §§ 1254, 1913, 1920; FRAP 39

Committee Comments:

No substantive change from prior Court Rule 17.1 is intended.

39.2 Schedule of Fees and Costs

Pursuant to 28 U.S.C. § 1913, a uniform schedule of fees and costs is prescribed from time to time by the Judicial Conference of the United States. An up-to-date schedule can be found as an annotation to 28 U.S.C. § 1913 in the United States Code, the United States Code Annotated, and West's *Federal Civil Judicial Procedure and Rules* manual.

Source: 1988 Court Rule 17.2

Cross-references: 28 U.S.C. § 1913; FRAP 39

Committee Comments:

The provisions of prior Court Rule 17.2 that were repetitive of 28 U.S.C. § 1913 and FRAP 3(b) and 24(a) have been deleted. The provisions of prior Court Rule 17.2 regarding the costs of printed opinions have been moved to 3rd Cir. LAR 36.2.

39.3 Taxation of Reproduction Costs

The cost of printing or otherwise producing necessary copies of briefs and appendices shall be taxable as follows:

(a) Number of Briefs. Costs will be allowed for ten (10) copies of each brief plus two (2) copies for each party separately represented, unless the court shall direct a greater number of briefs to be filed.

(b) Number of Appendices. Costs will be allowed for four (4) copies of the appendix plus one (1) copy for each party separately represented, unless the court shall direct a greater number of appendices to be filed.

(c) Costs of Reproduction of Briefs and Appendices. In taxing costs for printed or photocopied briefs and appendices, the clerk shall tax costs at the following rates, or at the actual cost, whichever is less, depending upon the manner of reproduction or photocopying:

(1) Reproduction (whether by offset or typography):

Reproduction per page (for 20 copies or less)	$ 4.00
Covers (for 20 copies or less)	$50.00
Binding per copy	$ 4.00
Sales tax	Applicable Rate

(2) Photocopying (whether in house or commercial):

Reproduction per page per copy	$ .10
Binding per copy	$ 4.00
Covers (for 20 copies or less)	$40.00
Sales Tax	Applicable Rate

(3) In the event a party subsequently corrects deficiencies in either a brief or appendix pursuant to 3rd Cir. LAR Misc. 107.3 and that party prevails on appeal, costs which were incurred in order to bring the brief or appendix into compliance may not be allowed.

(d) Other Costs. No other costs associated with briefs and appendices, including the costs of typing, word processing, and preparation of tables and footnotes, shall be allowed for purposes of taxation of costs.

Source: 1988 Court Rule 20.1

Cross-references: 28 U.S.C. § 1920; F.R.A.P. 39

Committee Comments:

Sales tax will be included in the costs only when actually paid to a commercial photocopying service. No substantive change from prior Court Rule 20.1 is intended.

39.4 Filing Date; Support for Bill of Costs

(a) The court shall deny untimely bills of cost unless a motion showing good cause is filed with the bill.

(b) Parties shall submit the itemized and verified bill of costs on a standard form to be provided by the clerk.

(c) An answer to objections to a bill of costs may be filed within 10 days of service of the objections.

Source: 1988 Court Rules 20.2, 20.3

Cross-references: FRAP 39

Committee Comments:

The portions of prior Court Rules 20.2 and 20.3 that were repetitive of FRAP 39 have been deleted. The rule now specifically allows for an answer to objections, a codification of existing practice. Otherwise, no substantive change from prior Court Rules 20.2 and 20.3 is intended.

(As amended Nov. 1997; Nov. 1999, eff. Jan. 1, 2000.)

LAR 40.0. PETITION FOR PANEL REHEARING

40.1 Required Attachments to Petition for Panel Rehearing

(a) A petition seeking panel rehearing shall include as an exhibit a copy of the panel's judgment, order, and opinion, if any, as to which rehearing is sought.

(b) An original and three (3) copies of a petition for panel rehearing shall be filed unless otherwise directed by the court.

Source: New provision

Cross-references: F.R.A.P. 35, 40

Committee Comments:

This is a new provision designed to create parallel provisions for petitions for panel rehearing and rehearing en banc. It is not intended to alter the provisions of IOP 9.5.1 which provide that an unlabeled petition will be construed as requesting both panel rehearing and rehearing en banc.

(Added Nov. 1999, eff. Jan. 1, 2000.)

LAR 45.0. DUTIES OF CLERKS

45.1 Office—Where Kept

The Clerk's Office shall be kept in the United States Courthouse in the city of Philadelphia.

Source: 1988 Court Rule 5.1

Cross-references: FRAP 45

Committee Comments:

No substantive change from prior Court Rule 5.1 is intended.

45.2 Daily Listing of Cases

The clerk shall prepare, under the direction of the court, a list for each session of the court, on which so far as practicable each case shall be listed for argument or submission on a day certain during the week.

Source: 1988 Court Rule 12.2

Cross-references: FRAP 34, 45; 3rd Cir. LAR 34.1

Committee Comments:

Language describing the clerk's method of preparing the argument lists has been deleted. Otherwise, no substantive change from prior Court Rule 12.2 is intended.

(As amended Nov. 1997.)

LAR 46.0. ATTORNEYS

46.1 Admission

(a) Except as the court otherwise directs, practice before the court shall be limited to the members of the bar of this court. Admission to the bar of this court shall be governed by the provisions of FRAP 46 and such other requirements as the court may adopt from time to time, provided, however, that (i) the applicant shall be familiar with the contents of the Federal Rules of Civil Procedure, Criminal Procedure, and Appellate Procedure, as well as with the Local Appellate Rules and Internal Operating Procedures of this court, and (ii) the applicant has read and understood those provisions of the above documents dealing with briefs, motions and appendices. The fee for admission shall be determined by order of the court and shall be payable to the clerk as trustee. All funds received from such applications shall be deposited in the Administrative Fund of the court designated for this purpose.

(b) Unless the court otherwise directs, an attorney shall apply for admission to the bar of this court when the attorney enters an appearance, or at such time as a motion, brief, or other document is filed in this court. An attorney who will argue the appeal, if not previously admitted to the bar of this court, may apply for admission on or before the date of oral argument. Forms prescribed by the court for purpose of admission may be obtained from the clerk of this court.

(c) Any applicant for admission to the bar of this court may be admitted in open court on oral motion, on motion before a single judge of this court, or as the court may otherwise from time to time determine. However, qualified applicants to the bar of this court not previously admitted and who will argue the appeal shall be admitted in open court on oral motion.

(d) An applicant for admission to the bar of this court may be admitted on written or oral motion of a member of the bar of this court or a circuit or district judge of this circuit.

(e) The initial brief filed by each party with the court shall contain a certification that at least one of the attorneys whose names appear on the brief is a member of the bar of this court, or has filed an application for admission pursuant to this rule.

Source: 1988 Court Rule 9.1

Cross-references: FRAP 46; 3rd Cir. LAR 28.3(a); Third Circuit Attorney Disciplinary Rules

Committee Comments:

No substantive change from prior Court Rule 9.1 is intended. It is not intended that current practice permitted by law be changed.

46.2 Entry Of Appearance

Within ten (10) days of notification of the docketing of a case, counsel for the appellant or petitioner shall file a written appearance which shall include an address where notices and papers may be mailed to or served upon him or her. The entry of appearance form shall be served on all parties. Not later than ten days after the docketing of the appeal, counsel for all parties in the trial court or agency below and any other persons entitled to participate in the proceedings as appellees or respondents and desiring to do so, shall file similar written appearances. Any such party or other person on whose behalf counsel fails to file a written appearance within the time fixed by this rule will not be entitled to receive notices or copies of briefs and appendices until a written appearance has been entered for such party. A party desiring to appear without counsel may so notify the clerk of this court in writing and shall be deemed to appear pro se in which case the pro se party must be served directly with copies of notices, motions, and briefs.

Source: 1988 Court Rule 9.2

Cross-references: FRAP 46

Committee Comments:

No substantive change from prior Court Rule 9.2 is intended.

46.3 Entry Of Appearance By Eligible Law Students

(a) Eligibility

(1) An eligible law student may enter an appearance in this court on behalf of any indigent prisoner in any civil rights or habeas corpus matter. An indigent who was confined at the commencement of the district court action shall be considered an "indigent prisoner" for purposes of this rule, even though the prisoner may have been subsequently released. The person on whose behalf the student is appearing must indicate in writing his or her consent to that appearance and a supervising lawyer must also indicate in writing his or her approval of that appearance.

(2) In each case the written consent and approval referred to above shall be filed in the record of the case and shall be brought to the attention of the court.

(3) An eligible law student may engage in other activities under the general supervision of a member of the bar of this court outside the personal presence of that lawyer for the purpose of preparation of briefs, abstracts, and other documents to be filed in this court, but such documents must be signed by the supervising lawyer.

(4) An eligible law student may participate in oral argument in this court but only in the presence of the supervising lawyer, who shall be prepared to supplement any written or oral statement made by the student.

(b) Requirements and Limitations.

In order to make an appearance pursuant to this rule, the law student must:

(1) Be duly enrolled in a law school approved by the American Bar Association.

(2) Have completed legal studies amounting to at least four semesters, or the equivalent if the school is on some basis other than a semester basis.

(3) Be certified by the dean of his or her law school as being of good character and competent legal ability, and as being adequately trained to perform as an eligible law student under this rule.

(4) Be introduced to this court by an attorney admitted to practice in this court and take the following oath or affirmation in open court:

"I, [name], do swear (or affirm) that I will support the Constitution of the United States, and that, in practicing as an eligible law student under 3rd Cir. LAR 46.3 I shall conduct myself strictly in accordance with the terms of that rule and according to law."

(5) Neither ask for nor receive any compensation or remuneration of any kind from the person on whose behalf the law student renders service, but this shall not prevent a lawyer, legal aid bureau, law school, public defender agency, or the government from paying compensation to the eligible law student, nor shall it prevent any agency from making such charges for its services as it may otherwise properly require.

(6) Certify in writing that the law student has read and is familiar with the rules of professional conduct governing attorneys practicing in the jurisdiction of the supervising attorney.

(c) Certification

(1) The certification of a student by the law school dean shall be filed with the clerk of court and, unless it is sooner withdrawn, shall remain in effect until the expiration of eighteen (18) months after it is filed, or until the announcement of the results of the first bar examination of the state where the student's law school is located following the student's graduation, whichever is earlier. For any student who passes that examination or who is admitted to the bar without taking an examination, the certification shall continue in effect until the date the student is admitted to the bar. The student shall be responsible for advising the clerk in writing of any change in status or event affecting the student's certification.

(2) The certification may be withdrawn by the dean at any time by mailing a notice to that effect to the clerk of the court. It is not necessary that the notice state the cause for withdrawal.

(3) The certification may be terminated by this court at any time without notice or hearing and without any showing of cause.

(d) Supervision. The member of the bar under whose supervision an eligible law student does any of the things permitted by this rule shall:

(1) Be a lawyer in good standing of the bar of this court.

(2) Assume personal professional responsibility for the student's guidance in any work undertaken and for supervising the quality of the student's work.

(3) Assist the student to the extent the supervising lawyer considers it necessary.

Source: 1988 Court Rule 9.3

Cross-references: FRAP 46; Third Circuit Attorney Disciplinary Rules

Committee Comments:

The Model Rules of Professional Responsibility replace the Canons of Professional Ethics. No substantive change from prior Court Rule 9.3 is intended.

46.4 Signing Papers

All papers, motions and briefs must be signed by an attorney or by a party appearing pro se.

Source: Fed.R.Civ.P. 11

Cross-references: LAR 28.4

Committee Comments:

This rule is derived from Fed.R.Civ.P. 11 which requires signatures on all papers. The signing of documents is important because it constitutes a certificate by the attorney or party that he or she has read the pleading or brief to ensure that it complies with all federal and local rules. The requirement is interpreted broadly and the attorney of record may designate another person to sign the brief. If a party is represented by multiple counsel, the signature from only one attorney of record is required.

(As amended Nov. 1997; eff. Jan. 1, 2002.)

LAR 47.0. RULES BY COURTS OF APPEALS

47.1 Advisory Committee

Any proposed change in the Third Circuit Local Appellate Rules shall be forwarded for comment to the Lawyers Advisory Committee, which constitutes the advisory committee for the study of the rules of practice as required by 28 U.S.C. § 2077(b).

Source: None

Cross-references: 28 U.S.C. § 2077(b)

Committee Comments:

The 1988 amendments to the Judicial Code provide for the appointment of an advisory committee to study, inter alia, local rules of practice. 3rd Cir. LAR 47.1 specifies the Lawyers Advisory Committee (LAC) as the statutorily-required review committee, and specifies that any proposed changes in these rules shall be studied by the LAC before they are adopted.

(As amended Nov. 1997.)

LAR 48.0. SPECIAL MASTERS

48.1 Special Masters

The court may appoint a master to hold hearings, if necessary, and make recommendations as to any auxiliary matter requiring a factual determination in the court of appeals. If the master is not a court officer, the compensation to be allowed to the master shall be fixed by the court, and shall be charged upon such of the parties as the court may direct.

Source: None

Cross-references: FRAP 48

Committee Comments:

New provision. This rule is intended to formalize by rule the court's practice of appointing special masters to resolve factual questions where appropriate and needed by the court.

(As amended Nov. 1997.)

MISCELLANEOUS LOCAL APPELLATE RULES

LAR MISC. 101.0. CONSTITUTION OF THE COURT—PANELS—QUORUM

101.1 The Court—Judges Who Constitute It

The court consists of the circuit judges in regular active service. The circuit justice and other justices and judges so designated or assigned by the chief judge are eligible to sit as judges of the court.

Source: 1988 Court Rule 2.1

Cross-references: None

Committee Comments:

Prior Court Rule 2.1 has no counterpart in FRAP and is therefore classified as Miscellaneous. No substantive change from prior Court Rule 2.1 is intended.

101.2 Quorum—Adjournment In Absence Of—By Whom Adjourned

A majority of the number of judges authorized to constitute the court or a panel thereof shall constitute a quorum. If a quorum does not attend on any day appointed for holding a session of the court or a panel thereof, any judge who does attend may adjourn the court or panel, or, in the absence of any judges, the clerk may adjourn the court or panel.

Source: 1988 Court Rule 2.5

Cross-references: 28 U.S.C. § 46(d)

Committee Comments:

Prior Court Rule 2.5 has no counterpart in FRAP and is therefore classified as Miscellaneous. All references in the prior rule to "divisions" of this court have been changed to "panels." Otherwise, no substantive change from prior Rule 2.5 is intended.

(As amended Nov. 1997.)

LAR MISC. 102.0. SESSIONS

102.1 Sessions—When And Where Held

(a) Stated sessions of the court or of its panels shall be held at Philadelphia or at another place within the circuit commencing on such dates each month as the court shall designate, and in the Virgin Islands commencing at such dates as the court shall designate. Pursuant to request of the parties or order of the court, a Virgin Islands case may be heard at another place in the circuit. The stated sessions of the court in the Virgin Islands shall be held in Charlotte Amalie in even-numbered years and in Christiansted in odd-numbered years unless the court directs otherwise.

(b) Special sessions may be held at any time or place within the circuit when so ordered by the court.

Source: 1988 Court Rules 3.2 and 3.3

Cross-references: None

Committee Comments:

Prior Court Rules 3.2 and 3.3 have no counterpart in F.R.A.P. and are therefore classified as Miscellaneous. The rule has been revised to give the court the option to schedule its Virgin Islands sessions in months other than April and December. A reference to the "divisions" of this court has been changed to "panels." Otherwise, no substantive change from prior Court Rules 3.2 and 3.3 is intended. The rule has been revised so that the court may sit at other places within the circuit and may, in appropriate circumstances, reverse the place or alter the timing of the Virgin Islands sitting.

(As amended Nov. 1997; Nov. 1999, eff. Jan. 1, 2000; eff. Jan. 1, 2002.)

LAR MISC. 103.0. MARSHAL, CRIER, AND OTHER OFFICERS

103.1 Who Shall Attend Court

A crier and, if requested, the marshal of the district in which the sessions of the court are held shall be in attendance during the sessions of the court.

Source: 1988 Court Rule 6.1

Cross-references: None

Committee Comments:

Prior Court Rule 6.1 has no counterpart in FRAP and is therefore classified as Miscellaneous. A reference to "divisions" of this court has been changed to "panels." Otherwise, no substantive change from prior Court Rule 6.1 is intended.

(As amended Nov. 1997.)

LAR MISC. 104.0. COURT LIBRARIES

104.1 Regulations Governing Use Of Libraries

The law libraries shall be open during such hours as are reasonable to satisfy the needs of the court, and shall be governed by such regulations as the librarian, with the approval of the court's library committee, may from time to time make effective.

Source: 1988 Court Rule 7.3

Cross-references: None

Committee Comments:

Prior Court Rule 7.3 has no counterpart in FRAP and is therefore classified as Miscellaneous. No substantive change from prior Court Rule 7.3 is intended.

(As amended Nov. 1997.)

LAR MISC. 105.0. JUDICIAL CONFERENCE OF THE THIRD CIRCUIT

105.1 Attendance At Invitations To The Conference

In addition to judicial participants, attendance at the Judicial Conference of the Third Circuit may be open at the discretion of the chief judge to any member of the bar of any court within the circuit interested in the work of the courts and the administration of justice in the circuit.

Source: 1988 Court Rule 18.2

Cross-references: 28 U.S.C. § 333

Committee Comments:

Prior Court Rule 18.2 has no counterpart in F.R.A.P. and is therefore classified as Miscellaneous. The rule has been revised to reflect the court's open invitation policy.

(As amended Nov. 1997; Nov. 1999, eff. Jan. 1, 2000; eff. Jan. 1, 2002.)

LAR MISC. 106.0. FILING OF PAPERS UNDER SEAL

106.1 Necessity; Grand Jury Matters; Previously Impounded Records; Unsealing

(a) Generally. With the exception of matters relating to grand jury investigations, filing of papers under seal without prior court approval is discouraged. If a party believes a portion of a brief or other papers merits treatment under seal, the party shall file a motion setting forth with particularity the reasons why sealing is deemed necessary. Any other party may file objections, if any, within seven (7) days. A motion to seal must explain the basis for sealing and specify the desired duration of the sealing order. If discussion of confidential material is necessary to support the motion to seal, the motion may be filed provisionally under seal. Rather than automatically requesting the sealing of an entire brief, motion, or other filing, litigants should consider whether argument relating to sealed materials may be contained in separate sealed supplemental brief, motion or filings. Sealed documents must not be included in a regular appendix, but may be submitted in a separate, sealed volume of the appendix. In addressing material under seal (except for the presentencing report) in an unsealed brief or motion or oral argument counsel are expected not to disclose the nature of the sealed material and to apprise the court that the material is sealed.

(b) Grand Jury Matters. In matters relating to grand jury investigations, when there is inadequate time for a party to file a motion requesting permission to file papers under seal, the party may file briefs and other papers using initials or a John or Jane Doe designation to avoid disclosure of the identity of the applicant or the subject matter of the grand jury investigation. Promptly thereafter, the party shall file a motion requesting permission to use such a designation. All responsive briefs and other papers shall follow the same format until further order of the court.

(c) Records Impounded in the District Court.

(1) Criminal Cases and Cases Collaterally Attacking Convictions. Motions, briefs, other papers, and any other part of the record related to any grand jury investigation, presentence report, statement of reasons for the sentence and other similar material in a criminal case or a case collaterally attacking a conviction (cases under 28 U.S.C. §§ 2241, 2254, 2255), which were filed with the district court under seal pursuant to statute, rule or an order of impoundment, and which constitute part of the record transmitted to this court, shall remain subject to the district court's impoundment order and shall be placed under seal by the clerk of this court until further order of this court. In cases in which impounded documents other than grand jury materials, presentence reports, statements of reasons for judgment, or other documents required to be sealed by statute or rule, are included in the record sent to this court, the party seeking to have the document sealed shall file a motion within 21 days of receiving notice of the docketing of the appeal in this court, explaining the basis for sealing and specifying the desired duration of the sealing order. If discussion of confidential material is necessary to support the motion to seal, the motion may be filed provisionally under seal.

(2) Civil Cases. When the district court impounds part or all of the papers in a civil case, they will remain under seal in this court for thirty (30) days after the filing of the notice of appeal to give counsel an opportunity to file a motion to continue the impoundment, setting forth the reasons therefor. A motion to continue impoundment must explain the basis for sealing and specify the desired duration of the sealing order. If discussion of confidential material is necessary to support the motion to seal, the motion may be filed provisionally under seal. If a motion to continue impoundment is filed, the documents shall remain sealed until further order of this court.

Source: 1988 Court Rule 21.3

Cross-references: 3rd Cir. LAR 30.3

Committee Comments:

Prior Court Rule 21.3 has no counterpart in F.R.A.P. and is therefore classified as Miscellaneous. The rule has been revised to place an affirmative obligation to file a motion on the party in a civil matter who wishes to continue the sealing of papers on appeal. The archiving center will not accept sealed documents, which presents storage problems for the court. The rule has been amended to require the parties to specify how long documents must be kept under seal after the case is closed.

(As amended Nov. 1997; eff. Jan. 1, 2002.)

LAR MISC. 107.0. SANCTIONS

107.1 Dismissal Of Appeal For Failure To Pay Certain Fees

(a) The clerk is authorized to dismiss the appeal if the appellant does not pay the docketing fee within fourteen (14) days after docketing, as prescribed by 3rd Cir. LAR 3.3.

(b) The appellant's failure to comply with 3rd Cir. LAR 11.1 regarding transcription fees shall be grounds for dismissal of the appeal.

Source: 1988 Court Rules 15.1, 28.1

Cross-references: FRAP 3(a), 11; 3rd Cir. LAR 3.3

Committee Comments:

For the convenience of counsel, all rules relating to sanctions are included in 3rd Cir. LAR Misc. 107.0. Where these rules have some counterpart in FRAP, they are included in both the corresponding 3rd Cir. LAR and Misc. 107.0. Where they have no counterpart in FRAP, they are included in 3rd Cir. LAR Misc. 107.0 only. Only the parts of prior Court Rules 15.1 and 28.1 setting forth sanctions have been included here. No substantive change from prior Court Rules 15.1 and 28.1 is intended.

107.2 Dismissal For Failure To Prosecute

(a) When an appellant fails to comply with the Federal Rules of Appellate Procedure or the Local Appellate Rules of this court, the clerk shall issue written notice to counsel or to the appellant who appears *pro se* that upon the expiration of fourteen (14) days from the date of the notice, the appeal may be dismissed for want of prosecution unless appellant remedies the deficiency within that time. If the deficiency is not remedied within this period, the clerk is authorized to dismiss the appeal for want of prosecution and issue a certified copy thereof to the clerk of the district court as the mandate. The appellant shall not be entitled to remedy the deficiency after the appeal is dismissed except by order of the court. A motion to set aside such an order must be justified by the showing of good cause and may not be filed after ten (10) days of the date of dismissal. If the appeal is one taken from the District Court of the Virgin Islands, an additional ten (10) days shall be added to the time limits specified in this paragraph.

(b) Notwithstanding subsection (a), if an appellant fails to comply with the Federal Rules of Appellate Procedure and the Local Appellate Rules with respect to the timely filing of a brief and appendix, at any time after the seventh day following the due date, the clerk is authorized to dismiss the appeal for want of timely prosecution. The procedure to be followed in requesting an order to set aside dismissal of the appeal is the same as that set forth in subsection (a).

Source: 1988 Court Rule 28.2

Cross-references: FRAP 3(a)

Committee Comments:

Court Rule 28.2 has no counterpart in FRAP and is therefore classified as Miscellaneous. No substantive change from prior Court Rule 28.2 is intended.

107.3 Non-Conforming Motion, Brief or Appendix

If a motion, brief, or appendix submitted for filing does not comply with F.R.A.P. 27–32 or 3rd Cir. L.A.R. 27.0–32.0, the clerk shall file the document, but notify the party of the need to promptly correct the deficiency. The clerk shall also cite this rule and indicate to the defaulting party how he or she failed to comply. In the event a party subsequently corrects the deficiencies in either a brief or appendix pursuant to this rule and that party prevails on appeal, costs which were incurred in order to bring the brief or appendix into compliance may not be allowed. If the party fails or declines to correct the deficiency, the clerk shall refer the defaulting document, any motion or answer by the party, and pertinent correspondence to a judge of this court for review. If the court finds that the party continues not to be in compliance with the rules despite the notice by the clerk, the court may, in its discretion, impose sanctions as it may deem appropriate, including but not limited to the dismissal of the appeal, striking of the document, imposition of costs or disciplinary sanctions upon counsel.

Source: 1988 Court Rule 21.4

Cross-references: F.R.A.P. 3(a), 30(b)(2), 38; 3rd Cir. L.A.R. 27.0–32.0

Committee Comments:

Court Rule 21.4 has no counterpart in F.R.A.P. and is therefore classified as Miscellaneous. No substantive change from prior Court Rule 21.4 is intended.

107.4 Sanctions Pursuant to F.R.A.P. 30(b)(2)

(a) The court, *sua sponte* by Rule to Show Cause or on the motion of any party, may impose sanctions in the form of denial of all or some of the costs of the appeal upon finding that any party has unreasonably and vexatiously caused the inclusion of materials in an appendix that are unnecessary for the determination of the issues presented on appeal.

(b) A party filing such a motion shall do so not later than ten (10) days after a bill of costs has been served. The movant shall submit with the motion an itemized statement specifically setting forth, by name and appendix page number, the item or items that the movant asserts were unnecessarily included in the appendix.

(c) Any party against whom sanctions are requested may file an answer to the motion or Rule to Show Cause, which shall be filed within ten (10) days after service of the motion or Rule to Show Cause.

Source: 1988 Court Rule 20.4

Cross-references: F.R.A.P. 30(b)(2); 3rd Cir. L.A.R. 30.5

Committee Comments:

This Miscellaneous Rule is identical to 3rd Cir. L.A.R. 30.5. No substantive change from prior Court Rule 20.4 is intended.

(As amended Nov. 1997; Nov. 1999, eff. Jan. 1, 2000.)

LAR MISC. 108.0. APPLICATIONS FOR ATTORNEY'S FEES AND EXPENSES

108.1 Application For Fees

(a) Except as otherwise provided by statute, all applications for an award of attorney's fees and other expenses relating to a case filed in this court, regardless of the source of authority for assessment, shall be filed within thirty (30) days after the entry of this court's judgment, unless a timely petition for rehearing or suggestion for rehearing en banc has been filed, in which case a request for attorney's fees shall be filed within fourteen (14) days after the court's disposition of such petition or suggestion. Such application shall be filed with the clerk in the time set forth above whether or not the parties seek further action in the case or further review from any court.

(b) The court shall strictly adhere to the time set forth above and grant exceptions only in extraordinary circumstances.

(c) The application shall include a short statement of the authority pursuant to which the party seeks the award. The application shall also show the nature and extent of services rendered and the amount sought, including an itemized statement in affidavit form from the attorney stating the actual time expended and the rate at which fees are computed, together with a statement of expenses for which reimbursement is sought.

Source: 1988 Court Rule 27.1

Cross-references: None

Committee Comments:

Prior Court Rule 27.1 has no counterpart in FRAP and is therefore classified as Miscellaneous. No substantive change from prior Court Rule 27.1 is intended. LAR Misc. 108.3 addresses claims for attorney's fees and expenses under the Criminal Justice Act, 18 U.S.C. § 3006A.

108.2 Objections To Applications For Fees

Written objections to an allowance of attorney's fees, setting forth specifically the basis for objection, shall be filed within ten (10) days after service of the application. Thereafter, the court may, when appropriate, either refer the application to the district court or agency where the case originated or refer the application to a master.

Source: 1988 Court Rule 27.2

Cross-references: FRAP 48; 3rd Cir. LAR 48.0

Committee Comments:

Prior Court Rule 27.2 has no counterpart in FRAP and is therefore classified as Miscellaneous. No substantive change from prior Court Rule 27.2 is intended.

108.3 Fee Applications Under 18 U.S.C. § 3006A

All claims for attorney's fees and reimbursement for expenses reasonably incurred by counsel in representing a defendant under the Criminal Justice Act, 18 U.S.C. § 3006A, shall be filed with the clerk no later than 45 days after the conclusion of the attorney's representation. Such claims shall be itemized and prepared on prescribed forms.

Source: 1988 Court Rule 30.1

Cross-references: 18 U.S.C. § 3006A; Third Circuit Criminal Justice Act Plan, Chapter 4(2) (1991)

Committee Comments:

Prior Court Rule 30.1 has no counterpart in FRAP and is therefore classified as Miscellaneous. No substantive change from prior Court Rule 30.1 is intended.

(As amended Nov. 1997.)

LAR MISC. 109.0. COUNSEL IN DIRECT CRIMINAL APPEALS

109.1 Trial Counsel to Continue Representation on Appeal

Trial counsel in criminal cases, whether retained or appointed, are expected to continue on appeal absent extraordinary circumstances. After the entry of an order of judgment, counsel will not be permitted to withdraw from a direct criminal appeal without specific leave of this court. Trial counsel not members of the bar of this court shall promptly move for admission pursuant to 3rd Cir. LAR 46.1.

Source: None

Cross-references: None

Committee Comments:

New provision. 3rd Cir. LAR Misc. 109.1 is designed to remind trial counsel in criminal cases that they are expected to continue the representation of their clients through appeal. "Trial counsel" includes counsel who have represented a client at pretrial, plea or sentencing proceedings.

109.2 Motions by Trial Counsel To Withdraw Representation

(a) Where, upon review of the district court record, trial counsel is persuaded that the appeal presents no issue of even arguable merit, trial counsel may file a motion to withdraw and supporting brief pursuant to *Anders v. California*, 386 U.S. 738, 87 S.Ct. 1396, 18 L.Ed.2d 493 (1967), which shall be served upon the appellant and the United States. The United States shall file a brief in response. Appellant may also file a brief in response *pro se*. After all briefs have been filed, the clerk will refer the case to a merits panel. If the panel agrees that the appeal is without merit, it will grant trial counsel's *Anders* motion, and dispose of the appeal without appointing new counsel. If the panel finds arguable merit to the appeal, it will discharge current counsel, appoint substitute counsel, restore the case to the calendar, and order supplemental briefing.

(b) In cases in which a motion to withdraw filed by counsel appointed under the Criminal Justice Act has been granted after the filing of a brief pursuant to *Anders v. California*, 386 U.S. 738, 87 S.Ct. 1396, 18 L.Ed.2d 493 (1967), the court in its decision determining the case may state that the issues presented in the appeal lack legal merit for purposes of counsel filing a petition for writ of certiorari in the Supreme Court. In such a case counsel shall be under no obligation to file a petition. In all other cases in which counsel appointed under the Criminal Justice Act is of the opinion, in his or her professional judgment, that no issues are present which warrant the filing of a petition for writ of certiorari in the Supreme Court, counsel shall promptly file with the court of appeals a motion stating that opinion with particularity and requesting leave to withdraw. *See Austin v. United States*, 513 U.S. 5, 115 S.Ct. 380, 115 S.Ct. 380, 130 L.Ed.2d 219 (1994). Any such motion shall be served on the appellant and the United States.

(c) If the court is of the opinion in a case in which counsel has been appointed under the Criminal Justice Act that there are no issues present which warrant the filing of a petition for writ of certiorari, the court may include a statement to that effect in its decision and counsel may thereafter file the appropriate motion to withdraw. Any such motion shall be served on the appellant and the United States. The absence of a statement by the court with respect to the merit of issues which might be presented to the Supreme Court shall not be construed as an indication of the opinion of the court of appeals of merit or lack of merit of any issue.

Source: None

Cross-references: Third Circuit Criminal Justice Act Plan, Chapter 3

Committee Comments:

New provision. 3rd Cir. LAR Misc. 109.2 sets out for the first time the procedure by which trial counsel may withdraw from a non-meritorious criminal appeal pursuant to *Anders v. California*, 386 U.S. 738, 87 S.Ct. 1396, 18 L.Ed.2d 493 (1967). Addition of sections (b) and (c) was made in response to *Austin v. United States*, 513 U.S. 5, 115 S.Ct. 380, 130 L.Ed.2d 219 (1994).

(As amended Nov. 1997.)

LAR MISC. 110.0. CERTIFICATION OF QUESTIONS OF STATE LAW

110.1 Certification of Questions of State Law

When the procedures of the highest court of a state provide for certification to that court by a federal court of questions arising under the laws of that state which will control the outcome of a case pending in the federal court, this court, sua sponte or on motion of a party, may certify such a question to the state court in accordance with the procedures of that court, and will stay the case in this court to await the state court's decision whether to accept the question certified. The certification will be made after the briefs are filed in this court. A motion for certification shall be included in the moving party's brief.

(Added Nov. 1997.)

LAR MISC. 111.0. DEATH PENALTY CASES

111.1 Scope

This rule, in conjunction with all other applicable rules, shall govern all cases in which this court is required to rule on the imposition of the death penalty. The rule shall be applicable to direct criminal appeals, appeals from the grant or denial of a motion to vacate sentence or a petition for writ of habeas corpus, appeals from the grant or denial of requests for stay or injunctive relief, applications under 28 U.S.C. § 2244 and/or § 2255, and original petitions for writ of habeas corpus.

Source: 1988 Court Rule 29 (Introductory Paragraph)

Cross-references: 18 U.S.C. § 3731, 28 U.S.C. §§ 2254, 2255; Federal Rules of Appellate Procedure; 3rd Cir. LAR; 3rd Cir. Internal Operating Procedures

Committee Comments:

Prior Court Rule 29 (Introductory Paragraph) has no counterpart in FRAP and is therefore classified as Miscellaneous. 3rd Cir. LAR Misc. 111.1 broadens the scope of the prior rule to provide for review of death sentences imposed on federal as well as state prisoners. Where applicable, 3rd Cir. LAR Misc. 111.2–111.7 are similarly amended to reflect the broadened scope of 3rd Cir.Misc. 111.0.

111.2 Preliminary Requirements

(a) In aid of this court's potential jurisdiction, each party in any proceeding filed in any district court in this circuit challenging the imposition of a sentence of death pursuant to a federal or state court judgment shall file a "Certificate of Death Penalty Case" with any initial pleading filed in the district court. A certificate shall also be filed by the U.S. Attorney upon return of a verdict of death in a federal criminal case. The certificate will include the following information: names, addresses, and telephone numbers of parties and counsel; if set, the proposed date of execution of sentence; and the emergency nature of the proceedings. Upon docketing, the clerk of the district court will transmit a copy of the certificate, together with a copy of the petition, to the clerk of this court.

(b) Upon entry of an appealable order in the district court, the clerk of the district court and appellant's counsel will prepare the record for appeal. The record will be transmitted to this court within five (5) days after the filing of a notice of appeal from the entry of an appealable order under 18 U.S.C. § 3731, 28 U.S.C. § 1291, or 28 U.S.C. § 1292(a)(1), unless the appealable order is entered within fourteen (14) days of the date of a scheduled execution, in which case the record shall be transmitted immediately by expedited delivery.

(c) Upon the entry of a warrant or order setting an execution date in any case within the geographical boundaries of this circuit, and in aid of this court's potential jurisdiction, the clerk is directed to monitor the status of the execution and any pending litigation and to establish communications with all parties and relevant state and/or federal courts. Without further order of this court, the clerk may direct parties to lodge with this court up to five copies of (1) relevant portions of previous state and/or federal court records, or the entire record, and (2) pleadings, briefs, and transcripts of any ongoing proceedings.

Source: 1988 Court Rule 29.1

Cross-references: 18 U.S.C. § 3731, 28 U.S.C. §§ 1291, 1292

Committee Comments:

Prior Court Rule 29.1 has no counterpart in F.R.A.P. and is therefore classified as Miscellaneous. The prior rule's general reference to a "certificate providing specific information" has been changed to the more specific "Certificate of Death Penalty Case" to reflect current practice. Subsection (c) directs the clerk to establish lines of communication with the sentencing court and other concerned parties and to authorize the filing of papers and court records in advance of the court's jurisdiction. This section has been added because some parties in recent cases have challenged the clerk's authority to request information in the absence of a docketed appeal. Because early warning is critical, the court expressly delegates this authority to the clerk pursuant to this local rule.

111.3 Review of Direct Criminal Appeals, Petitions for Writs of Habeas Corpus and Motions to Vacate Sentence

(a) In all such cases, the district court shall articulate the reasons for its disposition of the case in a written opinion, which shall be expeditiously prepared and filed, or by an oral opinion from the bench, which shall be promptly transcribed.

(b) The district court shall state whether a certificate of appealability is granted or denied at the time a final decision is entered on the merits of a claim seeking relief under 28 U.S.C. § 2254 or 2255. If the district court grants the certificate of appealability, it shall state the issues that merit the granting of the certificate and it shall also grant a stay pending disposition of the appeal except as provided in 28 U.S.C. § 2262.

(c) The denial of a certificate of appealability by the district court will not delay consideration by this court of a motion for stay or review of the merits. If the court grants a certificate of appealability, it may thereafter affirm, reverse or remand without further briefing under I.O.P. 10.6 or may direct full briefing and oral argument.

Source: 1988 Court Rule 29.2

Cross-references: 28 U.S.C. § 2254

Committee Comments:

Subsection (c) is intended to clarify this court's practice with respect to certificates of appealability in death penalty cases. In accordance with *Barefoot v. Estelle,* 463 U.S. 880 (1982), the court of appeals may consider, in addition to whether there has been a substantial showing of the denial of a constitutional right, the severity of the sentence in determining whether a certificate of appealability should be issued. Technical changes were made to conform to the Antiterrorism and Effective Death Penalty Act. This rule takes no position on the question of whether a district court can grant or deny a certificate of appealability.

111.4 Motion for Stay of Execution of a Federal or state Court Judgment and Motions to Vacate Orders Granting a Stay

(a) Except as provided in 28 U.S.C. § 2262, motions for stay of execution and motions to vacate stay orders may be filed in docketed requests for certificate of appealability, applications to file a second or successive petition, or appeals from the denial of injunctive relief. No such motion may be entertained unless a case has been docketed in this court. If a stay application is submitted to this court before a district court decision is entered, the clerk shall transmit the motion to the panel designated to hear and dispose of the case.

(b) Documents Required. The movant shall file the original and three (3) copies of a motion and serve all parties. Legible copies of the documents listed in I–x* below must be attached to the motion. If time does not permit, the motion may be filed without attachments, but the movant shall file the necessary copies as soon as possible.

(1) The complaint or petition to the district court;

(2) Each brief or memorandum of authorities filed by both parties in the district court;

(3) The opinion giving the reasons advanced by the district court for granting or denying relief;

(4) The district court judgment granting or denying relief;

(5) The application to the district court for a stay;

(6) The district court order granting or denying a stay, and the statement of reasons for its action;

(7) The certificate of appealability or, if there is none, the order denying a certificate of appealability;

(8) A copy of each state or federal court opinion or judgment in cases in which appellant was a party involving any issue presented to this court or, if the ruling was not made in a written opinion or judgment, a copy of the relevant portions of the transcripts;

(9) A copy of the docket entries of the district court; and

(10) Notice of appeal.

(c) Emergency Motions. Emergency motions or applications, whether addressed to the court or to an individual judge, shall ordinarily be filed with the clerk rather than an individual circuit judge. If time does not permit the filing of a motion or application in person, by mail, or by wire, counsel may communicate with the clerk or a single judge of this court and thereafter shall file the motion with the clerk in writing as promptly as possible. The motion, application, or oral communication shall contain a brief account of the prior actions of this court or judge to which the motion or application, or a substantially similar or related petition for relief, has been submitted.

* So in original. Probably should read "(1)–(10)".

Source: 1988 Court Rule 29.3

Cross-references: 28 U.S.C. § 2251; FRAP 8

Committee Comments:

Prior Court Rule 29.3 has no counterpart in FRAP and is therefore classified as Miscellaneous. Except where necessary to reflect the expansion of this rule to reach federal prisoners, no substantive change from prior Court Rule 29.3 is intended.

111.5 Statement of the Case; Exhaustion; Issues Presented

In addition to requirements set forth in 3rd Cir. LAR 28 with respect to the contents of motions and briefs, any application, motion, or brief that may result in either a disposition on the merits or the grant or denial of a stay of execution shall include:

(a) A statement of the case delineating precisely the procedural history of the case;

(b) With respect to state habeas corpus petitions brought pursuant to 28 U.S.C. § 2254, a statement of exhaustion with respect to each issue presented to the district court indicating whether it has been exhausted and if not, what circumstances exist that may justify an exception to the exhaustion requirement.

(c) The parties shall fully address every issue presented to this court. Supplemental briefing will be permitted only by order of this court.

Source: 1988 Court Rule 29.4

Cross-references: None

Committee Comments:

Prior Court Rule 29.4 has no counterpart in FRAP and is therefore classified as Miscellaneous. Except where necessary to reflect the expansion of this rule to reach federal prisoners, no substantive change from prior Court Rule 29.4 is intended.

111.6 Consideration Of Merits

The panel to which an appeal has been assigned shall consider and expressly rule on the merits before vacating or denying a stay of execution.

Source: 1988 Court Rule 29.5

Cross-references: None

Committee Comments:

None

111.7 Determination of Causes by the Court En Banc

(a) Filing. The filing of petitions seeking hearing or rehearing by the court en banc shall be governed by FRAP 35 and 3rd Cir. LAR 35. However, because of the difficulty of delivering petitions seeking hearing or rehearing by the court en banc to the judges of the court, the parties are hereby notified that due to these logistical considerations any such petition filed within 48 hours of a scheduled execution may not be delivered to the judges of the court in sufficient time for adjudication prior to the time of the scheduled execution. Petitions for rehearing by the court en banc filed within 48 hours of a scheduled execution shall be processed and distributed by the normal means of delivery used by the court unless the panel handling the case has entered an order for expedited voting in accordance to subsection (b) of this rule.

(b) Consideration. Consideration of a petition seeking hearing or rehearing by the court en banc will be in accordance with the procedures specified in the court's Internal Operating Procedures except that if an execution is scheduled, the original panel which has determined the matter may, upon a majority vote, direct that the time normally allowed for voting to request answers or to grant the petition may be reduced to a time specified by the panel. Upon the entry of an order by the panel reducing the time for voting, the clerk shall immediately transmit the petition and the order to the court by the most expedient means available.

(c) Stays. Generally the court will not enter a stay of execution solely to allow additional time for counsel to prepare, or for the court to consider, a petition for rehearing or for rehearing by the court en banc except as follows:

(1) A stay may be granted in order to allow time for counsel to prepare, or for the court to consider, a petition for rehearing upon majority vote of the original panel. Such a vote will be based upon a determination that there is a reasonable possibility that a majority of the active members of the court would vote to grant rehearing by the court en banc and whether there is a substantial possibility of reversal of its decision, in addition to a likelihood that irreparable harm will result if the decision is not stayed.

(2) In the event that four judges vote to direct the filing of answers to a petition seeking rehearing by the court en banc, the presiding judge of the merits panel will enter a stay.

(3) A stay entered in accordance with 3rd Cir. LAR 8.2 in a direct appeal of a conviction or sentence in a criminal case in which the district court has imposed a sentence of death will remain in effect until the court's mandate issues. The mandate will ordinarily not issue until such time that the time for filing a petition for rehearing has expired, or if such a petition has been filed, until the petition has been determined.

(d) No petition for rehearing shall be filed from the denial of a petition seeking authorization under 28 U.S.C. § 2244 or § 2255 to file a second or successive habeas corpus petition under § 2254 or motion to vacate sentence under § 2255.

Source: 6th Cir. Rule 28(k), 11th Cir. IOP 35–11.8 [LAR Misc. 111.7(a)]; 4th Cir. IOP 22.3(b) [LAR Misc. 111.7(c)]; 5th Cir. IOP 8.11 [LAR Misc. 111.7(c)(1)]

Cross-references: FRAP 35 and 40; 3rd Cir. LAR 35; Third Circuit Internal Operating Procedures, Chapter 9 (1994)

Committee Comments:

New Provision. Although the extraordinary nature of death penalty cases is recognized, this section must be read in conjunction with 3rd Cir. LAR 35.4 in which it is emphasized that the court does not favor requests for hearing or rehearing en banc. Because 28 U.S.C. § 2244(b)(3)(D) prohibits the filing of a petition for rehearing from the denial of an application seeking permission to file a second or successive § 2254 or § 2255 petition, there is no conflict with Rule 25(a), FRAP, which states that the clerk may not reject a paper "solely because it is not presented in proper form." The rejection of such a petition for rehearing is not for form, but is required by statute.

111.8 Post–Judgment Motions

(a) Mandate: The panel may order that the mandate of the court issue forthwith or after such time as it may fix.

(b) Stays of Execution: In ruling on a motion for stay to permit the filing and consideration of a petition for writ of certiorari, the panel shall determine whether there is a reasonable probability that the United States Supreme Court would consider the underlying issues sufficiently meritorious to grant the petition.

Source: 1988 Court Rule 29.6

Cross-references: None

Committee Comments:

No substantive change from prior Court Rule 29.6 is intended.

111.9 Second or Successive Petitions

The procedures of LAR 22.5 shall apply to the filing of a petition seeking authorization under 28 U.S.C. § 2244 or 2255 to file a second or successive habeas corpus petition under § 2254 or motion to vacate sentence under § 2255 in a death penalty case.

Source: LAR 22.5

Cross-references: 28 U.S.C. §§ 2244, 2254, and 2255

Committee Comments:

This rule makes clear that the procedures for filing a second or successive petition under 28 U.S.C. § 2244 set forth in LAR 22.5 also apply in death penalty cases and insures that the court will have the documents necessary to decide such petitions.

(As amended Nov. 1997; Nov. 1999, eff. Jan. 1, 2000.)

LAR MISC. 112.0 PETITIONS FOR WRIT OF CERTIORARI TO THE SUPREME COURT OF THE VIRGIN ISLANDS

112.1 Considerations Governing Review on Certiorari

(a) Review on writ of certiorari is not a matter of right, but of judicial discretion, and will be granted only when there are special and important reasons therefor. The following, while neither controlling nor limiting the court's discretion, indicate the character of reasons that will be considered.

(1) The Supreme Court of the Virgin Islands has decided a question in a way that conflicts with applicable decisions of this court, other appellate courts, or the United States Supreme Court.

(2) The Supreme Court of the Virgin Islands has so far departed from the accepted and usual course of judicial proceedings, or so far sanctioned such a departure by a lower court, as to call for an exercise of this court's powers of review.

(3) The Supreme Court of the Virgin Islands has decided an important question of federal or territorial law that has not been, but should be, decided by this court.

(4) The Supreme Court of the Virgin Islands was without jurisdiction of the case, or where, because of disqualifications or other reason, the decision of the Supreme Court of the Virgin Islands lacks the concurrence of the required majority of qualified non-recused judges.

(b) A petition for a writ of certiorari will rarely be granted when the asserted error consists of erroneous findings of fact or the misapplication of a properly stated rule of law. A petition for writ of certiorari that raises any issue or relies on any material fact that was omitted from or misstated in the opinion of the Supreme Court of the Virgin Islands will normally not be considered, unless the omission or misstatement was called to the attention of the Supreme Court of the Virgin Islands in a petition for rehearing. All other issues and facts may be presented in the petition for a writ of certiorari without the necessity of filing a petition for rehearing.

112.2 Petition for Writ of Certiorari—How Sought

(a) In both civil and criminal cases, review of a final decision of the Supreme Court of the Virgin Islands may be sought pursuant to 48 U.S.C. 1613 by filing a petition for a writ of certiorari with the Clerk of the United States Court of Appeals for the Third Circuit within sixty (60) days from the entry of judgment sought to be reviewed on the docket of the Supreme Court of the Virgin Islands. A petition filed by an incarcerated person will be deemed filed when placed in the prison mail system; the petition must be accompanied by a statement under penalty of perjury stating the date the petition was placed in the prison mail system and stating that first-class postage has been pre-paid. In all other cases, the petition must be received by the Clerk in Philadelphia by the sixtieth day.

(b) Petitioner must file, with proof of service, an original and three copies of the petition for writ of certiorari. Petitioner must serve one copy of the petition for writ of certiorari on each of the parties to the proceedings in the Supreme Court of the Virgin Islands. When filing the petition, petitioner must pay the docketing fee, which shall be the same as the fee charged for an original proceeding such as a petition for writ of mandamus or petition for review of an agency order, in the Court of Appeals. Counsel for the petitioner must enter an appearance within ten days of filing a petition.

(c) Parties interested jointly may file a joint petition. A petitioner not shown on the petition at the time of filing may not later join in that petition.

(d) If a petition for rehearing of the final decision of the Supreme Court of the Virgin Islands is timely filed pursuant to the Rules of the Supreme Court of the Virgin Islands or if that court sua sponte considers rehearing, the time for filing the petition for writ of certiorari shall run from entry of the order denying the petition or, if rehearing is granted, from entry of the order on rehearing.

112.3 Cross-Petitions for Certiorari

(a) Unless a rule specifies a different procedure for a cross-petition for certiorari, the rules for a petition for certiorari apply to cross-petitions.

(b) A cross-petition for a writ of certiorari may be filed within twenty-one (21) days after the first petition was filed. When filing the cross-petition, cross-petitioner must pay the docketing fee. The cross-petitioner must serve one copy of the petition on each of the parties to the proceedings in the Supreme Court of the Virgin Islands.

(c) A cross-petitioner need not duplicate the appendix filed by petitioner.

112.4 Extension of Time to File Petitions

(a) A circuit judge, for good cause shown, may extend the time for filing a petition for writ of certiorari or cross-petition for a period not exceeding thirty (30) days. Any application for extension of time within which to file a petition for writ of certiorari must set out the grounds on which the jurisdiction of this court is invoked, must identify the judgment sought to be reviewed and have appended thereto a copy of the opinion, and must set forth with specificity the reasons justifying an extension. An untimely petition for writ of certiorari must be accompanied by a motion for extension of time. However, an application for extension of time to file a petition for certiorari ordinarily will not be granted, if filed less than five (5) days before the expiration of the time to file a petition.

112.5 Denominating Parties

(a) The party filing the first petition for the writ of certiorari shall be denominated the petitioner; petitioner's denomination in the appeal or other proceeding before the Supreme Court and the Superior Court of the Virgin Islands must be included in the first paragraph of the statement of the case.

(b) Parties to the proceeding in the court whose judgment is sought to be reviewed are deemed parties in this court and shall be denominated respondents, unless the petitioner notifies the clerk of this court in writing of petitioner's belief that one or more of the parties below has no interest in the outcome of the petition. A copy of such notice must be served on all parties to the proceeding in the Supreme Court of the Virgin Islands. A party noted as no longer interested may remain a party by notifying the clerk in writing within ten (10) days from the date of service of petitioner's notice, with service on all other parties, that the party has an interest in the petition. Each respondent's denomination in the proceedings before the Supreme Court and the Superior Court of the Virgin Islands must be included in the petition for writ of certiorari in the first paragraph of the statement of the case. Any respondent who supports the position of a petitioner must meet the time schedule for filing responsive papers.

(c) A party who files a cross-petition for certiorari is denominated as respondent/cross-petitioner.

112.6 The Petition for Writ of Certiorari

(a) The petition for writ of certiorari must contain, in the following order:

(1) a table of contents;

(2) a table of authorities, including citations to the relevant constitutional provisions, treaties, statutes, ordinances, and regulations;

(3) a concise statement of the ground on which the jurisdiction of this court is invoked, with citations to applicable statutes and stating relevant facts establishing the finality of the order. The jurisdictional statement must also include the date of entry of the judgment sought to be reviewed, the date of any orders respecting rehearing, and, in the case of a cross-petition for a writ of certiorari, the date of the filing of the petition for a writ of certiorari;

(4) a concise statement, with citations to appropriate statutes, of the basis of jurisdiction of the Supreme Court of the Virgin Islands and of the Superior Court of the Virgin Islands;

(5) the questions presented for review, expressed concisely in relation to the circumstances of the case. The statement of the questions should not be argumentative or repetitious. The statement of a question presented will be deemed to comprise every subsidiary question fairly included therein. Only the questions set forth in the petition or fairly included therein will be considered by the court;

(6) a concise statement of the case containing the facts material to the consideration of the questions presented. The first paragraph of the statement of the case must specify the denomination of each of the parties as they appeared in the Supreme Court of the Virgin Islands and the Superior Court of the Virgin Islands. The statement of the case must specify, with appropriate citation to the record, the stage in the proceedings, both in the Superior Court and the Supreme Court of the Virgin Islands, at which the questions sought to be reviewed were raised and the ruling thereon;

(7) a direct and concise argument amplifying the reasons why the questions for review are important enough to warrant issuance of the writ; and

(8) a short conclusion, which must include a statement of the specific relief requested if the writ of certiorari is granted.

(b) All contentions in support of a petition for writ of certiorari must be set forth in the body of the petition, as provided by this rule. No separate brief in support of a petition for a writ of certiorari will be received, and the clerk will refuse to file any petition for a writ of certiorari to which is annexed or appended any supporting brief.

(c) Any reason for expedited treatment or request for interim relief must be made by separate motion. The requirement in Rule 8, F.R.A.P., that a request for stay or injunction pending appeal must first be made to the court below will be strictly enforced. Any motion for stay or injunction must attach the order of the Supreme Court of the Virgin Islands disposing of the motion for stay or injunction made to it in the first instance.

112.7 Appendix

(a) An original and three copies of an appendix must be filed with the petition. The appendix must contain in the following order:

(1) copies of all docket entries, opinions, orders, findings of fact, and conclusions of law, whether written or oral (if recorded and transcribed), delivered upon the rendering of the judgment or decree by the Supreme Court of the Virgin Islands; and

(2) copies of any applicable local statutes, ordinances, and regulations.

(b) The above documents in subparagraphs (1) and (2) may be bound with the petition provided they do not exceed 75 pages.

(c) Cross-petitioners need not duplicate materials filed by the petitioner.

(d) Respondents wishing to file materials in addition to those filed by petitioner must file a motion for permission to file a supplemental appendix.

112.8 Brief in Opposition—in Support—Reply—Supplemental Briefs

(a) Within thirty (30) days of receipt of a petition for writ of certiorari, a respondent may file an original and three copies, with certificate of service, of an opposing brief. In addition to the merits of the questions presented, the brief should address whether the issues identified by the petitioner are suitable for review. The respondent may agree that the petition for certiorari should be granted because the case presents an important question, yet argue that the decision of the Supreme Court of the Virgin Islands is correct.

(b) A respondent supporting the position of the petitioner must file a response supporting the petition with 20 days of the opening of the case. Parties who file no document will not qualify for any relief from the court.

(c) If no response is received within the time prescribed, it will be assumed that the party does not wish to participate and will no longer receive notices from the clerk or be entitled to service of documents from the other parties. The clerk may direct a party to file a response. Ordinarily, a petition for certiorari will not be granted unless a response has been filed or requested.

(d) No motion by a respondent to dismiss a petition for writ of certiorari will be received. Objections to the jurisdiction of the court to grant the writ of certiorari may be included in the brief in opposition.

(e) Petitioner may file an original and three copies, with certificate of service, of a reply brief addressed to arguments first raised in the brief in opposition within fourteen (14) days of receipt of respondent's brief.

(f) Motions for extensions of time to file a brief are governed by Third Circuit L.A.R. 31.4.

(g) No supplemental filings may be made by any party except as provided in Rule 28(j), F.R.A.P.

112.9 Format and Length

(a) The typeface, page size, margins, line spacing, binding, and text style of a petition for writ of certiorari and responses must be in compliance with Rule 32(a), F.R.A.P. and Third Circuit L.A.R. 32.1. The cover of a petition for writ of certiorari must be blue; the cover of respondent's brief must be red; the cover of a reply brief must be gray.

(b) A proportionately spaced petition for a writ of certiorari and response must not exceed 5,600 words, exclusive of the table of contents and table of authorities. A reply brief must not exceed 2,300 words.

112.10 Disposition of a Petition for Writ of Certiorari

(a) The petition and any responses shall be referred to a motions panel for disposition. If a petition for writ of certiorari is granted, the clerk will issue a briefing schedule and the case shall proceed as other appeals in accordance with the Federal Rules of Appellate Procedure and Local Appellate Rules but with review limited to the questions on which the writ of certiorari was granted.

112.11 Record on Review

(a) The record on review shall consist of the record presented to the Supreme Court of the Virgin Islands.

(b) Within thirty (30) days of an order granting a writ of certiorari, the Clerk of the Supreme Court of the Virgin Islands must file a certified copy of the docket entries in lieu of the record with the Clerk of the Court of Appeals. The filing of the certified docket entries with the Court of Appeals constitutes the filing of the record.

112.12 Rehearings

(a) Rules 35 and 40, F.R.A.P., govern petitions for rehearing an order denying a petition for writ of certiorari.

(b) The grounds for a petition for rehearing of an order denying a petition for writ of certiorari are limited to intervening circumstances of substantial or controlling effect or to other substantial grounds. A petitioner must certify that the petition is restricted to the grounds specified in this paragraph and that it is presented in good faith and not for delay. This certification is in lieu of that required by Third Circuit L.A.R. 35.1.

(c) No response to a petition for rehearing will be received unless requested by the court, but no petition will be granted without an opportunity to submit a response.

(d) Consecutive petitions for rehearings will not be received.

112.13 Costs

(a) Each party shall bear its own costs in a proceeding seeking a writ of certiorari, unless the court either sua sponte or following a motion directs that costs be taxed under Rule 38, F.R.A.P., for a vexatious or frivolous petition. If the writ is granted and the case proceeds to briefing and decision, costs may be taxed as in Rule 39, F.R.A.P.

112.14 Applicability of the Federal Rules of Appellate Procedure

(a) The Federal Rules of Appellate Procedure, to the extent that they are not inconsistent with any statutory provisions or these rules, may be applied to a proceeding seeking a writ of certiorari.

(Eff. Dec. 1, 2007.)

ORDER ESTABLISHING A TEMPORARY LOCAL RULE FOR ELECTRONIC FILING OF PETITIONS FOR REHEARING

A pilot program for the electronic transmission of petitions for rehearing by the Court has been established pursuant to Rule 25(a)(2)(D), F.R.A.P. It is hereby ORDERED that the Court adopts this practice order pending possible consideration of adoption of a permanent rule.

A party may file a petition for rehearing by electronic transmission. The page limitation set forth in Rule 40(b), F.R.A.P. shall be strictly enforced. The judgment, order or opinion as to which rehearing is sought shall be attached as an exhibit to the petition. Petitions which are submitted electronically must be in Adobe.pdf format.

Service of the petition for rehearing submitted electronically may be by e-mail, fax, mail, or hand delivery. A party may serve the opposing party electronically **only** with the prior consent of the opposing party. If electronic service is utilized, the filing party must note in the certificate of service that the opposing party consented to electronic service.

The filing party must include a certificate of service which complies with Rule 25(d), F.R.A.P clearly stating the manner and date of service.

The filing party will complete an Electronic Filing of Petition for Rehearing form which may be obtained at: www.ca3.uscourts.gov under Information and Forms and Petitions for Rehearing. The form shall be included as a separate attachment in the transmission to the Clerk.

The address for filing the petitions for rehearing is: petitions_rehearing@ca3.uscourts.gov

The Re: line or Subject Line for the message shall be the case number for the Court of Appeals.

The filing party will forward one hard copy of the petition for rehearing with an original signature and the Electronic Petition for Rehearing form to the Clerk by overnight mail.

The Clerk will review the petition when received for compliance with the rules. If it is determined that the petition does not comply with the applicable rules, the filing party will be notified electronically of any deficiency and directed to take corrective action. The opposing parties will be notified in the same manner as indicated in the certificate of service. If the deficiency is the absence of a certificate of service, then the parties will be notified by mail.

Petitions for rehearing submitted electronically which are in compliance with the applicable rules will be filed as of the date of receipt by the Clerk's e-mail system.

A party may electronically file the following motions with the petition for rehearing: 1) motion to file petition for rehearing out of time; 2) motion to file petition for rehearing with excess pagination; and 3) motion for leave to attach exhibits to the petition. The above motions must be submitted in Adobe.pdf format as a separate attachment to the transmission. The filing party will include one hard copy of the motion along with the petition for rehearing and the Electronic Petition for Rehearing form which are being sent to the Clerk by overnight mail. All other motions, including motions for extension of time to file a petition for rehearing, must be submitted in the traditional manner.

No questions or other communications shall be included with the electronic transmission of the petition for rehearing. If a party has a question regarding these procedures such questions shall be directed to the Clerk in writing through regular mail or by telephoning the Clerk's office at 215–597–2995.

Effective March 3, 2003.

APPENDIX I. INTERNAL OPERATING PROCEDURES OF THE UNITED STATES COURT OF APPEALS FOR THE THIRD CIRCUIT

Effective October 27, 1997

Including Amendments Received Through August 15, 2008

INTRODUCTION

A. Objectives.

These "Internal Operating Procedures" (IOPs) cover the essential processes of this court from the distribution of the briefs to the final termination of the appeal and are designed:

(1) To insure that appeals are processed as expeditiously as possible consistent with the careful discharge of appellate responsibilities;

(2) To insure decisional stability and avoid intracircuit conflict of decisions by providing a means for the panel system to operate efficiently and at the same time provide that a holding of a published opinion of the court may not be overruled without the approval of a majority of the en banc court;

(3) To insure the opportunity for contributions by every active judge to every decision of precedential or institutional significance; and

(4) To maintain the highest degree of collegiality among the judges.

B. Implementation.

These IOPs implement:

(1) Statutory mandates;

(2) The Federal Rules of Appellate Procedure;

(3) The Third Circuit Local Appellate Rules (LAR); and

(4) The customs and traditions of this court.

(Effective October 27, 1997.)

CHAPTER 1. BRIEFS AND PREPARATION

IOP 1.1 Prior to Panel Sitting.

Briefs and appendices are distributed sufficiently in advance to afford at least four (4) full weeks' study in chambers prior to the panel sitting. In special circumstances, such as expedited cases, the panel may unanimously agree to a shorter reading period. Except where typewritten briefs have been permitted, two sets of briefs and one appendix, two if available, are furnished to each chambers. At the termination of the case, the briefs and appendices need not be returned to the Clerk. Generally, fully briefed cases are randomly assigned by the Clerk to a three-judge panel.

IOP 1.2 Responsibility of Panel Prior to Scheduled Sitting.

This court has the tradition of carefully reading briefs and reviewing appendices prior to oral argument or conference. Inherent in Local Appellate Rule 34.1 is the understanding that each judge will read the briefs and review the appendices a minimum of eleven (11) days before the first day of the panel sitting. (Effective October 27, 1997.)

CHAPTER 2. ORAL ARGUMENT

IOP 2.1 Determination in Panel Cases.

The panel determines whether there will be oral argument and the amount of time allocated. There is oral argument if it is requested by at least one judge. Each judge communicates his or her views to the other panel members. No later than eleven (11) days before the first day of the panel sitting, the presiding judge furnishes the Clerk with the panel's determinations in accordance with the maximum request, up to twenty (20) minutes per side, of any single judge. Usually, fifteen (15) minutes per side is allotted. A request for oral argument beyond twenty (20) minutes a side is determined by a majority of the panel.

IOP 2.2 Determination in Cases En Banc.

There is oral argument in an en banc case if it is requested by at least one judge of the en banc court. No later than eleven (11) days before the en banc sitting, the Chief Judge or, in his or her absence, the presiding judge, furnishes the Clerk with the court's determination in accordance with the maximum request, up to thirty (30) minutes per side, of any judge. A request for oral argument beyond thirty (30) minutes a side is determined by a majority of the en banc court. Ordinarily, thirty (30) minutes per side will be allocated and an amicus will not argue unless at least four (4) members of the en banc court vote otherwise.

IOP 2.3 Failure to Notify Presiding Judge.

Should a judge fail to notify other panelists orally or in writing of his or her views prior to noon of the eleventh day before the panel sitting, the presiding judge assumes that the non-notifying judge agrees to be bound by the determinations of the other two judges or of the presiding judge, as the case may be.

IOP 2.4 Suggested Criteria for Oral Argument.

2.4.1 Experience discloses that judges usually find oral argument unnecessary when:

(a) The issue is tightly constrained, not novel, and the briefs adequately cover the arguments;

(b) The outcome of the appeal is clearly controlled by a decision of the Supreme Court or this court; or

(c) The state of the record will determine the outcome and the sole issue is either sufficiency of the evidence, the adequacy of jury instructions, or rulings as to admissibility of evidence, and the briefs adequately refer to the record.

2.4.2 Experience discloses that judges usually vote for oral argument when:

(a) The appeal presents a substantial and novel legal issue;

(b) The resolution of an issue presented by the appeal will be of institutional or precedential value;

(c) A judge has questions to ask counsel to clarify an important legal, factual, or procedural point;

(d) A decision, legislation, or an event subsequent to the filing of the last brief may significantly bear on the case; or

(e) An important public interest may be affected.

2.4.3 The foregoing criteria shall not be construed to limit any judge's discretion in voting for oral argument.

IOP 2.5 Notice to Counsel.

No later than ten (10) days prior to the first day of the panel sitting, the Clerk communicates to counsel in each case listed the names of the members of the panel and whether the case is to be orally argued.

(Effective October 27, 1997.)

CHAPTER 3. COMPOSITION OF PANELS AND ORDER OF PRECEDENCE

IOP 3.1 Composition of Panel.*

Unless there is a judicial emergency, each panel includes either two active judges of this court or one active judge and one senior judge of this court.

IOP 3.2 Presiding Judge.

The chief judge is the presiding judge. In the absence of the chief judge, the presiding judge is that judge of this court in active service next in precedence. See 28 U.S.C. § 45(b). Other active circuit judges sit in order of precedence based on the seniority of their commissions, followed by senior circuit judges and visiting judges.

IOP 3.3 Entering Court.

The panel assembles in the robing room approximately five (5) minutes prior to the opening of court. The judges enter the courtroom from the robing room in the reverse order of precedence. The next ranking judge is stationed to the right of the presiding judge facing the courtroom from the bench. All remain standing until the presiding judge sits.

(Effective October 27, 1997; amended effective January 1, 2000; July 1, 2002.)

*Publisher's Note. On June 27, 2006, the Court entered the following order: In the matter of Composition of Panels: IT APPEARING that this court is authorized fourteen (14) judgeships, but currently has only eleven (11) active judges [and] recently this court has lost two senior judges by reason of death, IT IS HEREBY ORDERED that I.O.P. 3.1's requirement that panels be composed of at least one active judge of the court is suspended for cases decided after June 30, 2006 until June 30, 2007 provided that the panel contained one active judge when the case was assigned.

CHAPTER 4. PANEL CONFERENCE PROCEDURE

IOP 4.1 Tentative Views.

After a case has been argued or submitted to a panel of the court, a conference is held to exchange tentative views as to the decision. The judges express views and tentative votes in reverse order of precedence. By unanimous agreement of the panel, conferences in submitted cases may be held by telephone or views may be exchanged by electronic mail prior to the submission date.

IOP 4.2 Opinion Assignment.

Following discussion and tentative votes, the presiding judge assigns those cases in which opinions of the court are to be drafted to the judges of the panel for preparation of the opinion of the court. If the panel is divided in its views and the presiding judge does not concur in the decision of the majority, the assignment is made by that member of the majority who is the ranking active judge of this court.

(Effective October 27, 1997.)

CHAPTER 5. OPINIONS

IOP 5.1 Forms of Opinions.

There are two forms of opinions: precedential and not precedential. A majority of the panel determines whether an opinion is designated as precedential or not precedential, unless a majority of the active judges of the court decides otherwise. The face of an opinion states whether it is precedential or not precedential.

IOP 5.2 Precedential Opinions.

An opinion, whether signed or per curiam, is designated as precedential and printed as a slip opinion when it has precedential or institutional value.

IOP 5.3 Not Precedential Opinions.

An opinion, whether signed or per curiam, that appears to have value only to the trial court or the parties is designated as not precedential and is not printed as a slip opinion but, unless otherwise provided by the court, it is posted on the court's internet website. A not precedential opinion may be issued without regard to whether the panel's decision is unanimous and without regard to whether the panel affirms, reverses, or grants other relief.

IOP 5.4 Listing of Counsel and Judge.

Counsel are listed on all precedential opinions and on not precedential opinions if the case was argued. The name of the district judge or magistrate judge is listed on all opinions.

IOP 5.5 Preparation and Circulation of Opinions.

5.5.1 By Author. The authoring judge prepares a draft opinion in accordance with the decision of the panel at conference, but the author may express any different views reached after subsequent study of the case. The opinion will set forth the reasons supporting the court's decision.

5.5.2 Circulation Within Panel. After the draft opinion has been prepared, the authoring judge circulates it, to the other two members of the panel with a request for approval or suggestions they may desire to make with respect to the draft opinion. Answering this request is given the highest priority by the other two judges, who shall communicate in writing their approval or disapproval within eight (8) days of receipt of the opinion. Absent a request for additional time, failure to respond within that time period shall be deemed an approval of the opinion as drafted. Because it is the opinion of the court, other members of the panel are free to make any suggestions relating to the modification of, addition to, or subtraction from the proposed text. Where a textual revision or addition is suggested, the suggesting judge submits his or her modification in specific language capable of being inserted into the opinion. When one of the other two judges approves, it becomes the proposed opinion of the court. Should the other panel members disagree with the author's draft, the opinion is reassigned by either the presiding judge or the ranking judge in active service who is a member of the panel's majority.

5.5.3 Time Schedule for Panel Drafting and Circulating Opinions; Reassignments.

(a) 60–day period for draft opinion writing. It is the aspirational goal of the court that, except in complex cases, the authoring judge transmit to the panel a draft opinion within sixty (60) days after assignment or after close of any supplemental briefing or other factors suspending the drafting process

(b) 45–day period to file concurring or dissenting opinion. If, after a second panel member approves the draft opinion, the third panel member desires to separately concur or dissent, the judge not joining in the opinion notifies the author promptly and transmits his or her separate opinion to the panel within forty-five (45) days after the second judge's approval is received. Panel opinions are not considered to be completed until each member has an opportunity to revise his or her opinion in response to those of other panel members.

5.5.4 To Non-panel Active Judges. Drafts of unanimous not precedential opinions do not circulate to non-panel judges. Drafts of precedential opinions and not precedential opinions that are not unanimous are circulated to all active judges of the court after the draft opinion has been approved by all three panel members, concurring or dissenting opinions have been transmitted, or all members of the panel have had the time set forth in IOP 5.6.3 to write separate opinions. Absent a request for additional time, if the third judge has not timely responded, the draft opinion is circulated to the active judges of the court with the notation added to the opinion that the third judge has not joined in the opinion. Non-panel active judges must notify the authoring judge within eight (8) days if they desire en banc consideration. The circulation to non-panel active judges contains a request for notification if there is a desire for en banc consideration. Although senior judges do not have a vote en banc, senior judges may choose to receive circulating opinions.

5.5.5 En banc Cases. The time schedule set forth in IOP 5.5. 2 and 5.5.3 is also followed in en banc cases, except that judges will give preparation of en banc opinions priority over preparation of panel opinions.

IOP 5.6 Filing of Opinions.

If, eight (8) days after the opinion is transmitted for circulation, insufficient votes for rehearing are received, the authoring judge transmits the original typescript to the Clerk for filing and notifies the author of any separate opinion to do likewise. The failure of a panel member to concur or dissent or to file a timely opinion does not delay the filing of the majority opinion or the entry of the judgment of this court.

IOP 5.7 Citations.

The court by tradition does not cite to its not precedential opinions as authority. Such opinions are not regarded as precedents that bind the court because they do not circulate to the full court before filing.

(Effective October 27, 1997; amended effective January 1, 2000; March 1, 2002; July 1, 2002.)

CHAPTER 6. JUDGMENT ORDERS

IOP 6.1 Panel Unanimity.

A case may be terminated in this court by a judgment order upon the unanimous decision of the panel.

IOP 6.2 Criteria.

6.2.1 A judgment order is filed when the panel unanimously determines to affirm the judgment or order of the district court or decision of the Tax Court, enforce or deny review of a decision or order of an administrative agency, or dismiss the appeal or petition for review for lack of jurisdiction or otherwise, and determines that a written opinion will have no precedential or institutional value.

6.2.2 A judgment order may be used when:

(a) The judgment of the district court is based on findings of fact which are not clearly erroneous;

(b) Sufficient evidence supports a jury verdict;

(c) Substantial evidence on the record as a whole supports a decision or order of an administrative agency;

(d) No error of law appears;

(e) The district court did not abuse its discretion on matters addressed thereto; or

(f) The court has no jurisdiction.

IOP 6.3 Form of Order.

6.3.1 A judgment order affirming the district court in a direct criminal appeal includes a statement of those issues raised by appellant and considered by the panel.

6.3.2 A judgment order may state that the case is affirmed by reference to the opinion of the district court or decision of the administrative agency and may contain one or more references to cases or other authorities.

IOP 6.4 Procedure.

6.4.1 At conference the panel decides whether the case requires an opinion or a judgment order. If the latter, the judge assigned to prepare the order furnishes other members of the panel with copies of the proposed order. The panel members indicate their approval either on a copy which is provided by the order writer or by signifying approval in writing by electronic mail or otherwise.

6.4.2 The order writer promptly arranges for filing the original with the Clerk.

(Effective October 27, 1997.)

CHAPTER 7. ORDERS REVERSING OR REMANDING

IOP 7.1 Retention of Jurisdiction.

When a panel deems it appropriate for this court to retain jurisdiction without disposing of the appeal and to remand the case to the district court, such as for correction or modification of the record pursuant to Fed.R.App.P. 10(e) or for consideration of a settlement reached on appeal, the panel may do so and hold the appeal in abeyance. In such an instance, the panel has discretion to retain assignment of the case or return it to the Clerk for reassignment upon its return.

IOP 7.2 Assignment Following Remand.

When an appeal is filed in a case which has previously been remanded, the Clerk will assign the appeal to a panel in the regular course unless directed otherwise by the Chief Judge after consultation with the original panel.

IOP 7.3 Reversal or Remand.

In some instances when a panel reverses or remands a case to the district court and it is not feasible to write an opinion, usually because the matter requires immediate attention, the court enters a dispositive order setting forth briefly the reasons for its action. Such an order does not circulate to the non-panel judges.

(Effective October 27, 1997.)

CHAPTER 8. PANEL REHEARING

IOP 8.1 Petition.

A petition for panel rehearing is sent to the members of the panel, including senior judges or visiting judges, with the request that they notify the authoring judge within ten (10) days of the date of the Clerk's letter forwarding the petition whether they vote to grant the petition or desire that an answer be filed. A judge who does not desire panel rehearing or the filing of an answer is not expected to respond.

IOP 8.2 Request for Answer.

If any member of the majority timely notifies the other members of the panel that an answer is desired, the author, if an active or senior judge of this court, enters an order directing the filing of an answer within fourteen (14) days. The Clerk forwards the answer to the panel members with the request that they notify the authoring judge within ten (10) days if they vote to grant the petition. A judge who does not desire panel rehearing is not expected to respond.

IOP 8.3 Disposition.

8.3.1 The author, if an active or senior judge of this court, enters an order granting panel rehearing if two members of the panel vote for panel rehearing, and vacates the panel's opinion and the judgment entered thereon. Otherwise, the author enters the order denying panel rehearing. If the author is a visiting judge or justice, the ranking active judge of this court on the panel majority receives responses to the petition, communicates with the Clerk, signs the necessary orders, and has all the administrative responsibility set forth in this IOP. A senior judge of this court who was the authoring judge handles all administrative responsibility on matters on which that judge has a vote but may choose to request the ranking active judge on the panel majority to undertake such administrative responsibility.

8.3.2 Any member of the panel may file an opinion sur denial of the petition for panel rehearing and direct its publication. When the panel grants a petition for rehearing and a petition for rehearing en banc is also pending, the judge who entered the order following panel rehearing notifies the active judges of the disposition, and whether the petition for rehearing is moot or if any further vote is required.

(Effective October 27, 1997; amended effective January 1, 2000.)

CHAPTER 9. EN BANC CONSIDERATION

IOP 9.1 Policy of Avoiding Intracircuit Conflict of Precedent.

It is the tradition of this court that the holding of a panel in a precedential opinion is binding on subsequent panels. Thus, no subsequent panel overrules the holding in a precedential opinion of a previous panel. Court en banc consideration is required to do so.

IOP 9.2 Hearing En Banc.

Initial en banc hearing is extraordinary; it is ordered only when a majority of the active judges who are not disqualified, provided that the judges who are not disqualified constitute a majority of the judges who are in regular active service, determines that the case is controlled by a prior decision of the court which should be reconsidered and the case is of such immediate importance that exigent circumstances require initial consideration by the full court.

IOP 9.3 Criteria for Rehearing En Banc.

9.3.1 This court strictly follows the precept of Fed. R.App.P. 35(a) and Local Appellate Rule 35.4 that rehearing en banc is not favored and will not be ordered unless consideration by the full court is necessary to secure or maintain uniformity of its decisions or the proceeding involves a question of exceptional importance.

9.3.2 This court does not ordinarily grant rehearing en banc when the panel's statement of the law is correct and the controverted issue is solely the application of the law to the circumstances of the case.

9.3.3 Rehearing en banc is ordinarily not granted when the only issue presented is one of state law.

IOP 9.4 Court Originated Rehearing En Banc.

9.4.1 If, during the eight-day circulation of draft opinions pursuant to IOP 5.5.2 and 5.7, a majority of the active judges who are not disqualified, provided that the judges who are not disqualified constitute a majority of the judges who are in regular active service, votes that the case be considered en banc, the Chief Judge enters an order for rehearing en banc.

9.4.2 If, during the eight-day period for circulation of draft opinions, one judge has timely voted for rehearing, another judge may obtain an extension of time to consider en banc rehearing by circulating a letter asking that the time for voting be extended for a period not to exceed five (5) working days beyond the eight-day time period. This request results in an automatic extension. Irrespective of the number of such requests, the voting time automatically is extended this one period only, unless the Chief Judge, upon application, grants a further extension of time. In death penalty cases, the times set forth herein may be reduced pursuant to Local Appellate Rule Misc. 111.7(b).

9.4.3 During the circulation of draft opinions, a judge who does not desire rehearing or who has no comment is not expected to respond. The active judge who has written a dissenting opinion is presumed to have voted for rehearing en banc absent a notification in writing to the contrary.

IOP 9.5 Rehearing En Banc on Petition by Party.

9.5.1 It is presumed that a petition for rehearing before the panel or suggestion for en banc rehearing filed by a party as provided by Fed.R.App.P. 40(a) or 35(b) requests both panel rehearing and rehearing en banc, unless the petition for panel rehearing under Rule 40(a) states explicitly that it does not request en banc rehearing under Rule 35(b).

9.5.2 When a petition for rehearing is filed, a copy of the petition is transmitted by the Clerk to each member of the panel which heard and decided the case and to the other active judges of the court with a request that they respond to the authoring judge if they desire rehearing or an answer. When the author is not an active member of the court, the Clerk requests that responses be directed to the ranking active judge of the majority. Any member of the panel majority may direct the Clerk to request an answer.

9.5.3 Pursuant to 28 U.S.C. § 46(c), only active judges of this court may vote for rehearing en banc. Therefore, rehearing en banc shall be ordered only upon the affirmative votes of a majority of the judges of this court in regular active service who are not disqualified, provided that the judges who are not disqualified constitute a majority of the judges who are in regular active service.

9.5.4 An active judge who does not communicate with the authoring judge concerning rehearing within ten (10) days after the date of the Clerk's letter transmitting the petition for rehearing is presumed not to desire rehearing en banc or that an answer be filed. In death penalty cases, the times set forth herein may be reduced pursuant to Local Appellate Rule Misc. 111.7(b).

9.5.5 If, during the ten-day period for circulation of petitions for rehearing, one judge has timely voted for rehearing, another judge may obtain an extension of time to consider en banc rehearing by circulating a letter asking that the time for voting be extended for a period not to exceed five (5) working days beyond the ten-day time period. This request results in an automatic extension. Irrespective of the number of such requests, the voting time automatically is extended this one period only, unless the Chief Judge, upon application, grants a further extension of time. In death penalty cases, the times set forth herein may be reduced pursuant to Local Appellate Rule Misc. 111.7(b).

9.5.6 If four active judges vote to request an answer to the petition or if there are a total of four votes for an answer or for rehearing, provided that there is at least one vote for an answer, the authoring judge enters an order directing such an answer within fourteen (14) days from the date of the order. The Clerk forwards the answer to the active judges with the request that they notify the authoring judge within ten (10) days if they vote to grant the petition. A judge who does not desire rehearing is not expected to respond. Copies of the answer are sent as a courtesy to any senior judge or visiting judge who was a member of the panel which heard and decided the case. In death penalty cases, the times set forth herein may be reduced pursuant to Local Appellate Rule Misc. 111.7(b).

9.5.7 The authoring judge enters an order denying rehearing before the panel, and denying rehearing en banc if a majority of the active judges who are not disqualified, provided that the judges who are not disqualified constitute a majority of the judges who are in regular active service, does not vote for rehearing. Separate orders may be entered if appropriate. When the panel grants a petition for rehearing and a petition for rehearing en banc is also pending, the judge who enters the order granting panel rehearing notifies the active judges of the vacatur of the panel opinion, and all action on the petition for rehearing en banc is suspended. Following panel rehearing, the authoring judge notifies the active judges of the disposition and whether any further vote on the petition for rehearing en banc is required.

9.5.8 If there is a dissent from the denial of rehearing and no dissenting opinion is filed, a notation will be added to the dispositive order, at the affirmative request of the dissenting judge, that "Judge _____ would grant rehearing by the court en banc."

Any active judge may file an opinion sur denial of the petition and direct its publication.

9.5.9 If a majority of the active judges of the court who are not disqualified, provided that the judges who are not disqualified constitute a majority of the judges who are in regular active service, votes for rehearing en banc, the Chief Judge enters an order which grants rehearing as to one or more of the issues, vacates the panel's opinion in full or in part and the judgment entered thereon, and assigns the case to the calendar for rehearing en banc.

IOP 9.6 Procedure.

9.6.1 If the author is a visiting judge, justice, or a senior circuit judge, the ranking active or senior judge of this court on the panel majority receives responses to the petition, communicates with the Clerk, signs the necessary orders, and has all the administrative responsibility set forth in this IOP.

9.6.2 An en banc hearing is held only at a regularly scheduled en banc session of the court, unless a majority of the active judges who are not disqualified, provided that the judges who are not disqualified constitute a majority of the judges who are in regular active service, votes to expedite.

9.6.3 The Chief Judge, when requested by a majority of the en banc court, directs the Clerk to advise counsel to submit supplemental briefs on specific issues or to be prepared to discuss at oral argument any other relevant issues.

9.6.4 A senior judge of this court may elect, pursuant to 28 U.S.C. § 46(c), to participate as a member of the en banc court reviewing a decision of a panel on which the senior judge was a member. That election may be made by letter to the Clerk, with copies to all active judges, covering all cases on which the senior judge may thereafter sit, or may be made on a case by case basis. Any judge participating in an en banc poll, hearing, or rehearing while in regular active service who subsequently takes senior status may elect to continue participating in the final resolution of the case.

(Effective October 27, 1997; amended effective January 1, 2000; July 1, 2002.)

CHAPTER 10. MOTION PRACTICE

IOP 10.1 Motion Panels.

A panel is available to receive motions at all times. The Chief Judge, with the consent of the court, designates standing motions panels (SMPs) to receive from the Clerk motions in cases which have not been sent to merits panels.

IOP 10.2 Distribution.

10.2.1 Insofar as possible, the Clerk equalizes the number of motions and emergency motions sent to each SMP.

10.2.2 When an emergency motion is filed, the movant may be directed by the Clerk to deliver by hand or by transmission via facsimile copies of the moving papers that day to each member of the SMP designated by the Clerk at the chambers where the judge is stationed or at such other place as may be designated.

10.2.3 Motions on non-emergency matters are distributed to the SMPs as they are complete; i.e., when responses have been filed and any necessary briefing completed.

IOP 10.3 Procedure.

10.3.1 Each standing motions panel sets its own procedures for conference and disposition. The presiding judge of each standing motions panel enters the order, generally on the motion form supplied by the Clerk, or requests another judge to do so. The order notes a dissenting vote on request of the dissenting judge.

10.3.2 When a certificate of appealability is granted on behalf of an indigent appellant pursuant to 28 U.S.C. § 2254 or § 2255, the Clerk appoints counsel for the appellant unless the court instructs otherwise.

10.3.3 A motion for reconsideration or rehearing of any standing motions panel or merits panel decision on a motion, other than a case-dispositive ruling, is referred only to that standing motions panel or merits panel and not to the court en banc. A petition for rehearing of a case-dispositive ruling is referred to the court en banc according to the procedures for petitions for rehearing. Non-case-dispositive rulings by either the merits panel or standing motions panel are referred to the court en banc only if the panel so orders.

10.3.4 The standing motions panel determines whether there shall be oral argument on a motion in the same manner as for an appeal.

10.3.5 A motion panel may grant a motion to dismiss an appeal. If the motion seeks dismissal for lack of jurisdiction, and the panel votes not to grant the motion, the motion is referred by order, without decision and without prejudice, to the merits panel.

10.3.6 A certification under 28 U.S.C. § 1292(b) by a motions panel does not in any manner bind or restrict the merits panel.

IOP 10.4 Motions Referred to Clerk.

The court may refer to the Clerk for disposition any category of motion other than those which are case-dispositive or which by statute or rule must be decided by judges.

IOP 10.5 Single-Judge Motions.

10.5.1 A single judge may entertain and may grant or deny any request for relief which, under the Federal Rules for Appellate Procedure or an applicable statute, may properly be sought by motion, except that a single judge may not dismiss or otherwise determine an appeal or other proceeding. The action of a single judge may be reviewed by the court.

10.5.2 Without limiting IOP 10.5.1, this court as a matter of practice refers to a single judge, the following motions:

(a) stay pending appeal or mandamus (generally only in emergency situations);

(b) stay of mandate or recall of the mandate;

(c) motion for appointment of counsel whether pursuant to § 1915 or under the Criminal Justice Act;

(d) approval of transcripts at government expense in criminal and civil cases;

(e) motions to withdraw;

(f) motions to expedite;

(g) motions to intervene;

(h) motions to compel the ordering of transcripts; and

(i) motions to unseal or seal.

IOP 10.6 Summary Action.

The court, *sua sponte* or upon motion by a party, may take summary action affirming, reversing, vacating, modifying, setting aside, or remanding the judgment, decree, or order appealed from; dismissing an appeal; granting or denying a petition for review; or granting or refusing enforcement of the order of an administrative agency if it clearly appears that no substantial question is presented or that subsequent precedent or a change in circumstances warrants such action. Before taking summary action, the court will afford the parties an opportunity to submit argument in support of or in opposition to such disposition if briefs on the merits have not already been filed. Summary action may be taken only by unanimous vote of the panel. If a motion panel determines that summary action is not appropriate at that time, it may, in lieu of denial, refer the matter to the merits panel without decision and without prejudice.

IOP 10.7 Motions Related to Cases Assigned to Merits Panels.

10.7.1 Motions related to cases assigned to merits panels are generally granted or denied by the presiding judge if they are merely administrative and unrelated to the disposition, unless the presider believes reference to the entire panel is appropriate.

10.7.2 Motions related to scheduling cases for argument are always referred to the entire panel.

IOP 10.8 Post–Decision Motions.

10.8.1 Unless the Clerk has been designated to act thereon, a motion for extension of time for filing a petition for rehearing or for leave to file out of time is referred to the author, who has authority to grant an extension of time. If the authoring judge votes to deny, the motion is referred to the entire panel for disposition.

10.8.2 A motion for stay of mandate or for the recall of the mandate, or certified judgment in lieu thereof, is processed as in IOP 10.8.1. It is the practice of this court not to grant such a motion unless the failure to grant a stay affects a substantive right of the applicant. Inasmuch as a stay of mandate is ordinarily not a requirement for filing a petition for a writ of certiorari, a motion for such a stay is not referred to the panel unless the failure to grant a stay affects a substantive right of the applicant.

10.8.3 A motion to amend the judgment of the court is referred to the panel.

10.8.4 A motion to extend time to file a bill of costs is determined by the Clerk. An appeal from the Clerk's ruling is referred to the authoring judge, unless the author was a visiting judge, in which case it is referred to the ranking active judge who voted with the majority.

10.8.5 A motion for the approval of a fee under the Criminal Justice Act is referred to the authoring judge.

10.8.6 If the author is a visiting judge, the ranking active judge of this court on the panel majority receives responses to the motion, communicates with the Clerk, signs the necessary orders, and has all the administrative responsibility set forth in this IOP. Senior judges on this court may choose to request the ranking active judge on the panel majority to undertake the above administrative responsibilities.

10.8.7 A remand from the Supreme Court is referred to the panel which decided the matter or to the court en banc, as the case may be.

IOP 10.9 Certification of Questions of State Law.

When a panel has certified a question of state law under LAR Misc. 110.0, the presider shall promptly notify all the other judges of the court by sending a copy of the question certified, and shall circulate the response received.

(Effective October 27, 1997; amended effective July 1, 2002.)

CHAPTER 11. RECUSAL OR DISQUALIFICATION OF JUDGES

IOP 11.1 Procedure.

11.1.1 Before cases are sent to a panel, the Clerk transmits copies of the docket sheets and disclosure statements to each judge who responds promptly informing the Clerk of those cases in which the judge is recused.

11.1.2 Each judge may submit to the Clerk in writing those circumstances which would generally require a recusal, including names of businesses in which the judge or family members have a financial interest, names of lawyer relatives whose names may appear as counsel in the appeals, and names of law firms on whose cases the judge does not sit.

11.1.3 A judge who finds it necessary to recuse after distribution of briefs or a motion immediately notifies other members of the panel and the Chief Judge or the active judge next in precedence if the Chief Judge is recused. The Chief Judge, or the judge next in precedence, names a substitute and reconstitutes the panel. A written order is not necessary for the reconstitution of any panel. The substituted judge on any panel is open to opinion assignments on the same basis as original panel members.

IOP 11.2 Circumstances.

11.2.1 The provisions of 28 U.S.C. § 455 and 28 U.S.C. § 144 re recusal are fully incorporated here.

11.2.2 (a) With respect to "financial interest" as used in 28 U.S.C. § 455, ownership of a small percentage of the outstanding shares of a publicly traded corporation which is a member of a trade association that is a party to the lawsuit is not a "financial interest" in the subject matter in controversy or in a party to the proceeding unless the owner has an interest that can be substantially affected by the outcome of the proceeding.

(b) Ownership of a small percentage of the outstanding shares of a publicly traded corporation that is listed as a creditor of the bankrupt who is a party to the lawsuit is not a "financial interest" in the subject matter in controversy or in a party to the proceeding unless the owner has an interest that can be substantially affected by the outcome of the proceeding.

(c) An insurance policy issued to a judge or a member of his or her family is not a "financial interest" in the insurance company.

(Effective October 27, 1997.)

CHAPTER 12. VISITING JUDGES

The Circuit Executive is charged with the responsibility of assisting the visiting judges and arranges for chambers, provides advance notification of these Internal Operating Procedures, arranges for a secretary, if necessary, and in general tends to the visitor's other needs.

(Effective October 27, 1997.)

CHAPTER 13. STAFF ATTORNEYS

Staff attorneys based in Philadelphia work under the supervision of the clerk and chief deputy for the Legal Division. They provide legal research and assistance to the court as directed.

(Effective October 27, 1997; amended effective July 1, 2002.)

CHAPTER 14. SENIOR JUDGE LAW CLERK VOLUNTEERS

Senior judges may volunteer use of their law clerks to assist active judges, especially in matters which can be carried out in a senior judge's chambers. Senior judges may also volunteer use of their law clerks to assist the Staff Attorneys Office in carrying out its responsibilities. A senior judge who takes an extended absence from chambers usually notifies the active judges that his or her law clerks are available, unless the law clerks will be fully occupied with court work during that period.

(Effective October 27, 1997.)

CHAPTER 15. DEATH PENALTY CASES

IOP 15.1 Docketing and Briefing.

Upon receipt of the required statement pursuant to Local Appellate Rule Misc. 111.2(a), the clerk of this court shall establish a file and monitor the progress of any such case through the district court. At an appropriate time, the clerk may tentatively assign the case to a special panel. If no appeal is filed, the tentatively assigned panel will be returned to the pool of unassigned death penalty panel combinations.

Upon the filing of any notice of appeal, request for certificate of appealability, 28 U.S.C. § 2253(c)(1) and/or for stay, the Clerk may establish, at the direction of the panel to which the case is assigned, a schedule for briefing and disposition on the merits.

IOP 15.2 Panel Assignments.

The Clerk will use a computer program to randomly select a panel from a pool of all possible three-judge combinations consisting of circuit judges in active service and those judges who have taken senior status and have indicated their willingness to hear death penalty cases. The computer program will be designed to use all possible three-judge combinations and to minimize the possibility of assignment of any judge to successive panels. The Clerk will be responsible for maintaining the program and for making any adjustments necessitated by vacancies and appointments. Ordinarily, a case will be assigned to a single panel for all proceedings to final order. Separate appeals concerning the same petitioner that are filed in close proximity may be assigned to the same panel. In the event of the unavailability or disqualification of a member of a special panel, a new panel will be randomly selected by the computer, excluding any judges unavailable or disqualified. Any unused panel will be returned to the pool for future reassignment. The Chief Judge periodically may address any imbalance in the caseload.

IOP 15.3 Stays, Tentative Assignments.

If a stay application is filed in this court before a district court decision has been entered, the Clerk shall forward the motion to a special panel. Whether or not a stay application has been filed, if no ruling has been made ten (10) days before the time scheduled for execution of the judgment, the case shall tentatively be assigned to a panel, which will be kept advised of the status of the case, the name of the district judge before whom it is pending, and the scheduled time of execution of the judgment.

IOP 15.4 Hearings or Rehearing En Banc.

Where the court has voted to grant hearing or rehearing en banc, the Chief Judge may specifically order briefing or schedule oral argument as necessary.

IOP 15.5 Notice to Supreme Court.

The Clerk shall notify the Clerk of the Supreme Court when a case involving the suspension or stay of execution of the judgment of a state or federal court is filed, and shall thereafter maintain communication with both the district court and the Supreme Court.

(Effective October 27, 1997; amended effective January 1, 2000; July 1, 2002.)

CHAPTER 16. SAMPLE FORMS

IOP 16.1 Judgment Order—Civil Cases.

JUDGMENT ORDER

After consideration of all contentions raised by appellant, it is

ADJUDGED AND ORDERED that the judgment of the district court be and is hereby affirmed. Costs taxed against appellant.

By the Court,

____

Chief Judge/Circuit Judge

Attest:

____

Clerk

Dated:

IOP 16.2 Judgment Order—Criminal Cases.

JUDGMENT ORDER

After considering the contentions raised by appellant, to-wit, that the court erred: (1) in refusing to charge on the testimony of an accomplice as requested by appellant; (2) in admitting hearsay testimony of a witness; and (3) in refusing to grant a motion of acquittal on the theory of insufficiency of evidence, it is

ADJUDGED AND ORDERED that the judgment of the district court be and is hereby affirmed.

IOP 16.3 Dismissal for Lack of Jurisdiction.

ORDER OR JUDGMENT ORDER

After consideration of all contentions raised by the appellant and concluding that this court has no jurisdiction because the appeal is premature, *see Griggs v. Provident Consumer Discount Co.*, 459 U.S. 56, 103 S.Ct. 400, 74 L.Ed.2d. 225 (1982), it is

ADJUDGED AND ORDERED that the appeal be and is hereby dismissed without prejudice to the filing of a timely appeal.

Costs taxed against appellant.

16.4 Dismissal for Lack of Certification Under Fed.R.Civ.P. 54(b). When the appeal is dismissed because of lack of certification under Fed.R.Civ.P. 54(b), an order of dismissal ordinarily contains language similar in form to:

> The appeal will be dismissed without prejudice to the right of appellant to apply to the district court for a determination and direction under Fed. R.Civ.P. 54(b). However, we express no opinion as to whether the determination and direction should be made, this being a matter within the discretion of the district court. If the determination and direction are made within thirty (30) days, a new appeal may come before us on the present briefs and record supplemented to show subsequent proceedings.

(Effective October 27, 1997.)

APPENDIX II. RULES OF ATTORNEY DISCIPLINARY ENFORCEMENT OF THE UNITED STATES COURT OF APPEALS FOR THE THIRD CIRCUIT

RULE 1. DEFINITIONS

1. "The Court" means the United States Court of Appeals for the Third Circuit.

2. "Another Court" means any court of the United States, the District of Columbia, or any state, territory or commonwealth of the United States.

3. "Serious Crime" means any felony or any lesser crime involving false swearing, misrepresentation, fraud, willful failure to file income tax returns, deceit, bribery, extortion, misappropriation, theft, or an attempt or a conspiracy or solicitation of another to commit such a lesser crime.

4. "Standing Committee" means this Court's Standing Committee on Attorney Discipline.

(Effective March 1991.)

RULE 2. GROUNDS FOR DISCIPLINE

A member of the bar of this Court may be disciplined by this Court as a result of

1. conviction in another court of a serious crime;

2. disbarment or suspension by another court, whether or not with the attorney's consent, or the resignation from the bar of another court while an investigation into allegations of misconduct is pending;

3. conduct with respect to this Court which violates the Federal Rules of Appellate Procedure, the Rules or Internal Operating Procedures of this Court, or orders or other instructions of the Court; or

4. any other conduct unbecoming a member of the bar of this Court.

(Effective March 1991.)

RULE 3. DISCIPLINARY SANCTIONS; ASSESSMENTS UNDER 28 U.S.C. § 1927 AND F.R.A.P. 38

1. Discipline may consist of disbarment, suspension from practice before this Court, monetary sanction, removal from the roster of attorneys eligible for appointment as Court-appointed counsel, reprimand, or any other sanction that the Court or a panel thereof may deem appropriate. Disbarment is the presumed discipline for conviction of a serious crime. Disbarment is also the presumed discipline when an attorney has resigned from the bar of another court while an investigation into allegations of misconduct is pending. The identical discipline imposed by another court is presumed appropriate for discipline imposed as a result of that other court's suspension or disbarment of an attorney. A monetary sanction imposed on disciplinary grounds is the personal responsibility of the attorney disciplined, and may not be reimbursed by a client directly or indirectly. Notice to that effect is sent to the client by the Clerk whenever a monetary sanction is imposed.

2. Assessments of damages, costs, expenses or attorneys' fees under 28 U.S.C. § 1927 or Federal Rule of Appellate Procedure 38 are not disciplinary sanctions within the meaning of these Rules and proceedings with respect thereto are not governed by these Rules.

(Effective March 1991.)

RULE 4. DISCIPLINE IMPOSED BY A PANEL OF THE COURT AND BY THE STANDING COMMITTEE ON ATTORNEY DISCIPLINE

1. A panel of the Court may impose any sanction other than suspension or disbarment in accordance with Rule 5.

2. Any matter of attorney discipline in which suspension or disbarment may be considered as an appropriate sanction is referred to the Court's Standing Committee on Attorney Discipline or, in the case of an uncontested matter, to its chairperson. The Standing Committee consists of three circuit judges, at least two of whom shall be active judges, who are appointed by the Chief Judge for three-year, staggered terms. The Chief Judge designates one of the three to serve as chairperson. If any member of the Standing Committee is unable to hear a particular matter, the Chief Judge designates another circuit judge as a member of the committee to hear that matter provided, however, that not less than two active judges shall hear a particular matter. After such a reference, any discipline may be imposed in accordance with Rules 6 through 10.

(Effective March 1991.)

RULE 5. PANEL PROCEDURE

Before imposing any disciplinary sanction, a panel notifies the attorney of the alleged conduct which may justify the imposition of discipline and affords the attorney an opportunity to be heard, in writing or in person at the option of the panel. If an attorney who has been afforded an opportunity to be heard in writing files a timely written application to appear before the panel in person, the panel schedules a hearing for that purpose. An application is timely if filed within eight (8) days of the date of the notice affording the opportunity to be heard in writing.

(Effective March 1991.)

RULE 6. NOTIFICATIONS OF CONVICTION OR DISCIPLINE IMPOSED BY ANOTHER COURT

1. A member of the bar of this Court shall notify the Clerk within ten (10) days if he or she is convicted of a serious crime, if he or she is disbarred or suspended by another court, or if he or she resigns or is disbarred by consent from the bar of another court while an investigation into allegations of misconduct is pending.

2. The Clerk refers to the Standing Committee all information received by him or her concerning disbarments, suspensions, resignations during the pendency of misconduct investigations, and other conduct sufficient to cast doubt upon the continuing qualification of a member of the bar of this Court to practice before it.

(Effective March 1991.)

RULE 7. INITIATION OF DISCIPLINARY PROCEEDINGS

1. When a member of the bar of this Court is suspended or disbarred by another court, or has resigned from the bar of another court during the pendency of a misconduct investigation, the suspension for the same period as imposed in the other court, disbarment or resignation, as the case may be, is immediately and automatically effective in this Court and the Chairperson of the Standing Committee enters an order imposing the aforesaid discipline, but failure to enter an order does not affect the effective date of the suspension or disbarment. For purposes of this rule, a resignation during the pendency of a misconduct investigation shall be deemed a disbarment. The entry of the said order is, however, without prejudice to the attorney moving before this Court for reinstatement. When the order of the chairperson is entered it is sent to the attorney by certified mail to his or her last known address and includes a copy of the order on which the discipline imposed in this Court is based, and of these rules. If a reinstatement proceeding is instituted, the Standing Committee, or any two members thereof, may reinstate the attorney as a member of the bar of this Court on a temporary basis on good cause being shown. Any application for reinstatement, whether or not it includes an application for temporary reinstatement, shall be supported by an affidavit of the attorney of good cause as to why the discipline imposed in the other court should not be imposed in this Court. The application may include such other materials as the attorney deems appropriate. After the application is filed, the matter is treated as a contested proceeding under Rule 10.

2. Upon receipt of a certified copy of a judgment or other court record demonstrating that a member of the bar of this Court has been convicted of a serious crime, unless the attorney is automatically disciplined as provided in paragraph (1) of this Rule, the Clerk issues an order to show cause why the Court should not impose upon the attorney the presumed discipline described in Rule 3. The notice is sent by certified mail, orders that any response be filed within thirty (30) days, and directs that the attorney complete and return to the Clerk within that time a declaration of the names and addresses of the other bars to which he or she is admitted using the form supplied by the Clerk, whether or not the attorney chooses otherwise to respond to the notice. The Clerk also sends a copy of the judgment, order, or other court record and these Rules.

3. When the Standing Committee determines that cause may exist for the suspension or disbarment of an attorney pursuant to Rule 2.3 or Rule 2.4, one of its members or the Clerk issues an order to show cause why such discipline should not be imposed by this Court. This order is sent by certified mail, sets forth the alleged conduct that is the subject of this proceeding and the reason this conduct may justify such discipline, directs that a response be filed within thirty (30) days, requires the submission of a declaration as described in paragraph (2) of this Rule, and is accompanied by a copy of these Rules.

4. Once an order to show cause has been issued pursuant to paragraph (2) or (3) of this Rule, the Standing Committee may decline to accept a resignation from the lawyer and continue the proceeding in accordance with these Rules.

(Effective March 1991.)

RULE 8. SUSPENSION DURING PENDENCY OF A DISCIPLINARY PROCEEDING

1. Upon receiving a certified copy of a judgment of conviction of a member of the bar of this Court of a serious crime or upon receiving a notice from such an attorney that he or she has been convicted of such a crime, the Standing Committee may summarily issue an order suspending the attorney's privilege to practice before this Court pending the determination of appropriate discipline.

2. The Court or the Standing Committee, after notice and an opportunity to be heard, may suspend an attorney's privilege to practice before this Court during the course of any disciplinary investigation and proceeding.

(Effective March 1991.)

RULE 9. UNCONTESTED PROCEEDINGS

1. If an attorney fails to timely respond to an order to show cause in a case in which a presumptive discipline is specified in Rule 3 or if an attorney consents to imposition of the presumptive discipline, the Clerk notifies the Chairperson of the Standing Committee who enters an order imposing the presumptive discipline.

2. Any member of the bar of this Court who is the subject of an investigation by this Court into allegations of misconduct may consent to disbarment by filing with the Clerk an affidavit stating that the attorney desires to consent to disbarment and that:

(a) the attorney's consent is freely and voluntarily rendered; the attorney is not being subjected to coercion or duress; the attorney is fully aware of the implications of so consenting;

(b) the attorney is aware that there is a presently pending proceeding involving allegations that there exist grounds for the attorney's discipline the nature of which the attorney shall specifically set forth; and

(c) the attorney acknowledges that he or she cannot successfully defend in the pending proceeding.

(Effective March 1991.)

RULE 10. CONTESTED PROCEEDINGS

1. If an attorney's response to an order to show cause specifically requests to be heard in person in defense or in mitigation, or if an attorney moves for reinstatement pursuant to Rule 7.1, and specifically requests to be heard in person in defense or in mitigation, the Standing Committee sets the matter for a prompt hearing before it. The attorney is given at least thirty (30) days notice of the time, date and place of the hearing. Prior to the hearing, the attorney is afforded the opportunity to inspect all documents which the Standing Committee has obtained in its investigation. At the hearing, the Standing Committee enters upon the record the order to show cause, the response, and such evidence as it considers relevant to the issues posed for resolution and the attorney is afforded the opportunity to cross-examine any witnesses called by the Standing Committee and to introduce evidence in defense or mitigation. The hearing is transcribed.

2. If an attorney's response to an order to show cause or motion for reinstatement does not specifically request to be heard in person, the Standing Committee prepares a record consisting of the order to show cause, the response, the relevant documents, and a summary of the other relevant information obtained by the Standing Committee in its investigation. If the record so prepared contains any information not reflected in the order to show cause and the response, the attorney is afforded the opportunity to inspect the record and to file an additional response within ten (10) days of the date of the notice of his or her opportunity to inspect.

3. Based solely on the record created pursuant to paragraphs (1) or (2) of this Rule, the Standing Committee prepares a Report and Recommendation setting forth its findings of fact and recommending whether, and if so what, discipline should be imposed. A copy of the Report and Recommendation is promptly sent to the attorney who is afforded the opportunity to file exceptions within twenty (20) days of the date thereof. The Report and Recommendation, any exceptions thereto, and the record are then submitted to the active members of the Court who make a final decision by a majority vote based solely on those documents.

4. A certified copy of a judgment of conviction for any crime shall be conclusive evidence of the commission of that crime in any disciplinary proceeding instituted against an attorney based upon the conviction. If the conviction is subsequently reversed or vacated, any discipline imposed on the basis thereof will be promptly reviewed by the Standing Committee and the Court upon submission of a certified copy of the relevant mandate.

5. A certified copy of a judgment or order demonstrating that a member of the bar of this Court has been disbarred or suspended by another court is accepted as establishing that the conduct for which the discipline was imposed in fact occurred and that the discipline imposed was appropriate unless it appears:

(a) that the procedure was so lacking in notice or opportunity to be heard as to constitute a deprivation of due process; or

(b) that there was such an infirmity of proof establishing the misconduct as to give rise to the clear conviction that this Court could not, consistent with its duty, accept as final the conclusion on that subject; or

(c) that the imposition of the same discipline by this Court would result in grave injustice; or

(d) that the misconduct established is deemed by this Court to warrant substantially different discipline.

6. A member of the bar of this Court to whom an order to show cause is issued pursuant to Rule 7 has the right to have counsel at all stages of the proceeding.

7. The Standing Committee may compel by subpoena the attendance of witnesses, including the attorney whose conduct is the subject of the proceeding, and the production of pertinent documents. If a hearing is held, the Standing Committee will compel by subpoena the attendance of any witness and the production of any document reasonably designated by the attorney as relevant to his or her defense.

(Effective March 1991.)

RULE 11. NOTIFICATION OF DISCIPLINE IMPOSED

Unless directed otherwise, within ten (10) days of the imposition of discipline by this Court or a panel thereof upon a member of its bar, the Clerk notifies the attorney and all other courts before whom the attorney is admitted to practice and the National Disciplinary Data Bank, enclosing a certified copy of the order imposing discipline.

(Effective March 1991.)

RULE 12. REINSTATEMENT

1. An attorney suspended for six (6) months or less is automatically reinstated at the end of the period of suspension upon the filing of an affidavit of compliance with the provisions of the order. An attorney suspended for more than six (6) months or disbarred may not resume practice until reinstated by order of the Court.

2. An attorney who has been disbarred may not apply for reinstatement until the expiration of five (5) years from the effective date of the disbarment.

3. No petition for reinstatement may be filed within one (1) year following an adverse determination on the attorney's petition for reinstatement.

4. The Clerk refers petitions for reinstatement to the Standing Committee. If the Standing Committee is satisfied that reinstatement is appropriate based upon the findings of another court or otherwise, it recommends to the Court that the petition be granted. If the Standing Committee is not so satisfied or if the matter is returned to it by the Court, the Standing Committee schedules a prompt hearing on the petition. At the hearing, the petitioner has the burden of demonstrating by clear and convincing evidence that he or she has the moral qualifications, competency, and learning in the law required for admission to practice before this Court and that his or her resumption of the practice of law will not be detrimental to the integrity and standing of the bar or to the administration of justice, or subversive of the public interest. The Standing Committee submits its Report and Recommendation, together with any exception thereto filed within twenty (20) days of the issuance thereof, to all active members of the Court who act upon the petition by a majority vote.

5. A reinstatement may be on such terms and conditions as the Court directs. If the attorney has been disbarred or suspended for five (5) years or more, this may include certification by the bar examiners of a state or other jurisdiction of the attorney's successful completion of an examination for admission to practice.

(Effective March 1991.)

RULE 13. APPOINTMENT OF COUNSEL

The Standing Committee may at any time appoint counsel to investigate or prosecute a disciplinary matter or to represent an indigent attorney instructed to show cause. The Court prefers to appoint as prosecuting counsel the disciplinary agency of the highest court of the state in which the attorney maintains his or her principal office. However, if the state disciplinary agency declines appointment, or the Court deems other counsel appropriate, it may appoint any other member of the bar as prosecuting counsel. Counsel appointed either for prosecution or defense will be compensated for his or her services as the Standing Committee shall direct.

(Effective March 1991.)

RULE 14. ACCESS TO DISCIPLINARY INFORMATION

1. A disciplinary proceeding before a panel conducted pursuant to Rule 4.1 and Rule 5 is public except:

(a) for deliberations of the panel;

(b) to the extent otherwise ordered by the panel.

2. Prior to the imposition of a suspension or disbarment or the issuance of a Report and Recommendation of the Standing Committee recommending a sanction other than a private reprimand, whichever shall first occur, the proceeding is confidential, except that the pendency, subject matter, and status of an investigation may be disclosed by the Court or the Standing Committee if:

(a) the respondent has waived confidentiality;

(b) the proceeding is based upon allegations which include the conviction of a crime;

(c) the proceeding is based upon allegations that have become generally known to the public; or

(d) there is a need to notify another person or organization in order to protect the public, the administration of justice, or the legal profession.

3. Upon the imposition of a suspension or disbarment, the issuance of a Report and Recommendation of the Standing Committee recommending a sanction other than a private reprimand, or the filing of a petition for reinstatement, the proceeding is public, except for:

(a) deliberations of the Standing Committee or the Court;

(b) information with respect to which a protective order has been entered under paragraph (4) of this Rule.

When a proceeding becomes public under this paragraph, any order to show cause why discipline should not be imposed, any record created by the Standing Committee pursuant to Rule 10.1 or 10.2, and any Report and Recommendation of the Standing Committee are docketed in the Clerk's office and are accessible to the public in the same manner as other records of the Court. Other documents previously created by or in the possession of the Standing Committee or prosecuting counsel do not become public records and are not accessible to the public.

4. In order to protect the interests of a complainant, witness, third party, or the attorney, a panel or the Standing Committee may, upon application and for good cause shown, issue a protective order prohibiting the disclosure of specific information and direct that the proceedings be conducted so as to implement the order.

5. A request for nonpublic information other than that authorized for disclosure under paragraph (2) of this Rule shall be denied unless the request is from one of the following agencies:

(a) an agency authorized to investigate qualifications for admission to practice;

(b) an agency authorized to investigate qualifications for government employment, including a committee or similar group authorized to investigate qualifications for judicial position; or

(c) a lawyer disciplinary enforcement agency.

If a panel or the Standing Committee decides to provide the nonpublic information requested, and if the attorney has not signed a waiver permitting the requesting agency to obtain nonpublic information, the attorney is notified in writing at his or her last known address that the information has been requested and by whom, together with a copy of the information proposed to be released to the requesting agency. The panel or the Standing Committee releases the information to the requesting agency eight (8) days after the mailing of the notice unless the attorney has satisfied the panel or the Standing Committee that there is good cause to withhold the requested information.

If an otherwise authorized requesting agency has not obtained a waiver from the attorney to obtain nonpublic information, and requests that the information be released without giving notice to the attorney, the requesting agency shall certify that:

(a) the request is made in furtherance of an ongoing investigation;

(b) the information is essential to that investigation; and

(c) disclosure of the existence of the investigation to the lawyer would seriously prejudice that investigation.

6. Except with respect to the content of his or her own testimony, each participant in a proceeding under these rules shall maintain the confidentiality mandated by this Rule.

(Effective March 1991.)

Rule 15. DISABILITY INACTIVE STATUS

1. There is hereby created a disability inactive status for an attorney whose mental or physical condition prevents the attorney from competently representing the interest of the attorney's clients.

2. An attorney is immediately and automatically transferred to disability inactive status upon proof being received by the Court that:

(a) the attorney has been declared incompetent in a judicial proceeding; or

(b) the attorney has been involuntarily committed because of incapacity or disability; or

(c) during a disciplinary or criminal proceeding the attorney alleges an incapability to assist in the defense due to mental or physical incapability; or

(d) the attorney has been placed on a disability inactive or equivalent status by another court.

3. If an attorney is immediately and automatically transferred to disability inactive status but desires to contest the transfer, the attorney institutes reinstatement proceedings which are conducted as though instituted under Rule 7.1. By bringing such a proceeding, the attorney waives the doctor-patient privilege (and other similar privileges) regarding the disability.

4. If the Standing Committee determines that cause may exist to place an attorney on disability inactive status and the attorney is not immediately and automatically transferred to such status under paragraph (2) of this Rule, the Standing Committee institutes proceedings which shall be conducted as though instituted under Rule 7.3. In these proceedings Rule 14 shall be applicable.

5. An attorney on disability inactive status may file a petition for reinstatement on the basis that the disability has been removed and the attorney is fit to resume the practice of law. The filing of a petition for reinstatement waives the doctor-patient privilege (and other similar privileges) regarding the disability. The attorney states in the petition the name and address of each physician, psychologist, and/or psychiatrist who has examined or treated the attorney and any hospital or other institution in which the attorney has been examined or treated since the attorney's transfer to disability inactive status, as well as the attorney's current status in all bars to which the attorney was or is admitted. A petition for reinstatement is treated in the same manner as a petition for reinstatement filed under Rule 12 by an attorney suspended for more than six (6) months.

6. An attorney raising the defense of current mental or physical disability in a disciplinary proceeding waives the doctor-patient privilege (and other similar privileges) regarding the disability. Furthermore, if the defense of current mental or physical disability is raised, the court may order an examination of the attorney by a court-appointed physician.

(Effective March 1991.)

APPENDIX III. RULES FOR JUDICIAL–CONDUCT AND JUDICIAL–DISABILITY PROCEEDINGS

PREFACE

These Rules were promulgated by the Judicial Conference of the United States, after public comment, pursuant to 28 U.S.C. §§ 331 and 358, to establish standards and procedures for addressing complaints filed by complainants or identified by chief judges, under the Judicial Conduct and Disability Act, 28 U.S.C. §§ 351–364.

ARTICLE I. GENERAL PROVISIONS

RULE 1. SCOPE

These Rules govern proceedings under the Judicial Conduct and Disability Act, 28 U.S.C. §§ 351–364 (the Act), to determine whether a covered judge has engaged in conduct prejudicial to the effective and expeditious administration of the business of the courts or is unable to discharge the duties of office because of mental or physical disability.

(Adopted Mar. 11, 2008, eff. Apr. 10, 2008.)

Commentary on Rule 1

In September 2006, the Judicial Conduct and Disability Act Study Committee, appointed in 2004 by Chief Justice Rehnquist and known as the "Breyer Committee," presented a report, known as the "Breyer Committee Report," 239 F.R.D. 116 (Sept. 2006), to Chief Justice Roberts that evaluated implementation of the Judicial Conduct and Disability Act of 1980, 28 U.S.C. §§ 351–364. The Breyer Committee had been formed in response to criticism from the public and the Congress regarding the effectiveness of the Act's implementation. The Executive Committee of the Judicial Conference directed the Judicial Conference Committee on Judicial Conduct and Disability to consider the recommendations made by the Breyer Committee and to report on their implementation to the Conference.

The Breyer Committee found that it could not evaluate implementation of the Act without establishing interpretive standards, Breyer Committee Report, 239 F.R.D. at 132, and that a major problem faced by chief judges in implementing the Act was the lack of authoritative interpretive standards. Id. at 212–15. The Breyer Committee then established standards to guide its evaluation, some of which were new formulations and some of which were taken from the "Illustrative Rules Governing Complaints of Judicial Misconduct and Disability," discussed below. The principal standards used by the Breyer Committee are in Appendix E of its Report. Id. at 238.

Based on the findings of the Breyer Committee, the Judicial Conference Committee on Judicial Conduct and Disability concluded that there was a need for the Judicial Conference to exercise its power under Section 358 of the Act to fashion standards guiding the various officers and bodies who must exercise responsibility under the Act. To that end, the Judicial Conference Committee proposed rules that were based largely on Appendix E of the Breyer Committee Report and the Illustrative Rules.

The Illustrative Rules were originally prepared in 1986 by the Special Committee of the Conference of Chief Judges of the United States Courts of Appeals, and were subsequently revised and amended, most recently in 2000, by the predecessor to the Committee on Judicial Conduct and Disability. The Illustrative Rules were adopted, with minor variations, by circuit judicial councils, to govern complaints under the Judicial Conduct and Disability Act.

After being submitted for public comment pursuant to 28 U.S.C. § 358(c), the present Rules were promulgated by the Judicial Conference on March 11, 2008.

RULE 2. EFFECT AND CONSTRUCTION

(a) Generally. These Rules are mandatory; they supersede any conflicting judicial-council rules. Judicial councils may promulgate additional rules to implement the Act as long as those rules do not conflict with these Rules.

(b) Exception. A Rule will not apply if, when performing duties authorized by the Act, a chief judge, a special committee, a judicial council, the Judicial Conference Committee on Judicial Conduct and Disability, or the Judicial Conference of the United States expressly finds that exceptional circumstances render application of that Rule in a particular proceeding manifestly unjust or contrary to the purposes of the Act or these Rules.

(Adopted Mar. 11, 2008, eff. Apr. 10, 2008.)

Commentary on Rule 2

Unlike the Illustrative Rules, these Rules provide mandatory and nationally uniform provisions governing the substantive and procedural aspects of misconduct and disability proceedings under the Act. The mandatory nature of these Rules is authorized by 28 U.S.C. § 358(a) and (c). Judicial councils retain the power to promulgate rules consistent with these Rules. For example, a local rule may authorize the electronic distribution of materials pursuant to Rule 8(b).

Rule 2(b) recognizes that unforeseen and exceptional circumstances may call for a different approach in particular cases.

RULE 3. DEFINITIONS

(a) Chief Judge. "Chief judge" means the chief judge of a United States Court of Appeals, of the United States Court of International Trade, or of the United States Court of Federal Claims.

(b) Circuit Clerk. "Circuit clerk" means a clerk of a United States court of appeals, the clerk of the United States Court of International Trade, the clerk of the United States Court of Federal Claims, or the circuit executive of the United States Court of Appeals for the Federal Circuit.

(c) Complaint. A complaint is:

(1) a document that, in accordance with Rule 6, is filed by any person in his or her individual capacity or on behalf of a professional organization; or

(2) information from any source, other than a document described in (c) (1), that gives a chief judge probable cause to believe that a covered judge, as defined in Rule 4, has engaged in misconduct or may have a disability, whether or not the information is framed as or is intended to be an allegation of misconduct or disability.

(d) Court of Appeals, District Court, and District Judge. "Courts of appeals," "district court," and "district judge," where appropriate, include the United States Court of Federal Claims, the United States Court of International Trade, and the judges thereof.

(e) Disability. "Disability" is a temporary or permanent condition rendering a judge unable to discharge the duties of the particular judicial office. Examples of disability include substance abuse, the inability to stay awake during court proceedings, or a severe impairment of cognitive abilities.

(f) Judicial Council and Circuit. "Judicial council" and "circuit," where appropriate, include any courts designated in 28 U.S.C. § 363.

(g) Magistrate Judge. "Magistrate judge," where appropriate, includes a special master appointed by the Court of Federal Claims under 42 U.S.C. § 300aa–12(c).

(h) Misconduct. Cognizable misconduct:

(1) is conduct prejudicial to the effective and expeditious administration of the business of the courts. Misconduct includes, but is not limited to:

(A) using the judge's office to obtain special treatment for friends or relatives;

(B) accepting bribes, gifts, or other personal favors related to the judicial office;

(C) having improper discussions with parties or counsel for one side in a case;

(D) treating litigants or attorneys in a demonstrably egregious and hostile manner;

(E) engaging in partisan political activity or making inappropriately partisan statements;

(F) soliciting funds for organizations; or

(G) violating other specific, mandatory standards of judicial conduct, such as those pertaining to restrictions on outside income and requirements for financial disclosure.

(2) is conduct occurring outside the performance of official duties if the conduct might have a prejudicial effect on the administration of the business of the courts, including a substantial and widespread lowering of public confidence in the courts among reasonable people.

(3) does not include:

(A) an allegation that is directly related to the merits of a decision or procedural ruling. An allegation that calls into question the correctness of a judge's ruling, including a failure to recuse, without more, is merits-related. If the decision or ruling is alleged to be the result of an improper motive, e.g., a bribe, ex parte contact, racial or ethnic bias, or improper conduct in rendering a decision or ruling, such as personally derogatory remarks irrelevant to the issues, the complaint is not cognizable to the extent that it attacks the merits.

(B) an allegation about delay in rendering a decision or ruling, unless the allegation concerns an improper motive in delaying a particular decision or habitual delay in a significant number of unrelated cases.

(i) Subject Judge. "Subject judge" means any judge described in Rule 4 who is the subject of a complaint.

(Adopted Mar. 11, 2008, eff. Apr. 10, 2008.)

Commentary on Rule 3

Rule 3 is derived and adapted from the Breyer Committee Report and the Illustrative Rules.

Unless otherwise specified or the context otherwise indicates, the term "complaint" is used in these Rules to refer both to complaints identified by a chief judge under Rule 5 and to complaints filed by complainants under Rule 6.

Under the Act, a "complaint" may be filed by "any person" or "identified" by a chief judge. See 28 U.S.C. § 351(a) and (b). Under Rule 3(c)(1), complaints may be submitted by a person, in his or her individual capacity, or by a professional organization. Generally, the word "complaint" brings to mind the commencement of an adversary proceeding in which the contending parties are left to present the evidence and legal arguments, and judges play the role of an essentially passive arbiter. The Act, however, establishes an administrative, inquisitorial process. For example, even absent a complaint under Rule 6, chief judges are expected in some circumstances to trigger the process—"identify a complaint," see 28 U.S.C. § 351(b) and Rule 5—and conduct an investigation without becoming a party. See 28 U.S.C. § 352(a); Breyer Committee Report, 239 F.R.D. at 214; Illustrative

Rule 2(j). Even when a complaint is filed by someone other than the chief judge, the complainant lacks many rights that a litigant would have, and the chief judge, instead of being limited to the "four corners of the complaint," must, under Rule 11, proceed as though misconduct or disability has been alleged where the complainant reveals information of misconduct or disability but does not claim it as such. See Breyer Committee Report, 239 F.R.D. at 183–84.

An allegation of misconduct or disability filed under Rule 6 is a "complaint," and the Rule so provides in subsection (c)(1). However, both the nature of the process and the use of the term "identify" suggest that the word "complaint" covers more than a document formally triggering the process. The process relies on chief judges considering known information and triggering the process when appropriate. "Identifying" a "complaint," therefore, is best understood as the chief judge's concluding that information known to the judge constitutes probable cause to believe that misconduct occurred or a disability exists, whether or not the information is framed as, or intended to be an accusation. This definition is codified in (c)(2).

Rule 3(e) relates to disability and provides only the most general definition, recognizing that a fact-specific approach is the only one available.

The phrase "prejudicial to the effective and expeditious administration of the business of the courts" is not subject to precise definition, and subsection (h)(1) therefore provides some specific examples. Although the Code of Conduct for United States Judges may be informative, its main precepts are highly general; the Code is in many potential applications aspirational rather than a set of disciplinary rules. Ultimately, the responsibility for determining what constitutes misconduct under the statute is the province of the judicial council of the circuit subject to such review and limitations as are ordained by the statute and by these Rules.

Even where specific, mandatory rules exist—for example, governing the receipt of gifts by judges, outside earned income, and financial disclosure obligations—the distinction between the misconduct statute and the specific, mandatory rules must be borne in mind. For example, an inadvertent, minor violation of any one of these Rules, promptly remedied when called to the attention of the judge, might still be a violation but might not rise to the level of misconduct under the statute. By contrast, a pattern of such violations of the Code might well rise to the level of misconduct.

An allegation can meet the statutory standard even though the judge's alleged conduct did not occur in the course of the performance of official duties. The Code of Conduct for United States Judges expressly covers a wide range of extra-official activities, and some of these activities may constitute misconduct. For example, allegations that a judge solicited funds for a charity or participated in a partisan political event are cognizable under the Act.

On the other hand, judges are entitled to some leeway in extra-official activities. For example, misconduct may not include a judge being repeatedly and publicly discourteous to a spouse (not including physical abuse) even though this might cause some reasonable people to have diminished confidence in the courts. Rule 3(h)(2) states that conduct of this sort is covered, for example, when it might lead to a "substantial and widespread" lowering of such confidence.

Rule 3(h)(3)(A) tracks the Act, 28 U.S.C. § 352(b)(1)(A)(ii), in excluding from the definition of misconduct allegations "[d]irectly related to the merits of a decision or procedural ruling." This exclusion preserves the independence of judges in the exercise of judicial power by ensuring that the complaint procedure is not used to collaterally attack the substance of a judge's ruling. Any allegation that calls into question the correctness of an official action of a judge—without more—is merits-related. The phrase "decision or procedural ruling" is not limited to rulings issued in deciding Article III cases or controversies. Thus, a complaint challenging the correctness of a chief judge's determination to dismiss a prior misconduct complaint would be properly dismissed as merits-related—in other words, as challenging the substance of the judge's administrative determination to dismiss the complaint—even though it does not concern the judge's rulings in Article III litigation. Similarly, an allegation that a judge had incorrectly declined to approve a Criminal Justice Act voucher is merits-related under this standard.

Conversely, an allegation—however unsupported—that a judge conspired with a prosecutor to make a particular ruling is not merits-related, even though it "relates" to a ruling in a colloquial sense. Such an allegation attacks the propriety of conspiring with the prosecutor and goes beyond a challenge to the correctness—"the merits"—of the ruling itself. An allegation that a judge ruled against the complainant because the complainant is a member of a particular racial or ethnic group, or because the judge dislikes the complainant personally, is also not merits-related. Such an allegation attacks the propriety of arriving at rulings with an illicit or improper motive. Similarly, an allegation that a judge used an inappropriate term to refer to a class of people is not merits-related even if the judge used it on the bench or in an opinion; the correctness of the judge's rulings is not at stake. An allegation that a judge treated litigants or attorneys in a demonstrably egregious and hostile manner while on the bench is also not merits-related.

The existence of an appellate remedy is usually irrelevant to whether an allegation is merits-related. The merits-related ground for dismissal exists to protect judges' independence in making rulings, not to protect or promote the appellate process. A complaint alleging an incorrect ruling is merits-related even though the complainant has no recourse from that ruling. By the same token, an allegation that is otherwise cognizable under the Act should not be dismissed merely because an appellate remedy appears to exist (for example, vacating a ruling that resulted from an improper ex parte communication). However, there may be occasions when appellate and misconduct proceedings overlap, and consideration and disposition of a complaint under these Rules may be properly deferred by a chief judge until the appellate proceedings are concluded in order to avoid, inter alia, inconsistent decisions.

Because of the special need to protect judges' independence in deciding what to say in an opinion or ruling, a somewhat different standard applies to determine the merits-relatedness of a non-frivolous allegation that a judge's language in a ruling reflected an improper motive. If the judge's language was relevant to the case at hand—for example a statement that a claim is legally or factually "frivolous"—then the judge's choice of language is presumptively merits-related and excluded, absent evidence apart from the ruling itself suggesting an improper motive. If, on the other hand, the challenged language does not seem relevant on its face, then an additional inquiry under Rule 11 is necessary.

With regard to Rule 3(h)(3)(B), a complaint of delay in a single case is excluded as merits-related. Such an allegation may be said to challenge the correctness of an official action of the judge—in other words, assigning a low priority to deciding the particular case. But, by the same token, an allegation of a habitual pattern of delay in a significant number of unrelated cases, or an allegation of deliberate delay in a single case arising out of an illicit motive, is not merits-related.

The remaining subsections of Rule 3 provide technical definitions clarifying the application of the Rules to the various kinds of courts covered.

RULE 4. COVERED JUDGES

A complaint under these Rules may concern the actions or capacity only of judges of United States courts of appeals, judges of United States district courts, judges of United States bankruptcy courts, United States magistrate judges, and judges of the courts specified in 28 U.S.C. § 363.

(Adopted Mar. 11, 2008, eff. Apr. 10, 2008.)

Commentary on Rule 4

This Rule tracks the Act. Rule 8(c) and (d) contain provisions as to the handling of complaints against persons not covered by the Act, such as other court personnel, or against both covered judges and noncovered persons.

ARTICLE II. INITIATION OF A COMPLAINT

RULE 5. IDENTIFICATION OF A COMPLAINT

(a) Identification. When a chief judge has information constituting reasonable grounds for inquiry into whether a covered judge has engaged in misconduct or has a disability, the chief judge may conduct an inquiry, as he or she deems appropriate, into the accuracy of the information even if no related complaint has been filed. A chief judge who finds probable cause to believe that misconduct has occurred or that a disability exists may seek an informal resolution that he or she finds satisfactory. If no informal resolution is achieved or is feasible, the chief judge may identify a complaint and, by written order stating the reasons, begin the review provided in Rule 11. If the evidence of misconduct is clear and convincing and no informal resolution is achieved or is feasible, the chief judge must identify a complaint. A chief judge must not decline to identify a complaint merely because the person making the allegation has not filed a complaint under Rule 6. This Rule is subject to Rule 7.

(b) Noncompliance with Rule 6(d). Rule 6 complaints that do not comply with the requirements of Rule 6(d) must be considered under this Rule.

(Adopted Mar. 11, 2008, eff. Apr. 10, 2008.)

Commentary on Rule 5

This Rule is adapted from the Breyer Committee Report, 239 F.R.D. at 245–46.

The Act authorizes the chief judge, by written order stating reasons, to identify a complaint and thereby dispense with the filing of a written complaint. See 28 U.S.C. § 351(b). Under Rule 5, when a chief judge becomes aware of information constituting reasonable grounds to inquire into possible misconduct or disability on the part of a covered judge, and no formal complaint has been filed, the chief judge has the power in his or her discretion to begin an appropriate inquiry. A chief judge's decision whether to informally seek a resolution and/or to identify a complaint is guided by the results of that inquiry. If the chief judge concludes that there is probable cause to believe that misconduct has occurred or a disability exists, the chief judge may seek an informal resolution, if feasible, and if failing in that, may identify a complaint. Discretion is accorded largely for the reasons police officers and prosecutors have discretion in making arrests or bringing charges. The matter may be trivial and isolated, based on marginal evidence, or otherwise highly unlikely to lead to a misconduct or disability finding. On the other hand, if the inquiry leads the chief judge to conclude that there is clear and convincing evidence of misconduct or a disability, and no satisfactory informal resolution has been achieved or is feasible, the chief judge is required to identify a complaint.

An informal resolution is one agreed to by the subject judge and found satisfactory by the chief judge. Because an informal resolution under Rule 5 reached before a complaint is filed under Rule 6 will generally cause a subsequent Rule 6 complaint alleging the identical matter to be concluded, see Rule 11(d), the chief judge must be sure that the resolution is fully appropriate before endorsing it. In doing so, the chief judge must balance the seriousness of the matter against the particular judge's alacrity in addressing the issue. The availability of this procedure should encourage attempts at swift remedial action before a formal complaint is filed.

When a complaint is identified, a written order stating the reasons for the identification must be provided; this begins the process articulated in Rule 11. Rule 11 provides that once the chief judge has identified a complaint, the chief judge, subject to the disqualification provisions of Rule 25, will perform, with respect to that complaint, all functions assigned to the chief judge for the determination of complaints filed by a complainant.

In high-visibility situations, it may be desirable for the chief judge to identify a complaint without first seeking an informal resolution (and then, if the circumstances warrant, dismiss or conclude the identified complaint without appointment of a special committee) in order to assure the public that the allegations have not been ignored.

A chief judge's decision not to identify a complaint under Rule 5 is not appealable and is subject to Rule 3(h)(3)(A), which excludes merits-related complaints from the definition of misconduct.

A chief judge may not decline to identify a complaint solely on the basis that the unfiled allegations could be raised by one or more persons in a filed complaint, but none of these persons has opted to do so.

Subsection (a) concludes by stating that this Rule is "subject to Rule 7. " This is intended to establish that only: (i) the chief judge of the home circuit of a potential subject judge, or (ii) the chief judge of a circuit in which misconduct is alleged to have occurred in the course of official business while the potential subject judge was sitting by designation, shall have the power or a duty under this Rule to identify a complaint.

Subsection (b) provides that complaints filed under Rule 6 that do not comply with the requirements of Rule 6(d), must be considered under this Rule. For instance, if a complaint has been filed but the form submitted is unsigned, or the truth of the statements therein are not verified in writing under penalty of perjury, then a chief judge must nevertheless consider the allegations as known information, and proceed to follow the process described in Rule 5(a).

RULE 6. FILING A COMPLAINT

(a) Form. A complainant may use the form reproduced in the appendix to these Rules or a form designated by the rules of the judicial council in the circuit in which the complaint is filed. A complaint form is also available on each court of appeals' website or may be obtained from the circuit clerk or any district court or bankruptcy court within the circuit. A form is not necessary to file a complaint, but the complaint must be written and must include the information described in (b).

(b) Brief Statement of Facts. A complaint must contain a concise statement that details the specific facts on which the claim of misconduct or disability is based. The statement of facts should include a description of:

(1) what happened;

(2) when and where the relevant events happened;

(3) any information that would help an investigator check the facts; and

(4) for an allegation of disability, any additional facts that form the basis of that allegation.

(c) Legibility. A complaint should be typewritten if possible. If not typewritten, it must be legible. An illegible complaint will be returned to the complainant with a request to resubmit it in legible form. If a resubmitted complaint is still illegible, it will not be accepted for filing.

(d) Complainant's Address and Signature; Verification. The complainant must provide a contact address and sign the complaint. The truth of the statements made in the complaint must be verified in writing under penalty of perjury. If any of these requirements are not met, the complaint will be accepted for filing, but it will be reviewed under only Rule 5(b).

(e) Number of Copies; Envelope Marking. The complainant shall provide the number of copies of the complaint required by local rule. Each copy should be in an envelope marked "Complaint of Misconduct" or "Complaint of Disability." The envelope must not show the name of any subject judge.

(Adopted Mar. 11, 2008, eff. Apr. 10, 2008.)

Commentary on Rule 6

The Rule is adapted from the Illustrative Rules and is self-explanatory.

RULE 7. WHERE TO INITIATE COMPLAINTS

(a) Where to File. Except as provided in (b),

(1) a complaint against a judge of a United States court of appeals, a United States district court, a United States bankruptcy court, or a United States magistrate judge must be filed with the circuit clerk in the jurisdiction in which the subject judge holds office.

(2) a complaint against a judge of the United States Court of International Trade or the United States Court of Federal Claims must be filed with the respective clerk of that court.

(3) a complaint against a judge of the United States Court of Appeals for the Federal Circuit must be filed with the circuit executive of that court.

(b) Misconduct in Another Circuit; Transfer. If a complaint alleges misconduct in the course of official business while the subject judge was sitting on a court by designation under 28 U.S.C. §§ 291–293 and 294(d), the complaint may be filed or identified with the circuit clerk of that circuit or of the subject judge's home circuit. The proceeding will continue in the circuit of the first-filed or first-identified complaint. The judicial council of the circuit where the complaint was first filed or first identified may transfer the complaint to the subject judge's home circuit or to the circuit where the alleged misconduct occurred, as the case may be.

(Adopted Mar. 11, 2008, eff. Apr. 10, 2008.)

Commentary on Rule 7

Title 28 U.S.C. § 351 states that complaints are to be filed with "the clerk of the court of appeals for the circuit." However, in many circuits, this role is filled by circuit executives. Accordingly, the term "circuit clerk," as defined in Rule 3(b) and used throughout these Rules, applies to circuit executives.

Section 351 uses the term "the circuit" in a way that suggests that either the home circuit of the subject judge or the circuit in which misconduct is alleged to have occurred is the proper venue for complaints. With an exception for judges sitting by designation, the Rule requires the identifying or filing of a misconduct or disability complaint in the circuit in which the judge holds office, largely based on the administrative perspective of the Act. Given the Act's emphasis on the future conduct of the business of the courts, the circuit in which the judge holds office is the appropriate forum because that circuit is likely best able to influence a judge's future behavior in constructive ways.

However, when judges sit by designation, the non-home circuit has a strong interest in redressing misconduct in the course of official business, and where allegations also involve a member of the bar—ex parte contact between an attorney and a judge, for example—it may often be desirable to have the judicial and bar misconduct proceedings take place in the same venue. Rule 7(b), therefore, allows transfer to, or filing or identification of a complaint in, the non-home circuit. The proceeding may be transferred by the judicial council of the filing or identified circuit to the other circuit.

RULE 8. ACTION BY CLERK

(a) Receipt of Complaint. Upon receiving a complaint against a judge filed under Rule 5 or 6, the circuit clerk must open a file, assign a docket number according to a uniform numbering scheme promulgated by the Judicial Conference Committee on Judicial Conduct and Disability, and acknowledge the complaint's receipt.

(b) Distribution of Copies. The clerk must promptly send copies of a complaint filed under Rule 6 to the chief judge or the judge authorized to act as chief judge under Rule 25(f), and copies of complaints filed under Rule 5 or 6 to each subject judge. The clerk must retain the original complaint. Any further distribution should be as provided by local rule.

(c) Complaints Against Noncovered Persons. If the clerk receives a complaint about a person not holding an office described in Rule 4, the clerk must not accept the complaint for filing under these Rules.

(d) Receipt of Complaint about a Judge and Another Noncovered Person. If a complaint is received about a judge described in Rule 4 and a person not holding an office described in Rule 4, the clerk must accept the complaint for filing under these Rules only with regard to the judge and must inform the complainant of the limitation.

(Adopted Mar. 11, 2008, eff. Apr. 10, 2008.)

Commentary on Rule 8

This Rule is adapted from the Illustrative Rules and is largely self-explanatory.

The uniform docketing scheme described in subsection (a) should take into account potential problems associated with a complaint that names multiple judges. One solution may be to provide separate docket numbers for each subject judge. Separate docket numbers would help avoid difficulties in tracking cases, particularly if a complaint is dismissed with respect to some, but not all of the named judges.

Complaints against noncovered persons are not to be accepted for processing under these Rules but may, of course, be accepted under other circuit rules or procedures for grievances.

RULE 9. TIME FOR FILING OR IDENTIFYING A COMPLAINT

A complaint may be filed or identified at any time. If the passage of time has made an accurate and fair investigation of a complaint impractical, the complaint must be dismissed under Rule 11(c)(1)(E).

(Adopted Mar. 11, 2008, eff. Apr. 10, 2008.)

Commentary on Rule 9

This Rule is adapted from the Act, 28 U.S.C. §§ 351, 352(b)(1)(A)(iii), and the Illustrative Rules.

RULE 10. ABUSE OF THE COMPLAINT PROCEDURE

(a) Abusive Complaints. A complainant who has filed repetitive, harassing, or frivolous complaints, or has otherwise abused the complaint procedure, may be restricted from filing further complaints. After giving the complainant an opportunity to show cause in writing why his or her right to file further complaints should not be limited, a judicial council may prohibit, restrict, or impose conditions on the complainant's use of the complaint procedure. Upon written request of the complainant, the judicial council may revise or withdraw any prohibition, restriction, or condition previously imposed.

(b) Orchestrated Complaints. When many essentially identical complaints from different complainants are received and appear to be part of an orchestrated campaign, the chief judge may recommend that the judicial council issue a written order instructing the circuit clerk to accept only a certain number of such complaints for filing and to refuse to accept further ones. The clerk must send a copy of any such order to anyone whose complaint was not accepted.

(Adopted Mar. 11, 2008, eff. Apr. 10, 2008.)

Commentary on Rule 10

This Rule is adapted from the Illustrative Rules.

Rule 10(a) provides a mechanism for a judicial council to restrict the filing of further complaints by a single complainant who has abused the complaint procedure. In some instances, however, the complaint procedure may be abused in a manner for which the remedy provided in Rule 10(a) may not be appropriate. For example, some circuits have been inundated with submissions of dozens or hundreds of essentially identical complaints against the same judge or judges, all submitted by different complainants. In many of these instances, persons with grievances against a particular judge or judges used the Internet or other technology to orchestrate mass complaint-filing campaigns against them. If each complaint submitted as part of such a campaign were accepted for filing and processed according to these Rules, there would be a serious drain on court resources without any benefit to the adjudication of the underlying merits.

A judicial council may, therefore, respond to such mass filings under Rule 10(b) by declining to accept repetitive complaints for filing, regardless of the fact that the complaints are nominally submitted by different complainants. When the first complaint or complaints have been dismissed on the merits, and when further, essentially identical submissions follow, the judicial council may issue a second order noting that these are identical or repetitive complaints, directing the circuit clerk not to accept these complaints or any further such complaints for filing, and directing the clerk to send each putative complainant copies of both orders.

ARTICLE III. REVIEW OF A COMPLAINT BY THE CHIEF JUDGE

RULE 11. REVIEW BY THE CHIEF JUDGE

(a) Purpose of Chief Judge's Review. When a complaint is identified by the chief judge or is filed, the chief judge must review it unless the chief judge is disqualified under Rule 25. If the complaint contains information constituting evidence of misconduct or disability, but the complainant does not claim it as such, the chief judge must treat the complaint as if it did allege misconduct or disability and give notice to the subject judge. After reviewing the complaint, the chief judge must determine whether it should be:

(1) dismissed;

(2) concluded on the ground that voluntary corrective action has been taken;

(3) concluded because intervening events have made action on the complaint no longer necessary; or

(4) referred to a special committee.

(b) Inquiry by Chief Judge. In determining what action to take under Rule 11(a), the chief judge may conduct a limited inquiry. The chief judge, or a designee, may communicate orally or in writing with the complainant, the subject judge, and any others who may have knowledge of the matter, and may review transcripts or other relevant documents. In conducting the inquiry, the chief judge must not determine any reasonably disputed issue.

(c) Dismissal.

(1) *Allowable grounds.* A complaint must be dismissed in whole or in part to the extent that the chief judge concludes that the complaint:

(A) alleges conduct that, even if true, is not prejudicial to the effective and expeditious administration of the business of the courts and does not indicate a mental or physical disability resulting in inability to discharge the duties of judicial office;

(B) is directly related to the merits of a decision or procedural ruling;

(C) is frivolous;

(D) is based on allegations lacking sufficient evidence to raise an inference that misconduct has occurred or that a disability exists;

(E) is based on allegations which are incapable of being established through investigation;

(F) has been filed in the wrong circuit under Rule 7; or

(G) is otherwise not appropriate for consideration under the Act.

(2) *Disallowed grounds.* A complaint must not be dismissed solely because it repeats allegations of a previously dismissed complaint if it also contains material information not previously considered and does not constitute harassment of the subject judge.

(d) Corrective Action. The chief judge may conclude the complaint proceeding in whole or in part if:

(1) an informal resolution under Rule 5 satisfactory to the chief judge was reached before the complaint was filed under Rule 6, or

(2) the chief judge determines that the subject judge has taken appropriate voluntary corrective action that acknowledges and remedies the problems raised by the complaint.

(e) Intervening Events. The chief judge may conclude the complaint proceeding in whole or in part upon determining that intervening events render some or all of the allegations moot or make remedial action impossible.

(f) Appointment of Special Committee. If some or all of the complaint is not dismissed or concluded, the chief judge must promptly appoint a special committee to investigate the complaint or any relevant portion of it and to make recommendations to the judicial council. Before appointing a special committee, the chief judge must invite the subject judge to respond to the complaint either orally or in writing if the judge was not given an opportunity during the limited inquiry. In the chief judge's discretion, separate complaints may be joined and assigned to a single special committee. Similarly, a single complaint about more than one judge may be severed and more than one special committee appointed.

(g) Notice of Chief Judge's Action; Petitions for Review.

(1) *When special committee is appointed.* If a special committee is appointed, the chief judge must notify the complainant and the subject judge that the matter has been referred to a special committee and identify the members of the committee. A copy of the order appointing the special committee must be sent

to the Judicial Conference Committee on Judicial Conduct and Disability.

(2) *When chief judge disposes of complaint without appointing special committee.* If the chief judge disposes of the complaint under Rule 11(c), (d), or (e), the chief judge must prepare a supporting memorandum that sets forth the reasons for the disposition. Except as authorized by 28 U.S.C. § 360, the memorandum must not include the name of the complainant or of the subject judge. The order and the supporting memorandum, which may be one document, must be provided to the complainant, the subject judge, and the Judicial Conference Committee on Judicial Conduct and Disability.

(3) *Right of petition for review.* If the chief judge disposes of a complaint under Rule 11(c), (d), or (e), the complainant and subject judge must be notified of the right to petition the judicial council for review of the disposition, as provided in Rule 18. If a petition for review is filed, the chief judge must promptly transmit all materials obtained in connection with the inquiry under Rule 11(b) to the circuit clerk for transmittal to the judicial council.

(h) Public Availability of Chief Judge's Decision. The chief judge's decision must be made public to the extent, at the time, and in the manner provided in Rule 24.

(Adopted Mar. 11, 2008, eff. Apr. 10, 2008.)

Commentary on Rule 11

Subsection (a) lists the actions available to a chief judge in reviewing a complaint. This subsection provides that where a complaint has been filed under Rule 6, the ordinary doctrines of waiver do not apply. A chief judge must identify as a complaint any misconduct or disability issues raised by the factual allegations of the complaint even if the complainant makes no such claim with regard to those issues. For example, an allegation limited to misconduct in fact-finding that mentions periods during a trial when the judge was asleep must be treated as a complaint regarding disability. Some formal order giving notice of the expanded scope of the proceeding must be given to the subject judge.

Subsection (b) describes the nature of the chief judge's inquiry. It is based largely on the Breyer Committee Report, 239 F.R.D. at 243–45. The Act states that dismissal is appropriate "when a limited inquiry . . . demonstrates that the allegations in the complaint lack any factual foundation or are conclusively refuted by objective evidence." 28 U.S.C. § 352(b)(1)(B). At the same time, however, Section 352(a) states that "[t]he chief judge shall not undertake to make findings of fact about any matter that is reasonably in dispute." These two statutory standards should be read together, so that a matter is not "reasonably" in dispute if a limited inquiry shows that the allegations do not constitute misconduct or disability, that they lack any reliable factual foundation, or that they are conclusively refuted by objective evidence.

In conducting a limited inquiry under subsection (b), the chief judge must avoid determinations of reasonably disputed issues, including reasonably disputed issues as to whether the facts alleged constitute misconduct or disability, which are ordinarily left to a special committee and the judicial council. An allegation of fact is ordinarily not "refuted" simply because the subject judge denies it. The limited inquiry must reveal something more in the way of refutation before it is appropriate to dismiss a complaint that is otherwise cognizable. If it is the complainant's word against the subject judge's—in other words, there is simply no other significant evidence of what happened or of the complainant's unreliability—then there must be a special-committee investigation. Such a credibility issue is a matter "reasonably in dispute" within the meaning of the Act.

However, dismissal following a limited inquiry may occur when the complaint refers to transcripts or to witnesses and the chief judge determines that the transcripts and witnesses all support the subject judge. Breyer Committee Report, 239 F.R.D. at 243. For example, consider a complaint alleging that the subject judge said X, and the complaint mentions, or it is independently clear, that five people may have heard what the judge said. Id. The chief judge is told by the subject judge and one witness that the judge did not say X, and the chief judge dismisses the complaint without questioning the other four possible witnesses. Id. In this example, the matter remains reasonably in dispute. If all five witnesses say the judge did not say X, dismissal is appropriate, but if potential witnesses who are reasonably accessible have not been questioned, then the matter remains reasonably in dispute. Id.

Similarly, under (c)(1)(A), if it is clear that the conduct or disability alleged, even if true, is not cognizable under these Rules, the complaint should be dismissed. If that issue is reasonably in dispute, however, dismissal under (c)(1)(A) is inappropriate.

Essentially, the standard articulated in subsection (b) is that used to decide motions for summary judgment pursuant to Fed. R. Civ. P. 56. Genuine issues of material fact are not resolved at the summary judgment stage. A material fact is one that "might affect the outcome of the suit under the governing law," and a dispute is "genuine" if "the evidence is such that a reasonable jury could return a verdict for the nonmoving party." *Anderson v. Liberty Lobby*, 477 U.S. 242, 248 (1986). Similarly, the chief judge may not resolve a genuine issue concerning a material fact or the existence of misconduct or a disability when conducting a limited inquiry pursuant to subsection (b).

Subsection (c) describes the grounds on which a complaint may be dismissed. These are adapted from the Act, 28 U.S.C. § 352(b), and the Breyer Committee Report, 239 F.R.D. at 239–45. Subsection (c)(1)(A) permits dismissal of an allegation that, even if true, does not constitute misconduct or disability under the statutory standard. The proper standards are set out in Rule 3 and discussed in the Commentary on that Rule. Subsection (c)(1)(B) permits dismissal of complaints related to the merits of a decision by a subject judge; this standard is also governed by Rule 3 and its accompanying Commentary.

Subsections (c)(1)(C)–(E) implement the statute by allowing dismissal of complaints that are "frivolous, lacking sufficient evidence to raise an inference that misconduct has occurred, or containing allegations which are incapable of being established through investigation." 28 U.S.C. § 352(b)(1)(A)(iii).

Dismissal of a complaint as "frivolous," under Rule 11(c)(1)(C), will generally occur without any inquiry beyond the face of the complaint. For instance, when the allegations are facially incredible or so lacking in indicia of reliability that no further inquiry is warranted, dismissal under this subsection is appropriate.

A complaint warranting dismissal under Rule 11(c)(1)(D) is illustrated by the following example. Consider a complainant who alleges an impropriety and asserts that he knows of it because it was observed and reported to him by a person who is identified. The judge denies that the event occurred. When contacted, the source also denies it. In such a case, the chief judge's proper course of action may turn on whether the source had any role in the allegedly improper conduct. If the complaint was based on a lawyer's statement that he or she had an improper ex parte contact with a judge, the lawyer's denial of the impropriety might not be taken as wholly persuasive, and it would be appropriate to conclude that a real factual issue is raised. On the other hand, if the complaint quoted a disinterested third party and that disinterested party denied that the statement had been made, there would be no value in opening a formal investigation. In such a case, it would be appropriate to dismiss the complaint under Rule 11(c)(1)(D).

Rule 11(c)(1)(E) is intended, among other things, to cover situations when no evidence is offered or identified, or when the only identified source is unavailable. Breyer Committee Report, 239 F.R.D. at 243. For example, a complaint alleges that an unnamed attorney told the complainant that the judge did X. Id. The subject judge denies it. The chief judge requests that the complainant (who does not purport to have observed the judge do X) identify the unnamed witness, or that the unnamed witness come forward so that the chief judge can learn the unnamed witness's account. Id. The complainant responds that he has spoken with the unnamed witness, that the unnamed witness is an attorney who practices in federal court, and that the unnamed witness is unwilling to be identified or to come forward. Id. at 243–44. The allegation is then properly dismissed as containing allegations that are incapable of being established through investigation. Id.

If, however, the situation involves a reasonable dispute over credibility, the matter should proceed. For example, the complainant alleges an impropriety and alleges that he or she observed it and that there were no other witnesses; the subject judge denies that the event occurred. Unless the complainant's allegations are facially incredible or so lacking indicia of reliability warranting dismissal under Rule 11(c)(1)(C), a special committee must be appointed because there is a material factual question that is reasonably in dispute.

Dismissal is also appropriate when a complaint is filed so long after an alleged event that memory loss, death, or changes to unknown residences prevent a proper investigation.

Subsection (c)(2) indicates that the investigative nature of the process prevents the application of claim preclusion principles where new and material evidence becomes available. However, it also recognizes that at some point a renewed investigation may constitute harassment of the subject judge and should be foregone, depending of course on the seriousness of the issues and the weight of the new evidence.

Rule 11(d) implements the Act's provision for dismissal if voluntary appropriate corrective action has been taken. It is largely adapted from the Breyer Committee Report, 239 F.R.D. 244–45. The Act authorizes the chief judge to conclude the proceedings if "appropriate corrective action has been taken." 28 U.S.C. § 352(b)(2). Under the Rule, action taken after the complaint is filed is "appropriate" when it acknowledges and remedies the problem raised by the complaint. Breyer Committee Report, 239 F.R.D. at 244. Because the Act deals with the conduct of judges, the emphasis is on correction of the judicial conduct that was the subject of the complaint. Id. Terminating a complaint based on corrective action is premised on the implicit understanding that voluntary self-correction or redress of misconduct or a disability is preferable to sanctions. Id. The chief judge may facilitate this process by giving the subject judge an objective view of the appearance of the judicial conduct in question and by suggesting appropriate corrective measures. Id. Moreover, when corrective action is taken under Rule 5 satisfactory to the chief judge before a complaint is filed, that informal resolution will be sufficient to conclude a subsequent complaint based on the identical conduct.

"Corrective action" must be voluntary action taken by the subject judge. Breyer Committee Report, 239 F.R.D. at 244. A remedial action directed by the chief judge or by an appellate court without the participation of the subject judge in formulating the directive or without the subject judge's subsequent agreement to such action does not constitute the requisite voluntary corrective action. Id. Neither the chief judge nor an appellate court has authority under the Act to impose a formal remedy or sanction; only the judicial council can impose a formal remedy or sanction under 28 U.S.C. § 354(a)(2). Id. Compliance with a previous council order may serve as corrective action allowing conclusion of a later complaint about the same behavior. Id.

Where a judge's conduct has resulted in identifiable, particularized harm to the complainant or another individual, appropriate corrective action should include steps taken by that judge to acknowledge and redress the harm, if possible, such as by an apology, recusal from a case, or a pledge to refrain from similar conduct in the future. Id. While the Act is generally forward-looking, any corrective action should, to the extent possible, serve to correct a specific harm to an individual, if such harm can reasonably be remedied. Id. In some cases, corrective action may not be "appropriate" to justify conclusion of a complaint unless the complainant or other individual harmed is meaningfully apprised of the nature of the corrective action in the chief judge's order, in a direct communication from the subject judge, or otherwise. Id.

Voluntary corrective action should be proportionate to any plausible allegations of misconduct in the complaint. The form of corrective action should also be proportionate to any sanctions that a judicial council might impose under Rule 20(b), such as a private or public reprimand or a change in case assignments. Breyer Committee Report, 239 F.R.D at 244–45. In other words, minor corrective action will not suffice to dispose of a serious matter. Id.

Rule 11(e) implements Section 352(b)(2) of the Act, which permits the chief judge to "conclude the proceeding," if "action on the complaint is no longer necessary because of intervening events," such as a resignation from judicial office. Ordinarily, however, stepping down from an administrative post such as chief judge, judicial-council member, or court-committee chair does not constitute an event rendering unnecessary any further action on a complaint alleging judicial misconduct. Breyer Committee Report, 239 F.R.D. at 245. As long as the subject of the complaint performs judicial duties, a complaint alleging judicial misconduct must be addressed. Id.

If a complaint is not disposed of pursuant to Rule 11(c), (d), or (e), a special committee must be appointed. Rule 11(f) states that a subject judge must be invited to respond to the complaint before a special committee is appointed, if no earlier response was invited.

Subject judges, of course, receive copies of complaints at the same time that they are referred to the chief judge, and they are free to volunteer responses to them. Under Rule 11(b), the chief judge may request a response if it is thought necessary. However, many complaints are clear candidates for dismissal even if their allegations are accepted as true, and there is no need for the subject judge to devote time to a defense.

The Act requires that the order dismissing a complaint or concluding the proceeding contain a statement of reasons and that a copy of the order be sent to the complainant. 28 U.S.C. § 352(b). Rule 24, dealing with availability of information to the public, contemplates that the order will be made public, usually without disclosing the names of the complainant or the subject judge. If desired for administrative purposes, more identifying information can be included in a non-public version of the order.

When complaints are disposed of by chief judges, the statutory purposes are best served by providing the complainant with a full, particularized, but concise explanation, giving reasons for the conclusions reached. See also Commentary on Rule 24, dealing with public availability.

Rule 11(g) provides that the complainant and subject judge must be notified, in the case of a disposition by the chief judge, of the right to petition the judicial council for review. A copy of a chief judge's order and memorandum, which may be one document, disposing of a complaint must be sent by the circuit clerk to the Judicial Conference Committee on Judicial Conduct and Disability.

ARTICLE IV. INVESTIGATION AND REPORT BY SPECIAL COMMITTEE

RULE 12. COMPOSITION OF SPECIAL COMMITTEE

(a) Membership. Except as provided in (e), a special committee appointed under Rule 11(f) must consist of the chief judge and equal numbers of circuit and district judges. If the complaint is about a district judge, bankruptcy judge, or magistrate judge, then, when possible, the district-judge members of the committee must be from districts other than the district of the subject judge. For the courts named in 28 U.S.C. § 363, the committee must be selected from the judges serving on the subject judge's court.

(b) Presiding Officer. When appointing the committee, the chief judge may serve as the presiding officer or else must designate a committee member as the presiding officer.

(c) Bankruptcy Judge or Magistrate Judge as Adviser. If the subject judge is a bankruptcy judge or magistrate judge, he or she may, within 14 days after being notified of the committee's appointment, ask the chief judge to designate as a committee adviser another bankruptcy judge or magistrate judge, as the case may be. The chief judge must grant such a request but may otherwise use discretion in naming the adviser. Unless the adviser is a Court of Federal Claims special master appointed under 42 U.S.C. § 300aa–12(c), the adviser must be from a district other than the district of the subject bankruptcy judge or subject magistrate judge. The adviser cannot vote but has the other privileges of a committee member.

(d) Provision of Documents. The chief judge must certify to each other member of the committee and to any adviser copies of the complaint and statement of facts in whole or relevant part, and any other relevant documents on file.

(e) Continuing Qualification of Committee Members. A member of a special committee who was qualified to serve when appointed may continue to serve on the committee even though the member relinquishes the position of chief judge, active circuit judge, or active district judge, as the case may be, but only if the member continues to hold office under Article III, Section 1, of the Constitution of the United States, or under 28 U.S.C. § 171.

(f) Inability of Committee Member to Complete Service. If a member of a special committee can no longer serve because of death, disability, disqualification, resignation, retirement from office, or other reason, the chief judge must decide whether to appoint a replacement member, either a circuit or district judge as needed under (a). No special committee appointed under these Rules may function with only a single member, and the votes of a two-member committee must be unanimous.

(g) Voting. All actions by a committee must be by vote of a majority of all members of the committee.

(Adopted Mar. 11, 2008, eff. Apr. 10, 2008.)

Commentary on Rule 12

This Rule is adapted from the Act and the Illustrative Rules.

Rule 12 leaves the size of a special committee flexible, to be determined on a case-by-case basis. The question of committee size is one that should be weighed with care in view of the potential for consuming the members' time; a large committee should be appointed only if there is a special reason to do so.

Although the Act requires that the chief judge be a member of each special committee, 28 U.S.C. § 353(a)(1), it does not require that the chief judge preside. Accordingly, Rule 12(b) provides that if the chief judge does not preside, he or she must designate another committee member as the presiding officer.

Rule 12(c) provides that the chief judge must appoint a bankruptcy judge or magistrate judge as an adviser to a special committee at the request of a bankruptcy or magistrate subject judge.

Subsection (c) also provides that the adviser will have all the privileges of a committee member except a vote. The adviser, therefore, may participate in all deliberations of the committee, question witnesses at hearings, and write a separate statement to accompany the special committee's report to the judicial council.

Rule 12(e) provides that a member of a special committee who remains an Article III judge may continue to serve on the committee even though the member's status otherwise changes. Thus, a committee that originally consisted of the chief judge and an equal number of circuit and district judges, as required by the law, may continue to function even though changes of status alter that composition. This provision reflects the belief that stability of membership will contribute to the quality of the work of such committees.

Stability of membership is also the principal concern animating Rule 12(f), which deals with the case in which a special committee loses a member before its work is complete. The Rule permits the chief judge to determine whether a replacement member should be appointed. Generally, appointment of a replacement member is desirable in these situations unless the committee has conducted evidentiary hearings before the vacancy occurs. However, cases may arise in which a committee is in the late stages of its work, and in which it would be difficult for a new member to play a meaningful role. The Rule also preserves the collegial character of the committee process by prohibiting a single surviving member from serving as a committee and by providing that a committee of two surviving members will, in essence, operate under a unanimity rule.

Rule 12(g) provides that actions of a special committee must be by vote of a majority of all the members. All the members of a committee should participate in committee decisions. In that circumstance, it seems reasonable to require that committee decisions be made by a majority of the membership, rather than a majority of some smaller quorum.

RULE 13. CONDUCT OF AN INVESTIGATION

(a) Extent and Methods of Special-Committee Investigation. Each special committee must determine the appropriate extent and methods of the investigation in light of the allegations of the complaint. If, in the course of the investigation, the committee has cause to believe that the subject judge may have engaged in misconduct or has a disability that is beyond the scope of the complaint, the committee must refer the new matter to the chief judge for action under Rule 5 or Rule 11.

(b) Criminal Conduct. If the committee's investigation concerns conduct that may be a crime, the committee must consult with the appropriate prosecutorial authorities to the extent permitted by the Act to avoid compromising any criminal investigation. The committee has final authority over the timing and extent of its investigation and the formulation of its recommendations.

(c) Staff. The committee may arrange for staff assistance to conduct the investigation. It may use existing staff of the judicial branch or may hire special staff through the Director of the Administrative Office of the United States Courts.

(d) Delegation of Subpoena Power; Contempt. The chief judge may delegate the authority to exercise the committee's subpoena powers. The judicial council or special committee may institute a contempt proceeding under 28 U.S.C. § 332(d) against anyone who fails to comply with a subpoena.

(Adopted Mar. 11, 2008, eff. Apr. 10, 2008.)

Commentary on Rule 13

This Rule is adapted from the Illustrative Rules.

Rule 13, as well as Rules 14, 15, and 16, are concerned with the way in which a special committee carries out its mission. They reflect the view that a special committee has two roles that are separated in ordinary litigation. First, the committee has an investigative role of the kind that is characteristically left to executive branch agencies or discovery by civil litigants. 28 U.S.C. § 353(c). Second, it has a formalized fact-finding and recommendation-of-disposition role that is characteristically left to juries, judges, or arbitrators. Id. Rule 13 generally governs the investigative stage. Even though the same body has responsibility for both roles under the Act, it is important to distinguish between them in order to ensure that appropriate rights are afforded at appropriate times to the subject judge.

One of the difficult questions that can arise is the relationship between proceedings under the Act and criminal investigations. Rule 13(b) assigns responsibility for coordination to the special committee in cases in which criminal conduct is suspected, but gives the committee the authority to determine the appropriate pace of its activity in light of any criminal investigation.

Title 28 U.S.C. § 356(a) provides that a special committee will have full subpoena powers as provided in 28 U.S.C. § 332(d). Section 332(d)(1) provides that subpoenas will be issued on behalf of judicial councils by the circuit clerk "at the direction of the chief judge of the circuit or his designee." Rule 13(d) contemplates that, where the chief judge designates someone else as presiding officer of a special committee, the presiding officer also be delegated the authority to direct the circuit clerk to issue subpoenas related to committee proceedings. That is not intended to imply, however, that the decision to use the subpoena power is exercisable by the presiding officer alone. See Rule 12(g).

RULE 14. CONDUCT OF HEARINGS BY SPECIAL COMMITTEE

(a) Purpose of Hearings. The committee may hold hearings to take testimony and receive other evidence, to hear argument, or both. If the committee is investigating allegations against more than one judge, it may hold joint or separate hearings.

(b) Committee Evidence. Subject to Rule 15, the committee must obtain material, nonredundant evidence in the form it considers appropriate. In the committee's discretion, evidence may be obtained by committee members, staff, or both. Witnesses offering testimonial evidence may include the complainant and the subject judge.

(c) Counsel for Witnesses. The subject judge has the right to counsel. The special committee has discretion to decide whether other witnesses may have counsel present when they testify.

(d) Witness Fees. Witness fees must be paid as provided in 28 U.S.C. § 1821.

(e) Oath. All testimony taken at a hearing must be given under oath or affirmation.

(f) Rules of Evidence. The Federal Rules of Evidence do not apply to special-committee hearings.

(g) Record and Transcript. A record and transcript must be made of all hearings.

(Adopted Mar. 11, 2008, eff. Apr. 10, 2008.)

Commentary on Rule 14

This Rule is adapted from Section 353 of the Act and the Illustrative Rules.

Rule 14 is concerned with the conduct of fact-finding hearings. Special-committee hearings will normally be held only after the investigative work has been completed and the committee has concluded that there is sufficient evidence to warrant a formal fact-finding proceeding. Special-committee proceedings are primarily inquisitorial rather than adversarial. Accordingly, the Federal Rules of Evidence do not apply to such hearings. Inevitably, a hearing will have something of an adversary character. Nevertheless, that tendency should be moderated to the extent possible. Even though a proceeding will commonly have investigative and hearing stages, committee members should not regard themselves as prosecutors one day and judges the next. Their duty—and that of their staff—is at all times to be impartial seekers of the truth.

Rule 14(b) contemplates that material evidence will be obtained by the committee and presented in the form of affidavits, live testimony, etc. Staff or others who are organizing the hearings should regard it as their role to present evidence representing the entire picture. With respect to testimonial evidence, the subject judge should normally be called as a committee witness. Cases may arise in which the judge will not testify voluntarily. In such cases, subpoena powers are available, subject to the normal testimonial privileges. Although Rule 15(c) recognizes the subject judge's statutory right to call witnesses on his or her own behalf, exercise of this right should not usually be necessary.

RULE 15. RIGHTS OF SUBJECT JUDGE

(a) Notice.

(1) *Generally.* The subject judge must receive written notice of:

(A) the appointment of a special committee under Rule 11(f);

(B) the expansion of the scope of an investigation under Rule 13(a);

(C) any hearing under Rule 14, including its purposes, the names of any witnesses the committee intends to call, and the text of any statements that have been taken from those witnesses.

(2) *Suggestion of additional witnesses.* The subject judge may suggest additional witnesses to the committee.

(b) Report of the Special Committee. The subject judge must be sent a copy of the special committee's report when it is filed with the judicial council.

(c) Presentation of Evidence. At any hearing held under Rule 14, the subject judge has the right to present evidence, to compel the attendance of witnesses, and to compel the production of documents. At the request of the subject judge, the chief judge or the judge's designee must direct the circuit clerk to issue a subpoena to a witness under 28 U.S.C. § 332(d)(1). The subject judge must be given the opportunity to cross-examine committee witnesses, in person or by counsel.

(d) Presentation of Argument. The subject judge may submit written argument to the special committee and must be given a reasonable opportunity to present oral argument at an appropriate stage of the investigation.

(e) Attendance at Hearings. The subject judge has the right to attend any hearing held under Rule 14 and to receive copies of the transcript, of any documents introduced, and of any written arguments submitted by the complainant to the committee.

(f) Representation by Counsel. The subject judge may choose to be represented by counsel in the exercise of any right enumerated in this Rule. As provided in Rule 20(e), the United States may bear the costs of the representation.

(Adopted Mar. 11, 2008, eff. Apr. 10, 2008.)

Commentary on Rule 15

This Rule is adapted from the Act and the Illustrative Rules.

The Act states that these Rules must contain provisions requiring that "the judge whose conduct is the subject of a complaint ... be afforded an opportunity to appear (in person or by counsel) at proceedings conducted by the investigating panel, to present oral and documentary evidence, to compel the attendance of witnesses or the production of documents, to cross-examine witnesses, and to present argument orally or in writing." 28 U.S.C. § 358(b)(2). To implement this provision, Rule 15(e) gives the judge the right to attend any hearing held for the purpose of receiving evidence of record or hearing argument under Rule 14.

The Act does not require that the subject judge be permitted to attend all proceedings of the special committee. Accordingly, the Rules do not give a right to attend other proceedings—for example, meetings at which the committee is engaged in investigative activity, such as interviewing persons to learn whether they ought to be called as witnesses or examining for relevance purposes documents delivered pursuant to a subpoena duces tecum, or meetings in which the committee is deliberating on the evidence or its recommendations.

RULE 16. RIGHTS OF COMPLAINANT IN INVESTIGATION

(a) Notice. The complainant must receive written notice of the investigation as provided in Rule 11(g)(1). When the special committee's report to the judicial council is filed, the complainant must be notified of the filing. The judicial council may, in its discretion, provide a copy of the report of a special committee to the complainant.

(b) Opportunity to Provide Evidence. If the committee determines that the complainant may have evidence that does not already exist in writing, a representative of the committee must interview the complainant.

(c) Presentation of Argument. The complainant may submit written argument to the special committee. In its discretion, the special committee may permit the complainant to offer oral argument.

(d) Representation by Counsel. A complainant may submit written argument through counsel and, if permitted to offer oral argument, may do so through counsel.

(e) Cooperation. In exercising its discretion under this Rule, a special committee may take into account the degree of the complainant's cooperation in preserving the confidentiality of the proceedings, including the identity of the subject judge.

(Adopted Mar. 11, 2008, eff. Apr. 10, 2008.)

Commentary on Rule 16

This Rule is adapted from the Act and the Illustrative Rules.

In accordance with the view of the process as fundamentally administrative and inquisitorial, these Rules do not give the complainant the rights of a party to litigation, and leave the complainant's role largely to the discretion of the special committee. However, Rule 16(b) provides that, where a special committee has been appointed and it determines that the complainant may have additional evidence, the complainant must be interviewed by a representative of the committee. Such an interview may be in person or by telephone, and the representative of the committee may be either a member or staff.

Rule 16 does not contemplate that the complainant will ordinarily be permitted to attend proceedings of the special committee except when testifying or presenting oral argument. A special committee may exercise its discretion to permit the complainant to be present at its proceedings, or to permit the complainant, individually or through counsel, to participate in the examination or cross-examination of witnesses.

The Act authorizes an exception to the normal confidentiality provisions where the judicial council in its discretion provides a copy of the report of the special committee to the complainant and to the subject judge. 28 U.S.C. § 360(a)(1). However, the Rules do not entitle the complainant to a copy of the special committee's report.

In exercising their discretion regarding the role of the complainant, the special committee and the judicial council should protect the confidentiality of the complaint process. As a consequence, subsection (e) provides that a special committee may consider the degree to which a complainant has cooperated in preserving the confidentiality of the proceedings in determining what role beyond the minimum required by these Rules should be given to that complainant.

RULE 17. SPECIAL–COMMITTEE REPORT

The committee must file with the judicial council a comprehensive report of its investigation, including findings and recommendations for council action. The report must be accompanied by a statement of the vote by which it was adopted, any separate or dissenting statements of committee members, and the record of any hearings held under Rule 14. A copy of the report and accompanying statement must be sent to the Judicial Conference Committee on Judicial Conduct and Disability.

(Adopted Mar. 11, 2008, eff. Apr. 10, 2008.)

Commentary on Rule 17

This Rule is adapted from the Illustrative Rules and is self-explanatory. The provision for sending a copy of the special-committee report and accompanying statement to the Judicial Conference Committee is new.

ARTICLE V. JUDICIAL–COUNCIL REVIEW

RULE 18. PETITIONS FOR REVIEW OF CHIEF JUDGE DISPOSITIONS UNDER RULE 11(C), (D), OR (E)

(a) Petitions for Review. After the chief judge issues an order under Rule 11(c), (d), or (e), a complainant or subject judge may petition the judicial council of the circuit to review the order. By rules promulgated under 28 U.S.C. § 358, the judicial council may refer a petition for review filed under this Rule to a panel of no fewer than five members of the council, at least two of whom must be district judges.

(b) When to File; Form; Where to File. A petition for review must be filed in the office of the circuit clerk within 35 days of the date on the clerk's letter informing the parties of the chief judge's order. The petition should be in letter form, addressed to the circuit clerk, and in an envelope marked "Misconduct Petition" or "Disability Petition." The name of the subject judge must not be shown on the envelope. The letter should be typewritten or otherwise legible. It should begin with "I hereby petition the judicial council for review of . . ." and state the reasons why the petition should be granted. It must be signed.

(c) Receipt and Distribution of Petition. A circuit clerk who receives a petition for review filed within the time allowed and in proper form must:

(1) acknowledge its receipt and send a copy to the complainant or subject judge, as the case may be;

(2) promptly distribute to each member of the judicial council, or its relevant panel, except for any member disqualified under Rule 25, or make available in the manner provided by local rule, the following materials:

(A) copies of the complaint;

(B) all materials obtained by the chief judge in connection with the inquiry;

(C) the chief judge's order disposing of the complaint;

(D) any memorandum in support of the chief judge's order;

(E) the petition for review; and

(F) an appropriate ballot;

(3) send the petition for review to the Judicial Conference Committee on Judicial Conduct and Disability. Unless the Judicial Conference Committee requests them, the clerk will not send copies of the materials obtained by the chief judge.

(d) Untimely Petition. The clerk must refuse to accept a petition that is received after the deadline in (b).

(e) Timely Petition Not in Proper Form. When the clerk receives a petition filed within the time allowed but in a form that is improper to a degree that would substantially impair its consideration by the judicial council—such as a document that is ambiguous about whether it is intended to be a petition for review—the clerk must acknowledge its receipt, call the filer's attention to the deficiencies, and give the filer the opportunity to correct the deficiencies within 21 days of the date of the clerk's letter about the deficiencies or within the original deadline for filing the petition, whichever is later. If the deficiencies are corrected within the time allowed, the clerk will proceed according to paragraphs (a) and (c) of this Rule. If the deficiencies are not corrected, the clerk must reject the petition.

(Adopted Mar. 11, 2008, eff. Apr. 10, 2008.)

Commentary on Rule 18

Rule 18 is adapted largely from the Illustrative Rules.

Subsection (a) permits a subject judge, as well as the complainant, to petition for review of a chief judge's order dismissing a complaint under Rule 11(c), or concluding that appropriate corrective action or intervening events have remedied or mooted the problems raised by the complaint pursuant to Rule 11(d) or (e). Although the subject judge may ostensibly be vindicated by the dismissal or conclusion of a complaint, a chief judge's order may include language disagreeable to the subject judge. For example, an order may dismiss a complaint, but state that the subject judge did in fact engage in misconduct. Accordingly, a subject judge may wish to object to the content of the order and is given the opportunity to petition the judicial council of the circuit for review.

Subsection (b) contains a time limit of thirty-five days to file a petition for review. It is important to establish a time limit on petitions for review of chief judges' dispositions in order to provide finality to the process. If the complaint requires an investigation, the investigation should proceed; if it does not, the subject judge should know that the matter is closed.

The standards for timely filing under the Federal Rules of Appellate Procedure should be applied to petitions for review. See Fed. R. App. P. 25(a)(2)(A) and (C).

Rule 18(e) provides for an automatic extension of the time limit imposed under subsection (b) if a person files a petition that is rejected for failure to comply with formal requirements.

RULE 19. JUDICIAL–COUNCIL DISPOSITION OF PETITIONS FOR REVIEW

(a) Rights of Subject Judge. At any time after a complainant files a petition for review, the subject judge may file a written response with the circuit clerk. The clerk must promptly distribute copies of the response to each member of the judicial council or of the relevant panel, unless that member is disqualified under Rule 25. Copies must also be distributed to the chief judge, to the complainant, and to the Judicial Conference Committee on Judicial Conduct and Disability. The subject judge must not otherwise communicate with individual council members about the matter. The subject judge must be given copies of any communications to the judicial council from the complainant.

(b) Judicial–Council Action. After considering a petition for review and the materials before it, a judicial council may:

(1) affirm the chief judge's disposition by denying the petition;

(2) return the matter to the chief judge with directions to conduct a further inquiry under Rule 11(b) or to identify a complaint under Rule 5;

(3) return the matter to the chief judge with directions to appoint a special committee under Rule 11(f); or

(4) in exceptional circumstances, take other appropriate action.

(c) Notice of Council Decision. Copies of the judicial council's order, together with any accompanying memorandum in support of the order or separate concurring or dissenting statements, must be given to the complainant, the subject judge, and the Judicial Conference Committee on Judicial Conduct and Disability.

(d) Memorandum of Council Decision. If the council's order affirms the chief judge's disposition, a supporting memorandum must be prepared only if the judicial council concludes that there is a need to supplement the chief judge's explanation. A memorandum supporting a council order must not include the name of the complainant or the subject judge.

(e) Review of Judicial–Council Decision. If the judicial council's decision is adverse to the petitioner, and if no member of the council dissented on the ground that a special committee should be appointed under Rule 11(f), the complainant must be notified that he or she has no right to seek review of the decision. If there was a dissent, the petitioner must be informed that he or she can file a petition for review under Rule 21(b) solely on the issue of whether a special committee should be appointed.

(f) Public Availability of Judicial–Council Decision. Materials related to the council's decision must be made public to the extent, at the time, and in the manner set forth in Rule 24.

(Adopted Mar. 11, 2008, eff. Apr. 10, 2008.)

Commentary on Rule 19

This Rule is largely adapted from the Act and is self-explanatory.

The council should ordinarily review the decision of the chief judge on the merits, treating the petition for review for all practical purposes as an appeal. The judicial council may respond to a petition by affirming the chief judge's order, remanding the matter, or, in exceptional cases, taking other appropriate action.

RULE 20. JUDICIAL–COUNCIL CONSIDERATION OF REPORTS AND RECOMMENDATIONS OF SPECIAL COMMITTEES

(a) Rights of Subject Judge. Within 21 days after the filing of the report of a special committee, the subject judge may send a written response to the members of the judicial council. The judge must also be given an opportunity to present argument through counsel, written or oral, as determined by the council. The judge must not otherwise communicate with council members about the matter.

(b) Judicial–Council Action.

(1) *Discretionary actions.* Subject to the judge's rights set forth in subsection (a), the judicial council may:

(A) dismiss the complaint because:

(i) even if the claim is true, the claimed conduct is not conduct prejudicial to the effective and expeditious administration of the business of the courts and does not indicate a mental or physical disability resulting in inability to discharge the duties of office;

(ii) the complaint is directly related to the merits of a decision or procedural ruling;

(iii) the facts on which the complaint is based have not been established; or

(iv) the complaint is otherwise not appropriate for consideration under 28 U.S.C. §§ 351–364.

(B) conclude the proceeding because appropriate corrective action has been taken or intervening events have made the proceeding unnecessary.

(C) refer the complaint to the Judicial Conference of the United States with the council's recommendations for action.

(D) take remedial action to ensure the effective and expeditious administration of the business of the courts, including:

(i) censuring or reprimanding the subject judge, either by private communication or by public announcement;

(ii) ordering that no new cases be assigned to the subject judge for a limited, fixed period;

(iii) in the case of a magistrate judge, ordering the chief judge of the district court to take action specified by the council, including the initiation of removal proceedings under 28 U.S.C. § 631(i) or 42 U.S.C. § 300aa–12(c)(2);

(iv) in the case of a bankruptcy judge, removing the judge from office under 28 U.S.C. § 152(e);

(v) in the case of a circuit or district judge, requesting the judge to retire voluntarily with the provision (if necessary) that ordinary length-of-service requirements will be waived; and

(vi) in the case of a circuit or district judge who is eligible to retire but does not do so, certifying the disability of the judge under 28 U. S.C. § 372(b) so that an additional judge may be appointed.

(E) take any combination of actions described in (b)(1)(A)–(D) of this Rule that is within its power.

(2) *Mandatory actions.* A judicial council must refer a complaint to the Judicial Conference if the council determines that a circuit judge or district judge may have engaged in conduct that:

(A) might constitute ground for impeachment; or

(B) in the interest of justice, is not amenable to resolution by the judicial council.

(c) Inadequate Basis for Decision. If the judicial council finds that a special committee's report, recommendations, and record provide an inadequate basis for decision, it may return the matter to the committee for further investigation and a new report, or it may conduct further investigation. If the judicial council decides to conduct further investigation, the subject judge must be given adequate prior notice in writing of that decision and of the general scope and purpose of the additional investigation. The judicial council's conduct of the additional investigation must generally accord with the procedures and powers set forth in Rules 13 through 16 for the conduct of an investigation by a special committee.

(d) Council Vote. Council action must be taken by a majority of those members of the council who are not disqualified. A decision to remove a bankruptcy judge from office requires a majority vote of all the members of the council.

(e) Recommendation for Fee Reimbursement. If the complaint has been finally dismissed or concluded under (b)(1)(A) or (B) of this Rule, and if the subject judge so requests, the judicial council may recommend that the Director of the Administrative Office of the United States Courts use funds appropriated to the Judiciary to reimburse the judge for reasonable expenses incurred during the investigation, when those expenses would not have been incurred but for the requirements of the Act and these Rules. Reasonable expenses include attorneys' fees and expenses related to a successful defense or prosecution of a proceeding under Rule 21(a) or (b).

(f) Council Action. Council action must be by written order. Unless the council finds that extraordinary reasons would make it contrary to the interests of justice, the order must be accompanied by a memorandum setting forth the factual determinations on which it is based and the reasons for the council action. The order and the supporting memorandum must be provided to the complainant, the subject judge, and the Judicial Conference Committee on Judicial Conduct and Disability. The complainant and the subject judge must be notified of any right to review of the judicial council's decision as provided in Rule 21(b).

(Adopted Mar. 11, 2008, eff. Apr. 10, 2008.)

Commentary on Rule 20

This Rule is largely adapted from the Illustrative Rules.

Rule 20(a) provides that within twenty-one days after the filing of the report of a special committee, the subject judge may address a written response to all of the members of the judicial council. The subject judge must also be given an opportunity to present oral argument to the council, personally or through counsel. The subject judge may not otherwise communicate with council members about the matter.

Rule 20(c) provides that if the judicial council decides to conduct an additional investigation, the subject judge must be given adequate prior notice in writing of that decision and of the general scope and purpose of the additional investigation. The conduct of the investigation will be generally in accordance with the procedures set forth in Rules 13 through 16 for the conduct of an investigation by a special committee. However, if hearings are held, the council may limit testimony or the presentation of evidence to avoid unnecessary repetition of testimony and evidence before the special committee.

Rule 20(d) provides that council action must be taken by a majority of those members of the council who are not disqualified, except that a decision to remove a bankruptcy judge from office requires a majority of all the members of the council as required by 28 U.S.C. § 152(e). However, it is inappropriate to apply a similar rule to the less severe actions that a judicial council may take under the Act. If some members of the council are disqualified in the matter, their disqualification should not be given the effect of a vote against council action.

With regard to Rule 20(e), the judicial council, on the request of the subject judge, may recommend to the Director of the Administrative Office of the United States Courts that the subject judge be reimbursed for reasonable expenses, including attorneys' fees, incurred. The judicial council has the authority to recommend such reimbursement where, after investigation by a special committee, the complaint has been finally dismissed or concluded under subsection (b)(1)(A) or (B) of this Rule. It is contemplated that such reimbursement may be provided for the successful prosecution or defense of a proceeding under Rule 21(a) or (b), in other words, one that results in a Rule 20(b)(1)(A) or (B) dismissal or conclusion.

Rule 20(f) requires that council action normally be supported with a memorandum of factual determinations and reasons and that notice of the action be given to the complainant and the subject judge. Rule 20(f) also requires that the notification to the complainant and the subject judge include notice of any right to petition for review of the council's decision under Rule 21(b).

ARTICLE VI. REVIEW BY JUDICIAL CONFERENCE COMMITTEE ON CONDUCT AND DISABILITY

RULE 21. COMMITTEE ON JUDICIAL CONDUCT AND DISABILITY

(a) Review by Committee. The Committee on Judicial Conduct and Disability, consisting of seven members, considers and disposes of all petitions for review under (b) of this Rule, in conformity with the Committee's jurisdictional statement. Its disposition of petitions for review is ordinarily final. The Judicial Conference of the United States may, in its sole discretion, review any such Committee decision, but a complainant or subject judge does not have a right to this review.

(b) Reviewable Matters.

(1) *Upon petition.* A complainant or subject judge may petition the Committee for review of a judicial-council order entered in accordance with:

(A) Rule 20(b)(1)(A), (B), (D), or (E); or

(B) Rule 19(b)(1) or (4) if one or more members of the judicial council dissented from the order on the ground that a special committee should be appointed under Rule 11(f); in that event, the Committee's review will be limited to the issue of whether a special committee should be appointed.

(2) *Upon Committee's initiative.* At its initiative and in its sole discretion, the Committee may review any judicial-council order entered under Rule 19(b)(1) or (4), but only to determine whether a special committee should be appointed. Before undertaking the review, the Committee must invite that judicial council to explain why it believes the appointment of a special committee is unnecessary, unless the reasons are clearly stated in the judicial council's order denying the petition for review. If the Committee believes that it would benefit from a submission by the subject judge, it may issue an appropriate request. If the Committee determines that a special committee should be appointed, the Committee must issue a written decision giving its reasons.

(c) Committee Vote. Any member of the Committee from the same circuit as the subject judge is disqualified from considering or voting on a petition for review. Committee decisions under (b) of this Rule must be by majority vote of the qualified Committee members. If only six members are qualified to vote on a petition for review, the decision must be made by a majority of a panel of five members drawn from a randomly selected list that rotates after each decision by a panel drawn from the list. The members who will determine the petition must be selected based on committee membership as of the date on which the petition is received. Those members selected to hear the petition should serve in that capacity until final disposition of the petition, whether or not their term of committee membership has ended. If only four members are qualified to vote, the Chief Justice must appoint, if available, an ex-member of the Committee or, if not, another United States judge to consider the petition.

(d) Additional Investigation. Except in extraordinary circumstances, the Committee will not conduct an additional investigation. The Committee may return the matter to the judicial council with directions to undertake an additional investigation. If the Committee conducts an additional investigation, it will exercise the powers of the Judicial Conference under 28 U.S.C. § 331.

(e) Oral Argument; Personal Appearance. There is ordinarily no oral argument or personal appearance before the Committee. In its discretion, the Committee may permit written submissions from the complainant or subject judge.

(f) Committee Decisions. Committee decisions under this Rule must be transmitted promptly to the Judicial Conference of the United States. Other distribution will be by the Administrative Office at the direction of the Committee chair.

(g) Finality. All orders of the Judicial Conference or of the Committee (when the Conference does not exercise its power of review) are final.

(Adopted Mar. 11, 2008, eff. Apr. 10, 2008.)

Commentary on Rule 21

This Rule is largely self-explanatory.

Rule 21(a) is intended to clarify that the delegation of power to the Judicial Conference Committee on Judicial Conduct and Disability to dispose of petitions does not preclude review of such dispositions by the Conference. However, there is no right to such review in any party.

Rules 21(b)(1)(B) and (b)(2) are intended to fill a jurisdictional gap as to review of dismissals or conclusions of complaints under Rule 19(b)(1) or (4). Where one or more members of a judicial council reviewing a petition have dissented on the ground that a special committee should have been appointed, the complainant or subject judge has the right to petition for review by the Committee but only as to that issue. Under Rule 21(b)(2), the Judicial Conference Committee on Judicial Conduct and Disability may review such a dismissal or conclusion in its sole discretion, whether or not such a dissent occurred, and only as to the appointment of a special committee. No party has a right to such review, and such review will be rare.

Rule 21(c) provides for review only by Committee members from circuits other than that of the subject judge. To avoid tie votes, the Committee will decide petitions for review by rotating panels of five when only six members are qualified. If only four members are qualified, the Chief Justice must appoint an additional judge to consider that petition for review.

Under this Rule, all Committee decisions are final in that they are unreviewable unless the Judicial Conference, in its discretion, decides to review a decision. Committee decisions, however, do not necessarily constitute final action on a complaint for purposes of Rule 24.

RULE 22. PROCEDURES FOR REVIEW

(a) Filing a Petition for Review. A petition for review of a judicial-council decision may be filed by sending a brief written statement to the Judicial Conference Committee on Judicial Conduct and Disability, addressed to:

Judicial Conference Committee on Judicial Conduct and Disability

Attn: Office of General Counsel

Administrative Office of the United States Courts

One Columbus Circle, NE

Washington, D.C. 20544

The Administrative Office will send a copy of the petition to the complainant or subject judge, as the case may be.

(b) Form and Contents of Petition for Review. No particular form is required. The petition must contain a short statement of the basic facts underlying the complaint, the history of its consideration before the appropriate judicial council, a copy of the judicial council's decision, and the grounds on which the petitioner seeks review. The petition for review must specify the date and docket number of the judicial-council order for which review is sought. The petitioner may attach any documents or correspondence arising in the course of the proceeding before the judicial council or its special committee. A petition should not normally exceed 20 pages plus necessary attachments.

(c) Time. A petition must be submitted within 63 days of the date of the order for which review is sought.

(d) Copies. Seven copies of the petition for review must be submitted, at least one of which must be signed by the petitioner or his or her attorney. If the petitioner submits a signed declaration of inability to pay the expense of duplicating the petition, the Administrative Office must accept the original petition and must reproduce copies at its expense.

(e) Action on Receipt of Petition for Review. The Administrative Office must acknowledge receipt of a petition for review submitted under this Rule, notify the chair of the Judicial Conference Committee on Judicial Conduct and Disability, and distribute the petition to the members of the Committee for their deliberation.

(Adopted Mar. 11, 2008, eff. Apr. 10, 2008.)

Commentary on Rule 22

Rule 22 is self-explanatory.

ARTICLE VII. MISCELLANEOUS RULES

RULE 23. CONFIDENTIALITY

(a) General Rule. The consideration of a complaint by the chief judge, a special committee, the judicial council, or the Judicial Conference Committee on Judicial Conduct and Disability is confidential. Information about this consideration must not be disclosed by any judge or employee of the judicial branch or by any person who records or transcribes testimony except as allowed by these Rules. In extraordinary circumstances, a chief judge may disclose the existence of a proceeding under these Rules when necessary to maintain public confidence in the federal judiciary's ability to redress misconduct or disability.

(b) Files. All files related to complaints must be separately maintained with appropriate security precautions to ensure confidentiality.

(c) Disclosure in Decisions. Except as otherwise provided in Rule 24, written decisions of the chief judge, the judicial council, or the Judicial Conference Committee on Judicial Conduct and Disability, and dissenting opinions or separate statements of members of the council or Committee may contain information and exhibits that the authors consider appropriate for inclusion, and the information and exhibits may be made public.

(d) Availability to Judicial Conference. On request of the Judicial Conference or its Committee on Judicial Conduct and Disability, the circuit clerk must furnish any requested records related to a complaint. For auditing purposes, the circuit clerk must provide access to the Committee to records of proceedings under the Act at the site where the records are kept.

(e) Availability to District Court. If the judicial council directs the initiation of proceedings for removal of a magistrate judge under Rule 20(b)(1)(D)(iii), the circuit clerk must provide to the chief judge of the district court copies of the report of the special committee and any other documents and records that were before the judicial council at the time of its decision. On request of the chief judge of the district court, the judicial council may authorize release to that chief judge of any other records relating to the investigation.

(f) Impeachment Proceedings. If the Judicial Conference determines that consideration of impeachment may be warranted, it must transmit the record of all relevant proceedings to the Speaker of the House of Representatives.

(g) Subject Judge's Consent. If both the subject judge and the chief judge consent in writing, any materials from the files may be disclosed to any person. In any such disclosure, the chief judge may require that the identity of the complainant, or of witnesses in an investigation conducted by a chief judge, a special committee, or the judicial council, not be revealed.

(h) Disclosure in Special Circumstances. The Judicial Conference, its Committee on Judicial Conduct and Disability, or a judicial council may authorize disclosure of information about the consideration of a complaint, including the papers, documents, and transcripts relating to the investigation, to the extent that disclosure is justified by special circumstances and is not prohibited by the Act. Disclosure may be made to judicial researchers engaged in the study or evaluation of experience under the Act and related modes of judicial discipline, but only where the study or evaluation has been specifically approved by the Judicial Conference or by the Judicial Conference Committee on Judicial Conduct and Disability. Appropriate steps must be taken to protect the identities of the subject judge, the complainant, and witnesses from public disclosure. Other appropriate safeguards to protect against the dissemination of confidential information may be imposed.

(i) Disclosure of Identity by Subject Judge. Nothing in this Rule precludes the subject judge from acknowledging that he or she is the judge referred to in documents made public under Rule 24.

(j) Assistance and Consultation. Nothing in this Rule precludes the chief judge or judicial council acting on a complaint filed under the Act from seeking the help of qualified staff or from consulting other judges who may be helpful in the disposition of the complaint.

(Adopted Mar. 11, 2008, eff. Apr. 10, 2008.)

Commentary on Rule 23

Rule 23 was adapted from the Illustrative Rules.

The Act applies a rule of confidentiality to "papers, documents, and records of proceedings related to investigations conducted under this chapter" and states that they may not be disclosed "by any person in any proceeding," with enumerated exceptions. 28 U.S.C. § 360(a). Three questions arise: Who is bound by the confidentiality rule, what proceedings are subject to the rule, and who is within the circle of people who may have access to information without breaching the rule?

With regard to the first question, Rule 23(a) provides that judges, employees of the judicial branch, and those persons involved in recording proceedings and preparing transcripts are obliged to respect the confidentiality requirement. This of course includes subject judges who do not consent to identification under Rule 23(i).

With regard to the second question, Rule 23(a) applies the rule of confidentiality broadly to consideration of a complaint at any stage.

With regard to the third question, there is no barrier of confidentiality among a chief judge, judicial council, the Judicial Conference, and the Judicial Conference Committee on Judicial Conduct and Disability. Each may have access to any of the confidential records for use in their consideration of a referred matter, a petition for review, or monitoring the administration of the Act. A district court may have similar access if the judicial council orders the district court to initiate proceedings to remove a magistrate judge from office, and Rule 23(e) so provides.

In extraordinary circumstances, a chief judge may disclose the existence of a proceeding under these Rules. The disclosure of such information in high-visibility or controversial cases is to reassure the public that the federal judiciary is capable of redressing judicial misconduct or disability. Moreover, the confidentiality requirement does not prevent the chief judge from "communicat[ing] orally or in writing with ... [persons] who may have knowledge of the matter," as part of a limited inquiry conducted by the chief judge under Rule 11(b).

Rule 23 recognizes that there must be some exceptions to the Act's confidentiality requirement. For example, the Act requires that certain orders and the reasons for them must be made public. 28 U.S.C. § 360(b). Rule 23(c) makes it explicit that memoranda supporting chief judge and council orders, as well as dissenting opinions and separate statements, may contain references to information that would otherwise be confidential and that such information may be made public. However, subsection (c) is subject to Rule 24(a) which provides the general rule regarding the public availability of decisions. For example, the name of a subject judge cannot be made public in a decision if disclosure of the name is prohibited by that Rule.

The Act makes clear that there is a barrier of confidentiality between the judicial branch and the legislative. It provides that material may be disclosed to Congress only if it is believed necessary to an impeachment investigation or trial of a judge. 28 U.S.C. § 360(a)(2). Accordingly, Section 355(b) of the Act requires the Judicial Conference to transmit the record of the proceeding to the House of Representatives if the Conference believes that impeachment of a subject judge may be appropriate. Rule 23(f) implements this requirement.

The Act provides that confidential materials may be disclosed if authorized in writing by the subject judge and by the chief judge. 28 U.S.C. § 360(a)(3). Rule 23(g) implements this requirement. Once the subject judge has consented to the disclosure of confidential materials related to a complaint, the chief judge ordinarily will refuse consent only to the extent necessary to protect the confidentiality interests of the complainant or of witnesses who have testified in investigatory proceedings or who have provided information in response to a limited inquiry undertaken pursuant to Rule 11. It will generally be necessary, therefore, for the chief judge to require that the identities of the complainant or of such witnesses, as well as any identifying information, be shielded in any materials disclosed, except insofar as the chief judge has secured the consent of the complainant or of a particular witness to disclosure, or there is a demonstrated need for disclosure of the information that, in the judgment of the chief judge, outweighs the confidentiality interest of the complainant or of a particular witness (as may be the case where the complainant is delusional or where the complainant or a particular witness has already demonstrated a lack of concern about maintaining the confidentiality of the proceedings).

Rule 23(h) permits disclosure of additional information in circumstances not enumerated. For example, disclosure may be appropriate to permit a prosecution for perjury based on testimony given before a special committee. Another example might involve evidence of criminal conduct by a judge discovered by a special committee.

Subsection (h) also permits the authorization of disclosure of information about the consideration of a complaint, including the papers, documents, and transcripts relating to the investigation, to judicial researchers engaged in the study or evaluation of experience under the Act and related modes of judicial discipline. The Rule envisions disclosure of information from the official record of complaint proceedings to a limited category of persons for appropriately authorized research purposes only, and with appropriate safeguards to protect individual identities in any published research results that ensue. In authorizing disclosure, the judicial council may refuse to release particular materials when such release would be contrary to the interests of justice, or that constitute purely internal communications. The Rule does not envision disclosure of purely internal communications between judges and their colleagues and staff.

Under Rule 23(j), chief judges and judicial councils may seek staff assistance or consult with other judges who may be helpful in the process of complaint disposition; the confidentiality requirement does not preclude this. The chief judge, for example, may properly seek the advice and assistance of another judge who the chief judge deems to be in the best position to communicate with the subject judge in an attempt to bring about corrective action. As another example, a new chief judge may wish to confer with a predecessor to learn how similar complaints have been handled. In consulting with other judges, of course, the chief judge should disclose information regarding the complaint only to the extent the chief judge deems necessary under the circumstances.

RULE 24. PUBLIC AVAILABILITY OF DECISIONS

(a) General Rule; Specific Cases. When final action has been taken on a complaint and it is no longer subject to review, all orders entered by the chief judge and judicial council, including any supporting memoranda and any dissenting opinions or separate statements by members of the judicial council, must be made public, with the following exceptions:

(1) if the complaint is finally dismissed under Rule 11(c) without the appointment of a special committee, or if it is concluded under Rule 11(d) because of voluntary corrective action, the publicly available materials must not disclose the name of the subject judge without his or her consent.

(2) if the complaint is concluded because of intervening events, or dismissed at any time after a special committee is appointed, the judicial council must determine whether the name of the subject judge should be disclosed.

(3) if the complaint is finally disposed of by a privately communicated censure or reprimand, the publicly available materials must not disclose either the name of the subject judge or the text of the reprimand.

(4) if the complaint is finally disposed of under Rule 20(b)(1)(D) by any action other than private censure or reprimand, the text of the dispositive order must be included in the materials made public, and the name of the subject judge must be disclosed.

(5) the name of the complainant must not be disclosed in materials made public under this Rule unless the chief judge orders disclosure.

(b) Manner of Making Public. The orders described in (a) must be made public by placing them in a publicly accessible file in the office of the circuit clerk or by placing the orders on the court's public website. If the orders appear to have precedential value, the chief judge may cause them to be published. In addition, the Judicial Conference Committee on Judicial Conduct and Disability will make available on the Federal Judiciary's website, www.uscourts.gov, selected illustrative orders described in paragraph (a), appropriately redacted, to provide additional information to the public on how complaints are addressed under the Act.

(c) Orders of Judicial Conference Committee. Orders of this Committee constituting final action in a complaint proceeding arising from a particular circuit will be made available to the public in the office of the clerk of the relevant court of appeals. The Committee will also make such orders available on the Federal Judiciary's website, www.uscourts.gov. When authorized by the Committee, other orders related to complaint proceedings will similarly be made available.

(d) Complaints Referred to the Judicial Conference of the United States. If a complaint is referred to the Judicial Conference under Rule 20(b)(1)(C) or 20(b)(2), materials relating to the complaint will be made public only if ordered by the Judicial Conference.

(Adopted Mar. 11, 2008, eff. Apr. 10, 2008.)

Commentary on Rule 24

Rule 24 is adapted from the Illustrative Rules and the recommendations of the Breyer Committee.

The Act requires the circuits to make available only written orders of a judicial council or the Judicial Conference imposing some form of sanction. 28 U.S.C. § 360(b). The Judicial Conference, however, has long recognized the desirability of public availability of a broader range of orders and other materials. In 1994, the Judicial Conference "urge[d] all circuits and courts covered by the Act to submit to the West Publishing Company, for publication in Federal Reporter 3d, and to Lexis all orders issued pursuant to [the Act] that are deemed by the issuing circuit or court to have significant precedential value to other circuits and courts covered by the Act." Report of the Proceedings of the Judicial Conference of the United States, Mar. 1994, at 28. Following this recommendation, the 2000 revision of the Illustrative Rules contained a public availability provision very similar to Rule 24. In 2002, the Judicial Conference again voted to encourage the circuits "to submit non-routine public orders disposing of complaints of judicial misconduct or disability for publication by on-line and print services." Report of the Proceedings of the Judicial Conference of the United States, Sept. 2002, at 58. The Breyer Committee Report further emphasized that "[p]osting such orders on the judicial branch's public website would not only benefit judges directly, it would also encourage scholarly commentary and analysis of the orders." Breyer Committee Report, 239 F.R.D. at 216. With these considerations in mind, Rule 24 provides for public availability of a wide range of materials.

Rule 24 provides for public availability of orders of the chief judge, the judicial council, and the Judicial Conference Committee on Judicial Conduct and Disability and the texts of any memoranda supporting their orders, together with any dissenting opinions or separate statements by members of the judicial council. However, these orders and memoranda are to be made public only when final action on the complaint has been taken and any right of review has been exhausted. The provision that decisions will be made public only after final action has been taken is designed in part to avoid public disclosure of the existence of pending proceedings. Whether the name of the subject judge is disclosed will then depend on the nature of the final action. If the final action is an order predicated on a finding of misconduct or disability (other than a privately communicated censure or reprimand) the name of the judge must be made public. If the final action is dismissal of the complaint, the name of the subject judge must not be disclosed. Rule 24(a)(1) provides that where a proceeding is concluded under Rule 11(d) by the chief judge on the basis of voluntary corrective action, the name of the subject judge must not be disclosed. Shielding the name of the subject judge in this circumstance should encourage informal disposition.

If a complaint is dismissed as moot, or because intervening events have made action on the complaint unnecessary, after appointment of a special committee, Rule 24(a)(2) allows the judicial council to determine whether the subject judge will be identified. In such a case, no final decision has been rendered on the merits, but it may be in the public interest—particularly if a judicial officer resigns in the course of an investigation—to make the identity of the judge known.

Once a special committee has been appointed, and a proceeding is concluded by the full council on the basis of a remedial order of the council, Rule 24(a)(4) provides for disclosure of the name of the subject judge.

Finally, Rule 24(a)(5) provides that the identity of the complainant will be disclosed only if the chief judge so orders. Identifying the complainant when the subject judge is not identified would increase the likelihood that the identity of the subject judge would become publicly known, thus circumventing the policy of nondisclosure. It may not always be practicable to shield the complainant's identity while making public disclosure of the judicial council's order and supporting memoranda; in some circumstances, moreover, the complainant may consent to public identification.

RULE 25. DISQUALIFICATION

(a) General Rule. Any judge is disqualified from participating in any proceeding under these Rules if the judge, in his or her discretion, concludes that circumstances warrant disqualification. If the complaint is filed by a judge, that judge is disqualified from participating in any consideration of the complaint except to the extent that these Rules provide for a complainant's participation. A chief judge who has identified a complaint under Rule 5 is not automatically disqualified from considering the complaint.

(b) Subject Judge. A subject judge is disqualified from considering the complaint except to the extent that these Rules provide for participation by a subject judge.

(c) Chief Judge Not Disqualified from Considering a Petition for Review of a Chief Judge's Order. If a petition for review of a chief judge's order entered under Rule 11(c), (d), or (e) is filed with the judicial council in accordance with Rule 18, the chief judge is not disqualified from participating in the council's consideration of the petition.

(d) Member of Special Committee Not Disqualified. A member of the judicial council who serves on a special committee, including the chief judge, is not disqualified from participating in council consideration of the committee's report.

(e) Subject Judge's Disqualification After Appointment of a Special Committee. Upon appointment of a special committee, the subject judge is automatically disqualified from participating in any proceeding arising under the Act or these Rules as a member of any special committee, the judicial council of the circuit, the Judicial Conference of the United States, and the Judicial Conference Committee on Judicial Conduct and Disability. The disqualification continues until all proceedings on the complaint against the subject judge are finally terminated with no further right of review.

(f) Substitute for Disqualified Chief Judge. If the chief judge is disqualified from participating in consideration of the complaint, the duties and responsibilities of the chief judge under these Rules must be assigned to the most-senior active circuit judge not disqualified. If all circuit judges in regular active service are disqualified, the judicial council may determine whether to request a transfer under Rule 26, or, in the interest of sound judicial administration, to permit the chief judge to dispose of the complaint on the merits. Members of the judicial council who are named in the complaint may participate in this determination if necessary to obtain a quorum of the judicial council.

(g) Judicial–Council Action When Multiple Judges Are Disqualified. Notwithstanding any other provision in these Rules to the contrary,

(1) a member of the judicial council who is a subject judge may participate in its disposition if:

(A) participation by one or more subject judges is necessary to obtain a quorum of the judicial council;

(B) the judicial council finds that the lack of a quorum is due to the naming of one or more judges in the complaint for the purpose of disqualifying that judge or judges, or to the naming of one or more judges based on their participation in a decision excluded from the definition of misconduct under Rule 3(h)(3); and

(C) the judicial council votes that it is necessary, appropriate, and in the interest of sound judicial administration that one or more subject judges be eligible to act.

(2) otherwise disqualified members may participate in votes taken under (g)(1)(B) and (g)(1)(C).

(h) Disqualification of Members of the Judicial Conference Committee. No member of the Judicial Conference Committee on Judicial Conduct and Disability is disqualified from participating in any proceeding under the Act or these Rules because of consultations with a chief judge, a member of a special committee, or a member of a judicial council about the interpretation or application of the Act or these Rules, unless the member believes that the consultation would prevent fair-minded participation.

(Adopted Mar. 11, 2008, eff. Apr. 10, 2008.)

Commentary on Rule 25

Rule 25 is adapted from the Illustrative Rules.

Subsection (a) provides the general rule for disqualification. Of course, a judge is not disqualified simply because the subject judge is on the same court. However, this subsection recognizes that there may be cases in which an appearance of bias or prejudice is created by circumstances other than an association with the subject judge as a colleague. For example, a judge may have a familial relationship with a complainant or subject judge. When such circumstances exist, a judge may, in his or her discretion, conclude that disqualification is warranted.

Subsection (e) makes it clear that the disqualification of the subject judge relates only to the subject judge's participation in any proceeding arising under the Act or these Rules as a member of a special committee, judicial council, Judicial Conference, or the Judicial Conference Committee. The Illustrative Rule, based on Section 359(a) of the Act, is ambiguous and could be read to disqualify a subject judge from service of any kind on each of the bodies mentioned. This is undoubtedly not the intent of the Act; such a disqualification would be anomalous in light of the Act's allowing a subject judge to continue to decide cases and to continue to exercise the powers of chief circuit or district judge. It would also create a substantial deterrence to the appointment of special committees, particularly where a special committee is needed solely because the chief judge may not decide matters of credibility in his or her review under Rule 11.

While a subject judge is barred by Rule 25(b) from participating in the disposition of the complaint in which he or she is named, Rule 25(e) recognizes that participation in proceedings arising under the Act or these Rules by a judge who is the subject of a special committee investigation may lead to an appearance of self-interest in creating substantive and procedural precedents governing such proceedings; Rule 25(e) bars such participation.

Under the Act, a complaint against the chief judge is to be handled by "that circuit judge in regular active service next senior in date of commission." 28 U.S.C. § 351(c). Rule 25(f) provides that seniority among judges other than the chief judge is to be determined by date of commission, with the result that complaints against the chief judge may be routed to a former chief judge or other judge who was appointed earlier than the chief judge. The Rules do not purport to prescribe who is to preside over meetings of the judicial council. Consequently, where the presiding member of the judicial council is disqualified from participating under these Rules, the order of precedence prescribed by Rule 25(f) for performing "the duties and responsibilities of the chief circuit judge under these Rules" does not apply to determine the acting presiding member of the judicial council. That is a matter left to the internal rules or operating practices of each judicial council. In most cases the most senior active circuit judge who is a member of the judicial council and who is not disqualified will preside.

Sometimes a single complaint is filed against a large group of judges. If the normal disqualification rules are observed in such a case, no court of appeals judge can serve as acting chief judge of the circuit, and the judicial council will be without appellate members. Where the complaint is against all circuit and district judges, under normal rules no member of the judicial council can perform the duties assigned to the council under the statute.

A similar problem is created by successive complaints arising out of the same underlying grievance. For example, a complainant files a complaint against a district judge based on alleged misconduct, and the complaint is dismissed by the chief judge under the statute. The complainant may then file a complaint against the chief judge for dismissing the first complaint, and when that complaint is dismissed by the next senior judge, still a third complaint may be filed. The threat is that the complainant will bump down the seniority ladder until, once again, there is no member of the court of appeals who can serve as acting chief judge for the purpose of the next complaint. Similarly, complaints involving the merits of litigation may involve a series of decisions in which many judges participated or in which a rehearing en banc was denied by the court of appeals, and the complaint may name a majority of the judicial council as subject judges.

In recognition that these multiple-judge complaints are virtually always meritless, the judicial council is given discretion to determine: (1) whether it is necessary, appropriate, and in the interest of sound judicial administration to permit the chief judge to dispose of a complaint where it would otherwise be impossible for any active circuit judge in the circuit to act, and (2) whether it is necessary, appropriate, and in the interest of sound judicial administration, after appropriate findings as to need and justification are made, to permit subject judges of the judicial council to participate in the disposition of a petition for review where it would otherwise be impossible to obtain a quorum.

Applying a rule of necessity in these situations is consistent with the appearance of justice. See, e.g., In re Complaint of Doe, 2 F.3d 308 (8th Cir. Jud. Council 1993) (invoking the rule of necessity); In re Complaint of Judicial Misconduct, No. 91–80464 (9th Cir. Jud. Council 1992) (same). There is no unfairness in permitting the chief judge to dispose of a patently insubstantial complaint that names all active circuit judges in the circuit.

Similarly, there is no unfairness in permitting subject judges, in these circumstances, to participate in the review of a chief judge's dismissal of an insubstantial complaint. The remaining option is to assign the matter to another body. Among other alternatives, the council may request a transfer of the petition under Rule 26. Given the administrative inconvenience and delay involved in these alternatives, it is desirable to request a transfer only if the judicial council determines that the petition is substantial enough to warrant such action.

In the unlikely event that a quorum of the judicial council cannot be obtained to consider the report of a special committee, it would normally be necessary to request a transfer under Rule 26.

Rule 25(h) recognizes that the jurisdictional statement of the Judicial Conference Committee contemplates consultation between members of the Committee and judicial participants in proceedings under the Act and these Rules. Such consultation should not automatically preclude participation by a member in that proceeding.

RULE 26. TRANSFER TO ANOTHER JUDICIAL COUNCIL

In exceptional circumstances, a chief judge or a judicial council may ask the Chief Justice to transfer a proceeding based on a complaint identified under Rule 5 or filed under Rule 6 to the judicial council of another circuit. The request for a transfer may be made at any stage of the proceeding before a reference to the Judicial Conference under Rule 20(b)(1)(C) or 20(b)(2) or a petition for review is filed under Rule 22. Upon receiving such a request, the Chief Justice may refuse the request or select the transferee judicial council, which may then exercise the powers of a judicial council under these Rules.

(Adopted Mar. 11, 2008, eff. Apr. 10, 2008.)

Commentary on Rule 26

Rule 26 is new; it implements the Breyer Committee's recommended use of transfers. Breyer Committee Report, 239 F.R.D. at 214–15.

Rule 26 authorizes the transfer of a complaint proceeding to another judicial council selected by the Chief Justice. Such transfers may be appropriate, for example, in the case of a serious complaint where there are multiple disqualifications among the original council, where the issues are highly visible and a local disposition may weaken public confidence in the process, where internal tensions arising in the council as a result of the complaint render disposition by a less involved council appropriate, or where a complaint calls into question policies or governance of the home court of appeals. The power to effect a transfer is lodged in the Chief Justice to avoid disputes in a council over where to transfer a sensitive matter and to ensure that the transferee council accepts the matter.

Upon receipt of a transferred proceeding, the transferee council shall determine the proper stage at which to begin consideration of the complaint—for example, reference to the transferee chief judge, appointment of a special committee, etc.

RULE 27. WITHDRAWAL OF COMPLAINTS AND PETITIONS FOR REVIEW

(a) Complaint Pending Before Chief Judge. With the chief judge's consent, a complainant may withdraw a complaint that is before the chief judge for a decision under Rule 11. The withdrawal of a complaint will not prevent a chief judge from identifying or having to identify a complaint under Rule 5 based on the withdrawn complaint.

(b) Complaint Pending before Special Committee or Judicial Council. After a complaint has been referred to a special committee for investigation and before the committee files its report, the complainant may withdraw the complaint only with the consent of both the subject judge and either the special committee or the judicial council.

(c) Petition for Review. A petition for review addressed to a judicial council under Rule 18, or the Judicial Conference Committee on Judicial Conduct and Disability under Rule 22 may be withdrawn if no action on the petition has been taken.

(Adopted Mar. 11, 2008, eff. Apr. 10, 2008.)

Commentary on Rule 27

Rule 27 is adapted from the Illustrative Rules and treats the complaint proceeding, once begun, as a matter of public business rather than as the property of the complainant. Accordingly, the chief judge or the judicial council remains responsible for addressing any complaint under the Act, even a complaint that has been formally withdrawn by the complainant.

Under subsection 27(a), a complaint pending before the chief judge may be withdrawn if the chief judge consents. Where the complaint clearly lacked merit, the chief judge may accordingly be saved the burden of preparing a formal order and supporting memorandum. However, the chief judge may, or be obligated under Rule 5, to identify a complaint based on allegations in a withdrawn complaint.

If the chief judge appoints a special committee, Rule 27(b) provides that the complaint may be withdrawn only with the consent of both the body before which it is pending (the special committee or the judicial council) and the subject judge. Once a complaint has reached the stage of appointment of a special committee, a resolution of the issues may be necessary to preserve public confidence. Moreover, the subject judge is given the right to insist that the matter be resolved on the merits, thereby eliminating any ambiguity that might remain if the proceeding were terminated by withdrawal of the complaint.

With regard to all petitions for review, Rule 27(c) grants the petitioner unrestricted authority to withdraw the petition. It is thought that the public's interest in the proceeding is adequately protected, because there will necessarily have been a decision by the chief judge and often by the judicial council as well in such a case.

RULE 28. AVAILABILITY OF RULES AND FORMS

These Rules and copies of the complaint form as provided in Rule 6(a) must be available without charge in the office of the clerk of each court of appeals, district court, bankruptcy court, or other federal court whose judges are subject to the Act. Each court must also make these Rules and the complaint form available on the court's website, or provide an Internet link to the Rules and complaint form that are available on the appropriate court of appeals' website.

(Adopted Mar. 11, 2008, eff. Apr. 10, 2008.)

RULE 29. EFFECTIVE DATE

These Rules will become effective 30 days after promulgation by the Judicial Conference of the United States.

(Adopted Mar. 11, 2008, eff. Apr. 10, 2008.)

APPENDIX

Complaint Form

Judicial Council of the ______ Circuit

COMPLAINT OF JUDICIAL MISCONDUCT OR DISABILITY

To begin the complaint process, complete this form and prepare the brief statement of facts described in item 5 (below). The Rules for Judicial-Conduct and Judicial-Disability Proceedings, adopted by the Judicial Conference of the United States, contain information on what to include in a complaint (Rule 6), where to file a complaint (Rule 7), and other important matters. The rules are available in federal court clerks' offices, on individual federal courts' Web sites, and on www.uscourts.gov.

Your complaint (this form and the statement of facts) should be typewritten and must be legible. For the number of copies to file, consult the local rules or clerk's office of the court in which your complaint is required to be filed. Enclose each copy of the complaint in an envelope marked "COMPLAINT OF MISCONDUCT" or "COMPLAINT OF DISABILITY" and submit it to the appropriate clerk of court. **Do not put the name of any judge on the envelope.**

1. Name of Complainant: ______________________
   Contact Address: ______________________
   ____
   Daytime telephone: (____) ______________________

2. Name(s) of Judge(s): ______________________
   Court: ______________________

3. Does this complaint concern the behavior of the judge(s) in a particular lawsuit or lawsuits?
   [ ] Yes [ ] No
   If "yes," give the following information about each lawsuit:
   Court: ______________________
   Case Number: ______________________
   Docket number of any appeal to the ____ Circuit: ______________________
   Are (were) you a party or lawyer in the lawsuit?
   [ ] Party [ ] Lawyer [ ] Neither

If you are (were) a party and have (had) a lawyer, give the lawyer's name, address, and telephone number:

____

____

____

4. Have you filed any lawsuits against the judge?
[ ] Yes [ ] No
If "yes," give the following information about each such lawsuit:
Court: ______________________
Case Number: ______________________
Present status of lawsuit: ______________________
Name, address, and telephone number of your lawyer for the lawsuit against the judge:

____

____

____

Court to which any appeal has been taken in the lawsuit against the judge:

____

Docket number of the appeal: ______________________
Present status of the appeal: ______________________

5. **Brief Statement of Facts.** Attach a brief statement of the specific facts on which the claim of judicial misconduct or disability is based. Include what happened, when and where it happened, and any information that would help an investigator check the facts. If the complaint alleges judicial disability, also include any additional facts that form the basis of that allegation.

6. **Declaration and signature:**

I declare under penalty of perjury that the statements made in this complaint are true and correct to the best of my knowledge.

(Signature)______________________ (Date)______________

(Adopted Mar. 11, 2008, eff. Apr. 10, 2008.)

INDEX TO THE THIRD CIRCUIT RULES

LOCAL CIVIL AND CRIMINAL RULES OF THE UNITED STATES DISTRICT COURT FOR THE DISTRICT OF NEW JERSEY

Revised Effective April 1, 1997

Including Amendments Received Through August 15, 2008

Research Note

These rules may be searched electronically on Westlaw in the NJ-RULES database; updates to these rules may be found on Westlaw in NJ-RULESUPDATES. For search tips, and a detailed summary of database content, consult the Westlaw Scope Screen of each database.

LOCAL CRIMINAL RULES

APPENDICES

STANDING ORDERS AND POLICIES

ELECTRONIC CASE FILING

INTRODUCTION—1984 REVISION

The General Rules of the United States District Court for the District of New Jersey have undergone a complete revision for the first time in many years. The catalyst for this project was a request in the autumn of 1983 from then Chief Judge Collins J. Seitz of the Court of Appeals for the Third Circuit, who requested that we assess our local rules to determine whether there was strict compliance with the Federal Rules of Civil, Criminal and Appellate Procedure. To that end, the Court asked the United States District Court Lawyers Advisory Committee to undertake the evaluation and, in addition, advise the Court as to those rules which the Committee felt could be revised in order to simplify practice before the United States District Court as well as comply with the spirit of Rule 1 of the Federal Rules of Civil Procedure requiring that "rules shall be construed to secure the just, speedy, and inexpensive determination of every action."

A committee of Court officials was appointed to work with the Lawyers Advisory Committee. The full Committee was composed of the following:

Donald A. Robinson, Esquire, Chairman
Jonathan L. Goldstein, Esquire
Joseph H. Kenney, Esquire
Joseph H. Markowitz, Esquire
William J. O'Shaughnessy, Esquire
The Honorable John F. Gerry, U.S.D.J.
The Honorable Dickinson R. Debevoise, U.S.D.J.
Honorable John W. Bissell, U.S.D.J.
Honorable Jerome B. Simandle, U.S.M.
Allyn Z. Lite, Esquire, Clerk of the Court

The Committee notified the bar of its project and sought comments as to which rules the bar wished to see modified and what changes should be made. The Committee considered the responses from the bar and presented to the Court a proposed new rule book. The Conference of Judges of the United States District Court tentatively adopted the rules pending their initial publication and further comment from the bar. Unless such comment creates the need for further major revision, it is expected that the new rules will be effective on October 1, 1984.

The Court wishes to extend its appreciation to the members of the Lawyer's Advisory Committee for their exceptional efforts in bringing this project to completion. An undertaking of this magnitude simply would not have been possible without the experience, concern, sensitivity and professionalism of the members of the Committee. The entire bar is in their debt.

CLARKSON S. FISHER

Chief Judge
For the Court

Newark, New Jersey
October 1, 1984

FOREWORD—1997 REVISION

Pursuant to Congressional mandate (P.L. 103–317), this Court, during the past six months, has divided its General Rules into Local Civil Rules and Local Criminal Rules, renumbered to correspond to their counterparts in the Federal Rules of Civil and Criminal Procedure. Those Local Rules without a counterpart were assigned numbers in the 100s (court administration), 200s (arbitration), 300s (mediation) and 400s (medical coverage). This Court and the Lawyers Advisory Committee appointed a special subcommittee to undertake this project, comprised of Judge John W. Bissell, Magistrate Judge John J. Hughes, Rosemary Alito, Esq., Allyn Z. Lite, Esq., and Daniel R. Guadalupe, Esq. Gann Law Books of Newark, N.J., provided invaluable assistance in generating both the drafts reviewed by the subcommittee and this Court and the final product which the Court's Board of Judges has adopted. Gann's important contributions also include the Conversion Tables, Source References and Renumbering Committee's Comments which accompanied the drafts of the renumbered Local Civil and Criminal Rules.

After publication of the final draft in February 1997 in the New Jersey Law Journal and the New Jersey Lawyer, all comments from the bar and the public were considered and any final modifications incorporated into the present product which Court adopted, effective April 1, 1997. The Board of Judges renews its thanks to the Lawyers Advisory Committee, the Renumbering Committee and Gann Law Books for their significant contributions to the important project of renumbering the Local Rules of this Court.

ANNE E. THOMPSON
Chief Judge

Trenton, New Jersey
April 1, 1997

LOCAL CIVIL RULES

CIV. RULE 1.1. RULES OF PROCEDURE; SCOPE OF THESE RULES

(a) The following Rules supplement the Federal Rules of Civil Procedure, the Federal Rules of Criminal Procedure and the Supplemental Rules of Practice for certain Admiralty and Maritime Claims, and are applicable in all proceedings when not inconsistent therewith.

(b) These Rules shall be considered as rules for the government of the Court and conduct of causes, and shall be construed consistent with the Civil Justice Reform Act of 1990 to secure a just determination, simplicity in procedure, fairness in administration and the elimination of unjustifiable expense and delay.

(c) Any references to specific statutes, regulations and rules in these Rules reflect the enumeration of those statutes, regulations and rules as of April 1, 1997 and are intended to incorporate by reference subsequent enactments and promulgations governing the same subject matter.

Source: L.Civ.R. 1.1(a)—G.R. 1.A. (sentence 1); L.Civ.R. 1.1(b)—G.R. 1.A. (sentence 2); L.Civ.R. 1.1(c)—new.

[Effective April 1, 1997.]

CIV. RULE 1.2. DEFINITIONS

The following definitions apply to terms used throughout these Rules unless specifically employed otherwise in any particular Rule:

"Attorney General" means the Attorney General of the United States.

"Chief Judge" means the Chief Judge of this Court or the Chief Judge's authorized designee.

"Clerk" means the Clerk of this Court or an authorized Deputy Clerk.

"Code of Judicial Conduct" means the Code of Judicial Conduct of the American Bar Association.

"Court" means the United States District Court for the District of New Jersey.

"District" means the District of New Jersey, the boundaries of which include the entire State of New Jersey.

"Government" means the Government of the United States of America.

"Governmental party" means the United States of America, any state, commonwealth or territory, any county, municipal or public entity, or any agency, department, unit, official or employee thereof.

"IRS" means the Internal Revenue Service of the Department of the Treasury, United States of America.

"Judge" means a United States District Judge sitting in this District.

"Magistrate Judge" means a United States Magistrate Judge sitting in this District.

"Marshal" means the United States Marshal for this District, a Deputy Marshal or other authorized designee.

"State" means the State of New Jersey or, if specifically so indicated, any other state of the United States of America.

"Supreme Court" means the Supreme Court of the United States.

"Third Circuit" means the United States Court of Appeals for the Third Circuit.

"United States Attorney" means the United States Attorney for the District of New Jersey or an authorized Assistant United States Attorney.

Source: G.R. 1.B.

[Effective April 1, 1997.]

CIV. RULE 4.1. SERVICE OF PROCESS

The Clerk is authorized to sign and enter orders specially appointing a United States Marshal, Deputy United States Marshal, or other person or officer to serve process when such appointments are required or requested pursuant to Fed. R. Civ. P. 4(c).

Source: G.R. 9.C.

[Effective April 1, 1997; Amended effective March 9, 2007.]

CIV. RULE 5.1. SERVICE AND FILING OF PLEADINGS AND OTHER PAPERS

(a) Service of all papers other than the initial summons and complaint shall be made in the manner specified in Fed.R.Civ.P. 5(b).

(b) Except where otherwise provided by these Rules (or the Federal Rules of Civil Procedure), proof of service of all papers required or permitted to be served shall be filed in the Clerk's office promptly and in any event before action is taken thereon by the Court or the parties. The proof shall show the date and manner of service and may be by written acknowledgment of service, by certificate of a member of the bar of this Court, by affidavit of the person who served the papers, or by any other proof satisfactory to the Court. Failure to make the required proof of service does not affect the validity of the service; the Court may at any time allow the proof of service to be amended or supplied unless it clearly appears that to do so would result in material prejudice to the substantive rights of any party.

(c) Except in an emergency, no papers shall be left with or mailed to a Judge for filing, but all pleadings shall be filed with the Clerk of the Court.

(d) When papers are filed, the Clerk shall endorse thereon the date and time of filing.

(e) Parties shall furnish to the Clerk forthwith, upon demand, all necessary copies of any pleading, judgment or order, or other matter of record in a cause, so as to permit the Clerk to comply with the provisions of any statute or rule. Plaintiff or plaintiff's attorney, upon filing a complaint, and defendant or defendant's attorney, upon filing a notice of removal pursuant to 28 U.S.C. § 1446, shall furnish to the Clerk a completed civil cover sheet and four (4) copies of such pleading in addition to any copies required to be filed under the Federal Rules of Civil Procedure. All such copies of the notice of removal shall also include a copy of all papers required to be filed under 28 U.S.C. § 1446(a). Upon receipt, the Clerk shall transmit one copy to the Judge to whom the case is assigned.

(f) Any papers received by the Clerk without payment of such fees as may be fixed by statute or by the Judicial Conference of the United States for the filing thereof shall be marked "received" and the date and time of receipt shall be noted thereon.

Source: L.Civ.R. 5.1(a)—G.R. 9.A.; L.Civ.R. 5.1(b)—G.R. 9.B.; L.Civ.R. 5.1(c)—G.R. 8.D.; L.Civ.R. 5.1(d)—G.R. 8.C.; L.Civ.R. 5.1(e)—G.R. 8.E., G.R. 10.A.

[Effective April 1, 1997; amended effective March 14, 2001.]

CIV. RULE 5.2. ELECTRONIC SERVICE AND FILING DOCUMENTS

Papers served and filed by electronic means in accordance with procedures promulgated by the Court are, for purposes of Federal Rule of Civil Procedure 5, served and filed in compliance with the local civil and criminal rules of the District of New Jersey.*

Adopted January 5, 2004.

* **Publisher's Note:** See the Electronic Case Filing Policies and Procedures following Standing Orders.

CIV. RULE 5.3. PROTECTIVE ORDERS AND PUBLIC ACCESS UNDER CM/ECF

(a) Scope of Rule

(1) This rule shall govern any request by a party to seal, or otherwise restrict public access to, any materials filed with the Court or utilized in connection with judicial decision-making. This rule shall also govern any request by a party or parties to seal, or otherwise restrict public access to, any judicial proceedings.

(2) As used in this rule, "materials" include pleadings as well as documents of any nature and in any medium. "Judicial proceedings" include hearings and trials but do not include conferences in chambers.

(3) This rule shall not apply to any materials or judicial proceedings which must be sealed pursuant to statute or other law.

(4) Subject to this rule and to statute or other law, all materials and judicial proceedings are matters of public record and shall not be sealed.

(b) Discovery Materials

(1) Notwithstanding this rule, parties may enter into written agreements to keep materials produced in discovery confidential and to return or destroy such materials as agreed by parties and as allowed by law.

(2) Parties may submit to a Judge or Magistrate Judge an agreed-on form of order which embodies a written agreement as described above. Any such form of order must be accompanied by an affidavit or attorney certification filed electronically under the designation "affidavit/certification in support of discovery confidentiality order." The affidavit or attorney certification shall describe (a) the nature of the materials to be kept confidential, (b) the legitimate private or public interests which warrant confidentiality and (c) the clearly defined and serious injury that would result should the order not be entered. The affidavit or attorney certification shall be available for public review.

(3) No form of order submitted by parties shall supersede the provisions of this rule with regard to the filing of materials or judicial proceedings. The form of order may, however, provide for the return or destruction of discovery materials as agreed by parties. The form of order shall be subject to modification by a judge or magistrate judge at any time.

(4) Any order under this section shall be filed electronically under the designation "discovery confidentiality order."

(5) Any dispute regarding the entry of, or the confidentiality of discovery materials under, any order under this section shall be brought before a Magistrate Judge pursuant to L. Civ. R. 37.1(a)(1).

(c) Motion to Seal or Otherwise Restrict Public Access

(1) Any request by a party or parties to seal, or otherwise restrict public access to, any materials or judicial proceedings shall be made by formal motion pursuant to L. Civ. R. 7.1. Any such motion shall be filed electronically under the designation "motion to seal materials" or "motion to seal judicial proceedings," and shall be returnable on the next available return date.

(2) Any motion to seal or otherwise restrict public access shall be available for review by the public. The motion papers shall describe (a) the nature of the materials or proceedings at issue, (b) the legitimate private or public interests which warrant the relief sought, (c) the clearly defined and serious injury that would result if the relief sought is not granted, and (d) why a less restrictive alternative to the relief sought is not available. Proposed Findings of Fact and Conclusions of Law shall be submitted with the motion papers in the proposed order required by (c)(5) below.

(3) Any materials deemed confidential by a party or parties and submitted with regard to a motion to seal or otherwise restrict public access shall be filed under the designation "confidential materials" and shall remain sealed until such time as the motion is decided.

(4) Any interested person may move to intervene pursuant to Fed. R. Civ. P. 24 (b) before the return date of any motion to seal or otherwise restrict public access.

(5) Any order or opinion on any motion to seal or otherwise restrict public access shall include findings on the factors set forth in (c)(2) above as well as other findings required by law and shall be filed electronically under the designation "order or opinion to seal." Such orders and opinions may be redacted. Unredacted orders and opinions may be filed under seal, either electronically or in other medium.

(6) Notwithstanding the above, on emergent application of a party or parties or sua sponte, a Judge or Magistrate Judge may seal or otherwise restrict public access to materials or judicial proceedings on a temporary basis. The Judge or Magistrate Judge shall do so by order which sets forth the basis for the temporary relief and which shall be filed electronically under the designation "temporary order to seal." Any interested person may move pursuant to L. Civ. R. 7.1 and Fed. R. Civ. P. 24 (b) to intervene, which motion shall be made returnable on the next available return date.

(d) Settlement Agreements

(1) No party or parties shall submit a proposed settlement agreement for approval by a Judge or Magistrate Judge unless required to do so by statute or other law or for the purpose of retaining jurisdiction.

(2) Any settlement agreement filed with the Court or incorporated into an order shall, absent an appropriate showing under federal law, be deemed a public record and available for public review.

(e) Dockets. No docket shall be sealed. However, entries on a docket may be sealed pursuant to the provisions of this rule.

(f) Web Site. The Clerk shall maintain for public review on the official Court PACER Site a consolidated report which reflects all motions, orders, and opinions described in this rule.

(g) Effective Date. This Rule shall be effective as of the date of adoption and shall apply to all motions to seal or otherwise restrict public access made after that date.

Adopted February 24, 2005. Amended March 9, 2007.

EXPLANATORY NOTE
LOCAL CIVIL RULE 5.3

History. In June of 2004, the Board of Judges was presented with a Lawyers Advisory Committee recommendation for the adoption of a local civil rule that would provide for public (i.e., press) notice of requests to seal, among other things, documents and proceedings. Several months before, in February of 2004, the District of New Jersey implemented CM/ECF (Case Management/Electronic Case Filing). This allowed the electronic filing of pleadings, motions, briefs, etc., under descriptive "events." CM/ECF also allowed remote access to dockets and filed materials as well as the creation of compilations or reports on the events.

Recognizing that CM/ECF might have a significant impact on what the Lawyers Advisory Committee recommended, the Board of Judges deferred the recommendation. Thereafter, the proposed local civil rule in its current form ("the Rule") was drafted. It was reviewed on an informal basis by representatives of the Administrative Office of the United States Courts and the Federal Judicial Center. It was also reviewed by Professor Laurie Kratky Dore of Drake University Law School in Des Moines, Iowa. Professor Dore is the author of a leading article on confidentiality, "Secrecy by Consent: The Use and Limits of Confidentiality in the Pursuit of Settlement," 74 Notre Dame L. Rev. 283 (1999), and of "Settlement, Secrecy, and Judicial Discretion: South Carolina's New Rules Governing the Sealing of Settlements," 55 S.C. L. Rev. 791 (2004). The Rule was circulated among members of the Committee on Rules on Practice and Procedure of the Board of Judges and thereafter submitted to the Lawyers Advisory Committee. The Rule is intended to reflect Supreme Court and Third Circuit law and does not set forth in detail all standards established by precedent.

Subparagraph (a)(1). This subparagraph describes the scope of the Rule. It applies to any application to seal materials filed with the Court, materials utilized in connection with judicial decision-making, or judicial proceedings. The use of the phrase, "otherwise restrict public access," as used in the Rule, is intended to address any application which might seek less than the complete sealing of materials or proceedings. The phrase, "in connection with judicial decision-making," is intended to exclude, among other things, letters to judges which are not substantive in nature. See, for the definition of a "judicial record", In re Cendant Corp., 260 F.3d 183 (3d Cir. 2001), and for the distinction between discovery and nondiscovery pretrial motions, Leucadia, Inc. v. Applied Extrusion Technologies, Inc., 998 F.2d 157 (3d Cir.1993).

Subparagraph (a)(2). This subparagraph defines "materials" and "judicial proceedings." The definitions are intended to be broad and to allow for the development of case law. For that reason, the word "materials" is used rather than "judicial records," the latter approaching a term of art. Note that judicial proceedings are not intended to encompass in-chambers conferences.

Subparagraph (a)(3). The purpose of this subparagraph is to make clear that the rule is not intended to affect any "statute or other law" that mandates sealing of materials or judicial proceedings (for example, amended Section 205 (c)(3) of the E–Government Act of 2002, Pub. L. No. 107–347, and the qui tam provisions of the False Claims Act, 31 U.S.C. § 3729, et seq.).

Subparagraph (a)(4). The right of public access to filed materials and judicial proceedings derives from the First Amendment and federal common law. Consistent with this right, this subparagraph establishes a presumption in favor of public access.

Subparagraph (b). In keeping with the comprehensive nature of the Rule, this subparagraph is intended to apply to unfiled discovery materials and to be consistent with footnote 17 of Pansy v. Borough of Stroudsburg, 23 F.3d 772 (3d Cir. 1994): "because of the benefits of umbrella protective orders in cases involving large-scale discovery, the court may construct a broad protective order upon a threshold showing by the movant of good cause. ***. After delivery of the documents, the opposing party would have the opportunity to indicate precisely which documents it believed not to be confidential, and the party seeking to maintain the seal would have the burden to proof with respect to those documents." 23 F.3d at 787, n.17 (citation omitted). As a general proposition, there is no right of public access to unfiled discovery materials. See, e.g., Seattle Times Co. v. Rhinehart, 467 U.S. 20 (1984); Estate of Frankl v. Goodyear Tire and Rubber and Co., 181 N.J. 1 (2004) (per curiam). This subparagraph, however, is not intended to prohibit any interested person from seeking access to such materials.

Subparagraph (b)(1) recognizes the above proposition, allows parties to enter into agreements such as that contemplated by Pansy, and also allows materials to be returned or destroyed. See, with regard to "Agreements on Return or Destruction of Tangible Evidence," ABA Section on Litigation Ethical Guidelines for Settlement Negotiations, Guideline 4.2.4 (August 2002).

Subparagraph (b)(2). This subparagraph describes the procedure which parties must follow in submitting blanket protective orders. Consistent with Pansy, there must be a showing by affidavit or certification of "good cause" and specific information must be provided. The affidavit or certification must also be available for public review. The intent of subparagraph (b)(2) is to allow parties to describe the materials in issue in categorical fashion and thus to avoid document-by-document description. This subparagraph does not go in greater detail as to the contents of the affidavit or certification. The sufficiency of an affidavit or certification is a matter for individual determination by a Judge or Magistrate Judge.

Subparagraph (b)(3). This subparagraph is intended to make plain the distinction between blanket protective orders and orders for the sealing of materials filed with the Court. Blanket protective orders should not include a provision that allows materials to be filed under seal with the Court.

Subparagraph (b)(4). This subparagraph, together with subparagraph (b)(2), describes "events" for purposes of CM/ECF. Affidavits or certifications in support of blanket protective orders as well as the protective orders should be electronically filed using these events.

Subparagraph (b)(5). This subparagraph contemplates that disputes may arise with regard to the terms of blanket protective orders and the designation of materials under such orders. Should such disputes arise, the parties are directed to the procedure set forth in Local Civil Rule 37.1(a)(1) for the resolution of discovery disputes. The Rule is not intended to be applicable to materials submitted with regard to discovery disputes.

Subparagraph (c). This subparagraph establishes the procedure by which applications must be made to seal or otherwise restrict public access to filed materials or judicial proceedings. Such applications may be made in advance of, as part of, or parallel with substantive motions.

Subparagraph (c)(1). This subparagraph provides that any such application must be made by formal motion.

Subparagraph (c)(2). This subparagraph provides that any motion must be available for public access and must set forth, at a minimum, certain specified information.

Subparagraph (c)(3). Under Third Circuit precedent, the filing of otherwise confidential material may make that material a public record and subject to public access. See, e.g., Bank of America Nat'l Trust and Savings Ass'n v. Hotel Rittenhouse Assoc., 800 F.2d 339 (3d Cir. 1988). This subparagraph is intended to allow confidential materials to be filed and remain under seal until a motion to seal or otherwise restrict public access is ruled on. Otherwise, arguably confidential materials would be "transmuted "into materials presumptively subject to public access. See Gambale v. Deutsche Bank AG, 377 F.3d 133, 143 n.8 (2d Cir. 2004).

Subparagraph (c)(4). "[T]he procedural device of permissive intervention is appropriately used to enable a litigant who was not an original party to an action to challenge protective or confidentiality orders entered in that action." Pansy, 23 F.3d at 778. Consistent with Pansy, this subparagraph allows a person to move to intervene pursuant to Rule 24 of Federal Rules of Civil Procedure before a motion to seal or to otherwise restrict public access is returnable. This subparagraph is not intended to foreclose any subsequent motion to modify or vacate an order.

Subparagraph (c)(5). This subparagraph serves two functions. First, it identifies the "event" corresponding to a sealing order or opinion, as subparagraph (c)(1) identifies events for sealing motions. Subparagraph (c)(5) also reminds Judges and Magistrate Judges that, as appropriate, opinions and orders on motions to seal or otherwise restrict public access may be filed in redacted and unredacted form.

Subparagraph (c)(6). This subparagraph is patterned after Section 7(a) of the Vermont Rules for Public Access to Court Records. It is intended to address emergent applications by parties where there may be a legitimate need for a temporary sealing order (for example, when an ex parte seizure order is sought in a trademark infringement action). The subparagraph identifies the appropriate CM/ECF event and also provides for motions to intervene.

Subparagraph (d). As a general proposition, settlement agreements are not presented to Judges or Magistrate Judges for "approval." Such approval has no legal significance. See, e.g., Pascarella v. Bruck, 190 N.J. Super. 118 (App. Div. 1983). Moreover, judicial approval of a settlement may make that settlement a public record and subject to public access. See Jessup v. Luther, 277 F.3d 926 (7th Cir. 2002). For these reasons, subparagraph (d)(1) proves that settlement agreements will not be approved by Judges or Magistrate Judges unless such approval is required by law (for example, in class actions or actions involving infants). Subdivision (d)(1) does, however, provide for judicial approval of a settlement if the intent of the parties in seeking that approval is to have the Court retain jurisdiction to enforce a settlement agreement. See, e.g., Kokkonen v. Guardian Life Ins. Co., 511 U.S. 375 (1994). Subdivision (d)(2) provides that, once filed with the Court or incorporated in an order, a settlement agreement becomes a public record and subject to public access absent an appropriate showing.

Subparagraph (e). Dockets are sources of basic information about civil actions and are historically public records. See, e.g., United States v. Criden, 675 F.2d 550 (3d Cir. 1982). Thus, this subparagraph provides that dockets will not be sealed but that, consistent with the Rule, specific docket entries may be. See Webster Groves School Dist. v. Pulitzer Publishing Co., 898 F.2d 1371 (8th Cir. 1990).

Subparagraph (f). This subdivision requires the Clerk to maintain a report which reflects all motions, order and opinions described in the Rule. The intent of this subparagraph is that reports be generated based on the "events" referred to in the Rule and be available to the general public through PACER.

SUPPLEMENTAL EXPLANATORY NOTE

After publication on December 20, 2004, several comments were received. These comments led to the addition of language in the Explanatory Note (History and subparagraphs (b), (b)(5), (c) and (c)(4)) intended to clarify the intent of the Rule. Subparagraph (d)(2) of the Rule and the accompanying Explanatory Note were revised to reflect that the appropriate standard may derive from other than Fed. R.Civ.P. 26(c). Finally, a new subparagraph (g) was added to the Rule.

CIV. RULE 6.1. EXTENSIONS OF TIME AND CONTINUANCES

(a) Each application for an extension of time shall:

(1) be made in writing;

(2) be served prior to the expiration of the period sought to be extended; and

(3) disclose in the application the date service of process was effected and all similar extensions previously obtained.

(b) The time within which to answer or reply may, before its first expiration and with or without notice, be extended once for a period not to exceed 15 days on order granted by the Clerk. Any other proposed extension of time must be presented to the Court for consideration.

(c) A motion to postpone or continue a trial on the grounds of absence of a witness or evidence shall be made upon affidavit showing the nature and materiality of the expected testimony or evidence, and that diligent effort has been made to secure the witness or evidence. If the testimony or the evidence would be admissible at the trial, and the adverse party stipulates that it shall be considered as actually given at the trial, there shall be no postponement or continuance.

Source: G.R. 13.

[Effective April 1, 1997.]

CIV. RULE 7.1. APPLICATION AND MOTION PRACTICE

(a) No Prefiling Applications. No applications will be entertained by a Judge or Magistrate Judge in any action until the action has been filed, allocated and assigned.

(b) All Motions.

(1) Unless a Judge or Magistrate Judge advises the attorneys otherwise, all motions, regardless of their complexity and the relief sought, shall be presented and defended in the manner set forth in L.Civ.R. 7.1.

(2) The Notice of Motion and all papers in support of or in opposition to the motion, including briefs, must be filed electronically with the Clerk.

(3) Motions filed electronically by ECF Registered Users shall also comply with the Policies and Procedures that govern Electronic Case Filing for the District of New Jersey.

(4) The procedure for requesting and scheduling oral argument is set forth in L. Civ. R. 78.1.

(c) Motion Days.

(1) The regular motion days for all vicinages are set forth in L.Civ.R. 78.1. All applications, other than applications under L.Civ.R. 65.1, by notice of motion or otherwise, shall be made returnable before the Judge or Magistrate Judge to whom the case has been assigned on the first regular motion day which is at least 24 days after the date of filing.

(2) If a motion is noticed for any day other than a regular motion day, unless such day has been fixed by the Court, the Clerk shall list the disposition of the motion for the next regular motion day and notify all parties of the change in date.

(d) Filing Motion Papers.

(1) No application will be heard unless the moving papers and a brief, prepared in accordance with L.Civ.R. 7.2, and proof or acknowledgment of service on all other parties, are filed with the Clerk at least 24 days prior to the noticed motion day. The brief shall be a separate document for submission to the Court, and shall note the motion day on the cover page.

(2) The brief and papers in opposition to a motion, specifying the motion day on the cover page, with proof or acknowledgment of service thereof on all other parties, must be filed with the Clerk at least 14 days prior to the original motion day, unless the Court otherwise orders, or an automatic extension is obtained pursuant to L.Civ.R. 7.1(d)(5).

(3) If the moving party chooses to file papers in reply, those papers including a reply brief specifying the motion day on the cover page, with proof or acknowledgment of service thereof on all other parties, must be filed with the Clerk at least seven calendar days prior to the motion day. No reply papers shall be filed on a motion for reconsideration pursuant to L.Civ.R. 7.1(i) or on a cross-motion, unless the Court otherwise orders.

(4) In lieu of filing any brief pursuant to L.Civ.R. 7.1(d)(1), (2) or (3), a party may file a statement that no brief is necessary and the reasons therefor.

(5) The motion day of a dispositive motion may be adjourned once by a party opposing the motion, without the consent of the moving party, the Court, or the Clerk. To obtain the automatic extension a party must file with the Clerk, and serve upon all other parties, a letter invoking the provisions of this rule before the date on which opposition papers would otherwise be due under L.Civ.R. 7.1(d)(2). That letter shall set forth the new motion day, which shall be the next available motion day following the originally noticed date. All parties opposing the motion shall file

their opposition papers at least 14 days prior to the new motion day, and the moving party shall file its reply papers, if any, at least seven calendar days prior to the new motion day. No other extension of the time limits provided in L.Civ.R. 7.1(d)(2) and (3) shall be permitted without an Order of the Court, and any application for such an extension shall advise the Court whether other parties have or have not consented to such request.

(6) No sur-replies are permitted without permission of the Judge or Magistrate Judge to whom the case is assigned.

(7) The Court may reject any brief or other paper not filed within the time specified.

(e) Preparation of Order. All filed motions shall have annexed thereto a proposed order. If the proposed order does not adequately reflect the Court's ruling, the prevailing party, if directed by the Court, shall submit an order within five calendar days of the ruling on the motion on notice to all other parties. Unless the Court otherwise directs, if no specific objection to that order with reasons therefor is received within seven calendar days of its receipt by the Court, the order may be signed. If such an objection is made, the matter may be listed for hearing at the discretion of the Court.

(f) Motions Regarding Additional Pleadings. Upon filing of a motion for leave to file an amended complaint or answer, a complaint in intervention, or other pleading requiring leave of Court, the moving party shall attach to the motion a copy of the proposed pleading or amendments and retain the original until the Court has ruled. If leave to file is granted, the moving party shall file the original forthwith.

(g) Courtesy Copies. In addition to the filing of all papers, including briefs, in support of or in opposition to a motion, the filer must submit forthwith to the Judge's or Magistrate Judge's chambers one courtesy copy of each filed paper or brief in paper form, unless otherwise directed by the judicial officer. These documents shall be clearly marked as courtesy copies.

(h) Cross–Motion. A cross-motion related to the subject matter of the original motion may be filed by the party opposing the motion together with that party's opposition papers and may be noticed for disposition on the same day as the original motion, as long as the opposition papers are timely filed. Upon the request of the original moving party, the Court may enlarge the time for filing a brief and/or papers in opposition to the cross-motion and adjourn the original motion day. The provisions of L.Civ.R. 7.1(d)(5) apply to dispositive cross-motions.

(i) Motions for Reconsideration. A motion for reconsideration shall be served and filed within 10 business days after the entry of the order or judgment on the original motion by the Judge or Magistrate Judge. A brief setting forth concisely the matter or controlling decisions which the party believes the Judge or Magistrate Judge has overlooked shall be filed with the Notice of Motion.

Source: L.Civ.R. 7.1(a)—G.R. 12.E.; L.Civ.R. 7.1(b)(1)—G.R. 12.C. (paragraph 1); L.Civ.R. 7.1(b)(2)—G.R. 12.C. (paragraph 4); L.Civ.R. 7.1(b)(3)—G.R. 12.C. (paragraph 3); L.Civ.R. 7.1(c)—G.R. 12.C. (paragraphs 5–8); L.Civ.R. 7.1(d)(1)—G.R. 12.C. (paragraph 9); L.Civ.R. 7.1(d)(2)—G.R. 12.H.; L.Civ.R. 7.1(e)—G.R. 12.C. (paragraph 10); L.Civ.R. 7.1(f)—G.R. 12.N.; L.Civ.R. 7.1(g)—G.R. 12.I.

[Effective April 1, 1997. Amended effective March 31, 1999; February 24, 2005; January 2, 2008.]

CIV. RULE 7.2. AFFIDAVITS AND BRIEFS

(a) Affidavits shall be restricted to statements of fact within the personal knowledge of the affiant. Argument of the facts and the law shall not be contained in affidavits. Legal arguments and summations in affidavits will be disregarded by the Court and may subject the affiant to appropriate censure, sanctions or both.

(b) Any brief shall include a table of contents and a table of authorities and shall not exceed 40 ordinary typed or printed pages (15 pages for any reply brief submitted under L.Civ.R. 7.1(d)(3) and any brief in support of or in opposition to a motion for reconsideration submitted under L.Civ.R. 7.1(i)), excluding pages required for the table of contents and authorities. Briefs of greater length will only be accepted if special permission of the Judge or Magistrate Judge is obtained prior to submission of the brief.

(c) All briefs shall be in black lettering on paper size 8.5 × 11 inches. All margins shall be not less than one-inch on sides, top, and bottom.

(d) Each page of a brief shall contain double-spaced text and/or single spaced footnotes or inserts. Typeface shall be in 12–point non-proportional font (such as Courier New 12) or an equivalent 14–point proportional font (such as Times New Roman 14). If a 12–point proportional font is used instead, the page limits shall be reduced by 25 percent (e.g., the 40 page limit becomes 30 pages in this font). Footnotes shall be printed in the same size of type utilized in the text.

Amended: December 22, 1999, April 19, 2000; January 2, 2008.

Source: L.Civ.R. 7.2(a)—G.R. 27.A.; L.Civ.R. 7.2(b)—G.R. 27.B.

[Effective April 1, 1997; amended effective April 19, 2000; January 2, 2008.]

CIV. RULE 8.1. PLEADING DAMAGES

A pleading which sets forth a claim for relief in the nature of unliquidated money damages shall state in the ad damnum clause a demand for damages generally without specifying the amount. Upon service of a written request by another party, the party filing the pleading shall within 10 days after service thereof furnish the requesting party with a written statement of the amount of damages claimed, which statement shall not be filed except on court order. Nothing stated herein shall relieve the party filing the pleading of the necessity of alleging the requisite jurisdictional amount in controversy, where applicable.

Source: G.R. 8.G.

[Effective April 1, 1997.]

CIV. RULE 9.1. SPECIAL MATTERS—REVIEW OF SOCIAL SECURITY MATTERS

(a) In an action to review a determination of the Commissioner of Social Security denying a claim for benefits under the Social Security Act, 42 U.S.C. § 405(g), hereafter "Social Security case," the following procedure shall apply:

(1) Defendant shall timely file an answer to the complaint, along with a copy of the certified administrative record, and shall simultaneously serve the answer and a copy of the certified administrative record upon plaintiff.

(2) Within 14 days, to encourage early and amicable resolution of Social Security matters, plaintiff shall serve upon defendant's counsel a statement setting forth plaintiff's primary contentions or arguments as to why plaintiff is entitled to relief. A copy of this statement shall also be sent to the Court. Defendant shall notify plaintiff within 30 days whether it agrees that plaintiff is entitled to relief. If the parties agree upon a resolution of a Social Security matter, the parties shall proceed in accordance with L.Civ.R. 41.1(b).

(3) Plaintiff shall serve upon defense counsel a brief (conforming to the requirements of L. Civ. R. 7.2(b)) with a cover letter, within 60 days after the answer was filed. Plaintiff shall send a copy of the cover letter, without the brief, to the Deputy Clerk of the Judge to whom the case is assigned. Plaintiff's brief shall set forth all errors which plaintiff contends entitle him or her to relief. The brief shall also contain, under the appropriate heading and in the order here indicated:

(A) A statement of the issues presented for review, set forth in separate numbered paragraphs.

(B) A statement of the case. This statement should indicate briefly the course of the proceeding and its disposition at the administrative level.

(C) A statement of facts with references to the administrative record.

(D) An argument. The argument may be preceded by a summary. The argument shall be divided into sections separately treating each issue and must set forth the contentions of plaintiff with respect to the issues presented and reasons therefor. Each contention must be supported by specific reference to the portion of the record relied upon and by citations to statutes, regulations and cases supporting plaintiff's position. Citations to unreported district court opinions must be accompanied by a copy of the opinion. If plaintiff has moved for remand to the Commissioner for further proceedings, the argument in support thereof must set forth good cause for remand. Furthermore, if the remand is for the purpose of taking additional evidence, such evidence must be attached to the brief and accompanied by a showing that the new evidence is material and that there is good cause for the failure to incorporate such evidence into the record in a prior proceeding. Further, if such evidence is in the form of a consultation examination sought at Government expense, plaintiff must make a proffer of the nature of the evidence to be obtained.

(E) A short conclusion stating the relief sought.

(4) Defendant shall serve upon plaintiff an original and two copies of a brief with a cover letter within 30 days after receipt of plaintiff's brief. Defendant shall send a copy of the cover letter, without the brief to the Deputy Clerk of the Judge to whom the case is assigned. Defendant's brief shall respond specifically to each issue raised by plaintiff and shall conform to the requirements set forth above for plaintiff's brief, except that a statement of the issues and a statement of the case need not be made unless defendant is dissatisfied with plaintiff's statement thereof.

(5) Plaintiff may serve upon defendant a brief in reply to the brief of defendant within 10 days after receipt of defendant's brief.

(6) Within 5 days of service of plaintiff's reply brief or within 10 days of plaintiff's receipt of defendant's brief (if no reply brief is submitted by plaintiff), the plaintiff shall file with the Clerk of the Court the originals plus one copy of the following documents (and shall send a copy of the transmittal letter to the defendant and to the Judge to whom the case is assigned):

(i) Plaintiff's brief;

(ii) Defendant's brief; and

(iii) Plaintiff's reply brief, if any.

(b) All Social Security cases will be handled by the court on written briefs unless the briefing requirements in L. Civ. R. 9.1(a) have not been timely met or a demand for oral argument is approved. Failure to timely prepare the documents in L. Civ. R. 9.1(a) may result in the imposition of sanctions by the Court.

Source: G.R. 48.

[Effective April 1, 1997. Amended effective June 22, 1999; February 20, 2002.]

CIV. RULE 9.2. SPECIAL MATTERS—ADMIRALTY AND MARITIME RULES FOR THE UNITED STATES DISTRICT COURT FOR THE DISTRICT OF NEW JERSEY

LOCAL ADMIRALTY AND MARITIME RULE (a). SCOPE, CITATION AND DEFINITIONS

LAMR (a)(1) Scope. These local admiralty and maritime rules apply only to civil actions that are governed by the Supplemental Rules for Certain Admiralty and Maritime Claims (Supplemental Rule or Rules). All other local rules are applicable in these cases, but to the extent that another local rule is inconsistent with the applicable local admiralty and maritime rules, the local admiralty and maritime rules shall govern.

LAMR (a)(2) Citation. The local admiralty and maritime rules may be cited by the letters "LAMR" and the lower case letters and numbers in parentheses that appear at the beginning of each section. The lower case letter is intended to associate the local admiralty and maritime rule with the Supplemental Rule that bears the same capital letter.

LAMR (a)(3) Definitions. As used in the local admiralty and maritime rules, "Court" means a United States District Court; "judicial officer" means a United States District Judge or a United States Magistrate Judge; "Clerk of Court" means the Clerk of the District Court and includes Deputy Clerks of Court; and "Marshal" means the United States Marshal and includes Deputy Marshals.

[Effective April 1, 1997.]

LOCAL ADMIRALTY AND MARITIME RULE (b). MARITIME ATTACHMENT AND GARNISHMENT

LAMR (b)(1) Affidavit That Defendant Is Not Found Within the District. The affidavit required by Supplemental Rule B(1) to accompany the complaint shall list the efforts made by and on behalf of plaintiff to find and serve the defendant within the District.

LAMR (b)(2) Use of State Procedures. When the plaintiff invokes a state procedure in order to attach or garnish under Fed.R.Civ.P. 4(e), the process of attachment or garnishment shall so state.

[Effective April 1, 1997.]

LOCAL ADMIRALTY AND MARITIME RULE (c). ACTIONS IN REM: SPECIAL PROVISIONS

LAMR (c)(1) Intangible Property. The summons issued pursuant to Supplemental Rule C(3) shall direct the person having control of intangible property to show cause no later than 10 days after service why the intangible property should not be delivered to the Court to abide further order of the Court. A judicial officer for good cause shown may lengthen or shorten the time. Service of the summons shall have the effect of an arrest of the intangible property and bring it within the control of the Court. Upon order of the Court, the person who is served may deliver or pay over to the Clerk of Court the intangible property proceeded against to the extent sufficient to satisfy the plaintiff's claim. If such delivery or payment is made, the person served is excused from the duty to show cause.

LAMR (c)(2) Publication of Notice of Action and Arrest. The notice required by Supplemental Rule C(4) shall be published by the plaintiff once in a newspaper of general circulation in the city or county where the property has been seized. The notice shall contain:

(a) The Court, title and number of the action;

(b) The date of arrest;

(c) The identity of the property arrested;

(d) The name, address, and telephone number of the attorney for plaintiff;

(e) A statement that the claim of a person who is entitled to possession or who claims an interest pursuant to Supplemental Rule C(6) must be filed with the Clerk and served on the attorney for plaintiff within 10 days after publication;

(f) A statement that an answer to the complaint must be filed and served within 20 days after the claim is filed, and that otherwise, default may be entered and condemnation ordered;

(g) A statement that motions to intervene under Fed.R.Civ.P. 24 by persons claiming maritime liens or other interests and claims for expenses of administration under LAMR(e)(10)(b) shall be filed within a time fixed by the Court; and

(h) The name, address and telephone number of the Marshal.

LAMR (c)(3) Notice Requirements.

(a) *Default Judgments.* A party seeking a default judgment in an action in rem must satisfy the Judge that due notice of the action and arrest of the property has been given (1) by publication as required in LAMR (c)(2), and (2) by service of the complaint and warrant of arrest upon the Master or other person having custody of the property. (3) If the defendant property is a vessel documented under the laws of the United States, plaintiff must attempt to notify all persons identified as having an interest in the vessel in the United States Coast Guard Certificate of Ownership. (4) If the defendant property is a vessel numbered as provided in the Federal Boat Safety Act, plaintiff must attempt to notify the owner as named in the records of the issuing authority.

(b) *Ship Mortgage Act.* For purposes of the Ship Mortgage Act, 46 U.S.C. § 31301 et seq., notice to the Master of a vessel, or the person having physical custody thereof, by service of the warrant of arrest and complaint shall be deemed compliance with the notice requirements of such Act, as to all persons, except as to those who have recorded a notice of claim of lien.

(c) *Mailing.* The notification requirement is satisfied by mailing copies of the warrant of arrest and complaint to the person's address using any form of mail requiring a return receipt.

LAMR (c)(4) Entry of Default and Default Judgment. After the time for filing a claim or answer has expired, the plaintiff may move for entry of default under Fed.R.Civ.P. 55(a). Default will be entered upon showing by affidavit or certificate of counsel that:

(a) Notice has been given as required in LAMR (c)(3)(a)(1) and (2), and

(b) Notice has been attempted as required by LAMR (c)(3)(a)(3) and (4), where appropriate, and

(c) The time for filing a claim or answer has expired, and

(d) No one has appeared to claim the property.

The plaintiff may move for judgment under Fed. R.Civ.P. 55(b) at any time after default has been entered.

[Effective April 1, 1997.]

LOCAL ADMIRALTY AND MARITIME RULE (d). POSSESSORY, PETITORY, AND PARTITION ACTIONS

LAMR (d) Return Date. In an action under Supplemental Rule D, a judicial officer may order that the claim and answer be filed on a date earlier than 20 days after arrest. The order may also set a date for expedited hearing of the action.

[Effective April 1, 1997.]

LOCAL ADMIRALTY AND MARITIME RULE (e). ACTIONS IN REM AND QUASI IN REM: GENERAL PROVISIONS

LAMR (e)(1) Itemized Demand for Judgment. The demand for judgment in every complaint filed under Supplemental Rule B or C shall allege the dollar amount of the debt or damages for which the action was commenced. The demand for judgment shall also allege the nature of other items of damage.

LAMR (e)(2) Salvage Action Complaints. In an action for a salvage award, the complaint shall allege the dollar value of the vessel, cargo, freight, and other property salved, and the dollar amount of the award claimed.

LAMR (e)(3) Verification of Pleadings. Every complaint in Supplemental Rule B, C, and D actions shall be verified upon oath or solemn affirmation or in the form provided by 28 U.S.C. § 1746, by a party or by an authorized officer of a corporate party. If no party or authorized corporate officer is readily available, verification of a complaint may be made by an agent, attorney in fact, or attorney of record, who shall state the sources of the knowledge, information and belief contained in the complaint; declare that the document verified is true to the best of that knowledge, information, and belief; state why verification is not made by the party or an authorized corporate officer; and state that the affiant is authorized so to verify. A verification not made by a party or authorized corporate officer will be deemed to have been made by the party as if verified personally. If the verification was not made by a party or authorized corporate officer, any interested party may move, with or without requesting a stay, for the personal oath of a party or an authorized corporate officer, which shall be procured by commission or as otherwise ordered.

LAMR (e)(4) Review by Judicial Officer. Unless otherwise required by the judicial officer, the review of complaints and papers called for by Supplemental Rules B(1) and C(3) does not require the affiant party or attorney to be present. Any complaint presented to a judicial officer for review shall be accompanied by a form of order to the Clerk which, upon signature by the judicial officer, shall direct the arrest, attachment, or garnishment sought by the applicant.

LAMR (e)(5) Instructions to the Marshal. The party who requests a warrant of arrest or process of attachment or garnishment shall provide instructions to the Marshal.

LAMR (e)(6) Property in Possession of United States Officer. When the property to be attached or arrested is in the custody of an employee or officer of the United States, the Marshal will deliver a copy of the complaint and warrant of arrest or summons and process of attachment or garnishment to that officer or employee if present, and otherwise to the custodian of the property. The Marshal will instruct the officer or employee or custodian to retain custody of the property until ordered to do otherwise by a judicial officer.

LAMR (e)(7) Security for Costs. In an action under the Supplemental Rules, a party may move upon notice to all parties for an order to compel an adverse party to post security for costs with the Clerk pursuant to Supplemental Rule E(2)(b). Unless otherwise ordered, the amount of security shall be $500. The party so notified shall post the security within five days after the order is entered. A party who fails to post security when due may not participate further in the proceedings. A party may move for an order increasing the amount of security for costs.

LAMR (e)(8) Adversary Hearing. An adversary hearing following arrest or attachment or garnishment under Supplemental Rule E(4)(f) shall be conducted by the Court within three court days after a request for such hearing, unless otherwise ordered.

LAMR (e)(9) Security Deposit for Seizure of Vessels. The party(ies) who seek(s) arrest or attachment of a vessel or property aboard a vessel shall deposit with the Marshal $4000 for vessels more than 65 feet in length overall or $500 for vessels 65 feet in length overall or less. For the arrest or attachment of intangible property, there shall be deposited with the Marshal $500. A check drawn upon the attorney's account of a member of the bar of this Court, or of a law firm having members who are admitted to the bar of this Court, shall be accepted by the Marshal as payment. These deposits shall be used to cover the expenses of the Marshal including, but not limited to, dockage, keepers, maintenance, and insurance. The party(ies) shall advance additional sums from time to time as requested by the Marshal to cover the estimated expenses until the property is released or disposed of as provided in Supplemental Rule E.

LAMR (e)(10) Intervenor's Claims and Sharing of Marshal's Fees and Expenses.

(a) *Intervention Before Sale.* When a vessel or other property has been arrested, attached, or garnished, and is in the hands of the Marshal or custodian substituted therefor, anyone having a claim against the vessel or property is required to present the claim by filing an intervening complaint under Fed.R.Civ.P. 24, and not by filing an original complaint, unless otherwise ordered by a judicial officer. An order permitting intervention may be signed ex parte at the time of filing the motion, subject to the right of any party to object to such intervention within 15 days after receipt of a copy of the motion and proposed pleading. Upon signing of an order permitting intervention the Clerk shall forthwith deliver a conformed copy of the intervening complaint to the Marshal, who shall deliver the copy to the vessel or custodian of the property. Intervenors shall thereafter be subject to the rights and obligations of parties, and the vessel or property shall stand arrested, attached, or garnished by the intervenor. An intervenor shall not be required to advance a security deposit to the Marshal for seizure of a vessel as required by LAMR (e)(9). Release of property arrested, attached, or garnished by an intervenor shall be done in accordance with Supplemental Rule E.

(b) *Sharing Marshal's Fees and Expenses Before Sale.* Upon motion by any party, security deposits may be ordered to be paid or shared by any party who has arrested, attached, or garnished a vessel or property aboard a vessel in amounts or proportions to be determined by a judicial officer.

(c) *Intervention After Sale.* After ratification of sale and payment of the purchase price, any person having a claim against the vessel or property that arose before ratification must present the same by intervening complaint, pursuant to LAMR (e)(10)(a), against the proceeds of the sale and may not proceed against the vessel unless the Court shall otherwise order for good cause shown. Where an intervening complaint prays service of process, the filing of such intervening complaint with the Clerk shall be deemed to be a claim against such proceeds without the issuance of in rem process, unless the Court shall otherwise order for good cause shown. The Court shall allow a period of at least 30 days after due ratification of the sale for the submission of such claims.

LAMR (e)(11) Custody of Property.

(a) *Safekeeping of Property.* When a vessel or other property is brought into the Marshal's custody by arrest or attachment, the Marshal shall arrange for adequate safekeeping, which may include the placing of keepers on or near the vessel. A substitute custodian in place of the Marshal may be appointed by order of the Court.

(b) *Employment of Vessel's Officers and Crew by Marshal.* All officers and members of the crew employed on a vessel of 750 gross tons or more shall be deemed employees of the Marshal for the period of 120 hours after the attachment or arrest of the vessel unless the Marshal, pursuant to a court order, has notified the officers and members of the crew that they are not so employed or unless the vessel is released from attachment or arrest. If the vessel is not released within 120 hours, the Marshal shall, on request of the seizing party, immediately thereafter designate which, if any, officers and members of the crew he or she is continuing to employ to preserve the vessel and shall promptly notify the remaining officers and members of the crew that they are no longer in his or her employ and are no longer in the service of the vessel and are free to depart from the vessel. The notice required by the preceding sentence shall be by written notice posted in a prominent place in each of the mess rooms or dining salons used by the officers and unlicensed personnel aboard the vessel.

(c) *Normal Vessel Operations and Movement of the Vessel.* Following arrest, attachment, or garnishment of a vessel or property aboard a vessel, normal vessel operations shall be permitted to commence or continue unless otherwise ordered by the Court. No movement of the vessel shall take place unless authorized by order of a judicial officer.

(d) *Procedure for Filing Claims by Suppliers for Payment of Charges.* A person who furnishes supplies or services to a vessel, cargo, or other property in custody of the Court who has not been paid and claims the right to payment as an expense of administration shall submit an invoice to the Clerk in the form of a verified claim within the time period set by the Court for intervention after sale pursuant to LAMR (e)(10)(c). The supplier must serve copies of the claim on the Marshal, substitute custodian if one has been appointed, and all parties of record. The Court may consider the claims individually or schedule a single hearing for all claims.

LAMR (e)(12) Sale of Property.

(a) *Notice.* Notice of sale of property in action in rem shall be published under such terms and conditions as set by the Court.

(b) *Payment of Bid.* These provisions apply unless otherwise ordered in the order of sale: The person whose bid is accepted shall immediately pay the Marshal the full purchase price if the bid is $1000 or less. If the bid exceeds $1000, the bidder shall immediately pay a deposit of at least $1000 or 10% of the bid, whichever is greater, and shall pay the balance within three days after the day on which the bid was accepted. If an objection to the sale is filed within that three-day period, the bidder is excused from paying the balance of the purchase price until three court days after the sale is confirmed. Payment shall be made in cash, by certified check or by cashier's check.

(c) *Default.* If the successful bidder does not pay the balance of the purchase price within the time allowed, the bidder is deemed to be in default. In such a case, the judicial officer may accept the second highest bid or arrange a new sale. The defaulting bidder's deposit shall be forfeited and applied to any additional costs incurred by the Marshal because of the default, the balance being retained in the Registry of the Court awaiting its order.

(d) *Report of Sale by Marshal.* At the conclusion of the sale, the Marshal shall forthwith file a written report with the Court of the fact of sale, the date, the price obtained, the name and address of the successful bidder, and any other pertinent information.

(e) *Time and Procedure for Objection to Sale.* An interested person may object to the sale by filing a written objection with the Clerk within three court days following the sale, serving the objection on all parties of record, the successful bidder, and the Marshal, and depositing such sum with the Marshal as determined by him or her to be sufficient to pay the expense of keeping the property for at least seven days. Payment to the Marshal shall be in cash, certified check or cashier's check.

(f) *Confirmation of Sale.* A sale shall be confirmed by order of the Court within five court days, but no sooner than three court days, after the sale. If an objection to the sale has been filed, the Court shall hold a hearing on the confirmation of the sale. The Marshal shall transfer title to the purchaser upon the order of the Court.

(g) *Disposition of Deposits.*

(1) Objection Sustained. If an objection is sustained, sums deposited by the successful bidder will be returned to the bidder forthwith. The sum deposited by the objector will be applied to pay the fees and expenses incurred by the Marshal in keeping the property until it is resold, and any balance remaining shall be returned to the objector. The objector will be reimbursed for the expense of keeping the property from the proceeds of a subsequent sale.

(2) Objection Overruled. If the objection is overruled, the sum deposited by the objector will be applied to pay the expense of keeping the property from the day the objection was filed until the day the sale is confirmed, and any balance remaining will be returned to the objector forthwith.

LAMR (e)(13) Discharge of Stipulations for Value and Other Security. When an order is entered in any cause marking the case dismissed or settled, the entry shall operate as a cancellation of all stipulations for value or other security provided to release the property seized that were filed in the case, unless otherwise provided in the order or by the Court.

[Effective April 1, 1997.]

LOCAL ADMIRALTY AND MARITIME RULE (f). LIMITATION OF LIABILITY

LAMR (f) Security for Costs. The amount of security for costs under Supplemental Rule F(1) shall be $250, and it may be combined with the security for value and interest, unless otherwise ordered.

Source: G.R. 5.

[Effective April 1, 1997.]

CIV. RULE 10.1 FORM OF PLEADINGS

(a) The initial pleading, motion, or other paper of any party filed in any cause other than criminal actions in this Court shall state in the first paragraph the street and post office address of each named party to the case or, if the party is not a natural person, the address of its principal place of business. If a pleading, motion, or other initial paper submitted for filing in a case does not contain the street and post office address of counsel, their client(s) or unrepresented parties, it may be struck by the Clerk and returned to the submitting party by the Clerk unless a statement why the client's address cannot be provided at this time is presented. Counsel and/or unrepresented parties must advise the Court of any change in their or their client's address within five days of being apprised of such change by filing a notice of said change with the Clerk. Failure to file a notice of address change may result in the imposition of sanctions by the Court.

(b) All papers to be filed in any cause or proceeding in this Court shall be plainly printed or typewritten, without interlineations or erasures which materially deface them; shall bear the docket number and the name of the Judge assigned to the action or proceeding; and shall have endorsed upon the first page the name, office, post office address, and telephone number of the attorney of record for the filing party. All papers shall be in black lettering on reasonably heavy paper size 8.5 × 11 inches; carbon copies shall not be used.

Source: L.Civ.R. 10.1(a)—G.R. 8.A.; L.Civ.R. 10.1(b)—G.R. 8.B.

[Effective April 1, 1997; Amended effective March 9, 2007.]

CIV. RULE 11.1. SIGNING OF PLEADINGS

In each case, the attorney of record who is a member of the bar of this Court shall personally sign all papers submitted to the Court or filed with the Clerk.

Source: G.R. 8.B.

[Effective April 1, 1997.]

CIV. RULE 11.2. VERIFICATION OF PETITIONS AND INITIAL CERTIFICATIONS

Except where otherwise provided by law, every petition shall be verified and, whenever possible, by the person on whose behalf it is presented. In case the same shall be verified by another, the affiant shall state in the affidavit the reasons such person does not make the verification and the affiant's authority for making it. The initial pleading, motion or other paper of any party filed in any case in this Court, other than a criminal action, shall be accompanied by a certification as to whether the matter in controversy is the subject of any other action pending in any court, or of any pending arbitration or administrative proceeding, and, if so, the certification shall identify each such action, arbitration or administrative proceeding, and all parties thereto.

Source: G.R. 14.

[Effective April 1, 1997; amended effective April 30, 1998.]

CIV. RULE 11.3. APPLICATIONS FOR FED.R.CIV.P. 11 SANCTIONS

All applications for sanctions pursuant to Fed. R.Civ.P. 11 shall be filed with the Clerk prior to the entry of final judgment notwithstanding the provisions of any other Rule of this Court.

Source: G.R. 12.L.

[Effective April 1, 1997.]

CIV. RULE 16.1. PRETRIAL CONFERENCES; SCHEDULING; CASE MANAGEMENT

(a) Scheduling Conferences—Generally.

(1) Conferences pursuant to Fed.R.Civ.P. 16 shall be conducted, in the first instance, by the Magistrate Judge, unless the Judge otherwise directs. The initial conference shall be scheduled within 60 days of filing of an initial answer, unless deferred by the Magistrate Judge due to the pendency of a dispositive or other motion.

(2) The Magistrate Judge may conduct such other conferences as are consistent with the circumstances of the particular case and this Rule and may revise any prior scheduling order for good cause.

(3) At each conference each party not appearing pro se shall be represented by an attorney who shall have full authority to bind that party in all pretrial matters.

(4) The Magistrate Judge may, at any time he or she deems appropriate or at the request of a party, conduct a settlement conference. At each such conference attorneys shall ensure that parties are available, either in person or by telephone, and as the Magistrate Judge directs, except that a governmental party may be represented by a knowledgeable delegate.

(5) Conferences shall not be conducted in those civil cases described in L.Civ.R. 72.1(a)(3)(C) unless the Magistrate Judge so directs.

(b) Scheduling and Case Management Orders.

(1) At or after the initial conference, the Magistrate Judge shall, after consultation with counsel, enter a scheduling order which may include, but need not be limited to, the following:

(A) dates by which parties must move to amend pleadings or add new parties;

(B) dates for submission of experts' reports;

(C) dates for completion of fact and expert discovery;

(D) dates for filing of dispositive motions after due consideration whether such motions may be brought at an early stage of proceedings (i.e., before completion of fact discovery or submission of experts' reports);

(E) a pretrial conference date; and

(F) any designation of the case for arbitration, mediation, appointment of a special master or other special procedure.

The scheduling order may further include such limitations on the scope, method or order of discovery as may be warranted by the circumstances of the particular case to avoid duplication, harassment, delay or needless expenditure of costs.

(2) [Deleted by order of September 23, 1997].

(3) The Magistrate Judge shall advise each party of the provisions of L.Civ.R. 73.1(a).

(4) In a civil action arising under 18 U.S.C. §§ 1961–1968, the Judge or Magistrate Judge may require a RICO case statement to be filed and served in the form set forth in Appendix O.

(c) Initial Conferences—L.Civ.R. 201.1 Arbitration Cases. At the initial conference in cases assigned to arbitration pursuant to L.Civ.R. 201.1(c) the Magistrate Judge shall enter a scheduling order as contemplated by L.Civ.R. 16.1(b) except that no pretrial date shall be set. Only an initial conference shall be conducted prior to a demand for trial de novo pursuant to L.Civ.R. 201.1(g), except that the Magistrate Judge may conduct one or more additional conferences if a new party or claim is added, or an unanticipated event occurs affecting the schedule set at the initial conference.

(d) [Deleted by order of September 23, 1997].

(e) Trial Briefs. Trial briefs shall be served upon counsel and delivered to the Court as directed in the pretrial order or otherwise.

(f) Conference to Resolve Case Management Disputes.

(1) Counsel shall confer to resolve any case management dispute. Any such dispute not resolved shall be presented by telephone conference call or letter to the Magistrate Judge. This presentation shall precede any formal motion.

(2) Cases in which a party appears pro se shall not be subject to L.Civ.R. 16.1(f)(1) unless the Magistrate Judge so directs. In such cases case management disputes shall be presented by formal motion consistent with L.Civ.R. 16.1(g).

(g) Case Management—Motions.

(1) Case management motions must be accompanied by an affidavit certifying that the moving party has conferred with the opposing party in a good faith effort to resolve by agreement the issues raised by the motion without the intervention of the Court and that the parties have been unable to reach agreement. The affidavit shall set forth the date and method of communication used in attempting to reach agreement.

(2) L.Civ.R. 7.1 shall apply to case management motions, except that the following schedule shall be followed. No such motion shall be heard unless the appropriate papers are received at the Clerk's office, at the place of allocation of the case, at least 24 days prior to the date noticed for argument. No opposition shall be considered unless appropriate answering papers are received at the Clerk's office, at the place of allocation of the case, and a copy thereof delivered to the Magistrate Judge to whom the motion is assigned, at least 14 days prior to the date originally noticed for argument, unless the Magistrate Judge otherwise directs. No reply papers shall be allowed except with the permission of the Magistrate Judge. Unless oral argument is to be heard under L.Civ.R. 16.1(g)(3), the Magistrate Judge may decide the motion on the basis of the papers received when the deadline for submitting opposition has expired.

(3) No oral argument shall be heard except as permitted expressly by the Magistrate Judge assigned to hear the motion. In the event oral argument is required, the parties shall be notified by the Court. Oral argument may be conducted in open court or by telephone conference, at the discretion of the Magistrate Judge. Any party who believes that a case management motion requires oral argument shall request it in the notice of motion or in response to the notice of motion, and so notify the Court in writing at the time the motion or opposition thereto is filed.

Source: L.Civ.R. 16.1(a)—G.R. 15.A.; L.Civ.R. 16.1(b)—G.R. 15.B.3–6; L.Civ.R. 16.1(c)—G.R. 15.C.; L.Civ.R. 16.1(d)—G.R. 15.D.; L.Civ.R. 16.1(e)—G.R. 27.C.; L.Civ.R. 16.1(f)—G.R. 15.E.2–3; L.Civ.R. 16.1(g)—G.R. 15.F.1, 3–4.

[Effective April 1, 1997, amended September 23, 1997.]

CIV. RULE 24.1. NOTICE OF CLAIM OF UNCONSTITUTIONALITY

(a) If, at any time prior to the trial of an action in which neither the United States nor any officer, agency or employee thereof is a party, a party to the action questions the constitutionality of an act of Congress, such party (to enable the Court to comply with 28 U.S.C. § 2403(a)) shall forthwith, upon the filing of any pleading which raises the question, notify the Judge to whom the action is assigned, in writing, of the existence of said question, identifying: (1) the title and docket number of the action; (2) the statute challenged; and (3) why it is claimed that the statute is unconstitutional. If memoranda have been served discussing the constitutional question, two copies of each memorandum shall be forwarded with the notification.

(b) If, at any time prior to the trial of an action in which neither the State of New Jersey nor any officer, agency or employee thereof is a party, a party to the action questions the constitutionality of any State statute, such party (to enable the Court to comply with 28 U.S.C. § 2403(b)) shall forthwith, upon the filing of any pleading which raises the question, notify the Judge to whom the action is assigned, in writing, of the existence of said question identifying: (1) the title and docket number of the action; (2) the statute challenged; and (3) why it is claimed that the statute is unconstitutional. If memoranda have been served discussing the constitutional question, two copies of each memorandum shall be forwarded with the notification.

Source: G.R. 32.

[Effective April 1, 1997.]

CIV. RULE 24.2. STATUTORY COURT

Where, pursuant to law, an action must be heard by a District Court composed of three Judges, two from this Court and one from the Third Circuit, the procedure to be followed by counsel in filing pleadings and submitting briefs will be as follows:

(a) All pleadings are to be filed with the Clerk in quadruplicate, the original becoming part of the Clerk's file, the three copies to be distributed by the Clerk to the members of the Statutory Court.

(b) Six copies of briefs are to be submitted. Unless otherwise directed by the Court, they are to be delivered to the Clerk for distribution to the members of the Statutory Court.

Source: G.R. 33.

[Effective April 1, 1997.]

CIV. RULE 26.1. DISCOVERY

(a) Discovery—Generally. All parties shall conduct discovery expeditiously and diligently.

(b) Meeting of Parties, Discovery Plans, and Initial Disclosures

(1) The requirements currently codified in Fed. R.Civ.P. 26(a) and (f) pertaining to required disclosures, meetings of parties, and submission of discovery plans, shall apply to all civil cases filed after December 1, 1993 and to all civil cases pending on December 1, 1993 that have not had their initial scheduling conference prior to January 20, 1994; except that these requirements shall not apply to those civil cases described in L.Civ.R. 72.1(a)(3)(C) in which scheduling conferences are not normally held, unless the judicial officer otherwise directs. The judicial officer may modify or suspend these requirements in a case for good cause.

(2) The initial meeting of parties as required in Fed.R.Civ.P. 26(f) shall be convened at least 21 days before the initial scheduling conference, and the proposed discovery plan under Fed.R.Civ.P. 26(f)(1)-(4) shall be generated at that meeting and delivered to the Magistrate Judge within 14 days after the meeting of parties. The parties shall submit their Fed.R.Civ.P. 26(f) discovery plan containing the parties' views and proposals regarding the following:

(a) Any changes in timing, form, or requirements of mandatory disclosures under Fed. R.Civ.P. 26(a);

(b) The date on which mandatory disclosures were or will be made;

(c) The anticipated substantive scope of discovery, including both discovery relevant to the claims and defenses and discovery relevant to the subject matter of the dispute;

(d) Whether any party will likely request or produce computer-based or other digital information, and if so, the parties' discussions of the issues listed under the Duty to Meet and Confer in L.Civ.R. 26.1(d)(3) below;

(e) Date by which discovery should be completed;

(f) Any needed change s in limitations imposed by the Federal Rules of Civil Procedure, local rule, or standing order;

(g) Any orders, such as data preservation orders, protective orders, etc., which should be entered;

(h) Proposed deadline for joining other parties and amending the pleadings;

(i) Proposed deadline for completing discovery;

(j) Propose d dates for filing motions and for trial;

(k) Whether the case is one which might be resolved in whole or in part by voluntary arbitration (pursuant to L.Civ.R. 201.1 or otherwise), mediation (pursuant to L.Civ.R. 301.1 or otherwise), appointment of a special master or other special procedure.

The parties shall make their initial disclosures under Fed.R.Civ.P. 26(a)(1) within 10 days after the initial meeting of the parties, unless otherwise stipulated or directed by the Court. Such discovery plans and disclosures shall not be filed with the Clerk.

(c) Discovery Materials

(1) Initial and expert disclosure materials under Fed.R.Civ.P. 26(a)(1) and 26(a)(2), transcripts of depositions, interrogatories and answers thereto, requests for production of documents or to permit entry onto land and responses thereto, and requests for admissions and answers thereto shall not be filed until used in a proceeding or upon order of the

Court. However, all such papers must be served on other counsel or parties entitled thereto under Fed. R.Civ.P. 5 and 26(a)(4).

(2) Pretrial disclosure materials under Fed. R.Civ.P. 26(a)(3) shall be incorporated by reference into the order entered after any final pretrial conference under Fed.R.Civ.P. 16(d).

(3) In those instances when such discovery materials are properly filed, the Clerk shall place them in the open case file unless otherwise ordered.

(4) The party obtaining any material through discovery is responsible for its preservation and delivery to the Court if needed or ordered. It shall be the duty of the party taking a deposition to make certain that the officer before whom it was taken has delivered it to that party for preservation and to the Court as required by Fed.R.Civ.P. 30(f)(1) if needed or so ordered.

(d) Discovery of Digital Information Including Computer-Based Information

(1) Duty to Investigate and Disclose. Prior to a Fed.R.Civ.P. 26(f) conference, counsel shall review with the client the client's information management systems including computer-based and other digital systems, in order to understand how information is stored and how it can be retrieved. To determine what must be disclosed pursuant to Fed.R.Civ.P. 26(a)(1), counsel shall further review with the client the client's information files, including currently maintained computer files as well as historical, archival, back-up, and legacy computer files, whether in current or historic media or formats, such as digital evidence which may be used to support claims or defenses. Counsel shall also identify a person or persons with knowledge about the client's information management systems, including computer-based and other digital systems, with the ability to facilitate, through counsel, reasonably anticipated discovery.

(2) Duty to Notify. A party seeking discovery of computer-based or other digital information shall notify the opposing party as soon as possible, but no later than the Fed.R.Civ.P. 26(f) conference, and identify as clearly as possible the categories of information which may be sought. A party may supplement its request for computer-based and other digital information as soon as possible upon receipt of new information relating to digital evidence.

(3) Duty to Meet and Confer. During the Fed. R.Civ.P. 26(f) conference, the parties shall confer and attempt to agree on computer-based and other digital discovery matters, including the following:

(a) Preservation and production of digital information; procedures to deal with inadvertent production of privileged information; whether restoration of deleted digital information may be necessary; whether back up or historic legacy data is within the scope of discovery; and the media, format, and procedures for producing digital information;

(b) Who will bear the costs of preservation, production, and restoration (if necessary) of any digital discovery.

(e) Protective Orders. Procedures for discovery-related protective orders are set forth in L.Civ.R. 5.3.

Source: L.Civ.R. 26.1(a)—G.R. 15.E.1; L.Civ.R. 26.1(b)—G.R. 15.B.1–2; L.Civ.R. 26.1(c)—G.R. 15.G.

[Effective April 1, 1997; amended effective March 14, 2001; October 6, 2003; February 24, 2005.]

CIV. RULE 27.1. DEPOSITIONS FOR USE IN A FOREIGN COUNTRY

(a) A person desiring to take the deposition of a witness who resides or may be found within the District for use in a judicial proceeding pending in a foreign country may apply ex parte to the Court for an appropriate order. If the deposition is to be taken upon written interrogatories, a copy of the interrogatories shall be annexed to the application. If the court of the foreign country has appointed a person to take the deposition, the order shall designate that person commissioner unless there be good cause for withholding such designation. If no such appointment has been made and designation of a commissioner is requested, the order shall designate a person authorized to administer oaths by the laws of the United States or of the State of New Jersey.

(b) The entry of such an order is sufficient authorization for the issuance by the Clerk of subpoenas for the persons named or described therein. Wherever applicable, the Federal Rules of Civil Procedure, including provisions for punishment of contempt for disobeying a subpoena, shall govern the taking of such depositions.

Source: L.Civ.R. 27.1(a)—G.R. 45.A; L.Civ.R. 27.1(b)—G.R. 45.B.

[Effective April 1, 1997.]

CIV. RULE 28.1. LETTERS ROGATORY

A party seeking execution of Letters Rogatory shall comply with the provisions of the Hague Convention, 28 U.S.C. § 1781 et seq.

Source: G.R. 45.C.

[Effective April 1, 1997.]

CIV. RULE 33.1. INTERROGATORIES

(a) Interrogatories shall be so arranged that after each separate question or request, there shall appear a blank space reasonably calculated to enable the answering party to have the answer to the interrogatory typed in. Each question shall be answered separately in the space allowed. If the space allowed shall not be sufficient for the answer, the answering party may insert additional pages or retyped pages repeating each question in full, followed by the answer in such manner that the final document shall have each interrogatory immediately succeeded by the separate answer thereto.

(b) If the person who verifies the answers to interrogatories does not have personal knowledge of the information contained in the answers, that person shall, for each answer not verified by personal knowledge, identify the person or persons from whom the information was obtained or, if the source of the information is documentary, provide a full description including the location thereof.

(c) Where a claim of privilege is asserted in responding or objecting to any discovery requested in interrogatories and information is not provided on the basis of such assertion, the party asserting the privilege shall in the response or objection identify the nature of the privilege (including work product) which is being claimed and if the privilege is being asserted in connection with a claim or defense governed by state law, set forth the state privilege rule being invoked. When any privilege is claimed, the party asserting it shall indicate, as to the information requested, whether (a) any documents exist, or (b) any oral communications took place.

Source: L.Civ.R. 33.1(a)—G.R. 16.A.; L.Civ.R. 33.1(b)—G.R. 16.B.; L.Civ.R. 33.1(c)—G.R. 16.C.

[Effective April 1, 1997.]

CIV. RULE 34.1. REQUESTS FOR PRODUCTION OF DOCUMENTS

Where a claim of privilege is asserted in responding or objecting to any discovery requested in requests for documents, and information is not provided on the basis of such assertion, the party asserting the privilege shall in the response or objection identify the nature of the privilege (including work product) which is being claimed and if the privilege is being asserted in connection with a claim or defense governed by state law, set forth the state privilege rule being invoked. When any privilege is claimed, the party asserting it shall indicate, as to the information requested, whether any such documents exist.

Source: G.R. 16.A.

[Effective April 1, 1997.]

CIV. RULE 36.1. REQUESTS FOR ADMISSION

(a) Requests for admission shall be so arranged that after each separate request, there shall appear a blank space reasonably calculated to enable the answering party to have the answer to the request for admission typed in. Each request shall be answered separately in the space allowed. If the space allowed shall not be sufficient for the answer, the answering party may insert additional pages or retyped pages repeating each request for admission in full, followed by the answer in such manner that the final document shall have each request for admission immediately succeeded by the separate answer thereto.

(b) Where a claim of privilege is asserted in responding or objecting to any requests for admission, and information is not provided on the basis of such assertion, the party asserting the privilege shall in the response or objection identify the nature of the privilege (including work product) which is being claimed and if the privilege is being asserted in connection with a claim or defense governed by state law, set forth the state privilege rule being invoked. When any privilege is claimed, the party asserting it shall indicate, as to the information requested, whether (a) any documents exist, or (b) any oral communications took place.

Source: L.Civ.R. 36.1(a)—G.R. 16.A.; L.Civ.R. 36.1(b)—G.R. 16.B.

[Effective April 1, 1997.]

CIV. RULE 37.1. DISCOVERY MOTIONS

(a) Conference to Resolve Disputes.

(1) Counsel shall confer to resolve any discovery dispute. Any such dispute not resolved shall be presented by telephone conference call or letter to the Magistrate Judge. This presentation shall precede any formal motion.

(2) Cases in which a party appears pro se shall not be subject to L.Civ.R. 37.1(a)(1) unless the Magistrate Judge so directs. In such cases discovery disputes shall be presented by formal motion consistent with L.Civ.R. 37.1(b).

(b) Discovery Motions.

(1) Discovery motions must be accompanied by an affidavit certifying that the moving party has conferred with the opposing party in a good faith effort to resolve by agreement the issues raised by the motion without the intervention of the Court and that the parties have been unable to reach agreement. The affidavit shall set forth the date and method of communication used in attempting to reach agreement.

(2) Discovery motions shall have annexed thereto copies of only those pertinent portions of depositions, interrogatories, demands for admission and responses, etc., which are the subject matter of the motion.

(3) L.Civ.R. 7.1 shall apply to discovery motions, except that the following schedule shall be followed. No such motion shall be heard unless the appropriate

papers are received at the Clerk's office, at the place of allocation of the case, at least 24 days prior to the date noticed for argument. No opposition shall be considered unless appropriate answering papers are received at the Clerk's office, at the place of allocation of the case, and a copy thereof delivered to the Magistrate Judge to whom the motion is assigned, at least 14 days prior to the date originally noticed for argument, unless the Magistrate Judge otherwise directs. No reply papers shall be allowed except with the permission of the Magistrate Judge. Unless oral argument is to be heard under L.Civ.R. 37.1(b)(4), the Magistrate Judge may decide the motion on the basis of the papers received when the deadline for submitting opposition has expired.

(4) No oral argument shall be heard except as permitted expressly by the Magistrate Judge assigned to hear the motion. In the event oral argument is required, the parties shall be notified by the Court. Oral argument may be conducted in open court or by telephone conference, at the discretion of the Magistrate Judge. Any party who believes that a discovery motion requires oral argument shall request it in the notice of motion or in response to the notice of motion, and so notify the Court in writing at the time the motion or opposition thereto is filed.

Source: L.Civ.R. 37.1(a)—G.R. 15.E.2–3; L.Civ.R. 37.1(b)—G.R. 15.F.

[Effective April 1, 1997.]

CIV. RULE 37.2. APPLICATIONS FOR FED.R.CIV.P. 37 SANCTIONS

All applications for sanctions pursuant to Fed. R.Civ.P. 37 shall be filed with the Clerk prior to the entry of final judgment notwithstanding the provisions of any other Rule of this Court.

Source: G.R. 12.L.

[Effective April 1, 1997.]

CIV. RULE 38.1. JURY DEMAND

If a demand for jury trial under Fed.R.Civ.P. 38(b) is endorsed upon a pleading, the title of the pleading shall include the words "and Demand for Jury Trial" or the equivalent.

Source: G.R. 8.F.

[Effective April 1, 1997.]

CIV. RULE 40.1 ALLOCATION AND ASSIGNMENT OF CASES

(a) Allocation. Each civil case shall be allocated by the Clerk of the Court to Camden, Newark or Trenton at the time it is commenced. The Clerk shall consider the residence of the defendant, the convenience of litigants, counsel and witnesses, and the place where the cause of action arose. The vicinage allocated shall be the location of trial and of all proceedings in the case, unless changed by order of the Court.

(b) Assignment.

(1) After allocation, and subject to the supervision of the Chief Judge, each case shall be assigned forthwith to a Judge by the Clerk or the Deputy charged with such duty.

(2) If it appears that any matter requires immediate attention and the Judge to whom an action has been or would be assigned is not or will not be available, the Clerk or Deputy charged with such duty, under direction of the Chief Judge, shall assign the matter either permanently or temporarily to an available Judge.

(c) Related Cases. When a civil action: (1) relates to any property included in a case already pending in this Court; (2) grows out of the same transaction as any case already pending in this Court; or (3) involves the validity or infringement of any patent, copyright or trademark which is involved in a case already pending in this Court, counsel shall at the time of filing the action inform the Clerk of such fact. Whenever possible, such action shall be assigned to the same Judge to whom the pending related action is assigned.

(d) Notice and Objection. Promptly after allocation and assignment of a civil case, the Clerk shall notify both the parties or their counsel and the Judge of such allocation and assignment. Objections to either the allocation or the assignment of a civil case shall be made before the Chief Judge, on notice to opposing counsel and to the Judge to whom the case has been assigned.

(e) Reallocation and Reassignment. Disposition of any objections submitted under paragraph (d) above, and any other reallocation or reassignment of any case, shall be upon order of the Chief Judge.

Source: L.Civ.R. 40.1(a)—G.R. 11.A.; L.Civ.R. 40.1(b)—G.R. 11.B.; L.Civ.R. 40.1(c)—G.R. 11.C.; L.Civ.R. 40.1(d)—G.R. 11.D.; L.Civ.R. 40.1(e)—G.R. 11.F.

[Effective April 1, 1997; amended effective March 3, 1998.]

CIV. RULE 41.1. DISMISSAL OF INACTIVE CASES

(a) Civil cases, other than bankruptcy matters, which have been pending in the Court for more than 120 days without any proceedings having been taken therein must be dismissed for lack of prosecution by the Court (1) on its own motion, or (2) on notice from the Clerk to all parties who have appeared, unless good cause is shown with the filing of an affidavit from counsel of record or the unrepresented party. Notice shall be provided by the Clerk of either action contemplated above under sub-paragraphs (1) and (2) to counsel, their client(s) and/or unrepresented persons who have appeared.

(b) When a case has been settled, counsel shall promptly notify the Clerk and the Court, thereafter confirming the same in writing. Within 15 days of such notification, counsel shall file all papers necessary to terminate the case. Upon failure of counsel to do so, the Clerk shall prepare an order for submission to the Court dismissing the action, without costs, and without prejudice to the right to reopen the action within 60 days upon good cause shown if the settlement is not consummated.

Source: G.R. 30.

[Effective April 1, 1997.]

CIV. RULE 42.1. CONSOLIDATION OF CASES

A motion to consolidate two or more civil cases pending upon the docket of the Court shall be filed in the cases bearing the earliest docket number. That motion shall be adjudicated by the Judge to whom that case is assigned. A copy of the moving papers shall be served upon all parties in each case to which the consolidation motion applies. For each such case other than that in which the motion for consolidation is filed, counsel for the moving party shall submit to the Clerk for docketing a copy of the cover letter accompanying the filing of the motion.

Source: G.R. 30.

[Adopted effective March 3, 1998.]

CIV. RULE 44.1. SEAL

The seal of this Court shall consist of the upward-flying eagle, front presentation, with wings and legs outstretched, and the words, "United States District Court for the District of New Jersey," in the outer rim surrounding same.

Source: G.R. 2.

[Effective April 1, 1997.]

CIV. RULE 47.1. PETIT JURORS

(a) The selection, qualification, summoning, exemption or excuse from service of petit jurors shall be governed by the Plan of Implementation adopted by the Court pursuant to 28 U.S.C. § 1861, et seq. The Plan is available for inspection at the office of the Clerk.

(b) In any case where each side is entitled to an equal number of peremptory challenges, these challenges shall alternate one by one, with the plaintiff in a civil case exercising the first challenge.

(c) In any case where there is more than one defendant, in the event the Court allows defendants additional peremptory challenges, the order of challenge will be established by the Court.

(d) The passing of a peremptory challenge by any party shall not constitute a waiver of the right thereafter to exercise the same against any juror, unless all parties pass successive challenges.

(e) No attorney or party to an action shall personally or through any investigator or other person acting for such attorney or party, directly or indirectly interview, examine or question any juror, relative, friend or associate thereof during the pendency of the trial or with respect to the deliberations or verdict of the jury in any action, except on leave of Court granted upon good cause shown.

Source: L.Civ.R. 47.1(a)—G.R. 19.A.; L.Civ.R. 47.1(b)—G.R. 20.A.; L.Civ.R. 47.1(c)—G.R. 20.C.; L.Civ.R. 47.1(d)—G.R. 20.E.; L.Civ.R. 47.1(e)-G.R. 19.B.

[Effective April 1, 1997.]

CIV. RULE 47.2. ASSESSMENT OF JURY COSTS

All counsel in civil cases must seriously discuss the possibility of settlement a reasonable time prior to trial. The trial Judge may, in his or her discretion, assess any party or attorney with the costs of jury attendance if a case is settled after the jury has been summoned or during the trial, the amount to be paid to the Clerk. For the purpose of interpreting this paragraph, a jury is considered summoned for trial as of noon of the business day prior to the designated date of the trial.

Source: G.R. 20.G.

[Effective April 1, 1997.]

CIV. RULE 48.1. CIVIL JURY

In all civil jury actions, except as otherwise expressly required by law, the jury shall consist of not fewer than six and not more than 12 members, and all jurors shall participate in the verdict to the extent authorized by Fed.R.Civ.P. 48.

Source: G.R. 20.F.

[Effective April 1, 1997.]

CIV. RULE 48.2. TAKING OF CIVIL VERDICT

In all civil jury cases the Court need not call any party or attorney, nor need any party be present or represented when the jury returns into court with its verdict. In all cases, unless the contrary affirmatively appears of record, it will be presumed that the parties either were present or, by their voluntary absence, waived their presence.

Source: G.R. 21.

[Effective April 1, 1997.]

CIV. RULE 52.1. ORAL OPINIONS

When an oral opinion is given in lieu of a written opinion and is transcribed, the reporter shall submit it to the Judge for revision before it is filed.

Source: G.R. 28.

[Effective April 1, 1997.]

CIV. RULE 54.1. COSTS

(a) Within 30 days after the entry of a judgment allowing costs, or within 30 days of the filing of an order dispositive of the last of any timely-filed post-trial motions, whether or not an appeal has been filed, the prevailing party shall serve on the attorney for the adverse party and file with the Clerk a Bill of Costs and Disbursements, together with a notice of motion when application will be made to the Clerk to tax the same.

(b) Such Bill of Costs shall precisely set forth each item thereof, so that the nature of the charge can be readily understood, and shall be verified by the attorney for the applicant, stating that (1) the items are correct, (2) the services were actually and necessarily performed, and (3) the disbursements were necessarily incurred in the action or proceeding. Counsel shall append to the verified Bill of Costs copies of all invoices in support of the request for each item.

(c) Counsel are directed to review 28 U.S.C. § 1927 regarding counsel's liability for excessive costs.

(d) The notice of motion shall specify the hour and date when application to the Clerk to tax the costs will be made, which shall not be less than one nor more than three days from the date of the notice if personal service is made and, if service is made by mail, not less than four nor more than six days from the date the notice is deposited in the mail.

(e) Upon failure of the prevailing party to comply with this Rule, all costs shall be waived.

(f) At or before the hearing the adverse party may file specific objections to claimed items of cost with a statement of the grounds for objection, supported by affidavits or other evidence.

(g) Unless otherwise ordered by the Court, the Clerk shall observe the following general rules in taxing costs:

(1) The fees of witnesses for actual and proper attendance shall be allowed, whether such attendance was voluntary or procured by subpoena. The rates for witness fees, mileage and subsistence are fixed by statute (see 28 U.S.C. § 1821). Witness fees and subsistence are taxable only for the reasonable period during which the witness was within the District. Subsistence to the witness under 28 U.S.C. § 1821 is allowable if the distance from the courthouse to the residence of the witness is such that mileage fees would be greater than subsistence fees if the witness were to return to his or her residence from day to day.

(2) The reasonable fee of a competent interpreter is taxable if the fee of the witness involved is taxable. Fees, salaries, expenses and costs of an interpreter are taxable as provided by 28 U.S.C. §§ 1827 and 1828. Fees for translation of documents are taxable only if those documents are received in evidence or filed with the Clerk for use in a proceeding.

(3) Witness fees shall not be allowed to parties to an action, but officers and employees of a party shall not be considered to be parties solely because of such relationship.

(4) Where costs are taxed in favor of multiple parties there shall be no apportionment of costs by the Clerk.

(5) In actions in which a counsel fee is allowed by the Court, such fee shall be in lieu of the statutory attorney's docket fee.

(6) The cost of a reporter's transcript is allowable only (A) when specifically requested by the Judge, master, or examiner, or (B) when it is of a statement by the Judge to be reduced to a formal order, or (C) if required for the record on appeal. Mere acceptance by the Court of a submitted transcript does not constitute a request. Copies of transcripts for an attorney's own use are not taxable in the absence of a prior order of the Court. All other transcripts of hearings, pretrials and trials will be considered by the Clerk to be for the convenience of the attorney and not taxable as costs.

(7) In taxing costs, the Clerk shall allow all or part of the fees and charges incurred in the taking and transcribing of depositions used at the trial under Fed.R.Civ.P. 32. Fees and charges for the taking and transcribing of any other deposition shall not be taxed as costs unless the Court otherwise orders. Counsel's fees, expenses in arranging for taking a deposition and attending the taking of a deposition are not taxable, except as provided either by statute or by the Federal Rules of Civil Procedure. Fees for the witness at the taking of a deposition are taxable at the same rate as for attendance at trial. (See L.Civ.R. 54.1(g)(1).) The witness need not be under subpoena.

(8) The reasonable premiums or expenses paid on undertakings, bonds or security stipulations shall be allowed where furnished by reason of express requirement of the law or a rule of court, by an order of the Court, or where necessarily required to enable a party to receive or preserve some right accorded the party in the action or proceeding.

(9) The fees for exemplification and copies of papers are taxable when (A) the documents are admitted into evidence or necessarily attached to a document required to be filed and served in support of a dispositive motion, and (B) they are in lieu of originals which are not introduced at the request of opposing counsel. The cost of copies submitted in lieu of originals because of convenience to offering counsel or his or her client is not taxable. The cost of copies obtained for counsel's own use is not taxable.

(10) The reasonable expense of preparing visual aids including, but not limited to, maps, charts, photographs, motion pictures and kindred material, is taxable as costs when such visual aids are admitted into evidence. It is advisable to obtain a court order at a pretrial conference before incurring the expense of preparation of such visual aids. Expenses incurred in the preparation of models are not taxable as costs even though the models are admitted into evidence without obtaining a court order before incurring the expense.

(h) A dissatisfied party may appeal to the Court upon written notice of motion served within five days of the Clerk's action, as provided in Fed.R.Civ.P. 54(d).

Source: G.R. 23.

[Effective April 1, 1997.]

CIV. RULE 54.2. COMPENSATION FOR SERVICES RENDERED AND REIMBURSEMENT OF EXPENSES

(a) Affidavits: Content. In all actions in which a counsel fee is allowed by the Court or permitted by statute, an attorney seeking compensation for services or reimbursement of necessary expenses shall file with the Court an affidavit within 30 days of the entry of judgment or order, unless extended by the Court, setting forth the following:

(1) the nature of the services rendered, the amount of the estate or fund in court, if any, the responsibility assumed, the results obtained, any particular novelty or difficulty about the matter, and other factors pertinent to the evaluation of the services rendered;

(2) a record of the dates of services rendered;

(3) a description of the services rendered on each of such dates by each person of that firm including the identity of the person rendering the service and a brief description of that person's professional experience;

(4) the time spent in the rendering of each of such services; and

(5) the normal billing rate for each of said persons for the type of work performed.

The time spent by each individual performing services shall be totalled at the end of the affidavit. Computerized time sheets, to the extent that they reflect the above, may be utilized and attached to any such affidavit showing the time units expended.

Reimbursement for actual, not estimated, expenses may be granted if properly itemized.

(b) Affidavits: Fee Agreements. Applications for the allowance of counsel fees shall include an affidavit describing all fee agreements and setting forth both the amount billed to the client for fees and disbursements and the amount paid.

(c) Exceptions Authorized. In appropriate circumstances, including but not limited to those where counsel fees are sought as sanctions in connection with discovery and other pretrial motions, the Judge or Magistrate Judge to whom the application is directed may order that any one or more of the items enumerated in L.Civ.R. 54.2(a) and (b) will not be required.

(d) Application for Attorney's Fees and Petitions for Leave to Appeal Determination of Attorney's Fees Under the Provisions of the Equal Access to Justice Act.

(1) A party applying for an award of attorney's fees and expenses under 28 U.S.C. § 2412(d)(1)(B), as amended, in actions filed prior to October 1, 1984, shall submit the required information on the applicable form, which is available at the Clerk's office. A party applying for fees and expenses shall identify the specific position of the Government which the party alleges was not substantially justified.

(2)(A) A petition for leave to appeal an agency fee determination, pursuant to 5 U.S.C. § 504(c)(2), shall be filed with the Clerk within 30 days after the entry of the agency's order with proof of service on all other parties to the agency's proceedings.

(B) The petition shall contain a copy of the order to be reviewed and any findings of fact, conclusions of law and opinion relating thereto, a statement of the facts necessary to an understanding of the petition, and a memorandum showing why the petition for permission to appeal should be granted. An answer shall be filed within 30 days after service of the petition, together with a reply memorandum. The application and any answer shall be submitted without further briefing and oral argument unless otherwise ordered.

(C) Appeals to review fee determinations otherwise contemplated by the Equal Access to Justice Act shall be filed pursuant to the applicable statutes and these Rules.

Source: G.R. 46.

[Effective April 1, 1997.]

CIV. RULE 54.3. PREPAYMENT OF CLERK'S AND MARSHAL'S FEES

(a) Except as otherwise directed by the Court, the Clerk shall not be required to enter any suit, file any paper, issue any process or render any other service for which a fee is prescribed by statute or by the Judicial Conference of the United States, nor shall the Marshal be required to serve the same or perform any service, unless the fee therefor is paid in advance. The Clerk shall receive any such papers in accordance with L.Civ.R. 5.1(f).

(b) In all actions in which the fees of the Clerk and Marshal are not required by law to be paid in advance, and in which a poor suitor or a seaman prevails either by judgment or settlement, no dismissal or satisfaction of judgment shall be filed or entered until all of the fees of the Clerk and Marshal are paid.

Source: G.R. 10.

[Effective April 1, 1997.]

CIV. RULE 56.1. SUMMARY JUDGMENT MOTIONS

On motions for summary judgment, each side shall furnish a statement which sets forth material facts as to which there exists or does not exist a genuine issue. Briefs submitted upon such motions regarding review of Social Security matters shall be governed by L.Civ.R. 9.1.

Source: G.R. 12.G.

[Effective April 1, 1997.]

CIV. RULE 58.1. ENTRY OF JUDGMENTS AND ORDERS

(a) In all cases in which the Clerk is required to prepare the judgment pursuant to Fed.R.Civ.P. 58(1), it shall be submitted to the Court for signature and entered forthwith.

(b) In all cases contemplated by Fed.R.Civ.P. 58(2) and when the Court makes any judgment as defined in Fed.R.Civ.P. 54(a), the prevailing party shall, within five days after determination, submit a judgment or order to the Court on notice to his or her adversary. Unless the Court otherwise directs, if no specific objection to that judgment or order with reasons therefor is received from the adversary within seven days of receipt of the prevailing party's judgment or order, the judgment or order may be signed by the Court. If such an objection is made, the matter may be listed for hearing at the discretion of the Court.

Source: G.R. 22.

[Effective April 1, 1997.]

CIV. RULE 65.1. APPLICATIONS FOR EMERGENCY RELIEF

(a) Any party may apply for an order requiring an adverse party to show cause why a preliminary injunction should not issue, upon the filing of a verified complaint or verified counterclaim or by affidavit during the pendency of the action. No order to show cause to bring on a matter for hearing will be granted except on a clear and specific showing by affidavit or verified pleading of good and sufficient reasons why a procedure other than by notice of motion is necessary. An order to show cause which is issued at the beginning of the action may not, however, serve as a substitute for a summons which shall issue in accordance with Fed.R.Civ.P. 4. The order to show cause may include temporary restraints only under the conditions set forth in Fed.R.Civ.P. 65(b).

(b) Applications for orders to show cause, and for consent and ex parte orders, shall be made by delivering the proposed orders and supporting papers to the Clerk, who shall promptly deliver each application to the Judge to whom the case has been assigned. No application will be entertained by a Judge in any action until the action has been filed, allocated and assigned.

(c) The order shall provide for service upon the opposing party of the order together with all supporting papers, as specified by the Court.

(d) All applications for provisional remedies or a writ of habeas corpus or any other emergency relief may be made at any time to the Judge to whom the case has been assigned.

Source: L.Civ.R. 65.1(a)—G.R. 12.A., paragraph 1; L.Civ.R. 65.1(b), sentence 1—G.R. 12.A. (paragraph 2); L.Civ.R. 65.1(b), sentence 2—G.R. 12.E.; L.Civ.R. 65.1(c)—G.R. 12.A., paragraph 3; L.Civ.R. 65.1(d)—G.R. 12.B.

[Effective April 1, 1997.]

CIV. RULE 65.1.1. SECURITY AND SURETIES

(a) Deposit in Lieu of Surety. In lieu of surety in any case there may be deposited with the Clerk lawful United States currency, certificates of deposit issued by a bank licensed to do business in the United States, negotiable bonds approved by the Court or notes of the United States. If certificates of deposit, negotiable bonds or notes are deposited, the depositor shall execute the agreement required by 31 U.S.C. § 9303, authorizing the Clerk to collect or sell the bonds or notes in the event of default. In the case of certificates of deposit, the depositor shall notify the banking institution that the depositor's rights in the certificate of deposit have been assigned to the Clerk, United States District Court, and the banking institution shall acknowledge such notification to the Clerk. Unless ordered otherwise, the Clerk automatically shall reinvest the certificate of deposit at the maturity date at the then-prevailing rate of interest.

(b) Attorney Shall Not Provide Surety. No attorney shall tender his or her own funds or otherwise personally serve as surety for costs in any suit pending in the Court, except by special leave of the Court.

Source: L.Civ.R. 65.1.1(a)—G.R. 35.A.1; L.Civ.R. 65.1.1(b)—G.R. 35.D.

[Effective April 1, 1997.]

CIV. RULE 66.1. RECEIVERSHIPS

(a) Pursuant to Fed.R.Civ.P. 66, this Rule is promulgated for the administration of estates by receivers or similar officers appointed by the Court. Other than in administration of estates, any civil action in which the appointment of a receiver or similar officer is sought, or which is brought by or against such an officer, is to be governed by the Federal Rules of Civil Procedure and by these Rules.

(b) The appointment or discharge of a receiver appointed either ex parte or pending a final hearing shall, as nearly as possible, follow procedures set forth in Fed.R.Civ.P. 65. The Court may require any receiver appointed to furnish a bond in such amount as deemed appropriate.

(c) Upon appointment of a custodial or statutory receiver or similar officer, the Court shall designate one or more banking institutions as depositories in which shall be deposited, until the further order of the Court, all funds obtained by the receiver. A certified copy of the order shall be filed with each depository. Funds so deposited shall be withdrawn only by check or warrant, serially numbered, signed by the receiver. Each check or warrant shall have written on its face the abbreviated title and docket number of the case and a brief statement of the purpose for the disbursement. The receiver shall keep a record of all checks drawn and shall be responsible for determining the propriety of each disbursement.

(d) Every receiver appointed pursuant to this Rule shall within 60 days after appointment file with the Clerk an inventory of the entire estate committed to his or her care, and of the manner in which funds of the estate are invested or deposited. If authorized to continue the operation of a business the receiver shall, on or before the 15th day of every month following appointment, file with the Clerk a report and summary of such operation based on sound accounting principles, showing all accruals and containing a statement of income and of profit and loss for the preceding month. If not authorized to continue the operation of a business the receiver shall, on or before the 15th day of the month following appointment and every three months thereafter (or more frequently if ordered by the Court), file with the Clerk a schedule of receipts and disbursements for such period and a statement from each depository showing the balance on hand.

(e) In settling the final account, every receiver shall be charged with the property shown in the initial inventory and with all amounts collected in addition thereto and shall state the expenditures, other credits and balance on hand. The receiver shall set forth the manner in which such balance is invested and all changes in the assets with which he or she is charged which have accrued during the period covered by the account.

(f) When an order is entered approving the final account of and discharging a receiver, the Court may authorize the destruction or other disposition of the books, papers and records of the business or property for which the receiver acted and may fix a date after which the receiver may destroy the financial papers and records on hand relating to his or her administration. No destruction shall be authorized by order unless it appears that notice of the application for such an order has been given to all parties in interest and to the Commissioner of IRS, Washington, D.C.; the District Director of IRS, Newark, N.J.; United States Attorney, Newark, N.J.; the State of New Jersey, Division of Taxation, Trenton, N.J.; and the Attorney General for the State of New Jersey, Trenton, N.J.

(g) No receiver may employ an attorney, counsel or accountant except upon order of the Court supported by an affidavit of the receiver setting forth the necessity for the employment and an affidavit of the proposed attorney, counsel or accountant claiming no interest in the suit or any of the parties thereto in any way which would disqualify that person from serving the receiver in good faith as a fiduciary for all of the beneficial owners and creditors of the estate.

(h) In fixing the compensation of a receiver, attorney, accountant, auctioneer or other officer, the Court shall consider the value of the actual services rendered and the pain, trouble and risk incurred by them in the discharge of their duties relative to the estate and shall be guided by the standards fixed for compensation of such officers in connection with proceedings under the Bankruptcy Code.

Source: G.R. 34.

[Effective April 1, 1997.]

CIV. RULE 67.1. DEPOSIT IN COURT

(a) Deposit in Court Pursuant to Fed.R.Civ.P. 67.

(1) *Receipt of Funds.*

(A) No money shall be sent to the Court or its officers for deposit into the Court's Registry without a court order by the Judge assigned to the case.

(B) Unless otherwise directed, all registry funds ordered to be paid into Court or received by its officers in any case pending or adjudicated shall be deposited with the Treasurer of the United States in the name and to the credit of this Court pursuant to 28 U.S.C. § 2041 through depositories designated by the Treasury to accept such deposit on its behalf.

(C) The party or attorney making the deposit or transferring funds to the Court's Registry shall personally serve the order permitting the deposit or transfer on the Clerk, the Chief Deputy Clerk or the Chief Financial Deputy Clerk. Failure to personally serve a copy of the order to invest shall release the Clerk and any Deputy Clerk from any liability for the loss of interest which could have been earned on the funds.

(2) *Orders Directing Investment of Registry Funds by Clerk.*

(A) Where, by stipulation of the parties and approval of the Court, funds on deposit with the Court are to be placed in some interest-bearing form, the Court Registry Investment System (C.R.I.S.) administered through the United States District Court for the Southern District of Texas shall be the investment mechanism authorized. (See Form of Required Order at Appendix D).

(B) Funds deposited in each case under C.R.I.S. will be "pooled" together with those on deposit with the Treasury to the credit of other courts in the C.R.I.S. and used to purchase Treasury Securities which will be held at the Federal Reserve Bank of Dallas/Houston Branch, in a safekeeping, interest-bearing account in the name and to the credit of the Clerk of the United States District Court for the Southern District of Texas, hereby designated Custodian for the C.R.I.S. for this District Court.

(C) An account for each case will be established in the C.R.I.S. titled in the name of the case giving rise to the investment in the system. Income received from fund investments will be distributed to each case based on the ratio which each account's principal and income has to the aggregate principal and income total in the fund each week. Weekly reports showing the income earned and the principal amounts contributed in each case will be prepared and distributed to each court participating in C.R.I.S. and made available to counsel on request.

(3) *Registry Investment Fee.*

(A) The custodian shall deduct a miscellaneous schedule fee for the handling of those registry funds invested in interest-bearing accounts, as authorized by the Judicial Conference of the United States and by Standing Order of this Court dated June 30, 1989, as amended November 30, 1990, of 10% of the income earned on an account and any subsequent deposit of new principal while invested in the C.R.I.S.

(B) No additional fee shall be assessed with respect to investments for which a fee has already been deducted prior to the establishment of C.R.I.S. in this District.

(4) *Transition from Former Investment Procedure.*

(A) The Clerk is directed to develop a systematic method of redemption of all existing investments and their transfer to C.R.I.S.

(B) Parties not wishing to transfer existing investment instruments into C.R.I.S. may seek leave to transfer them to the litigants or their designees on motion and approval by order of the Judge assigned to a specific case.

(b) Orders Relating to the Disbursement of Court Funds.

(1) Before any proposed order for disbursement of monies from the Registry of the Court is submitted to or considered by a Judge, the order first shall be approved as to form and content by the Clerk and contain the Clerk's endorsement thereon.

(2) The Clerk will not calculate interest on court registry funds invested in interest bearing accounts whenever accrued interest is to be apportioned between parties or partial payments are to be made from the investment. Counsel of record for a prevailing party(ies) shall consult with the Clerk to ascertain the amount of interest accrued to date before applying (preferably by consent) to the Court for an order to disburse funds, including interest, from the Court's Registry.

(3) The Clerk shall deduct a miscellaneous schedule fee for the handling of those registry funds invested in interest bearing accounts, as authorized by the Judicial Conference of the United States and by Standing Order of this Court dated June 30, 1989, as amended November 30, 1990, of 10% of the income earned on an account and any subsequent deposit of new principal while invested in the Court's Registry.

(4) All disbursement orders shall provide for the signature of the Clerk in addition to that of the Judge, and shall state the following: "I recommend approval of the above order and declare that no lien or other claim against monies deposited in the Registry of the Court in this matter is on file in my office as of this date."

______________ ______________________

(Date) (Clerk)

(5) Failure of a party to personally serve the proposed order provided in L.Civ.R. 67.1(b)(1) upon the Clerk, Chief Deputy Clerk, Deputy-in-Charge, or Chief Financial Deputy shall relieve the Clerk from any liability for any lien on or other claim against the monies on deposit.

Source: L.Civ.R. 67.1(a)—G.R. 35.E.; L.Civ.R. 67.1(b)—G.R. 35.F.

[Effective April 1, 1997.]

CIV. RULE 69.1. MARSHAL'S VOUCHERS

In all cases of sales of property by the Marshal, the Marshal shall (a) annex to the return vouchers for all disbursements, and (b) make an affidavit that (1) the services charged were actually and necessarily performed, and (2) the disbursements paid were actually incurred as therein stated.

Source: G.R. 43.

[Effective April 1, 1997.]

CIV. RULE 72.1 UNITED STATES MAGISTRATE JUDGES

Each Magistrate Judge is authorized to perform all judicial duties assigned by the Court that are consistent with the Constitution and the laws of the United States which include, but are not limited to, the following:

(a) Duties in Civil Matters

(1) *Non–Dispositive Motions.* Hearing and determining any pretrial motion or other pretrial matter, other than those motions specified in L.Civ.R. 72.1(a)(2), in accordance with 28 U.S.C. § 636(b)(1)(A) and Fed. R. Civ. P. 72. An appeal from a Magistrate Judge's determination of such a non-dispositive motion shall be served and filed in accordance with L.Civ.R. 72.1(c)(1).

(2) *Dispositive Motions.* Hearing and conducting such evidentiary hearings as are necessary or appropriate and submitting to a Judge proposed findings of fact and recommendations for the disposition of motions for injunctive relief (including temporary restraining orders and preliminary injunctions), for judgment on the pleadings, for summary judgment, to dismiss or permit the maintenance of a class action, to dismiss for failure to state a claim upon which relief may be granted, to involuntarily dismiss an action, for judicial review of administrative determinations, for review of default judgments, and for review of prisoners' petitions challenging conditions of confinement, in accordance with 28 U.S.C. § 636(b)(1)(B) and (C) and Fed. R. Civ. P. 72. Any party may object to the Magistrate Judge's proposed findings, recommendations or report issued under this Rule by serving and filing an objection in accordance with L.Civ.R. 72.1(c)(2).

(3) *Civil Case Management*

(A) Exercising general supervision of the civil calendars of the Court, conducting calendar and status calls, and determining motions to expedite or postpone the trial of cases for the Judges.

(B) Conducting pretrial conferences as set forth in Fed. R. Civ. P. 16 and 26(f), which include but are not limited to scheduling, settlement, discovery, preliminary and final pretrial conferences, and entry of appropriate orders, including scheduling orders in accordance with L.Civ.R. 16.1 and Fed. R. Civ. P. 16.

(C) As part of the Magistrate Judge's general supervision of the civil calendar, the Magistrate Judge shall conduct scheduling conferences and enter scheduling orders in accordance with Fed. R. Civ. P. 16 in all civil cases except the following:

(i) all actions in which one of the parties appears pro se and is incarcerated;

(ii) all actions for judicial review of administrative decisions of Government agencies or instrumentalities where the review is conducted on the basis of the administrative record;

(iii) proceedings in bankruptcy, prize proceedings, sales to satisfy liens of the United States, and actions for forfeitures and seizures, for condemnation, or for foreclosure of mortgages;

(iv) proceedings for admission to citizenship or to cancel or revoke citizenship;

(v) proceedings for habeas corpus or in the nature thereof, whether addressed to Federal or State custody;

(vi) proceedings to compel arbitration or to confirm or set aside arbitration awards;

(vii) proceedings to compel the giving of testimony or production of documents under a subpoena or summons issued by an officer, agency or instrumentality of the United States not provided with authority to compel compliance;

(viii) proceedings to compel the giving of testimony or production of documents in this District in connection with discovery, or testimony de bene esse, or for perpetuation of testimony, for use in a matter pending or contemplated in another court;

(ix) proceedings for the temporary enforcement of orders of the National Labor Relations Board; and

(x) proceedings instituted for prosecution in a summary manner in the Superior Court of New Jersey and removed to this Court on diversity only.

(4) Conducting voir dire and selecting petit juries for the Court and, in the absence of the Judge, accepting petit jury verdicts in civil cases.

(5) Issuing subpoenas, writs of habeas corpus ad testificandum or habeas corpus ad prosequendum, or other orders necessary to obtain the presence of

parties or witnesses or evidence needed for court proceedings.

(6) Conducting proceedings for the collection of civil penalties of not more than $1000 assessed in accordance with 46 U.S.C. § 2302.

(7) Conducting examinations of judgment debtors, in accordance with Fed. R. Civ. P. 69.

(8) Reviewing petitions in civil commitment proceedings under Title III of the Narcotic Addict Rehabilitation Act.

(9) Issuing warrants or entering orders permitting entry into and inspection of premises, and/or seizure of property, in noncriminal proceedings, as authorized by law, when properly requested by the IRS or other governmental agencies.

(10) Serving as a special master in an appropriate civil action, pursuant to 28 U.S.C. § 636(b)(2) and Fed. R. Civ. P. 53. The Magistrate Judge may, where the parties consent, serve as a special master in any civil action without regard to the provisions of Fed. R. Civ. P. 53(b) and try the issues of any civil action. The entry of final judgment in the civil action, however, shall be made by a Judge or at the direction of a Judge with the consent of the parties.

(11) Administering oaths and affirmations and taking acknowledgments, affidavits, and depositions.

(12) Supervising proceedings conducted pursuant to 28 U.S.C. § 1782 with respect to foreign tribunals and to litigants before such tribunals.

(b) Duties in Proceedings for Post–Conviction Relief. A Magistrate Judge may exercise the powers enumerated in Rules 5, 8, 9 and 10 of the Rules Governing §§ 2254 and 2255 Proceedings, in accordance with the standards and criteria established in 28 U.S.C. § 636(b)(1).

(c) Appeals from Judgments and Other Orders

(1) *Appeals from Non–Dispositive Orders*

(A) Any party may appeal from a Magistrate Judge's determination of a non-dispositive matter within 10 days after the party has been served with a copy of the Magistrate Judge's order, unless a motion for reargument of the matter pursuant to L.Civ.R. 7.1(g) has been timely filed and served, in which case the time to appeal will begin to run when the parties are served with a copy of the Magistrate Judge's order rendering a determination on the merits of such a motion. Such party shall file with the Clerk and serve on all parties a written notice of appeal which shall specifically designate the order or part thereof appealed from and the basis for objection thereto. The notice of appeal shall be submitted for filing in the form of a notice of motion conforming with the requirements of L.Civ.R. 7.1. The party filing an appeal shall provide to the Court a transcript of that portion of the hearing before the Magistrate Judge wherein findings of fact were made, no later than 10 days before the return date of the motion. Any party opposing the appeal shall file a responsive brief at least 14 days prior to the date originally noticed for argument. A cross-appeal related to the subject matter of the original determination may be filed by the responding party together with that party's opposition and may be noticed for a hearing on the same date as the original appeal, as long as the responding papers are timely filed. A brief in reply to the cross-appeal may be filed at least seven days prior to the date originally noticed for argument. Each of the above periods may be altered by the Magistrate Judge or Judge. A Judge shall consider the appeal and/or cross-appeal and set aside any portion of the Magistrate Judge's order found to be clearly erroneous or contrary to law.

(B) Except as provided in (C) below, the filing of such a motion or cross-motion to appeal does not operate to stay the order pending appeal to a Judge. A stay of a Magistrate Judge's order pending appeal must be sought in the first instance from the Magistrate Judge whose order had been appealed, upon due notice to all interested parties.

(C) The Clerk shall take no action with respect to a Magistrate Judge's order for transfer of venue or denying a motion to seal under L. Civ. R. 5.3 until 15 days from the filing of such an order. In the event that a notice of appeal from such an order is filed within time allowed in the Rule, the Clerk shall take no action until the appeal is decided by the Judge.

(2) *Objections to Magistrate Judge's Proposed Findings, Recommendation or Report.* Any party may object to the Magistrate Judge's proposed findings, recommendations or report issued under this Rule within 10 days after being served with a copy thereof. Such party shall file with the Clerk and serve on all parties written objections which shall specifically identify the portions of the proposed findings, recommendations or report to which objection is made and the basis of such objection. Such party shall file with the Clerk a transcript of the specific portions of any evidentiary proceeding to which objection is made. A Judge shall make a de novo determination of those portions to which objection is made and may accept, reject, or modify, in whole or in part, the findings or recommendations made by the Magistrate Judge. The Judge, however, need not normally conduct a new hearing and may consider the record developed before the Magistrate Judge, making his or her own determination on the basis of that record. The Judge may also receive further evidence, recall witnesses or recommit the matter to the Magistrate Judge with instructions.

Source: L.Civ.R. 72.1(a)(1)-(2)—G.R. 40.A.1–2; L.Civ.R. 72.1(a)(3)-(9)—G.R. 40.A.4–10; L.Civ.R. 72.1(a)(10)-(12)—

G.R. 40.A.12–14; L.Civ.R. 72.1(b)—G.R. 40.C.; L.Civ.R. 72.1(c)(1)—G.R. 40.D.4; L.Civ.R. 72.1(c)(2)—G.R. 40.D.5.

[Effective April 1, 1997. Amended March 31, 1999; March 9, 2007.]

CIV. RULE 73.1. CIVIL TRIALS BY CONSENT BEFORE UNITED STATES MAGISTRATE JUDGES

(a) Where the parties consent, each Magistrate Judge is authorized to conduct a jury or nonjury trial in any civil action and order the entry of final judgment in accordance with 28 U.S.C. § 636(c) and Fed. R.Civ.P. 73–76. In the course of conducting proceedings in any civil action upon the consent of the parties, a Magistrate Judge may hear and determine any and all pretrial and post-trial motions including case-dispositive motions.

(b) The Clerk shall notify the parties in all civil cases that they may consent to have a Magistrate Judge conduct any or all proceedings in the case and order the entry of a final judgment. Such notice shall be mailed to the parties with the notice of the first pretrial conference.

(c) The Clerk shall not accept a consent form for filing unless it has been signed by all the parties in a case. Plaintiff shall be responsible for securing the execution and filing of such a consent form. No consent form will be made available, nor will its contents be made known to any Judge or Magistrate Judge, unless all stated parties have consented to the reference to a Magistrate Judge. No Magistrate Judge, Judge or other Court official may attempt to persuade or induce any party to consent to the reference of any matter to a Magistrate Judge. This Rule, however, shall not preclude a Judge or Magistrate Judge from informing the parties that they may have that option.

(d) The consent form shall be filed with the Clerk not later than 15 days after the date of the final pretrial conference.

(e) After the consent form has been executed and filed, the Clerk shall so advise the Judge to whom the case has been assigned. At the direction of the Judge, the Clerk shall prepare for the Judge's signature an order referring the case to a Magistrate Judge. Once the case has been referred, the Magistrate Judge shall have the authority to conduct any and all proceedings to which the parties have consented and to direct the Clerk to enter a final judgment in the same manner as if a Judge had presided.

(f) Upon the entry of judgment in a civil case disposed of by a Magistrate Judge on consent of the parties under authority of 28 U.S.C. § 636(c) and L.Civ.R. 73.1, an aggrieved party shall appeal directly to the Third Circuit in the same manner as an appeal from any other judgment of this Court.

Source: L.Civ.R. 73.1(a)—G.R. 40.A.3 (first paragraph); L.Civ.R. 73.1(b)—G.R. 40.A.3(a); L.Civ.R. 73.1(c)—G.R. 40.A.3(b); L.Civ.R. 73.1(d)—G.R. 40.A.3(c); L.Civ.R. 73.1(e)—G.R. 40.A.3(d); L.Civ.R. 73.1(f)—G.R. 40.D.2(a).

[Effective April 1, 1997.]

CIV. RULE 77.1. COURT SESSION

There shall be a regular continuous session of the Court at Camden, Newark and Trenton starting on the first business day of January, except for such holidays and recess periods as may be established.

Source: G.R. 3.A.

[Effective April 1, 1997.]

CIV. RULE 78.1. MOTION DAYS AND ORAL ARGUMENT

(a) Except during vacation periods of the Court, the regular motion days for all vicinages are the first and third Monday of each month. Whenever a regular motion day falls on a holiday, the motion day becomes the following non-holiday. The Clerk shall publish a list of all regular motion days for each calendar year, and corresponding filing deadlines, on the web site of the Court and in appropriate legal publications.

(b) All motions and other applications will be decided on the papers submitted unless: (1) a party requests oral argument and the request is granted by the Judge or Magistrate Judge; or (2) the Court, sua sponte, directs that oral argument be held. Any request for oral argument shall be clearly marked on the first page of the notice of motion and/or the brief filed by the party making such request. If oral argument is to be heard, the Court will so notify the parties and designate the day and time of the argument.

Source: G.R. 12.C. (paragraph 2).

[Effective April 1, 1997; amended effective February 24, 2005; January 2, 2008.]

CIV. RULE 79.1. CUSTODY OF ORIGINAL PAPERS, RECORDS AND EXHIBITS

(a) No original papers or records shall be taken from the Clerk's office or the courtroom (except in the custody of the Clerk) without an order from a Judge.

(b) Unless the Court otherwise directs, each exhibit admitted into evidence prior to disposition of any matter shall be held in the custody of the Clerk.

(c) Unless the Court otherwise directs in civil matters, the Clerk shall permit only the parties to the action or their attorneys to examine or copy exhibits in the Clerk's custody.

(d) At the conclusion of the trial or other disposition of a civil matter, the Clerk shall promptly return all exhibits to the attorney for the party on whose behalf they were introduced, except those pleadings from the Clerk's file marked as exhibits. The attorney to whom the exhibits are returned shall be responsible for their preservation until the time for appeal has passed, during the pendency of any appeal, or for six months, whichever period is longer, and shall make them available to any party or attorney for any party for the purpose of preparing the record or appendix on appeal.

(e) In the event that exhibits consist of heavy or bulky models or other material which cannot conveniently be mailed, the Clerk, in writing, shall notify the attorney who introduced such exhibits to remove them within 15 days and, upon the attorney's failure to do so, they shall be disposed of as the Clerk sees fit.

Source: L.Civ.R. 79.1(a)—G.R. 31; L.Civ.R. 79.1(b)—G.R. 26.A.; L.Civ.R. 79.1(c)—G.R. 26.B.; L.Civ.R. 79.1(d)—G.R. 26.C.; L.Civ.R. 79.1(e)—G.R. 26.E.

[Effective April 1, 1997.]

CIV. RULE 79.2. BRIEFS PART OF PUBLIC RECORD

Although not filed with the Clerk, all briefs, unless otherwise ordered by the Court, shall constitute parts of the public record, and it is the policy of the Court that counsel should, if reasonably feasible, provide to the media and members of the public access to a copy of the submitted briefs in pending actions for the purpose of review or copying at the requesting party's expense.

Source: G.R. 12.M.

[Effective April 1, 1997.]

CIV. RULE 79.3. ENTRY OF SATISFACTION OF JUDGMENTS AND DECREES

Satisfaction of a money judgment recovered in this District, or registered in this District pursuant to 28 U.S.C. § 1963, shall be entered by the Clerk, as follows:

(a) Upon the filing of a warrant of satisfaction executed and acknowledged by (1) the judgment-creditor or his or her attorney of record; or (2) the assignee of the judgment-creditor, with evidence of the assignment.

(b) Upon the filing of a warrant of satisfaction executed by the United States Attorney, if the judgment-creditor is the United States.

(c) Upon the registration of a certified copy of a satisfaction of the judgment entered in another district.

Source: G.R. 24.

[Effective April 1, 1997.]

CIV. RULE 79.4. FILING OF MANDATE

Upon the filing of a mandate or certified copy of the judgment in lieu thereof from an appellate court, the Clerk shall file and enter it and notify counsel for the parties. In the event that the mandate or judgment provides for costs or directs a disposition other than an affirmance, the prevailing party shall submit an order implementing the mandate or judgment.

Source: G.R. 25.

[Effective April 1, 1997.]

CIV. RULE 79.5. CLERK TO MAINTAIN LIST OF OFFICIAL NEWSPAPERS

There shall be maintained at each office of the Clerk a list of the newspapers designated by order of the Court as the official newspapers, within their respective counties, for the publication of all notices and orders under all statutes, rules, and general orders of the Supreme Court of the United States requiring or permitting this Court to designate newspapers for official publication. (See Appendix G for listing of official newspapers.)

Source: G.R. 42.

[Effective April 1, 1997.]

CIV. RULE 80.1. TRANSCRIPTS

(a) Rates of Official Reporters. The rates for transcripts furnished by the official court reporters shall be those fixed by order of the Court, pursuant to recommendations of the Judicial Conference of the United States, and filed with the Clerk. See Appendix F.

(b) Requests for Transcripts of Proceedings. To order transcripts of matters on appeal, appellant or counsel for appellant shall submit a Third Circuit Court of Appeals Transcript Purchase Order form to the office of the Clerk. Persons requesting transcripts of the record for purposes other than appeal shall submit a District of New Jersey Transcript Purchase Order to the office of the Clerk. Supplies of both of these forms are available at the office of the Clerk.

Source: G.R. 41.

[Effective April 1, 1997.]

CIV. RULE 81.1. NATURALIZATION

All applications to take the Oath of Allegiance to the United States under the Act of June 25, 1936, as amended, before being presented to the Court shall be referred to the Immigration and Naturalization Service, for the purpose of conducting preliminary hearings thereon by a designated officer of that Service, and the submission of findings and recommendations to the Court. All such applications shall be heard only on days fixed by the Court for the hearing of other naturalization matters.

Source: G.R. 37.

[Effective April 1, 1997.]

CIV. RULE 81.2 PETITIONS FOR HABEAS CORPUS AND MOTIONS UNDER 28 U.S.C. § 2255 IN NON–DEATH PENALTY CASES.

(a) Unless prepared by counsel, petitions to this Court for a writ of habeas corpus and motions under 28 U.S.C. § 2255 shall be in writing (legibly handwritten in ink or typewritten), signed by the petitioner or movant, on forms supplied by the Clerk. When prepared by counsel, the petition or motion shall follow the content of the forms.

(b) If the petition or motion is presented in forma pauperis it shall include an affidavit (attached to the back of the form) setting forth information which establishes that the petitioner or movant is unable to pay the fees and costs of the proceedings. Whenever a Federal, State, or local prisoner submits a civil rights complaint, petition for a writ of habeas corpus, or motion for relief under 28 U.S.C. § 2255 and seeks in forma pauperis status, the prisoner shall also submit an affidavit setting forth information which establishes that the prisoner is unable to pay the fees and costs of the proceedings and shall further submit a certification signed by an authorized officer of the institution certifying (1) the amount presently on deposit in the prisoner's prison account and, (2) the greatest amount on deposit in the prisoner's prison account during the six-month period prior to the date of the certification. The affidavit and certification shall be in the forms attached to and made a part of these Rules as Appendix P.

(c) If the prison account of any petitioner or movant exceeds $200, the petitioner or movant shall not be considered eligible to proceed in forma pauperis.

(d) The respondent shall file and serve his or her answer to the petition or motion not later than 45 days from the date on which an order directing such response is filed with the Clerk, unless an extension is granted for good cause shown. The answer shall include the respondent's legal argument in opposition to the petition or motion. The respondent shall also file, by the same date, a certified copy of all briefs, appendices, opinions, process, pleadings, transcripts and orders filed in the underlying criminal proceeding or such of these as may be material to the questions presented by the petition or motion.

(e) Upon entry of an appealable order, the Clerk and appellant's counsel will prepare the record for appeal. The record will be transmitted to the Third Circuit Court of Appeals within five days after the filing of a notice of appeal from the entry of an appealable order under 18 U.S.C. § 3731, 28 U. S.C. § 1291 or 28 U.S.C. § 1292(a)(1).

Source: G.R. 29.

Publisher's Note: The highlighted text in subsection (b) was suspended effective July 26, 2005; see notice dated July 26, 2005, post.

[Effective April 1, 1997; amended effective January 10, 2001; March 9, 2007.]

CIV. RULE 81.3. PETITIONS FOR HABEAS CORPUS AND MOTIONS UNDER 28 U.S.C. § 2255 IN DEATH PENALTY CASES.

(a) The following Local Civil Rule shall govern all petitions for a writ of habeas corpus and all motions under 28 U.S.C. § 2255 where the relief sought would affect a sentence of death previously imposed on the petitioner (hereinafter "capital case").

(b) Any petition for a writ of habeas corpus and any motion to vacate, set aside or correct a sentence under 28 U.S.C. § 2255 in a capital case must be accompanied by a cover sheet that lists:

(1) petitioner's full name and prisoner number; if prosecuted under a different name or alias that name must be indicated;

(2) name of person having custody of petitioner (warden, superintendent, etc.);

(3) petitioner's address;

(4) name of trial judge;

(5) court term and bill of information or indictment number;

(6) charges of which petitioner was convicted;

(7) sentence for each of the charges;

(8) plea entered;

(9) whether trial was by jury or to the bench;

(10) date of filing, docket numbers, dates of decision and results of any direct appeal of the conviction;

(11) date of filing, docket numbers, dates of decision and results of any state collateral attack on a state conviction including appeals;

(12) date of filing, docket numbers, dates of decision of any prior federal habeas corpus or § 2255 proceedings, including appeals; and

(13) name and address of each attorney who represented petitioner, identifying the stage at which the attorney represented the litigant.

(c) Any such petition or motion in a capital case:

(1) must list every ground on which the petitioner claims to be entitled to habeas corpus relief (or relief under 28 U.S.C. § 2255 for federal prisoners) followed by a concise statement of the material facts supporting the claims;

(2) must identify at what stage of the proceedings each claim was exhausted in state court if the petition seeks relief from a state court judgment;

(3) must contain a table of contents if the petition is more than 25 pages;

(4) may contain citation to legal authorities that form the basis of the claim.

(d) Petitioner must file, not later than 30 days after the date of the filing of the habeas corpus petition or the motion under 28 U.S.C. § 2255, in a capital case an original and one copy of a brief in support of the relief requested, which brief shall comply with the requirements of Local Civil Rule 7.2(b). The original brief shall be filed by the Clerk and the copy forwarded by the Clerk to the Judge assigned to the case.

(e) The petition/motion and brief together must not exceed 100 pages. Any such paper shall be served upon the respondent when it is filed with the Court.

(f) Within 60 days after being served with all papers, including the brief, filed by the petitioner/movant, the respondent shall file and serve a response which:

(1) must contain a table of contents if it is more than 25 pages;

(2) must include an original and one copy of a brief complying with the requirements of Local Civil Rule 7.2(b), which the Clerk shall file and process in the manner set forth in subsection (d) above; and

(3) must include a certified copy of all briefs, appendices, opinions, process, pleadings, transcripts and orders filed in the underlying criminal proceeding or such of these as may be material to the questions presented by the petition or motion.

(g) The response and brief required in sections (f) (1) and (2) above must not exceed 100 pages.

(h) Any reply to the response must be filed and served within 21 days of the filing of the response and may not exceed 30 pages.

(i) Upon motion (with notice to all adverse parties) and for good cause shown, the Judge may extend the page limits for any document.

(j) Upon motion (with notice to all adverse parties) and for good cause shown, the Judge may extend the time for filing any document. This provision does not enlarge the power of the Judge to extend the time for filing a petition under 28 U.S.C. § 2254 or a motion under 28 U.S.C. § 2255 beyond that permitted by applicable statutory and case law.

(k) All documents filed by any party under this rule must be succinct and must avoid repetition.

(*l*) Each petitioner in any habeas corpus proceeding or motion under 28 U.S.C. § 2255 in which the imposition of a death sentence is challenged shall file a "Certificate of Death Penalty Case" with the initial petition, motion or other pleading. This Certificate shall include the following information:

(1) names, addresses and telephone numbers of parties and counsel;

(2) if set, the proposed date of the execution of sentence; and

(3) the emergency nature of the proceedings.

(m) A Certificate of Death Penalty Case shall be filed with the Clerk by the United States Attorney for the District of New Jersey upon return of a verdict of death in a federal criminal case.

(n) Upon the entry of a warrant or order setting an execution date in any case within the geographical boundaries of this district, and in aid of this court's potential jurisdiction, the Clerk is directed to monitor the status of the execution and any pending litigation and to establish communication with all parties and relevant state and/or federal courts. Without further order of this Court, the Clerk may, prior to the filing of a petition, direct parties to lodge with this court (1) relevant portions of previous state and/or federal court records, or the entire record, and (2) pleadings, briefs, and transcripts of any ongoing proceedings. To prevent delay, the case may be assigned to a Judge, up to 14 days prior to the execution date. The identity of the Judge assigned shall not be disclosed until a petition is actually docketed.

(*o*) The assignment of death-penalty cases among the Judges of this Court (whether before or after a petition is docketed) shall be as follows: If habeas relief from a State conviction is sought, the Clerk shall allocate the case to the vicinage which encompasses the county in which the capital sentence was imposed and assign the case to the next District Judge on that vicinage's list of Judges to receive such cases. If relief from a federal conviction arising in this District is sought under 28 U.S.C. § 2255, the case shall be assigned to the District Judge who presided at the capital sentencing or in his or her unavailability to the next District Judge on that vicinage's list of Judges to receive such cases.

(p) In accordance with Third Circuit L.A.R. Misc. 111.3(a), at the time a final decision is entered, the court shall state whether a certificate of appealability is granted, the court must state the issues that merit the granting of a certificate and must also grant a stay pending disposition of the appeal, except as provided in 28 U.S.C. § 2262.

(q) Upon entry of an appealable order, the Clerk and appellant's counsel will prepare the record for appeal. The record will be transmitted to the Third Circuit Court of Appeals within five days after the filing of a notice of appeal from the entry of an appealable order under 18 U.S.C. § 3731, 28 U.S.C. § 1291 or 28 U.S.C. § 1292(a) (1), unless the appealable order is entered within 14 days of the date of the scheduled execution, in which case the record shall be transmitted immediately by an expedited means of delivery.

[Effective January 10, 2001.]

CIV. RULE 83.1. ADOPTION AND AMENDMENT OF LOCAL RULES

(a) The Court may, by action of the majority of the Judges of this Court, from time to time, after giving appropriate public notice and an opportunity for comment, amend these Rules. All such amendments shall be consistent with the United States Constitution. Federal statutory law, and the Federal Rules of Civil and Criminal Procedure. Any Rule or Rule amendment adopted pursuant to this Rule shall take effect upon the date specified by this Court and shall have such effect on pending proceedings as this Court may direct. All Rules of this Court shall remain in effect unless amended by the Court or abrogated by the Judicial Council of the Third Circuit. Copies of these Rules and any amendments thereto shall, upon their promulgation, be furnished to the Judicial Council of the Third Circuit, the Administrative Office of the United States Courts, and made available to the public.

(b) If the Court determines that there is an immediate need for a Rule or amendment to these Rules, it may promulgate such a Rule or Rule amendment without public notice and an opportunity for comment. The Court shall promptly thereafter afford such notice and opportunity for comment.

Source: L.Civ.R. 83.1(a)—G.R. 1.D.; L.Civ.R. 83.1(b)—G.R. 1.E.

[Effective April 1, 1997.]

CIV. RULE 83.2. RELAXATION OR MODIFICATION OF LOCAL RULES

(a) The Chief Judge may, after recommendation by the Lawyer's Advisory Committee and with the approval of the Court, authorize the relaxation, dispensation or modification of any Rule on a temporary basis. The effective period of any such authorization shall not exceed one year.

(b) Unless otherwise stated, any Rule may be relaxed or dispensed with by the Court if adherence would result in surprise or injustice.

Source: L.Civ.R. 83.2(a)—G.R. 1.C.; L.Civ.R. 83.2(b)—G.R. 1.A. (next to last sentence).

[Effective April 1, 1997.]

CIV. RULE 83.3. PROCEDURE IN THE ABSENCE OF RULE OR STATUTORY PROVISION

In the absence of any governing rule and/or if no procedure is especially prescribed, the Court and parties shall proceed in any lawful manner not inconsistent with the Constitution of the United States, the Federal Rules of Civil and Criminal Procedure, these Rules, or any applicable statute with the aims of securing a just determination, simplicity in procedure, fairness in administration and the elimination of unjustifiable expense and delay and of avoiding surprise and injustice. In such instances, the procedure and practice of the Courts of the State of New Jersey may be considered for guidance.

Source: G.R. 1.A. (second and last sentences); G.R. 44.

[Effective April 1, 1997.]

CIV. RULE 85.1. TITLE

These Rules may be known and cited as the Local Civil Rules of the United States District Court for the District of New Jersey and abbreviated as "L.Civ.R."

Source: G.R. 1.A. [by inference].

[Effective April 1, 1997.]

CIV. RULE 101.1 ADMISSION OF ATTORNEYS

(a) Scope of Admission. The bar of this Court shall consist of those persons heretofore admitted to practice in this Court and those who may hereafter be admitted in accordance with these Rules.

(b) New Jersey Attorneys. Any attorney licensed to practice by the Supreme Court of New Jersey may be admitted as an attorney at law on motion of a member of the bar of this Court, made in open court, and upon taking the prescribed oath and signing the roll. Any New Jersey attorney deemed ineligible to practice law by order of the New Jersey Supreme Court entered pursuant to New Jersey Court Rule 1:28–2(a) shall not be eligible to practice law in this Court during the period of such ineligibility. Any attorney licensed to practice by the Supreme Court of New Jersey who has resigned from the New Jersey bar shall be deemed to have resigned from the bar of this Court effective as of the same date as his/her resignation from the New Jersey bar.

(c) Appearance Pro Hac Vice; Local Counsel

(1) Any member in good standing of the bar of any court of the United States or of the highest court of any state, who is not under suspension or disbarment by any court and is ineligible for admission to the bar of this Court under L.Civ.R. 101.1(b), may in the discretion of the Court, on motion, be permitted to appear and participate in a particular case. The motion shall contain a statement certifying that no disciplinary proceedings are pending against the attorney in any jurisdiction and no discipline has previously been imposed on the attorney in any jurisdiction. If discipline has previously been imposed within the past five years, the certification shall state the date, jurisdiction, nature of the ethics violation and the penalty imposed. If proceedings are pending, the certification shall specify the jurisdiction, the charges and the likely time of their disposition. An attorney admitted pro hac vice shall have the continuing obligation during the period of such admission promptly to advise the court of the disposition made of pending charges or of the institution of new disciplinary proceedings.

(2) The order of the Court granting a motion to appear pro hac vice shall require the out-of-state attorney to make a payment to the New Jersey Lawyers' Fund for Client Protection as provided by New Jersey Court Rule 1:28–2(a). This payment shall be made for any year in which the admitted attorney continues to represent a client in a matter pending in this Court. A copy of the order shall be forwarded by the Clerk to the Treasurer of the Fund.

(3) The order of the Court granting a motion to appear pro hac vice shall require the out-of-state attorney to make a payment of $150.00 on each admission payable to the Clerk, USDC.

(4) If it has not been done prior to the granting of such motion, an appearance as counsel of record shall be filed promptly by a member of the bar of this Court upon whom all notices, orders and pleadings may be served, and who shall promptly notify his or her specially admitted associate of their receipt. Only an attorney at law of this Court may file papers, enter appearances for parties, sign stipulations, or sign and receive payments on judgments, decrees or orders. A lawyer admitted pro hac vice is deemed to have agreed to take no fee in any tort case in excess of New Jersey Court Rule 1:21–7 governing contingent fees.

(5) A lawyer admitted pro hac vice is within the disciplinary jurisdiction of this Court.

(d) Adherence to Schedules; Sanctions. All members of the bar of this Court and those specially permitted to participate in a particular action shall strictly observe the dates fixed for scheduling conferences, motions, pretrial conferences, trials or any other proceedings. Failure of counsel for any party, or of a party appearing pro se, to comply with this Rule may result in the imposition of sanctions, including the withdrawal of the permission granted under L.Civ.R. 101.1(c) to participate in the particular action. All applications for adjournment shall be made promptly and directed to the Judge or Magistrate Judge to whom the matter is assigned.

(e) Appearance by Patent Attorneys. Any member in good standing of the bar of any court of the United States or of the highest court of any state who is not eligible for admission to the bar of this Court under L.Civ.R. 101.1(b) may be admitted as an attorney at law, subject to the limitations hereinafter set forth, on motion of a member of the bar of this Court and upon taking the prescribed oath and signing the roll, provided such applicant has filed with the Clerk a verified application for admission as an attorney of this Court establishing that the applicant:

(1) is a member in good standing of the bar of any United States court or the highest court of any state for at least five years;

(2) has been admitted to practice as an attorney before the United States Patent Office and is listed on its Register of attorneys;

(3) has been continuously engaged in the practice of patent law as a principal occupation in an established place of business and office located in the State of New Jersey for at least two years prior to date of application; and

(4) has sufficient qualifications both as to prelegal and legal training to satisfy the Court.

No member admitted under L.Civ.R. 101.1(e) shall designate himself or herself other than as a patent attorney or patent lawyer, and that person's admission to practice before this Court shall be limited to cases solely arising under patent laws of the United States or elsewhere. Failure to continue to maintain an established place of business or office within the State for the practice of patent law shall, upon proof thereof to the Court, justify the striking of such attorney's name from the roll of patent attorneys established under this Rule. In any litigation, any patent attorney admitted under L.Civ.R. 101.1(e) shall be associated of record with a member of the bar of this Court admitted under L.Civ.R. 101.1(b). Nothing herein contained shall preclude any patent attorney from being admitted under L.Civ.R. 101.1(b) or (c).

(f) Appearance by Attorneys for the United States. An attorney admitted to practice in any United States District Court may practice before this Court in any proceeding in which he or she is representing the United States or any of its officers or agencies. If such attorney does not have an office in this District he or she shall designate the United States Attorney to receive service of all notices or papers in that action. Service upon the United States Attorney or authorized designee shall constitute service upon a government attorney who does not have an office in this District.

(g) Appearance by Professional Law Corporations. The provisions of this Rule shall extend to duly created professional law corporations, authorized to be formed under the law of the jurisdiction to which the attorney employed by the corporation shall have been admitted to practice, to the same extent as they apply to partnerships and other unincorporated law firms. In every case in which such a professional law corporation participates, all appearances and papers shall be in the full name of the corporation, including such designations as "Chartered," "Professional Association," "P.C.," and the like, and shall be executed on its behalf by an individual attorney qualified under this Rule and employed by it, as "Authorized Attorney." Both the corporate entity and its attorney employee shall be subject to all provisions of these Rules.

(h) Appearance by Supervised Law Students. With the Court's approval, an eligible law student may appear under supervision of an attorney on behalf of any person, including the United States Attorney, who has consented in writing.

(1) The attorney who supervises a student shall:

(A) be either a member of the bar of this Court who maintains a bona fide office in this District or an attorney permitted to practice before the courts of the State of New Jersey under N.J.R. 1:21–3(c).

(B) personally assume professional responsibility for the student's work;

(C) assist the student to the extent necessary;

(D) appear with the student in all proceedings before the Court; and

(E) file written consent to supervise the student.

(2) In order to appear, the student shall:

(A) be enrolled in a law school approved by the American Bar Association;

(B) have successfully completed legal studies amounting to at least two-thirds of the credits needed for graduation or the equivalent;

(C) be certified by either the dean or a faculty member of that law school as qualified to provide the legal representation permitted by these Rules (This certification may be withdrawn by the person so certifying at any time by mailing a notice to the Clerk, or upon termination by the Judge presiding in the case in which the student appears without notice or hearing and without a showing of cause. The loss of certification by action of a Judge shall not be considered a reflection upon the character or ability of the student.);

(D) be introduced to the Court by an attorney admitted to practice in this District;

(E) neither ask for nor receive from the client represented any compensation or remuneration of any kind for services rendered; but this limitation shall not prevent an attorney, legal aid bureau, law school, public defender agency, a State, or the United States from paying compensation to the eligible law student, nor shall it prevent any agency from making proper charges for its services;

(F) certify in writing that he or she is familiar and will comply with the Disciplinary Rules;

(G) certify in writing that he or she is familiar with the Federal procedural and evidentiary rules relevant to the action in which he or she is appearing.

(3) The law student, supervised in accordance with these Rules, may:

(A) appear as counsel in court or at other proceedings when written consent of the client (or of the United States Attorney when the client is the United States) and the supervising attorney have been filed, and when the Court has approved the student's request to appear in the particular case to the extent that the Judge presiding at the hearing or trial permits;

(B) prepare and sign motions, petitions, answers, briefs, and other documents in connection with any matter in which he or she has met the conditions of L.Civ.R. 101.1(h)(3)(A); each such document shall also be signed by the supervising attorney.

(4) Forms for designating compliance with this Rule are set forth in Appendix A1 and A2, and shall be available in the Clerk's office. Completed forms shall be filed with the Clerk.

(5) Participation by students under this Rule shall not be deemed a violation in connection with the rules for admission to the bar of any jurisdiction concerning practice of law prior to admission to that bar.

(i) Admission Fee. An attorney admitted to the bar of this Court shall pay an admission fee in the amount set by the Court. The Clerk shall collect such funds and maintain them in the manner set forth by the Court in the Plan for Administration and Operation of the Attorney's Admission Fee Account. Such funds are to be used for projects which the Court determines are for the benefit of the bench and bar in the administration of justice within the District.

(j) Appearance of Attorneys in Criminal Cases. This Rule does not govern the appearance of attorneys representing defendants in criminal cases.

Source: G.R. 4.

[Effective April 1, 1997. Amended August 4, 1998; March 31, 1999; March 22, 2005; March 9, 2007.]

CIV. RULE 102.1. WITHDRAWAL OF APPEARANCE

Unless other counsel is substituted, no attorney may withdraw an appearance except by leave of Court. After a case has been first set for trial, substitution and withdrawal shall not be permitted except by leave of Court.

Source: G.R. 18.

[Effective April 1, 1997.]

CIV. RULE 103.1. JUDICIAL ETHICS AND PROFESSIONAL RESPONSIBILITY

(a) The Rules of Professional Conduct of the American Bar Association as revised by the New Jersey Supreme Court shall govern the conduct of the members of the bar admitted to practice in this Court, subject to such modifications as may be required or permitted by Federal statute, regulation, court rule or decision of law.

(b) The Code of Judicial Conduct of the American Bar Association shall govern the conduct of the Judges of this Court, subject to such modifications as may be required or permitted by Federal statute, regulation, court rule or decision of law.

(c) The GUIDELINES FOR LITIGATION CONDUCT adopted by the American Bar Association's Section of Litigation in August 1998, are hereby adopted by this Court and incorporated into these Rules as Appendix R. These Guidelines have been adopted by this Court to encourage civility, courtesy and professionalism among the bench and the bar. They are purely aspirational in nature and are not to be used as a basis for litigation, liability, discipline, sanctions, or penalties of any type.

Source: G.R. 6.

[Effective April 1, 1997. Amended March 31, 1999.]

CIV. RULE 104.1. DISCIPLINE OF ATTORNEYS

The Court, in furtherance of its inherent power and responsibility to supervise the conduct of attorneys who are admitted to practice before it or admitted for the purpose of a particular proceeding (pro hac vice), promulgates the following Rules of Disciplinary Enforcement superseding all of its other Rules pertaining to disciplinary enforcement heretofore promulgated.

(a) Attorneys Convicted of Crimes.

(1) Upon the filing with this Court of a certified copy of a judgment of conviction demonstrating that any attorney admitted to practice before the Court has been convicted in any court of the United States, or the District of Columbia, or any state, territory, commonwealth or possession of the United States, of a serious crime as hereinafter defined, the Court shall enter an order immediately suspending that attorney, whether the conviction resulted from a plea of guilty or nolo contendere, or from a verdict after trial or otherwise, and regardless of the pendency of any appeal, until final disposition of a disciplinary proceeding to be commenced upon such conviction. A copy of such order shall immediately be served upon the attorney. Upon good cause shown, the Court may set aside such order when the interest of justice requires.

(2) The term "serious crime" shall include any felony and any lesser crime a necessary element of which, as determined by the statutory or common law definition of such crime in the jurisdiction where the judgment was entered, involves false swearing, misrepresentation, fraud, willful failure to file income tax returns, deceit, bribery, extortion, misappropriation, theft, or an attempt, conspiracy or solicitation of another to commit a "serious crime."

(3) A certified copy of a judgment of conviction of an attorney for any crime shall be conclusive evidence of the commission of that crime in any disciplinary proceeding instituted against that attorney based upon the conviction.

(4) Upon the filing of a certified copy of a judgment of conviction of an attorney for a serious crime, the Court shall, in addition to suspending that attorney in accordance with the provisions of this Rule, also refer the matter to counsel for the institution of a disciplinary proceeding before the Court in which the sole issue to be determined shall be the extent of the final discipline to be imposed as a result of the conduct resulting in the conviction, provided that a disciplinary proceeding so instituted will not be brought to final hearing until all direct appeals from the conviction are concluded.

(5) Upon the filing of a certified copy of a judgment of conviction of an attorney for a crime not constituting a serious crime, the Court may refer the matter to counsel for a recommendation as to what action, if any, should be taken, including the institution of a disciplinary proceeding before the Court; provided, however, that the Court may in its discretion make no reference with respect to convictions for minor offenses.

(6) An attorney suspended under the provisions of this Rule will be reinstated immediately upon the filing of a certificate demonstrating that the underlying conviction of a serious crime has been reversed but the reinstatement will not terminate any disciplinary proceeding then pending against the attorney, the disposition of which shall be determined by the Court on the basis of all available evidence pertaining to both guilt and the extent of discipline to be imposed.

(b) Discipline Imposed by Other Courts.

(1) Any attorney admitted to practice before this Court shall, upon being subjected to public discipline by any other court of the United States or the District of Columbia, or by a court of any state, territory, commonwealth or possession of the United States, promptly inform the Clerk of this Court of such action.

(2) Upon the filing of a certified or exemplified copy of a judgment or order demonstrating that an attorney admitted to practice before this Court has been disciplined by another court, this Court shall forthwith issue a notice directed to the attorney containing:

(A) a copy of the judgment or order from the other court; and

(B) an order to show cause directing that the attorney inform this Court within 30 days after service of that order upon the attorney, personally or by mail, of any claim by the attorney predicated upon the grounds set forth in L.Civ.R. 104.1(b)(4), that the imposition of the identical discipline by the Court would be unwarranted, and the reasons therefor.

(3) In the event the discipline imposed in the other jurisdiction has been stayed there, any reciprocal discipline imposed in this Court shall be deferred until such stay expires.

(4) Upon the expiration of 30 days from service of the notice issued pursuant to the provisions of L.Civ.R. 104.1(b)(2), this Court shall impose the identical discipline unless the respondent-attorney demonstrates or this Court finds that, upon the face of the record upon which the discipline in another jurisdiction is predicated, it clearly appears:

(A) that the procedure was so lacking in notice or opportunity to be heard as to constitute a deprivation of due process; or

(B) that there was such an infirmity of proof establishing the misconduct as to give rise to the clear conviction that this Court could not, consistent with its duty, accept as final the conclusion on that subject; or

(C) that the imposition of the same discipline by this Court would result in grave injustice; or

(D) that the misconduct established is deemed by this Court to warrant substantially different discipline.

Where this Court determines that any of said elements exist, it shall enter such other order as it deems appropriate.

(5) In all other respects, a final adjudication in another court that an attorney has been guilty of misconduct shall establish conclusively the misconduct for the purposes of a disciplinary proceeding in this Court.

(6) This Court may at any stage appoint counsel to prosecute the disciplinary proceedings.

(c) Disbarment on Consent or Resignation in Other Courts.

(1) Any attorney admitted to practice before this Court who shall be disbarred on consent or resign from the bar of any other court of the United States or the District of Columbia, or from the bar of any state, territory, commonwealth or possession of the United States, while an investigation into allegations of misconduct is pending, shall, upon the filing with this Court of a certified or exemplified copy of the judgment or order accepting such disbarment on consent or resignation, cease to be permitted to practice before this Court and be stricken from the roll of attorneys admitted to practice before this Court.

(2) Any attorney admitted to practice before this Court shall, upon being disbarred on consent or resigning from the bar of any other court of the United States or the District of Columbia, or from the bar of any state, territory, commonwealth or possession of the United States while an investigation into allegations of misconduct is pending, promptly inform the Clerk of this Court of such disbarment on consent or resignation.

(d) Standards for Professional Conduct.

(1) For misconduct defined in these Rules and for good cause shown, and after notice and opportunity to be heard, any attorney admitted to practice before this Court may be disbarred, suspended from practice before this Court, reprimanded or subjected to such other disciplinary action as the circumstances may warrant.

(2) An act or omission by an attorney admitted to practice before this Court, individually or in concert with any other person or persons, which violates the applicable Rules of Professional Conduct referred to in L.Civ.R. 103.1 shall constitute misconduct and be grounds for discipline whether or not the act or omission occurred in the course of an attorney-client relationship.

(e) Disciplinary Proceedings.

(1) Every attorney authorized to practice law or appearing before this Court, including those specially authorized for a limited purpose or in connection with a particular proceeding pursuant to L.Civ.R. 101.1, shall be subject to the disciplinary jurisdiction of this Court.

(2) When misconduct or allegations of misconduct which, if substantiated, would warrant discipline of an attorney, shall come to the attention of a Judge of this Court, and the applicable procedure is not otherwise mandated by these Rules, that Judge shall refer the matter in writing to the Chief Judge. The Chief Judge may refer the matter to the appropriate State disci-

plinary body or, if the Chief Judge concludes that further investigation is warranted, he or she shall direct the Clerk to refer the matter to an attorney ("investigating counsel") who is admitted to practice before this Court to conduct such an investigation in order to determine whether a formal order to show cause should issue.

(3) The Clerk's order of reference to investigating counsel and all other papers filed in the matter shall be placed under seal and shall remain under seal unless and until an order to show cause and complaint are issued under L.Civ.R. 104.1(e)(7), at which point an order shall be entered unsealing the entire file.

(4) Investigating counsel shall promptly, and with reasonable particularity, notify the respondent-attorney ("respondent") in writing of the pendency and nature of the investigation and solicit comments thereon in furtherance of the preliminary investigation. Every attorney, as set forth in L.Civ.R. 104.1(e)(1), has the affirmative obligation to cooperate in an investigation. Such cooperation shall include the production of documents and submission to interviews conducted by the investigating counsel as follows:

(A) Respondent shall serve upon investigating counsel a response to the inquiry within 30 days of service of the inquiry.

(B) Investigating counsel may conduct such discovery as is reasonable necessary to complete the investigation, which may include interviews of the respondent, depositions, requests for production of documents and requests for admissions.

(C) Respondent shall serve upon investigating counsel a response to any request for production of documents or request for admissions within 30 days of service of the request.

(D) The time within which to respond pursuant to (A) and (C) above may be extended by investigating counsel for good cause shown.

(E) If respondent fails to respond or otherwise fails to cooperate with investigating counsel, investigating counsel shall apply to the Chief Judge for appropriate relief which may include, but is not limited to, temporary suspension, pending compliance with this rule.

(F) Failure to cooperate may constitute an independent basis for the imposition of discipline unless it is based upon the proper assertion of a legal or constitutional right.

(5) *Conclusion of No Formal Disciplinary Proceeding.* Should investigating counsel conclude after investigation and review that a formal disciplinary proceeding should not be initiated against the respondent because (A) sufficient evidence of misconduct is not present, or (B) there is pending another proceeding against the respondent, the disposition of which in the judgment of the investigating counsel should be concluded before further action by this Court, or (C) any other valid reason exists, investigating counsel shall submit a report to the Chief Judge containing his or her findings and recommendations for disposition of the matter. If the Chief Judge concludes that no further action is required or that the matter should be deferred pending conclusion of another proceeding against the respondent, the Chief Judge shall instruct investigating counsel to so notify the respondent. If the Chief Judge concludes that further investigation is required he or she shall remand the matter to investigating counsel for further investigation in accordance with the Chief Judge's directive.

(6) *Conclusion of Discipline by Consent.* Should investigating counsel conclude after investigation and review that a private reprimand or public discipline should be issued to the respondent, and the respondent consents to the recommendation of investigating counsel, the investigating counsel shall submit a written report to the Chief Judge containing his or her findings and recommendations. If the Chief Judge approves the recommendation of investigating counsel, he or she shall submit the report to the full Court for review and disposition. If the Chief Judge or the full Court concludes that further investigation is required, the matter shall be remanded to investigating counsel for further investigation in accordance with the Chief Judge's or the full Court's directive. If the respondent does not consent to the issuance of either a private reprimand or public discipline as recommended by the investigating counsel, the investigating counsel shall proceed in accordance with the provisions of L.Civ.R. 104.1(e)(7).

(7) *Conclusion of Public Discipline.* Should investigating counsel conclude that sufficient evidence of misconduct exists warranting the imposition of public discipline, investigating counsel shall submit a written report and application to the Chief Judge for the issuance of a Complaint and an order to show cause signed by the Chief Judge requiring the respondent to show cause why such discipline should not be imposed.

(8) Upon the Chief Judge's issuance of a complaint and order to show cause as set forth in L.Civ.R. 104.1(e)(7), the respondent shall file an answer within 20 days of the receipt of the complaint and order to show cause. In the answer respondent may set forth all affirmative defenses, including all claims of mental and physical disability, if any, and whether they are alleged to be causally related to the offense charged. Within 30 days of the filing of an answer, the respondent and investigating counsel may serve demands for discovery.

(9) Upon the filing of a complaint and order to show cause, as set forth in L.Civ.R. 104.1(e)(7), the Chief Judge shall set the matter for prompt hearing before a Judge, provided, however, that if the disciplinary proceeding is predicated upon the complaint of a

Judge of this Court, the hearing shall be conducted before a different Judge appointed by the Chief Judge, or if the Chief Judge is the complainant, by the next active Judge senior in commission.

(10) The hearing referred to in L.Civ.R. 104.1(e)(9) shall be presented by the investigating counsel. A stenographic record shall be made of the proceeding. At the conclusion of the hearing, the Judge assigned to the matter shall submit his or her findings of fact, conclusions of law and recommendations, if any, to the full Court for action, with a copy to the respondent and to investigating counsel.

(11) The full Court shall review the findings of fact, conclusions of law and recommendations of the Judge designated by the Chief Judge to hear the matter, the transcript of the hearings and the briefs previously filed with the Court. The record may be supplemented by the filing of briefs pursuant to a schedule fixed by the Chief Judge for review on the record and briefs, without oral argument, by the full Court. The full Court shall take whatever action it deems appropriate including, but not limited to, the dismissal of the action, private reprimand, the issuance of a public reprimand, suspension or disbarment.

(12) If a respondent desires legal representation, but claims to be unable to retain counsel by reason of indigence, the respondent may make application to the Chief Judge for appointment of counsel. Upon exceptional circumstances having been shown, the Judge to whom the matter has been assigned shall designate an attorney who is admitted to practice before this Court to represent respondent in the matter.

(13) In furtherance of the investigation proceeding pursuant to L.Civ.R. 104.1(e)(4), investigating counsel may seek the issuance of a subpoena ad testificandum or a subpoena duces tecum by making an application to the Chief Judge. After an order to show cause has been issued by the Chief Judge pursuant to L.Civ.R. 104.1(e)(7), investigating counsel and respondent may seek the issuance of the aforesaid subpoenas by way of application to the Judge designated to hear the matter.

(14) The standard of proof in proceedings before the Judge designated to hear the matter and the full Court shall be clear and convincing evidence, and the burden of proof under that standard shall be on the investigating counsel.

(f) Disbarment on Consent While Under Disciplinary Investigation or Prosecution.

(1) Any attorney admitted to practice before this Court who is the subject of an investigation into or a pending proceeding involving allegations of misconduct may consent to disbarment, but only by delivering to this Court an affidavit stating that the attorney desires to consent to disbarment and that:

(A) the attorney's consent is freely and voluntarily rendered; the attorney is not being subjected to coercion or duress; the attorney is fully aware of the implications of such consent;

(B) the attorney is aware that there is presently pending an investigation or proceeding involving allegations that there exist grounds for the attorney's discipline, the nature of which the attorney shall specifically set forth;

(C) the attorney acknowledges that the material facts so alleged are true; and

(D) the attorney so consents because the attorney knows that if charges were predicated upon the matters under investigation, or if the proceeding were prosecuted, the attorney could not successfully defend.

(2) Upon receipt of the required affidavit, this Court shall enter an order disbarring the attorney signed by the Chief Judge, unless unavailable, at which time the order shall be signed by the next active Judge senior in commission.

(3) The order disbarring the attorney on consent shall be a matter of public record; however, the affidavit required by this Rule shall not be publicly disclosed or made available for use in any other proceeding except upon order of this Court.

(g) Reinstatement.

(1) *After Disbarment or Suspension.* An attorney suspended for three months or less shall be automatically reinstated at the end of the period of suspension upon filing with the Court an affidavit of compliance with the provisions of the order. An attorney suspended for more than three months or disbarred may not resume practice until reinstated by order of this Court.

(2) *Time of Application Following Disbarment.* A person who has been disbarred after hearing or by consent may not apply for reinstatement until the expiration of at least five years from the effective date of the disbarment.

(3) *Hearing on Application.* Filing, service and notice of the petition shall be in accordance with the rules and regulations promulgated by the Disciplinary Review Board appointed by the Supreme Court of New Jersey. See New Jersey Court Rule 1:20–21. Petitions for reinstatement under this Rule by a disbarred or suspended attorney shall be filed with the Clerk. Upon receipt of the petition, the Clerk shall refer the petition to counsel and shall assign the matter for prompt hearing before a Judge, provided however that if the disciplinary proceeding was predicated upon the complaint of a Judge of this Court the hearing shall be conducted before a different Judge appointed by the Chief Judge, or if the Chief Judge was the complainant, by the next active Judge senior in commission. The Judge assigned to the matter

shall, within 30 days after referral, schedule a hearing at which the petitioner shall have the burden of demonstrating by clear and convincing evidence that he or she has the moral qualifications, competency and learning in the law required for admission to practice law before this Court and that his or her resumption of the practice of law will not be detrimental to the integrity and standing of the bar or to the administration of justice, or subversive of the public interest.

(4) *Duty of Counsel.* In all proceedings upon a petition for reinstatement, cross-examination of the witnesses of the petitioner and the submission of evidence, if any, in opposition to the petition shall be conducted by counsel.

(5) *Conditions of Reinstatement.* If the petitioner is found unfit to resume the practice of law, the petition shall be dismissed. If the petitioner is found fit to resume the practice of law, the judgment shall reinstate that person, provided that the judgment may make reinstatement conditional upon the payment of all or part of the costs of the proceedings, and upon the making of partial or complete restitution to parties harmed by the petitioner whose conduct led to the suspension or disbarment. If the petitioner has been suspended or disbarred for five years or more, reinstatement may be conditioned, in the discretion of the Judge before whom the matter is heard, upon the furnishing of proof of competency and learning in the law, which proof may include certification by the bar examiners of a state or other jurisdiction of the attorney's successful completion of an examination for admission to practice subsequent to the date of suspension or disbarment.

(6) *Successive Petitions.* No petition for reinstatement under this Rule shall be filed within one year following an adverse judgment upon a petition for reinstatement filed by or on behalf of the same person.

(h) Attorneys Specially Admitted. Whenever an attorney applies to be admitted or is admitted to practice before this Court for purposes of a particular proceeding (pro hac vice), the attorney shall be deemed thereby to have conferred disciplinary jurisdiction upon this Court for any alleged misconduct of that attorney arising in the course of or in the preparation for such proceeding.

(i) Service of Papers and Other Notices. Service of an order to show cause instituting a formal disciplinary proceeding shall be made by personal service or by registered or certified mail addressed to the respondent at the address shown in the roll of attorneys of this Court or the most recent edition of the New Jersey Lawyers Diary and Manual. Service of any other papers or notices required by these Rules shall be deemed to have been made if such paper or notice is addressed to the respondent at the address shown on the roll of attorneys of this Court or the most recent edition of the New Jersey Lawyers Diary and Manual, or to the respondent's attorney at the address indicated in the most recent pleading or other document filed in the course of any proceeding.

(j) Appointment of Counsel. Whenever counsel is to be appointed pursuant to these Rules to investigate allegations of misconduct or prosecute disciplinary proceedings or in conjunction with a reinstatement petition filed by a disciplined attorney, this Court may appoint as counsel the disciplinary agency of the Supreme Court of New Jersey, or other disciplinary agency having jurisdiction. If no such disciplinary agency exists or such disciplinary agency declines appointment, or such appointment is clearly inappropriate, this Court shall appoint as counsel one or more members of the bar of this Court to investigate allegations of misconduct or to prosecute disciplinary proceedings under these Rules, provided, however, that the respondent may move to disqualify an attorney so appointed who is or has been engaged as an adversary of the respondent in any matter. Counsel, appointed under this paragraph or paragraph (e)(12) above, may not resign without permission from the Court.

(k) Payment of Fees and Costs. At the conclusion of any disciplinary investigation or prosecution under these Rules, counsel appointed by the Court to either investigate, prosecute or defend the respondent in these disciplinary proceedings shall submit to the Court an itemized affidavit of expenses incurred in the course of such disciplinary investigation or prosecution. Any such appointed counsel may also submit an itemized affidavit of fees, calculated at $75 per hour or such higher rate as may from time to time be allowable to counsel for indigent defendants under the federal Criminal Justice Act. Any attorney who is disciplined because of misconduct may be directed by the Court to pay all or part of the fees and expenses incurred by the Court and/or by any counsel appointed by the Court to investigate allegations of misconduct and/or to prosecute or defend the disciplinary proceedings. If the disciplinary proceedings result in the imposition of no discipline upon the respondent, counsel appointed to investigate and/or prosecute the proceedings may seek from the Court an order that his/her expenses be reimbursed from the Court's Attorney Admissions Fee Fund. If the respondent is determined to be indigent, any attorney appointed to either investigate, prosecute or defend the respondent may seek from the Court an order that his/her expenses be reimbursed from the Court's Attorney Admissions Fee Fund, without regard to whether the proceedings resulted in the imposition of discipline. Upon receipt of affidavits regarding attorneys fees as described above, the Court may, in exceptional circumstances and if specifically requested by the applicant, order payment from the Court's Attorney Admissions Fee Fund of all or part of the fees of any appointed counsel. Any of the foregoing applications shall be made to the Judge appointed pursuant to paragraph (e)(9) hereof or, if no such Judge has been appointed, to the Chief Judge.

(*l*) Duties of the Clerk.

(1) Upon being informed that an attorney admitted to practice before this Court has been convicted of any crime, the Clerk shall determine whether the clerk of the court in which such conviction occurred has forwarded a certificate of such conviction to this Court. If a certificate has not been so forwarded, the Clerk shall promptly obtain a certificate and file it with this Court.

(2) Upon being informed that an attorney admitted to practice before this Court has been subjected to discipline by another court, the Clerk shall determine whether a certified or exemplified copy of the disciplinary judgment or order has been filed with this Court, and, if not, the Clerk shall promptly obtain a certified or exemplified copy of the disciplinary judgment or order and file it with this Court.

(3) Whenever it appears that any person convicted of any crime or disbarred or suspended or censured or disbarred on consent by this Court is admitted to practice law in any other jurisdiction or before any other court, the Clerk shall, within 10 days of that conviction, disbarment, suspension, censure, or disbarment on consent, transmit to the disciplinary authority in such other jurisdiction, or for such other court, a certificate of the conviction or a certified copy of the judgment or order of disbarment, suspension, censure or disbarment on consent, as well as the last known office and residence addresses of the defendant or respondent.

(4) The Clerk shall also promptly notify the National Discipline Data Bank operated by the American Bar Association of any order imposing public discipline upon any attorney admitted to practice before this Court.

(m) Jurisdiction. Nothing contained in these Rules shall be construed to deny to this Court such powers as are necessary for the Court to maintain control over proceedings conducted before it, such as proceedings for contempt under Title 18 of the United States Code or under Fed. R. Crim. P. 42.

Source: L.Civ.R. 105.1(a)—G.R. 36.A; L.Civ.R. 105.1(b)—G.R. 36.B; L.Civ.R. 105.1(c)—G.R. 36.C; L.Civ.R. 105.1(d)—G.R. 36.E (first clause); L.Civ.R.105. 1(e)—G.R.36.E (second and third clauses); L.Civ.R. 105.1(f)—G.R. 36.F; L.Civ.R. 105.1(g)—G.R. 36.G.

[Effective April 1, 1997; amended effective March 14, 2001.]

CIV. RULE 105.1. EXTRAJUDICIAL STATEMENTS

(a) A lawyer representing a party in a civil matter triable to a jury shall not make any extrajudicial statement that a reasonable person would expect to be disseminated by means of public communication if the lawyer or other person knows or reasonably should know that it will have a substantial likelihood of causing material prejudice to an adjudicative proceeding.

(b) A statement referred to in L.Civ.R. 105.1(a) ordinarily is likely to have such an effect when it relates to:

(1) the character, credibility, reputation or criminal record of a party or witness, the identity of a witness, or the expected testimony of a party or witness;

(2) the performance or results of any examination or test, the refusal or failure of a person to submit to an examination or test, or the identity or nature of physical evidence expected to be presented; and

(3) information the lawyer knows or reasonably should know is likely to be inadmissible as evidence in a trial and would if disclosed create a substantial risk of prejudice to an impartial trial.

(c) Notwithstanding L.Civ.R. 105.1(a) and (b), a lawyer involved in the litigation of a matter may state without elaboration:

(1) the general nature of a claim or defense;

(2) the information contained in a public record;

(3) the scheduling or result of any step in litigation; and

(4) a request for assistance in obtaining evidence and the information necessary thereto.

(d) Nothing in this Rule is intended to preclude either the formulation or application of more restrictive rules relating to the release of any information about parties or witnesses in an appropriate case.

(e) Nothing in this Rule is intended to apply to the holding of hearings or the lawful issuance of reports by legislative, administrative or investigative bodies, nor to a reply by any attorney to charges of misconduct publicly made against that attorney.

(f) The Court's supporting personnel including, among others, the Marshal, Deputy Marshals, the Clerk, Deputy Clerks, bailiffs, court reporters and employees or subcontractors retained by the Court-appointed official reporters, probation officers and their staffs, and members of the Judges' staffs, are prohibited from disclosing to any person, without authorization by the Court, information relating to a proceeding that is not part of the public record of the Court. The disclosure of information concerning in camera arguments and hearings held in chambers or otherwise outside the presence of the public is also forbidden.

(g) The Court, on motion of any party or on its own motion, may issue a special order governing such matters as extrajudicial statements by parties and witnesses likely to interfere with the rights of a party to a fair trial by an impartial jury, the seating and conduct in the courtroom of spectators and news media representatives, the management and sequestration of jurors and witnesses, and any other matters which the Court may deem appropriate for inclusion in such an order.

Source: L.Civ.R. 105.1(a)—G.R. 36.A.; L.Civ.R. 105.1(b)—G.R. 36.B.; L.Civ.R. 105.1(c)—G.R. 36.C.; L.Civ.R. 105.1(d)—G.R. 36.E. (first clause); L.Civ.R. 105.1(e)—G.R. 36.E. (second and third clauses); L.Civ.R. 105.1(f)—G.R. 36.F.; L.Civ.R. 105(g)—G.R. 36.G.

[Effective April 1, 1997.]

CIV. RULE 201.1 ARBITRATION

(a) Certification of Arbitrators.

(1) The Chief Judge shall certify as many arbitrators as determined to be necessary under this Rule. Arbitrators shall be designated for terms of service up to three years, subject to extension at the discretion of the Chief Judge, and all such terms shall be staggered to provide orderly rotation of a portion of the membership of the panel of arbitrators.

(2) An individual may be designated to serve as an arbitrator if he or she: (a) has been for at least five years a member of the bar of the highest court of a State or the District of Columbia, (b) is admitted to practice before this Court, (c) is determined by the Chief Judge to be competent to perform the duties of an arbitrator, and (d) has participated in a training program (or the equivalent thereof) to the satisfaction of the Chief Judge.

(3) Each individual certified as an arbitrator shall take the oath or affirmation prescribed by 28 U.S.C. § 453 before serving as an arbitrator.

(4) A list of all persons certified as arbitrators shall be maintained in the office of the Clerk.

(5) Each arbitrator shall, for the purpose of performing his or her duties, be deemed a quasi-judicial officer of the Court.

(b) Designation of Compliance Judge. The Board of Judges shall designate a Judge or Magistrate Judge to serve as the compliance judge for arbitration. This compliance judge shall be responsible to the Board of Judges for administration of the arbitration program established by this Rule and shall be responsible for monitoring the arbitration processes; provided, however that the compliance judge shall not be responsible for individual case management.

(c) Compensation and Expenses of Arbitrators. An arbitrator shall be compensated $250 for service in each case assigned for arbitration. In the event that the arbitration hearing is protracted, the Court will entertain a petition for additional compensation. The fees shall be paid by or pursuant to an order of the Director of the Administrative Office of the United States Courts. Arbitrators shall not be reimbursed for actual expenses incurred by them in the performance of their duties under this Rule.

(d) Civil Cases Eligible for Compulsory Arbitration.

(1) *Compulsory Arbitration.* Subject to the exceptions set forth in L.Civ.R. 201.1(d)(2), the Clerk shall designate and process for compulsory arbitration any civil action pending before the Court where the relief sought consists only of money damages not in excess of $150,000 exclusive of interest and costs and any claim for punitive damages.

(2) *Exclusion from Compulsory Arbitration.* No civil action shall be designated or processed for compulsory arbitration if the claim therein is

(A) based on an alleged violation of a right secured by the Constitution of the United States; or

(B) jurisdictionally based, on whole or in part, on (i) 28 U.S.C. §1346(a)(1) (tax refund actions) or (ii) 42 U.S.C. § 405(g) (Social Security actions).

Upon filing its initial pleading a party may request that an otherwise eligible case not be designated or processed for compulsory arbitration if either circumstances encompassed within L.Civ.R. 201.1(e)(6) are present or other specific policy concerns exist which make formal adjudication, rather than arbitration, appropriate.

(3) *Presumption of Damages.* For the sole purpose of making the determination as to whether the damages are in excess of $150,000 as provided in L.Civ.R. 201.1(d)(1), damages shall be presumed in all cases to be $150,000 or less, exclusive of interest and costs and any claim for punitive damages, unless counsel of record for the plaintiff at the time of filing the complaint or counsel of record for any other party at the time of filing that party's first pleading, or any counsel within 30 days of the filing of a notice of removal, files with the Court a document signed by said counsel which certifies that the damages recoverable exceed the sum of $150,000 exclusive of interest and costs and any claim for punitive damages. The Court may disregard any certification filed under this Rule and require arbitration if satisfied that recoverable damages do not exceed $150,000. No provision of this Rule shall preclude an arbitrator from entering an award exceeding $150,000 based upon the proofs presented at the arbitration hearing; and an arbitrator's award may also include interest, costs, statutory attorneys' fees and punitive damages, if appropriate.

(e) Referral for Arbitration.

(1) After an answer is filed in a case determined eligible for arbitration, the Clerk shall send a notice to counsel setting forth the date and time for the arbitration hearing consistent with the scheduling order entered in the case and L.Civ.R. 201.1(e)(3). The notice

shall also advise counsel that they may agree to an earlier date for the arbitration hearing provided the Clerk is notified within 30 days of the date of the notice. In the event additional parties have been joined in the action, this notice shall not be sent until an answer has been filed by all such parties who have been served with process and are not in default.

(2) The arbitration hearing shall be held before a single arbitrator. The arbitrator shall be chosen by the Clerk from among the lawyers who have been certified as arbitrators by the Chief Judge. The arbitrator shall be scheduled to hear not more than three cases on a date or dates which shall be scheduled several months in advance.

(3) The Judge to whom the case has been assigned shall, at least 30 days prior to the date scheduled for the arbitration hearing, sign an order setting forth the date and time of the arbitration hearing and the name of the arbitrator designated to hear the case. In the event that a party has filed a motion to dismiss the complaint, for judgment on the pleadings, summary judgment or to join necessary parties, or proceedings are initiated under L.Civ.R. 201.1(e)(6), the Judge shall not sign the order required herein until the Court has ruled on the motion or order to show cause, but the filing of such a motion on or after the date of said order shall not stay arbitration unless the Judge so orders.

(4) The Plaintiff shall within 10 days upon receipt of the order appointing arbitrator send to the arbitrator a copies of any complaint, amended complaint and answers to counterclaim; counsel for each defendant shall, within 10 days upon receipt of this order, send to the arbitrator any answer, amended answer, counterclaim, cross-claim and answer hereto, any third-party complaint. Upon receipt of these materials, the arbitrator shall forthwith inform all parties, in writing, as to whether the arbitrator, or any firm or member of any firm with which he or she is affiliated has (either as a party or attorney), at any time within the past five years, been involved in litigation with or represented any party to the arbitration, or any agency, division or employee of such a party.

(5)(A) Statutory Disqualification. Persons selected to be arbitrators shall be disqualified for bias or prejudice as provided in 28 U.S.C. §144, and shall disqualify themselves in any action in which they would be required under 28 U.S.C. §455 to disqualify themselves if they were a justice, judge, or magistrate judge.

(B) Impartiality. An arbitrator shall be impartial and advise all parties of any circumstances bearing on possible bias, prejudice, or impartiality. Impartiality means freedom from favoritism or bias in word, action, and appearance.

(C) Conflicts of Interest and Relationships; Required Disclosures; Prohibitions.

i. An arbitrator must disclose to the parties and to the compliance judge any current, past, or possible future representation or consulting relationship with, or pecuniary interest in, any party or attorney involved in the arbitration.

ii. An arbitrator must disclose to the parties any close personal relationship or other circumstance which might reasonably raise a question as to the arbitrator's impartiality.

iii. The burden of disclosure rests on the arbitrator. All such disclosures shall be made as soon as practical after the arbitrator becomes aware of the interest or relationship. After appropriate disclosure, the arbitrator may serve if all parties so desire. If the arbitrator believes or perceives that there is a clear conflict of interest, the arbitrator shall withdraw irrespective of the expressed desires of the parties.

iv. In no circumstance may an arbitrator represent any party in any matter during the arbitration.

v. An arbitrator shall not use the arbitration process to solicit, encourage, or otherwise incur future professional services with any party.

(6) Either sua sponte, or upon a recommendation received from the arbitrator, or upon the application of a party, the Judge to whom the case is assigned may exempt from arbitration any action that would otherwise be arbitrable under this Rule if (a) it involves complex or novel legal issues, or (b) the legal issues predominate over the factual issues, or (c) other good cause is shown. When initiating such a review either sua sponte or upon recommendation of the arbitrator, the Judge may proceed pursuant to an order to show cause providing not less than 10 days notice to all parties of the opportunity to be heard. Any application by a party to exempt an action from arbitration shall be by formal motion pursuant to these Rules.

(f) Arbitration Hearing.

(1) The arbitration hearing shall take place on the date and at the time set forth in the order of the Court. The arbitrator is authorized to change the date and time of the hearing, provided the hearing is commenced within 30 days of the hearing date set forth in the Court's order. Any continuance beyond this 30-day period must be approved by the Judge to whom the action is assigned. The Clerk must be notified immediately of any continuance.

(2) Counsel for the parties shall report settlement of the action to the Clerk and to the arbitrator assigned to that action.

(3) The arbitration hearing may proceed in the absence of any party who, after notice, fails to be present. In the event that a party fails to participate

in the arbitration process in a meaningful manner, the arbitrator shall make that determination and shall support it with specific written findings filed with the Clerk. Thereupon, the Judge to whom the action is assigned shall conduct a hearing upon notice to all counsel and personal notice to any party adversely affected by the arbitrator's determination and may thereupon impose any appropriate sanctions, including, but not limited to, the striking of any demand for a trial de novo filed by that party.

(4) Fed. R. Civ. P. 45 shall apply to subpoenas for attendance of witnesses and the production of documentary evidence at an arbitration hearing under this Rule. Testimony at an arbitration hearing shall be under oath or affirmation.

(5) The Federal Rules of Evidence shall be used as guides to the admissibility of evidence. Copies or photographs of all exhibits, except exhibits intended solely for impeachment, must be marked for identification and delivered to adverse parties at least 10 days prior to the hearing and the arbitrator shall receive exhibits into evidence without formal proof unless counsel has been notified at least five days prior to the hearing that the adverse party intends to raise an issue concerning the authenticity of the exhibit. The arbitrator may refuse to receive into evidence any exhibit a copy or photograph of which has not been delivered to the adverse party, as provided herein.

(6) A party desiring to have a recording and/or transcript made of the arbitration hearing shall make all necessary arrangements for same and shall bear all expenses so incurred.

(g) Arbitration Award and Judgment. Within 30 days after the hearing is concluded, the arbitrator shall file under seal with the Clerk a written award, accompanied by a written statement or summary setting forth the basis for the award which shall also be filed under seal by the Clerk. Neither the Clerk nor any party or attorney shall disclose to any Judge to whom the action is or may be assigned the contents of the arbitration award except as permitted by 28 U.S.C. § 657(b). The arbitration award shall be unsealed and entered as the judgment of the Court after the time period for demanding a trial de novo, pursuant to L.Civ.R. 201.1(h), has expired, unless a party demands a trial de novo before the Court. The judgment so entered shall be subject to the same provisions of law, and shall have the same force and effect as a judgment of the Court in a civil action, except that it shall not be the subject of appeal. In a case involving multiple claims and parties, any separable part of an arbitration award may be the subject of a trial de novo if the aggrieved party makes a demand for same pursuant to L.Civ.R. 201.1(h) before the expiration of the applicable time period. If the aggrieved party fails to make a timely demand pursuant to L.Civ.R. 201.1(h), that part of the arbitration award shall become part of the final judgment with the same force and effect as a judgment of the Court in a civil action, except that it shall not be the subject of appeal.

(h) Trial De Novo.

(1) Any party may demand a trial de novo in the District Court by filing with the Clerk a written demand, containing a short and plain statement of each ground in support thereof, and serving a copy upon all counsel of record or other parties. Such a demand must be filed and served within 30 days after the arbitration award is filed and service is accomplished by a party pursuant to 28 U.S.C. § 657(a), or by the Clerk (whichever occurs first), except that in any action in which the United States or any employee or agency thereof is a party the time period within which any party therein may file and serve such a demand shall be 60 days.

(2) Upon the filing of a demand for a trial de novo, the action shall be placed on the calendar of the Court and treated for all purposes as if it had not been referred to arbitration, except that no additional pretrial discovery shall be permitted without leave of Court, for good cause shown. Any right of trial by jury that a party would otherwise have shall be preserved inviolate.

(3) The Magistrate Judge shall conduct a pretrial conference within 60 days of filing of a demand for a trial de novo.

(i) Guidelines for Arbitration. The Court, the Clerk, the parties, attorneys and arbitrators are hereby referred to the Guidelines for Arbitration (Appendix M to these Rules) for their information and guidance in civil actions arbitrated pursuant to this Rule.

Source: G.R. 49.

[Effective April 1, 1997. Amended March 31, 1999; amended effective April 19, 2000; July 5, 2001; amended March 9, 2007.]

CIV. RULE 301.1. MEDIATION

(a) Designation of Mediators.

(1) The Chief Judge shall designate as many mediators as determined to be necessary under this Rule. Mediators shall be designated for terms of service up to three years, subject to extension at the discretion of the Chief Judge, and such terms shall be staggered to provide orderly rotation of a portion of the membership of the panel of mediators.

(2) An individual may be designated to serve as a mediator if he or she:

(A) has been for at least five years a member of the bar of the highest court of a State or the District of Columbia;

(B) is admitted to practice before this Court;

(C) is determined by the Chief Judge to be competent to perform the duties of a mediator; and

(D) has participated in a training program (or the equivalent thereof) to the satisfaction of the Chief Judge.

(3) Each mediator shall, for the purpose of performing his or her duties, be deemed a quasijudicial officer of the Court.

(b) Designation of Compliance Judge. The Board of Judges shall designate a Judge or Magistrate Judge to serve as the compliance judge for mediation. This compliance judge shall be responsible to the Board of Judges for administration of the mediation program established by this Rule and shall entertain any procedural or substantive issues arising out of mediation.

(c) Compensation of Mediators. Each mediator designated to serve by the Chief Judge under L.Civ. R. 301.1 (a) shall be compensated $300 an hour for service in each civil action referred to mediation, which compensation shall be borne equally by the parties; notwithstanding this provision, the first three hours of service shall be without compensation. Where all parties select as a mediator a person not designated as a panel mediator under L. Civ. R. 301.1 (a), the parties and the mediator may, by written agreement, fix the amount and terms of the mediator's compensation.

(d) Civil Actions Eligible for Mediation. Each Judge and Magistrate Judge may, without the consent of the parties, refer any civil action to mediation. The parties in any civil action may, with consent of a Judge or Magistrate Judge, agree to mediation and, if such consent is given, select a mediator. Notwithstanding the above, no civil action described in L.Civ. R.72.1(a)(3)(C), may be referred to mediation.

(e) Mediation Procedure.

(1) Counsel and the parties in each civil action referred to mediation shall participate therein and shall cooperate with the mediator, who shall be designated by the compliance judge.

(2) Whenever a civil action is referred to mediation the parties shall immediately prepare and send to the designated mediator a position paper not exceeding 10 pages in length. The parties may append to their position papers essential documents only. Pleadings shall not be appended or otherwise submitted unless specifically requested by the mediator.

(3) Counsel and the parties (including individuals with settlement authority for specific individuals) shall attend all mediation sessions unless otherwise directed by the mediator.

(4) The mediator may meet with counsel and the parties jointly or ex parte. All information presented to the mediator shall be deemed confidential unless requested otherwise and shall not be disclosed by anyone, including the mediator, without consent, except as necessary to advise the Court of an apparent failure to participate. The mediator shall not be subject to subpoena by any party. No statements made or documents prepared for mediation shall be disclosed in any subsequent proceeding or construed as an admission.

(5) All proceedings (including motion practice and discovery) shall be stayed for a period of 90 days from the date a civil action is referred to mediation. Any application for an extension of the stay shall be made jointly by the parties and the mediator and shall be considered by the referring Judge or Magistrate Judge.

(f) Guidelines for Mediation. The Court, the Clerk, the parties, attorneys and mediators are hereby referred to the Guidelines for Mediation (Appendix Q to these Rules) for their information and guidance in civil actions referred to mediation pursuant to this Rule. Said Guidelines for Mediation shall have the same force and effect as the provisions of this Rule.

(g) Ethical Standards for Mediators.

(1) *Impartiality.* A mediator shall be impartial and advise all parties of any circumstances bearing on possible bias, prejudice, or impartiality. Impartiality means freedom from favoritism or bias in word, action, and appearance. Impartiality implies a commitment to aid all parties, as opposed to an individual party, in moving toward an agreement.

(A) A mediator shall maintain impartiality while raising questions for the parties to consider as to the reality, fairness, equity, and feasibility of proposed options for settlement.

(B) A mediator shall withdraw from mediation if the mediator believes the mediator can no longer be impartial.

(C) A mediator shall not accept or give a gift, request, favor, loan or any other item of value to or from a party, attorney, or any other person involved in and arising from any mediation process.

(2) *Conflicts of Interest and Relationships; Required Disclosures; Prohibitions.*

(A) A mediator must disclose to the parties and to the compliance judge any current, past, or possible future representation or consulting relationship with, or pecuniary interest in, any party or attorney involved in the mediation.

(B) A mediator must disclose to the parties any close personal relationship or other circumstance, in addition to those specifically mentioned in L.Civ.R. 301.1(g)(2)(A), which might reasonably raise a question as to the mediator's impartiality.

(C) The burden of disclosure rests on the mediator. All such disclosures shall be made as soon as practical after the mediator becomes aware of the interest or the relationship. After appropriate disclosure, the mediator may serve if all parties so desire. If the mediator believes or perceives that there is a clear conflict of interest, the mediator shall withdraw irrespective of the expressed desires of the parties.

(D) In no circumstance may a mediator represent any party in any matter during the mediation.

(E) A mediator shall not use the mediation process to solicit, encourage, or otherwise incur future professional services with any party.

(h) Grievance Procedure. Any grievance concerning the conduct of a mediator, attorney, or other participant in mediation shall be in writing to the compliance judge within 30 days from the event giving rise to the grievance. The compliance judge may investigate the grievance and take such action in response thereto as may be appropriate, upon due notice to all affected persons or entities.

Source: G.R. 49.

[Effective April 1, 1997; amended effective May 27, 1998; April 19, 2000; March 14, 2001; July 5, 2001; January 2, 2008.]

CIV. RULE 401.1. MEDIA COVERAGE

(a) The taking of photographs and operation of audio or videotape recorders in the courtroom or its environs and radio or television broadcasting from the courtroom or its environs, during the progress of and in connection with judicial proceedings, including proceedings before a Magistrate Judge, whether or not court is actually in session, is prohibited. Environs of the courtroom shall include the entire United States Courthouses at Camden, Newark and Trenton, including all entrances to and exits from said buildings. A Judge or Magistrate Judge may, however, permit the use of electronic or photographic means for the presentation of evidence or the perpetuation of a record.

(b) In the discretion of any Judge, broadcasting, photographing, audio or videorecording of investitive, naturalization or ceremonial proceedings in a courtroom may be permitted under such conditions as the Judge may prescribe.

Source: G.R. 36.H.

[Effective April 1, 1997.]

CIV. RULE 501.1 POSSESSION AND USE OF ELECTRONIC EQUIPMENT

(a) Objective. This policy establishes that "Electronic Devices," as defined herein may be brought into courthouses subject to all appropriate security screening and that such Electronic Devices must be rendered inoperable in courtrooms and judicial chambers, unless use is authorized in such areas by the presiding judicial officer. A significant goal of this policy is to create circuit-wide consistency for the benefit of the public, attorneys and employees.

(b) Scope. This policy identifies authorized devices, establishes the classes of individuals who may possess authorized devices, sets out the basis for exceptions to the policy, and specifies guidelines for security screening and establishing areas where use of electronic devices may be prohibited. The use of electronic devices in courthouses and courtrooms is subject to existing judiciary court policies regarding inappropriate and unauthorized activity, including U.S. Judicial Conference prohibition against "broadcasting, televising, recording or taking photographs in the courtroom and areas immediately adjacent thereto . . . "

(c) Exception. Nothing in this policy prevents a judge, on an individual case basis, and with adequate notification, from temporarily establishing a ban on all Electronic Devices to be carried into a courtroom.

(d) Explanation of Terms. Electronic Devices refers to those devices (both currently available as well as future technology) that have as their primary function wireless communication, the storage and retrieval of digitized data, and computer applications. The list of covered devices includes, but is not limited to, electronic devices that serve as cell phones, pagers, Palm Pilots/digital assistants, pocket computers, laptop computers, notebook computers, Blackberries, wireless network cards, and Internet cards or devices. Devices that serve only as cameras, audio recorders or video recorders are not covered by this policy, and remain subject to regulation by local court rules and orders.

(e) Authorization. Electronic Devices may be brought into the courthouse, whether in the possession of attorneys, jurors, court employees, public, or press. Unless specifically authorized by the presiding judicial officers, all Electronic Devices must be rendered inoperable before entering any courtroom or judicial chambers. Use of Electronic Devices shall remain subject to Judicial Conference and local court policies regarding inappropriate use and unauthorized activity.

Permission to carry these devices, with all of the sensitive data they may contain, into the courthouse, is intended as a convenience to those possessing such devices and to ease the burden on court security staff at building entrances. This policy is not to be construed as granting permission to use any of these devices.

(f) Enforcement

(1) *Physical Security.* Current policies regarding physical security will remain in effect. Security officers at courthouse entrances will screen all Electronic Devices for explosives, weapons, etc. Nothing in this

policy is intended to limit the authority of the security officers to determine the appropriate means of screening Electronic Devices and to bar the possession of any Electronic Device determined to pose a security threat.

(2) *Prohibited Uses.* Unless authorized by the presiding judicial officer, all Electronic Devices shall be rendered inoperable prior to entering any courtroom or judicial chambers. Courts may, by local rule or order, further restrict the use of any Electronic Devices inside the courthouse.

(A) Notification. Policies proscribing use of Electronic Devices, with appropriate penalties, will be prominently displayed in the courthouse, on the court's web site, and in mailings to potential jurors and grand jurors.

The court's employee handbook will clearly state the use policy pertaining to employees of the judiciary, including law clerks.

(B) Courtrooms. Unauthorized use of Electronic Devices in courtrooms will be addressed by courtroom security or court staff pursuant to local regulations.

(C) Jurors. Jurors in possession of Electronic Devices will surrender these devices to court staff prior to entering the jury room to commence deliberations.

(D) Grand Jurors. Grand jurors in possession of electronic devices will surrender these devices to court staff prior to entering the Grand Jury room.

(3) *Case–by–Case Exceptions.* In the event a judge temporarily establishes a complete ban of any Electronic Device for the duration of a trial, screening for possession of Electronic Devices will occur, if practicable, in close proximity to the relevant courtroom, with a portable screening station/magnetometer, or other appropriate device. Additional security staff should be requested for this function.

(4) *Court Security Officers*

(A) Physical Security. Court Security Officers (CSOs) will be responsible for physical screening of devices at courthouse entrances in accordance with policies established by the United States Marshal, and will be responsible for barring any Electronic Device determined to pose a security threat.

(B) Custodial Duties. CSOs will not have any custodial duties regarding the checking and storing of Electronic Devices except as may be required on a case-by-case temporary basis as outlined in § VI.(C) above.

(g) Implementation of This Policy. This policy will be implemented as a Standing Order of the Court with limited or unlimited duration as the court determines.

Publisher's Note: The italicized text of this rule was suspended pursuant to Standing Order 05–03 dated July 26, 2005; see post.

[Adopted effective April 30, 1998; Amended effective March 9, 2007.]

LOCAL CRIMINAL RULES

CR. RULE 1.1. SCOPE AND APPLICABILITY

The following Local Civil Rules are applicable to criminal cases tried in the District of New Jersey:

L.Civ.R. 1.1
L.Civ.R. 1.2
L.Civ.R. 5.1(b)–(e)
L.Civ.R. 6.1(a)(1)–(2)
L.Civ.R. 7.1(a)
L.Civ.R. 7.1(c)(1)
L.Civ.R. 7.1(e)
L.Civ.R. 7.1(g)
L.Civ.R. 7.1(i)
L.Civ.R. 7.2
L.Civ.R. 10.1(b)
L.Civ.R. 52.1
L.Civ.R. 54.1
L.Civ.R. 54.3(a)
L.Civ.R. 69.1
L.Civ.R. 77.1
L.Civ.R. 78.1
L.Civ.R. 79.1(a), (b) and (e)
L.Civ.R. 79.2
L.Civ.R. 79.4
L.Civ.R. 79.5
L.Civ.R. 80.1
L.Civ.R. 83.1
L.Civ.R. 83.2
L.Civ.R. 83.3
L.Civ.R. 102.1
L.Civ.R. 103.1
L.Civ.R. 104.1
L.Civ.R. 401.1

Source: New.

[Effective April 1, 1997; amended effective February 24, 2005.]

CR. RULE 5.1. UNITED STATES MAGISTRATE JUDGES

Each Magistrate Judge is authorized to perform all judicial duties assigned by the Court that are consistent with the Constitution and the laws of the United States which include, but are not limited to the following duties in criminal matters:

(a) Proceeding in matters involving misdemeanors and petty offenses in accordance with Fed.R.Crim.P. 58 and L.Cr.R. 58.1;

(b) Administering oaths and affirmations, imposing conditions of release under 18 U.S.C. § 3142, taking acknowledgments, affidavits, and depositions, and performing such functions related to bail as are described in L.Cr.R. 46.1.

(c) Receiving grand jury returns and issuing bench warrants, when necessary, for defendants named in an indictment.

(d) Exercising all the powers and duties conferred or imposed upon United States Commissioners by law.

(e) Receiving and filing complaints, issuing search warrants and arrest warrants and receiving their return. The approval of the United States Attorney or a designated Assistant shall be secured with respect to the contents of all proposed complaints and warrants.

(f) Conducting initial appearances and preliminary examinations.

(g) Conducting arraignments in accordance with Fed.R.Crim.P. 10, to the extent of taking a not guilty plea or noting a defendant's intention to plead guilty or nolo contendere, and ordering a presentence report in appropriate cases.

(h) Taking a plea and imposing sentence upon the transfer under Fed.R.Crim.P. 20 of any information or indictment charging a misdemeanor, if the defendant consents in writing to this procedure.

(i) Conducting proceedings in accordance with Fed. R.Crim.P. 40.

(j) Conducting proceedings for revocation or modification of probation in non-felony cases.

(k) Conducting extradition proceedings, in accordance with 18 U.S.C. § 3184.

(*l*) Issuing subpoenas, writs of habeas corpus ad testificandum or habeas corpus ad prosequendum, or other orders necessary to obtain the presence of parties or witnesses or evidence needed for court proceedings.

(m) Upon the request of the United States Attorney, authorizing the installation of pen register devices and executing orders directing telephone company assistance to the Government for such installation.

(n) Hearing and determining any criminal pretrial motion or other criminal pretrial matter, other than those motions specified in L.Cr.R. 5.1(*o*), in accordance with 28 U.S.C. § 636(b)(1)(A).

(*o*) In accordance with 28 U.S.C. § 636(b)(1)(B) and (C), conducting such evidentiary hearings as are necessary and appropriate, and submitting to a Judge proposed findings of fact and recommendations for the disposition of:

(1) applications for post-trial relief made by individuals convicted of criminal offenses; or

(2) motions to dismiss or quash an indictment or information made by a defendant, or to suppress evidence in a criminal case.

(3) Any party may object to the Magistrate Judge's proposed findings, recommendations or report issued under this Rule within 10 days after being served with a copy thereof, pursuant to the procedure set forth in L.Civ.R. 72.1(c)(2).

Source: L.Cr.R. 5.1 (first sentence)—G.R. 40; L.Cr.R. 5.1(a)—G.R. 40.B.2 and B.17 [by inference]; L.Cr.R. 5.1(b)—G.R. 40.B.3; L.Cr.R. 5.1(c)—G.R. 40.B.4; L.Cr.R. 5.1(d)—G.R. 40.B.5; L.Cr.R. 5.1(e)—G.R. 40.B.6; L.Cr.R. 5.1(f)—G.R. 40.B.7; L.Cr.R. 5.1(g)—G.R. 40.B.8; L.Cr.R. 5.1(h)—G.R. 40.B.9; L.Cr.R. 5.1(i)—G.R. 40.B.10; L.Cr.R. 5.1(j)—G.R. 40.B.11; L.Cr.R. 5.1(k)—G.R. 40.B.12; L.Cr.R. 5.1(*l*)—G.R. 40.B.13; L.Cr.R. 5.1(m)—G.R. 40.A.11; L.Cr.R. 5.1(n)—G.R. 40.B.14; L.Cr.R. 5.1(*o*)—G.R. 40.B.15.

[Effective April 1, 1997.]

CR. RULE 7.1. GRAND JURORS

The selection, qualification, summoning, exemption or excuse from service of grand jurors shall be governed by the Plan of Implementation adopted by the Court pursuant to 28 U.S.C. § 1861, et seq. The Plan is available for inspection at the office of the Clerk.

Source: G.R. 19.A.

[Effective April 1, 1997.]

CR. RULE 12.1. MOTIONS UNDER Fed.R.Crim.P. 12

Defenses or objections permitted pursuant to Fed. R.Crim.P. 12 shall be made before pleading or within 30 days thereafter unless the Court at the time of arraignment on application of counsel otherwise specifies, or unless good cause is shown.

Source: G.R. 12.F.

[Effective April 1, 1997.]

CR. RULE 18.1. ASSIGNMENT OF CRIMINAL CASES

(a) All criminal cases shall be assigned by the Clerk to a Judge of the vicinage where the alleged offense arose. The Clerk may, however, assign a criminal case to a Judge in a vicinage other than where the alleged offense arose, if necessary to balance the assigned case loads among the vicinages, employing such plan as the Court from time to time adopts for such assignments. The vicinage where the assigned Judge is sitting shall be the place of trial and all proceedings in the cause, unless changed by order of the Court. Any application for reassignment of a criminal matter to any Judge in a vicinage other than where the assigned Judge is sitting shall be made by notice of motion pursuant to L.Civ.R. 7.1, returnable before the Chief Judge.

(b) Reassignment of any case shall be upon the order of the Chief Judge.

Source: L.Cr.R. 18.1(a)—G.R. 11.E; L.Cr.R. 18.1(b)—G.R. 11.F.

[Effective April 1, 1997; amended effective March 14, 2001.]

CR. RULE 24.1. SELECTION AND IMPANELMENT OF TRIAL JURORS

(a) The selection, qualification, summoning, exemption or excuse from service of petit jurors shall be governed by the Plan of Implementation adopted by the Court pursuant to 28 U.S.C. § 1861, et seq. The Plan is available for inspection at the office of the Clerk.

(b) In any case where each side is entitled to an equal number of challenges, these challenges shall alternate one by one, with the Government exercising the first challenge.

(c) In criminal cases where the Government is entitled to six peremptory challenges and the defendant or defendants jointly to 10 peremptory challenges, the order of challenge shall be as follows:

Government 1
Defendant 2
Government 1
Defendant 2
Government 1
Defendant 2
Government 1
Defendant 2
Government 1
Defendant 1
Government 1
Defendant 1

(d) In any case where there is more than one defendant, in the event the Court allows defendants additional peremptory challenges, the order of challenge will be established by the Court.

(e) In challenging alternate jurors in a criminal case, such challenges shall alternate one by one with the Government exercising the first challenge.

(f) The passing of a peremptory challenge by any party shall not constitute a waiver of the right thereafter to exercise the same against any juror, unless all parties pass successive challenges.

(g) No attorney or party to an action shall personally or through any investigator or other person acting for such attorney or party, directly or indirectly interview, examine or question any juror, relative, friend or associate thereof during the pendency of the trial or with respect to the deliberations or verdict of the jury in any action, except on leave of Court granted upon good cause shown.

Source: L.Cr.R. 24.1(a)—G.R. 19.A.; L.Cr.R. 24.1(b)—G.R. 20.A.; L.Cr.R. 24.1(c)—G.R. 20.B.; L.Cr.R. 24.1(d)—G.R. 20.C.; L.Cr.R. 24.1(e)—G.R. 20.D.; L.Cr.R. 24.1(f)—G.R. 20.E.; L.Cr.R. 24.1(g)—G.R. 19.B.

[Effective April 1, 1997.]

CR. RULE 32.1. PROBATION

(a) Conditions. The "conditions of probation" set forth on any official probation form as may be approved for use in the United States District Courts shall be deemed included in the conditions of probation prescribed by the Court as to every defendant placed on probation. Copies of that form shall be signed by the probationer and one copy shall be delivered to the probationer by the probation office at the time the defendant is placed on probation.

(b) Records. No confidential records of this Court maintained by the probation office, including presentence and probation supervision records, shall be sought by any applicant except by written petition to this Court establishing with particularity the need for specific information in the records.

When a demand for disclosure or presentence and probation records is made by way of subpoena or other judicial process to a probation officer of this Court, the probation officer may file a petition seeking instruction from the Court with respect to responding to the subpoena. Whenever a probation officer is subpoenaed for such records, he or she shall petition the Court in writing for authority to release documentary records or produce testimony with respect to such confidential information. In either event no disclosure shall be made except upon an order issued by the Court.

Source: G.R. 39.

[Effective April 1, 1997.]

CR. RULE 41.1. MOTIONS UNDER Fed.R.Crim.P. 41

Defenses or objections permitted pursuant to Fed. R.Crim.P. 41(e) shall be made before pleading or within 30 days thereafter unless the Court at the time of arraignment on application of counsel otherwise specifies, or unless good cause is shown.

Source: G.R. 12.F.

[Effective April 1, 1997.]

CR. RULE 44.1. FORMAL WRITTEN APPEARANCE—CRIMINAL MATTERS

Unless appointed by a formal order of the Court, after the filing of an indictment or information the attorney for each defendant named therein shall promptly file with the Clerk a formal appearance in substantially the form set forth in Appendix B and mail a copy thereof to the United States Attorney.

Source: G.R. 17.

[Effective April 1, 1997.]

CR. RULE 46.1. RELEASE FROM CUSTODY

(a) Deposit in Lieu of Surety.

(1) In lieu of surety in any case there may be deposited with the Clerk lawful United States currency, certificates of deposit issued by a bank licensed to do business in the United States, negotiable bonds approved by the Court or notes of the United States. If certificates of deposit, negotiable bonds or notes are deposited, the depositor shall execute the agreement required by 31 U.S.C. § 9303, authorizing the Clerk to collect or sell the bonds or notes in the event of default. In the case of certificates of deposit, the depositor shall notify the banking institution that the depositor's rights in the certificate of deposit have been assigned to the Clerk, United States District Court, and the banking institution shall acknowledge such notification to the Clerk. Unless ordered otherwise, the Clerk automatically shall reinvest the certificate of deposit at the maturity date at the then-prevailing rate of interest.

(2) If such a deposit in a criminal proceeding is not forfeited for default upon the appearance bond and was made by the party required to give security, or is shown to the Court to be his or her property though deposited in another name, it may be applied successively to the satisfaction of: (a) pecuniary conditions imposed upon the grant of probation; (b) claims of the United States in the proceeding, such as fines, costs or costs of prosecution under 28 U.S.C. § 1918; and (c) fees and expenses of the Marshal and Clerk. Upon exoneration of the appearance bond, the balance of the deposit then remaining shall be returned to the depositor.

(b) Bail.

(1) *Security Required.* Unless otherwise specified, an order fixing bail in a stated amount will be deemed to require the execution of a bail bond or equivalent security.

(2) *Bail Review.* Bail fixed by a Magistrate Judge in this District may not be reviewed by the Court unless an application to modify has first been made to the Magistrate Judge who fixed bail. A Magistrate Judge shall hear the first bail review, including bail review after indictment, unless bail was previously set in open court by a Judge after hearing. If bail is set by a Judge after an adversary hearing, no Magistrate Judge shall hear any review of that bail without the specific authorization of the Judge setting the bail. Further review by a Judge shall be made upon the

record of the reasons for the bail set forth in writing by the Magistrate Judge, together with additional information that may be presented.

(3) *Hearing.* Upon request of the United States Attorney with regard to a particular defendant, the Clerk shall notify the United States Attorney at the time the defendant appears to satisfy the bail provisions set by the Magistrate Judge or Judge. Upon motion by the United States Attorney or by its own motion, the Court may hold a hearing at which any person who posts collateral or cash for the securing of any bond may be examined as to the sources of such cash or collateral. The Court shall refuse to accept such bond if there is reason to believe that such cash or collateral is from a source such that it will not reasonably assure the appearance of the defendant as required.

(4) *Posting Security.* When the release of a defendant is conditioned upon the deposit of cash or other security with the Court, such deposit shall be made with the Clerk.

(5) *Approval of Bonds and Sureties.* All bail bonds and witness signatures on personal surety bonds shall be approved by a Magistrate Judge or the Clerk, who will acknowledge the signatures of those persons having executed the bonds. Unless the Court otherwise directs, all bonds in noncapital criminal cases for appearance before the Court shall be presented to a Magistrate Judge or the Clerk for approval, and if approved by the Magistrate Judge immediately forwarded to the Clerk together with any money or certificates of deposit, negotiable bonds approved by the Court, or notes of the United States deposited as security.

(6) *Documentation—Review by United States Attorney.* Any documentation required by this Rule shall be promptly reviewed, if necessary, by the United States Attorney present at the office where the bail bond is being executed, who shall advise the judicial officer or the Clerk of his or her approval or disapproval of the documentation presented. If the documentation is disapproved, the United States Attorney shall specify to the Court the reason for disapproval.

(7) *Documentation—Disapproval by United States Attorney; Hearing.* At the request of an aggrieved party, the Court as soon as practicable shall set a hearing on the reasons for disapproval or the failure of the United States Attorney to respond.

(8) *Cancellation of Bond.* Subject to L.Cr.R. 46.1(a)(2), upon termination of a criminal proceeding and authorization from the United States Attorney, the Clerk shall cancel the appearance bond and, where there has been a deposit of money, negotiable bonds, certificates of deposit or notes of the United States, shall prepare an order for submission to the Court for the return of the money, bonds, certificates of deposit or notes to the depositor thereof.

(c) Refund of Bond Monies.

(1) Where a defendant's bond is secured by depositing cash with the Clerk pursuant to L.Cr.R. 46.1(a), the monies shall be refunded when the conditions of the bond have been performed, the defendant has been discharged from all obligations thereon, and the recognizance bond has been duly cancelled of record. If the sentence includes a fine or costs, however, any such fine or costs shall constitute a lien in favor of the United States on the amount deposited to secure the bond. No such lien shall attach when someone other than the defendant has deposited the cash and the refund is directed to someone other than the defendant.

(2) The depositor shall at the time of the deposit execute a certification indicating the name and address of the person to whom the cash is to be refunded. This shall be done on the form provided by the Clerk and appended to the bail bond. See Appendix C. The depositor may change the designation of the person to receive the refund only by filing an executed assignment of bail or a consent order.

(d) Sureties.

(1) All surety companies holding certificates of authority from the Secretary of the Treasury as acceptable sureties on Federal bonds, and which have appointed process agents for the District of New Jersey, are approved up to the amount for which they are respectively authorized by the Treasury Department as sureties on stipulations for cost or value, undertakings, bail bonds, and all other bonds required to be filed in the Court.

(2) Noncorporate sureties shall be required to annex to every bail bond an affidavit of justification executed on the form furnished by the Clerk.

(3) Unless the Court otherwise directs, the equity of a noncorporate surety offering real estate as security shall be determined to be the difference between the assessed valuation as shown by the last current tax bill and the existing mortgages and liens against the property. Such equity must be at least twice the amount of the bonds if the surety offering such bond is unmarried, or if husband and wife jointly sign the bonds as sureties, where the property is in either of their names. If a married person offers a bond as surety without the spouse joining, then the equity must be four times the amount of the bond.

(4) Only property held in fee simple shall be accepted, and where title is in the name of husband and wife as tenants by the entirety, their bond shall not be accepted unless both sign the same.

(5) All noncorporate sureties shall be required to exhibit at the time of the execution of the bond, deeds, last current tax receipts and personal identification prior to acceptance of any such surety.

(6) It shall be the duty of the officer accepting bail to acquaint a noncorporate surety with the conditions of suretyship as set forth in this Rule.

(7) In determining equity, the Court may consider market value of such real estate instead of its assessed valuation only upon formal application to the Court with notice to the attorney for each adversary party. All such applications shall be accompanied by not less than two affidavits.

(8) Property owned out of the District of New Jersey may be offered as surety on the same basis as set forth in L.Cr.R. 46.1(d)(3) and, if such property is accepted, it shall become the obligation of counsel for the defendant to perfect a lien on it in accordance with the law and rules of the courts in the jurisdiction where the property is located, and said counsel shall so certify to the Clerk.

(e) Attorney Shall Not Provide Bail. No attorney shall tender his or her own funds for use as bail, except by special leave of the Court.

Source: L.Cr.R. 46.1(a)—G.R. 35.A.; L.Cr.R. 46.1(b)—G.R. 35.B.; L.Cr.R. 46.1(c)—G.R. 35.C.1–2; L.Cr.R. 46.1(d)—G.R. 35.C.3–5; L.Cr.R. 46.1(e)–G.R. 35.D.

[Effective April 1, 1997.]

CR. RULE 53.1. CONDUCT IN THE COURTROOM

The Marshal or a designated Deputy Marshal shall, unless expressly excused by the presiding Judge, attend each criminal proceeding of the Court and shall exercise the powers granted to and discharge the duties set forth in 28 U.S.C. § 566 and in other applicable laws and rules as may be required by the Court.

Source: G.R. 3.B.

[Effective April 1, 1997.]

CR. RULE 55.1. RECORD OF PROCEEDINGS

(a) The Magistrate Judge disposing of a case involving a petty offense or a misdemeanor, as defined in the Federal criminal code, shall file with the Clerk a record of proceedings prepared on forms, dockets, etc., to be furnished by the Administrative Office of the United States Courts. The record of proceedings, with the original papers attached, shall be filed with the Clerk not later than 20 days following the date of final disposition.

(b) All fines collected or collateral forfeited shall be transmitted immediately to the Clerk.

(c) In all other cases, as soon as the defendant is discharged or after binding over, is either confined on final commitment or released on bail, except as provided in the Court's plan implementing the Criminal Justice Act, the Magistrate Judge is required within 20 days thereafter to transmit to the Clerk the file in the case including, if issued or received by the Magistrate Judge, the original complaint, warrant of arrest with the officer's return thereon, temporary and final commitments with returns thereon, and the completed transcript which consists of verbatim copies, carbon or otherwise, of all successive docket entries in the case.

Source: G.R. 40.B.16.

[Effective April 1, 1997.]

CR. RULE 55.2. CUSTODY AND DISPOSITION OF EXHIBITS

At the conclusion of a criminal matter, the Clerk shall promptly return to the United States Attorney all trial exhibits marked or introduced in evidence by the Government, except those pleadings from the Clerk's file that were marked as exhibits, and all supporting materials in the form of unused exhibits, contraband and grand jury material, including audio and videotapes held by the Clerk at the request of the Government. Any exhibit marked or introduced in evidence by a defendant in a criminal matter shall be returned to the attorney for the defendant at the conclusion of the matter. The attorney to whom the exhibits are returned shall be responsible for their preservation until the time for appeal has passed, during the pendency of any appeal, or for six months, whichever period is longer, and shall make them available to any party or attorney in the matter for the purpose of preparing the record or appendix on appeal. For the purpose of this Rule, a criminal matter is deemed concluded after a verdict is returned, or after a dispositive finding by the Court.

Source: G.R. 26.D.

[Effective April 1, 1997.]

CR. RULE 58.1. PROCEEDINGS IN MISDEMEANOR AND PETTY OFFENSE CASES

(a) Assignment of Misdemeanor and Petty Offense Cases. Upon the filing of an information or the return of an indictment, all misdemeanor cases shall be assigned by the Clerk to a Magistrate Judge, who shall proceed in accordance with the provisions of 18 U.S.C. § 3401. Upon the filing of a complaint or violation notice charging a petty offense, the Magistrate Judge by whom such complaint or violation notice is received shall open a Magistrate Judge's docket and proceed in the matter.

(b) Trial and Disposition of Misdemeanor and Petty Offense Cases. The Magistrate Judge is authorized to perform all judicial duties assigned by the Court in order to try persons accused of misdemeanors and petty offenses committed within this District in accordance with 18 U.S.C. § 3401 and 28 U.S.C. § 636 in jury and nonjury cases, order a presentence investigation report on any such person who is convicted or pleads guilty or nolo contendere, sentence such person, and determine requests for reduction of sentence of such person.

(c) Forfeiture of Collateral in Lieu of Appearance.

(1) In suitable petty offense or misdemeanor cases, a forfeiture of collateral security may be accepted in lieu of appearance as a disposition of the case.

(2) There shall be maintained at each office of the Clerk and Magistrate Judge a list of the offenses and fines applicable thereto for which a forfeiture of collateral security may be accepted. See Appendix E.

(3) Persons charged with offenses which do not appear on the list must appear for trial. A person who timely tenders the forfeiture of collateral security for an offense listed pursuant to L.Cr.R. 58.1(c)(2) will not be required to appear for trial by the authority issuing the violation notice.

(4) Amendments and revisions to the list of offenses and fines set forth in Appendix E may be made from time to time by the Court.

(d) Appeals From Judgments in Misdemeanor or Petty Offense Cases.

(1) A defendant may appeal a judgment of conviction by a Magistrate Judge in a misdemeanor or petty offense case by filing a notice of appeal with the Clerk within 10 days after entry of the judgment, and by serving a copy of the notice upon the United States Attorney. The scope of review upon appeal shall be the same as an appeal from a judgment of the District Court to the Third Circuit.

(2) In all such misdemeanor appeals, the appellant shall serve and submit a brief within 20 days of the filing of the notice of appeal. The appellee shall serve and submit a brief within 20 days after the receipt of a copy of appellant's brief. The appellant may serve and submit a reply brief within five days after receipt of the appellee's brief. All briefs shall conform to the requirements of L.Civ.R. 7.2(b). Fifty days after the filing of the notice of appeal, the Clerk shall place that appeal upon the calendar for hearing.

Source: L.Cr.R. 58.1(a)—G.R. 40.B.1; L.Cr.R. 58.1(b)—G.R. 40.B.2; L.Cr.R. 58.1(c)—G.R. 40.B.17; L.Cr.R. 58.1(d)—G.R. 40.D.1.

[Effective April 1, 1997.]

CR. RULE 60.1. TITLE

These Rules may be known and cited as the Local Criminal Rules of the United States District Court for the District of New Jersey and abbreviated as "L.Cr.R."

Source: G.R. 1.A. [by inference].

[Effective April 1, 1997.]

CR. RULE 101.1. EXTRAJUDICIAL STATEMENTS IN CRIMINAL PROCEEDINGS

(a) A lawyer representing a party with respect to a criminal matter, or any other proceeding that could result in incarceration, shall not make any extrajudicial statement that a reasonable person would expect to be disseminated by means of public communication if the lawyer or other person knows or reasonably should know that it will have a substantial likelihood of causing material prejudice to an adjudicative proceeding.

(b) A statement referred to in L.Cr.R. 101.1(a) ordinarily is likely to have such an effect when it relates to:

(1) the character, credibility, reputation or criminal record of a defendant, suspect in a criminal investigation or witness, the identity of a witness, or the expected testimony of a party or witness;

(2) the possibility of a plea of guilty to the offense or the existence or contents of any confession, admission or statement given by a defendant or suspect, or that person's refusal or failure to make a statement;

(3) the performance or results of any examination or test, the refusal or failure of a person to submit to an examination or test, or the identity or nature of physical evidence expected to be presented;

(4) any opinion as to the guilt or innocence of a defendant or suspect; or

(5) information the lawyer knows or reasonably should know is likely to be inadmissible as evidence in a trial and would if disclosed create a substantial risk of prejudice to an impartial trial.

(c) Notwithstanding L.Cr.R. 101.1(a) and (b), a lawyer involved in the investigation or prosecution of a matter may state without elaboration:

(1) the general nature of a charge or defense;

(2) the information contained in a public record;

(3) that an investigation of the matter is in progress, including the general scope of the investigation, the offense, claim or defense involved and, except when prohibited by law, the identity of the persons involved;

(4) the scheduling or result of any step in litigation;

(5) a request for assistance in obtaining evidence and the information necessary thereto;

(6) a warning of danger concerning the behavior of a person involved, when there is reason to believe that

there exists the likelihood of substantial harm to an individual or to the public interest;

(7) the identity, residence, occupation and family status of the accused;

(8) if the accused has not been apprehended, information necessary to aid in apprehension of that person;

(9) the fact, time and place of arrest; and

(10) the identity of investigating and arresting officers or agencies and the length of the investigation.

(d) The prohibitions set forth in L.Cr.R. 101.1(a), (b) and (c) pertain to all stages of criminal proceedings, including investigation before a grand jury, the post-arrest pretrial period, jury selection, and jury trial through verdict.

(e) Nothing in this Rule is intended to preclude either the formulation or application of more restrictive rules relating to the release of any information about juvenile or other offenders.

(f) Nothing in this Rule is intended to apply to the holding of hearings or the lawful issuance of reports by legislative, administrative or investigative bodies, nor to a reply by any attorney to charges of misconduct publicly made against that attorney.

(g) The Court's supporting personnel including, among others, the Marshal, Deputy Marshals, the Clerk, Deputy Clerks, bailiffs, court reporters and employees or subcontractors retained by the Court-appointed official reporters, probation officers and their staffs, and members of the Judges' staffs, are prohibited from disclosing to any person, without authorization by the Court, information relating to a pending grand jury proceeding or a criminal case that is not part of the public record of the Court. The disclosure of information concerning grand jury proceedings, in camera arguments and hearings held in chambers or otherwise outside the presence of the public is also forbidden.

(h) The Court, on motion of any party or on its own motion, may issue a special order governing such matters as extrajudicial statements by parties and witnesses likely to interfere with the rights of a party to a fair trial by an impartial jury, the seating and conduct in the courtroom of spectators and news media representatives, the management and sequestration of jurors and witnesses, and any other matters which the Court may deem appropriate for inclusion in such an order.

Source: L.Cr.R. 101.1(a)—G.R. 36.A.; L.Cr.R. 101.1(b)—G.R. 36.B.; L.Cr.R. 101.1(c)—G.R. 36.C.; L.Cr.R. 101.1(d)—G.R. 36.D.; L.Cr.R. 101.1(e)—G.R. 36.E. (first clause); L.Cr.R. 101.1(f)—G.R. 36.E. (second and third clauses); L.Cr.R. 101.1(g)—G.R. 36.F.; L.Cr.R. 101.1(h)—G.R. 36.G.
[Effective April 1, 1997.]

APPENDICES

APPENDIX A1. CLIENT'S & SUPERVISING ATTORNEY'S AUTHORIZATIONS FOR APPEARANCE BY LAW STUDENT

UNITED STATES DISTRICT COURT FOR THE DISTRICT OF NEW JERSEY

FORM TO BE COMPLETED BY THE CLIENT FOR WHOM A LAW STUDENT IS RENDERING SERVICES; OR IF THE SERVICES ARE RENDERED FOR THE GOVERNMENT, BY THE UNITED STATES ATTORNEY OR HIS OR HER AUTHORIZED REPRESENTATIVE.

I authorize ______, a law student, to appear in court or at other proceedings and to prepare documents on my behalf. I am aware that (he) (she) is not admitted to the bar and that (he) (she) will appear pursuant to the Student Practice Rule (L.Civ.R. 101.1(h)) of the District of New Jersey.

______________________ ______________________

(Date) (Signature of Client)

(If more than one client is involved, approvals from each shall be attached. If a class action is involved, approvals from class members named in the caption shall be attached.)

TO BE COMPLETED BY THE LAW STUDENT'S SUPERVISING ATTORNEY:

I will carefully supervise all of this student's work. I authorize this student to appear in court or at other proceedings and to prepare documents. I will accompany the student at such appearances and sign all documents prepared by the student. I personally assume professional responsibility for the student's work.

______________________ ______________________

(Date) (Signature of Attorney)

[Effective April 1, 1997.]

APPENDIX A2. FORM FOR DESIGNATING COMPLIANCE WITH THE STUDENT PRACTICE RULE

UNITED STATES DISTRICT COURT FOR THE
DISTRICT OF NEW JERSEY

FORM FOR DESIGNATING COMPLIANCE WITH THE STUDENT PRACTICE RULE OF THE DISTRICT OF NEW JERSEY

______________________	______________________
(Name of Student)	(Name of Supervising Attorney)
Address & Phone of Above:	Address & Phone of Above:
______________________	______________________
______________________	______________________
______________________	______________________

Name of Law School student is attending: ______________________

Number of credits student has successfully completed: ______________

Number of credits needed for graduation: ______________________

TO BE COMPLETED BY LAW STUDENT:

I certify that: I have successfully completed ______ credits of law school, I am familiar and will comply with the Code of Professional Responsibility of the American Bar Association as amended by the Supreme Court of New Jersey, and I am familiar with the Federal procedural and evidentiary rules relevant to the action in which I am appearing.

______________________	______________________
(Date)	(Student Signature)

TO BE COMPLETED BY THE DEAN OR A FACULTY MEMBER OF THE STUDENT'S LAW SCHOOL:

I certify that this student has successfully completed ______ credits law school work, and is, to the best of my knowledge, qualified to provide the legal representation permitted by the Local Civil and Criminal Rules of the United States District Court for the District of New Jersey.

______________________	______________________
(Date)	(Signature of Dean or Faculty Member)
	______________________
	(Position of Above)

[Effective April 1, 1997.]

APPENDIX B. CRIMINAL CASE APPEARANCE FORM

UNITED STATES DISTRICT COURT
DISTRICT OF NEW JERSEY

Criminal No. ______

United States
v.
John Doe

Appearance for Defendant(s)

I (We) hereby enter my (our) appearance as attorney(s) for the following named defendant(s).

____
Attorney(s)
By: ______________________________
(Member of Above Firm)

Date: ______________________________

____
Address
____
____
Phone

[Effective April 1, 1997.]

APPENDIX C. AFFIDAVIT BY OWNER OF CASH SECURITY

UNITED STATES DISTRICT COURT
DISTRICT OF NEW JERSEY

UNITED STATES OF AMERICA
v.

Case No. ______
Affidavit re Appearance Bond
(Cash Security)

AFFIDAVIT BY OWNER OF CASH SECURITY

I, ______, on oath say that I reside at ______ and that the $______ cash deposited as security on the foregoing bond is owned by me and is to be returned to me at the above address upon examination* of this bond.

I hereby subject said fund to the provisions of L.Cr.R 46.1 and consent and agree that in case of default or contumacy on the part of the principal, the Court may proceed summarily and render judgment against said cash security in accordance with my obligation herein and award execution thereon.

Sworn to and subscribed before me this __ day of ______, 20__

____
Deputy

____
Signature of Cash Security Owner

[Effective April 1, 1997.]

* Publishers Note: As in original. Probably should be "exoneration".

APPENDIX D. ORDER GRANTING MOTION TO DEPOSIT SUM OF MONEY WITH THE COURT

UNITED STATES DISTRICT COURT FOR THE DISTRICT OF NEW JERSEY

Civil No.

Plaintiff(s)

vs.

Defendant(s)

ORDER GRANTING MOTION TO DEPOSIT SUM OF MONEY WITH THE COURT

The above-entitled cause having come before the Court upon the ______ Motion to Deposit Sum of Money with the Court pursuant to Fed.R.Civ.P. 67 and L.Civ.R. 67.1, and the Court having considered the motion.

NOW, THEREFORE, it is on this ___ day of ______, 20__;

ORDERED that the Motion to Deposit Sum of Money with the Court shall be, and is hereby, granted; it is

FURTHER ORDERED that such sum, to wit; ______ dollars, be deposited by the Clerk into the Registry of this Court and then, as soon as the business of his or her office allows, the Clerk shall deposit these funds into the interest-bearing Court Registry Investment System (C.R.I.S.) administered by the Clerk of the United States District Court for the Southern District of Texas as Custodian, pursuant to L.Civ.R. 67.1(a)(2); it is

FURTHER ORDERED that sum of money so invested in the interest-bearing C.R.I.S. fund shall remain on deposit until further order of this Court at which time the funds, together with interest thereon, shall be retrieved by the Clerk and redeposited into the non-interest-bearing Registry of the Court for disposition pursuant to the further order of the Court; it is

FURTHER ORDERED that the Custodian deduct a miscellaneous schedule fee for the handling of registry funds, as authorized by the Judicial Conference of the United States and the Standing Order of this Court dated June 30, 1989, as amended November 30, 1990, of 10% of the income earned on this account and each subsequent deposit of new principal so deposited while invested in the C.R.I.S.; and it is

FURTHER ORDERED that a certified copy of this Order shall be by the ______________ personally served upon the Clerk of this Court, the Chief Deputy Clerk, or upon the Chief Financial Deputy Clerk.

____
UNITED STATES DISTRICT JUDGE

[Effective April 1, 1997.]

APPENDIX E. LIST OF PETTY OFFENSES AND MINIMUM FINES APPLICABLE THERETO PURSUANT TO L.Cr.R. 58.1(c)

[For current copy of Appendix E. List of Petty Offenses and Minimum Fines Applicable Thereto Pursuant to L.Cr.R. 58.1(c), contact Clerk of Court.]

APPENDIX F. TRANSCRIPT RATES

It is on this day of March, 2003,

ORDERED that the following rates be and hereby are established for transcripts furnished by the Official Court Reporters:

	Original	First Copy to Each Party	Each Add'l Copy to the Same Party
Ordinary Transcript A transcript to be delivered within 30 calendar days after receipt of order.	$3.30	$.83	$.55
Expedited Transcript A transcript to be delivered within seven calendar days after receipt of order.	4.40	.83	.55
Daily Transcript A transcript to be delivered following adjournment and prior to the normal opening hour of the Court on the following morning whether or not it actually be a court day.	5.50	1.10	.83
Hourly Transcript A transcript of proceedings ordered under unusual circumstances to be delivered within two hours.	6.60	1.10	.83
Realtime Transcript A draft unedited transcript produced by a certified realtime reporter as a byproduct of realtime to be delivered electronically during proceedings or immediately following adjournment.	2.75	1.10	

It is FURTHER ORDERED these amendments are effective April 15, 2003.

[Effective April 1, 1997; amended effective September 6, 2000; April 15, 2003.]

APPENDIX G. OFFICIAL NEWSPAPERS

The following have been designated as official newspapers, within their respective counties, for the publication of notices and orders under all statutes and under all rules and general orders of the Supreme Court of the United States requiring or permitting this Court to designate newspapers for official publications:

THE ASBURY PARK PRESS
3601 Highway 66
P.O. Box 1550
Neptune, NJ 07754-4818
Counties: Monmouth, Ocean

BURLINGTON COUNTY TIMES
4284 Route 130 North
Willingboro, NJ 08046
Counties: Burlington

THE COURIER-NEWS
1201 Route 22 West
P.O. Box 6600
Bridgewater, NJ 08807
Counties: Hunterdon, Middlesex, Somerset, Union

COURIER-POST
301 Cuthbert Boulevard
P.O. Box 5300
Cherry Hill, NJ 08002
Counties: Burlington, Camden, Gloucester

THE DAILY JOURNAL
891 East Oak Road
P.O. Box 1504
Vineland, NJ 08360
Counties: Atlantic, Cumberland, Salem

THE GLOUCESTER COUNTY TIMES
309 South Broad Street
Woodbury, NJ 08096-2488
Counties: Gloucester

THE STAR LEDGER
One Star Ledger Plaza
Newark, NJ 07102-1200
Atlantic, Bergen, Essex, Hudson, Hunterdon, Mercer, Monmouth, Morris, Somerset, Union, Warren

THE TIMES
500 Perry Street
P.O. Box 847
Trenton, NJ 08605
Counties: Burlington, Hunterdon, Mercer, Middlesex, Ocean

TODAY'S SUNBEAM
93 Fifth Street
Salem NJ 08079
Counties: Gloucester, Salem

THE TRENTONIAN
600 Perry Street
Trenton, NJ 08619
Counties: Burlington, Hunterdon, Mercer

HERALD NEWS
One Garrett Mountain Plaza
CN 473
West Paterson, NJ 07424
Counties: Bergen, Passaic

HOME NEWS TRIBUNE
35 Kennedy Boulevard
P.O. Box 1049
East Brunswick, NJ 08816
Counties: Middlesex, Somerset, Union

THE JERSEY JOURNAL
30 Journal Square
Jersey City, NJ 07306
Counties: Hudson

NEW JERSEY HERALD
2 Spring Street
P.O. Box 10
Newton, NJ 07860
Counties: Sussex

THE PRESS OF ATLANTIC CITY
Devins Lane
Pleasantville, NJ 08232-3806
Counties: Atlantic, Cape May, Cumberland, Gloucester, Ocean

THE RECORD
150 River Street
Hackensack, NJ 07601-7172
Counties: Bergen, some Morris, Passaic

LEGAL PUBLICATIONS

NEW JERSEY LAW JOURNAL
238 Mulberry Street
P.O. Box 20081
Newark, NJ 07101-6081
Weekly Publication Throughout New Jersey

NEW JERSEY LAWYER
2035 Lincoln Highway
Edison, NJ 08817
Weekly Publication Throughout New Jersey

[Effective April 1, 1997.]

APPENDIX H. APPOINTMENT OF ATTORNEYS IN PRO SE CIVIL ACTIONS

The following procedures shall govern the appointment of attorneys to represent pro se parties in civil actions who lack sufficient resources to retain counsel.

The following procedures shall not govern the appointment of attorneys to represent pro se petitioners seeking a writ of habeas corpus on the ground they are in custody in violation of the Constitution or laws or treaties of the United States pursuant to 28 U.S.C. § 2254, or to pro se petitioners moving to vacate, set aside or correct their sentences pursuant to 28 U.S.C. § 2255. The appointment of attorneys in such cases shall be governed instead by 18 U.S.C. § 3006A, and counsel furnishing representation in such cases shall be selected from a panel of attorneys designated by the Court pursuant to 18 U.S.C. § 3006A(b) and its Criminal Justice Act Plan.

1. **Civil Pro Bono Panel.** There shall be a panel of attorneys who are willing to accept appointment to represent pro se parties in civil actions when such parties lack the resources to retain counsel. Appointment shall be made by the Office of the Clerk in accordance with the written procedures there on file, except that in special circumstances the Judge may appoint counsel directly.

2. **Committee on Civil Pro Bono Litigation.** The Chief Judge shall annually appoint a committee on civil pro bono litigation to oversee the operation of the Pro Bono Panel. This Committee shall include at least one United States District Judge, one United States Magistrate Judge, and representatives of the District of New Jersey bar who practice primarily in federal courts. The Committee shall oversee the Civil Pro Bono Panel established herein, recruit new members to the Panel and expert witnesses willing to accept reduced fees, provide training opportunities for Panel members, and annually report to the Chief Judge on the operation and utilization of the panel, recruitment, and recommended changes for improving the operation of the Panel.

3. **Composition of the Civil Pro Bono Panel.** The Civil Pro Bono Panel will consist of the following:

a. *Attorney Instructors in Law School Clinical Programs.* An attorney working with a clinical program from a law school accredited by the American Bar Association and located in the District of New Jersey may apply to participate by completing the appropriate forms available from the Clerk. In the application the attorney shall set forth, among other things:

1. that the attorney is in good standing in the District of New Jersey;

2. the number of cases per calendar year the attorney is willing to accept for the clinical program;

3. the preference for appointment among the types of actions (e.g., social security appeals, inmate civil rights, other civil rights, and miscellaneous);

4. the number of students involved in the clinical program;

5. the ability of the attorney and the clinical program to represent non-English-speaking clients;

6. the name of the supervisor of the clinical program.

b. *Law Firms.* Law firms, including public interest law firms, may apply to participate in the panel as firms by completing an application which sets forth, among other things:

1. the number of appointed cases per calendar year in which the firm is willing to accept appointment;

2. the names of the participating attorneys;

3. the ability of participating attorneys to represent non-English-speaking clients;

4. the firm's preference for appointment among various types of actions;

5. the name of the firm's attorney who will serve as the panel liaison.

Any matter assigned to a firm shall be directed to that firm's panel liaison, who, in turn, shall assign the matter to an attorney with that firm. Appearance in the action may be entered by either the firm or the assigned attorney, at the firm's option. The liaison, however, shall inform the Clerk, in writing, of the name of the attorney actually handling the matter.

c. *Individual Attorneys.* Attorneys who are willing to accept appointment to represent pro se parties shall submit an application setting forth, among other things:

1. the number of appointed cases per calendar year the attorney is willing to accept;

2. a description of the attorney's prior civil trial experience, including number of trials and areas of experience;

3. whether the attorney is able to represent non-English-speaking clients;

4. the attorney's preference for appointment among various types of actions.

d. *Review of Applications.* The Committee on Civil Pro Bono Litigation shall review all applications received and shall appoint attorneys to the panel when appropriate. The Committee may remove an attorney or firm from the panel at any time.

e. *Amendment or Withdrawal.* Information on an application may be amended at any time by letter. An attorney or firm may by letter withdraw from the panel at any time, subject to paragraphs 5 (Relief from Appointment) and 6 (Responsibilities of the Appointed Attorney).

4. Appointment Procedure.

a. The Office of the Clerk shall advise and assist any party appearing pro se in filing an in forma pauperis affidavit. The Clerk shall notify every party who has been granted in forma pauperis status pursuant to 28 U.S.C. § 1915 and is appearing pro se of the opportunity to apply in writing to the assigned judge for the appointment of counsel. The Clerk shall enclose with such notice a copy of this Rule and a form application for appointment of counsel. If the party is an inmate and the case falls within a category for which this Court has provided that standard discovery shall occur, the Office of the Clerk shall provide the relevant forms to the party, who will be responsible for serving them, but no request for standard discovery shall issue in cases deemed frivolous under 28 U.S.C. § 1915A.

b. The Clerk shall identify each case in one of the following categories: social security appeals, employment discrimination actions, inmates' civil rights, other civil rights, and miscellaneous.

c. Upon the filing of an Application for Appointment of Counsel, the Judge or Magistrate Judge (hereinafter the term "Judge" also includes Magistrate Judges) to whom the action is assigned shall determine whether and when a panel attorney should be appointed to represent the pro se party. The Judge may also make this determination at any time sua sponte. In making this determination the Judge shall consider all relevant materials, including the standard discovery, if any, obtained by the litigant.

d. Whenever the assigned Judge concludes that appointment of counsel is warranted, the Judge shall refer the case to the Clerk for appointment of an attorney from the Civil Pro Bono Panel. In special circumstances, the Judge may appoint counsel directly, in which case the Judge shall notify the Clerk of that appointment. Assignment of cases to attorneys on the Civil Pro Bono Panel shall not be made without prior agreement by the attorney. Assignments to attorneys representing law school clinical programs will be made at appropriate times during the school's academic year.

e. The Clerk will select a law intern or attorney from the appropriate list unless the Judge orders appointment of a specific attorney. Assignments to law firms and attorneys will be made randomly throughout the year.

f. Before referring a case to a law firm or an attorney, the Clerk shall determine whether the litigant has any other case pending before the Court and whether an attorney has been appointed in such case. Where an appointed attorney is already representing the litigant in a prior action, such attorney is encouraged but not required to represent the litigant in the new action.

g. Once an attorney has agreed to accept an appointment, the Clerk shall immediately send written notice of the appointment to the selected law firm or attorney. Copies of the pleadings filed to date, any responses by the Department of Corrections to standard discovery served by a pro se inmate, and relevant correspondence and other documents shall accompany such notice. Upon receipt of such notice, the appointed attorney shall promptly review the matter and enter an appearance in the action.

h. The Clerk shall also send immediate written notice of the appointment, including the name, address, and telephone number of the appointed attorney, to the party for whom the appointment is made and to all other parties in the action.

5. Relief From Appointment.

a. An appointed attorney may apply to be relieved from appointment, on the following grounds:

(i) A conflict of interest precludes the attorney from representing the party;

(ii) the attorney believes that he or she is not competent to represent the party in the particular type of action assigned;

(iii) a personal incompatibility exists between the attorney and the party, or a substantial disagreement exists between the attorney and the party concerning litigation strategy; or

(iv) the attorney believes that the party is proceeding for the purposes of harassment or malicious injury, or that the party's claims or defenses are clearly unsupported by fact, are unwarranted under existing law, or cannot be supported by good faith argument to extend, modify, or reverse existing law.

b. If, at any time, the appointed attorney discovers that the party is or has become able to pay for legal services, the attorney shall bring this information to the attention of the assigned Judge. The Judge may thereupon relieve the attorney from the appointment and permit the party to retain another attorney, to proceed pro se or to continue with the appointed attorney, but on a paying basis.

c. Any attorney who seeks to be relieved from an appointment under 5a(i) or (ii) shall first make that request in writing to the client, setting forth the reasons therefor. If the client consents to the attorney's request to be relieved, the attorney, upon presenting such facts to the assigned Judge, shall be relieved.

d. If a client objects to an attorney's request to be relieved under 5a(i) or (ii), the attorney shall promptly submit his or her request in writing to the assigned Judge, along with a statement of the reasons for the request. The assigned Judge shall then decide whether to grant the request. Any request under this section, and the decision thereon, shall remain confidential and may not be made available to the other parties to the litigation.

e. If an application for relief from appointment is consented to or granted, the Judge may appoint or direct the Clerk to appoint another attorney from the panel to represent the party.

6. **Responsibilities of the Appointed Attorney.**

a. Upon receiving an appointment, the attorney shall promptly communicate with the newly represented party concerning the action.

b. If, after reviewing the file and initial conference with the pro se litigant, the attorney concludes that he or she [cannot accept] must withdraw from the appointment because of the grounds enumerated in Section 5a(iii) or (iv), the attorney shall file a Notice of Withdrawal with the Court, with proof of service upon the client, stating without identification of reasons that "grounds for relief from appointment under 5(a)(iii) or (iv) exist" and return the case to the Clerk.

c. The appointed attorney should discuss the merits of the dispute with the party and explore with the party the possibilities of resolving the dispute by other means, including but not limited to administrative remedies.

d. If, after consultation with the appointed attorney, the party decides to prosecute or defend the action, the appointed attorney shall proceed to represent the party in the action, unless or until the attorney-client relationship is terminated as provided herein.

7. **Discharge.** A party for whom an attorney has been appointed shall be permitted to relieve the attorney from the representation. The party may ask the Judge to discharge the attorney. Upon a showing by affidavit of satisfactory reasons, the Judge may appoint a new attorney.

8. **Expenses.** The appointed attorney or the firm with which he or she is affiliated may advance the expenses of the litigation. Appointed pro bono attorneys or firms may apply to the Judge during the litigation or within a reasonable period thereafter for reimbursement of costs reasonably incurred in connection with the litigation, not including attorneys' fees, to be paid from the Pro Bono Fund ("Fund") and the Attorneys' Admission Fee Account ("Account"). Reimbursement shall be granted to the extent that funds are available for this purpose in the Fund and Account for all expenses reasonably incurred and not reimbursed by the opposing party pursuant to an Order of the Court. It shall be irrelevant to the application for reimbursement whether the attorney's client prevailed.

a. The Court should generally approve motions by the appointed attorney or stipulations designed to reduce discovery expenses, such as taking depositions by other than use of a stenographic transcript, for example by tape recorder or telephone. See Fed. R. Civ. P. 30(b)(7).

b. To the extent practicable and where the client is a prisoner, pretrial proceedings in which the prisoner's participation is permitted shall be conducted by telephone, video conference, or other telecommunications technology without removing the prisoner from the facility in which he or she is confined. See 42 U.S.C. § 1997e(f)(1).

c. On request to the Clerk, the appointed attorney may use the Court's video conferencing facilities to communicate with a client who is a prisoner in a facility that has confidential video conferencing capabilities.

d. Appointed attorneys are encouraged to seek free or reduced costs for depositions from the National Court Reporters Association, and free or reduced cost expert reports and/or witnesses from a list which shall be maintained by the Committee on Civil Pro Bono Litigation and shall be available from the Clerk.

9. **Compensation for Services.**

a. If the action is one for which compensation for legal services may become available to the appointed attorney by statute and be deductible from any recovery, the Clerk shall furnish information regarding such facts to the pro se party at the time the appointment is made. The Clerk shall also inform the party that any statutory fee award may be made only by the Judge upon application of counsel.

b. Pro se litigants in social security disability cases shall be specifically advised by the Clerk that a statutory attorney's fee may be awarded to be paid from the award, if any, of retroactive disability benefits.

c. Upon appropriate application by the appointed attorney, the Judge may award attorney's fees to the appointed attorney or legal clinic for services rendered in the action, as authorized by applicable statute, regulation, rule, or other provision of law, and as the Judge deems just and proper.

10. Duration of Representation.

a. An appointed attorney shall represent the party in the action in the trial court from the date he or she enters an appearance until he or she has been relieved from appointment by the Court or until a final judgment is entered in the action and reasonable efforts are made to enforce the judgment. The attorney shall, if it is appropriate in his or her judgment or requested by the litigant, file a notice of appeal from a final judgment as well as any post-trial motions.

b. If the party wishes to take an appeal from a final judgment or appealable interlocutory order, of if such judgment or order is appealed by another party, or if the matter is remanded to an administrative forum, the appointed attorney is encouraged but not required to represent the party on the appeal and in any proceeding, judicial or administrative, that may ensure upon an order of remand. If the attorney declines to perform such additional services, the client and the Court shall be notified in writing.

11. Training. The Committee on Civil Pro Bono Litigation shall, in cooperation with the New Jersey Bar, organize and conduct educational programs and prepare educational materials to train and advise attorneys on the Civil Pro Bono Panel in the preparation and trial of the most common types of civil actions involving pro se parties brought before the Court.

12. Annual Review. At the end of each fiscal year, the Clerk of the Court shall report to the Chief Judge, the Board of Judges, and the members of the Committee on Civil Pro Bono Litigation the following statistics broken down by type and judicial assignment:

a. the number of civil cases filed in forma pauperis, excluding petitions filed pursuant to 28 U.S.C. §§ 2241, 2254, and 2255;

b. the number of applications for appointed counsel filed;

c. the number of orders of appointment entered;

d. the number of applications for withdrawal filed;

e. the number of applications for withdrawal granted;

f. the number of applications for withdrawal denied; and

g. the number of appointments made subsequent to withdrawal of counsel.

[Effective April 1, 1997; revised effective August 18, 1999.]

APPENDIX I. UNITED STATES DISTRICT COURT FOR THE DISTRICT OF NEW JERSEY CRIMINAL JUSTICE ACT PLAN

I. AUTHORITY

Pursuant to the Criminal Justice Act of 1964, as amended, ("CJA"), section 3006A of Title 18, United States Code, and the *Guidelines for the Administration of the Criminal Justice Act*, Volume VII, Guide to Judiciary Policies and Procedures ("CJA Guidelines"), the Judges of the United States District Court for the District of New Jersey adopt this Plan for furnishing representation in federal court for any person financially unable to obtain adequate representation in accordance with the CJA.

II. STATEMENT OF POLICY

A. Objectives.

1. The objective of this Plan is to attain the ideal of equality before the law for all persons. Therefore, this Plan shall be administered so that those accused of a crime, or otherwise eligible for services pursuant to the CJA, will not be deprived, because they are financially unable to pay for adequate representation, of any element of representation necessary to an adequate defense.

2. The further objective of this Plan is to particularize the requirements of the CJA, the Anti-Drug Abuse Act of 1988 (codified in part at section 848(q) of Title 21, United States Code), and the CJA Guidelines in a way that meets the needs of this District.

B. Compliance.

1. The Court, its Clerk, the Federal Public Defender Organization, and private attorneys appointed under the CJA shall comply with the CJA Guidelines approved by the Judicial Conference of the United States and/or its Committee on Defender Services and with this Plan.

2. Each private attorney shall be provided by the Clerk of the Court with a then-current copy of this Plan upon the attorney's first appointment under the CJA or designation as a member of the Panel of Private Attorneys under the Criminal Justice Act ("CJA Panel"). The Clerk shall maintain a current copy of the CJA Guidelines for the use of members of the CJA Panel and shall make known to such attorneys its availability.

III. DEFINITIONS

A. "Representation" includes counsel and investigative, expert, and other services.

B. "Appointed attorney" includes private attorneys, the Federal Public Defender, and staff attorneys of the Federal Public Defender Organization.

IV. PROVISION OF REPRESENTATION

A. Circumstance.

1. *Mandatory.* Representation shall be provided for any financially eligible person who:

a. is charged with a felony or with a Class A misdemeanor;

b. is a juvenile alleged to have committed an act of juvenile delinquency as defined in section 5031 of Title 18, United States Code;

c. is charged with a violation of probation, or faces a change of a term or condition of probation (unless the modification sought is favorable to the probationer and the government has not objected to the proposed change);

d. is under arrest, when such representation is required by law;

e. is entitled to appointment of counsel in parole proceedings;

f. is charged with a violation of supervised release or faces modification, reduction, or enlargement of a condition, or extension or revocation of a term of supervised release;

g. is subject to a mental condition hearing under chapter 313 of Title 18, United States Code;

h. is in custody as a material witness;

i. is seeking to set aside or vacate a death sentence under sections 2254 or 2255 of Title 28, United States Code;

j. is entitled to appointment of counsel in verification of consent proceedings pursuant to a transfer of an offender to or from the United States for the execution of a penal sentence under section 4109 of Title 18, United States Code;

k. is entitled to appointment of counsel under the Sixth Amendment to the Constitution; or

l. faces loss of liberty in a case and federal law requires the appointment of counsel.

2. *Discretionary.* Whenever a District Judge or Magistrate Judge determines that the interests of justice so require, representation may be provided for any financially eligible person who:

a. is charged with a petty offense (Class B or C misdemeanor, or an infraction) for which a sentence to confinement is authorized;

b. is seeking relief, other than to set aside or vacate a death sentence under sections 2241, 2254, or 2255 of Title 28, United States Code;

c. is charged with civil or criminal contempt and faces loss of liberty;

d. has been called as a witness before the grand jury, a Court, the Congress, or a federal agency or commission which has the power to compel testimony, and there is reason to believe, either prior to or during testimony, that the witness could be subject to a criminal prosecution, a civil or criminal contempt proceeding, or loss of liberty;

e. is proposed by the United States Attorney for processing under a pretrial diversion program;

f. is held for international extradition under chapter 209 of Title 18, United States Code. Representation may also be furnished for financially eligible persons in ancillary matters appropriate to the proceedings pursuant to subsection (c) of the CJA.

B. Waiver of Appointment of Counsel.

1. In the event that an otherwise eligible person desires to waive representation by counsel, the Magistrate Judge or District Judge shall present to him or her a written waiver form. If the person executes such waiver, it shall be filed. If the person waives representation by counsel but refuses to execute a written waiver, the Magistrate Judge or District Judge will note such fact on the record. If the person admits, or the Magistrate Judge or District Judge finds after appropriate inquiry, that he or she is financially able to obtain counsel but declines to do so, the Magistrate Judge or District Judge shall note such fact on the record.

2. In the event a person waives representation by counsel and a Magistrate Judge or District Judge deems representation necessary, and the person qualifies for appointed counsel and agrees to be represented at least in part, "standby" counsel shall be appointed to assist the person in his or her defense.

3. When a person waives representation by counsel and is financially eligible, the Magistrate Judge or District Judge may appoint counsel, under the Court's inherent authority, in the capacity of an expert or consultant to serve exclusively on behalf of the Court to protect the integrity and continuity of the proceedings.

C. When Counsel Shall Be Provided. Unless representation by counsel has been waived, counsel shall be provided to eligible persons as soon as feasible after they are taken into custody, when they appear before a Magistrate Judge or District Judge, when they are formally charged or notified of charges if formal charges are sealed, or when a Magistrate Judge or District Judge otherwise considers appointment of counsel appropriate under the CJA, whichever occurs earliest. If, at any stage of the proceeding, a Magistrate Judge or District Judge finds that a party — for whom counsel has not previously been appointed under this Plan but who has retained his or her own attorney — subsequently becomes financially unable to provide for continued representation, the Magistrate Judge or District Judge may appoint counsel for such party.

D. Number and Qualifications of Counsel.

1. *Number.* More than one attorney may be appointed in any case determined by the Court to be extremely difficult. In a capital case, at least two attorneys should be appointed.

2. *Qualifications.* Except as provided by Section 848(q)(7) of Title 21, United States Code, at least one attorney appointed in a capital case shall meet the qualification requirements set forth in sections 848(q)(5) and (6) of Title 21, United States Code. Pursuant to Section 848(q)(7), the presiding judicial officer, for good cause, may appoint an attorney who may not qualify under sections 848(q)(5) and (6), but who has the background, knowledge and experience necessary to represent the defendant properly in a capital case, giving due consideration to the seriousness of the possible penalty and to the unique and complex nature of the litigation.

E. Eligibility for Representation.

1. *Fact Finding.* The determination of eligibility for representation under the CJA is a judicial function to be performed by a District Judge or Magistrate Judge after making appropriate inquiry concerning the person's financial condition. The test for the appointment of counsel is not indigence; it is the financial inability of a party to secure competent representation and to obtain an adequate defense.

2. On the basis of such inquiry, if the District Judge or Magistrate Judge finds that the person is financially unable to obtain counsel, the District Judge or Magistrate Judge shall immediately direct his or her attention to the question of bail, adjourn the remainder of the proceeding forthwith, and appoint counsel as soon thereafter as is reasonably possible, as provided herein. Such appointment may be made retroactive to include any representation furnished pursuant to the Plan prior to appointment.

3. It shall be the duty of any person released on bail and for whom counsel is appointed to report to such appointed counsel at his or her office as promptly as possible, and not later than five days from the date of the Clerk's mailing of the order of appointment.

4. It shall be the duty of any attorney who is appointed to represent a person incarcerated at the time the appointment to communicate with that person at his or her place of incarceration as promptly as possible, and not later than five days from the date of the Clerk's mailing of the order of appointment.

5. No such person shall select his or her own counsel from the panel of attorneys, or otherwise. The selection of counsel shall be within the exclusive prov-

ince of the District Judge or Magistrate Judge as provided herein.

6. The District Judge or Magistrate Judge shall appoint separate counsel for persons having interests that cannot properly be represented by the same counsel, or when other good cause is shown.

7. The District Judge or Magistrate Judge may, in the interest of justice, substitute one or more appointed counsel for another at any stage of the proceedings before him or her.

8. Counsel appointed by a District Judge or Magistrate Judge shall represent the person in proceedings before the District Judge or Magistrate Judge and in all subsequent proceedings before the Court unless or until relieved by order of the District Judge or Magistrate Judge or the Court.

9. No counsel appointed hereunder shall seek or accept any fee from a person whom he or she represents. If, at any time after appointment, counsel obtains information that a client is financially able to make payment, in whole or in part, for legal or other services in connection with his or her representation, and the source of the attorney's information is not protected as a privileged communication, counsel shall advise the Court.

10. If, at any time after the appointment of counsel, the District Judge or Magistrate Judge finds that the person is financially able to obtain counsel, or make partial payment for his or her representation, the District Judge or Magistrate Judge may terminate the appointment of counsel or direct that payment by the person be made to the Court for deposit in the Treasury of the United States as a reimbursement under the provisions of Subsection (f) of the Act.

11. If at any stage of the proceedings the District Judge or Magistrate Judge shall find that a person for whom counsel has not been appointed previously under this Plan is financially unable to pay counsel whom he or she has retained, the District Judge or Magistrate Judge may appoint counsel in the same manner as hereinabove provided. Such appointment, if made from the panel of attorneys approved by the Court, may be made retroactive to include any representation furnished pursuant to the Plan prior to appointment.

12. If requested to do so by the person, counsel appointed under this Plan shall file a timely notice of appeal and shall continue to represent the person on appeal unless, or until, he or she is relieved by an appropriate order of the United States Court of Appeals for the Third Circuit.

V. FEDERAL PUBLIC DEFENDER ORGANIZATION

A. Establishment.

1. The Federal Public Defender Organization of the District of New Jersey, previously established in this district pursuant to the provisions of the Act, is hereby recognized as the Federal Public Defender Organization for this district.

2. The Federal Public Defender Organization shall be capable of providing legal services throughout the district and shall maintain offices in Newark, Trenton and Camden, New Jersey.

3. The Federal Public Defender shall be appointed for a term of four years, unless sooner removed by the Judicial Council of the Third Circuit for incompetency, misconduct in office, or neglect of duty.

4. The Federal Public Defender may appoint, without regard to the provisions of Title 5 governing appointments in the competitive service, full-time attorneys in such number as may be approved by the Judicial Council of the Third Circuit and other personnel in such numbers as may be approved by the Director of the Administrative Office of the United States Courts.

5. Neither the Federal Public Defender nor any staff attorney appointed by him or her may engage in the private practice of law.

B. Supervision of Defender Organization. The Federal Public Defender shall be responsible for the supervision and management of the Federal Public Defender Organization. Accordingly, the Federal Public Defender shall be appointed in all cases assigned to that Organization for subsequent assignment to staff attorneys at the discretion of the Federal Public Defender.

VI. COMPOSITION OF PANEL OF PRIVATE ATTORNEYS

A. Establishment of CJA Panel.

1. *Approval.* The existing previously established panel of attorneys who are eligible and willing to be appointed to provide representation under the Act is hereby recognized. The CJA Panel is to be reconstituted within six months of the adoption of this Plan. The Court shall review the recommendations of the Panel Selection and Management Committee, established pursuant to Appendix I to the Criminal Justice Act Plan, and approve attorneys for membership on the Panel who are competent to give effective representation to persons under the Criminal Justice Act. Members of the CJA Panel shall serve at the pleasure of the Court for a fixed term of years. The Court has established a separate panel for each of the Newark, Trenton and Camden vicinages. However, this division shall not prohibit the Court from appointing a panel member from one vicinage to serve in another vicinage nor prohibit the Court on the basis of geographic considerations from allowing a panel member to serve in more than one vicinage.

2. *Size.* The Court shall fix the size of the CJA Panel. The Panel shall be large enough to provide a sufficient number of experienced attorneys to handle the CJA caseload, yet small enough so that panel members will receive an adequate number of appointments to maintain their proficiency in federal criminal defense work, and thereby provide a high quality of representation. The Court may from time to time redetermine the size of the CJA Panel to achieve these goals.

3. *Organization.* The Plan for the Composition, Administration and Management of the Panel of Private Attorneys under the Criminal Justice Act is found at Appendix I to this CJA Plan.

4. *Ratio of Appointments.* Where practical and cost effective, private attorneys from the CJA Panel shall be appointed in a substantial proportion of the cases in which an accused is determined to be financially eligible for representation under the Act. "Substantial" shall usually be defined as approximately 25 percent of the appointments under the CJA annually throughout the district. A "case" should be deemed to be each proceeding actually docketed in the United States District Court. An Order granting a new trial should be deemed to initiate a new "case."

VII. REPRESENTATION IN STATE DEATH PENALTY HABEAS CORPUS PROCEEDINGS UNDER 28 U.S.C. § 2254

Appointment of Counsel. The court shall appoint the Office of the Public Defender for the State of New Jersey, the Federal Public Defender with his or her consent, or such other attorney who qualifies for appointment pursuant to section 848(q) of Title 21, United State Code, to represent financially eligible persons seeking habeas corpus relief in state death penalty proceedings under section 2254 of Title 28 United States Code.

VIII. DUTIES OF APPOINTED COUNSEL

A. Standards. The services to be rendered a person represented by appointed counsel shall be commensurate with those rendered if counsel were privately employed by the person.

B. Professional Conduct. Attorneys appointed pursuant to the CJA shall conform to the highest standards of professional conduct, as described in the American Bar Association's Model Rules of Professional Conduct, as revised by the New Jersey Supreme Court, subject to such modifications as may be required or permitted by federal statute, regulation, court rule or decision of law.

C. Compensation—Filing of Vouchers. Claims for compensation shall be submitted, on the appropriate CJA form, to the office of the Clerk of the Court. The Clerk of the Court shall review the claim form for mathematical and technical accuracy and for conformity with the *Guidelines for the Administration of the Criminal Justice Act* (Volume VII, *Guide to Judiciary Policies and Procedures*), and, if correct, shall forward the claim form for the consideration and action of the presiding District Judge or Magistrate Judge. The Court will exert its best efforts to avoid delays in reviewing payment vouchers and in submitting them for further processing.

D. No Receipt of Other Payment. Appointed counsel may not require, request, or accept any payment or promise of payment or any other valuable consideration for representation under the appointment, unless such payment is approved by Order of the Court.

E. Continuing Representation. Once counsel is appointed under the CJA, counsel shall continue the representation until the matter is closed, including filing appropriate notices of appeal, representation on appeal, or review by certiorari (as governed by the circuit CJA plan provisions concerning representation on appeal); until substitute counsel has filed a notice of appearance; until an Order has been entered allowing or requiring the person represented to proceed *pro se*; or until the appointment is terminated by Court Order.

IX. DUTIES OF LAW ENFORCEMENT AND RELATED AGENCIES

A. Presentation of Person for Appointment of Counsel. Federal law enforcement and prosecutorial agencies, probation officers, and pretrial services officers in this district, and those acting on their behalf, shall promptly ask any person who is in custody, or who otherwise may be entitled to counsel under the Act, whether he or she is financially able to secure representation, and shall, in such cases in which the person indicates that he or she is not able, notify the Federal Public Defender who shall discuss with the person the right to representation and right to appointed counsel, and if appointment of counsel seems likely, assist in the completion of a financial affidavit (CJA Form 23) and arrange to have the person promptly presented before a Magistrate Judge or District Judge of this court for determination of financial eligibility and appointment of counsel.

B. Pretrial Services Interview. Appointed counsel should be furnished to financially eligible defendants prior to the defendants being interviewed by a pretrial services or probation officer. If appointed counsel is not available within 30 minutes of notification of the defendant's arrival at the federal building, the pretrial services or probation officer may interview the defendant.

C. Notice of Indictment of Criminal Information. Upon the return or unsealing of an indictment, the filing of a criminal information, or the filing of a petition to modify or revoke probation, the United

States Attorney or the probation officer, as appropriate, immediately shall mail or otherwise deliver a copy of the document to appointed counsel, or to the defendant if he or she is without counsel, at the address shown on defendant's bond papers or to the jail in which the defendant is incarcerated.

X. MISCELLANEOUS

A. Forms. Standard forms, pertaining to the CJA and approved by the Judicial Conference of the United States or its Committee on Defender Services and prescribed and distributed by the Director of the Administrative Office of the United States Courts, shall be used, where applicable, in all proceedings under this Plan.

B. Amendments. Amendments to this Plan may be made from time to time, as adopted by a majority vote of the Judges of this Court. Any such amendment or amendments shall be subject to the approval of the Judicial Council of the Third Circuit, and shall become effective only upon and at the time of appropriate notice by it of such approval. The Clerk shall notify the Director of the Administrative Office of the United States Courts promptly of any and all amendments to this Plan as may be made.

C. Rules of Construction. It shall be the policy and practice of this Court to construe and apply this Plan in manner and effect consistent with the purposes and provisions of the Criminal Justice Act, as well as such modification of this Plan as may be made from time to time by the Judicial Council of the Third Circuit. Provisions not contained in the Plan shall be governed and controlled by the Criminal Justice Act.

D. Supersession. This Plan supersedes all prior Criminal Justice Act Plans of this Court.

XI. EFFECTIVE DATE

This Plan shall become effective when approved by the Judicial Council of the Third Circuit.

APPENDIX 1 TO THE CRIMINAL JUSTICE ACT PLAN. PLAN FOR THE COMPOSITION, ADMINISTRATION, AND MANAGEMENT OF THE PANEL OF PRIVATE ATTORNEYS UNDER THE CRIMINAL JUSTICE ACT

I. INTRODUCTION

Pursuant to the *Guidelines for the Administration of the Criminal Justice Act* and the District of New Jersey Criminal Justice Act Plan, the United States District Court for the District of New Jersey has established the following "Plan for the Composition, Administration, and Management of the Panel of Private Attorneys Under the Criminal Justice Act."

II. COMPOSITION OF PANEL OF PRIVATE ATTORNEYS

A. Panels.

1. *Approval.* The Court shall establish one panel of private attorneys (hereinafter referred to as the "CJA Panel") who are eligible and willing to be appointed to provide representation under the Criminal Justice Act. The Court shall approve attorneys for membership on the panel after receiving recommendations from the "Panel Selection and Management Committee," established pursuant to paragraph II(B) of this Plan. Any attorney aggrieved by the decision on his or her application may present a written grievance to the Committee for review and decision and that decision can be appealed to the Court.

2. *CJA Panel.*

A. Size. The CJA Panel established by the Court shall consist of one hundred (100) attorneys, divided by vicinage, with sixty (60) attorneys for the Newark vicinage, twenty (20) attorneys for the Trenton vicinage, and twenty (20) attorneys for the Camden vicinage. The division by vicinage shall not prohibit the Court where appropriate from appointing a panel member from one vicinage to serve in another vicinage, nor prohibit the Court on the basis of geographic considerations from allowing a panel member to serve in more than one vicinage. The Court may from time to time, on recommendation of the Panel Selection and Management Committee, redetermine the number of attorneys on the CJA Panel and/or the number of attorneys serving in each vicinage.

B. Term. Each panel member shall serve for a term of three (3) years, except that the initial panel shall serve staggered terms as follows: one-third of the members of the initial panel shall serve for one (1) year, another one-third shall serve for two (2) years, and the remaining one-third shall serve for three (3) years. Any member of the initial panel or subsequent panels whose term expires may be reappointed or replaced, as determined by the Panel Selection and Management Committee.

C. Eligibility.

i. General Requirements. Attorneys who serve on the CJA Panel must be members in good standing of the bar of this Court, and have demonstrated experience in, and knowledge of, the Federal Rules of Criminal and Appellate Procedure, the Federal Rules of Evidence, the Sentencing Guidelines, and the local rules of both the District and Circuit Courts.

ii. Specific Requirements for CJA Panel. All attorneys seeking initial membership on the CJA Panel must meet the following minimum eligibility requirements:

a. 1. at least two (2) years in a public defender or prosecutor's office, either state or federal *OR* at least three (3) years in private practice, during which time the attorney was involved in at least 20 criminal cases in either state or federal court, 5 of which were state or federal felony trials; AND

2. attendance at two (2) hours of seminar training on sentencing guideline topics within one year prior to the application; AND

3. attendance at two (2) hours of seminar training on federal criminal defense topics within two years prior to the application;

OR

b. 1. at least two (2) years admission to the bar during which time the attorney was involved in at least 5 criminal cases in either state or federal court, 1 of which was a state or federal felony trial; **AND**

2. participation in the CJA training program established in sections 2(D) and 3 of this Appendix; **AND**

3. participation in at least two (2) hours of seminar training on federal sentencing guidelines topics; **AND**

4. participation in at least four (4) hours of seminar training on topics relating to the defense of federal criminal cases.

D. Second Chair Training Procedure. On application and on reapplication, attorneys who indicate that they have had prior trial/guilty plea experience in federal court will also be asked to indicate whether they would be willing to accept a second chair. A list of attorneys expressing this willingness will be maintained by the Clerk of the Court in such manner that names can be provided on a rotating basis. The names of at least three attorneys willing to accept a second chair shall be provided to each applicant. Attorneys seeking membership on the CJA Panel who need second chair experience to meet their eligibility requirements will be responsible for calling both the Clerk of the Court and the attorney(s) with whom they wish to second chair.

All arrangements for the applicant's second chair experience shall be made between the applicant and the first chair attorney, except that: it shall be the responsibility of the first chair attorney to make the status of the second chair attorney clear to both the Court and his/her client; AND the second chair attorney shall not represent the client in any part of the trial or guilty plea and sentencing hearing unless specifically authorized in writing by the client on a form provided, a copy of said form signed by the client to be presented to the Court; AND second chair attorneys shall not be compensated in any way for the time spent as second chair.

At the completion of the second chair experience, the first chair attorney shall, if requested, provide certification in writing that the applicant second chaired the entire trial and/or guilty plea and sentencing hearing. It shall be the responsibility of the applicant to complete this requirement. Completion of the Second Chair Training Procedure shall require participation in at least 1 trial AND participation in 3 guilty plea and sentencing hearings.

Service as "second chair" does not guarantee admission of an attorney to the CJA Panel.

3. *CJA Training Panel.* The Panel Selection and Management Committee shall establish a "CJA Training Panel", consisting of attorneys who do not have the experience required for membership on the CJA Panel. Training Panel members may be assigned, by the Court, to assist members of the CJA Panel in a "second chair" capacity. Training Panel members are not eligible to receive appointments independently and shall not be eligible to receive compensation for their services in assisting CJA Panel members. Prior service on the CJA Training Panel is not a requirement for membership on the CJA Panel but may be used to fulfill the eligibility requirements outlined in section 2(C)ii(b)(2), above, of this Appendix, nor will service on the Training Panel guarantee admission of an attorney to the CJA Panel.

4. *Appointments.* Counsel furnishing representation under the Plan shall be selected from the panel of attorneys designated or approved by the Court or from the defender organization furnishing representation pursuant to the provisions in part III below.

5. *Appointment in Death Penalty Cases.* Pursuant to Title 18 U.S.C. § 3005, a defendant who is facing the possibility of the death penalty is entitled to the appointment of two attorneys, at least one of whom is learned in the law of capital punishment. In such a case, the Court is not limited to the CJA Panel list for its selection of the attorney learned in the law of capital cases, but may appoint counsel who satisfies the following minimum criteria:

i. unless appointment is made pursuant to § 6, below, an attorney must have been admitted to practice in the United States District Court for the District of New Jersey for not less than five (5) years; AND

ii. must have had not less than three (3) years experience in the actual trial of felony prosecutions in the District of New Jersey within the five (5) years prior to the application; AND

iii. must have attended a seminar on the topic of the death penalty within one (1) year of the application; AND

iv. must have had actual trial experience in state or federal court of a first degree murder case, capital or otherwise.

6. *Special Appointments.* When the District Judge presiding over the case, or the Chief Judge if a District Judge has not yet been assigned to the case, determines that the appointment of an attorney, who is not a member of the CJA Panel, is in the interest of justice, judicial economy or continuity of representation, or there is some other compelling circumstance warranting his or her appointment, the attorney may be admitted to the CJA Panel *pro hac vice* and appointed to represent the defendant. Consideration for preserving the integrity of the panel selection process suggests that such appointments should be made only in exceptional circumstances. Further, the attorney, who may or may not be admitted to practice and/or maintain an office in the district, should possess such qualities as would qualify him or her for admission to the CJA Panel in the ordinary course of panel selection.

7. *Removal From the CJA Panel.*

a. Removal from the CJA Panel shall be automatic upon proof made to the Chief Judge that a panel attorney has been convicted of any crime in either state or federal court carrying a possible maximum penalty of more than one (1) year imprisonment.

b. The Panel Selection and Management Committee may determine from time to time that, by reason of information received by the Committee, a panel member should be recommended for removal from the CJA Panel. In such instance, the panel member being considered for removal shall be asked to meet with the Panel Selection and Management Committee and shall be permitted to present information in his/her own behalf in response to the information received by the Committee.

A decision shall be rendered by the Panel Selection and Management Committee after it is satisfied that all relevant information has been received and shall be communicated in writing to the panel member, with reasons stated for the decision. The decision of the Committee can be appealed to the Court.

There is no presumption that because a client has alleged the ineffectiveness of his/her attorney in a collateral attack on his/her conviction, that attorney must be removed from the CJA Panel.

8. *Equal Opportunity.* All qualified attorneys shall be encouraged to participate in the furnishing of representation in CJA cases, without regard to race, color, religion, sex, age, national origin or disabling condition.

9. *Application.* Application forms for membership on the CJA Panel shall be made available, upon request, by the Clerk of the Court. Completed applications shall be submitted to the Clerk of the Court who will transmit the applications to the chairperson of the Panel Selection and Management Committee.

b. Panel Selection and Management Committee

1. *Membership.* A Panel Selection and Management Committee shall be established by the Court. The Committee shall consist of one District Judge from each vicinage, one Magistrate Judge from each vicinage, the Federal Public Defender or his/her designee, and four private attorneys. The President of the Association of the Federal Bar and the President of the Association of Criminal Defense Attorneys—New Jersey shall each designate two of the private attorneys to serve on the panel.

Except for the Federal Public Defender, each Committee member shall serve for a term of three years. At the conclusion of the first three year term, the member may be reappointed or replaced, but no member may serve more than two successive three year terms.

2. *Duties.*

a. The Panel Selection and Management Committee shall meet at least once a year to consider applications for vacancies on the CJA Panel. The Committee shall review the qualifications of applicants and recommend, for approval by the Court, those applicants best qualified to fill the vacancies.

Once a year, the Committee shall review the operation and administration of the CJA Panel over the preceding year, and recommend to the Court any changes deemed necessary or appropriate by the Committee regarding the appointment process and panel management. The Committee shall also inquire annually as to the continued availability and willingness of each panel member to accept appointments.

b. If, at any time during the course of a year, the number of vacancies due to resignation, removal, or death significantly decreases the size of the CJA Panel, the Committee shall solicit applications for the vacancies, convene a special meeting to review the qualifications of the applicants, and select prospective members for recommendation to the Court for approval. Members approved by the Court to fill mid-term vacancies shall serve until the expiration of the term that was vacated and shall be immediately eligible for reappointment.

c. Training. The Panel Selection and Management Committee through the Office of the Federal Public Defender, in conjunction with the Association of the Federal Bar and the Association of Criminal Defense Attorneys—New Jersey, will arrange annual training programs for new and experienced panel members. Members of the panel will be expected to attend such training programs.

III. SELECTION FOR APPOINTMENT

A. Maintenance of List. The Clerk of the Court shall maintain a current list of all attorneys included on the CJA Panel, with current office addresses and telephone numbers, as well as a statement of qualifications and experience. The Clerk shall furnish a copy of this list to each District Judge and Magistrate Judge. The Clerk shall also maintain a public record of assignments to private counsel, and, when appropriate, statistical data reflecting the proration of appointments between attorneys from the Federal Public Defender's Office and private attorneys.

B. Distribution of Appointments. CJA Panel attorneys are to be appointed in multi-defendant and conflict cases, or where the Federal Defender Office is otherwise unavailable and where it is appropriate to provide federal court experience to CJA Panel attorneys and satisfy the Ratio of Appointments requirement as outlined in section VI(A)(4) of the District of New Jersey Criminal Justice Act Plan.

C. Method of Selection. Appointments from the CJA Panel should be made on a rotational basis, subject to the Court's discretion to make exceptions due to the nature and complexity of the case, an attorney's experience, and geographical considerations. This procedure should result in a balanced distribution of appointments and compensation among the members of the CJA Panel and quality representation for each CJA defendant.

Upon the determination of a need for the appointment of counsel, the District Judge or Magistrate Judge shall notify the Clerk of Court of the need for counsel and the nature of the case. Where, based on the status of the distribution of cases (*See* Ratio of Appointment, CJA Plan, section VI(A)(4)), the Clerk of the Court determines that the appointment of an attorney from the CJA Panel is appropriate, the Clerk shall determine the name of the next panel member on the list who is available for appointment, and shall provide the name to the appointing District Judge or Magistrate Judge.

In the event of an emergency, i.e., weekend, holidays, or other non-working hours of the Clerk of the Court's office, the presiding District Judge or Magistrate Judge may appoint any attorney from the list. In all cases where members of the CJA Panel are appointed out of sequence, the appointing District Judge or Magistrate Judge shall notify the Clerk of the Court as to the name of the attorney appointed and the date of the appointment.

IV. COMPENSATION—FILING OF VOUCHERS

Claims for compensation shall be submitted on the appropriate CJA form to the office of the Clerk of the Court. The Clerk of the Court shall review the claim form for mathematical and technical accuracy, and for conformity with the *Guidelines for the Administration of the Criminal Justice Act* (Volume VII, *Guide to Judiciary Policies and Procedures)*, and, if correct, shall forward the claim form for consideration by and action of the presiding District Judge or Magistrate Judge.

It is acknowledged that in some cases reduction of the amount of compensation sought will be necessary or appropriate. In those cases, the procedure set forth in the balance of this section shall be followed.

In any case where the judicial officer intends to reduce the amount of payment requested in a trial level voucher, CJA counsel shall be notified of the amount of the intended reduction and the reasons for same, and may request an opportunity for review by the judicial officer. After review of any submission by appointed counsel, including his/her response to the judicial officer's reasons for the reduction, and the completion of any other steps deemed appropriate by the judicial officer, the judicial officer shall take action on the voucher consistent with the Plan, the CJA and the interests of justice.

The Third Circuit shall consider all vouchers submitted by appellate counsel.

Notice to CJA Panel Attorneys Regarding Availability of Investigative, Expert, and Other Services

Attorneys appointed to provide representation under the Criminal Justice Act, 18 U.S.C. § 3006A, may seek investigative, expert, and other services necessary for adequate representation, such services to be paid for out of funds appropriated for the administration of the Criminal Justice Act.

In addition to investigators, psychiatrists, psychologists and reporters, services other than counsel may include but are not necessarily limited to interpreters, neurologists, and laboratory experts in areas such as ballistics, fingerprinting, and handwriting.

Requests for authority to obtain subsection (e) services should be made to the presiding District Judge or Magistrate Judge (see cautionary note below). In order to prevent the possibility that an open hearing concerning a request for subsection (e) services will cause a defendant to reveal his or her defenses, these requests should be made by ex parte application. Guidelines promulgated by the Judicial Conference of the United States (Guidelines for the Administration of the Criminal Justice Act, Volume VII, Guide to Judiciary Policies and Procedures) provide that the applications shall be heard in camera, and not be revealed without the consent of the defendant. The Guidelines further state that such applications shall be placed under seal until the final disposition of the case in the trial court, subject to final order of the Court.

CAUTIONARY NOTE: Counsel should be aware of the limitations that apply to the obtaining of such services. PRIOR AUTHORIZATION MUST BE SECURED from the presiding judicial officer for all subsection (e) services where the cost of such services (exclusive of reimbursement for expenses) can only be paid if the presiding District Judge or Magistrate Judge certifies that payment in excess of $1,000 (excluding reimbursement for expenses) is necessary to provide for services of an unusual character or duration, and the amount of the excess payment is approved by the Chief Judge of the Circuit. Compensation for subsection (e) services should be claimed directly by the service provider on CJA form 21 "Authorization and Voucher for Expert and Other Services."

Further information about the availability of subsection (e) services and the procedures and limitations involved may be obtained from the Clerk of the Court. In addition, counsel should review both the Criminal Justice Act and the CJA Guidelines. A copy of the Guidelines is located in the office of the Clerk of the Court.

[Effective April 1, 1997; amended September 4, 1998.]

APPENDIX J. PLAN FOR PROMPT DISPOSITION OF CRIMINAL CASES

Final Plan Pursuant to Speedy Trial Act of 1974, As Amended 1979—18 U.S.C. § 3165(e)(3)

I. INTRODUCTORY MATERIAL

A. Adoption of Plan

Pursuant to the provisions of 18 U.S.C. § 3165, the United States District Court for the District of New Jersey adopts this District Plan, subject to approval in accordance with 18 U.S.C. § 3165(c). This District Plan was initially prepared by the District Planning Group, formulated according to the planning process authorized by 18 U.S.C. § 3168. Part II of this Plan shall be the District Plan for Disposition of Criminal cases as required by Fed.R.Crim.P. 50(b).

B. Planning Group

The Planning Group for the District of New Jersey is comprised of the following members:

Honorable Clarkson S. Fisher, Chief Judge

Honorable Frederick B. Lacey, United States District Judge

Honorable William J. Hunt, United States Magistrate

Robert J. Del Tufo, United States Attorney

Angelo W. Locascio, Clerk of Court

John F. McMahon, Federal Public Defender

Richard A. Levin, Private Attorney

John E. Keale, Private Attorney

Allyn Z. Lite, Private Attorney

John L. Costley, Jr., Chief Probation Officer

Samuel F. Naples, United States Marshal

Professor Livingston Baker, Reporter, Seton Hall University, School of Law

C. Availability of Copies of the Plan

Copies of the District Plan and of the recommendations of the Planning Group will be available for public inspection in the offices of the Clerk of the Court for the District of New Jersey.

II. STATEMENT OF TIME LIMITS AND PROCEDURES FOR ACHIEVING PROMPT DISPOSITION OF CRIMINAL CASES

Pursuant to the requirements of Fed.R.Crim.P. 50(b) the Speedy Trial Act of 1974 (18 U.S.C. Chapter 208), the Speedy Trial Act Amendments Act of 1979 (Pub.L. No. 96–43, 93 Stat. 327), and the Federal Juvenile Delinquency Act (18 U.S.C. §§ 5036, 5037), the Judges of the United States District Court for the District of New Jersey have adopted the following time limits and procedures to minimize undue delay and to further the prompt disposition of criminal cases and certain juvenile proceedings.

1. Applicability

(a) Offenses. The time limits set forth herein are applicable to all criminal offenses triable in this Court, including cases triable by United States Magistrate Judges, except for petty offenses as defined in the Federal criminal code. Except as specifically provided, they are not applicable to proceedings under the Federal Juvenile Delinquency Act.

(b) Persons. The time limits are applicable to persons * accused who have not been indicted or informed against as well as those who have, and the word "defendant" includes such persons unless the context indicates otherwise.

* The term "person" shall be interpreted to include any business or corporate type entity as well as natural persons.

2. Priorities in Scheduling Criminal Cases

Preference shall be given to criminal proceedings as far as practicable as required by Fed.R.Crim.P. 50(a). The trial of defendants in custody solely because they are awaiting trial and of high-risk defendants as defined in section 5 should be given preference over other criminal cases.

3. Time Within Which an Indictment or Information Must Be Filed

(a) Time Limits. If an individual is arrested or served with a summons and the complaint charges an offense to be prosecuted in this District, any indictment or information subsequently filed in connection with such charge shall be filed within 30 days of arrest or service.

(b) Measurement of Time Periods. If a person has not been arrested or served with a summons on a Federal charge, an arrest will be deemed to have been made at such time as the person (i) is held in custody solely for the purpose of responding to a Federal charge; (ii) is delivered to the custody of a Federal official in connection with a Federal charge; or (iii) appears before a judicial officer in connection with a Federal charge.

(c) Related Procedures.

(1) At the time of the earliest appearance before a judicial officer of a person who has been arrested for an offense not charged in an indictment or information, the judicial officer shall establish for the record the date on which the arrest took place.

(2) In the absence of a showing to the contrary, a summons shall be considered to have been served on the date of service shown on the return thereof.

4. Time Within Which Trial Must Commence

(a) Time Limits. The trial of a defendant shall commence not later than 70 days after the last to occur of the following dates:

(1) The date on which an indictment or information is filed in this District;

(2) The date on which a sealed indictment or information is unsealed; or

(3) The date of the defendant's first appearance before a judicial officer of this District.

(b) Retrial. Subject to the exclusions provided in 18 U.S.C. § 3161(h), where a new trial has been ordered by the District Court or a trial or new trial has been ordered by an appellate court, it shall commence at the earliest practicable time but, in any event, not later than 70 days after the finality of such order. When the defendant is to be retried following an appeal or collateral attack, if unavailability of witnesses or other factors resulting from passage of time shall make trial within 70 days impractical, the Court trying the case may extend such period for a total not to exceed 180 days from the date on which the order occasioning the retrial becomes final.

(c) Withdrawal of Plea. If a defendant enters a plea of guilty or nolo contendere to any or all charges in an indictment or information and is subsequently permitted to withdraw it, the time limit shall be determined for all counts as if the indictment or information were filed on the day the order permitting withdrawal of the plea became final.

(d) Superseding Charges. If, after an indictment or information has been filed, a complaint, indictment, or information is filed which charges the defendant with the same offense or with an offense required to be joined with that offense, the time limit applicable to the subsequent charge will be determined as follows:

(1) If the original indictment or information was dismissed on motion of the defendant before the filing of the subsequent charge, the time limit shall be determined without regard to the existence of the original charge.

(2) If the original indictment or information is pending at the time the subsequent charge is filed, the trial shall commence within the time limit for commencement of trial on the original indictment or information.

(3) If the original indictment or information was dismissed on motion of the United States Attorney before the filing of the subsequent charge, the trial shall commence within the time limit for commencement of trial on the original indictment or information, but the period during which the defendant was not under charges shall be excluded from the computations. Such period is the period between the dismissal of the original indictment or information and the date the time would have commenced to run on the subsequent charge had there been no previous charge.

If the subsequent charge is contained in a complaint, the formal time limit within which an indictment or information must be obtained on the charge shall be determined without regard to the existence of the original indictment or information, but earlier action may, in fact, be required if the time limit for commencement of trial is to be satisfied.

(e) Measurement of Time Periods. For the purposes of this section:

(1) If a defendant signs a written consent to be tried before a Magistrate Judge and no indictment or information charging the offense has been filed, the time limit shall run from the date of such consent.

(2) In the event of a transfer to this District under Fed.R.Crim.P. 20, the indictment or information shall be deemed filed in this District when the papers in the proceeding or certified copies thereof are received by the Clerk.

(3) A trial in a jury case shall be deemed to commence at the beginning of voir dire.

(4) A trial in a non-jury case shall be deemed to commence on the day the case is called, provided that some step in the trial procedure immediately follows.

(f) Related Procedures.

(1) At the time of the defendant's earliest appearance before a judicial officer of this District, the officer will take appropriate steps to assure that the defendant is represented by counsel and shall appoint counsel where appropriate under the Criminal Justice Act and Fed.R.Crim.P. 44. The Judicial officer will also inform the defendant of his or her rights under this Plan and pertinent legislation.

(2) The Court shall have sole responsibility for setting cases for trial after consultation with counsel. At the time of arraignment or as soon thereafter as is practicable, each case will be set for trial on a day certain or listed for trial on a weekly or other short-term calendar.

(3) Individual calendars shall be managed so that it will be reasonably anticipated that every criminal case set for trial will be reached during the week of original setting. A conflict in schedules of Assistant United States Attorneys or defense counsel will be grounds for a continuance or delayed setting only if approved by the Court and called to the Court's attention at the earliest practicable time.

(4) In the event that a complaint, indictment, or information is filed against a defendant charged in a pending indictment or information or in an indictment or information dismissed on motion of the United States Attorney, the trial on the new charge shall commence within the time limit for commencement of trial on the original indictment or information unless the Court finds that the new charge is not for the same offense charged in the original indictment or information or an offense required to be joined therewith.

(5) At the time of the filing of a complaint, indictment, or information described in the preceding Section 4(f)(4), the United States Attorney shall note on the cover

sheet if the new charge is for the same offense charged in the original indictment or information, or for an offense required to be joined therewith.

(6) At the time of the filing of a complaint, indictment, or information described in Section 4(f)(4), the United States Attorney shall give written notice to the Court of that circumstance and of his or her position with respect to the computation of the time limits.

(7) All pretrial hearings shall be conducted as soon after the arraignment as possible, consistent with the priorities of other matters on the Court's criminal docket.

(8) A defendant contending that the time within which trial should have commenced has passed, must move for dismissal as provided in 18 U.S.C. § 3162(a)(2) not less than 10 days before the scheduled trial date, unless the time within which trial should have commenced expires less than 10 days prior to the scheduled trial date, in which event the motion for dismissal must be made no later than the date defendant avers the trial should have commenced. Failure of the defendant to so move shall constitute a waiver of the rights set forth in 18 U.S.C. § 3162(a)(2), unless the Court, for good cause shown, permits the motion to be made and heard at a later date.

(9) Except for good cause shown, the Court may not extend the time for filing motions after plea under Fed.R.Crim.P. 12(c) beyond 10 days. Such motions will be heard and ruled upon promptly, so that the trial need not be delayed.

5. Defendants in Custody and High–Risk Defendants

(a) Time Limits. Notwithstanding any longer time periods that may be permitted under Sections 3 and 4, the following time limits will also be applicable to defendants in custody and high-risk defendants as herein defined:

(1) The trial of a defendant held in custody solely for the purpose of trial on a Federal charge shall commence within 90 days following the beginning of continuous custody.

(2) The trial of a high-risk defendant shall commence within 90 days of the designation as high-risk.

(b) Definition of "High–Risk Defendant." A high-risk defendant is one reasonably designated by the United States Attorney as posing a danger to himself or herself or any other person or to the community.

(c) Measurement of Time Periods. For the purposes of this section:

(1) A defendant is deemed to be in detention awaiting trial when he or she is arrested on a Federal charge or otherwise held for the purpose of responding to a Federal charge. Detention is deemed to be solely because the defendant is awaiting trial unless the person exercising custodial authority has an independent basis (not including a detainer) for continuing to hold the defendant.

(2) If a case is transferred pursuant to Fed.R.Crim.P. 20 and the defendant subsequently rejects disposition under Rule 20 or the Court declines to accept the plea, a new period of continuous detention awaiting trial will begin at that time.

(3) A trial shall be deemed to commence as provided in Sections 4(e)(3) and 4(e)(4).

(d) Related Procedures.

(1) If a defendant is being held in custody solely for the purpose of awaiting trial, the United States Attorney shall advise the Court at the earliest practicable time of the date of the beginning of such custody.

(2) The United States Attorney shall advise the Court at the earliest practicable time (usually at the hearing with respect to bail) if the defendant is considered by him or her to be high risk.

(3) If the Court finds that the filing of a "high-risk" designation as a public record may result in prejudice to the defendant, it may order the designation sealed for such period as is necessary to protect the defendant's right to a fair trial, but not beyond the time that the Court's judgment in the case becomes final. During the time the designation is under seal, it shall be made known to the defendant and his or her counsel but shall not be made known to other persons without the permission of the Court.

6. Exclusion of Time From Computations

(a) Applicability. In computing any time limit under Sections 3, 4 or 5, the periods of delay set forth in 18 U.S.C. § 3161(h) shall be excluded. Such periods of delay shall not be excluded in computing the minimum period for commencement of trial under Section 7. In determining excludable time under 18 U.S.C. § 3161(h)(1)(F), 90 days will be the maximum time excluded, unless the Court orders a hearing on the motion or additional extensions of time for filing briefs are specifically allowed by the Court. If the Court orders a hearing on the motion or additional extensions of time for filing briefs are allowed, the time consumed thereby shall be excluded only if the Court makes a specific and approximately contemporaneous determination that such delays are reasonably necessary to make the motion ready for judicial determination.

(b) Records of Excludable Time. The Clerk of the Court shall enter on the docket, in the form prescribed by the Administrative Office of the United States Courts, verifiable information received from any Federal criminal justice agency, the Court and/or the Magistrate Judge with respect to excludable periods of time for each criminal defendant. In any removal of a defendant from this District to another, under Fed.R.Crim.P. 40, the Magistrate Judge shall initially determine the amount of excludable time accrued from the time of arrest to the signing of the warrant of removal. This information shall be transmitted by the Clerk to the clerk of the transferee district. With respect to proceedings prior to the filing of an indictment or information, excludable time shall be reported to the Clerk by the United States Attorney on the criminal cover sheet appended to the indictment or information.

(c) Stipulations.

(1) The attorney for the Government and counsel for the defendant may at any time enter into stipulations with respect to the accuracy of the docket entries recording excludable time. The word "docket" for the purposes of this provision shall include all or any part of the docket assembly form issued by the Administrative Office of the United States Courts and is not limited to the proceedings' docket sheet.

(2) To the extent that the amount of time stipulated by the parties does not exceed the amount recorded on the docket for any excludable period of delay, the stipulation shall be conclusive as between the parties unless it has no basis in fact or law. It shall similarly be conclusive as to a co-defendant for the limited purpose of determining, under 18 U.S.C. § 3161(h)(7), whether time has run against the defendant entering into the stipulation.

(3) To the extent that the amount of time stipulated exceeds the amount recorded on the docket, the stipulation shall have no effect unless approved by the Court.

(d) Pre-indictment Procedures.

(1) In the event that the United States Attorney anticipates that an indictment or information will not be filed within the time limit set forth in Section 3, he or she may file a written motion with the Court for a determination of excludable time. In the event that the United States Attorney seeks a continuance under 18 U.S.C. § 3161(h)(8), he or she shall file a written motion with the Court requesting such a continuance.

(2) The motion of the United States Attorney shall state (i) the period of time proposed for exclusion, and (ii) the basis of the proposed exclusion. If the motion is

for a continuance under 18 U.S.C. § 3161(h)(8), it shall also state whether or not the defendant is being held in custody on the basis of the complaint. In appropriate circumstances, the motion may include a request that some or all of the supporting material be considered ex parte and in camera.

(3) The Court may grant a continuance under 18 U.S.C. § 3161(h)(8) for either a specific period of time or a period to be determined by reference to an event (such as recovery from illness) not within the control of the Government. If the continuance is to a date not certain, the Court shall require one or both parties to inform the Court promptly when and if the circumstances that justify the continuance no longer exist. In addition, the court shall require one or both parties to file periodic reports bearing on the continued existence of such circumstances. The Court shall determine the frequency of such reports in the light of the facts of the particular case.

(e) Post-Indictment Procedures.

(1) At each appearance of counsel before the Court, counsel shall examine the Clerk's records of excludable time for completeness and accuracy and shall bring to the Court's immediate attention any claim that the Clerk's record is in any way incorrect.

(2) In the event that the Court continues a trial beyond the time limit set forth in Section 4 or 5, the Court shall determine whether the limit may be recomputed by excluding time pursuant to 18 U.S.C. § 3161(h).

(3) If it is determined that a continuance is justified, the Court shall set forth its findings in the record, either orally or in writing. If the continuance is granted under 18 U.S.C. § 3161(h)(8), the Court shall also set forth its reasons for finding that the ends of justice served by granting the continuance outweigh the best interests of the public and the defendant in a speedy trial. If the continuance is to a date not certain, the Court shall require one or both parties to inform the Court promptly when and if the circumstances that justify the continuance no longer exist. In addition, the Court shall require one or both parties to file periodic reports bearing on the continued existence of such circumstances. The Court shall determine the frequency of such reports in the light of the facts.

(f) Motions.

Any motion filed prior to commencement of trial involving issues relating to the Speedy Trial Act of 1974, 18 U.S.C. § 3161 et seq., or this Plan, including but not limited to determinations of excludable time under § 3161(h), shall state concisely the movant's position and be accompanied by a brief prepared in accordance with the Local Criminal Rules of the Court.

7. Minimum Period for Defense Preparation

Unless the defendant consents in writing to the contrary, the trial shall not commence earlier than 30 days from the date on which the indictment or information is filed or, if later, from the date on which counsel first enters an appearance or on which the defendant expressly waives counsel and elects to proceed pro se. In circumstances in which the 70-day time limit for commencing trial on a charge in an indictment or information is determined by reference to an earlier indictment or information pursuant to Section 4(d), the 30-day minimum period shall also be determined by reference to the earlier indictment or information. When prosecution is resumed on an original indictment or information following a mistrial, appeal, or withdrawal of a guilty plea, a new 30-day minimum period will not begin to run. The Court will, in all cases, schedule trials so as to permit defense counsel adequate preparation time in the light of all the circumstances.

8. Time Within Which Defendant Should Be Sentenced

(a) Time Limit. A defendant shall ordinarily be sentenced within 45 days of the date of his or her conviction or plea of guilty or nolo contendere. The Court shall set a date for sentence at the time of defendant's conviction or plea of guilty or nolo contendere.

(b) Related Procedures. If the defendant and his or her counsel consent thereto, a presentence investigation may be commenced prior to a plea of guilty or nolo contendere or a conviction. The time during the pendency of the presentence investigation may be excludable pursuant to 18 U.S.C. § 3161(h)(8) upon such finding by the Court.

9. Juvenile Proceedings

(a) Time Within Which Trial Must Commence. An alleged delinquent who is in detention pending trial shall be brought to trial within 30 days of the date upon which such detention was begun, as provided in 18 U.S.C. § 5036.

(b) Time for Dispositional Hearing. If a juvenile is adjudicated delinquent, a separate dispositional hearing shall be held no later than 20 court days after trial, unless the Court has ordered further study of the juvenile in accordance with 18 U.S.C. § 5037(c).

10. Sanctions

(a) Dismissal or Release From Custody. Failure to comply with the requirements of Title 1 of the Speedy Trial Act may entitle the defendant to dismissal of the charges against him or her or to release from pretrial custody. Nothing in this Plan shall be construed to require that a case be dismissed or a defendant released from custody in circumstances in which such action would not be required by 18 U.S.C. §§ 3162 and 3164.

(b) High-Risk Defendants. A high-risk defendant whose trial has not commenced within the time limit set forth in 18 U.S.C. § 3164(b) shall, if the failure to commence trial was through no fault of the attorney for the Government, have his or her release conditions automatically reviewed. A high-risk defendant who is found by the Court to have intentionally delayed the trial of his or her case shall be subject to an order of the Court modifying his or her nonfinancial conditions of release under Chapter 207 of Title 18, U.S.C., to ensure that he or she shall appear at trial as required.

(c) Discipline of Attorneys. In a case in which counsel (1) knowingly allows the case to be set for trial without disclosing the fact that a necessary witness would be unavailable for trial, (2) files a motion solely for the purpose of delay which he or she knows is frivolous and without merit, (3) makes a statement for the purpose of obtaining a continuance which he or she knows to be false and which is material to the granting of the continuance, or (4) otherwise willfully fails to proceed to trial without justification consistent with 18 U.S.C. § 3161, the Court may punish such counsel as provided in 18 U.S.C. §§ 3162(b) and (c).

(d) Alleged Juvenile Delinquents. An alleged delinquent in custody whose trial has not commenced within the time limit set forth in 18 U.S.C. § 5036 shall be entitled to dismissal of his or her case pursuant to that section unless the Attorney General shows that the delay was consented to or caused by the juvenile or his or her counsel, or would be in the interest of justice in the particular case.

11. Monitoring Compliance With Time Limits

(a) Responsibilities of Clerk. In addition to maintaining such statistical data as is required to be maintained by the Administrative Office of the United States Courts, the Clerk will, from time to time, report to the Chief Judge on the status of the criminal docket within the District with specific emphasis upon (1) each case in which there is a failure to comply with any time limit set forth herein, and (2) each case in which sanctions were imposed.

(b) Responsibilities of United States Attorney.

(1) The United States Attorney will familiarize himself or herself with the scheduling procedures of each Judge and will assign or reassign cases in such manner that the Government will be ready for trial. A conflict in schedules of Assistant United States Attorneys will not be grounds for a continuance or delayed

setting except under circumstances approved by the Court and called to the Court's attention at the earliest practicable time.

(2) If the United States Attorney knows that a person charged with a criminal offense is serving a term of imprisonment in a Federal, State or other institution, or an institution of another jurisdiction, he or she shall, pursuant to 18 U.S.C. § 3161(j), promptly:

(i) Undertake to obtain the presence of the prisoner for plea and trial; or

(ii) When the Government is unable to obtain the presence of the defendant, to cause a detainer to be filed with the official having custody of the prisoner and request him or her to advise the prisoner of the detainer and to inform the prisoner of his or her rights under this Plan.

(3) If a defendant is being held in custody, either criminal or administrative, the United States Attorney shall be responsible for advising the Court, through notice to the Clerk, at the earliest practicable time of the date of the beginning of custody.

(4) The United States Attorney shall, within five days after the close of the reporting period, furnish each Judge, each Magistrate Judge, the Circuit Executive and the Clerk of the Court with a copy of the bi-weekly DJ–130 report of persons in custody. The report shall contain the docket number of the case, the name of the Judge or Magistrate Judge to whom the case has been assigned and a letter symbol of the vicinage to which the case is assigned, if known. The "reason for detention" column shall include an explanation in any case for which the defendant's status appears to be inconsistent with the time limits set forth in the Plan. As to all other criminal cases, the United States Attorney shall, on or before the fifth day of each month, furnish each Judge, each Magistrate Judge, the Circuit Executive and the Clerk of the Court with a report regarding each case in which the trial has not commenced within 60 days of the entering of the plea of not guilty. The report shall contain the docket number of the case, the name of the Judge or Magistrate Judge to whom the case has been assigned, the letter symbol of the vicinage to which the case is assigned and the reason for delay in the disposition of the case.

(5) The United States Attorney shall submit to each Judge and Magistrate Judge a separate report about each defendant in fugitive status assigned to that particular Judge or Magistrate Judge. The information shall set forth what efforts have been made, and are being made, to secure the presence of the fugitive defendant before the Court. If all logical leads have been reasonably pursued, it shall be sufficient that the fugitive status has been entered in the National Crime Information Center (NCIC). These reports shall be submitted at six month intervals after the defendant enters fugitive status. The contents of each report shall be sealed by the Court.

(c) Responsibilities of United States Marshal.

(1) The United States Marshal shall make, to the Clerk of the Court, a written daily report to include:

(i) The names, and reasons for detention, of all persons taken into custody during the preceding 24 hours.

(ii) Change of status of any person in custody.

(2) When a defendant is arrested out of the District on a warrant issued in this Court, the United States Marshal shall report the fact of the arrest in writing to the Clerk of the Court by the close of the working day on which he or she is made aware of the arrest.

(3) When a defendant is to be transferred pursuant to Fed.R.Crim.P. 40, the United States Marshal shall arrange to have the defendant transferred to this District as promptly as possible notwithstanding the fact that the defendant may be en route on a day on which the Federal offices are closed.

(d) Responsibilities of the Court. The Court has sole responsibility for controlling cases on the trial calendar. Each Judge and Magistrate Judge will schedule criminal trials at such time as may be necessary to assure prompt disposition of criminal cases. If it appears to the Chief Judge that, due to calendar congestion, sickness or disability of a Judge, that a particular criminal trial will not commence within the time limits set forth herein, the Chief Judge may make such adjustments, including the reassignment of cases, in accordance with the Local Criminal Rules of this Court in order to insure compliance with the Act.

The United States Attorney shall be informed of any case in which his or her office appears to be responsible for unnecessary delay.

12. Effective Dates

(a) The amendments to the Speedy Trial Act made by Public Law 96–43 became effective August 2, 1979. To the extent that this revision of the District's Plan does more than merely reflect the amendments, the revised Plan shall take effect upon approval of the reviewing panel designated in accordance with 18 U.S.C. § 3165(c). However, the dismissal sanction and the sanctions against attorneys authorized by 18 U.S.C. § 3162 and reflected in Sections 10(a) and (c) of this Plan shall apply only to defendants whose cases are commenced by arrest or summons on or after July 1, 1980, and to indictments and informations filed on or after that date.

(b) If a defendant was arrested or served with a summons before July 1, 1979, the time within which an information or indictment must be filed shall be determined under the Plan that was in effect at the time of such arrest or service.

(c) If a defendant was arraigned before August 2, 1979, the time within which the trial must commence shall be determined under the Plan that was in effect at the time of such arraignment.

(d) If a defendant was in custody on August 2, 1979, solely because he or she was awaiting trial, the 90-day period under Section 5 shall be computed from that date.

[Effective April 1, 1997.]

APPENDIX K. SCHEDULE OF FEES

The **Clerk of the District Court** is required to collect the following fees:

Commencing any civil case or proceeding other than an application for a writ of habeas corpus	$350.00
Application for a writ of habeas corpus	5.00
Filing a notice or petition of appeal in any case—fee includes docket fee of the United States Court of Appeals	455.00
Filing a Notice of Appeal to District Judge from a Judgment of Conviction by a Magistrate Judge in a Misdemeanor Case	32.00
Certificate of Search Each Name—	26.00
Certifying any document or paper	9.00
Exemplification of any document or paper	18.00
Filing any paper not in a case or proceeding	39.00
Registration of foreign judgment	39.00
Admission of attorney to practice (including certificate)	200.00
Duplicate Attorney Certificate of Admission	20.00
Certificate of Good Standing to Practice	15.00
Admission to Appear Pro Hac Vice (each case)	150.00
Copies made by Clerk (does not include certification) Per Page— Photographic (Xerox) copies	.50
Cassette Tapes of Proceedings	26.00
Comparing copies prepared by applicant (does not include certification) Per Page—	2.00
Retrieval of a Court Record from Federal Records Center or National Archives	45.00
Check Paid into the Court Which is Returned for Insufficient Funds	45.00
Commencing a civil case under Title III of Cuban Liberty and Democratic Solidarity (Liberated) Act of 1996 (This fee is in addition to the fee for commencing a civil case)	5,431.00

CHECKS AND MONEY ORDERS SHOULD BE MADE PAYABLE TO: CLERK, UNITED STATES DISTRICT COURT

[Effective April 1, 1997; amended effective January 1, 1998; February 1, 2001; July 1, 2001; October 1, 2002; November 1, 2003; June 1, 2004; February 7, 2005; March 22, 2005; April 9, 2006.]

APPENDIX L. APPLICATION FOR EXTENSION OF TIME TO REPLY

UNITED STATES DISTRICT COURT
DISTRICT OF NEW JERSEY

Civil Action No. ______

Application for an Extension of Time to Answer, Move or Otherwise Reply

(L.Civ.R. 6.1(b))

Application is hereby made for a Clerk's Order extending time within which defendant(s) ____

____

may answer, move or otherwise reply to Complaint filed by plaintiff(s) herein and it is represented that:

1. No previous extension has been obtained;
2. Service of Process was effected on ________; and
3. Time to Answer, Move or Otherwise Reply expires on ________(date)

____
Attorney for Defendant(s)

Address: ______________

____

ORDER

The above application is ORDERED GRANTED extended to ______ (date to be filled in by applicant counsel).

ORDER DATED ______

WILLIAM T. WALSH, Clerk

By: ______________

Deputy Clerk

[Effective April 1, 1997.]

APPENDIX M. GUIDELINES FOR ARBITRATION

TABLE OF CONTENTS

I. Case Management Responsibility of the Assigned District Judge.

The referral of civil actions to the Arbitration Program, pursuant to L. Civ. R. 201.1(d), does not divest the assigned District Judge and Magistrate Judge of the responsibility for exercising overall management control over a case during the pendency of the arbitration process, nor does it preclude the parties from filing pretrial motions or pursuing discovery.

The Arbitration Program has been revised to provide for a "compliance judge for arbitration." The duty of this judicial officer is to administer the arbitration program as a whole and to monitor the arbitration processes. Individual case management, however, remains at all times with the assigned District Judge or Magistrate Judge.

The management of cases referred to arbitration will continue to be subject to this Court's procedures regulating discovery and other pretrial matters, the applicable Federal Rules of Civil Procedure, and the Local Civil Rules of the Court. As in other cases, the dates for concluding pretrial discovery (including expert discovery) will be set at the scheduling conference under Fed. R. Civ. P. 16(b), and the parties will be required to complete all pretrial discovery before the arbitration hearing. Unlike other cases, these dates will not be extended except where a new party has been joined recently or an *exceptional* reason is presented to the Judge or Magistrate Judge. Extended discovery and the final pretrial conference will be eliminated. This means that approximately one (1) month following the filing of the last answer plus a 120–day discovery period, or at such other date as set by the scheduling order, the case will be set for arbitration through the Arbitration Clerk.

This procedure provides litigants with a prompt and less expensive alternative to the traditional courtroom trial and relieves the heavy burden of the constantly increasing case load. The Court intends for the resulting arbitration hearing to be similar in purpose to a bench trial but without the formality required by the Federal Rules of Evidence.

II. Arbitrator's Responsibility for Managing the Arbitration Hearing Process

A. Although the assigned District Judge retains overall responsibility for cases referred to the arbitration program, the Court delegates authority to the arbitrator to control and regulate the scope and duration of the arbitration hearing, including:

(1) Ruling upon the admissibility of testimonial evidence.

(2) Ruling upon the admissibility of documentary evidence.

(3) Ruling upon the admissibility of demonstrative evidence.

(4) Ruling upon objections to evidence.

(5) Ruling upon requests of counsel to excuse individual parties or authorized corporate representatives from attending the arbitration hearing.

(6) Commencing the hearing in the absence of a party.

(7) Limiting the time for presentation of evidence and summary arguments by a party.

(8) Compelling the presence of witnesses, if desirable.

(9) Swearing witnesses.

(10) Adjourning the arbitration hearing to a date certain, not to exceed 30 days from court order date, to accommodate lengthy proceedings or an unavailable witness whom the arbitrator determines to be essential to the proceedings.

(11) Preparing the Arbitration Award. The scope of delegation to the arbitrator does not include the powers to:

(1) Exercise civil or criminal contempt.

(2) Continue the hearing for an indefinite period.

B. Arbitrator as Adjudicator. The arbitrator's role is as a non-jury adjudicator of the facts based upon evidence and arguments presented at the arbitration hearing. The arbitrator is not a mediator, and the arbitrator shall not convene a settlement discussion at any point in the arbitration process unless all litigants have first explicitly requested the arbitrator to preside over settlement discussions. The arbitrator may decline the parties' request for a settlement discussion if the arbitrator believes that such participation would bring his or her own impartiality into question if the matter is arbitrated. The Court expects that the arbitrator and counsel shall strive at all times to preserve the essential functions of a finder of facts at a hearing which, though less formal than a trial, nonetheless inspires similar confidence in the objectivity and validity of the fact-finding process.

III. Suggested Format for the Presentation of Evidence at Arbitration Hearings

The Court intends that attorneys shall be prepared to present evidence through any combination of exhibits, affidavits, deposition transcripts, expert reports and, if desirable, live testimony. The Court further expects that testimonial evidence shall be limited to situations involving issues of credibility of witnesses. Evidence shall be presented primarily through the attorneys for the parties, who may incorporate arguments on such evidence in their presentation. Expert opinion may normally be presented through written reports, although live expert testimony is desirable where helpful to resolving profound differences of opinion between such experts through direct and cross-examination. In a general sense, the Court envisions this presentation process to be somewhat similar to a combination of opening and closing arguments augmented by live testimony where necessary to aid the arbitrator's fact-finding function.

In developing their arguments, counsel may present only factual representations supportable by reference to discovery materials; to a signed statement of a witness; to a stipulation; to a document; or by a representation that counsel personally spoke with the witness and is repeating what the witness stated.

Arbitrators and counsel are reminded that L.Civ.R. 201.1(f)(5) notes that the Federal Rules of Evidence shall be employed as a guide; however, the Rules should not be construed in a manner to preclude the presentation of evidence submitted by counsel in the fashion discussed above. L.Civ.R. 201.1(f)(5) further requires, "Copies of photographs of all exhibits, except exhibits intended solely for impeachment, must be marked for identification and delivered to adverse parties at least 10 days prior to the hearing...." To facilitate this exchange, counsel may obtain exhibit stickers from the Clerk's office. Copies of all exhibits exchanged must also be forwarded to the arbitrator at least 10 days prior to the hearing.

With respect to the admissibility and subsequent use of evidence offered at an arbitration hearing, counsel are reminded that L.Civ.R. 201.1(h)(2) provides:

"Upon the filing of a demand for trial de novo ... the action shall be placed on the calendar of the Court and treated for all purposes as if it had not been referred to arbitration..."

Therefore, neither the fact that the case was arbitrated nor the amount of the arbitrator's award is admissible. However, testimony given upon the record of the arbitration hearing may be used to impeach the credibility of a witness at any subsequent trial de novo. In light of the limitation placed by the Court upon the use of exhibits at subsequent Court proceedings, the arbitrator should return all exhibits to counsel at the conclusion of the arbitration hearing.

IV. Attendance of Parties; Participation in a "Meaningful Manner"

Although L.Civ.R. 201.1(f)(3) provides for the arbitration hearing to proceed in the absence of any party, the Court has determined that the attendance of the parties and/or corporate representatives is essential for the hearing to proceed in a meaningful manner. The goals of the arbitration program and the authority of the Court will be seriously undermined if a party were permitted to refuse to attend an arbitration hearing and then demand trial de novo. Accordingly the Court has, in the same Rule, allowed for the imposition of "appropriate sanctions, including, but not limited to, the striking of any demand for a trial de novo" filed by a party who fails to participate in the arbitration process in such a "meaningful manner." Failure by a party or counsel to follow these Guidelines will also be considered in determining whether there has been meaningful participation in the process.

V. Stenographic Transcript

A party desiring to have a recording and/or transcript made of the arbitration hearing shall make all necessary arrangements for same and shall bear all expenses so incurred.

VI. The Arbitration Procedure—A Summary

Upon receipt of the order referring the case to arbitration and appointing an arbitrator, counsel for plaintiff shall *promptly* forward to the arbitrator copies of *all pleadings* including any counterclaim or third party complaint and answers thereto. Thereafter, and at least *10 days* prior to the arbitration hearing, each counsel shall comply with L.Civ.R. 201.1(f)(5) by delivering to the arbitrator and to adverse counsel premarked copies of *all exhibits*, including expert reports and all portions of depositions and interrogatories, to which reference will be made at the hearing (but not including documents intended solely for impeachment). Failure to timely submit such exhibits may be deemed a failure to meaningfully participate in the process under L.Civ.R. 201.1(f)(3).

The arbitrator will have reviewed the pleadings prior to the arbitration hearing. At least one week prior to the scheduled date of the arbitration hearing, the arbitrator should conduct a conference call with the attorneys to determine whether live testimony will be necessary and who the witnesses will be.

The following is presented as an example of the agenda for a typical arbitration hearing; however, the arbitrator is empowered to define the scope and sequence of events at the hearing.

(1) Convening of the arbitration hearing and introduction of the arbitrator, counsel for the parties, and the parties.

(2) Brief procedural overview presented by the arbitrator.

(3) Opening statement by plaintiff's counsel.

(4) Opening statement by defendant's counsel.

(5) Presentation of evidence by plaintiff's counsel including, if desirable, live testimony.

(6) Presentation of evidence by defendant's counsel including, if desirable, live testimony.

(7) Summation by plaintiff's counsel.

(8) Summation by defendant's counsel.

(9) Adjournment of the arbitration hearing.

(10) Retirement of the arbitrator for deliberation and for documentation of the arbitration award.

VII. Scope of the Arbitration Award

The $150,000 limit of L.Civ.R. 201.1(d)(3) is jurisdictional for the purpose of referring cases to the program pursuant to L.Civ.R. 201.1. However, once a case has been referred to the program, the actual award need not be limited to $150,000. The arbitrator's award may also make provisions for interest and punitive damages if appropriate.

VIII. Processing the Arbitration Award

At the conclusion of the hearing, the arbitrator shall promptly file the award with the Clerk. When the award is filed, the Clerk's office will docket the fact of the award, leaving out the details, and mail a copy of the award and the arbitrator's written statement or summary setting forth the basis for the award to the arbitrator and counsel.

IX. Compensation of Arbitrators

In the event that an arbitration hearing is protracted, the District Judge to whom the matter is assigned may entertain a petition for additional compensation.

Although the Clerk's Office does not make any deductions from the compensation paid to arbitrators, it should be treated as ordinary income for tax purposes.

X. Alternative Dispute Resolution

After enactment of the Civil Justice Reform Act of 1990, then—General Rule 49 (now Local Civil Rule 201.1) was amended to provide for arbitration by consent of any civil action regardless of amount in controversy. Provision was also made for the parties to "consent to participation in any other form of alternative dispute resolution."

The Alternative Dispute Resolution Act of 1998 required the district courts to make at least one alternative dispute resolution "process" available to litigants. One such process could be arbitration by consent. However, the act placed limitations on civil actions that could be referred to arbitration by consent, including a maximum dollar "value" of $150,000.

This Court has a compulsory arbitration program with the same limitations as are imposed for arbitration by consent under the Alternative Dispute Resolution Act of 1998. Accordingly, "consent" to arbitration becomes meaningless when any eligible civil action would be subject to compulsory arbitration. This led to amendment of Local Civil Rule 201.1 to delete the "arbitration by consent" provision.

It *remains* the intent of the Court to encourage parties to choose a particular form of alternative dispute resolution. Parties may agree to participate in the mediation process prescribed in L. Civ. R. 301.1 or may participate in other forms of alternative dispute resolution such as, by way of example only, mini-trials or summary jury trials. Any such agreement between the parties must, however, be presented to the Judge or Magistrate Judge for approval, who shall consider it with due regard for the calendar and resources of the Court. Should the parties agree on some form of alternative dispute resolution, the District Judge may administratively terminate the civil action pending completion of the alternative dispute resolution procedure.

[Effective April 1, 1997; amended effective April 19, 2000.]

APPENDIX N. PROCEDURE FOR DISPOSITIVE AND COMPLEX MOTIONS—REPEALED

[Effective April 1, 1997. Amended March 31, 1999; September 27, 2000. Repealed effective February 24, 2005.]

APPENDIX O. OPTIONAL RICO CASE ORDER

UNITED STATES DISTRICT COURT
DISTRICT OF NEW JERSEY

Plaintiff(s)	:	
v.	:	Civil Action No. ______
Defendant(s)	:	

RICO CASE ORDER
18 U.S.C. §§ 1961–1968

The above-captioned case contains a civil RICO claim, which has been filed in this Court pursuant to 18 U.S.C. §§ 1961–1968. This order has been designed to establish a uniform and efficient procedure for processing this case.

The plaintiff shall file, within 30 days hereof, a RICO Case Statement. This Statement is equivalent to a supplemental pleading which shall include the facts the plaintiff is relying upon to initiate this RICO complaint as a result of the "reasonable inquiry" required by Fed.R.Civ.P. 11. In particular, this Statement shall be in a form which uses the numbers and letters set forth below, and shall state in detail and with specificity the following information:

1. State whether the alleged unlawful conduct is in violation of 18 U.S.C. § 1962(a), (b), (c) and/or (d).

2. List each defendant and state the alleged misconduct and basis of liability of each defendant.

3. List the alleged wrongdoers, other than the defendants listed above, and state the alleged misconduct of each wrongdoer.

4. List the alleged victims and state how each victim was allegedly injured.

5. Describe in detail the pattern of racketeering activity or collection of unlawful debts alleged for each RICO claim. A description of the pattern of racketeering shall include the following information:

   a. List the alleged predicate acts and the specific statutes which are allegedly violated;

   b. Provide the dates of the predicate acts, the participants in the predicate acts, and a description of the facts surrounding the predicate acts;

   c. If the RICO claim is based on the predicate offenses of wire fraud, mail fraud, or fraud in the sale of securities, provide the "circumstances constituting fraud or mistake [which] shall be stated with particularity." Fed.R.Civ.P. 9(b). Identify the time, place and contents of the alleged misrepresentations, and the identity of persons to whom and by whom the alleged misrepresentations were made;

   d. State whether there has been a criminal conviction in regard to the predicate acts;

   e. State whether civil litigation has resulted in a judgment in regard to the predicate acts;

   f. Describe how the predicate acts form a "pattern of racketeering activity"; and

   g. State whether the alleged predicate acts relate to each other as part of a common plan. If so, describe in detail.

6. State whether the existence of an "enterprise" is alleged within the meaning of 18 U.S.C. § 1961(4). If so, for each such enterprise, provide the following information:

a. State the names of the individuals, partnerships, corporations, associations or other legal entities, which allegedly constitute the enterprise;

b. Describe the structure, purpose, function and course of conduct of the enterprise;

c. State whether any defendants are employees, officers or directors of the alleged enterprise;

d. State whether any defendants are associated with the alleged enterprise;

e. State whether you are alleging that the defendants are individuals or entities separate from the alleged enterprise, or that the defendants are the enterprise itself, or members of the enterprise; and

f. If any defendants are alleged to be the enterprise itself, or members of the enterprise, explain whether such defendants are perpetrators, passive instruments, or victims of the alleged racketeering activity.

7. State and describe in detail whether you are alleging that the pattern of racketeering activity and the enterprise are separate or have merged into one entity.

8. Describe the alleged relationship between the activities of the enterprise and the pattern of racketeering activity. Discuss how the racketeering activity differs from the usual and daily activities of the enterprise, if at all.

9. Describe what benefits, if any, the alleged enterprise receives from the alleged pattern of racketeering.

10. Describe the effect of the activities of the enterprise on interstate or foreign commerce.

11. If the complaint alleges a violation of 18 U.S.C. § 1962(a), provide the following information:

a. State who received the income derived from the pattern of racketeering activity or through the collection of an unlawful debt; and

b. Describe the use or investment of such income.

12. If the complaint alleges a violation of 18 U.S.C. § 1962(b), describe in detail the acquisition or maintenance of any interest in or control of the alleged enterprise.

13. If the complaint alleges a violation of 18 U.S.C. § 1962(c), provide the following information:

a. State who is employed by or associated with the enterprise; and

b. State whether the same entity is both the liable "person" and the "enterprise" under § 1962(c).

c. Describe specifically how the defendant(s) participated in the operation or management of the enterprise.

14. If the complaint alleges a violation of 18 U.S.C. § 1962(d), describe in detail the alleged conspiracy.

15. Describe the alleged injury to business or property.

16. Describe the direct causal relationship between the alleged injury and the violation of the RICO statute.

17. List the damages sustained by reason of the violation of § 1962, indicating the amount for which each defendant is allegedly liable.

18. List all other Federal causes of action, if any, and provide the relevant statute numbers.

19. List all pendent state claims, if any.

20. Provide any additional information that you feel would be helpful to the Court in processing your RICO claim.

AND IT IS SO ORDERED this ___ day of _______, 20__.

____

[Signature of Judicial Officer]

[Effective April 1, 1997.]

APPENDIX P. APPLICATION TO PROCEED WITHOUT PREPAYMENT OF FEES AND AFFIDAVIT

AO 240 (1/94)

United States District Court
______________________ DISTRICT OF ______________________

Plaintiff

v.

Defendant

APPLICATION TO PROCEED WITHOUT PREPAYMENT OF FEES AND AFFIDAVIT

CASE NUMBER:

I, ______________ declare that I am the (check appropriate box)
☐ petitioner/plaintiff/movant ☐ other
in the above-entitled proceeding; that, in support of my request to proceed without being required to prepay fees, costs or give security therefore, I state that because of my poverty, I am unable to pay the costs of said proceeding or give security therefore; that I believe I am entitled to relief. The nature of my action, defense, or other proceeding or the issues I intend to present on appeal are briefly stated as follows:

In support of this application, I answer the following questions under penalty of perjury:

1. Are you currently incarcerated? ☐ Yes ☐ No (If "No" go to Part 2)
   If "Yes" state the place of your incarceration ______________
   Are you employed at the institution? ______ Do you receive any payment from the institution? ______
   Have the institution fill out the Certificate portion of this affidavit and attach a ledger sheet from the institution(s) of your incarceration showing at least the past six months' transactions.
2. Are you currently employed? ☐ Yes ☐ No
   a. If the answer is "Yes" state the amount of your take-home salary or wages and pay period and give the name and address of your employer.

   b. If the answer is "No" state the date of your last employment and the amount of your take-home salary or wages and pay period and the name and address of your last employer.

3. In the past 12 months have you received any money from any of the following sources?
   a. Business, profession or other self-employment ☐ Yes ☐ No
   b. Rent payments, interest or dividends ☐ Yes ☐ No
   c. Pensions, annuities or life insurance payments ☐ Yes ☐ No
   d. Disability or workers compensation payments ☐ Yes ☐ No
   e. Gifts or inheritances ☐ Yes ☐ No
   f. Any other sources ☐ Yes ☐ No

   If the answer to any of the above is "Yes" describe each source of money and state the amount received and what you expect you will continue to receive.
4. Do you have any cash or checking or savings accounts? ☐ Yes ☐ No
   If "Yes" state the total amount: ________
5. Do you own any real estate, stocks, bonds, securities, other financial instruments, automobiles or other valuable property? ☐ Yes ☐ No
   If "Yes" describe the property and state its value.

6. List the persons who are dependent on you for support, state your relationship to each person and indicate how much you contribute to their support.

I declare under penalty of perjury that the above information is true and correct.

____________________ ____

DATE SIGNATURE OF APPLICANT

CERTIFICATE
(Incarcerated applicants only)
(To be completed by the institution of incarceration)

I certify that the applicant named herein has the sum of $__________ on account to his/her credit at (name of institution) ____________________. I further certify that the applicant has the following securities to his/her credit ____________________ __________. I further certify that during the past six months the applicant's average balance was $__________.

____________________ ____

DATE SIGNATURE OF AUTHORIZED OFFICER

[Effective April 1, 1997.]

APPENDIX Q. GUIDELINES FOR MEDIATION

I. Case Management Responsibility of the Assigned Judicial Officers; Stay of Proceedings

Mediation is intended to afford litigants a less expensive alternative to traditional litigation. L.Civ.R. 301.1, which provides for both compulsory and voluntary mediation, is expected to conserve the resources of litigants which would otherwise be expended in discovery and to concentrate those resources on meaningful and intensive settlement negotiation. Mediation is also intended to conserve judicial resources, enabling Judges and Magistrate Judges to concentrate on cases which have not been referred to mediation. The Court expects and requires both litigants and their attorneys to participate in mediation in good faith.

Any case pending in the Court may be referred to mediation by the assigned Judge or Magistrate Judge. However, there are certain categories of cases (described in L.Civ.R.72.1(a)(3)(C)) which the Court has determined are not generally appropriate for mediation. Moreover, any pending case (other than in these categories) may be referred to mediation if all parties consent.

The referral of cases to mediation does not divest the assigned Judge and Magistrate Judge of the responsibility for exercising overall management control over a case during the pendency of the mediation process. However when a case is referred to mediation all proceedings (including pretrial motions or the pursuit of discovery) are stayed for a 90–day period. The purpose of this stay is to afford a reasonable period of time within which to reach a settlement. If it appears that it would be futile to continue mediation efforts before the stay expires the mediator may request that the case be restored to the active calendar forthwith.

When the stay expires, a case which has not been settled will be restored to the active calendar, protecting the parties from an extended (and unfruitful) stay. L.Civ.R. 301.1(e)(5) does provide that the parties and the mediator may make a joint application for an extension of the stay, thus recognizing that certain cases may need additional time for settlement. This application shall be made to and considered by the referring Judge or Magistrate Judge.

L.Civ.R. 301.1(b) provides for the designation of a "compliance judge for mediation." The duty of this judicial officer is to administer the mediation program and resolve procedural or substantive issues which might arise. Any such issue (including recusal of a mediator) may be brought to the attention of the compliance judge by either the parties or the mediator.

II. Mediator's Responsibility for Managing the Mediation Process

A. When a case is referred to mediation the compliance judge shall designate a mediator or co-mediators as may be appropriate. With the designation of a mediator the Court has delegated to him or her the authority to control and regulate the mediation process, including:

(1) Communicating with counsel to establish an expedited schedule for, among other things, the submission of position papers and the selection of dates for first and subsequent mediation sessions.

(2) Communicating on an ex parte basis.

(3) Determining and designating the appropriate representatives of parties, including individuals with settlement authority or other specific individuals, to attend mediation sessions.

B. The function of the mediator is to serve as a neutral facilitator of settlement. The mediator is expected to conduct the mediation process in an expeditious manner. Neither the parties nor the mediator may disclose any information presented during the mediation process without consent. The only exception to this rule of confidentiality is when disclosure may be necessary to advise the compliance judge of an apparent failure to participate in the mediation process.

Mediation, unlike arbitration, is not intended to be a fact-finding or decision-making process. Instead, the focus of mediation is to resolve the dispute between the parties. Resolution of that dispute may lead the parties and the mediator to explore questions of law or issues of fact beyond the scope of the pleadings or to reach settlements which go beyond the relief sought in the pleadings. In short, mediation is a flexible process which may be molded to fit the needs of a particular case. No specific procedures have been set for the mediator to follow. Instead, the intent of L.Civ.R. 301.1 is for the mediator to assist the parties to reach a negotiated settlement by conducting meetings, defining issues, defusing emotion and suggesting possible ways to resolve the dispute.

III. Attendance of Parties; Participation in a Meaningful Manner

The attendance of the parties or their representatives may be deemed by the mediator to be appropriate for mediation to proceed in a meaningful manner. Moreover, one of the goals of the mediation program is to involve both parties and attorneys more intimately. Likewise, the assurance of confidentiality furthers the intimate involvement of parties and attorneys as well as the frank and open discussion required for mediation to succeed. Accordingly, appropriate sanctions may be imposed on any party or attorney who fails to participate in a meaningful manner or to cooperate with the mediator or who breaches confidentiality.

IV. Compensation of Mediators

A. A mediator who is selected by the court or by the parties from the panel of mediators designated by the Chief Judge shall be compensated at the rate of $300.00 an hour except for the first three hours of his or her time, which shall not be compensated. The time incurred by a mediator in reviewing the submissions of the parties shall be included in the calculation of his or her time. The compensation, which shall be paid equally by the parties, may not be varied by the consent of the parties.

B. A mediator who is selected by the parties who is not a member of the panel of mediators designated by the Chief Judge may be compensated according to the amount and terms mutually agreed to by the mediator and the parties. Such agreement must be in writing.

V. Mediation by Consent

If all parties consent to have a case referred to mediation the parties may request the appointment of a mediator from the panel approved by the Chief Judge or may select any other individual or organization to serve as the mediator.

[Effective April 1, 1997; amended effective May 27, 1998; April 19, 2000; July 5, 2001; January 2, 2008.]

APPENDIX R. GUIDELINES FOR LITIGATION CONDUCT

Introduction

The widely-perceived, accelerating decline in professionalism—often denominated "civility"—has been the subject of increasing concern to the profession for many, years. Twice since 1988, the American Bar Association has urged adoption of, and adherence to, civility codes. What has been lacking, however, is an ABA-endorsed model code. The GUIDELINES FOR LITIGATION CONDUCT fill that void.

These GUIDELINES are consensus-driven and state nothing novel or revolutionary. They are purely aspirational and are not to be used as a basis for litigation, liability, discipline, sanctions or penalties of any type. The GUIDELINES are designed not to promote punishment but rather to elevate the tenor of practice—to set a voluntary, higher standard, "in the hope that," in the words of former ABA President John J. Curtin, "some progress might be made towards greater professional satisfaction."

The GUIDELINES FOR LITIGATION CONDUCT are modeled on the Standards for Professional Conduct adopted by the United States Court of Appeals for the Seventh Circuit, a set of proven aspirational standards. Chief United States District Judge Marvin E. Aspen of Chicago, architect of the Seventh Circuit Standards, has accurately observed that civility in the legal profession is inextricably linked to the manner in which lawyers are perceived by the public—and, therefore, to the deteriorating public confidence that our system of justice enjoys.

Deteriorating civility, in former ABA President Lee Cooper's words, "interrupts the administration of justice. It makes the practice of law less rewarding. It robs a lawyer of the sense of dignity and self-worth that should come from a learned profession. Not least of all, it . . . brings with it all the problems . . . that accompany low public regard for lawyers and lack of confidence in the justice system."

The problem of incivility is more pervasive, and insidious, than its impact on the legal profession alone. As Justice Anthony M. Kennedy has stressed:

Civility is the mark of an accomplished and superb professional, but it is more even than this. It is an end in itself. Civility has deep roots in the idea of respect for the individual.

The decline in civility is not limited to the legal profession, but this profession has been in the forefront of those addressing this problem. These GUIDELINES are offered in this spirit.

Gregory P. Joseph

Chair, 1997–1998
Section of Litigation
American Bar Association

Guidelines for Litigation Conduct

August 1998

Preamble

A lawyer's conduct should be characterized at all times by personal courtesy and professional integrity in the fullest sense of those terms. In fulfilling our duty to represent a client vigorously as lawyers, we will be mindful of our obligations to the administration of justice, which is a truth-seeking process designed to resolve human and societal problems in a rational, peaceful, and efficient manner.

A judge's conduct should be characterized at all times by courtesy and patience toward all participants. As judges we owe to all participants in a legal proceeding respect, diligence, punctuality, and protection against unjust and improper criticism or attack.

Conduct that may be characterized as uncivil, abrasive, abusive, hostile, or obstructive impedes the fundamental goal of resolving disputes rationally, peacefully, and efficiently. Such conduct tends to delay and often to deny justice.

The following Guidelines are designed to encourage us, judges and lawyers, to meet our obligations to each other, to litigants and to the system of justice, and thereby achieve the twin goals of civility and professionalism, both of which, are hallmarks of a learned profession dedicated to public service.

We encourage judges, lawyers and clients to make a mutual and firm commitment to these Guidelines.

We support the principles espoused in the following Guidelines, but under no circumstances should these Guidelines be used as a basis for litigation or for sanctions or penalties.

Lawyers' Duties to Other Counsel

1. We will practice our profession with a continuing awareness that our role is to zealously advance the legitimate interests of our clients. In our dealings with others we will not reflect the ill feelings of our clients. We will treat all other counsel, parties, and witnesses in a civil and courteous manner, not only in court, but also in all other written and oral communications. We will refrain from acting upon or manifesting bias or prejudice based upon race, sex, religion, national origin, disability, age, sexual orientation or socioeconomic status toward any participant in the legal process.

2. We will not, even when called upon by a client to do so, abuse or indulge in offensive conduct directed to other counsel, parties, or witnesses. We will abstain from disparaging personal remarks or acrimony toward other counsel, parties, or witnesses. We will treat adverse witnesses and parties with fair consideration.

3. We will not encourage or knowingly authorize any person under our control to engage in conduct that would be improper if we were to engage in such conduct.

4. We will not, absent good cause, attribute bad motives or improper conduct to other counsel.

5. We will not lightly seek court sanctions.

6. We will in good faith adhere to all express promises and to agreements with other counsel, whether oral or in writing, and to all agreements implied by the circumstances or local customs.

7. When we reach an oral understanding on a proposed agreement or a stipulation and decide to commit it to writing, the drafter will endeavor in good faith to state the oral understanding accurately and completely. The drafter will provide other counsel the opportunity to review the writing. As drafts are exchanged between or among counsel, changes from prior drafts will be identified in the draft

or otherwise explicitly brought to other counsel's attention. We will not include in a draft matters to which there has been no agreement without explicitly advising other counsel in writing of the addition.

8. We will endeavor to confer early with other counsel to assess settlement possibilities. We will not falsely hold out the possibility of settlement to obtain unfair advantage.

9. In civil actions, we will stipulate to relevant matters if they are undisputed and if no good faith advocacy basis exists for not stipulating.

10. We will not use any form of discovery or discovery scheduling as a means of harassment.

11. Whenever circumstances allow, we will make good faith efforts to resolve by agreement objections before presenting them to the court.

12. We will not time the filing or service of motions or pleadings in any way that unfairly limits another party's opportunity to respond.

13. We will not request an extension of time solely for the purpose of unjustified delay or to obtain unfair advantage.

14. We will consult other counsel regarding scheduling matters in a good faith effort to avoid scheduling conflicts.

15. We will endeavor to accommodate previously scheduled dates for hearings, depositions, meetings, conferences, vacations, seminars, or other functions that produce good faith calendar conflicts on the part of other counsel.

16. We will promptly notify other counsel and, if appropriate, the court or other persons, when hearings, depositions, meetings, or conferences are to be canceled or postponed.

17. We will agree to reasonable requests for extensions of time and for waiver of procedural formalities, provided our clients' legitimate rights will not be materially or adversely affected.

18. We will not cause any default or dismissal to be entered without first notifying opposing counsel, when we know his or her identity, unless the rules provide otherwise.

19. We will take depositions only when actually needed. We will not take depositions for the purposes of harassment or other improper purpose.

20. We will not engage in any conduct during a deposition that would not be appropriate in the presence of a judge.

21. We will not obstruct questioning during a deposition or object to deposition questions unless permitted under applicable law.

22. During depositions we will ask only those questions we reasonably believe are necessary, and appropriate, for the prosecution or defense of an action.

23. We will carefully craft document production requests so they are limited to those documents we reasonably believe are necessary, and appropriate, for the prosecution or defense of an action. We will not design production requests to place an undue burden or expense on a party, or for any other improper purpose.

24. We will respond to document requests reasonably and not strain to interpret requests in an artificially restrictive manner to avoid disclosure of relevant and non-privileged documents. We will not produce documents in a manner designed to hide or obscure the existence of particular documents, or to accomplish any other improper purpose.

25. We will carefully craft interrogatories so they are limited to those matters we reasonably believe are necessary, and appropriate, for the prosecution or defense of an action, and we will not design them to place an undue burden or expense on a party, or for any other improper purpose.

26. We will respond to interrogatories reasonably and will not strain to interpret them in an artificially restrictive manner to avoid disclosure of relevant and non-privileged information, or for any other improper purpose.

27. We will base our discovery objections on a good faith belief in their merit and will not object solely for the purpose of withholding or delaying the disclosure of relevant information, or for any other improper purpose.

28. When a draft order is to be prepared by counsel to reflect a court ruling, we will draft an order that accurately and completely reflects the court's ruling. We will promptly prepare and submit a proposed order to other counsel and attempt to reconcile any differences before the draft order is presented to the court.

29. We will not ascribe a position to another counsel that counsel has not taken.

30. Unless permitted or invited by the court, we will not send copies of correspondence between counsel to the court.

31. Nothing contained in these Guidelines is intended or shall be construed to inhibit vigorous advocacy, including vigorous cross-examination.

Lawyers' Duties to the Court

1. We will speak and write civilly and respectfully in all communications with the court.

2. We will be punctual and prepared for all court appearances so that all hearings, conferences, and trials may commence on time; if delayed, we will notify the court and counsel, if possible.

3. We will be considerate of the time constraints and pressures on the court and court staff inherent in their efforts to administer justice.

4. We will not engage in any conduct that brings disorder or disruption to the courtroom. We will advise our clients and witnesses appearing in court of the proper conduct expected and required there and, to the best of our ability, prevent our clients and witnesses from creating disorder or disruption.

5. We will not knowingly misrepresent, mis-characterize, misquote, or mis-cite facts or authorities in any oral or written communication to the court.

6. We will not write letters to the court in connection with a pending action, unless invited or permitted by the court.

7. Before dates for hearings or trials are set, or if that is not feasible, immediately after such date has been set, we will attempt to verify the availability of necessary participants and witnesses so we can promptly notify the court of any likely problems.

8. We will act and speak civilly to court marshals, clerks, court reporters, secretaries, and law clerks with an awareness that they, too, are an integral part of the judicial system.

Courts' Duties to Lawyers

1. We will be courteous, respectful, and civil to lawyers, parties, and witnesses. We will maintain control of the proceedings, recognizing that judges have both the obligation and the authority to insure that all litigation proceedings are conducted in a civil manner.

2. We will not employ hostile, demeaning, or humiliating words in opinions or in written or oral communications with lawyers, parties, or witnesses.

3. We will be punctual in convening all hearings, meetings, and conferences; if delayed, we will notify counsel, if possible.

4. In scheduling all hearings, meetings and conferences we will be considerate of time schedules of lawyers, parties, and witnesses.

5. We will make all reasonable efforts to decide promptly all matters presented to us for decision.

6. We will give the issues in controversy deliberate, impartial, and studied analysis and consideration.

7. While endeavoring to resolve disputes efficiently, we will be considerate of the time constraints and pressures imposed on lawyers by the exigencies of litigation practice.

8. We recognize that a lawyer has a right and a duty to present a cause fully and properly, and that a litigant has a right to a fair and impartial hearing. Within the practical limits of time, we will allow lawyers to present proper arguments and to make a complete and accurate record.

9. We will not impugn the integrity or professionalism of any lawyer on the basis of the clients whom or the causes which a lawyer represents.

10. We will do our best to insure that court personnel act civilly toward lawyers, parties, and witnesses.

11. We will not adopt procedures that needlessly increase litigation expense.

12. We will bring to lawyers' attention uncivil conduct which we observe.

Judges' Duties to Each Other

1. We will be courteous, respectful, and civil in opinions, ever mindful that a position articulated by another judge is the result of that judge's earnest effort to interpret the law and the facts correctly.

2. In all written and oral communications, we will abstain from disparaging personal remarks or criticisms, or sarcastic or demeaning comments about another judge.

3. We will endeavor to work with other judges in an effort to foster a spirit of cooperation in our mutual goal of enhancing the administration of justice.

[Effective March 31, 1999.]

STANDING ORDERS AND POLICIES

STANDING ORDER 08-1. RE: PETITIONS FOR RETROACTIVE APPLICATION OF NOVEMBER 1, 2007 AMENDMENT TO CRACK COCAINE OFFENSE LEVEL GUIDELINES

Pursuant to the provisions of the Criminal Justice Act, Title 18, U.S.C. §§ 3006A(a)(1) and (c), the Office of the Federal Public Defender for the District of New Jersey is hereby appointed to represent any defendant previously determined to have been entitled to appointment of counsel or who is now indigent or files a motion seeking relief, or whose name appears on lists supplied by the United States Sentencing Commission or the Administrative Office of the United States Courts, to determine whether that defendant may qualify to seek reduction of sentence and to present any motions or applications for reduction of sentence in accordance with the revised base offense levels for crack cocaine, U.S.S.G. § 2D1.1 and 18 U.S.C. § 3582(c)(2). This appointment is limited to cases affected or potentially affected by this retroactive amendment.

The U.S. Probation Office for the District of New Jersey is authorized to disclose redacted Presentence Reports that shall consist only of page one, the guidelines calculations and sentencing options paragraphs; and the FPD shall not be provided a complete copy of the Presentence Report without written permission by the Defendant, CJA counsel, or retained counsel, unless the Court otherwise directs.

IT IS SO ORDERED.

Dated: March 3, 2008.

STANDING ORDER 06-01. IN RE: EXTENDING THE SUSPENSION OF SOME REQUIREMENTS OF LOCAL CIVIL RULES 10.1(b); 81.2(b); AND 501.1

This Standing Order of the District of New Jersey is intended to address the suspension of certain Local Civil Rules on a temporary basis as contemplated by Local Civil Rule 83.2.

IT IS THEREFORE **ORDERED** THAT:

Pending a complete and formal review of Local Civil Rules 10.1(b), 81.2(b), and 501.1 by the Committee of Rules of Practice and Procedure and the Board of Judges, and with notice of opportunity for public comment to be given in the future, the Court determines that under 28 U.S.C. § 2071(e) and Local Civil Rule 83.2 there is an immediate need for extending the suspension of requirements in Local Civil Rules 10.1(b) (see Standing Order 05-4), 81.2(b) (see Order of July 26, 2005), and 501.1 (see Standing Order 05-3), and said requirements are hereby suspended nunc pro tunc as of July 26, 2006 for a period not to exceed one year and until further Order of this Court.

Dated: October 2, 2006.

STANDING ORDER 05-4. SUSPENSION OF SOME REQUIREMENTS OF LOCAL CIVIL RULE 10.1(b)

This Standing Order of the District of New Jersey is intended to address certain concerns regarding privacy and identity engendered by Local Civil Rule 10.1(b).

IT IS THEREFORE ORDERED THAT:

In light of the Court's concerns about privacy and identity intrusions under the current version of Local Civil Rule 10.1(b), and pending a complete formal review of Local Civil Rule 10.1 by the Committee of Rules of Practice and Procedure and the Board of Judges, and with notice and opportunity for public comment to be given in the future, the Court determines that under 28 U.S.C. § 2071(e) and Local Civil Rule 83.2 there is an immediate need for the suspension of the requirement in Local Civil Rule 10.1(b) that attorneys provide "the initials of their first and last name, and last four digits of the [attorney's] social security number" on filed documents, and said requirement is hereby suspended for a period not to exceed one year and until further order of this Court.

Dated: July 26, 2005.

STANDING ORDER 05-3. ADOPTION AND IMPLEMENTATION OF THE MODEL THIRD CIRCUIT ELECTRONIC DEVICE POLICY

This Standing Order of the District of New Jersey is intended to ensure compliance with the Model Circuit Electronic Device Policy which this Court adopted in September 2004.

IT IS THEREFORE ORDERED THAT:

In light of the Court's adoption and implementation of the Model Third Circuit Electronic Device Policy, a copy of which is attached hereto, and pending a complete formal review of Local Civil Rule 501.1 by the Committee of Rules of Practice and Procedure and the Board of Judges, and with notice and opportunity for public comment to be given in the future, the Court determines that under 28 U.S.C. § 2071(e) and Local Civil Rule 83.2 there is an immediate need for the suspension of Local Civil Rule 501.1 governing possession and use of Electronic Equipment, and said Rule is hereby suspended for a period not to exceed one year and until further order of this Court.

UNITED STATES DISTRICT COURT DISTRICT OF NEW JERSEY ELECTRONIC DEVICE POLICY

I. Objective. This policy establishes that "Electronic Devices," as defined herein, may be brought into courthouses subject to all appropriate security screening and that such Electronic Devices must be rendered inoperable in courtrooms and judicial chambers, unless use is authorized in such areas by the presiding judicial officer. A significant goal of this policy is to create circuit-wide consistency for the benefit of the public, attorneys, and employees.

II. Scope. This policy identifies authorized devices, establishes the classes of individuals who may possess authorized devices, sets out the basis for exceptions to the policy, and specifies guidelines for security screening and establishing areas where use of electronic devices may be prohibited. **The *use* of electronic devices in courthouses and courtrooms is subject to existing judiciary court policies regarding inappropriate and unauthorized activity,** including U.S. Judicial Conference prohibition against "broadcasting, televising, recording or taking photographs in the courtroom and areas immediately adjacent thereto . . . ."

III. Exception. Nothing in this policy prevents a judge, on an individual case basis, and with adequate notification, from temporarily establishing a ban on all Electronic Devices to be carried into a courtroom.

IV. Explanation of Terms. *Electronic Devices* refers to those devices (both currently available as well as future technology) that have as their primary function wireless communication, the storage and retrieval of digitized data, and computer applications.

The list of covered devices includes, but is not limited to, electronic devices that serve as cell phones, pagers, Palm Pilots/digital assistants, pocket computers, laptop computers, notebook computers, Blackberries, wireless network cards, and Internet cards or devices. Devices that serve only as cameras, audio recorders or video recorders are not covered by this policy, and remain subject to regulation by local court rules and orders.

V. Authorization. Electronic Devices may be brought into the courthouse, whether in the possession of attorneys, jurors, court employees, public, or press. Unless specifically authorized by the presiding judicial officers, all Electronic Devices shall remain subject to Judicial Conference and local court policies **regarding inappropriate *use* and unauthorized activity.**

Permission to carry these devices, with all of the sensitive data they may contain, into the courthouse, is intended as a convenience to those possessing such devices and to ease the burden on court security staff at building entrances. **This policy is not to be construed as granting permission to *use* any of these devices.**

VI. Enforcement.

A. *Physical Security.* Current policies regarding physical security will remain in effect. Security officers at courthouse entrances will screen all Electronic Devices for explosives, weapons, etc. Nothing in this policy is intended to limit the authority of the security officers to determine the appropriate means of screening Electronic Devices and to bar the possession of any Electronic Device determined to pose a security threat.

B. *Prohibited Uses.* Unless authorized by the presiding judicial officer, all Electronic Devices shall be rendered inoperable prior to entering any courtroom or judicial chambers. Courts may, by local rule or order, further restrict the use of any Electronic Devices inside the courthouse.

1. Notification. Policies prescribing *use* of Electronic Devices, with appropriate penalties, will be prominently displayed in the courthouse, on the court's web site, and in mailings to potential jurors and grand jurors.

2. Courtrooms. Unauthorized use of Electronic Devices in courtrooms will be addressed by courtroom security or court staff pursuant to local regulations.

3. Jurors. Jurors in possession of Electronic Devices will surrender these devices to court staff prior to entering the jury room to commence deliberations.

4. Grand jurors in possession of electronic devices will surrender these devices to court staff prior to entering the Grand Jury room.

C. *Case-by-Case Exceptions.* In the event a judge temporarily establishes a complete ban of any Electronic Device for the duration of a trial, screening for possession of Electronic Devices will occur, if practicable, in close proximity to the relevant courtroom, with a portable screening station/magnetometer, or other appropriate device. Additional security staff should be requested for this function.

D. *Court Security Officers.*

1. Physical Security. Court Security Officers (CSOs) will be responsible for physical screening of devices at courthouse entrances in accordance with policies established by the United States Marshal, and will be responsible for barring any Electronic Device determined to pose a security threat.

2. Custodial Duties. CSOs will not have any custodial duties regarding the checking and storing of Electronic Devices except as may be required on a case-by-case temporary basis as outlined in VI.(C) above.

E. *Implementation of This Policy* This policy will be implemented as a Standing Order of the Court with limited or unlimited duration as the Court determines.

Dated: July 26, 2005.

STANDING ORDER 05-2. MULTIPLE, UNRELATED DEFENDANTS IN MATTERS INVOLVING THE UNAUTHORIZED RECEPTION OF SATELLITE AND BROADCAST TRANSMISSIONS

This General Order of the District of New Jersey is intended to ensure compliance with Federal Rule of Civil Procedure 20(a) for permissive joinder of defendants. Rule 20(a) allows the permissive joinder of defendants where the claims "aris[e] out of the same transaction, occurrence, or series of transactions or occurrences." In this District, in actions where defendants are accused of receiving unauthorized broadcast and satellite transmissions, plaintiffs have typically been joining numerous defendants in a single case where there is no transactional relatedness. This is not permissible under Fed.R.Civ.P. 20(a) or any other rule, and shall not be done.

IT IS THEREFORE ORDERED THAT:

An attorney filing an action for the unauthorized reception of satellite and broadcast transmissions is obligated to meet the requirements of Rule 20(a) before joining numerous defendants in a single action and shall attest to his or her compliance in a certification accompanying the initial pleading, if more than one defendant is named.

Dated: May 6, 2005.

Policy on Privacy and Public Access to Electronic Criminal Case Files

Pursuant to the new Judicial Conference Policy on Privacy and Public Access to Electronic Criminal Case Files, documents filed in criminal cases after **November 1, 2004,** will be available to the public via the Court's electronic access system (PACER). The Court reminds counsel and litigants that the Electronic Case Filing System Policies and Procedures require that the filer of a document redact the following personal identifiers from the document, whether they file the document electronically or in paper form:

1) Social Security numbers to the last four digits;

2) financial account numbers to the last four digits;

3) names of minor children to the initials;

4) dates of birth to the year; and

5) home addresses to city and state.

The filer of the document has the sole responsibility for redacting this information from the document. The Clerk will not review each filing for redaction.

In compliance with the E-Government Act of 2002, a party wishing to file a document containing the personal data identifiers specified above may file an unredacted document under seal or file a reference list under seal. Either document shall be retained by the Court as part of the record. The Court may, however, also require the party to file a redacted copy for public access.

Additionally, because filings will be available electronically and may contain information implicating not only privacy but also personal security concerns, the Court encourages counsel and litigants to exercise caution when filing a document that contains any of the following information:

1) any personal identifying number, such as a driver's license number;

2) medical records, treatment and diagnosis;

3) employment history;

4) individual financial information;

5) proprietary or trade secret information;

6) information regarding an individual's cooperation with the government;

7) information regarding the victim of any criminal activity;

8) national security information;

9) sensitive security information as described in 49 U.S.C. § 114(s).

Counsel is strongly urged to share this notice with all clients so that an informed decision about the inclusion of certain materials may be made. **It is the sole responsibility of counsel and the parties to be sure that all documents and pleadings comply with the rules of this Court in connection with the redaction of personal identifiers.**

Dated: October 7, 2004.

STANDING ORDER IN RE GUIDELINE SENTENCING

IT IS on this 7th day of July, 2000, on the Court's own motion in accordance with the Sentencing Reform Act of 1984 and Rule 32 of the Federal Rules of Criminal Procedure, with respect to offenses committed on or after November 1, 1987;

ORDERED that the following Standing Order shall constitute the rule for guideline sentencing:

(a) Not less than 50 calendar days prior to the date set for sentencing, the probation officer shall disclose a preliminary presentence investigation report to the defendant and to counsel for the defendant and the government. Within 14 calendar days of receiving that report, the parties through their counsel shall communicate in writing to the probation officer and all other counsel (unless the Court provided otherwise) any objections they may have as to any material information, sentencing classification, sentencing guideline ranges and policy statements contained in or omitted from the report. If there are no such objections and the parties reach an agreement concerning all Sentencing Guidelines issues, adjustments, and departures, the probation officer shall be advised, and with the probation officer's concurrence, the parties may ask the Court to accelerate the schedule set for sentencing.

(b) After receiving objections, the probation officer may meet with the defendant, the defendant's counsel, and the attorney for the government to discuss those objections. The probation officer may also conduct a further investigation and revise the presentence report as appropriate.

(c) Not less than 25 calendar days prior to the date of the sentencing hearing, the probation officer shall submit the final presentence investigation report to the sentencing judge, the government, the defendant and all counsel. If resolution of counsel's objections makes it impossible to meet this deadline, the probation officer shall confer with the sentencing judge concerning a revision of the sentencing schedule. The report shall be accompanied by an addendum setting forth any objections counsel may have made that have not been resolved, together with the officer's comments thereon.

(d) Within 3 calendar days after the submission of the final presentence investigation report, the government and counsel for the defendant(s) shall confer to determine if an agreement can be reached concerning all Sentencing Guidelines issues, adjustments, and departures. If such agreement is made, the parties may ask the Court to accelerate the schedule set for sentencing.

(e) Except with regard to any objection made under subdivision (a) that has not been resolved, the final presentence investigation report may be accepted by the court as its findings of fact. The sentencing hearing, including the resolution of any objections to the presentence investigation report, shall be conducted in conformity with Rules 32(c)(1) and (c)(2) of the Federal Rules of Criminal Procedure.

(f)(1) Not less than 15 calendar days prior to the date for sentencing, the government shall submit its sentencing memorandum and any motions for departure to the Court, to the probation officer and to defense counsel. The motions for departure shall include motions based upon U.S.S.G § 5K1.1 and/or 18 U.S.C. § 3553(e). The sentencing memorandum shall include any arguments concerning the application of guideline adjustments.

(2) Not less than 10 calendar days before the date for sentencing, the defendant shall submit his/her sentencing memorandum and motions for departure to the Court, to the probation officer, and to the government. The sentencing memorandum shall include any response to the government's departure motions as well as any arguments concerning the application of guideline adjustments.

(3) Not less than 5 calendar days before the date for sentencing, the government shall submit any response to the defendant's downward departure motions or arguments concerning the application of any guideline adjustments, to the Court, to the probation officer, and to the defendant.

(4) Absent prior order of the Court, sentencing memoranda must exclude those matters excluded from the presentence report under Rule 32(b)(5) of the Federal Rules of Criminal Procedure.

(g) The time periods set forth in this Rule may be modified by the Court for good cause shown, except that the 50-day period set forth in subsection (a) may be diminished only with the consent of the defendant.

(h) Nothing in this Order requires the disclosure of any portions of the presentence report that are not disclosable under Rule 32 of the Federal Rules of Criminal Procedure; and, more particularly, pursuant to subsection (b)(6)(A) of that Rule, the Court directs that, unless the sentencing judge otherwise orders in an individual case, the probation officer shall not disclose his or her recommendation on the sentence to be imposed.

(i) The presentence report shall be deemed to have been disclosed when a copy of the report is physically delivered or 3 days after a copy of the report is mailed.

(j) Any and all references to counsel aforesaid are applicable to and include *pro se* litigants.

(k) This order supersedes this Court's prior Standing Orders of December 1, 1994, January 28, 1999 and February 11, 1999 and shall remain in full force and effect pending further modification as deemed necessary by the Court.

Dated: July 7, 2000.

ELECTRONIC DEVICE POLICY

I. Objective

This policy establishes that "Electronic Devices," as defined herein may be brought into courthouses subject to all appropriate security screening and that such Electronic Devices must be rendered inoperable in courtrooms and judicial chambers, unless use is authorized in such areas by the presiding judicial officer. A significant goal of this policy is to create circuit-wide consistency for the benefit of the public, attorneys and employees.

II. Scope

This policy identifies authorized devices, establishes the classes of individuals who may possess authorized devices, sets out the basis for exceptions to the policy, and specifies guidelines for security screening and establishing areas where use of electronic devices may be prohibited. **The *use* of electronic devices in courthouses and courtrooms is subject to existing judiciary court policies regarding inappropriate and unauthorized activity**, including U.S. Judicial Conference prohibition against "broadcasting, televising, recording or taking photographs in the courtroom and areas immediately adjacent thereto . . ."

III. Exception

Nothing in this policy prevents a judge, on an individual case basis, and with adequate notification, from temporarily establishing a ban on all Electronic Devices to be carried into a courtroom.

VI. Explanation of Terms

Electronic Devices refers to those devices (both currently available as well as future technology) that have as their primary function wireless communication, the storage and retrieval of digitized data, and computer applications.

The list of covered devices includes, but is not limited to, electronic devices that serve as cell phones, pagers, Palm Pilots/digital assistants, pocket computers, laptop computers, notebook computers, Blackberries, wireless network cards, and Internet cards or devices. Devices that serve only as cameras, audio recorders or video recorders are not covered by this policy, and remain subject to regulation by local court rules and orders.

V. Authorization

Electronic Devices may be brought into the courthouse, whether in the possession of attorneys, jurors, court employees, public, or press. Unless specifically authorized by the presiding judicial officers, all Electronic Devices must be rendered inoperable before entering any courtroom or judicial chambers. Use of Electronic Devices shall remain subject to Judicial Conference and local court policies **regarding inappropriate *use* and unauthorized activity**.

Permission to carry these devices, with all of the sensitive data they may contain, into the courthouse, is intended as a convenience to those possessing such devices and to ease the burden on court security staff at building entrances. **This policy is not to be construed as granting permission to *use* any of these devices.**

VI. Enforcement

A. Physical Security

Current policies regarding physical security will remain in effect. Security officers at courthouse entrances will screen all Electronic Devices for explosives, weapons, etc. Nothing in this policy is intended to limit the authority of the security officers to determine the appropriate means of screening Electronic Devices and to bar the possession of any Electronic Device determined to pose a security threat.

B. Prohibited Uses

Unless authorized by the presiding judicial officer, all Electronic Devices shall be rendered inoperable prior to entering any courtroom or judicial chambers. Courts may, by local rule or order, further restrict the use of any Electronic Devices inside the courthouse.

1. Notification

Policies proscribing ***use*** of Electronic Devices, with appropriate penalties, will be prominently displayed in the courthouse, on the court's web site, and in mailings to potential jurors and grand jurors.

The court's employee handbook will clearly state the use policy pertaining to employees of the judiciary, including law clerks.

2. Courtrooms

Unauthorized use of Electronic Devices in courtrooms will be addressed by courtroom security or court staff pursuant to local regulations.

3. Jurors

Jurors in possession of Electronic Devices will surrender these devices to court staff prior to entering the jury room to commence deliberations.

4. Grand Jurors

Grand jurors in possession of electronic devices will surrender these devices to court staff prior to entering the Grand Jury room.

C. Case–by–Case Exceptions

In the event a judge temporarily establishes a complete ban of any Electronic Device for the duration of a trial, screening for possession of Electronic Devices will occur, if practicable, in close proximity to the relevant courtroom, with a portable screening station/magnetometer, or other appropriate device. Additional security staff should be requested for this function.

D. Court Security Officers

1. Physical Security

Court Security Officers (CSOs) will be responsible for physical screening of devices at courthouse entrances in accordance with policies established by the United States Marshal, and will be responsible for barring any Electronic Device determined to pose a security threat.

2. Custodial Duties

CSOs will not have any custodial duties regarding the checking and storing of Electronic Devices except as may be required on a case-by-case temporary basis as outlined in § VI.(C) above.

E. Implementation of This Policy

This policy will be implemented as a Standing Order of the Court with limited or unlimited duration as the court determines.

Dated July 26, 2005.

ELECTRONIC CASE FILING

STANDING ORDER 05-1. ELECTRONIC CASE FILING

Effective January 31, 2005, electronic case filing will be mandatory for all civil and criminal cases other than pro se cases.

Requests by attorneys for an exemption to the mandatory policy will be considered for good cause hardship only, and will be reviewed on an individual basis by the Court. The Clerk's Office provides an electronic filing training program to assist attorneys filing electronically. Before seeking hardship exemption, attorneys are advised to participate in the training program or otherwise seek the assistance of the Clerk's Office.

Dated: January 31, 2005.

ELECTRONIC CASE FILING POLICIES AND PROCEDURES

1. Definitions.

(a) "*Electronic Filing System*" refers to the court's automated system that receives and stores documents filed in electronic form. The program is part of the CM/ECF (Case Management/Electronic Case Filing) software which was developed for the Federal Judiciary by the Administrative Office of the United States Courts.

(b) "*Filing User*" is an individual who has a court-issued login and password to file documents electronically.

(c) "*Notice of Electronic Filing*" is a notice automatically generated by the Electronic Filing System at the time a document is filed with the system, setting forth the time of filing, the name of the party and attorney filing the document, the type of document, the text of the docket entry, the name of the party and/or attorney receiving the notice, and an electronic link (hyperlink) to the filed document, which allows recipients to retrieve the document automatically.

(d) "*PACER*" (Public Access to Court Electronic Records) is an automated system that allows an individual to view, print, and download court docket information over the internet.

(e) "*PDF*" refers to Portable Document Format. A document file created with a word processor, or a paper document which has been scanned, must be converted to portable document format to be filed electronically with the court. Converted files contain the extension ".pdf."

(f) "*Proposed Order*" is a draft document submitted by an attorney for a judge's signature. A proposed order shall accompany a motion or other request for relief as an electronic attachment to the document.

(g) "*Document*" shall include pleadings, motions, briefs, memoranda, exhibits, certifications, declarations, affidavits, papers, orders, notices, and any other filing by or to the court.

(h) "*Technical Failure*" is defined as a malfunction of court owned/leased hardware, software, and/or telecommunications facility which results in the inability of a Filing User to submit a filing electronically. Technical failure does not include malfunctioning of a Filing User's equipment.

(i) "*In Paper Form*" is submitting a document in hard copy on paper.

2. Actions Subject to Electronic Case Filing. All civil, criminal, miscellaneous cases and documents filed in this court on or after January 5, 2004, will be entered into the court's Electronic Case Filing ("ECF") System in accordance with these Policies and Procedures ("Procedures"). Except as expressly provided in these Procedures and in exceptional circumstances, all documents shall be filed electronically.

3. Initial Papers. The filing of initial papers in civil cases, such as the complaint, notice of removal and the issuance and service of the summons, and, in criminal cases, the indictment, information, or complaint, including any superseders, warrant for arrest or summons, will be accomplished by filing in paper form accompanied with a disk or CD-ROM as stated in paragraph 5. In a case removed to the federal court, parties are requested to provide electronic copies of all documents previously filed in the state court.

4. Service of Process. Service of summons and complaint must be made under Federal Rule of Civil Procedure 4 and applicable Local Rules governing service.

5. Disk or CD-ROM. All documents submitted in paper form, including initial papers referenced in paragraph 3, must be accompanied by a disk or CD-ROM containing the signed document in PDF format.

6. Eligibility, Registration, Passwords. An attorney admitted to the Bar of this court, including attorneys authorized to represent the United States, may register as a Filing User by completing the prescribed registration form and submitting it to the Clerk of Court. Exceptions to this requirement are out-of-state attorneys who: 1) represent a party in an action transferred to New Jersey pursuant to an Order issued by the Judicial Panel on Multidistrict Litigation;[1] or 2) are retained to represent defendants in criminal cases. The form is available on the court's web site at *www.njd.uscourts.gov.* Registration as a Filing User constitutes consent to electronic service of all documents as provided in this order in accordance with the Federal Rules of Civil Procedure and the Federal Rules of Criminal Procedure.

When registering as an ECF Filing User, an attorney is certifying that he/she has completed the ECF tutorial on the court's web site or some other form of training. It is recommended that a PACER account be established, which can be accomplished by visiting the PACER web site at *http://pacer.psc.uscourts.gov.* After verification, the Filing User will receive an electronic notification of the user login and password. A Filing User shall protect the security of the User's password and immediately notify the court if the Filing User suspects that the password has been compromised.

A Filing User will promptly notify the court by e-mail to ecfchange@njd.uscourts.gov if there is a change in personal data, such as name, e-mail address, telephone number, etc., as required under Local Civil Rule 10.1.

The E–Filing Registration Form includes a field for the user's e-mail address. This e-mail address is essential in order to receive Notices of Electronic Filing. It can be the user's business or personal e-mail address. It can also be an e-mail address for another person designated to receive these Notices. If you change the e-mail address for receiving Notices of Electronic Filing, notify the Clerk's Office promptly by e-mail to ecfchange@njd.uscourts.gov.

Pro Se Parties—A party who is not represented by counsel must file papers with the clerk in the traditional manner in paper form.

A Pro Se party who is not incarcerated may request to receive filed documents electronically upon completion of a "Consent & Registration Form to Receive Documents Electronically." The form is available on the court's web site at www.njd.uscourts.gov.

7. Consequences of Electronic Filing. Electronic transmission of documents to the Electronic Filing System in accordance with these Policies and Procedures, together with the transmission of a Notice of Electronic Filing from the court, constitutes filing of the document for all purposes of the Federal Rules of Civil Procedure, the Federal Rules of Criminal Procedure, and the Local Rules of this court, and constitutes entry of the document on the docket kept by the clerk under Federal Rules of Civil Procedure 58 and 79 and Federal Rules of Criminal Procedure 49 and 55.

Before filing a scanned document with the court, a Filing User must verify its legibility.

When a document has been filed electronically, the official record of that document is the electronic recording as stored by the court, and the filing party is bound by the document filed. A document filed electronically is deemed filed on the date and time stated on the Notice of Electronic Filing from the court.

Filing a document electronically does not alter the filing deadline for that document. Electronic filing must be completed before midnight Eastern time in order to be considered timely filed that day. In accordance with Rule 6(e) of the Federal Rules of Civil Procedure and Rule 45(c) of the Federal Rules of Criminal Procedure, service by electronic means is treated the same as service by mail for the purposes of adding three (3) days to the prescribed period to respond.

8. Entry of Court Orders and Related Papers. All orders, decrees, judgments, and proceedings of the court entered or issued by the court will be filed in accordance with these Policies and Procedures, and such filing shall constitute entry on the docket kept by the clerk under Federal Rules of Civil Procedure 58 and 79 and Federal Rules of Criminal Procedure 55.

All orders will be filed electronically by the court or court personnel. An order filed electronically without the original signature of a judge shall have the same force and effect as if the judge had affixed a signature to a paper copy of the order and the order had been entered on the docket in the conventional manner.

The assigned judge or the clerk's office, if appropriate, may grant routine orders by a text-only docket entry for which a Notice of Electronic Filing will be generated. In such cases, no PDF document will be issued, and the text-only entry shall constitute the court's only order on the matter.

A Filing User submitting a proposed order to a motion should submit the document as an electronic attachment to the motion. Any other type of proposed order should be submitted in accordance with the procedure for a "Proposed Order" as outlined in the court's ECF User Manual.

9. Notice of Court Orders and Judgments. Immediately upon the entry of an order or judgment in an action, the clerk will transmit to Filing Users in the case, in electronic form, a Notice of Electronic Filing. Electronic transmission of the Notice of Electronic Filing constitutes the notice required by Federal Rules of Civil Procedure 77(d) and Federal Rules of Criminal Procedure 49(c).

10. Attachments and Exhibits. A Filing User must submit in electronic form all documents referenced as exhibits or attachments, including briefs, in accordance with the court's ECF User Manual, including file size limitations contained therein, unless otherwise ordered by the court. A Filing User shall submit as exhibits or attachments only those excerpts of the referenced documents that are directly germane to the matter under consideration by the court. Excerpt materials must be clearly and prominently identified as such. The court may require parties to file additional excerpts or the complete document.

11. Courtesy Copies. In addition to the electronic filing of all motion papers, including briefs, in support of or in opposition to a motion, the filer must submit forthwith to the Judge's or Magistrate Judge's chambers one courtesy copy of a filed paper or brief in paper form without disk or CD-ROM, unless otherwise directed by the judicial officer. These documents shall be clearly marked as courtesy copies.

12. Sealed Documents

(a) Sealing of Documents and Confidential Materials under Local Civil Rule 5.3. Effective September 1, 2005, the Court will no longer accept documents in civil cases in paper form for filing under seal. On or after that date, any such documents must be submitted electronically and must be submitted in compliance with Local Civil Rule 5.3.

Unless otherwise provided by federal law, nothing may be filed under seal unless an existing order so provides or 5.3(c)(3) is complied with. FAILURE TO COMPLY WITH LOCAL CIVIL RULE 5.3 MAY RESULT IN A WAIVER OF ANY OTHERWISE VALID BASIS FOR SEALING AND MAY RESULT IN THE DOCUMENT IN ISSUE BECOMING PUBLICLY AVAILABLE. Note, that any properly sealed document will, absent further order, be available to all other counsel of record in the particular civil action.

(b) Sealing of Criminal Documents. A document subject to a sealing order or order of confidentiality must be submitted in paper form, in an envelope clearly marked "sealed," and shall be accompanied by a disk or CD–ROM containing the document in PDF format for filing by the Clerk's Office. A motion to file a document under seal may be filed electronically, unless prohibited by law. The order of the court authorizing the filing of documents under seal may be filed electronically, unless prohibited by law. A paper copy of the sealing order must be attached to the documents under seal and be delivered to the clerk.

13. Exceptions to Electronic Filing.

(a) Permissive Exceptions

The following documents may be excluded from the Electronic Filing System and filed solely on paper:

(1) In cases where the record of an administrative proceeding (excluding Social Security Cases as referred to in paragraph 18) or other prior proceeding must be filed with the court, such record may be served and filed in hard copy without prior motion and order of the court.

(2) A party may move for permission to serve and file in paper form documents that cannot reasonably be scanned.

(b) Mandatory Exceptions

The following documents are excluded from the Electronic Filing System and shall be filed solely in paper form:

(1) ADMINISTRATIVE RECORDS IN SOCIAL SECURITY CASES

(2) TRANSCRIPTS (by Official Court Reporters/Electronic Sound Recording System)

(3) GRAND JURY MATTERS:

The following documents are examples of grand jury matters:

A) Minute Sheets of swearing in and empanelment;

B) Grand Jury Returns;

C) Voting Slips;

D) Motions to quash subpoenas and orders ruling on them;

E) Motions to enforce subpoenas and orders ruling on them;

F) Motions for immunity and orders ruling on them;

G) Motions for appointment of counsel and orders ruling on them.

(4) WARRANTS ISSUED:

The following are examples of types of warrants issued:

A) Seizure Warrants;

B) Search Warrants;

C) Pen Registers;

D) Wire Tap Orders;

(5) SENTENCING MEMORANDUMS.

14. Signatures.

(a) Attorney Signatures. The user login and password required to submit documents to the Electronic Filing System serve as the Filing User's signature on all electronic documents filed with the court. They serve as the signature for purposes of Federal Rules of Civil Procedure 11, all other Federal Rules of Civil Procedure, Federal Rules of Criminal Procedure, and the Local Rules of this court, and any other purpose for which a signature is required in connection with proceedings before the court.

An electronically filed document, or a document submitted on disk or CD–ROM, and in compliance with Local Civil Rules 10.1 and 11.1, must include a signature line with "s/," as shown below.

s/ Jennifer Doe

No Filing User or other person may knowingly permit or cause to permit a Filing User's password to be used by anyone other than an authorized agent of the Filing User.

(b) Multiple Signatures. A document requiring signatures of more than one party must be filed electronically either by: (1) submitting a scanned document containing all necessary signatures; or (2) in any other manner approved by the court.

(c) Non-Attorney Signatures. A document requiring the signature of a nonattorney must be filed electronically by: (1) submitting a scanned document containing all necessary signatures; or (2) in any other manner approved by the court.

15. Retention Requirements.

A document that is electronically filed and requires an original signature other than that of the Filing User must be maintained in paper form by the ECF Filing User and/or the firm representing the party on whose behalf the document was filed until one year after all periods for appeals expire. On request of the court, the ECF Filing User or law firm must provide the original document.

16. Service of Documents by Electronic Means.

(a) Service of Process

Nothing in these Procedures shall affect the manner of filing and service of complaints (including third-party complaints) and the issuance and service of summonses, which in all civil actions shall continue to be filed, issued and served in paper form and in conformance with the Federal Rules of Civil Procedure and the Local Rules of this Court.

(b) Other Types of Service:

(1) Filing User

Upon the electronic filing of a pleading or other document, the court's ECF System will automatically generate and send a Notice of Electronic Filing to all Filing Users associated with that case. Transmission of the Notice of Electronic Filing constitutes service of the filed document on Filing Users.

The Notice of Electronic Filing includes the time of filing, the name of the party and attorney filing the document, the type of document, the text of the docket entry, and an electronic link (hyperlink) to the filed document, allowing anyone receiving the notice by e-mail to retrieve the document automatically. If the Filing User becomes aware that the Notice of Electronic Filing was not transmitted successfully to a party, or that the notice is deficient, e.g., the electronic link to the document is defective, the filer shall serve the electronically filed document by e-mail, hand, facsimile, or by first-class mail postage prepaid immediately upon notification of the deficiency of the Notice of Electronic Filing. The submission of the Registration Form to the court constitutes consent to service of all papers via the court's electronic filing system as provided in Federal Rules of Civil Procedure 5(b) and 77(d), and the "Notice of Electronic Filing" that is automatically generated by the court's Electronic Filing System constitutes service of the filed document on Filing Users.

A certificate of service must be included with all documents filed electronically. The certification of service must indicate how service was accomplished, i.e., electronically and/or other means as provided in Federal Rule of Civil Procedure 5(b).

(2) Non ECF Filer

A Non ECF Filer is entitled to receive a paper copy of any electronically filed document from the party making such filing. Service of such paper copy must be made according to the Federal Rules of Civil Procedure, the Federal Rules of Criminal Procedure, the Local Rules of this court, and as set forth in the ECF User Manual.

(c) Time to Respond Under Electronic Service

In accordance with Rule 6(e) of the Federal Rules of Civil Procedure and Rule 45(c) of the Federal Rules of Criminal Procedure service by electronic means is treated the same as service by mail for the purposes of adding three (3) days to the prescribed period to respond.

17. Technical Failures.

The clerk shall deem the court's Electronic Case Filing web site to be subject to a technical failure if the site is unable to accept filings continuously or intermittently for more than one hour occurring after 12:00 noon (Eastern Time) that day. If a Filing User experiences technical failure, the document may be submitted to the court that day in an alternative manner, provided that it is accompanied by an affidavit of the Filing User's failed attempts to file electronically at least two times at least one hour apart after 12:00 noon. The following methods of filing are acceptable as a result of **only the court's** technical failure:

(a) In person, by bringing the document to the Clerk's Office on paper accompanied by a disk or CD–ROM which contains the document in PDF format;

(b) Via electronic mail in PDF attachment, sent to the e-mail address for technical failures listed in the ECF User Manual.

(c) Through facsimile transmission to the Clerk's Office where the presiding judicial officer is stationed. When a Filing User subject to technical failure submits a document by fax, the document shall be filed electronically on the next business day. Please refer to the fax numbers listed in the ECF User manual.

The initial point of contact for a Filing User experiencing technical difficulty filing a document electronically shall be the court's ECF Help Desk at the toll free numbers listed in the ECF User Manual. When possible, the clerk will provide notice of all such technical failures on the court's web site.

A Filing User who suffers prejudice as a result of a technical failure may seek appropriate relief from the court.

18. Public Access

A person may retrieve information from the Electronic Filing System at the court's Internet site, *ecf.njd.uscourts.gov*, by obtaining a PACER login and password. With the exception of social security cases, a person who has PACER access may retrieve docket sheets and documents in civil and criminal[2] cases. Retrieval of documents in **social security cases** [3] is limited and may only be accessed by counsel of record. Any case or document under seal shall not be available to the public through electronic or other means.

19. Sensitive Information

As the public may access certain case information over the internet through the court's Electronic Filing System, sensitive information should not be included in any document filed with the court unless such inclusion is necessary and relevant to the case. If sensitive information must be included, the following personal data identifiers **must** be partially redacted from the document, whether it is filed traditionally or electronically:

1) Social Security numbers to the last four digits;

2) financial account numbers to the last four digits;

3) names of minor children to the initials;

4) dates of birth to the year; and

5) home addresses to city and state.

In compliance with the E–Government Act of 2002, a party wishing to file a document containing the personal data identifiers specified above may either:

1) File an unredacted version of the document under seal, or;

2) File a redacted version of the document and file a reference list under seal. The reference list shall contain the complete personal identifier(s) and the redacted identifier(s) used in its (their) place in the filing. All references in the case to the redacted identifiers included in the reference list will be construed to refer to the corresponding complete personal data identifier. The reference list must be filed under seal, and may be amended as of right.

The court may still require the party to file a redacted copy for the public file. In addition, caution must be exercised when filing documents that contain the following:

1) Personal identifying numbers, such as a driver's license number;

2) Medical records, treatment, and diagnoses;

3) Employment history;

4) Individual financial information; and

5) Proprietary or trade secret information.

Additional items for criminal cases only:

6) Information regarding an individual's cooperation with the government;

7) Information regarding the victim of any criminal activity;

8) National security information; and

9) Sensitive security information as described in 49 U.S.C. § 114(s).

Counsel are strongly urged to share this information with all clients so that an informed decision about the inclusion of certain material may be made. If a redacted document is filed, it is the sole responsibility of counsel and the parties to be sure that pleadings and other papers comply with the rules and orders of this court requiring redaction of personal identifiers. The clerk will **not** review each filing for redaction.

Counsel and the parties are cautioned that failure to redact personal identifiers and/or the inclusion of irrelevant personal information in a document filed with the court may subject them to the full disciplinary and remedial power of the court, including sanctions pursuant to Federal Rule of Civil Procedure 11.

20. Correcting Docket Entries

Once a document is filed electronically, corrections to the docket can only be made by the Clerk's Office. The System will not permit the filing party to make changes to the document or docket entry once the transaction has been accepted. Only upon an Order of the Court can a document be removed or withdrawn from the ECF system.

Dated: December 2, 2003; amended effective March 24, 2005; September 1, 2005.

1 Pursuant to the General Rules of the Judicial Panel on Multidistrict Litigation, any attorney of record in any action transferred under Section 1407 may continue to represent his or her client in any district court of the United States to which such action is transferred; therefore, parties are not required to obtain local counsel in the district to which such action is transferred.

2 The Judicial Conference of the United States, has agreed to permit remote public access to electronic criminal case file documents filed after November 1, 2004.

3 Documents in social security cases may be excluded from the redaction requirement as they are not electronically available to the public over the Internet, pursuant to the privacy policy of the Judicial Conference of the United States.

CLERK'S NOTICE–ELECTRONIC CASE FILING

Dear Bar Member:

I am pleased to announce that the United States District Court for the District of New Jersey will be implementing electronic case filing on January 5, 2004. The Case Management/Electronic Case Filing (CM/ECF) system is browser-based and accessible over the Internet. CM/ECF is now running in many federal courts throughout the country. We are excited about the benefits this technology offers to the court and the bar, especially being able to file and view documents 24 hours a day from the convenience of your office or home.

Attorneys are encouraged to register and become e-filers in order to use this System. Registration forms are available at any of our three offices or on our web site at pacer.njd.uscourts.gov. It is highly recommended that you familiarize yourself with the Polices and Procedures that govern the use of this System. This document is available on our web site, along with other useful materials.

To utilize the full capabilities of this system, training is essential. Classes will be offered at each of our three courthouses. For your convenience, we've provided an on-line tutorial which can be accessed on our web site. On-site training can be arranged at your firm depending on the number of attendees and the availability of suitable facilities by calling 973–645–4439.

Please be advised that documents not filed electronically but filed in the traditional manner on paper must be accompanied by a disc or a CD containing the document in PDF format. This requirement will also become effective on January 5th.

CM/ECF represents a whole new way of doing business with the federal court. The real success of this system is a function of the number of lawyers who become registered users. We hope that you will take advantage of this new technology.

Sincerely,

William T. Walsh, Clerk

Effective January 5, 2004.

INDEX TO LOCAL CIVIL AND CRIMINAL RULES OF THE UNITED STATES DISTRICT COURT FOR THE DISTRICT OF NEW JERSEY

LOCAL RULES OF THE UNITED STATES BANKRUPTCY COURT FOR THE DISTRICT OF NEW JERSEY

Amended April 15, 1997

Including Amendments Received Through August 15, 2008

Research Note

These rules may be searched electronically on WESTLAW in the NJ-RULESS database; updates to these rules may be found on WESTLAW in NJ-RULESUPDATES. For search tips, and a detailed summary of database content, consult the WESTLAW Scope Screen of each database.

LOCAL FORMS

INTRODUCTION TO APRIL 15, 1997, AMENDMENTS

In accordance with the directive of the Judicial Conference of the United States and the provisions of Federal Rule of Bankruptcy Procedure 9029 and Federal Rule of Civil Procedure 83, the Local Rules of Bankruptcy Practice for the United States Bankruptcy Court for the District of New Jersey have been renumbered to correspond to their counterparts in the Federal Rules of Bankruptcy Procedure. The Advisory Committee on Bankruptcy Rules for the Judicial Conference of the United States approved a uniform numbering system for local bankruptcy rules.

The renumbering project involved the participation of members of this court and the Local Rules Subcommittee of the Lawyers Advisory Committee. This court acknowledges the efforts of Judge Kathryn C. Ferguson, U.S.B.J., who served as judicial liaison to the subcommittee; James J. Waldron, Clerk of the Bankruptcy Court; the members of the subcommittee: Karen Bezner, Esq., Nancy Isaacson, Esq., Rachael Lehr, Esq., and particularly Geraldine Ponto, Esq., who chaired the committee; and the analyst staff of the clerk's office composed of Andrew Kaczynski, Pat Meravi, Leanne Michalek, and Melissa Trugman. The Bankruptcy Court extends its appreciation to everyone involved in this project.

The final draft of the renumbered rules was submitted to the United States District Court for the District of New Jersey and was published in March 1997 in the *New Jersey Law Journal* and in the *New Jersey Lawyer.* These Rules have been approved by the United States District Court for the District of New Jersey. They are effective April 15, 1997.

FOR THE COURT,

WILLIAM H. GINDIN,

Chief Judge, United States Bankruptcy Court

April 15, 1997

D.N.J. LBR 1001–1. SCOPE OF RULES

(a) These rules shall be cited as the "District of New Jersey Local Bankruptcy Rules, D.N.J. LBR ____" (hereinafter "Local Rules" or "Rules") of the United States Bankruptcy Court for the District of New Jersey (hereinafter "Court"). These rules and the Local Civil Rules of the United States District Court for the District of New Jersey (hereinafter

"District Court Rules") shall be followed insofar as they are not inconsistent with the Bankruptcy Code (hereinafter "Code") and the Federal Rules of Bankruptcy Procedure (hereinafter "Fed.R.Bankr.P.") The forms appended hereto shall be known as the Local Bankruptcy Forms of the United States Bankruptcy Court for the District of New Jersey (hereinafter "Local Forms"). The local forms shall be used in the circumstances indicated by the titles to such forms.

(b) These rules shall be construed to secure the just, speedy and inexpensive determination of cases and proceedings in the Court. The application of these rules in any case or proceeding may be modified or relaxed by the Court in the interests of justice.

(c) From time to time, the Court may issue general orders and administrative procedures to supplement these Local Rules, copies of which may be obtained from the Clerk through the Court's web site, *www.njb.uscourts.gov.*

1997 Comment: Formerly Local Rule 1

2001 Comment: This Rule Amendment is intended to allow the Court to issue general orders to supplement the Local Rules, such as the Court's issuance of a general order to authorize the Court to establish practices and procedures for the filing, signing, and verification of documents by electronic means.

Reference: Fed.R.Bankr.P. 9029(a) Local Bankruptcy Rules

[April 15, 1997; amended May 30, 2001.]

D.N.J. LBR 1002-1. PETITION—GENERAL

(a) Content. In addition to the requirements of the Code, Federal Rules of Bankruptcy Procedure and Official Forms, every voluntary and, to the extent possible, involuntary petition shall contain the following information:

(1) The correct name, complete street address, city, state, and zip code of the debtor. The address stated on the petition shall be the actual location of the debtor's residence or principal place of business.

(2) In an individual petition, the correct full first, middle, and last name and the last four digits of the social security number of the debtor.

(3) In a business petition, the employer's identification number of the debtor.

(4) In a corporate petition, the signature of an officer or other authorized representative of the corporation.

(5) In a corporate petition, a copy of the corporate resolution authorizing the filing.

(6) In a partnership petition, a certification evidencing compliance with Fed.R.Bankr.P. 1004(a).

(b) Involuntary Petitions. In involuntary petitions, the above subdivisions (a)(1) through (3) apply.

1997 Comment: Subpart (a)(1) through (a)(7) is the former Local Rule 2(b)(1)(A) through (G); Subpart (b) is the former Local Rule 2(b)(2).

2003 Comment: Subpart (a)(7) is deleted as duplicative of Fed.R.Bankr.P. 1008.

2004 Comment: Subpart (a)(2) is amended to require the last four digits of a debtor's social security number on an individual petition, in accordance with the amendments to the Federal Rules of Bankruptcy Procedure and Official Forms which became effective December 1, 2003, implementing the Judicial Conference's policy on privacy and public access to case files. Pursuant to the amendment to Fed.R.Bank.P. 1007(f), an individual debtor must submit a verified statement that sets out the debtor's full social security number, or states that the debtor does not have a social security number. The statement is submitted, in accordance with instructions posted to the Court's website, but it is not filed in the case, and does not become a part of the Court record. Per the national rule amendment, the statement provides the information necessary to include on the service copy of the notice required under Rule 2002(a)(1). The corresponding amendment to Fed.R.Bankr.P. 1005 now provides that the caption of the petition include only the last four digits of the social security number.

References: 28 U.S.C. § 1930(a) Bankruptcy fees; 11 U.S.C. § 301 Voluntary cases; 11 U.S.C. § 302 Joint Cases; 11 U.S.C. § 303 Involuntary cases; Fed.R.Bankr.P. 1003 Involuntary Petition; Fed.R.Bankr.P. 1004 Partnership Petition; Fed.R.Bankr.P. 1005 Caption of Petition; Fed. R.Bankr.P. 1007 Lists, Schedules, and Statements, Time Limits; Fed.R.Bankr.P. 1008 Verification of Petitions and Accompanying Papers; Fed.R.Bankr.P. 9011 Signing and Verification of Orders; Official Form 1.

[April 15, 1997; amended effective July 2, 2003; August 1, 2004.]

D.N.J. LBR 1007-1. LISTS, SCHEDULES AND STATEMENTS [DELETED]

[April 15, 1997; deleted July 2, 2003.]

D.N.J. LBR 1007-2. MAILING—LIST OR MATRIX

(a) The matrix shall consist of an alphabetized mailing list of creditors (last name first, first name last), equity security holders, partners and other parties in interest with complete names and addresses, including zip codes. The matrix shall be filed with the petition, schedules and statement of affairs. The matrix shall be supplemented, to the extent required, by the filing of amended matrices containing only those additions in the amended schedules.

(b) The matrix shall be arranged in a single column on each page, left justified, with margins of at least 1 inch using one of the following standard typefaces or print styles in 10 or 12 point size:

(1) Courier

(2) Arial

(3) Times New Roman

(c) Each name and address block shall consist of no more than 5 lines with at least one blank line between each block. Each line shall be no more than 40 characters in length.

(d) A matrix containing 50 or more parties shall be submitted in the form of a computer diskette accompanied by a paper copy. The diskette shall be prepared in accordance with instructions provided by the clerk.

(e) A matrix submitted electronically shall be prepared in accordance with instructions provided by the clerk.

1997 Comment: Formerly Local Rule 2(c)(1)-(4)

2001 Comment: Subdivision (e) is intended to guide the procedure for submission of a matrix electronically.

Reference: Fed.R.Bankr.P. 1009 Amendments of Voluntary Petitions, Lists, Schedules and Statements; D.N.J. LBR 1009-1

[April 15, 1997; amended May 30, 2001; amended July 2, 2003.]

D.N.J. LBR 1009-1. AMENDMENTS TO LISTS AND SCHEDULES

(a) Amendment to List, Schedule or Statement. Whenever an amendment to the list of creditors, schedules or statement of affairs is filed pursuant to Fed. R. Bankr.P. 1009, the amendment must be verified by the debtor. The amendment shall include *only* the changes and shall indicate if changes are additions or deletions. The amendment must also be in compliance with **D.N.J. LBR 1007-2.**

(b) Addition of Creditor. Creditors added by amendment to the debtor's list of creditors or schedules, shall have 60 days from the date of entry of the Court's *Order Respecting Amendment to Schedule D, E or F or List of Creditors* or until the date specified in the Notice of the Meeting of Creditors under 11 U.S.C. § 341, whichever is later, to file a complaint objecting to the debtor's discharge under 11 U.S.C. § 727(a) and 1141(d) or to determine dischargeability of a debt under 11 U.S.C. § 523(c).

[April 15, 1997; amended July 2, 2003; August 1, 2008.]

Comment

1997 Comment: Formerly Local Rule 2(d).

2008 Comment: This rule is amended to supplement and formalize the Court's form Order Respecting Amendment in cases under Chapters 7, 11 and 13 which provides the added creditor 60 days from the date of entry of the Court's Order Respecting Amendment or the date specified in the Notice of the Meeting of Creditors whichever is later, to file a complaint objecting to discharge under 11 U.S.C. § 727(a) and 1141(d) or to determine the dischargeability of a debt under 11 U.S.C. § 523(c) if the debtor is an individual.

D.N.J. LBR 1019-1. CONVERSION—PROCEDURE FOLLOWING

(a) Upon conversion of a chapter 13 case to a case under chapter 7, the chapter 13 trustee shall distribute any funds on hand to the debtor unless otherwise ordered by the Court.

(b) Upon conversion of a chapter 13 case to a case under chapter 11, the chapter 13 trustee shall distribute any funds on hand to the debtor in possession or the chapter 11 trustee.

1997 Comment: Formerly Local Rule 34

Reference: 11 U.S.C. § 1307 Conversion or dismissal; Fed.R.Bankr.P. 1017(d) Dismissal or Conversion of Case; Suspension; 11 U.S.C. § 704 Duties of trustees; 11 U.S.C. § 1106 Duties of trustee and examiner; 11 U.S.C. § 1107 Rights, powers and duties of debtor in possession

[April 15, 1997; amended July 2, 2003.]

D.N.J. LBR 1073-1. ASSIGNMENT OF CASES

(a) For purposes of the division of business, the Court shall be divided into three units known as "vicinages," which shall consist of the counties served by such units in the three federal Courthouses in this District.

The Newark vicinage consists of Bergen, Essex, Hudson, Morris, Passaic, Sussex and Union Counties.

The Trenton vicinage consists of part of Burlington (except for the townships of Cinnaminson, Delran, Edgewater Park, Evesham (Marlton), Maple Shade, Moorestown, Mount Laurel, Palmyra, Riverside and Riverton), Hunterdon, Mercer, Middlesex, Monmouth, Ocean, Somerset, and Warren counties.

The Camden vicinage consists of Atlantic, part of Burlington (the townships of Cinnaminson, Delran, Edgewater Park, Evesham (Marlton), Maple Shade, Moorestown, Mount Laurel, Palmyra, Riverside and Riverton), Camden, Cape May, Cumberland, Gloucester and Salem counties.

(b) A petition commencing a case shall be filed in the vicinage in which the debtor resides if the debtor is an individual, or in which the debtor has its principal place of business within the District if the debtor is an entity other than an individual. The address stated on the petition shall be the actual location of the debtor's residence or principal place of business.

(c) All papers in a case shall be filed in the vicinage in which the case is pending.

(d) If the petition commencing a case states in writing that the case is related to another case which has been or is being filed in the same vicinage, the clerk shall assign the case to the judge to whom the lowest numbered related case has been assigned. All other case assignments shall be made by the random draw method used by the Court.

(e) An application to transfer a case from one judge to another, or from one vicinage to another, shall be made to the judge to whom the case has been assigned. The application shall be on notice to the debtor, any trustee, any secured creditors, and any official committees.

(f) If a case is dismissed, and, within 180 days of such dismissal, another bankruptcy case is filed as to the same debtor, the subsequent case shall be assigned to the same judge to whom the prior case was assigned.

1997 Comment: Formerly Local Rule 9

2002 Comment: This Rule amendment realigns the Newark Vicinage to include the Counties of Middlesex and Union.

2007 Comment: In accordance with the Court's General Order dated September 26, 2006, the Trenton Vicinage is realigned to include the County of Middlesex effective October 1, 2006.

Reference: Fed.R.Bankr.P. 5005 Filing and Transmittal of Papers

[April 15, 1997; amended effective July 1, 2002; August 1, 2007.]

D.N.J. LBR 2004-1. DEPOSITIONS AND EXAMINATION

(a) If a party from whom an examination or document production is sought under Fed.R.Bankr.P. 2004 agrees to appear for examination or to produce documents voluntarily, no subpoena or Court order is required.

(b) Any party in interest seeking to compel an examination or production of documents shall serve a subpoena pursuant to Fed.R.Bankr.P. 2004(c) without filing a motion or obtaining an order authorizing such examination or document production.

(c) A subpoena pursuant to subdivision (b) shall not set the examination or document production for less than 14 days after service of the subpoena except by agreement of the deponent.

(d) Upon motion of the deponent or any party in interest, the Court may quash or modify a subpoena pursuant to subdivision (b) for cause shown. The filing of such a motion prior to the date set for examination or document production shall stay the subpoena until the Court rules on the motion.

(e) If a deponent fails or refuses to comply with a subpoena served pursuant to subdivision (b) and has not filed a motion pursuant to subdivision (d), the party who obtained the subpoena may file a motion for an order directing such examination or document production under Fed.R.Bankr.P. 2004(a).

1997 Comment: Formerly Local Rule 16.

2002 Comment: Subsection (e) of this rule was amended. The amendments eliminated language that held that upon motion, a deponent could be held in contempt pursuant to Fed.R.Bankr.P. 9016 and Fed.R.Civ.P. 45(c) in the event of noncompliance with a subpoena. The issuing party remains free to file a motion to enforce the subpoena in the event of noncompliance. The party to be deposed remains free to file a motion to quash.

Reference: Fed.R.Bankr.P. 2005 Apprehension and Removal of Debtor to Compel Attendance for Examination; Fed.R.Bankr.P. 4002 Duties of Debtor; Fed.R.Bankr.P. 9001(5) General Definitions.

[April 15, 1997; amended September 18, 2002.]

D.N.J. LBR 2014-1. EMPLOYMENT OF PROFESSIONALS

(a) General Requirements. In addition to the requirements of Fed. R. Bankr. P. 2014, an application for an order approving employment of a professional person shall be served upon the debtor, the trustee, the secured creditors, the official committees, and parties requesting notice of all proceedings. Except to the extent that relief is otherwise governed by Fed. R. Bankr. P. 6003, any objection to such application shall be filed and served within 5 days of service of the application. A hearing may be conducted on the objection in the Court's discretion.

(b) Auctioneer Requirements.

(1) In addition to the requirements of Fed. R.Bankr.P. 2014, an application for employment of an auctioneer shall contain the following:

(A) the applicant's qualifications and previous experience as an auctioneer;

(B) a statement as to whether the auctioneer or its principals have ever been convicted of any criminal offense, other than motor vehicle violations;

(C) a description of the property to be sold and the location.

(2) The application shall be accompanied by a surety bond in favor of the United States of America in an amount at least equal to the anticipated sale proceeds or proof as to the existence of an adequate blanket bond. The surety bond shall be conditioned upon the faithful and prompt performance of the auctioneer's duties and the accounting for all monies and property which may come into the auctioneer's possession, control or custody and for compliance with rules, orders and judgments of the Court. The auctioneer shall certify that the bond is presently in effect, and will remain in effect through turnover of the auction proceeds.

1997 Comment: Subpart (a) is former Local Rule 6; subpart (b)(1) and (2) is former Local Rule 7(a) and (b).

Reference: 11 U.S.C. § 327 Employment of professional persons; 11 U.S.C. § 1103(a) Powers and duties of committees; D.N.J. LBR 2016-1, 6004-1, 6005-1

2008 Comment: Subpart (a) is amended to conform with the requirements of Fed. R. Bankr.P. 6003 which limits the granting of certain forms of relief, including the employment of professional persons, during the first 20 days after commencement of a case, unless granting of relief is necessary to avoid immediate and irreparable harm.

[April 15, 1997; amended August 1, 2008.]

D.N.J. LBR 2016-1. COMPENSATION OF PROFESSIONALS

(a) Except as set forth in (j)(3) below, this rule applies to any application for compensation and reimbursement of expenses from the bankruptcy estate by a professional person employed under 11 U.S.C. § 327.

(b) The statement of services rendered and itemization of expenses in an application for compensation shall contain:

(1) A copy of the order of retention or authorization.

(2) A copy of any administrative order pertaining to interim compensation.

(3) The dates of services rendered.

(4) The services rendered on each date and the identity of the person rendering the service.

(5) The time spent in the rendering of each service. Computer time sheets showing the time units may be attached to the application.

(6) The normal billing rate for each person.

(7) At the end of the application, a total of the time spent by each individual performing services.

(8) A list of actual, not estimated, expenses, summarized by category, such as computer assisted research (which shall not be more than the actual cost), outgoing facsimile transmissions, (which shall not exceed $1.00 per page, with no charge for incoming facsimiles), telephone charges, airfare, meals, lodging and photocopying (which shall not exceed $.20 per page).

(9) A narrative explanation of the nature of the work performed and the results achieved. The narrative portion of the application shall inform the court of circumstances that are not apparent from the activity descriptions or that the applicant wishes to bring to the attention of the Court, including, but not limited to, special employment terms, billing policies, expense policies, voluntary reductions, reasons for the use of multiple professionals for a particular activity, or reasons for substantial time billed relating to a specific activity.

(10) **D.N.J. Local Form 3** shall be filed with each application for compensation in excess of $10,000.

(c) A copy of each application for allowances shall be served on the United States Trustee at the time of filing.

(d) No Court appearance shall be required on applications for compensation unless an objection is filed and served.

(e) Professionals Retained on a Commission or Contingency Basis. A professional retained on a commission or contingency basis is exempt from the requirements of subdivisions (b)(3), (4), (5), (6), (8) and (10).

(f) Appraisers. Except where a flat fee is sought, the statement of services rendered and itemization of expenses in an application for fees or expenses for appraisers shall comply with subsection (b) of this rule. Appraisers shall include in the application the value of the appraised assets.

(g) Auctioneers. An auctioneer shall be allowed those expenses approved by the Court and, in addition, commissions on net proceeds of sale, not to exceed: 10% of the first $50,000; 7% of the next $50,000; 5% of the next $50,000; and 3% of all amounts above $150,000.

(h) Interim Applications in Chapter 11 Cases. Authorization for allowance of compensation at intervals more frequent than is permitted by 11 U.S.C. § 331, must be sought by a motion brought under the Court's General Order Adapting Guidelines Governing Procedures for Payment of Interim Compensation and Reimbursement of Expenses to Professionals.

(i) Final Applications in Chapter 11 Cases. All applications for compensation shall be filed within 90 days after the order confirming the plan becomes a final order, or such compensation request shall be deemed waived.

(j) Special Requirements in Chapter 13 Cases.

(1) *Debtor's Attorney, Generally.* If the fee of the attorney for the debtor disclosed pursuant to Fed. R. Bankr. P. 2016(b) exceeds $3,500, the attorney for the debtor shall file and serve on the Chapter 13 trustee and the debtor an application for allowances not less than 7 days before the confirmation hearing.

(2) *Supplemental Fees.*

(A) For supplemental fee applications of up to $2,000 per application, the attorney for the debtor may submit **D.N.J. Local Forms 13** and **14.** Such applications shall be served on the Chapter 13 trustee and the debtor. If the supplemental fee application is for an amount in excess of $1,000, the clerk shall issue notice of hearing as required by Fed. R. Bankr. P. 2002(a)(6) for a date on which Chapter 13 cases are heard.

(B) Any other supplemental fee applications shall be filed in accordance with subsection (a) of this rule and shall be served on the Chapter 13 trustee and the debtor. If the supplemental fee application is for an amount in excess of $1,000, the clerk shall issue notice of hearing as required by Fed. R. Bankr. P. 2002(a)(6) for a date on which Chapter 13 cases are heard.

(C) Supplemental fee applications shall be submitted not more than once every 90 days.

(3) *Residential Mortgagee's Post–Petition Preconfirmation Attorney's Fees in Proof of Claim; Waiver of and Bar to Fee–Based Claims;*

A) A residential mortgagee's proof of claim, as initially filed or as amended, may include a claim for properly reimbursable attorney's fees and costs for post-petition preconfirmation attorney's services, in an amount not to exceed $400.00 in lieu of the attorney filing an application for compensation under D.N.J. LBR 2016–1.

B) Reimbursement hereunder is permitted *only* if the following conditions are met:

(1) The residential mortgagee has actually incurred post-petition preconfirmation attorney's fees and costs for properly reimbursable services of at least the amount sought in the proof of claim, and the services performed are separately enumerated therein;

(2) The claim is for services of an attorney admitted to practice before this Court pursuant to D.N.J. LBR 2090–1, who shall be identified in the proof of claim;

(3) The attorney's fees will not be split or shared with any other entity; and

(4) The underlying mortgage documents provide for payment of attorney's fees by the debtor under the circumstances of the debtor's Chapter 13 case, and such fee is not contrary to 11 U.S.C. § 506(b) or applicable non-bankruptcy law.

C) That portion of a residential mortgagee's proof of claim seeking reimbursement of attorney's fees hereunder shall be considered prima facie evidence of the validity and amount thereof in accordance with Fed. R. Bankr. P. 3001(f). Any party in interest may object to the allowance of the claim pursuant to 11 U.S.C. section 502(a), Fed. R. Bankr.P. 3007 and D.N.J. LBR 3007–1.

D) The proof of claim must include the following statement in conjunction with any request for reimbursement of attorney's fees: "This reimbursement is requested pursuant to D.N.J. LBR 2016–1(j)(3) and the claimant certifies that all the requirements for allowance of this fee have been met."

E) Any other D.N.J. LBR 2016–1 fee application for post-petition preconfirmation attorney's services and costs on behalf of the residential mortgagee in a Chapter 13 case shall not include those services and costs allowed pursuant to this subsection (j)(3).

F) Any and all post-petition preconfirmation claims based upon the attorney's fees and costs incurred in a Chapter 13 case by the residential mortgagee which are not applied for pursuant to this subsection (j)(3) or more generally pursuant to D.N.J. LBR 2016–1, shall be deemed waived, and the residential mortgagee shall be estopped and barred from claiming such fees and costs at any time, whether in the Chapter 13 case or otherwise.

1997 Comment: Subparts (a) and (b), and (d) through (h) are former Local Rule 8(a) through (g); subpart (c) is former Local Rule 7(c); subpart (i) is the former Local Rule 25(c); subpart (j) is former Local Rule 33.

2001 Comment: Subpart (j) amended March 8, 2001; amendments include increasing the fee dollar amount from $1,500.00 to $2,000.00 and the addition of paragraphs (2), (3) and (4).

2004 Comment: Subsection (i) is amended to add reference to the Court's *General Order Adopting Guidelines Governing Procedures for Payment of Interim Compensation and Reimbursement of Expenses to Professionals* which was implemented on March 31, 2003, and posted to the Court's web site, as one of four General Orders comprising the Court's Chapter 11 Initiative. The General Orders and related Guidelines governing Chapter 11 practice in this district are referenced at D.N.J. LBR 3016–1(e).

Subsection (j)(5) is added for Chapter 13 cases, exempting from the requirements of this Local Rule, a real estate broker or debtor's real estate attorney duly retained pursuant to D.N.J. LBR 2014–1 and whose fees are approved in an order authorizing debtor to sell real property and pay certain professional fees at closing, pursuant to D.N.J. LBR 6004–1(b).

2005 Comment: Subpart (j) is amended effective August 1, 2005, to increase the fee dollar amount from $2,000 to $2,500.

2006 Comment: This rule has been substantially amended with respect to information requirements relating to compensation requests in order to aid the court in determining whether the time spent in a case, or any portion thereof, was actual, reasonable and necessary. It emphasizes activity descriptions based upon general project categories. New subdivision (b)(10) requires professionals seeking allowance of fees in excess of $10,000, except as provided in subsection (g), to submit a summary on D.N.J. Local Form 3, which has been amended to provide greater substantive detail regarding the types of services rendered by the professional and with respect to which fees are sought. New subdivision (b)(9) expands upon the nature of the narrative portion of the application to the extent that it is intended to serve a heightened informational purpose with respect to expenses incurred and for which reimbursement is sought. Subdivision (j)(1) is amended to increase the fee dollar amount above which the debtor must file an application for allowances in Chapter 13 cases, from $2,500 to $3,500. Subdivision (j)(2) is amended to permit the attorney for the debtor in Chapter 13 cases to submit D.N.J. Local Forms 13 and 14 for supplemental fee applications of up to $2,000 per application. Subdivision (j)(2)(c) is further amended to permit the filing of supplemental fee applications in Chapter 13 cases not more than once every 90 days. With the exception of subdivision (j) regarding special requirements concerning fees in Chapter

13 cases that will become effective in cases filed on or after August 1, 2006, this rule as amended shall apply to applications for compensation and expenses in cases filed on or after October 1, 2006. For cases filed before October 1, 2006, applicants may submit D.N.J. Local Form 3 in accordance with this amendment at their option.

Reference: 11 U.S.C. § 327 Employment of professional persons; 11 U.S.C. § 328 Limitation on compensation of professional persons; 11 U.S.C. § 330 Compensation of officers; 11 U.S.C. § 504 Sharing of compensation; Fed. R.Bankr.P. 2013 Public Record of Compensation Awarded to Trustees, Examiners, and Professionals; Fed.R.Bankr.P. 2014 Employment of Professional Persons; D.N.J. LBR 2014-1, 2016-1, 6004-1, 6005-1

2008 Comment: Subsection (j)(3) is added for Chapter 13 cases to allow a residential mortgagee to include in a proof of claim, attorney's fees in the amount of $400.00 or less, for standard post-petition preconfirmation legal services rendered in the Chapter 13 case such as legal work relating to the filing of a proof of claim, reviewing the Chapter 13 plan, and filing an objection to the plan, without the need to file an application for allowance in accordance with D.N.J. LBR 2016-1. The amendment requires the residential mortgagee to specify the services performed in connection with the attorney's fees requested.

This subsection pertains to the procedural requirements for including in the proof of claim, a claim for post-petition preconfirmation attorney's fees and costs, which are deemed to have prima facie validity pursuant to Fed. R. Bankr.P. 3001(f) subject to the right of a party in interest to file an objection to the claim in the normal course pursuant to 11 U.S.C. section 502(a), Fed. R. Bankr.P. 3007 and D.N.J. LBR 3007-1.

The residential mortgagee's attorney's fees may be, absent objection, added to the arrears to be cured through the plan pursuant to 11 U.S.C. § 1322(e). In cases in which it is proposed in a plan to cure a default with respect to a residential mortgage in which a foreclosure judgment has been obtained, the amount of attorney's fees that may be sought may be limited by New Jersey Court Rule 4:42-9. In cases in which the plan does not propose to cure a default, a residential mortgagee's proof of claim may include post-petition preconfirmation attorney's fees pursuant to 11 U.S.C. section 506(b), to the extent that the creditor is oversecured. In such cases, absent objection, the secured claim may be increased by the amount of the attorney's fees.

[April 15, 1997; amended March 8, 2001; amended effective July 2, 2003; August 1, 2004, August 1, 2005; October 1, 2006; August 1, 2008.]

D.N.J. LBR 2090-1. ATTORNEYS—ADMISSION TO PRACTICE

(a) The bar of this Court shall consist of any attorney admitted to practice before the United States District Court for the District of New Jersey.

(b) Attorneys may seek admission pro hac vice by application on 5 days notice to the debtor, any committee, the United States Trustee, and any other party as the Court may direct. The application must be accompanied by this Court's form order for admission pro hac vice as found on the Court's website (www.njb.uscourts.gov).

1997 Comment: Formerly Local Rule 10, as amended.

2006 Comment: This rule is amended to supplement the Court's *General Order Respecting Amendment of D.N.J. L.Civ.R. 101.1(c)(3) Requiring Payment on Each Pro Hac Vice Admission to the Clerk of the District Court* (entered on December 14, 2005) which requires inter alia, use of the form order for Admission Pro Hac Vice.

Reference: D.N.J.L.Civ.R. 101.1 Admission of Attorneys

[April 15, 1997; amended effective August 1, 2006.]

D.N.J. LBR 3003-1. FILING PROOF OF CLAIM OR EQUITY SECURITY INTEREST IN CHAPTER 11 REORGANIZATION CASES

(a) A proof of claim or interest required under Fed.R.Bankr.P. 3003(c)(2) shall be filed within 90 days after the first date set for the meeting of creditors called pursuant to § 341(a) of the Code.

(b) A proof of claim arising from rejection of executory contracts or unexpired leases shall be filed within the later of:

(1) 30 days after the date of rejection; or

(2) 90 days after the first date set for the meeting of creditors called pursuant to § 341(a).

1997 Comment: Formerly Local Rule 26

2006 Comment: This rule is amended to supplement the Court's *General Order Respecting Amendment of D.N.J. L.Civ.R. 101(c)(3) Requiring Payment on Each Pro Hac Vice Admission to the Clerk of the District Court* (entered on December 14, 2005) which requires inter alia, use of the form order for Admission Pro Hac Vice.

Reference: 11 U.S.C. § 365 Executory contracts and unexpired leases; 11 U.S.C. § 501 Filing of proofs of claim or interests; Fed.R.Bankr.P. 3001 Proof of Claim; Fed. R.Bankr.P. 3002 Filing Proof of Claim or Interest

[April 15, 1997.]

D.N.J. LBR 3003-2. FILING REQUEST FOR PAYMENT OF ADMINISTRATIVE EXPENSE CLAIM IN CHAPTER 11 REORGANIZATION OR CHAPTER 7 LIQUIDATION CASES

(a) In a Chapter 11 case, absent an administrative expense claims bar date, or a provision in a confirmed plan or confirmation order directing the filing of administrative expense claims by a date certain, a request for payment of an administrative expense, permitted under § 503(a) of the Code, may be filed at any time prior to confirmation of a plan. In a Chapter 7 case, a request for payment of an administrative expense may be filed at any time prior to any administrative expense claims bar date set by the Court.

(b) A request for payment of an administrative expense shall be filed in accordance with D.N.J. Local Bankruptcy Form 24.

(c) The filing of a request for payment of an administrative expense in accordance with D.N.J. Local Bankruptcy Form 24 shall not result in the scheduling of a hearing on the request, but shall result in the registry of the claim on the claims docket. In order to have a hearing scheduled to consider payment of any administrative expense claim, a claimant must file a motion to compel payment in accordance with D.N.J. LBR 9013-1.

(d) This Rule shall not apply to any application or request by a professional retained pursuant to a Court order in a Chapter 11 case or a Chapter 7 case for payment of fees and expenses incurred post-petition. Any such application or request by a professional for payment of administrative fees and expenses must comply with D.N.J. LBR 2016-1.

2006 Comment: This rule is new. It sets forth the time and form within which requests for payment of administrative expense claims must be filed in a Chapter 11 case or a Chapter 7 case. This Rule does not apply to requests by a professional for compensation which are governed by D.N.J. LBR 2016-1.

[August 1, 2006.]

D.N.J. LBR 3007-1. CLAIMS—OBJECTIONS

(a) All motions with respect to chapter 11 claims shall be filed within 60 days after confirmation.

(b) All motions with respect to chapter 13 claims shall be filed within 60 days after the later of confirmation of the plan or the filing of the claim or amended claim.

1997 Comment: Subpart (a) was formerly Local Rule 24(c); subpart (b) was formerly Local Rule 32.

Reference: 11 U.S.C. § 502(b) Allowance of claims or interests; Fed.R.Bankr.P. 3008 Reconsideration of Claims

[April 15, 1997.]

D.N.J. LBR 3011-1. UNCLAIMED FUNDS

(a) Unclaimed distributions shall be deposited into the Registry without court order. The deposit shall be accompanied by a list of the payees and the amounts. All other deposits and all withdrawals shall require court order. Such orders shall specify the amount deposited or withdrawn and shall state the name, address and tax identification number of any entity to which funds are paid.

(b) Unclaimed funds deposited into the Registry may be withdrawn by a motion to recover unclaimed funds brought before the judge before whom the case is pending or, if the case has been closed, the chief judge in accordance with this rule.

(1) The motion must be brought by:

(A) an attorney at law admitted to practice before the United States District Court for the District of New Jersey or admitted pro hac vice in accordance with the provisions of Local Civil Rule 101.1 of the District Court for the District of New Jersey;

(B) the claimant or its legal successor; or

(C) the assignee of the claimant or its legal successor.

(2) The notice of motion shall include:

(A) a certification setting forth the reason for the application, including an explanation of the reason the funds were not collected originally;

(B) proof of the right to the original payment;

(C) identification of the claimant by: social security number, employer's tax identification number, certification of the claimant's authority, or similar proof; and

(D) proof of any name change or succession to any right to receive funds.

(3) Service of the notice of motion shall be upon the original claimant, any assignee thereof, the trustee in a pending case or, if known, the trustee at the time the case was closed or, if same not be known, the United States Trustee; service shall be by certified mail, return receipt requested.

(4) Appearance shall be necessary on the return date of the motion unless the applicant is the original entity entitled to the funds and no objection has been filed.

(5) All remittances shall be made payable to the claimant or the claimant and an attorney at law admitted to practice before this court.

1997 Comment: Subpart (a) was formerly the entire text of D.N.J. LBR 3011-1.

1998 Comment: Subpart (b) is new.

Reference: D.N.J. LBR 7067-1

[April 15, 1997; amended April, 1998.]

D.N.J. LBR 3015-1. CHAPTER 13 PLAN

(a) The Debtor shall file a Chapter 13 Plan on Local Form 8.

(b) Only motions to avoid judicial liens under 11 U.S.C. § 522(f) and to avoid liens and reclassify claims in whole or in part may be filed within the plan. If the Plan proposed contains such motions, the Debtor must, within twenty days of the date of entry on the docket of the Notice of Hearing on Confirmation of Plan, serve each potentially affected creditor with a copy of the Plan and Chapter 13 Plan Transmittal Letter that conforms with Local Form 22. The Debtor shall file a Proof of Service of compliance with this section at least seven days prior to the scheduled Confirmation Hearing. The Plan and transmittal letter shall be served in the manner provided for service by Fed.Rule Bankr. Proc. 9014

1997 Comment: Formerly Local Rule 30

2003 Comment: This rule is amended to implement the use of Local Form 8 — Chapter 13 Plan and Motions and Local Form 22 — Chapter 13 Plan Transmittal Letter.

Reference: 11 U.S.C. § 1321 Filing of plan; 11 U.S.C. § 1322 Contents of plan; D.N.J. LBR 3015-2

[April 15, 1997; amended July 2, 2003.]

D.N.J. LBR 3015-2. CHAPTER 13 AMENDMENTS TO PLAN

(a) A modification of a plan filed before confirmation which does not adversely affect creditors will be considered by the Court at the confirmation hearing scheduled for the original plan, if the modification is filed and served on the chapter 13 trustee at least 3 days before the confirmation hearing.

(b) A modification of a plan which adversely affects creditors requires notice pursuant to Fed.R.Bankr.P. 2002(b).

(c) If a plan is modified, the entire plan shall be refiled and shall indicate in its title which modified plan is being filed, such as "First Modified Plan."

1997 Comment: Formerly Local Rule 31

Reference: 11 U.S.C. § 1323 Modification of plan before confirmation; 11 U.S.C. § 1324 Confirmation hearing; D.N.J. LBR 3015-1

[April 15, 1997.]

D.N.J. LBR 3015-3. CHAPTER 13 CONFIRMATION

The attorney for a debtor, or a pro se debtor, shall appear at the confirmation hearing. The debtor is not required to appear if represented by an attorney.

1997 Comment: Formerly Local Rule 35

Reference: 11 U.S.C. § 1324 Confirmation hearing; 11 U.S.C. § 1325 Confirmation of plan

[April 15, 1997.]

D.N.J. LBR 3015-6. OBJECTIONS TO CONFIRMATION OF CHAPTER 13 PLAN

(a) An objection to confirmation of the plan shall be filed with the court and served upon the debtor, debtor's attorney, the chapter 13 trustee, and any other party in interest at least seven (7) days prior to the confirmation hearing date set in the *Notice of Hearing on Confirmation of Plan* **or** *Notice of Modification of Chapter 13 Plan*, whichever occurs later.

(b) Except as provided in subsection (c) of this rule, a proof of claim filed that asserts a claim that is greater than, either the scheduled amount of the claim or the amount of the claim as designated in the plan serves as an objection to confirmation as to the amount of the claim, without appearance by the creditor at the confirmation hearing. The proof of claim shall be served in accordance with subsection (a) of this rule. The creditor shall file a proof of service prior to the scheduled confirmation hearing. The plan may be confirmed using the amount asserted in the proof of claim. The right of the debtor to file an objection to the allowance of a claim pursuant to D.N.J. LBR 3007-1 is preserved, without the need for oral or written reservation at confirmation.

(c) Where a motion to avoid liens or partially avoid liens has been filed in the plan, a proof of claim filed that asserts a secured claim that is greater than the amount to be paid in the plan serves as opposition to the motion and serves as an objection to confirmation. The proof of claim shall be served in accordance with subsection (a) of this rule. The creditor shall file a proof of service prior to the scheduled confirmation hearing. In order to prosecute the objection, the creditor must appear at the confirmation hearing, which shall be the hearing on the motion. Failure to appear to prosecute the objection may result in the motion being granted and the plan being confirmed pursuant to the terms as set forth in the plan.

2001 Comment: This rule is new; it sets forth the time within which objections to confirmation of the chapter 13 plan must be filed and served.

2003 Comment: This rule is amended to eliminate reference to the Chapter 13 Summary of Plan.

2005 Comment: Subsection (b) is added to allow a creditor's proof of claim in an amount different from that set forth in a debtor's Chapter 13 Plan to constitute an objection to confirmation. No further objection to confirmation of the Chapter 13 Plan need be filed. The proof of claim must be served upon the debtor, debtor's attorney, the chapter 13 trustee and any other party in interest, at least seven days prior to the confirmation hearing date set in the Notice of Hearing on Confirmation or Notice of Modification of Chapter 13 Plan whichever occurs first. Confirmation of the Chapter 13 Plan may occur using the amount listed in the creditor's proof of claim. The right of the Debtor to file an objection to the allowance of a claim pursuant to D.N.J. LBR 3007-1, Claims—Objections, for 60 days post confirmation is preserved, without the need for oral or written reservation at confirmation.

2006 Comment: Subsection (b) is amended to clarify that where a proof of claim asserts a claim that is greater than either the scheduled amount of the claim or the amount of the claim as designated in the plan, the plan may be confirmed using the amount asserted in the proof of claim without the need for an appearance by the creditor at the confirmation hearing. By operation of the rule, the debtor's right to object to the claim is reserved for 60 days after confirmation. Subsection (c) is added to clarify and highlight that where a plan includes a motion to avoid liens or partially avoid liens, a proof of claim filed that asserts a secured claim that is greater than the amount to be paid in the plan serves as opposition to the motion and serves as an objection to confirmation. In order to prosecute the objection, the creditor must appear at the confirmation hearing, as the failure to do so may result in the plan being confirmed pursuant to the terms as set forth in the plan, including the relief sought by the motion.

[Effective March 8, 2001; amended July 2, 2003; August 1, 2005; August 1, 2006.]

D.N.J. LBR 3016-1. CHAPTER 11 PLAN

(a) A plan proponent shall review all claims prior to filing a plan.

(b) Effective Date. Unless a plan provides otherwise, its effective date shall be the date on which the order of confirmation becomes final.

(c) Format of Plan. In addition to the requirements of § 1123 of the Code, a plan shall contain:

(1) A title indicating whether the plan is one of reorganization or liquidation.

(2) A table of contents.

(3) Definitions.

(4) Clearly numbered articles or sections.

(5) A signature of the proponent and the date thereof.

(d) Modification of Plan. If a chapter 11 plan is modified, the entire modified plan shall be refiled and shall indicate in its title its relationship to the original plan and any previous modification, such as "First Modified Plan of Reorganization."

(e) Pursuant to D.N.J. LBR 1001-1(c), the Court has issued the following General Orders and related Guidelines governing the Chapter 11 practice in this District:

(1) General Order Governing Procedures for Complex Chapter 11 Cases;

(2) General Order Adopting Guidelines Governing First Day Matters;

(3) General Order Adopting Guidelines Governing Procedures for Payment of Interim Compensation and Reimbursement of Expenses To Professionals;

(4) General Order Adopting Guidelines for Financing Requests.

Copies of the General Orders and related Guidelines may be obtained from the Clerk through the Court's web site: *www.njb.uscourts.gov*.

1997 Comment: Formerly Local Rule 20.

2004 Comment: Subsection (e) is added to formally reference within the Court's Local Rules, the four General Orders and related Guidelines comprising the Chapter 11 Initiative implemented by the Court on March 31, 2003.

References: 11 U.S.C. § 1128 Confirmation hearing; D.N.J. LBR 1001-1, 3016-2, 3018-2.

[April 15, 1997; amended effective July 2, 2003; August 1, 2004.]

D.N.J. LBR 3016-2. DISCLOSURE STATEMENT—GENERAL

(a) A plan proponent shall review all claims prior to filing a disclosure statement.

(b) A disclosure statement shall state the number and amount of claims of each class to which the proponent intends to object.

(c) If a chapter 11 disclosure statement is modified, the entire modified disclosure statement shall be refiled and shall indicate in its title its relationship to the original disclosure statement and any previous modification, such as "First Modified Disclosure Statement."

1997 Comment: Subparts (a) and (b) formerly Local Rule 24(a) and (b). Subpart (c) formerly Local Rule 21. Former Local Rule 24(c) has been renumbered under D.N.J. LBR 3007-1.

Reference: 11 U.S.C. § 1125 Postpetition disclosure and solicitation; Fed.R.Bankr.P. 3019 Modification of Accepted Plan Before Confirmation in a Chapter 9 Municipality or a Chapter 11 Reorganization Case; D.N.J. LBR 3016-1

[April 15, 1997; amended July 2, 2003.]

D.N.J. LBR 3018-2. ACCEPTANCE/REJECTION OF PLANS

Unless the Court directs otherwise, ballots shall be filed with the attorney for the plan proponent. At or before the chapter 11 confirmation hearing, the plan proponent shall file a certification of balloting, under penalty of perjury, summarizing both the numbers and amounts of acceptances and rejections in each class, and certifying to their timely filing. The ballots shall be retained by the party completing the certification for a period of two years from the time of closing of the case. A copy of the certification shall be served on the debtor, debtor in possession, trustee, if any, United States Trustee and any committee appointed pursuant to the Code, any party having filed a notice of appearance in the case, and such other persons as the Court may direct.

1997 Comment: Formerly Local Rule 22

2004 Comment: This rule is amended as a result of the Court's transition to Case Management/Electronic Case Filing (CM/ECF). This amendment requires that unless the Court directs otherwise, ballots are to be filed with the attorney for the plan proponent. At or before the chapter 11 confirmation hearing, the certification of balloting is then filed with the Court, under penalty of perjury, by the party with whom ballots have been filed. The party filing the certification must certify to both the numbers and amounts of acceptances and rejections in each class, as well as to the timely filing of same. The ballots are to be retained by the party with whom they have been filed for a period of two years from the date of case closing, and need not be filed with the Court. This amendment also conforms with the requirements of Official Form 14 (Ballot for Accepting or Rejecting Plan) which allows for mailing of the ballot to the attorney for the plan proponent.

Reference: 11 U.S.C. § 1126 Acceptance of plan

[April 15, 1997; amended effective August 1, 2004.]

D.N.J. LBR 3021-1. DISTRIBUTION—UNDER PLAN (CH. 11)

(a) If a plan provides for distribution of property but does not designate a disbursing agent, the Court may designate a disbursing agent. The terms of any compensation to a disbursing agent shall be set forth in the plan or the order of the Court that directs the appointment of the disbursing agent.

(b) The disbursing agent shall maintain funds for distribution to creditors and equity holders in a special account established for the exclusive purpose of making such distribution and shall make disbursements from such account only by check imprinted with the case name and the disbursing agent's name.

(c) If the plan requires the disbursing agent to maintain funds for more than 30 days, those funds shall be held in interest-bearing accounts or certificates, and interest earned shall inure to the benefit of creditors and equity holders, unless otherwise directed by the Court.

(d) Within 60 days after the initial distribution under any plan, the disbursing agent shall file and serve on the debtor, the plan proponent if other than the debtor, any official committee, and other parties as the Court may direct, a report of initial distribution utilizing Local Form 7. The disbursing agent shall serve reports of any subsequent distributions on the parties named above. These subsequent reports shall not be filed.

(e) Unless the plan provides otherwise, the time period for return of unclaimed security, money, or other property in accordance with § 347(b) of the Code shall be 90 days from the date of distribution.

1997 Comment: Formerly Local Rule 23

Reference: 11 U.S.C. § 1123 Contents of plan; Fed. R.Bankr.P. 3020(a) Deposit; Confirmation of Plan in a Chapter 9 Municipality or a Chapter 11 Reorganization Case

[April 15, 1997.]

D.N.J. LBR 3022-1. FINAL REPORT/DECREE (CH. 11)

(a) The clerk shall close a chapter 11 case 180 days after entry of a final order confirming a plan.

(b) On motion of a party in interest filed and served within the time period set forth in subsection (a) above, the Court may for cause extend the time for closing the case.

1997 Comment: Formerly Local Rule 25(a) and (b)

Reference: 11 U.S.C. § 350 Closing and reopening cases

[April 15, 1997.]

D.N.J. LBR 4001-1. AUTOMATIC STAY—RELIEF FROM

(a) No court appearances are required for uncontested motions relating to the automatic stay.

(b) To contest a motion relating to the automatic stay in a Chapter 13 case, the Debtor shall file and serve upon the creditor and the Chapter 13 Standing Trustee, a Chapter 13 Debtor's Certification in Opposition to Creditor's Motion of Certification of Default on Local Form 23 at least seven (7) days before the return date if filed in opposition to a Motion for Relief from the Automatic Stay; and within 10 days of the filing of a Creditor's Certification of Default under an Order Resolving Motion to Vacate Stay and/or Dismiss with Conditions.

(c) In addition to the requirements of D.N.J. LBR 9013-1 through 9013-3, every motion for relief from the automatic stay shall be accompanied by a certification or affidavit and supporting exhibits which shall contain the following:

(1) Copies of all documents upon which the movant will rely at the time of the hearing including, where applicable, all notes, bonds, recorded mortgages with the stamped dates of recordation, security agreements, filed financing statements with the stamped dates of filing, and assignments.

(2) Where applicable, a statement of amount due, including a breakdown of the following categories:

(A) Unpaid principal.

(B) Accrued interest from a specific date.

(C) Late charges from a specific date to a specific date.

(D) Attorneys' fees.

(E) Advances for taxes, insurance and the like.

(F) Unearned interest.

(G) Per diem interest.

(H) Any other charges.

(I) Total post-petition arrearages.

(J) Date of last payment.

(3) In all cases in which the relief sought is dependent upon the secured creditor proving the amount secured by a mortgage on real estate owned by the debtor, the movant shall attach to the certification in support of its notice of motion Local Form No. 15

("Calculation of Amounts Due"). In chapter 13 cases in which the relief sought is based upon a secured creditor's claim that the debtor has failed to make all post-petition payments due under the terms of the mortgage, security agreement or lease in issue, the movant shall attach to its certification in support of its notice of motion Local Form No. 16 ("Post-Petition Payment History Note and Mortgage") or Local Form No. 16A ("Post-Petition Payment History Vehicle Loan/ Lease"). Local Form Nos. 15, 16 and 16A shall be certified by the secured creditor.

(d) Any appraisals shall be filed and served with the moving and answering papers.

(e) Failure to oppose a request for adjournment of a hearing on a motion for relief from the automatic stay shall be deemed to be consent to continuation of the automatic stay until the new hearing date without a Court order under § 362(e) of the Code.

(f) Notwithstanding D.N.J. LBR 9013-1(j)(1), a consent order in lieu of a motion under Code § 362(d) in a chapter 11 case can be filed without the written consent of the 20 largest unsecured creditors if no committee of unsecured creditors has been appointed. In such event, the 20 largest unsecured creditors shall be served with the application and consent order and shall have 5 days to file and serve an objection. If a committee of unsecured creditors has been appointed, its written consent must be affixed to a consent order in lieu of a motion under Code § 362(d).

1997 Comment: Subparts (a) through (d) (except (b)(3)) are former Local Rule 3(i)(1)-(4). Subpart (e) is new (April 1997) and is derived from former Local Rule 3(k)(2).

2000 Comment: Subpart (b)(3) was added.

2005 Comment: Subpart (a) is amended to eliminate the appearance requirement for uncontested motions relating to the automatic stay. Subpart (b) was added to provide that the creditor's stay relief motion will be deemed uncontested and the creditor's appearance at the hearing will not be required unless the debtor files a Chapter 13 Debtor's Certification in Opposition to Creditor's Motion or Certification of Default on Local Form 23 within the time periods prescribed by this subpart. Pursuant to the Court's General Order Relating to Motions For Relief From the Automatic Stay; And Requiring The Filing of Chapter 13 Debtor's Certification in Opposition to Creditor's Motion or Certification of Default and Related Forms entered on January 4, 2005, secured creditors are required to accept debtors' post petition payments, and to apply those payments to debtors' accounts; any such acceptance is without any prejudice to, waiver of, or estoppel as to the position of secured creditors in disputes with debtors, including payment and accounting disputes.

2006 Comment: Subpart (c)(3) is amended to maintain and clarify the current requirement that the information contained in Local Forms 15 ("Calculation of Amounts Due"), 16 ("Post-Petition Payment History Note and Mortgage") and 16A ("Post-Petition Payment History Vehicle Loan/ Lease") be certified by the secured creditor with personal knowledge of the calculation or payment history set forth therein, or a custodian of the secured creditor's records or other similarly qualified and authorized person having access to those records.

Reference: 11 U.S.C. § 361 Adequate Protection.

[April 15, 1997; amended January 2000; August 1, 2005; August 1, 2006.]

D.N.J. LBR 5005-1. FILING AND TRANSMITTAL OF PAPERS

Electronic filing is authorized subject to general orders and administrative procedures as issued by the Court. In cases in which electronic filing is utilized, documents shall be filed, signed, or verified by means that are consistent with any general orders issued by the Court.

2001 Comment: This Rule is new and provides the general authority for electronic filing as authorized under Fed. R.Bankr.P. 5005(a)(2).

Reference: Fed.R.Bankr.P. 5005(2)(a).

[Effective May 30, 2001.]

D.N.J. LBR 5005-2. FILING PAPERS—NUMBER OF COPIES

An original and one copy of the petition, statement of financial affairs and schedules are required for filing in hard copy in cases under Chapters 7, 9, 11, 12 and 13.

Only the originally filed petition, statement of financial affairs and schedules are required for filing electronically in cases under Chapter 7, 9, 11, 12 and 13.

1997 Comment: Formerly Local Rule 2(b)(3)

2003 Comment: This rule is amended to recognize the reduced number of copies of petitions, statements of financial affairs and schedules required due to the implementation of the Court's Electronic Case Filing System (ECF).

[April 15, 1997; amended July 2, 2003.]

D.N.J. LBR 5005-3. FILING PAPERS—SIZE OF PAPERS

All petitions, pleadings, schedules and other papers shall be of standard letter size (8½ × 11 inches).

1997 Comment: Formerly part of Local Rule 2(a)(1)

[April 15, 1997.]

D.N.J. LBR 5011-1. WITHDRAWAL OF REFERENCE

A motion for withdrawal of the reference of a case or proceeding shall be filed in the bankruptcy court in the form and manner prescribed by Local Civil Rules 5.1, 7.1, 10.1, 11.1 and 78.1 of the District Court Rules. All such motions are then to be immediately transmitted to the district court.

1997 Comment: Formerly Local Rule 14

Reference: 28 U.S.C. § 157 Procedures; Fed.R.Bankr.P. 5005(c) Filing and Transmittal of Papers

[April 15, 1997.]

D.N.J. LBR 5071-1. CONTINUANCE

(a) An adjournment request shall be made no later than 3 days before the hearing date. Before requesting an adjournment, the requesting party shall attempt to obtain the consent of the other parties and inform the Court of their position, including the reasons for any opposition.

(b) If a request cannot be presented to the Court within the time period provided in (a), the parties shall appear on the hearing date. The adjournment request will be considered at that time.

1997 Comment: Formerly Local Rule 11

Reference: Fed.R.Bankr.P. 9006(a) Time

[April 15, 1997.]

D.N.J. LBR 6004-1. SALE OF ESTATE PROPERTY

(a) The trustee, debtor in possession, or an authorized representative shall attend and monitor the bidding process at all auctions of estate property.

(b) In a Chapter 13 case, an Information for Notice of Private Sale of Real Property may include a request to pay at closing, the fees or commissions of a duly retained real estate broker or debtor's real estate attorney.

1997 Comment: Formerly Local Rule 7(f).

2004 Comment: Subsection (b) is added in conjunction with the 2004 amendment to D.N.J. LBR 2016-1(j)(5) which allows, exclusively in a Chapter 13 case, a real estate broker or debtor's real estate attorney, retained pursuant to D.N.J. LBR 2014-1, to include a request for reasonable fees to be paid upon closing, in the debtor's Information for Notice of Private Sale. The notice of private sale pursuant to Fed. R.Bankr.P. 2002(a) will include the requested real estate broker's commission as a percentage of the sale price, and/or the debtor's real estate attorney's fee, as well as the date of the respective orders of appointment. A request for approval of a section 363(f) sale requires the filing of a motion (Fed.R.Bank.P. 6004(a)), in addition to the Information for Notice of Private Sale (2002(a)). Moreover, where debtor's counsel seeks entry of an order authorizing debtor to sell real property and pay certain professionals at closing, a motion will accompany the filing of the Information for Notice of Private Sale. The Court retains its discretion, on a case-by-case basis, to require the filing of an application for fees and expenses pursuant to D.N.J. LBR 2016-1, setting forth a statement of services rendered and itemization of expenses incurred by the real estate broker or debtor's closing attorney.

[April 15, 1997; amended effective August 1, 2004.]

D.N.J. LBR 6005-1. APPRAISERS AND AUCTIONEERS

(a) No auctioneer shall be directly or indirectly interested in the sale or purchase of any of the assets or property of the estate being administered.

(b) In all sales at public auction the personal property shall first be offered in bulk. After the bidding in bulk is completed, the property shall be offered for sale in lots set forth in the original lotting and selling sheets. Copies of lotting and selling sheets shall be available for prospective purchasers the day of the sale.

(c) Upon completion of the sale, the auctioneer shall deliver to the trustee or debtor in possession all cash or its equivalent received from the sale and the original selling or lotting sheets. The auctioneer shall be liable for the collection and payment of the proceeds of sale. The original selling sheets shall contain an itemized statement of the property offered for sale, the names and addresses of the bulk bidders and the amounts of the bids, the name and address of the highest bidder for each lot, the price bid or received for each lot and the total amount bid or received for all lots.

(d) No property shall be delivered to the successful bidder until payment of the balance of the bid price. All funds collected by the auctioneer on the date of delivery shall be promptly remitted to the trustee or debtor in possession, together with a list setting forth the amount of each payment and from whom such payment was received.

(e) A successful bidder shall deposit with the auctioneer the required percentage deposit as announced before the sale. All deposits and final payments shall be made in cash, certified check or bank check. The terms of sale shall be announced by the trustee or auctioneer before the sale. All advertisements shall specify the conditions, including the monetary terms of the sale.

1997 Comment: Formerly Local Rule 7(d), (e), (g), (h), and (i)

Reference: D.N.J. LBR 2016-1, 6004-1

[April 15, 1997.]

D.N.J. LBR 6007-1. ABANDONMENT

A trustee or debtor in possession seeking approval to abandon property of the estate may file a Notice of Intent to Abandon on Local Form No. 5 or 6. The clerk shall send notice in accordance with Fed. R.Bankr.P. 6007 of the proposed abandonment.

Comment: Formerly Local Rule 15

Reference: 11 U.S.C. § 554 Abandonment of property of the estate

[April 15, 1997.]

D.N.J. LBR 7001–1. ADVERSARY PROCEEDINGS—GENERAL

A party or attorney filing a complaint or third party complaint shall prepare a summons and notice of pretrial conference conforming to Form B250B of the Director of the Administrative Office as authorized by Fed.R.Bankr.P. 9009 and shall deliver the complaint and summons to the clerk for the issuance of the summons and notice of pretrial conference.

Comment: Formerly Local Rule 2(e)(1)

Reference: Fed.R.Civ.P. 4 Summons; Fed.R.Civ.P. 16 Pretrial Conferences, Scheduling, Management; Fed. R.Bankr.P. 7004 Process, Service of Summons, Complaint; Fed.R.Bankr.P. 7016 Pretrial Procedure; Formulating Issues

[April 15, 1997.]

D.N.J. LBR 7003–1. COVER SHEET

Each complaint shall have attached an official bankruptcy cover sheet, Form B–104, which shall be provided by the clerk on request.

1997 Comment: Formerly Local Rule 2(e)(2)

[April 15, 1997.]

D.N.J. LBR 7005–1. SERVICE AND FILING OF PLEADINGS AND OTHER PAPERS—ELECTRONIC CASE FILING SYSTEM

(a) Participants in the Court's electronic case filing system (ECF), by accepting a login and password from the Court, waive their right to service by personal service or first class mail and agree to electronic service, except with regard to service of process of a summons and complaint in an adversary proceeding under Fed.R.Bankr.P. 7004 and the initiating motion in a contested matter under Fed.R.Bankr.P. 9014.

(b) A party may make service upon a Participant in the Court's electronic case filing system under Fed. R.Civ.P. 5(b)(2)(D) made applicable to bankruptcy cases pursuant to Fed.R.Bankr.P. 7005, through the Notice of Electronic Filing automatically generated by the Court's transmission facilities.

2003 Comment: The December 2001 amendment to Fed. R.Civ.P. 5(b)(2)(D) requires the promulgation of a local rule if a court wants to authorize parties to use its transmission facilities to make electronic service.

Express written consent to electronic service through the Court's transmission facilities as further required by Fed. R.Civ.P. 5(b)(2)(D) is provided by the Participant's signature on the Court's ECF registration form.

[July 2, 2003. Amended effective August 1, 2004.]

D.N.J. LBR 7026–1. DISCOVERY—GENERAL

The provisions of Local Civil Rules 26.1 and 37.1 of the District Court Rules may be applied in adversary proceedings in the discretion of the Court.

Comment: Formerly Local Rule 5

[April 15, 1997.]

D.N.J. LBR 7055–1. ENTRY OF DEFAULT AND DEFAULT JUDGMENT

(a) Entry of Default. To obtain entry of default pursuant to Fed. R. Civ. P. 55(a), the party moving for entry of default shall file with the Clerk of the Court an application requesting entry of default, together with a supporting affidavit listing all defaulting parties and alleging the following:

(1) The party against whom default is sought has been properly served with a summons and a complaint.

(2) The party has failed to plead or otherwise defend within the allowed time and that time has run.

(3) The party has not requested or has not been granted an extension of time to plead or otherwise defend.

(b) Entry of Default Judgment. In addition to the filing of an application requesting entry of default, along with supporting affidavit, the party seeking the entry of a default judgment shall file with the Clerk of the Court an application for default judgment containing the following:

(1) A request to enter default judgment.

(2) An affidavit in support of default judgment, executed by an individual having personal knowledge of the facts set forth therein, which sets forth with specificity each element of at least one cause of action asserted in the initial pleading. The supporting affidavit must comply with 50 App. U.S.C. § 520 regarding defendant's military status. The affidavit must also allege that the defendant is not an infant or incompetent person, unless represented in the action by a general guardian, committee, conservator, or other such representative who has appeared in the action.

(3) Appropriate documentary evidence to support the allegations in the affidavit.

(4) A proposed form of judgment.

(c) Notice. Notice shall be served in accordance with Fed. R. Civ. P. 55(b)(2).

(d) Proof Hearing. Chambers shall advise the party seeking entry of a default judgment of the time and date of a proof hearing, if required.

1999 Comment: This new rule is intended to amplify and clarify the procedures to obtain the entry of default and default judgment pursuant to Fed. R. Civ. P. 55(a) and (b), respectively, made applicable to adversary proceedings pursuant to Fed. R. Bankr. P. 7055. Compliance with this new Rule should ease the burdens on both Chambers and the Clerk's office by reducing the number of nonconforming pleadings which must be returned to counsel with remedial instructions.

Subdivisions (a) and (b) detail the content of the pleadings and supporting documentation required to obtain the entry of default and a default judgment.

Subdivision (d) is intended to clarify that a default judgment may be entered upon the submission of pleadings and supporting documentation conforming to the provisions of the Rule, without a proof hearing, unless the Court notifies counsel that a proof hearing is required.

References: Fed. R. Bankr. P. 7054 Judgment; Costs; Fed. R. Bankr. P. 7055 Default; 50 App. U.S.C. § 520 Default Judgments; Affidavits; Bonds; Attorneys For Persons in Service

[January 1999.]

D.N.J. LBR 7067-1. REGISTRY FUND

(a) Registry funds maintained pursuant to 28 U.S.C. § 2041 shall include, but shall not be limited to:

(1) Unclaimed distributions in chapter 7, 12 or 13 cases remaining unpaid 90 days after the final distribution.

(2) Monies to be held in escrow pending resolution of a particular dispute before the Court.

(b) Unclaimed distributions shall be deposited into the Registry without court order. The deposit shall be accompanied by a list of the payees and the amounts. All other deposits and all withdrawals shall require court order. Such orders shall specify the amount deposited or withdrawn and shall state the name, address and tax identification number of any entity to which funds are paid.

(c) An order requiring the deposit of funds shall be served personally by the movant upon the clerk, chief deputy clerk, deputy-in-charge, or chief financial deputy. The movant shall also verify that the clerk has deposited the funds.

(d) In accordance with 28 U.S.C. § 1930(b) and 56 F.R. 56356, the Clerk shall collect a fee of 10% of all income earned on funds in the Registry when the funds total less than $100,000,000. On amounts exceeding $100,000,000, the 10% fee shall be reduced by one percent for each increment of $50,000,000 over the initial $100,000,000. The fee will be collected in pro rata amounts prior to ordered disbursements. The amount collected at any such time shall be 10% of that proportion of total accrued interest which equals the claimant's proportion of principal in the account.

Comment: Formerly Local Rule 12

Reference: 11 U.S.C. § 347(a) Unclaimed property; Fed. R.Bankr.P. 3011 Unclaimed Funds in a Chapter 7 Liquidation, Chapter 12 Family Farmer's Debt, and Chapter 13 Individual's Debt Adjustment Cases

[April 15, 1997.]

D.N.J. LBR 8006-1. DESIGNATION OF RECORD—APPEAL

If an appellant fails to timely file the designation and statement required by Fed.R.Bankr.P. 8006, the clerk shall file a certification of such failure with the clerk of the District Court and serve same upon all parties to the appeal.

1997 Comment: Formerly Local Rule 13.

Reference: Fed.R.App.P. 16 Appeal in Bankruptcy Case from a Final Judgment, Order or Decree of a District Court or a Bankruptcy Appellate Panel; Fed.R.Bankr.P. 8007 Completion and Transmittal of Record; Docketing of the Appeal

[April 15, 1997.]

D.N.J. LBR 9004-1. PAPERS—REQUIREMENTS OF FORM

All petitions, pleadings, schedules and other documents filed in paper form, shall be legibly typewritten, printed or reproduced. The papers shall be of standard weight and shall have an upper margin of not less than 1½ inches. No such document may be stapled or similarly fastened so as to cause punctures in the paper.

1997 Comment: Formerly Local Rule 2(a)(1)

2001 Comment: This Rule amendment is intended to facilitate the imaging process when utilized in conjunction with the electronic case filing system.

[April 15, 1997; amended May 30, 2001.]

D.N.J. LBR 9004-2. CAPTION—PAPERS, GENERAL

(a) All papers, including motions, complaints, orders, judgments, letters, and briefs shall set forth a caption, and the title shall include a specific reference to the subject of the paper and shall state the hearing date as follows: "Hearing Date: ______, 20___."

(b) All papers shall set forth the case number, chapter, initials of judge assigned and, when applicable, the adversary proceeding number. In the case of motions, the notice of motion and any answering papers shall state below the hearing date either "oral argument requested" or "oral argument waived."

(c) All pleadings commencing with the original petition shall contain in the top left margin the typewritten or printed name, address, telephone number, the initials of the first and last names and the last 4 digits of the social security number of the attorney of record for the filing party, and the identity of the party represented, or, if a party is appearing pro se, the typewritten or printed name, address and telephone number of such party.

1997 Comment: Formerly Local Rule 2(a)(2), (3), and (4)

2001 Comment: This Rule amendment substitutes reference to the year "20___" for the year "19___".

[April 15, 1997; amended May 30, 2001.]

D.N.J. LBR 9013-1. MOTION PRACTICE

(a) General Provisions. An application to the Court for an order requiring notice and opportunity for hearing shall be by motion. Every motion shall state the time and place returnable; the grounds upon which it is made, and the nature of the relief sought. A motion shall be deemed uncontested unless responsive papers are timely filed in accordance with subdivision (d). A proposed form of order shall accompany the moving papers, except as provided in D.N.J. LBR 9072-1(b).

(b) Scheduling. An application by motion except in a chapter 13 case shall be made returnable on a regular motion day before the judge to whom the case has been assigned. The regular motion day shall be Monday for all three vicinages. A motion in a chapter 13 case shall be made returnable on a date assigned by the Court. A motion not timely filed pursuant to subdivision (c) will be scheduled for the next motion day.

(c) Time and Place of Filing. All moving papers shall be filed in the vicinage of the case. Such papers shall be filed and served at least 20 days before the return date, except as provided in Fed. R. Bankr. P. 3007.

(d) Responsive Papers; Cross-Motions.

(1) All answering papers and cross-motions shall be filed and served at least 7 days before the return date. All cross motions shall be deemed contested. No motion shall be designated as a cross motion unless it is related to the original motion.

(2) All reply papers, as well as answering papers to a cross-motion, shall be filed and served at least 4 days before the return date. Upon the request of a party, the Court may enlarge the time for the filing of answering and reply papers.

(e) Orders Shortening Time. An application under Fed. R. Bankr. P. 9006(c) for an order shortening time for hearing on a motion shall be submitted with the moving papers in a form substantially the same as Local Forms 1 and 2. Use of orders to show cause shall be limited to adversary proceedings in accordance with D.N.J. LBR 9075-1.

(f) Oral Argument. Unless a party requests oral argument or the Court otherwise directs, all motions shall be decided on the papers. All parties must state their intentions regarding oral argument in the moving or answering papers.

(g) Telephone Conference. The Court, on its own motion or on a party's request, may direct argument of any motion by telephone conference without Court appearance. A verbatim record shall be made of all such telephone arguments.

(h) Motion for Reconsideration. A motion for reconsideration shall be filed within 10 days of the entry of the Court's order or judgment on the original motion. The motion shall be filed with a memorandum setting forth concisely the matters or controlling decisions which the movant believes constitute cause for reconsideration. A timely motion for reconsideration shall be deemed to be a motion under Fed. R. Bankr. P. 8002(b).

(i) Testimony. Unless the Court authorizes or directs otherwise prior to the return date, no testimony shall be taken on a motion except by certification or affidavit under Fed. R. Civ. P. 43(e) and Fed. R. Bankr. P. 9017. Notwithstanding the foregoing, live testimony may be taken on a motion under Code § 363(c) or § 364 without prior authorization from the Court.

(j) Consent Order in Lieu of Motion.

(1) Requests to the Court for an order on which all parties who are entitled to notice have affixed their written consent may be presented by application without motion or hearing. The application shall explain the grounds for entry of the order.

(2) Notwithstanding subsection (j)(1) of this rule, a consent order in lieu of a motion under Code § 363(e) in a chapter 11 case can be filed without the written consent of the 20 largest unsecured creditors if no committee of unsecured creditors has been appointed. In such event, the 20 largest unsecured creditors shall be served with the application and consent order and shall have 5 days to serve an objection. The proponent of the consent order must simultaneously submit a separate certification of service to the Court indicating service on the 20 largest unsecured creditors. If a committee of unsecured creditors has been appointed, its written consent must be affixed to a consent order in lieu of a motion under Code § 363(e).

(k) Duty to Confer. If a motion is contested, the movant shall confer with the respondent prior to the hearing to determine whether a consent order may be entered disposing of the motion, or, in the alternative, to stipulate the resolution of as many issues as possible.

(*l*) Duty to Report Settlement or Withdrawal. If a motion is settled or withdrawn, the movant shall inform the Court immediately by telephone, and send written confirmation promptly thereafter.

(m) Any motion seeking relief from the automatic stay, the use, sale or lease of property or the assumption, rejection or assignment of executory contracts and unexpired leases shall specifically state in the caption of the motion whether the movant seeks a waiver of the 10 day stay of the effectiveness of any proposed order for the relief sought under Federal Rules of Bankruptcy Procedure 4001(a)(3), 6004(g) or 6006(d). The movant shall bear the burden of establishing cause for the waiver of the 10 day stay provisions and shall detail the cause in its moving papers.

1997 Comment: Formerly Local Rule 3(a) through (h), and (j) through (m).

1999 Comment: Subsection (h) of this rule was amended. The amendment substituted the word "entry" for the word "filing" in the first sentence to be consistent with the federal rules of civil and bankruptcy procedure.

2004 Comment: Subsection (j)(2) is amended to require that the proponent of the consent order, in lieu of motion under Code § 363(e) in a Chapter 11 case, simultaneously submit a separate certification of service to the Court indicating service on the 20 largest unsecured creditors, where the consent order in lieu of motion is filed, without the written consent of the 20 largest unsecured creditors if no committee of unsecured creditors has been appointed, and the 20 largest unsecured creditors have been served with the application and consent order providing 5 days to file and serve an objection.

2008 Comment: Subsection (d) of this rule is amended to require that the proponent of a reply or answer to a cross-motion file and serve such papers at least 4 days before the return date of the original motion.

Reference: Fed. R. Bankr. P. 5005 Filing and Transmittal of Papers; Fed. R. Bankr. P. 9006 Time; Fed. R. Bankr. P. 9014 Contested Matters; Fed. R. Bankr. P. 9001(7) and 9021.

[April 15, 1997; amended January 1999; amended effective July 2, 2003; August 1, 2004; August 1, 2008.]

D.N.J. LBR 9013-2. BRIEFS AND MEMORANDA OF LAW

All moving papers, answering papers, and cross-motions shall include a brief, or a statement that no brief is necessary and the reasons therefor. The brief shall be a separate document.

1997 Comment: This rule is new [April 1997] and is derived from Local Rule 3(c) and (d).

2001 Comment: This Rule amendment is intended to maintain and clarify the current requirement that a brief is to be a separate document whether submitted electronically or in paper form.

[April 15, 1997; amended May 30, 2001.]

D.N.J. LBR 9013-3. CERTIFICATE OF SERVICE—MOTIONS

(a) All moving papers, answering papers, and cross motions, including those filed electronically, must be supported by a certificate of service. The certificate of service shall identify the relationship to the case of each party served.

(b) Where service is accomplished through the Notice of Electronic Filing pursuant to D.N.J. LBR 7005-1(b) upon a Participant in the Court's electronic case filing system, the certificate of service must indicate that the document was electronically filed and the manner in which the party was served.

(c) The certificate of service shall be a separate document.

1997 Comment: This rule is new [April 1997] and is derived from Local Rule 3(c) and (d).

1998 Comment; The second sentence of this rule was added [April 1998]. It is intended to facilitate the court's meaningful review of the certification of service. The service list should identify the name of the party served, the address of the party served, and the party's relationship to the case. For example:

John Doe, Esq.	Jane Doe
123 Main Street	456 Main Street
Anytown, USA 12345	Anytown, USA 12345
Attorney for Secured Creditor	Unsecured Creditor
Big Bank, N.A.	

2001 Comment: This Rule amendment is intended to clarify that where electronic case filing is utilized, a certificate of service may be filed subsequent to the filing of the moving papers, answering papers, and cross motions.

2004 Comment: This Rule amendment specifies that the Court requires a certificate of service to be filed with respect to documents filed electronically indicating the manner in which the party was served. It also requires the certificate of service to be a separate document, thereby precluding inclusion of the certificate within the pleading.

Reference: Fed.R.Civ.P. 5 Service and Filing of Pleadings and Other Papers; Fed.R.Bankr.P. 7005 Service and Filing of Pleadings and Other Papers

[April 15, 1997; amended effective April, 1998; May 30, 2001; August 1, 2004.]

D.N.J. LBR 9015-1. JURY TRIALS

Where a party to a case or proceeding demands a trial by jury, the party making the demand shall, within 90 days after serving the demand, (i) file with the Clerk of the Bankruptcy Court the consent of all parties to trial by jury in the Bankruptcy Court, (ii) move pursuant to D.N.J. LBR 5011-1 for withdrawal of the reference of the case or proceeding by the District Court, or (iii) move to extend the time. The failure of a party to file or move as required by this rule constitutes a waiver by the party of trial by jury.

[July 2, 2003.]

D.N.J. LBR 9019-2. ALTERNATIVE DISPUTE RESOLUTION (ADR)

(a) Register of Mediators.

(1) The clerk shall maintain a register of eligible individuals who wish to serve as mediators.

(2) An individual may be eligible for appointment to the register upon the filing of an application for appointment to the register demonstrating the qualifications of the individual as mediator and satisfactory completion of such training as may be required from time to time by the Court.

(3) The register of eligible mediators shall be reviewed and approved by the Court periodically and shall be posted by the clerk in each vicinage.

(b) Compensation of Mediators.

(1) Mediators shall be compensated at the rate of two hundred dollars ($200) per hour, unless otherwise ordered by the Court.

(2) In the event that the parties to mediation and the mediator agree on an hourly rate in excess of or less than two hundred ($200) dollars, the order of referral for mediation shall indicate the agreed hourly rate of the mediator, if in the opinion of the Court such rate is reasonable.

(3) The parties shall share the charges of the mediator equally, unless otherwise provided in the order allowing the mediator's compensation.

(4) A mediator seeking compensation shall comply with the requirements of D.N.J. LBR 2016–1(a).

(5) A copy of the mediator's application for compensation shall be served on each party to the mediation.

(c) Referral to Mediation.

(1) An adversary proceeding or contested matter may be referred to mediation either by joint request of the parties or by the Court at a status conference or other hearing.

(2) Where the parties consent to mediation, they shall file an application and consent order, as allowed by D.N.J. LBR 9013–1(j), requesting referral to mediation and designating a mutually acceptable mediator and alternate selected from the current register. If the parties are unable to agree on a mediator and alternate, the application shall request selection by the Court from the current register.

(3) Where mediation is directed by the Court, on its own motion, the parties shall confer and attempt to designate a mutually acceptable mediator and alternate from the current register. If the parties cannot agree, the Court shall appoint a mediator and alternate.

(d) Mediation Procedure.

(1) *Conflicts.* Within 5 days of receipt of the referral order, the mediator shall determine whether he or she is disqualified. Disqualification shall include, but not be limited to, acting as trustee in the case or in the case of an insider or affiliate of the debtor. If the mediator determines that he or she is disqualified, the mediator shall promptly file a notice of disqualification, serving copies on the parties and the alternate, and the alternate shall become the mediator.

(2) *Time and Place.* The mediator shall fix a time and place for the mediation conferences which are reasonably convenient for the parties and shall serve written notice of the initial conference at least 15 days before the return date. The conference shall be commenced as early as practicable, and in any event not more than 45 days following the entry of the referral order. Upon consent of all parties, the mediator may adjourn the conference and inform the Court, in writing, of the need for adjournment and the new date(s).

(3) *Information Statement.* Each party shall prepare an information statement which shall contain the following:

(A) A copy of the pleading setting forth the party's cause of action or defense;

(B) A list of all witnesses upon which the party would rely at trial, and a summary of their expected testimony;

(C) Copies of the principal exhibits upon which the party would rely at trial; and

(D) A statement, not exceeding 3 pages, of the principal rules of law upon which the party relies.

Where an exhibit is voluminous, a *summary* may be provided. The submission of a *summary* of expected testimony shall constitute a certification by the attorney that he or she, or other counsel of record for the party, has personally spoken with the witness or has reviewed a written statement of the witness, deposition transcript, or interrogatory answers signed by the witness, and believes in good faith that the witness will testify substantially in conformity with the *summary*.

The information statement shall be served on the mediator and all parties at least 7 calendar days before the initial conference. The information statement shall not be filed, shall not be construed as a pleading, shall not satisfy any discovery obligation, and shall not limit the evidence the parties may use at trial, if mediation does not result in settlement. No responsive or supplemental statements shall be permitted.

(4) *Attendance by Attorneys.* The attorney with primary responsibility for representation in the proceeding or matter to be mediated shall personally attend the conference(s). Attorneys shall be prepared to discuss in detail and in good faith the following:

(A) All liability issues;

(B) All damages issues; and

(C) Authorized parameters for settlement.

(5) *Attendance by Parties.* An individual party who resides within the vicinage of the case shall

personally attend the mediation conference(s) unless excused by the mediator for cause. A party, other than an individual, whose principal place of business is located in the vicinage of the case shall attend the mediation conference(s) through a representative with authority to negotiate. All other parties shall be available for consultation with their attorneys and the mediator by telephone.

(6) *Caucus.* The mediator shall decide which parties and/or attorneys shall be present, and the nature of any caucus sessions.

(7) *Failure to Attend.* A party's willful failure to attend the mediation conference(s) shall be reported to the Court by the mediator and may result in the imposition of sanctions by the Court.

(8) *Privilege.* All proceedings or writings of the mediation conference, including the information statement, mediator's settlement recommendation, and any statement made by any party, attorney or other participant, shall in all respects be privileged and not reported, recorded, placed in evidence, communicated to the Court or jury, where applicable, or construed for any purpose as an admission against interest.

(9) *Settlement Recommendations.* The mediator may, but need not, make oral or written recommendations for settlement. Attorneys shall confer with their parties to review the mediator's recommendations and to determine whether a consent order or stipulation may be entered disposing of the adversary proceeding or contested matter or resolving as many issues as possible.

(e) Completion of Mediation. Upon completion of the mediation conference(s), the mediator shall inform the Court, in writing, whether the parties have reached agreement to settle the adversary proceeding or contested matter. If settlement has been reached, the mediator shall direct the preparation of a consent order or stipulation containing the terms of settlement, which shall be filed.

1997 Comment: Formerly Local Rule 17.

2002 Comment: Subsections (b)(1) and (b)(2) of this rule were amended. The amendments increased the mediators hourly rate of compensation from one hundred and fifty ($150) to two hundred dollars ($200) per hour.

[April 15, 1997; amended September 18, 2002.]

D.N.J. LBR 9072-1. ORDERS—PROPOSED

(a) Any order or judgment must be a separate document. The title of an order or judgment shall identify the nature of the relief granted.

(b) The Court may approve standard forms of order and judgment pursuant to Fed.R.Bankr.P. 9021. When a decision by the Court is identical to that provided in any such standard form of order or judgment, and includes no additional relief or ruling, the clerk shall prepare, sign and enter an order or judgment on the appropriate form as directed by the Court. Where use of a standard form of order or judgment is required under this subdivision, there shall be no substitution for, or modification or supplementation of such form without the express consent of the Court.

(c) Except as provided in subdivision (b), if the ruling on a motion or application differs from that reflected in any proposed orders which have been submitted, the prevailing party or applicant shall file and serve a revised form of order within 5 days of the Court's decision. If the prevailing party or applicant fails to do so, any other party may file and serve such form of order.

(d) If all parties consent to the form of an order submitted under subdivision (c), the correspondence transmitting such order shall so state in bold face or upper case type, and such order shall be signed and entered in the discretion of the court. In all other cases under subdivision (c), all parties served with such order shall have 5 days to file and serve an objection and alternative form of order. A hearing may be conducted on the objection in the Court's discretion.

(e) Any proposed order seeking relief from the automatic stay, the use, sale or lease of property or the assumption, rejection or assignment of executory contracts and unexpired leases shall not include a waiver of the 10 day stay provisions provided in Federal Rules of Bankruptcy Procedure 4001(a)(3), Interim Rule 6004(h), or Federal Rule of Bankruptcy Procedure 6006(d) unless cause for relief from the stay is specifically plead in the moving papers. The caption of the proposed order must state the order waives the 10 day stay provisions contained in the applicable Federal Rule.

1997 Comment: Formerly Local Rule 4

2001 Comment: This Rule amendment substitutes the phrase "shall be signed and entered in the discretion of the court" for the phrase "shall be signed and entered forthwith."

Reference: D.N.J. LBR 4001-1(d) Automatic Stay—Relief From; Fed.R.Bankr.P. 9022 Notice of Judgment or Order

[April 15, 1997; amended May 30, 2001; amended July 2, 2003; August 1, 2007.]

D.N.J. LBR 9072-2. ORDERS PROPOSED—ELECTRONIC CASE FILING SYSTEM

(a) Orders submitted under D.N.J. LBR 9072-1(c) shall be directed to the presiding judge's electronic mail box designated for this purpose. The address box of the electronic mail shall reflect the names of the parties served. If any party is not served electronically, the filer must serve a copy of the order on that party conventionally and indicate such service in the electronic correspondence directed to the presiding judge's electronic mail box.

(b) Pursuant to the requirements of D.N.J. LBR 9072-1(d), if all parties consent to the form of an order submitted electronically, the electronic correspondence transmitting such order shall so state in bold face or upper case type, and such order shall be signed and entered in the discretion of the court. In all other cases under subdivision (a), all parties served with such order shall have 5 days to submit and serve an objection and alternative form of order to the presiding judge's electronic mail box. A hearing may be conducted on the objection in the Court's discretion.

2001 Comment: This Rule is new and is intended to provide a procedure for orders submitted by electronic means under D.N.J. LBR 9072-1(c).

[Effective May 30, 2001.]

D.N.J. LBR 9075-1. EMERGENCY ORDERS

Use of orders to show cause shall be limited to adversary proceedings in which immediate injunctive relief is requested.

1997 Comment: Formerly part of Local Rule 3(e)

Reference: Fed.R.Bank.P. 7001 Scope of Rules Part VII.

[April 15, 1997.]

LOCAL FORMS

D.N.J. LOCAL FORM 1. APPLICATION FOR ORDER SHORTENING TIME PERIOD FOR NOTICE UNDER Fed.R.Bankr.P. 9006(c)(1)

UNITED STATES BANKRUPTCY COURT
DISTRICT OF NEW JERSEY

IN RE:)
)
) CASE NO.:
) CHAPTER: ______
)
DEBTOR(S))
______________________)

APPLICATION FOR ORDER SHORTENING TIME PERIOD FOR NOTICE UNDER FED.R.BANKR.P. 9006(c)(1)

The application of ______________ respectfully represents:

1. [State applicant's relationship to case.]

2. [State reasons for application. Cause must be shown to shorten time. State date(s) requested.]

3. Reduction of the time period in question is not prohibited under Fed. R.Bankr.P. 9006(c)(2) and the rules listed therein.

WHEREFORE, applicant requests entry of the order submitted herewith.

____

APPLICANT

Date:

[April 15, 1997.]

D.N.J. LOCAL FORM 2. ORDER SHORTENING TIME PERIOD FOR NOTICE AND SETTING HEARING

UNITED STATES BANKRUPTCY COURT
DISTRICT OF NEW JERSEY

UNITED STATES BANKRUPTCY COURT
DISTRICT OF NEW JERSEY

Caption in Compliance with D.N.J.LBR 9004–2(c)

In Re:	Case No:	________
	Adv. No:	________
	Hearing Date:	________
	Judge:	________

ORDER SHORTENING TIME PERIOD
FOR NOTICE AND SETTING HEARING

The relief set forth on the following pages, numbered two (2) through two (2) is hereby ORDERED.

Upon consideration of the application of ______________ for notice under Fed. R.Bankr.P. 9006(c)(1), and for cause shown, it is

ORDERED as follows:

1. The time period required by Local Bankruptcy Rule 9013–1 or Fed. R.Bankr.P. 2002 or other rule for notice of hearing on _________ is hereby shortened as set forth herein.

2. Hearing shall be conducted on the aforesaid motion/application on _________, 20____ at ____ ___.m. in the United States Bankruptcy Court ______________, Courtroom No. ____.

3. True copies of this order, the application for it, and the moving papers shall be served upon ______________

☐ fax, ☐ overnight mail,
☐ e-mail, ☐ hand delivery,
☐ regular mail,

and within

☐ _______ day(s) of the date hereof, or
☐ on the same date as the order.

4. Immediate telephone notice of entry of this order shall also be given to said parties.

5. Any objections to said motion/application:

☐ shall be filed and served so as to be received no later than ________

☐ may be presented at the hearing.

6. ☐ Court appearances will be required to prosecute said motion/application and any objections.

☐ Any Objector may appear by telephone at the hearing.

☐ The hearing will be held by telephone conference call, to be arranged by the applicant.

[April 15, 1997; revised May 23, 2002; revised April 6, 2004; June 1, 2006.]

D.N.J. LOCAL FORM 3. D.N.J. 2016–1, FEE APPLICATION COVER SHEET

UNITED STATES BANKRUPTCY COURT
DISTRICT OF NEW JERSEY

D.N.J. 2016–1, FEE APPLICATION COVER SHEET

IN RE: ______________________ APPLICANT: ______________

CASE NO: ____________________ CLIENT: ________________
CHAPTER: ____________________ CASE FILED: ____________

COMPLETION AND SIGNING OF THIS FORM CONSTITUTES A CERTIFICATION UNDER PENALTY OF PERJURY, PURSUANT TO 28 U.S.C. SECTION 1746.

RETENTION ORDER(S) ATTACHED

SECTION I
FEE SUMMARY

INTERIM FEE APPLICATION NO. ___ OR FINAL FEE APPLICATION ___

	FEES	EXPENSES
TOTAL PREVIOUS FEE REQUESTED:	$	$
TOTAL FEES ALLOWED TO DATE:	$	$
TOTAL RETAINER (IF APPLICABLE)	$	$
TOTAL HOLDBACK (IF APPLICABLE)	$	$
TOTAL RECEIVED BY APPLICANT	$	$

NAME OF PROFESSIONAL & TITLE	YEAR ADMITTED (OR YEARS OF PROFESSIONAL SERVICE)	HOURS	RATE	FEE
1.				
2.				
3.				
4.				
5.				
6.				
7.				

FEE TOTALS—PAGE 2 ________
DISBURSEMENTS TOTALS—PAGE 3 ________

TOTAL FEE APPLICATION ________

[Page 2]

SECTION II
SUMMARY OF SERVICES

SERVICES RENDERED	HOURS	FEE
a) Asset Analysis and Recovery		
b) Asset Disposition		
c) Business Operations		
d) Case Administration		
e) Claims Administration and Objections		
f) Employee Benefits/Pensions		
g) Fee/Employment Applications		
h) Fee/Employment Objections		
i) Financing		
j) Litigation (Other than Avoidance Action Litigation)		
k) Avoidance Action Litigation		
l) Meetings of Creditors		
m) Plan and Disclosure Statement		
n) Relief from Stay Proceedings		
o) Regulatory Compliance		
p) Travel		
q) Accounting/Auditing		
r) Business Analysis		
s) Corporate Finance and Valuation		
t) Data Analysis		
u) Litigation Consulting		
v) Reconstruction Accounting		
w) Tax Issues		
x) Other (specify category)		
SERVICES TOTAL:		

[Page 3]

SECTION III
SUMMARY OF DISBURSEMENTS

DISBURSEMENTS	AMOUNT
a) Computer Assisted Legal Research	
b) Facsimile (with rates) No. of Pages ____ Rate per Page ____ (Max. $1.00/pg.)	
c) Long Distance Telephone	
d) In-House Reproduction No. of Pages ____ Rate per Page ____ (Max. 20¢/pg.)	
e) Outside Reproduction	
e) Postage	
f) Outside Research ____________________ ____________________ ____________________	
g) Filing/Court Fees	
h) Court Reporting	
i) Travel	
j) Courier & Express Carriers (e.g., Federal Express)	

k) Postage

l) Other (Explain)

DISBURSEMENTS TOTAL:

[Page 4]

SECTION IV
CASE HISTORY

(NOTE: Items 3–6 are not applicable to applications under 11 U.S.C. § 506)

(1) DATE CASE FILED:

(2) CHAPTER UNDER WHICH CASE WAS COMMENCED:

(3) DATE OF RETENTION:
(ANNEX COPY OF ORDER(S))
IF LIMIT ON NUMBERS OF HOURS OR OTHER LIMITATIONS TO RETENTION, SET FORTH:

(4) SUMMARIZE IN BRIEF THE BENEFITS TO THE ESTATE AND ATTACH SUPPLEMENTS AS NEEDED:

(5) ANTICIPATED DISTRIBUTION TO CREDITORS:
(A) ADMINISTRATION EXPENSES:
(B) SECURED CREDITORS:
(C) PRIORITY CREDITORS:
(D) GENERAL UNSECURED CREDITORS:

(6) FINAL DISPOSITION OF CASE AND PERCENTAGE OF DIVIDEND PAID TO CREDITOR (IF APPLICABLE):

I certify under penalty of perjury that the foregoing is true and correct.

SIGNATURE OF APPLICANT DATE

[April 15, 1997; amended effective August 1, 2006.]

D.N.J. LOCAL FORM 4. ACCOUNTANT FEE APPLICATION COVER SHEET [REDACTED]

[April 15, 1997; Redacted effective August 1, 2006.]

D.N.J. LOCAL FORM 5. CHAPTER 7 INFORMATION FOR NOTICE OF ABANDONMENT

UNITED STATES BANKRUPTCY COURT
DISTRICT OF NEW JERSEY

TO: JAMES J. WALDRON, CLERK CASE NO. ____________
IN RE:

CHAPTER 7

INFORMATION FOR NOTICE OF ABANDONMENT

__________, Trustee has filed a notice of intention to abandon certain property described below as being of inconsequential value to the estate. If any creditor or other party in interest has an objection to the proposed abandonment, the objection and a request for a hearing on such application shall be in writing, served upon the trustee and filed with the Clerk of the United States Bankruptcy Court.

Such objection and request shall be filed with the Clerk and served upon the trustee no later than (*date to be fixed by the Court*).

In the event an objection is timely filed a hearing thereon will be held on (*time and location to be fixed by the Court*).

If no objection is filed with the Clerk and served upon the trustee on or before (*date to be fixed by the Court*) the abandonment will take effect on (*date to be fixed by Court*).

The description of the property and the liens and exemptions claimed are as follows:

DESCRIPTION OF PROPERTY TO BE ABANDONED	LIENS ON THE PROPERTY OF THE DEBTOR (INCLUDING AMOUNT CLAIMED DUE)	AMOUNT OF EQUITY CLAIMED AS EXEMPT BY THE DEBTOR

Request for additional information about the property to be abandoned should be directed to:

NAME: ____________
ADDRESS: ____________
TELEPHONE NO: ____________

SUBMITTED BY: ____________ POSITION: ____________ PHONE: ____________
DATED: ____________

[April 15, 1997.]

D.N.J. LOCAL FORM 6. CHAPTER 11 INFORMATION FOR NOTICE OF ABANDONMENT

UNITED STATES BANKRUPTCY COURT
DISTRICT OF NEW JERSEY

TO: JAMES J. WALDRON, CLERK CASE NO. ______
IN RE:

CHAPTER 11
INFORMATION FOR NOTICE OF ABANDONMENT

______, debtor-in-possession (or trustee in the above captioned case), has filed a notice of intention to abandon certain property described below as being of inconsequential value to the estate.

If any creditor or other party in interest has an objection to the proposed abandonment, the objection and a request for a hearing on such application shall be in writing, served upon the trustee and filed with the Clerk of the United States Bankruptcy Court.

Such objection and request shall be filed with the Clerk and served upon the person named below no later than (*date to be fixed by the Court*).

In the event an objection is timely filed a hearing thereon will be held on (*time and location to be fixed by the Court*).

If no objection is filed with the Clerk and served upon the person named below on or before (*date to be fixed by the Court*) the abandonment will take effect on (*date to be fixed by the Court*).

The description of the property and the liens and exemptions claimed are as follows:

DESCRIPTION OF PROPERTY TO BE ABANDONED	LIENS ON THE PROPERTY OF THE DEBTOR (INCLUDING AMOUNT CLAIMED DUE)	AMOUNT OF EQUITY CLAIMED AS EXEMPT BY THE DEBTOR

Request for information about the property to be abandoned should be directed to:

NAME: ______
ADDRESS: ______
TELEPHONE NO: ______

SUBMITTED BY: ______ POSITION: ______ PHONE: ______
DATED: ______

[April 15, 1997.]

D.N.J. LOCAL FORM 7. REPORT OF INITIAL DISTRIBUTION

UNITED STATES BANKRUPTCY COURT
DISTRICT OF NEW JERSEY

IN RE:)
) CASE NO.
)
)
Debtor(s))
______________________________________)

REPORT OF INITIAL DISTRIBUTION

_______ PLAN CONFIRMED _______ PLAN NOT CONFIRMED

If the plan was confirmed and the case is still in Chapter 11, what percentage dividend was (or is to be) paid under the plan to the general unsecured class of creditors: _____%.

If future payments are contemplated under Chapter 11 plan but percentage of dividend is not determinable check here: _____

A. FEES AND EXPENSES:

$______ Trustee's Statutory Compensation
(if applicable)
______ Fee for Attorney for Trustee
______ Other Professionals Fees and All Expenses
(Including Fee for Attorney for Debtor; Itemize on Schedule A)

B. DISTRIBUTIONS:

$______ Secured Creditors (itemize exh. D)
______ Priority Creditors (itemize exh. E)
______ Unsecured Creditors (itemize exh. F)
______ Other (itemize on Schedule A)
______ Equity Security Holders
______ Debtor

$______ TOTAL DISTRIBUTIONS (SUM OF A & B)

SCHEDULE A

Fees Paid to Other Professionals:	FEES
____________________	$__________
____________________	__________
____________________	__________
____________________	__________
____________________	__________

Expenses Paid to Other Professionals:	EXPENSES
____________________	$__________
____________________	__________
____________________	__________
____________________	__________
____________________	__________

Distribution to Others:	DISTRIBUTION
____________________	$__________
____________________	__________
____________________	__________
____________________	__________

I certify under penalty of perjury that the information provided on this form is true and correct to the best of my knowledge, information and belief.

____________	____________	____________
DATE	NAME	TITLE

EXHIBIT D

SECURED CLAIMS

* Indicate claim number if Proof of Claim or "S" for a Scheduled Claim

CLAIMANT ALPHABETICALLY	*CLAIM NO. IF APPLICABLE	AMOUNT SCHEDULED OR CLAIMED	AMOUNT PAID

PAGE 1 OF ___

(CONTINUE TO A SEPARATELY MARKED PAGE IF NEEDED)

EXHIBIT E

PRIORITY CLAIMS

* Indicate claim number if Proof of Claim or "S" for a Scheduled Claim

CLAIMANT ALPHABETICALLY	*CLAIM NO. IF APPLICABLE	AMOUNT SCHEDULED OR CLAIMED	AMOUNT PAID

PAGE 1 OF ___

(CONTINUE TO A SEPARATELY MARKED PAGE IF NEEDED)

EXHIBIT F

UNSECURED CLAIMS

* Indicate claim number if Proof of Claim or "S" for a Scheduled Claim

CLAIMANT ALPHABETICALLY	*CLAIM NO. IF APPLICABLE	AMOUNT SCHEDULED OR CLAIMED	AMOUNT PAID

PAGE 1 OF ___

(CONTINUE TO A SEPARATELY MARKED PAGE IF NEEDED)

[April 15, 1997.]

D.N.J. LOCAL FORM 8. CHAPTER 13 PLAN AND MOTIONS

UNITED STATES BANKRUPTCY COURT
DISTRICT OF NEW JERSEY

IN RE: CASE NO.: ____________________
JUDGE: ____________________
(Debtor) CHAPTER: 13

CHAPTER 13 PLAN AND MOTIONS

___ Original ___ Modified/Notice Required ___ Modified/No Notice Required

☐ Discharge Sought
☐ No Discharge Sought

Date: ______________

THE DEBTOR HAS FILED FOR RELIEF UNDER CHAPTER 13
OF THE BANKRUPTCY CODE.

YOUR RIGHTS WILL BE AFFECTED.

You should have received from the court a separate Notice of the Hearing on Confirmation of Plan, which contains the date of the confirmation hearing on the Plan proposed by the Debtor. This document is the actual Plan proposed by the Debtor to adjust debts. You should read these papers carefully and discuss them with your attorney. Anyone who wishes to oppose any provision of this Plan or any motion included in it must file a written objection within the time frame stated in the Notice. **This Plan may be confirmed and become binding, and included motions may be granted without further notice or hearing, unless written objection is filed before the deadline stated in the Notice.**

YOU SHOULD FILE A PROOF OF CLAIM BY THE DEADLINE STATED IN THE NOTICE TO RECEIVE DISTRIBUTIONS UNDER ANY PLAN THAT MAY BE CONFIRMED, EVEN IF THE PLAN REFERS TO YOUR CLAIM

1. PAYMENT AND LENGTH OF PLAN

a. The Debtor shall pay $______ per ______ to the Chapter 13 Trustee, starting on ______ for approximately ______ months.

b. The Debtor shall make plan payments to the Trustee from the following sources:

___ Future Earnings

___ Other sources of funding (describe source, amount and date when funds are available) __________

___ Sale or refinance of the following assets on or before __________.

c. Adequate protection payments will be made in the amount of $______ to be paid to the Chapter 13 Trustee and disbursed pre-confirmation to ________ (creditor).

d. Adequate protection payments will be made in the amount of $______ to be paid directly by the Debtor(s) outside of the Plan, pre-confirmation to ________ (creditor).

2. PRIORITY CLAIMS (INCLUDING ADMINISTRATIVE EXPENSES)

All allowed priority claims will be paid in full unless the creditor agrees otherwise:

Creditor	Type of Priority	Amount to be Paid

3. SECURED CLAIMS

a. Curing Default and Maintaining Payments

The Debtor shall pay to the Trustee (as part of the Plan) allowed claims for arrearages on monthly obligations and the Debtor shall pay directly to the creditor (outside the Plan) monthly obligations due after the bankruptcy filing as follows:

Creditor	Collateral or Type of Debt	Arrearage	Interest Rate on Arrearage	Amount to be Paid to Creditor (In Plan)	Regular Monthly Payment (Outside Plan)

b. Modification

1.) The Debtor values collateral as indicated below. If the claim may be modified under Section 1322(b)(2), the secured creditor shall be paid the amount listed as the "Value of the Creditor Interest in Collateral," plus interest as stated. The portion of any allowed claim that exceeds that value shall be treated as an unsecured claim. If a secured claim is identified as having "NO VALUE" it shall be treated as an unsecured claim.

Creditor	Collateral	Scheduled Debt	Total Collateral Value	Superior Liens	Value of Creditor Interest in Collateral	Annual Interest Rate	Total Amount to Be Paid

2.) Where the Debtor retains collateral and completes the Plan, payment of the full amount of the allowed secured claim shall discharge the corresponding lien.

c. Surrender

Upon confirmation, the stay is terminated as to surrendered collateral. The Debtor surrenders the following collateral:

Creditor	Collateral to be Surrendered	Value of Surrendered Collateral	Remaining Unsecured Debt

d. Secured Claims Unaffected by the Plan

The following secured claims are unaffected by the Plan:

e. Secured Claims to be paid in full through the Plan

Creditor	Collateral	Total Amount to be Paid through the Plan

4. UNSECURED CLAIMS

a. **Not separately classified** Allowed non-priority unsecured claims shall be paid:

___ Not less than $_____ to be distributed pro rata

___ Not less than _____ percent

___ Pro rata distribution from any remaining funds

b. **Separately Classified Unsecured Claims** shall be treated as follows:

Creditor	Basis for Separate Classification	Treatment	Amount to be Paid

5. EXECUTORY CONTRACTS AND UNEXPIRED LEASES

All executory contracts and unexpired leases are rejected, **except** the following, which are **assumed:**

Creditor	Nature of Contract or Lease	Treatment by Debtor

6. MOTIONS

NOTE: All Plans including motions must be served separately in accordance with D.N.J. LBR 3015–1. Proof of Service of compliance with this requirement must be filed with the Clerk of Court.

Where a motion to avoid liens or partially avoid liens has been filed in the plan, a proof of claim filed that asserts a secured claim that is greater than the amount to be paid in the plan serves as opposition to the motion, and serves as an objection to confirmation. The proof of claim shall be served in accordance with D.N.J. LBR 3015–6(a). The creditor shall file a proof of service prior to the scheduled confirmation hearing. In order to prosecute the objection, the creditor must appear at the confirmation hearing, which shall be the hearing on the motion. Failure to appear to prosecute the objection may result in the motion being granted and the plan being confirmed pursuant to the terms as set forth in the plan.

a. **Motion to Avoid Liens under 11 U.S.C. Section 522(f).** The Debtor moves to avoid the following liens that impair exemptions:

Creditor	Nature of Collateral	Type of Lien	Amount of Lien	Value of Collateral	Amount of Claimed Exemption	Sum of All Other Liens Against the Property	Amount of Lien to be Avoided

b. **Motion to Void Liens and Reclassify Claim from Secured to Completely Unsecured.** The Debtor moves to reclassify the following claims as unsecured and to void liens on collateral consistent with Part 3 above:

Creditor	Collateral	Amount of Lien to be Reclassified

c. **Motion to Partially Void Liens and Reclassify Underlying Claims as Partially Secured and Partially Unsecured.** The Debtor moves to reclassify the following claims as partially secured and partially unsecured, and to void liens on collateral consistent with Part 3 above:

Creditor	Collateral	Amount to be Deemed Secured	Amount to be Reclassified as Unsecured

7. **OTHER PLAN PROVISIONS**

a. **Vesting of Property of the Estate** Property of the Estate shall revest in the Debtor:

___ Upon Confirmation
___ Upon Discharge

b. **Payment Notices** Creditors and Lessors provided for in Sections 3, 5 or 6 may continue to mail customary notices or coupons to the Debtor notwithstanding the automatic stay.

c. **Order of Distribution** The Trustee shall pay allowed claims in the following order:

1) Trustee Commissions
2) ___________
3) ___________
4) ___________

d. **Post-petition claims** The Trustee ☐ is, ☐ is not authorized to pay post-petition claims filed pursuant to 11 U.S.C. Section 1305(a) in the amount filed by the post-petition claimant.

Date ______________ ______________________
Attorney for the Debtor

I certify under penalty of perjury that the foregoing is true and correct.

Date ______________ ______________________
Debtor

Date ______________ ______________________
Joint Debtor

February 20, 2004; Revised effective May 23, 2006; June 20, 2006.

D.N.J. LOCAL FORM 9. CHAPTER 7 INFORMATION FOR NOTICE OF SETTLEMENT OF CONTROVERSY

UNITED STATES BANKRUPTCY COURT
DISTRICT OF NEW JERSEY

TO: JAMES J. WALDRON, CLERK CASE NO. ______________
IN RE:

CHAPTER 7

INFORMATION FOR NOTICE OF SETTLEMENT OF CONTROVERSY

__________, Trustee proposes to settle a claim and/or action, the nature of which is described below.

If any creditor or other party in interest has an objection to the settlement, the objection and request for a hearing on such objection shall be in writing, served upon the person named below and filed with the Clerk of the United States Bankruptcy Court.

Such objection and request shall be filed with the Clerk and served upon the person named below no later than (*date to be fixed by the Court*).

In the event an objection is timely filed a hearing thereon will be held on (*date and location will be supplied by the Court*).

If no objection is filed with the Clerk and served upon the person named below on or before twenty days from the date of this notice, the settlement will be consummated as proposed on or after twenty-five days from the date of this notice.

The nature of action and the terms of the settlement are as follows:

NATURE OF ACTION	PERTINENT TERMS OF THE SETTLEMENT

Request for additional information about the nature of the action or the terms of the settlement should be directed to:

NAME: ______________________________
ADDRESS: ______________________________
TELEPHONE NO: ______________________________

SUBMITTED BY: __________ POSITION: __________ PHONE: __________
DATED: __________

[April 15, 1997.]

D.N.J. LOCAL FORM 10. CHAPTER 11 INFORMATION FOR NOTICE OF SETTLEMENT OF CONTROVERSY

UNITED STATES BANKRUPTCY COURT
DISTRICT OF NEW JERSEY

TO: JAMES J. WALDRON, CLERK CASE NO. ______________
IN RE:

CHAPTER 11

INFORMATION FOR NOTICE OF SETTLEMENT
OF CONTROVERSY

__________, debtor-in-possession, [or Trustee in the above captioned case], proposes to settle an action, the nature of which is described below.

If any creditor or other party in interest has an objection to the settlement, the objection and request for a hearing on such objection shall be in writing, served upon the person named below and filed with the Clerk of the United States Bankruptcy Court.

Such objection and request shall be filed with the Clerk and served upon the person named below no later than (*date to be fixed by the Court*).

In the event an objection is timely filed a hearing thereon will be held on (*date and location of hearing will be supplied by the Court*).

If no objection is filed with the Clerk and served upon the person named below on or before twenty days from the date of this notice, the settlement will be consummated as proposed on or after twenty-five days from the date of this notice.

The nature of action and the terms of the settlement are as follows:

NATURE OF ACTION	PERTINENT TERMS OF THE SETTLEMENT

Request for additional information about the nature of the action or the terms of the settlement should be directed to:

NAME: ______________________________
ADDRESS: ______________________________
TELEPHONE NO: ______________________________

SUBMITTED BY: __________ POSITION: __________ PHONE: __________
DATED: ______________

[April 15, 1997.]

D.N.J. LOCAL FORM 11. INFORMATION FOR NOTICE OF PUBLIC SALE BY THE TRUSTEE

UNITED STATES BANKRUPTCY COURT
DISTRICT OF NEW JERSEY

TO: JAMES J. WALDRON, CLERK CASE NO. ________
IN RE:

____

INFORMATION FOR NOTICE OF PUBLIC SALE
BY THE TRUSTEE

________, Trustee proposes to sell certain property of the estate as described below.

If any creditor or other party in interest has an objection to the public sale, the objection and a request for a hearing shall be in writing, served upon the trustee and filed with the Clerk of the United States Bankruptcy Court.

Such objection and request shall be filed with the Clerk and served upon the trustee no later than (*date to be fixed by Court*).

In the event an objection is timely filed a hearing thereon will be held on (*date to be fixed by the Court*) at (*location of hearing to be fixed by the Court*).

If no objection to the public sale is filed with the Clerk and served upon the Trustee as required above on or before (*date to be fixed by Court*), the sale will be held:

(*location, date and time of sale*)
____

Unless otherwise stated the public sale will be free and clear of all liens. Liens, if any be claimed, will attach to the proceeds of the public sale and the validity and extent of such liens will be determined at a later time.

All sales will be for cash or equivalent, payable at 25% at the time bid is made for personal property and 10% at the time bid is made for real estate with balance payable in full on approval of sale or delivery. The Trustee reserves the right to reject any and all bids or to withdraw any item of property from the sale at any time before the sale is completed.

DESCRIPTION OF THE PROPERTY TO BE SOLD

____
____
____
____
____
____
____
____
____

SUBMITTED BY: ________________
ADDRESS: ________________
TELEPHONE NO: ________________ DATED: ________________

[April 15, 1997.]

D.N.J. LOCAL FORM 12. INFORMATION FOR NOTICE OF PRIVATE SALE BY THE TRUSTEE

UNITED STATES BANKRUPTCY COURT
DISTRICT OF NEW JERSEY

TO: JAMES J. WALDRON, CLERK CASE NO. ______________
IN RE:

INFORMATION FOR NOTICE OF PRIVATE SALE
BY THE TRUSTEE

_________, Trustee proposes to sell certain property of the estate to the persons and on the terms described below.

If any creditor or other party in interest has an objection to the sale, the objection and a request for a hearing on such objection shall be in writing, served upon the trustee and filed with the Clerk of the United States Bankruptcy Court.

Such objection and request shall be filed with the Clerk and served upon the trustee no later than (*date to be fixed by Court*).

In the event an objection is timely filed a hearing thereon will be held on (*time and place to be fixed by the Court*).

If no objection to the public sale is filed with the Clerk and served upon the Trustee as required above on or before (*date to be fixed by Court*), the sale will be consummated as proposed on (*date to be fixed by the Court*).

The property to be sold, the proposed purchaser and the sale price are:

____
____
____
____
____
____
____
____
____
____
____
____

Higher and better offers will be received. They must be in writing and filed with the Clerk prior to the date set for filing objections.

Request for information about the property to be sold, the prospective purchaser, the price to be paid and other matters should be directed to:

NAME: ______________________________
ADDRESS: ______________________________
TELEPHONE NO: ______________________________

SUBMITTED BY: __________ POSITION: __________ PHONE: __________
DATED: __________

[April 15, 1997.]

D.N.J. LOCAL FORM 13. CERTIFICATION OF DEBTOR'S COUNSEL SUPPORTING SUPPLEMENTAL CHAPTER 13 FEE

UNITED STATES BANKRUPTCY COURT
DISTRICT OF NEW JERSEY

In re

Case No.: ________

Debtor(s). Judge: ________

____

CERTIFICATION OF DEBTOR'S COUNSEL SUPPORTING SUPPLEMENTAL CHAPTER 13 FEE

For time incurred in Chapter 13 cases prior to August 1, 2006, for which supplemental fees are sought, you must utilize the alternate version of Local Form 13 as has been designated for that purpose on the Court's web site: www.njb.uscourts.gov.

________, Esquire, hereby certifies as follows:

1. I represented the debtor in connection with the following proceeding in debtor's chapter 13 case:

___ Prosecution of motion on behalf of debtor. $500

Nature of motion: ______________

____

Hearing date(s): ______________

____

___ Defense of motion on behalf of debtor (Including filing Objection to Creditor's or Trustee's Certification of Default. $400
Nature of motion: ______________

____

Hearing date(s): ______________

____

___ Additional court appearance(s). (Not to exceed three). $100
Purpose: ______________

____

Hearing date(s): ______________

____

___ Filing and appearance on modified Chapter 13 Plan. $300

___ Preparation of Wage Order. $100

___ Preparation and filing of Amendments to Schedules D, E, F or List of Creditors. $100

___ Preparation and filing of other amended schedules. $100

___ Preparation and filing of Application for Retention of Professional. $200

___ Preparation and filing of Notice of Sale or Settlement of Controversy. $100

NON-STANDARD FEES

Do not combine standard and non-standard fees for the same motion or service. If you believe the standard fee is inappropriate for services in a particular instance, you must request only non-standard fees for that particular service.

Describe non-standard services in detail, and attach a time detail (including applicable hourly rates) as Exhibit A: ______________________

____

____

____

Describe non-standard expenses in detail: ______________________

____

____

____

2. To date, in this case:

I have applied for fees (including original retainer) in the amount of: ________

To date, I have received: ________

3. I seek compensation for services rendered in the amount of $ ___ payable:

________ through the chapter 13 plan as an administrative priority.

________ outside the plan.

4. ☐ This allowance will not impact on plan payments.
☐ This allowance will impact on plan payments.

Present plan: $ _____ per month for _____ months.

Proposed Plan: $ _____ per month for _____ months.

I certify that I have not filed any fee application within the last 90 days.

I certify under penalty of perjury that the foregoing is true and correct.

Dated: ________________ ________________

Signature of applicant

[March 1998; revised January 2001; October 2, 2002; June 17, 2005; August 1, 2006.]

D.N.J. LOCAL FORM 14. ORDER GRANTING SUPPLEMENTAL CHAPTER 13 FEES

UNITED STATES BANKRUPTCY COURT
DISTRICT OF NEW JERSEY

UNITED STATES BANKRUPTCY COURT
DISTRICT OF NEW JERSEY

Caption in Compliance with D.N.J.LBR 9004–2(c)

In Re:	Case No:
	Chapter 13
	Hearing Date:
	Judge:

ORDER GRANTING SUPPLEMENTAL CHAPTER 13 FEES

The relief set forth on the following pages, numbered two (2) through _____ is hereby ORDERED.

The applicant having certified that legal work supplemental to basic Chapter 13 services has been rendered, and no objections having been raised:

ORDERED that _______, the applicant, is allowed a fee of $_______ for services rendered and expenses in the amount of $_______ for a total of $_______. The allowance shall be payable:

____ through the Chapter 13 plan as an administrative priority.

____ outside the plan.

The debtor's monthly plan is modified to require a payment of $_____ per month for ____ months to allow for payment of the aforesaid fee.

[March 1998; revised January 2001; May 23, 2002; October 2, 2002.]

D.N.J. LOCAL FORM 15. CERTIFICATION RE CALCULATION OF AMOUNTS DUE NOTE AND MORTGAGE DATED ______

UNITED STATES BANKRUPTCY COURT
DISTRICT OF NEW JERSEY

UNITED STATES BANKRUPTCY COURT
DISTRICT OF NEW JERSEY

Caption in Compliance with D.N.J.LBR 9004–2(c)

In Re:

Case No:

Chapter:

Hearing Date:

Judge:

CERTIFICATION RE CALCULATION OF AMOUNTS DUE
NOTE AND MORTGAGE DATED ________

________ of full age, employed as _______ by ________, hereby certifies the following information:

Recorded on _______, in _______ County, in Book ______ at Page __________
Property Address: ______________________________
Mortgage Holder: ______________________________

I. PAYOFF STATEMENT

Unpaid Principal Balance .... $ __________
Interest from ________ to ________ .... __________
(Interest rate = ___% per year; $_____ per day x ___ days)
Late Charges from ___ to ___($___/mo. x ___ mos.) 0.00
Attorney's fees and costs as of ____________ .... __________
Advances through ______________________ for:
Real Estate Taxes .... $ __________
Insurance premiums .... __________
M.I.P. .... __________
Inspections .... __________
Winterizing/Securing .... __________
Sub-Total of Advances .... $ __________
Less Escrow Monies .... (__________)
Net Advances .... $ 0.00 $ 0.00

Interest on advances from ______ to ______ .... __________

Other charges (specify) .... ______
Less unearned interest .... (______)
TOTAL DUE AS OF __/__/__ .... $ 0.00

II. EQUITY ANALYSIS (When appropriate)

Estimated fair market value of real estate (as of ________) ...... $ ______ *

Liens on the real estate:

1. Real estate taxes as of ________ .... $ ______
2. First Mortgage (principal and interest) as of ______ .... $ ______
3. Second Mortgage (principal and interest) as of ______ .... $ ______
4. Other (specify on separate exhibit) .... $ ______

TOTAL LIENS .... $(0.00) $(0.00)
APPARENT EQUITY AS OF __/__/__ .... $ 0.00**

* Source: ________ (e.g. appraisal, tax bill/assessment, contract of sale, debtor's schedules, etc.)
** If negative, insert zero (0).

I certify under penalty of perjury that the foregoing is true and correct.

______________________________ ______________________________
(Date of signature) Signature

[Effective January 2000; Revised effective May 1, 2006.]

D.N.J. LOCAL FORM 16. CERTIFICATION RE POST-PETITION PAYMENT HISTORY ON THE NOTE AND MORTGAGE DATED ______

CERTIFICATION RE POST-PETITION PAYMENT HISTORY ON THE NOTE AND MORTGAGE DATED ______

UNITED STATES BANKRUPTCY COURT
DISTRICT OF NEW JERSEY
Caption in Compliance with D.N.J. LBR 9004-2(c)

In Re:

Case No.: ______

Chapter: ______

Hearing Date: ______

Judge: ______

Recorded on ______, in ______ County, in Book ______ at Page ______
Property Address: ______
Mortgage Holder: ______
Mortgage(s)/Debtor(s): ______

POST-PETITION PAYMENTS (Petition filed on __/ __/ __)

Amount Due	Date Payment Was Due	How Payment Was Applied (Mo./Yr.)	Amount Received	Date Payment Received	Check or Money Order Number
1.					
2.					
3.					
4.					
5.					
6.					
7.					
8.					
9.					
10.					
TOTAL 0.00			0.00		

[Continue on attached sheets if necessary.]

MONTHLY PAYMENTS PAST DUE: ______ x $______ (MONTHLY PAYMENT $ LATE CHARGE) = $______ AS OF ____/____/____.

Each current monthly payment is comprised of:
(Attach sheets if payment amounts varies from figures set forth below.)

Principal . . . . $ ______
Interest . . . . ______
R.E. Taxes . . . . ______
Insurance . . . . ______
Late Charge . . . . ______
Other . . . . ______ (Specify) ______)
TOTAL . . . . $ ______0.00______

If the monthly payment has changed during the pendency of the case, please explain (attach separate sheet(s) if necessary):

____

____

____

PRE-PETITION ARREARS: ___/_____/_____ to _____/_____/_____

(____mos. x $________/mo. = $ 0.00)

I certify under penalty of perjury that the foregoing is true and correct.

__________________________ __________________________

Date of signature Signature

[Effective January 2000; amended effective August 1, 2006.]

D.N.J. LOCAL FORM 16A. POST–PETITION PAYMENT HISTORY ON VEHICLE LOAN/LEASE

UNITED STATES BANKRUPTCY COURT
DISTRICT OF NEW JERSEY
Caption in Compliance with D.N.J.LBR 9004–2(c)

In Re:

Case No: ____________

Hearing Date: ____________

Chapter: ____________

Judge: ____________

CERTIFICATION OF SECURED CREDITOR REGARDING POST–PETITION PAYMENT HISTORY ON VEHICLE LOAN/LEASE

Vehicle lender/lessor: ____________

Vehicle description: ____________

POST–PETITION PAYMENTS RECEIVED (Petition filed on ________)

Amount due	Date Payment due	Date payment Received	Amount received	How payment applied (mo./yr)	Type of payment (See Legend below)
1.					
2.					
3.					
4.					
5.					
6.					
7.					
8.					
9.					
10.					
11.					
12.					
Total 0.00			0.00		

(Continue on attached sheets if necessary)

Monthly payments past due @ $______ per month from ______ to ________: $ ________

Plus miscellaneous amounts due:

Late Charges: $ ________
Repossession fees: $ ________
Extension fees: $ ________
Other: $ ________

TOTAL POST–PETITION PAST DUE $0.00

______

Pre-petition arrears: ______ to ______

(___ months x $______ per month = $ 0.00

Legend: MP = monthly payment; EXF = Extension fee; LC = Late Charge
O = Other*

*specify other payments received

I certify under penalty of perjury that the foregoing is true and correct.

______________________________	______________________________
Date of Signature	Signature

May 13, 2003; Revised effective August 1, 2006.

D.N.J. LOCAL FORM 17. ORDER TO EMPLOYER TO PAY TO THE CHAPTER 13 STANDING TRUSTEE

UNITED STATES BANKRUPTCY COURT%
DISTRICT OF NEW JERSEY

UNITED STATES BANKRUPTCY COURT
DISTRICT OF NEW JERSEY
Caption in Compliance with D.N.J.LBR 9004–2(c)

In Re:	Case No:
	Hearing Date:
	Judge:

ORDER TO EMPLOYER TO PAY THE CHAPTER 13 TRUSTEE

The relief set forth on the following pages, numbered two (2) through 3 is hereby ORDERED.

The above-named debtor has filed a proceeding under Chapter 13 of Title 11 of the United States Code. The debtor's future earnings have been submitted to the jurisdiction of this Court, in furtherance of the debtor's Chapter 13 plan.

NOW, THEREFORE, PURSUANT to 11 U.S.C. § 1325(c) and § 105, IT IS ORDERED that, until further order of this Court, the employer or other party providing income to said debtor shall deduct from the earnings or income of said debtor the following sums each pay period, beginning on the next pay day following receipt of this order, and shall deduct the same amount for each pay period thereafter, including any period for which the debtor receives periodic or lump sum payment for or on account of vacation, termination or other benefits, arising out of present or past employment of the debtor, and to forthwith remit the sum so deducted to the Chapter 13 Standing Trustee.

Debtor's Employer and Address:

Trustee to Whom Payments Must be Forwarded:

Amount to be Deducted and paid Per Pay Period:

Monthly ☐ Bi–Weekly ☐ Weekly ☐ $______

IT IS FURTHER ORDERED that the employer or other party making payments shall note the debtor's name and bankruptcy case number on the checks to the trustee.

IT IS FURTHER ORDERED that said employer or other party shall notify said trustee and mortgagee(s) if the earnings or income of said debtor are terminated, and the reasons for such termination.

IT IS FURTHER ORDERED that all earnings and wages of the debtor, except the amounts required to be withheld by the provisions of any laws of the United

States, the laws of any State or political subdivision, or by any insurance, pension or union dues agreement between employer and the debtor, or by the order of this court, shall be paid to the debtor in accordance with employer's usual payroll procedure.

IT IS FURTHER ORDERED that no deduction for or on account of any garnishment, wage assignment, credit union or other purpose not specifically authorized by this Court shall be made from the earnings of said debtor.

IT IS FURTHER ORDERED that an order dismissing the debtor's bankruptcy case shall constitute a termination of the requirement to make payments under this order.

IT IS FURTHER ORDERED that this order supersedes previous orders, if any, made to the subject employer or other party in this case.

IT IS FURTHER ORDERED that the attorney for the debtor shall serve copies of this order on the employer or other party, the trustee, and the mortgagee(s) within five days.

[Effective January 2001; revised May 23, 2002.]

IT IS A VIOLATION OF 15 U.S.C. § 1674 AND N.J.S.A. 2A:170–90.4 FOR AN EMPLOYER TO DISCHARGE AN EMPLOYEE OR TAKE ANY OTHER DISCIPLINARY ACTION BECAUSE OF A WAGE GARNISHMENT. AN EMPLOYER VIOLATING SAID STATUTES IS SUBJECT TO FINES AND IMPRISONMENT.

D.N.J. LOCAL FORM 18. DISCLOSURE STATEMENT PURSUANT TO SECTION 1125

Attorney Name
Firm Name
Firm Address
Firm Telephone No.
Attorneys for ______
By: Names of Responsible Individual Attorney(s) (Attorney Code)

UNITED STATES BANKRUPTCY COURT
FOR THE DISTRICT OF NEW JERSEY

In re:	) Chapter 11
	)
NAME OF DEBTOR,	) Case No. ______(___)
	)
Debtor.	)

____[1] DISCLOSURE STATEMENT PURSUANT TO SECTION 1125 OF THE BANKRUPTCY CODE DESCRIBING ____[2] CHAPTER 11 PLAN PROPOSED BY ____[3]

PLEASE READ THIS DISCLOSURE STATEMENT CAREFULLY. THIS DISCLOSURE STATEMENT CONTAINS INFORMATION THAT MAY BEAR UPON YOUR DECISION TO ACCEPT OR REJECT THIS ____[4] PLAN OF REORGANIZATION. THE PLAN PROPONENT BELIEVES THAT THIS PLAN OF REORGANIZATION IS IN THE BEST INTEREST OF THE CREDI-

TORS AND THAT THE PLAN IS FAIR AND EQUITABLE. THE PROPONENT URGES THAT THE VOTER ACCEPT THE PLAN.

Dated:

Proponent ____________

By: ____________

I. INTRODUCTION

____[5] is the Debtor in a Chapter 11 bankruptcy case. On ____[6], ____[7] commenced a bankruptcy case by filing ____[8] Chapter 11 ____[9] petition under the United States Bankruptcy Code ("Code"), 11 U.S.C. § 101, et seq., Chapter 11 of the Code allows the Debtor, and under some circumstances, creditors and other parties in interest, to propose a plan of reorganization ("Plan"). The Plan may provide for the Debtor to reorganize by continuing to operate, to liquidate by selling assets of the estate, or a combination of both. ____[10] is the party proposing the Plan sent to you in the same envelope as this document. THE DOCUMENT YOU ARE READING IS THE DISCLOSURE STATEMENT FOR THE PLAN WHICH IS ANNEXED HERETO AS EXHIBIT A.

This is a ____[11] plan. In other words, the Proponent seeks to accomplish payments under the Plan by ____[12].

A. Purpose of This Document. This Disclosure Statement summarizes what is in the Plan, and tells you certain information relating to the Plan and the process the Court follows in determining whether or not to confirm the Plan.

READ THIS DISCLOSURE STATEMENT CAREFULLY IF YOU WANT TO KNOW ABOUT:

(1) WHO CAN VOTE OR OBJECT,

(2) THE PROPOSED TREATMENT OF YOUR CLAIM (i.e., what your claim will receive if the Plan is confirmed), AND HOW THIS TREATMENT COMPARES TO WHAT YOU WOULD RECEIVE IN LIQUIDATION,

(3) THE HISTORY OF THE DEBTOR AND SIGNIFICANT EVENTS DURING THE BANKRUPTCY,

(4) WHAT THE COURT WILL CONSIDER WHEN DECIDING WHETHER TO CONFIRM THE PLAN,

(5) THE EFFECT OF CONFIRMATION, AND

(6) THE FEASIBILITY OF THE PLAN.

This Disclosure Statement cannot tell you everything about your rights. You should consider consulting your own lawyer to obtain more specific advice on how this Plan will affect you and what is the best course of action for you.

Be sure to read the Plan as well as the Disclosure Statement. If there are any inconsistencies between the Plan and the Disclosure Statement, the Plan provisions will govern.

Code Section 1125 requires a Disclosure Statement to contain "adequate information" concerning the Plan. The term "adequate information" is defined in Code Section 1125(a) as "information of a kind, and in sufficient detail," about a debtor and its operations "that would enable a hypothetical reasonable investor typical of holders of claims or interests" of the debtor to make an informed judgment about accepting or rejecting the Plan. The Bankruptcy Court ("Court") has determined that the information contained in this Disclosure Statement is adequate, and it has approved this document in accordance with Code Section 1124.

This Disclosure Statement is provided to each creditor whose claim has been scheduled by the Debtor or who has filed a proof of claim against the Debtor and to each interest holder of record as of the date of approval of this Disclosure Statement. Under the Bankruptcy Code, your acceptance of the Plan may not be solicited unless you receive a copy of this Disclosure Statement prior to or concurrently with such solicitation.

B. Confirmation Procedures.

Persons Potentially Eligible to Vote on the Plan. In determining acceptance of the Plan, votes will only be counted if submitted by a creditor whose claim is duly scheduled by the Debtor as undisputed, non-contingent and unliquidated, or who, prior to the hearing on confirmation of the Plan, has filed with the Court a proof of claim which has not been disallowed or suspended prior to computation of the votes on the Plan. All shareholders of record as of the date of approval of this Disclosure Statement may vote on the Plan. The Ballot Form that you received does not constitute a proof of claim. If you are uncertain whether your claim has been correctly scheduled, you should check the Debtor's Schedules, which are on file at the office of the Clerk of the Bankruptcy Court located at: United States Bankruptcy Court, U.S. Court House, (insert address). The Clerk of the Bankruptcy Court will not provide this information by telephone.

THE COURT HAS NOT YET CONFIRMED THE PLAN DESCRIBED IN THIS DISCLOSURE STATEMENT. IN OTHER WORDS, THE TERMS OF THE PLAN ARE NOT YET BINDING ON ANYONE. HOWEVER, IF THE COURT LATER CONFIRMS THE PLAN, THEN THE PLAN WILL BE BINDING ON THE DEBTOR AND ON ALL CREDITORS AND INTEREST HOLDERS IN THIS CASE.

1. **Time and Place of the Confirmation Hearing.** The hearing at which the Court will determine whether to confirm the Plan will take place on _____[13], at ___ [A.M./P.M.], in Courtroom ____, [Insert Courthouse Name], [Insert Full Court Address, City, State, Zip Code].

2. **Deadline For Voting For or Against the Plan.** If you are entitled to vote, it is in your best interest to timely vote on the enclosed ballot and return the ballot in the enclosed envelope to _____[14].

Your ballot must be received by _____[15] or it will not be counted.

3. **Deadline For Objecting to the Confirmation of the Plan.** Objections to the confirmation of the Plan must be filed with the Court and served upon _____[16] by _____[17].

4. **Identity of Person to Contact for More Information Regarding the Plan.** Any interested party desiring further information about the Plan should contact _____[18].

C. Disclaimer. The financial data relied upon in formulating the Plan is based on _____[19]. The information contained in this Disclosure Statement is provided by _____[20]. The Plan Proponent represents that everything stated in the Disclosure Statement is true to the Proponent's best knowledge.

PLEASE NOTE THAT THE APPROVAL OF THIS DISCLOSURE STATEMENT BY THE BANKRUPTCY COURT DOES NOT CONSTITUTE A RULING ON THE MERITS, FEASIBILITY OR DESIRABILITY OF THE PLAN.

II. BACKGROUND

A. Description and History of the Debtor's Business.

The Debtor is a _____[21].

The Debtor is in the business of _____[22].

The Debtor has been in this business since _____[23].

B. Principals/Affiliates of Debtor's Business. _____[24].

C. Management of the Debtor Before and During the Bankruptcy. _____[25].

D. Events Leading to Chapter 11 Filing. Here is a brief summary of the circumstances that led to the filing of this Chapter 11 case: _____[26].

E. Significant Events During the Bankruptcy.

1. Bankruptcy Proceedings. The following is a chronological list of significant events which have occurred during this case: _____[27].

The Court has approved the employment of the following professionals: _____[28].

Currently, the following significant adversary proceedings and motions are still pending: _____[29].

2. Other Legal Proceedings. In addition to the proceedings discussed above, the Debtor is currently involved in the following non-bankruptcy legal proceedings: _____[30].

3. Actual and Projected Recovery of Preferential or Fraudulent Transfers[31]. _____[32] is estimated to be realized from the recovery of fraudulent and preferential transfers. The following is a summary of the fraudulent conveyance and preference actions filed or to be filed in this case: _____[33].

4. Procedures Implemented to Resolve Financial Problems. In an effort to remedy the problems that led to the bankruptcy filing, Debtor has implemented the following procedures: _____[34].

5. Current and Historical Financial Conditions _____[35]. (Include description, valuation, means for valuation and documentary support for the valuation approach taken.)

(For historical data, attach last monthly operating report filed by debtor.)

III. SUMMARY OF THE PLAN OF REORGANIZATION

A. What Creditors and Interest Holders Will Receive Under the Proposed Plan. The Plan classifies claims and interests in various classes. The Plan states whether each class of claims or interests is impaired or unimpaired. The Plan provides the treatment each class will receive.

B. Unclassified Claims. Certain types of claims are not placed into voting classes. They are not considered impaired and they do not vote on the Plan because they are automatically entitled to specific treatment provided for them in the Bankruptcy Code. As such, the Proponent has not placed the following claims in a class:

1. Administrative Expenses and Fees. Administrative expenses are claims for fees, costs or expenses of administering the Debtor's Chapter 11 case which are allowed under Code Section 507(a)(1), including all professional compensation requests pursuant to Sections 330 and 331 of the Code. The Code requires that all administrative expenses including fees payable to the Bankruptcy Court and the Office of the United States Trustee which were incurred during the pendency of the case must be paid on the Effective Date of the Plan, unless a particular claimant agrees to a different treatment.[36]

The following chart lists all of the Debtor's unpaid administrative fees and expenses ("Compensation"), an estimate of future professional fees and other administrative claims and fees and their treatment under the Plan[37]:

NAME	AMOUNT ESTIMATED	TREATMENT	TYPE OF CLAIM
Clerk's Office Fees		Paid in full on Effective Date	
Office of U.S. Trustee Fees		Paid in full on Effective Date	
TOTAL			

Court Approval of Professional Compensation Required: Pursuant to the Bankruptcy Code, the Court must rule on all professional compensation and expenses listed in this chart before the compensation and expenses will be owed. The professional in question must file and serve a properly noticed fee application for compensation and reimbursement of expenses and the Court must rule on the application. Only the amount of compensation and reimbursement of expenses allowed by the Court will be owed and required to be paid under this Plan as an administrative claim.

Each professional person who asserts a further administrative claim that accrues before the confirmation date shall file with the Bankruptcy Court, and serve on all parties required to receive notice, an application for compensation and reimbursement of expenses no later than thirty (30) days after the Effective Date of the Plan. Failure to file such an application timely shall result in the professional person's claim being forever barred and discharged. Each and every other person asserting an administrative claim shall be entitled to file a motion for allowance of the asserted administrative claim within ninety days of the Effective Date of the Plan, or such administrative claim shall be deemed forever barred and discharged. No motion or application is required to fix the fees payable to the Clerk's Office or Office of the United States Trustee. Such fees are determined by statute.

As indicated above, the Debtor will need to pay _____[38] worth of administrative claims and fees on the Effective Date of the Plan unless a claimant has agreed to be paid later or the Court has not yet ruled on the claim.

2. Priority Tax Claims. Priority tax claims are certain unsecured income, employment and other taxes described by Code Section 507(a)(8).[39] The Code requires that each holder of such a Section 507(a)(8) priority tax claim receive the present value of such claim in deferred cash payments, over a period not exceeding six years from the date of the assessment of such tax.

The following chart lists all of the Debtor's Section 507(a)(8)[40] priority tax claims and their treatment under the Plan:

Description	Amount Owed	Treatment[41]
• Name = • Type of tax = • Date tax assessed =		• Pymt interval[42] = • Pymt amt/interval[43] = • Begin date[44] = • End date[45] = • Interest Rate % [46]= • Total Payout Amount __% [47]=
• Name = • Type of tax = • Date tax assessed =		• Pymt interval = • Pymt amt/interval = • Begin date = • End date = • Interest Rate % = • Total Payout Amount __% =

C. Classified Claims and Interests.

1. Classes of Secured Claims. Secured claims are claims secured by liens on property of the estate. The following chart lists all classes of creditors containing the holders of the Debtor's secured pre-petition claims and their treatment under this Plan[48]:

CLASS#	DESCRIPTION	INSIDERS (Y/N)	IMPAIRED (Y/N)	TREATMENT
	Secured Claim of: • Name = • Collateral description = • Collateral value = • Claimed Priority of security int. = • Principal owed = • Pre-pet. arrearage amount = • Post-pet. arrearage amount = • Total claim amount =		49	• Pymt interval = • Pymt amt/interval = • Balloon pymt 50= • Begin date = • End date = • Interest rate % = • Total payout __% 51 = • Treatment of lien =
	Secured Claim of: • Name = • Collateral description = • Collateral value = • Claimed Priority of security int. = • Principal owed = • Pre-pet. arrearage amount = • Post-pet. arrearage amount = • Total claim amount =			• Pymt interval = • Pymt amt/interval = • Balloon pymt = • Begin date = • End date = • Interest rate % = • Total payout __% = • Treatment of lien =

2. Classes of Priority Unsecured Claims. Certain priority claims that are referred to in Code Sections 507(a)(3), (4), (5), (6), and (7)[52] are required to be placed in classes. These types of claims are entitled to priority treatment as follows: the Code requires that each holder of such a claim receive cash on the Effective Date equal to the allowed amount of such claim. However, a class of unsecured priority claim holders may vote to accept deferred cash payments of a value, as of the Effective Date, equal to the allowed amount of such claims.

The following chart lists all classes containing Debtor's 507(a)(3), (a)(4), (a)(5), (a)(6), and (a)(7)[53] priority unsecured claims and their treatment under this Plan:

CLASS#	DESCRIPTION	IMPAIRED (Y/N)	TREATMENT
	Priority unsecured claim pursuant to 54 • Total amt of claims = 55		• Paid in full in cash on Effective Date56
	Priority unsecured claim pursuant to 57 • Total amt of claims = 58		• Paid in full in cash on Effective Date

3. Class of General Unsecured Claims. General unsecured claims are uncollateralized claims not entitled to priority under Code Section 507(a). The following chart identifies this Plan's treatment of the class containing all of Debtor's general unsecured claims:

CLASS#	DESCRIPTION	IMPAIRED (Y/N)	TREATMENT
	General unsecured claims • Total amt of claims =	59	• Pymt interval = • Pymt amt/interval = • Begin date = • End date = • Interest rate % = • Total payout60 __% =

4. Class(es) of Interest Holders. Interest holders are the parties who hold ownership interest (i.e., equity interest) in the Debtor. If the Debtor is a corporation, entities holding preferred or common stock in the Debtor are interest holders. If the Debtor is a partnership, the interest holders include both general and limited partners. If the Debtor is an individual, the Debtor is the interest holder. The following chart identifies the Plan's treatment of the class[61] of interest holders:

CLASS#	DESCRIPTION	IMPAIRED (Y/N)	TREATMENT
	Interest holders	[62]	

D. Means of Effectuating the Plan.

1. Funding for the Plan. The Plan will be funded by the following: _____[63].

2. Post-confirmation Management _____[64].

3. Disbursing Agent. _____[65] shall act as the disbursing agent for the purpose of making all distributions provided for under the Plan. The Disbursing Agent shall be compensated as set forth in the Plan.

E. Other Provisions of the Plan.

1. Executory Contracts and Unexpired Leases. The Plan provides that all Executory Contracts and Unexpired Leases, except for those specifically assumed by the Debtor in writing or previously assumed by Court Order, shall be deemed rejected. All proofs of claim with respect to claims arising from said rejection must be filed with the Bankruptcy Court within the earlier of (i) the date set forth for filing claims in any order of the Bankruptcy Court approving such rejection or (ii) thirty (30) days after the Confirmation Date. Any such claims, proofs of which are not filed timely, will be barred forever from assertion.

2. Changes in Rates Subject to Regulatory Commission Approval. This Debtor is/is not subject to governmental regulatory commission approval of its rates.[66]

3. Retention of Jurisdiction. The Court will retain jurisdiction as provided in Section _______ of the Plan.

4. Procedures for Resolving Contested Claims. The Debtor and/or the Disbursing Agent shall have 60 days subsequent to confirmation to object to the allowance of claims. The Proponent has reviewed the claims that have been filed. The Proponent intends to object or cause the Disbursing Agent to object to the following number and amounts of claims in each class.[67]

5. Effective Date. *The Plan will become effective on the Effective Date which is the date on which the order of confirmation becomes final.*[68]

6. Modification. The Plan Proponent may alter, amend or modify the Plan at any time prior to the Confirmation Date and thereafter as provided in Section 1127(b) of the Bankruptcy Code.

F. Tax Consequences of Plan. CREDITORS AND INTEREST HOLDERS CONCERNED WITH HOW THE PLAN MAY AFFECT THEIR TAX LIABILITY SHOULD CONSULT WITH THEIR OWN ACCOUNTANTS, ATTORNEYS, AND/OR ADVISORS. The following disclosure of possible tax consequences is intended solely for the purpose of alerting readers to possible tax issues this Plan may present to the Debtor. The Proponent CANNOT and DOES NOT represent that the tax consequences contained below are the only tax consequences of the Plan because the Tax Code embodies many complicated rules which make it difficult to state completely and accurately all the tax implications of any action.

The following are the tax consequences that the Plan will have on the Debtor's tax liability: _____[69]

G. Risk Factors. The following discussion is intended to be a non-exclusive summary of certain risks attendant upon the consummation of the Plan. You are encouraged to supplement this summary with your own analysis and evaluation of the Plan and Disclosure Statement, in their entirety, and in consultation with your own advisors. Based on the analysis of the risks summarized below, the Plan Proponent believes that the Plan is viable and will meet all requirements of confirmation:

IV. CONFIRMATION REQUIREMENTS AND PROCEDURES

PERSONS OR ENTITIES CONCERNED WITH CONFIRMATION OF THIS PLAN SHOULD CONSULT WITH THEIR OWN ATTORNEYS BECAUSE THE LAW ON CONFIRMING A PLAN OF REORGANIZATION IS VERY COMPLEX. The following discussion is intended solely for the purpose of alerting readers about basic confirmation issues, which they may wish to consider, as well as certain deadlines for filing claims. The proponent CANNOT and DOES NOT represent that the discussion contained below is a complete summary of the law on this topic.

Many requirements must be met before the Court can confirm a Plan. Some of the requirements include that the Plan must be proposed in good faith, that creditors or interest holders have accepted the Plan, that the Plan pays creditors at least as much as creditors would receive in a Chapter 7 liquidation, and that the Plan is feasible. These requirements are not the only requirements for confirmation.

A. Who May Vote or Object.

1. Who May Object to Confirmation of the Plan. Any party in interest may object to the confirmation of the Plan, but as explained below not everyone is entitled to vote to accept or reject the Plan.

2. Who May Vote to Accept/Reject the Plan. A creditor or interest holder has a right to vote for or against the Plan if that creditor or interest holder has a claim that is both (1) allowed or allowed for voting purposes and (2) classified in an impaired class.

a. What Is an Allowed Claim/Interest. As noted above, a creditor or interest holder must first have an allowed claim or interest to have the right to vote. Generally, any proof of claim or interest will be allowed, unless a party in interest brings a motion objecting to the claim. When an objection to a claim or interest is filed, the creditor or interest holder holding the claim or interest cannot vote unless the Court, after notice and hearing, either overrules the objection or allows the claim or interest for voting purposes.

THE BAR DATE FOR FILING A PROOF OF CLAIM IN THIS CASE WAS ______[70].

A creditor or interest holder may have an allowed claim or interest even if a proof of claim or interest was not timely filed. A claim is deemed allowed if (1) it is scheduled on the Debtor's schedules and such claim is not scheduled as disputed, contingent, or unliquidated, and (2) no party in interest has objected to the claim. An interest is deemed allowed if it is scheduled and no party in interest has objected to the interest.

b. What Is an Impaired Claim/Interest. As noted above, an allowed claim or interest only has the right to vote if it is in a class that is impaired under the Plan. A class is impaired if the Plan alters the legal, equitable, or contractual rights of the members of that class. For example, a class comprised of general unsecured claims is impaired if the Plan fails to pay the members of that class 100% of their claim plus interest.

In this case, the Proponent believes that classes ______[71] are impaired and that holders of claims in each of these classes are therefore entitled to vote to accept or reject the Plan. The Proponent believes that classes ______[72] are unimpaired and that holders of claims in each of these classes therefore do not have the right to vote to accept or reject the Plan. Parties who dispute the Proponent's characterization of their claim or interest as being impaired or unimpaired may file an objection to the Plan contending that the Proponent has incorrectly characterized the class.

3. Who Is Not Entitled to Vote. The following four types of claims are not entitled to vote: (1) claims that have been disallowed; (2) claims in unimpaired classes; (3) claims entitled to priority pursuant to Code Section 507(a)(1), (a)(2), and (a)(8)[73]; and (4) claims in classes that do not receive or retain any value under the Plan. Claims in unimpaired classes are not entitled to vote because such classes are deemed to have accepted the Plan. Claims entitled to priority pursuant to Code Section 507(a)(1), (a)(2), and (a)(7) are not entitled to vote because such claims are not placed in classes and they are required to receive certain treatment specified by the Code. Claims in classes that do not receive or retain any value under the Plan do not vote because such classes are deemed to have rejected the Plan. EVEN IF YOUR CLAIM IS OF THE TYPE DESCRIBED ABOVE, YOU MAY STILL HAVE A RIGHT TO OBJECT TO THE CONFIRMATION OF THE PLAN.

4. **Who Can Vote in More Than One Class.** A creditor whose claim has been allowed in part as a secured claim and in part as an unsecured claim is entitled to accept or reject a Plan in both capacities by casting one ballot for the secured part of the claim and another ballot for the unsecured claim.

5. **Votes Necessary to Confirm the Plan.** If impaired classes exist, the Court cannot confirm the Plan unless (1) at least one impaired class has accepted the Plan without counting the votes of any insiders within that class, and (2) all impaired classes have voted to accept the Plan, unless the Plan is eligible to be confirmed by "cramdown" on non-accepting classes, as discussed later in Section (IV.A.8.).

6. **Votes Necessary for a Class to Accept the Plan.** A class of claims is considered to have accepted the Plan when more than one-half (½) in number and at least two-thirds (⅔) in dollar amount of the allowed claims that actually voted, voted in favor of the Plan. A class of interests is considered to have accepted the Plan when at least two-thirds (⅔) in amount of the allowed interest-holders of such class which actually voted, voted to accept the Plan.

7. **Treatment of Nonaccepting Classes.** As noted above, even if all impaired classes do not accept the proposed Plan, the Court may nonetheless confirm the Plan if the nonaccepting classes are treated in the manner required by the Code. The process by which nonaccepting classes are forced to be bound by the terms of the Plan is commonly referred to as "cramdown". The Code allows the Plan to be "crammed down" on nonaccepting classes of claims or interests if it meets all consensual requirements except the voting requirements of Section 1129(a)(8) and if the Plan does not "discriminate unfairly" and is "fair and equitable" toward each impaired class that has not voted to accept the Plan as referred to in 11 U.S.C. § 1129(b) and applicable case law.

8. **Request for Confirmation Despite Nonacceptance by Impaired Class(es).** The party proposing this Plan asks the Court to confirm this Plan by cramdown on impaired classes if any of these classes do not vote to accept the Plan.

B. Liquidation Analysis. Another confirmation requirement is the "Best Interest Test", which requires a liquidation analysis. Under the Best Interest Test, if a claimant or interest holder is in an impaired class and that claimant or interest holder does not vote to accept the Plan, then that claimant or interest holder must receive or retain under the Plan property of a value not less than the amount that such holder would receive or retain if the Debtor were liquidated under Chapter 7 of the Bankruptcy Code.

In a Chapter 7 case, the Debtor's assets are usually sold by a Chapter 7 trustee. Secured creditors are paid first from the sales proceeds of properties on which the secured creditor has a lien. Administrative claims are paid next. Next, unsecured creditors are paid from any remaining sales proceeds, according to their rights to priority. Unsecured creditors with the same priority share in proportion to the amount of their allowed claims. Finally, interest holders receive the balance that remains after all creditors are paid, if any.

In order for the Court to be able to confirm this Plan, the Court must find that all creditors and interest holders who do not accept the Plan will receive at least as much under the Plan as such holders would receive under a Chapter 7 liquidation. The Plan Proponent maintains that this requirement is met here for the following reasons: ____[74].

Below is a demonstration, in balance sheet format, that all creditors and interest holders will receive at least as much under the Plan as such creditor or interest holder would receive under a Chapter 7 liquidation:

Assets[75]

Real Property		$_____
Minus: 1st Mortgage	$_____	
2nd Mortgage	$_____	
Any exemption	$_____	
Costs of sale	$_____	
Net equity		$_____
Personal Property [segregate by type]		$_____
Total assets		$_____

Liabilities

Priority Claims:		
Chapter 7 admin. expenses	$_____	
Chapter 11 admin. expenses	$_____	
Other priority claims	$_____	
Total priority claims		$_____
Amount available for unsecured claims (total assets minus priority claims)		$_____
Total unsecured claims		$_____
Estimated dividend in Chapter 7 (amount available—unsecured claims)		_____%

C. Feasibility. Another requirement for confirmation involves the feasibility of the Plan, which means that confirmation of the Plan is not likely to be followed by the liquidation or the need for further financial reorganization of the Debtor or any successor to the Debtor under the Plan, unless such liquidation or reorganization is proposed in the Plan.

There are at least two important aspects of a feasibility analysis. The first aspect considers whether the Debtor will have enough cash on hand on the Effective Date of the Plan to pay all the claims and expenses that are entitled to be paid on such date. The Plan Proponent maintains that this aspect of feasibility is satisfied as illustrated here:

Cash Debtor will have on hand by Effective Date[76]	$_____
To Pay: Administrative claims	-_____
To Pay: Statutory costs & charges	-_____
To Pay: Other Plan Payments due on Effective Date	-_____
Balance after paying these amounts	$_____

The sources of the cash Debtor will have on hand by the Effective Date, as shown above are:

$_____	Cash in DIP Account now
+_____	Additional cash DIP will accumulate from net earnings between now and Effective Date
+_____	Borrowing
+_____	Capital Contributions
+_____	Other
$_____	Total[77]

Borrowing is from _____[78] and will be paid back as follows: _____[79].

The second aspect considers whether the Proponent will have enough cash over the life of the Plan to make the required Plan payments.

The Proponent believes that this second aspect of the feasibility requirement is met for the following reasons: _____[80].

In summary, the Plan proposes to pay _____[81] each _____[82]. As Debtor's financial projections demonstrate, Debtor will have an average cash flow, after paying operating expenses and postconfirmation taxes, of _____[83] each _____[84] for the life of the Plan. The final Plan payment is expected to be paid on _____[85]. The Plan Proponent contends that Debtor's financial projections are feasible in light of the financial records maintained by the Debtor prior to and during the pendency of the bankruptcy case. As shown by Debtor's historical financial statements, Debtor's average _____[86] cash flow, after paying operating expenses and post-confirmation taxes, in the three years preceding the filing of this bankruptcy case is _____[87]. Debtor's average _____[88] cash flow, after paying operating expenses and post-confirmation taxes, during the bankruptcy case is _____[89]. Furthermore, as discussed earlier in the Disclosure Statement at Section (II.E.4), Debtor has implemented procedures to _____[90].

Accordingly, the Plan Proponent believes, on the basis of the foregoing, that the Plan is feasible.

V. EFFECT OF CONFIRMATION OF PLAN

A. Discharge. The Plan provides that upon confirmation of the Plan, the Debtor shall be discharged of liability for payment of debts incurred before confirmation of the Plan, to the extent specified in 11 U.S.C. § 1141. However, any liability imposed by the Plan will not be discharged. If Confirmation of the Plan does not occur or if, after Confirmation occurs, the Debtor elects to terminate the Plan, the Plan shall be deemed null and void. In such event, nothing contained in the Plan shall be deemed to constitute a waiver or release of any claims against the Debtor or its estate or any other persons, or to prejudice in any manner the rights of the Debtor or its estate or any person in any further proceeding involving the Debtor or its estate. The provisions of the Plan shall be binding upon Debtor, all Creditors and all Equity Interest Holders, regardless of whether such Claims or Equity Interest holders are impaired or whether such parties accept the Plan, upon Confirmation thereof.

B. Revesting of Property in the Debtor. Except as provided in the Plan, the confirmation of the Plan revests all of the property of the estate in the Debtor.

C. Modification of Plan. The Proponent may modify the Plan at any time before confirmation. However, the Court may require a new disclosure statement and/or revoting on the Plan if Proponent modifies the plan before confirmation.

The Proponent may also seek to modify the Plan at any time after confirmation so long as (1) the Plan has not been substantially consummated and (2) the Court authorizes the proposed modification after notice and a hearing. Proponent further reserves the right to modify the treatment of any Allowed Claims at any time after the Effective Date of the Plan upon the consent of the Creditor whose Allowed Claim treatment is being modified, so long as no other Creditors are materially adversely affected.

D. Post–Confirmation Conversion/Dismissal. A creditor or party in interest may bring a motion to convert or dismiss the case under Section 1112(b), after the Plan is confirmed, if there is a default in performance of the Plan or if cause exists under Section 1112(b). If the Court orders the case converted to Chapter 7 after the Plan is confirmed, then all property that had been property of the Chapter 11 estate, and that has not been disbursed pursuant to the Plan, will revest in the Chapter 7 estate, and the automatic stay will be reimposed upon the revested property only to the extent that relief from stay was not previously granted by the Court during this case.

Quarterly fees pursuant to 28 U.S.C. § 1930(a)(6) continue to be payable to the Office of the United States Trustee post-confirmation until such time as the case is converted, dismissed, or closed pursuant to a final decree.[91]

Date: ______

____

Name of Plan Proponent

[Effective January 2001; Revised effective June 1, 2006.]

---

1 Put which version of Disclosure Statement (Original, First Amended, Second Amended Disclosure Statement). Do not use the term "Modified" when describing any version subsequent to the Original.

2 D.N.J. LBR 3016–1(b)(1) and 3016–2(c) require that title indicate whether the plan is one of reorganization or liquidation and that any modified plan indicate its relationship to the original.

3 Insert identity of Plan Proponent (Debtor, Trustee, Official Committee of Unsecured Creditors, etc.).

4 Insert what Plan is being described (original, First Amended, Second Amended, etc.).

5 Debtor's name.

6 Petition date.

7 Insert the applicable information, depending on who filed the petition:

(a) Debtor's name

(b) Names of the petitioning creditors

8 Insert one of the following:

(a) a voluntary

(b) an involuntary

9 If case was commenced in a chapter other than Chapter 11 and later converted to Chapter 11, so state and state date of conversion to Chapter 11.

10 Proponent's name.

11 Insert the applicable phrases:

(a) liquidating

(b) reorganizing

(c) combined liquidating and reorganizing

12 Provide a brief summary of how Proponent proposes to fund the Plan. If applicable, include statement that this plan is a joint plan, or is otherwise related to a plan in another bankruptcy case, or is a consensual plan between one or more parties to this Chapter 11 case.

13 Date of the confirmation hearing.

14 The address of the Clerk's Office or name and address of claims processing agent, if one has been retained should be inserted here. If Proponent also wants to receive a copy of the ballot. Proponent should provide that a copy be sent to the Proponent and include name, address, and telephone number of the Plan Proponent or Counsel to the Plan Proponent. A second envelope should be provided for this purpose.

If applicable, the Disclosure Statement should indicate that there are two or more competing plans, and should tell readers to look at their ballots for special instructions on marking them. The ballots should be modified to contain any applicable special instructions.

15 Deadline for receipt of ballots. (**Note:** This date will be provided by the Court at the hearing where the Court approves the Disclosure Statement.)

16 Name and address of the Plan Proponent or Counsel to the Plan Proponent.

17 Deadline for filing and serving any objection to the confirmation of the Plan. (**Note:** This date will be provided to you by the Court at the hearing where the Court approves the Disclosure Statement.)

18 Name, address, and telephone number of Plan Proponent or Counsel to the Plan Proponent. In cases where there is a creditor's committee, include the name, address and telephone number of counsel for the creditor's committee.

19 Insert documents such as Debtor's books and records, financial statements such as projections, appraisals, and evaluations, as well as who provided these documents.

20 Identify by name and title the party providing the financial information (i.e., corporate officer, managing agent, accountant, accounting firm, bookkeeper, etc.). Accountants who assist clients in the preparation of financial statements should consult *Statement of Position 90–7, Financial Reporting by Entities in Reorganization Under the Bankruptcy Code*, dated November 19, 1990 and prepared by the AICPA Task Force on Financial Reporting by Entities in Reorganization Under the Bankruptcy Code.

21 Insert the applicable phrase:

(a) corporation

(b) partnership

(c) individual

(**Note:** If the Debtor is an entity that is not listed above, provide a description of Debtor's entity and verify that such an entity is eligible to be a debtor.)

22 Type of business conducted by the Debtor (if applicable).

Note: For example, if the Debtor is in the business of developing real estate, the following should be listed:

(a) The location of the properties/lots

(b) The size of the lots

(c) The stage of the development for each lot

(d) The type of development, e.g., commercial, industrial or residential

If the Debtor is a manufacturer or service provider, the following should be listed:

(a) The type of products manufactured or services provided

(b) The location of Debtor's business

If the Debtor is in the business of renting real estate, the following should be listed:

(a) Location of the building(s)

(b) Size of the building(s)

(c) Current occupancy rate(s)

(d) Type(s) of building, e.g., residential, commercial, industrial

(e) Debtor's interest in the building(s) being leased

If the Debtor is an individual, the following should be listed:

(a) Debtor's employer and description of the employer's type of business

(b) Length of Debtor's employment

(c) Debtor's position, including title, number of hours worked, salaried or hourly

(d) Description of Debtor's duties

(e) Amount of Debtor's compensation

If Debtor is no longer in business, the above information should still be provided with respect to Debtor's business immediately preceding the bankruptcy. The date Debtor ceased to conduct business should also be provided.

23 Approximate date and year debtor's business commenced.

24 Detailed list of the names and identity of Debtor's principals and affiliates. Include the amount of compensation currently paid to principals and affiliates.

Note: For example, if Debtor is a corporation, the following must be listed:

(a) Key members of the board of directors.

(b) Key officers of the corporation.

(c) Key shareholders and their respective percentage interest.

If Debtor is a partnership, the following must be provided:

(a) Identity of all general partners since the inception of the partnership

(b) Identity of all current limited partners.

(c) If the general partner is a corporation, the board members, officers and shareholders must be listed.

25 List key management of the Debtor before the bankruptcy petition was filed and list key management of the Debtor during the course of the bankruptcy. Also disclose compensation and other key terms of employment agreements with bankruptcy key management.

26 Discuss the specific events and dates which led the debtor to file bankruptcy. (**Note:** A statement to the effect that the recession caused debtor's business to fail is not specific enough.) Proponent must disclose the receipt of any notices from any governmental agency relating in any manner to actual or potential liability on the part of the Debtor for any environment or toxic waste hazards, whether or not occurring on the Debtor's premises.

27 In chronological order, list the significant events and orders that have been entered in this case and the entry dates of the orders. Also, give a brief description of the proceedings that led to the entry of the orders.

28 Detailed list of the professionals who have obtained Court approval of their employment, including (1) the professional's name, (2) scope of employment, and (3) date Court approved the employment and (4) estimate of amount owed.

29 Brief description of the following: (1) each significant adversary proceeding or motion that is still pending, including objections to claims, (2) the status of each matter, (3) the effects winning or losing the matter will have on the Plan, and (4) the anticipated cost of pursuing or defending the matter.

30 Brief description of the following: (1) each significant matter that is still pending in other courts, (2) status of each matter, (i.e., whether the matter is stayed), (3) effect the outcome of the matter will have on the Plan, and (4) the anticipated cost of pursuing or defending the matter.

31 If no preference or fraudulent conveyance actions exist and none are expected to be filed, then insert an affirmative statement to that effect and delete the rest of the text under this heading.

32 Estimated total recovery in dollar amount from avoiding preferential and fraudulent transfers and anticipated total expense of pursuing those matters.

33 Provide a brief summary of each fraudulent conveyance or preference action. For each action, include the name of the defendant, summary of the underlying facts, status of the action, and the estimated amount of recovery.

34 Describe post-petition efforts made by the Debtor to remedy the problems that led to the filing of bankruptcy. (**Note:** Be specific.) Also describe the goals Debtor had in mind when implementing these procedures (e.g., save costs, increase profits.)

35 The Proponent should provide a textual discussion pertaining to the Debtor's historical current financial condition. This discussion should inform the reader about the Debtor's current income and expenses and whether Debtor's operations, if any, are currently profitable and whether the Debtor is current with post-petition expenses. If not, the Proponent should include a schedule of post-petition obligations. Each document shall identify (i) the accounting method used (e.g., cash or accrual), (ii) whether the financial statements are prepared in conformity with generally accepted accounting principles, and (iii) if the financial statements have been audited.

36 If professional(s) have agreed to payment over time, state the precise terms and payment schedule (e.g. $____ per month over ____ months).

37 For each chart, add more rows to the tables as necessary.

38 Total amount of administrative claims to be paid on Effective Date.

39 Denominated as Section 507(a)(7) for bankruptcy cases filed before October 22, 1994.

40 Denominated as Section 507(a)(7) for bankruptcy cases filed before October 22, 1994.

41 Section 507(a)(7)[now renumbered 507(a)(8) for cases filed after October 22, 1994] describing certain priority tax claims. All 507(a)(7) tax claims must be fully paid within 6 years from the date of assessment. Only unsecured tax claims of the kind described by 11 U.S.C. § 507(a)(7)[8] should be inserted here.

42 Identify the proposed payment interval (e.g., monthly, quarterly, yearly).

43 Amount of payment per payment interval.

44 The date Plan payments will commence.

45 The date Plan payments will end.

46 The interest rate paid to a Section 507(a)(8) priority tax claimant should be consistent with the rate provided by 26 U.S.C. § 6621.

47 Total percentage of claim proposed to be paid to claimant over the life of the Plan plus total dollar amount to be paid to the claimant over life of the Plan.

48 Each secured claim should be placed in a separate class, unless the secured claims have identical collateral, priority, and terms of indebtedness.

Begin numbering the classes with the number "1". The subsequent class should be numbered with the number "2". Do not use subclasses, *e.g.*, 1.1, 1.2, etc.

49 If this class is Not Impaired, put the following in the box: "Not Impaired; claims in this class are not entitled to vote on Plan, class is deemed to have accepted Plan."

If this class is Impaired, put the following in the box: "Impaired; claims in this class are entitled to vote on the Plan"; unless this class is not retaining or receiving any value under the Plan. In this latter case only, put "Impaired, and claims in this case are deemed to have rejected Plan."

50 Balloon payment amount, if any.

51 Total percent of claim proposed to be paid to claimant over the life of the Plan plus total dollar amount to be paid to claimant over the life of the Plan.

52 Omit reference to 507(a)(7) (alimony/child support priority) if case was filed before October 22, 1994 because priority would not exist for cases filed before that date.

53 Omit reference to 507(a)(7) (alimony/child support priority) if case was filed before October 22, 1994 because priority would not exist for cases filed before that date.

54 Insert one of the following:

A. 11 U.S.C. § 507(a)(3)

B. 11 U.S.C. § 507(a)(4)

C. 11 U.S.C. § 507(a)(5)

D. 11 U.S.C. § 507(a)(6)

55 Total amount of claims in this class.

56 If the Plan does not provide for cash payment in full on Effective Date, Plan Proponent must be able to prove that this class has accepted deferred payments pursuant to 11 U.S.C. § 1129(a)(9) before the Plan can be confirmed.

57 Insert one of the following:

(a) 11 U.S.C. § 507(a)(3)

(b) 11 U.S.C. § 507(a)(4)

(c) 11 U.S.C. § 507(a)(5)

(d) 11 U.S.C. § 507(a)(6)

58 Total amount of claims in this class.

59 If this class is Not Impaired, put the following in the box: "Not Impaired; claims in this class are not entitled to vote on Plan, class is deemed to have accepted Plan."

If this class is Impaired, put the following in the box: "Impaired; claims in this class are entitled to vote on the Plan"; unless this class is not retaining or receiving any value under the Plan. In this latter case only, put "Impaired, and claims in this class are deemed to have rejected Plan."

60 Total percent of claim proposed to be paid to claimant over the life of the Plan plus total dollar amount to be paid to claimant over the life of Plan.

61 If there is more than one class of equity holders (e.g., preferred stock and common stock), put each in a separate class and change "class" to "classes".

62 If this class is Not Impaired, put the following in the box: "Not Impaired; claims in this class are not entitled to vote on Plan, class is deemed to have accepted Plan."

If this class is Impaired, put the following in the box: "Impaired; claims in this class are entitled to vote on the Plan"; unless this class is not retaining or receiving any value under the Plan. In this latter case only, put "Impaired, and claims in this class are deemed to have rejected Plan."

63 Describe the source of funding for this Plan. Be specific and consistent with the information set forth in Section [IV.C.]

A. If property of the estate is being sold and 11 U.S.C. § 1129 (b)(2)(A)(ii) applies, then explain how that section impacts on the rights of a lienholder at a sale of the property.

B. If a buyer of the property has already been identified, then disclose the financial solvency of the proposed buyer.

64 For each entity who will be involved in post-confirmation management, state or explain the following:

A. Identity

B. Post-confirmation managerial duties

C. Amount of compensation paid pre-petition, paid currently, and to be paid postconfirmation

D. Key terms of employment agreements

E. Description of expertise

65 Name and identity of disbursing agent.

66 See 11 U.S.C. § 1129(a)(6). This section is only applicable if Debtor's business is regulated by a governmental regulatory commission. Examples include certain transportation companies and public utility companies. If Debtor is not regulated by a governmental commission, insert an affirmative statement to that effect in the Disclosure Statement. If debtor is regulated, state this and Plan must comply with 11 U.S.C. § 1129(a)(6).

67 D.N.J. LBR 3016–2(a) and (b) require the Proponent to review all claims prior to filing a Disclosure Statement and Plan and to set forth in the Disclosure Statement the number and amount of claims in each class to which the Proponent intends to object.

68 D.N.J. LBR 3016–1(a) establishes this date as the effective date unless the Proponent specifies an alternate date.

69 State the expected tax consequences of the Plan. For example, tax ramifications may include such issues as capital gains on the sale of real property and operating loss-carry forwards.

Note: If the Proponent has no idea of what such consequences might be, then the document must disclose that fact and why it is so. Few situations exist where the tax liability should not be considered because any tax liability would affect distribution to creditors. Tax considerations might affect the likelihood of continued successful post-confirmation operation of the Debtor and may also affect the feasibility analysis. For these reasons, the Proponent should know the tax consequences of the Plan.

70 Bar date for filing proof of claim.

Note: In most bankruptcy cases it is necessary that a bar date for filing proofs of claim and interest has passed before creditors and interest holders may vote on the Plan. Knowing which claims and interests have been allowed will allow the Plan Proponent to easily determine who is entitled to vote. Also, without knowing the amount and nature of the claims against the estate, it is impossible to complete a precise liquidation analysis and difficult to determine whether the Plan is feasible.

If the claims bar date has not yet passed, the motion for order approving the disclosure statement should explain why the disclosure statement and plan are proposed now instead of after the claim bar date.

71 Classes that are impaired.

72 Classes that are unimpaired. (For cases filed after October 22, 1994 please note that the Bankruptcy Reform Act of 1994 deleted Section 1124(3). Therefore, creditors who receive cash in full equal to their allowed claim by the effective date would be considered impaired under the Bankruptcy Reform Act of 1994.)

73 Denominated as 507(a)(7) for bankruptcy case filed before October 22, 1994.

74 Insert the following reasons, if applicable:

A. The liquidation value of the "x" is less than its fair market value because _____.

(**Note:** Be specific when justifying the difference between liquidation value and fair market value. State the basis for your justification.)

B. In a chapter 7 case, a trustee is appointed and entitled to compensation from the bankruptcy estate in an amount not to exceed 25% of the first $5,000 of all moneys disbursed, 10% on any amount over $5,000 but less than $50,000, 5% on any amount over $50,000 but not in excess of $1 million, and 3% on all amounts over $1 million. In this case, the trustee's compensation is estimated to equal "x".

C. A Chapter 7 recovery is less because the Debtor is permitted to exempt a certain amount of the sales proceeds before unsecured creditors are paid anything. (**Note:** Be specific when relying on Debtor's claimed exemptions. List each exempt property, the code section which entitles the Debtor to the claimed exemption, and the amount of each exemption.)

Note: If Debtor is a partnership then Section 723(a) provides that the general partners of the partnership are liable for any deficiency of property of the estate to pay in full all allowed claims. Therefore, the Proponent must disclose the financial condition of the individual general partners from whom Chapter 7 trustee could seek to collect if this was a Chapter 7 case.

75 The disclosure statement should reflect the method of valuation—i.e., appraisal, cost, etc.

76 Explain sources of cash Debtor will have on Effective Date if Debtor does not currently have sufficient cash on hand to pay all claims that must be paid on the Effective Date.

77 Total must match figure shown above as "Cash debtor will have on hand by Effective Date."

78 Insert person or entity from whom funds are being borrowed.

79 Explain how loan will be paid back (example, lender has agreed it will not be paid until all Plan payments are completed and then will be paid at $_____ per month at _____% until paid in full). If gift instead of borrowing, change "Borrowing" to "Gift" and state amount will never be repaid.

80 Explain the sources of future revenues which Debtor will have both to operate and make deferred payments under the Plan. Cross reference Financial Projection and attach as an exhibit.

81 Total amount of Plan Payments to be made each payment interval.

[82] Plan payment interval (e.g. monthly, yearly, quarterly).

[83] Average cash flow per Plan payment interval, after paying operating expenses and postconfirmation taxes for the entire duration of the Plan.

[84] Plan payment interval.

[85] The last Plan payment date.

[86] Payment interval (e.g., monthly, yearly, quarterly).

[87] Amount of actual average cash flow per Plan payment interval, after paying operating expenses and post-confirmation taxes, for the three years preceding the filing of this bankruptcy case.

[88] Plan payment interval (e.g., monthly, yearly, quarterly).

[89] Debtor's average cash flow per Plan payment interval, after paying operating expenses and post-confirmation taxes, during the bankruptcy case.

[90] Select one:

1. decrease costs
2. increase costs
3. decrease costs and increase income

[91] Counsel should be aware that as long as the case remains open, quarterly fees to the United States Trustee continue. Counsel should take steps to make sure that an Order closing the case is entered at the appropriate time to avoid having these fees continue unnecessarily.

D.N.J. LOCAL FORM 19. CHAPTER 11 REORGANIZATION PLAN

Name of Attorneys
Attorneys' Address
Attorneys' Telephone and Fax Numbers
Attorneys for Debtor/Plan Proponent
By: Name of Responsible Individual Attorney(s) (Attorney Code)

____

IN THE MATTER OF:	UNITED STATES BANKRUPTCY COURT FOR THE DISTRICT OF NEW JERSEY ____[1] VICINAGE
DEBTOR.	CHAPTER 11 CASE NO.[2]

PLAN OF ____[3]

Debtor/Plan Proponent respectfully submits its Plan of Reorganization pursuant to Chapter 11, Title 11 of the United States Code, in the form annexed hereto and made a part hereof.

NAME OF DEBTOR/PLAN PROPONENT

BY: ______________________

DATED:

I. INTRODUCTION

____[4] ("Debtor") is the debtor in a Chapter 11 bankruptcy case. On ____[5], ____[6] commenced a bankruptcy case by filing ____[7] Chapter 11 petition under the United States Bankruptcy Code ("Bankruptcy Code "), 11 U.S.C. § 101 et seq. This document is the Chapter 11 plan ("Plan") proposed by ____[8] ("Proponent"). Sent to you in the same envelope as this document is the Disclosure Statement which has been approved by the United States Bankruptcy Court for the District of New Jersey (the "Court"), and which is provided to help you understand the Plan.

This is a _____[9] plan. In other words, the Proponent seeks to accomplish payments under the Plan by _____[10]. The Effective Date of the proposed Plan is _____[11].

II. CLASSIFICATION AND TREATMENT OF CLAIMS AND INTERESTS

A. General Overview. As required by the Bankruptcy Code, the Plan classifies claims and interests in various classes according to their right to priority of payments as provided in the Bankruptcy Code. The Plan states whether each class of claims or interests is impaired or unimpaired. The Plan provides the treatment each class will receive under the Plan.

B. Definitions.

Scope of Definitions. For purposes of this Plan, except as expressly otherwise provided or unless the context otherwise requires, all capitalized terms not otherwise defined shall have the meanings assigned to them in this Section of the Plan. In all references herein to any parties, persons, entities, or corporations, the use of any particular gender or the plural or singular number is intended to include the appropriate gender or number as the text may require.

1. **Administrative Expense** shall mean any cost or expense of administration of the Chapter 11 case allowable under Section 507(a) of the Bankruptcy Code, including, without limitation, any actual and necessary expenses of preserving the estate of the Debtor, any actual and necessary expense of operating the business of the Debtor, any indebtedness or obligation incurred or assumed by the Debtor in connection with the conduct of its business or for the acquisition or lease of property or the rendition of services to the Debtor, all allowances of compensation and reimbursement of expenses, any fees or charges assessed against the estate of any Debtor under Chapter 123, Title 28, of the United States Code, and the reasonable fees and expenses incurred by the Proponent in connection with the proposal and confirmation of this Plan.

2. **Allowed** when used as an adjective preceding the words "Claims" or "Equity Interest", shall mean any Claim against or Equity Interests of the Debtor, proof of which was filed on or before the date designated by the Bankruptcy Court as the last date for filing proofs of claim or Equity Interest against such Debtor, or, if no proof of claim or Equity Interest is filed, which has been or hereafter is listed by the Debtor as liquidated in amount and not disputed or contingent and, in either case, a Claim as to which no objection to the allowance thereof has been interposed with the applicable period of limitations fixed by the Plan, the Bankruptcy Code, the Federal Rules of Bankruptcy Procedure, Local Rules, or as to which any objection has been interposed and such Claim has been allowed in whole or in part by a Final Order. Unless otherwise specified in the Plan, "Allowed Claim" and "Allowed Equity Interest" shall not, for purposes of computation of distributions under the Plan, include interest on the amount of such Claim or Equity Interest from and after the Petition Date.

3. **Allowed Administrative Expense** shall mean any Administrative Expense allowed under Section 507(a)(1) of the Bankruptcy Code.

4. **Allowed Unsecured Claim** shall mean an Unsecured Claim that is or has become an Allowed Claim.

5. **Bankruptcy Code** shall mean the Bankruptcy Reform Act of 1978, as amended, and as codified in Title 11 of the United States Code.

6. **Bankruptcy Court** shall mean the United States Bankruptcy Court for the District of New Jersey having jurisdiction over the Chapter 11 Case and, to the extent of any reference made pursuant to 28 U.S.C. Section 158, the unit of such District Court constituted pursuant to 28 U.S.C. Section 151.

7. **Bankruptcy Rules** shall mean the rules and forms of practice and procedure in bankruptcy, promulgated under 28 U.S.C. Section 2075 and also referred to as the Federal Rules of Bankruptcy Procedure.

8. **Business Day** means and refers to any day except Saturday, Sunday, and any other day on which commercial banks in New Jersey are authorized by law to close.

9. **Chapter 11 Case** shall mean a case under Chapter 11 of the Bankruptcy Code in which _____[12] is the Debtor.

10. **Claim** shall mean any right to payment from the Debtor whether or not such right is reduced to judgment, liquidated, unliquidated, fixed, contingent, matured, unmatured, disputed, undisputed, legal, equitable, secured, or unsecured; or any right to an equitable remedy for breach of performance if such breach gives rise to a right of payment from the Debtor whether or not such right to an equitable remedy is reduced to judgment, fixed, contingent, matured, unmatured, disputed, undisputed, secured, or unsecured. All claims as such term is defined in section 101(5) of the Bankruptcy Code.

11. **Class** shall mean a grouping of substantially similar Claims or Equity Interests for common treatment thereof pursuant to the terms of this Plan.

12. **Code** shall mean Title 11 of the United States Code, otherwise known as the Bankruptcy Code.

13. **Confirmation** shall mean the entry of an Order by this Court approving the Plan in accordance with the provisions of the Bankruptcy Code.

14. **Confirmation Hearing** shall mean a hearing conducted before the Bankruptcy Court for the purpose of considering confirmation of the Plan.

15. **Confirmation Order** shall mean an Order of the Bankruptcy Court confirming the Plan in accordance with the provisions of Chapter 11 of the Bankruptcy Code.

16. **Creditor** shall mean any person that has a Claim against the Debtor that arose on or before the Petition Date or a Claim against the Debtor's estate of any kind specified in section 502(g), 502(h) or 502(i) of the Bankruptcy Code. This includes all persons, corporations, partnerships, or business entities holding claims against the Debtor.

17. **Debt** means, refers to and shall have the same meaning ascribed to it in Section 101(12) of the Code.

18. **Debtor** shall mean _____[13].

19. **Disbursing Agent** shall mean the _____[14] or any party appointed by and subject to Court approval, which shall effectuate this Plan and hold and distribute consideration to be distributed to holders of Allowed Claims and Allowed Equity Interests pursuant to the provisions of the Plan and Confirmation Order.

20. **Disclosure Statement** means and refers to the Disclosure Statement filed by the Debtor as required pursuant to Section 1125, et seq. of the Bankruptcy Code.

21. **Effective Date** shall mean the day on which the Confirmation Order becomes a Final Order.

22. **Equity Interest Holder** shall mean the holder of an equity interest in the Debtor.

23. **Equity Interest** shall mean any interest in the Debtor represented by stock, warrants, options, or other rights to purchase any shares of stock in the Debtor.

24. **Final Order** shall mean an order of the Bankruptcy Court or a court of competent jurisdiction to hear appeals from the Bankruptcy Court which, not having been reversed, modified, or amended, and not being stayed, and the time to appeal from which or to seek review or rehearing of which having expired, has become final and is in full force and effect.

25. **Impaired** when used as an adjective preceding the words "Class of Claims" or "Class of Equity Interest", shall mean that the Plan alters the legal, equitable, or contractual rights of the member of that class.

26. **Person** shall mean an individual, a corporation, a partnership, an association, a joint stock company, a joint venture, an estate, a trust, an unincorporated organization, or a government or any political subdivision thereof or other entity.

27. **Petition Date** shall mean the date on which the Debtor filed this petition for relief commencing the Chapter 11 Case.

28. **Plan** shall mean the Plan of Reorganization filed in these Proceedings, together with any additional modifications and amendments.

29. **Priority Non–Tax Claim** shall mean a Claim entitled to priority under sections 507(a)(2),(3), (4), (5), (6) or (7) of the Bankruptcy Code, but only to the extent it is entitled to priority in payment under any such subsection.

30. **Priority Tax Creditor** shall mean a Creditor holding a priority tax claim.

31. **Priority Tax Claim** shall mean any Claim entitled to priority in payment under section 507(a)(8) of the Bankruptcy Code, but only to the extent it is entitled to priority under such subsection.

32. **Proceedings** shall mean the Chapter 11 Case of the Debtor.

33. **Professional Persons** means and refers to all attorneys, accountants, appraisers, consultants, and other professionals retained or to be compensated pursuant to an Order of the Court entered under Sections 327, 328, 330, or 503(b) of the Bankruptcy Code.

34. **Professional Claim** means and refers to a claim by any and all professionals as provided for in Sections 327, 328, 330 and 503(b) of the Bankruptcy Code.

35. **Proponent** means _____[15].

36. **Reorganized Debtor** means the Debtor after confirmation of the Plan.

37. **Secured Claim** means and refers to a Claim which is secured by a valid lien, security interest, or other interest in property in which the Debtor has an interest which has been perfected properly as required by applicable law, but only to the extent of the value of the Debtor's interest in such property, determined in accordance with Section 506(a) of the Bankruptcy Code.

38. **Unsecured Claim** shall mean any Claim against the Debtor which arose or which is deemed by the Bankruptcy Code to have arisen prior to the Petition Date for such Debtor, and which is not (i) a secured claim pursuant to Section 506 of the Bankruptcy Code, as modified by section 1111(b) of the Bankruptcy Code, or (ii) a Claim entitled to priority under sections 503 or 507 of the Bankruptcy Code. "Unsecured Claim" shall include all Claims against the Debtor that are not expressly otherwise dealt with in the Plan.

39. **Other Definitions**, a term used and not defined herein but that is defined in the Bankruptcy Code shall have the meaning set forth therein. The words "herein", "hereof", "hereto," "hereunder", and others of similar import refer to the Plan as a whole and not to any particular section, subsection, or clause contained in the Plan. Moreover some terms defined herein are defined in the section in which they are used.

C. Unclassified Claims. Certain types of claims are not placed into voting classes; instead they are unclassified. They are not considered impaired and they do not vote on the Plan because they are automatically entitled to specific treatment provided for them in the Bankruptcy Code. As such, the Proponent has not placed the following claims in a class. The treatment of these claims is provided below.

1. Administrative Expenses and Fees. Administrative expenses are claims for costs or expenses of administering the Debtor's Chapter 11 case which are allowed under Code Section 503(b). Fees payable to the Clerk of the Bankruptcy Court and the Office of the United States Trustee were also incurred during the Chapter 11

Case. The Code requires that all administrative expenses be paid on the Effective Date of the Plan, unless a particular claimant agrees to a different treatment.

Court Approval of Professional Compensation and Expenses Required: The Court must approve all professional compensation and expenses. Each professional person requesting compensation in the case pursuant to Sections 327, 328, 330, 331, 503(b) or 1103 of the Bankruptcy Code shall file an application for allowance of final compensation and reimbursement of expenses not later than ninety (90) days after the Confirmation Date. Nothing herein shall prohibit each professional person from requesting interim compensation during the course of this case pending Confirmation of this Plan. No motion or application is required to fix fees payable to the Clerk's Office or the Office of the United States Trustee, as those fees are determined by statute.

2. Priority Tax Claims. Priority tax claims are certain unsecured income, employment and other taxes described by Code Section 507(a)(8). The Code requires, and thus this Plan provides, that each holder of such a 507(a)(8) priority tax claim receives the present value of such claim in deferred cash payments, over a period not exceeding six years from the date of the assessment of such tax.

D. Classified Claims and Interests.

1. Classes of Secured Claims. Secured claims are claims secured by liens on property of the estate. The following represent all classes containing Debtor's secured pre-petition claims and their treatment under this Plan:

Insert Chart Appearing in Disclosure Statement and State Whether Each Class of Secured Claims Is Impaired or Unimpaired.

2. Priority Non–Tax Claims. Certain priority non-tax claims that are referred to in Code Sections 507(a)(3), (4), (5), (6), and (7) are entitled to priority treatment. These claims are to be treated as follows:

There may need to be a separate class for different categories of Non–Tax Priority Claims since they may receive different treatment under the Plan. See 11 U.S.C. § 1129(a)(9)(B)(i) and (ii). Insert chart appearing in Disclosure Statement and state whether each Class of Non–Tax Priority Claim is impaired or unimpaired.

3. Class of General Unsecured Claims. General unsecured claims are unsecured claims not entitled to priority under Code Section 507(a). These claims are to be treated as follows: Insert Chart Appearing in Disclosure Statement and State Whether the Class of Unsecured Creditors is Impaired or Unimpaired.

4. Class(es) of Equity Interest Holders. The members of this class will be treated as follows:

Insert Chart Appearing in Disclosure Statement and State Whether the Class(es) of Equity Interest Holders are Impaired or Unimpaired.

E. Acceptance or Rejection of Plan. Each impaired class of Creditors with claims against the Debtor's estate shall be entitled to vote separately to accept or reject the Plan. A class of Creditors shall have accepted the Plan if the Plan is accepted by at least two-thirds in the aggregate dollar amount and more than one-half in number of holders of the allowed Claims of such class that have accepted or rejected the Plan. In the event that any impaired class of Creditors or Interest holders shall fail to accept the Plan in accordance with Section 1129(a) of the Bankruptcy Code, the Proponent reserves the right to request that the Bankruptcy Court confirm the Plan in accordance with Section 1129(b) of the Bankruptcy Code.

F. Means of Effectuating the Plan.

1. Funding for the Plan. The Plan will be funded by the following: ____[16].

2. Post–Confirmation Management. ____[17]

3. Disbursing Agent. ____[18] ("Disbursing Agent") shall act as the disbursing agent for the purpose of making all distributions provided for under the Plan. The

Disbursing Agent shall serve _____[19] bond and shall receive _____[20] for distribution services rendered and expenses incurred pursuant to the Plan.

III. TREATMENT OF MISCELLANEOUS ITEMS

A. Executory Contracts and Unexpired Leases.

1. Assumptions. The following are the unexpired leases and executory contracts to be assumed as obligations of the reorganized Debtor under this Plan:

[*Insert*]

On the Effective Date, each of the unexpired leases and executory contracts listed above shall be assumed as obligations of the reorganized Debtor. The Order of the Court confirming the Plan shall constitute an Order approving the assumption of each lease and contract listed above. If you are a party to a lease or contract to be assumed and you object to the assumption of your lease or contract, you must file and serve your objection to the Plan within the deadline for objecting to the confirmation of the Plan.

2. Rejections. On the Effective Date, all executory contracts not assumed shall be deemed to be rejected.

The order confirming the Plan shall constitute an order approving the rejection of the lease or contract. If you are a party to a contract or lease to be rejected and you object to the rejection of your contract or lease, you must file and serve your objection to the Plan within the deadline for objecting to the confirmation of the Plan. See Disclosure Statement for the specific date.

THE BAR DATE FOR FILING A PROOF OF CLAIM BASED ON A CLAIM ARISING FROM THE REJECTION OF A LEASE OR CONTRACT IS _____[21].

Any claim based on the rejection of an executory contract or unexpired lease will be barred if the proof of claim is not timely filed, unless the Court later orders otherwise.

B. Changes in Rates Subject to Regulatory Commission Approval. This Debtor _____[22] subject to governmental regulatory commission approval of its rates.

C. Retention of Jurisdiction. The Court shall retain jurisdiction of this case pursuant to the provisions of Chapter 11 of the Bankruptcy Code, pending the final allowance or disallowance of all Claims affected by the Plan, and to make such orders as are necessary or appropriate to carry out the provisions of this Plan.

In addition, the Court shall retain jurisdiction to implement the provisions of the Plan in the manner as provided under Section 1142, sub-paragraphs (a) and (b) of the Bankruptcy Code. If the Court abstains from exercising, or declines to exercise jurisdiction, or is otherwise without jurisdiction over any matter set forth in this Section, or if the Debtor or the reorganized debtor elect to bring an action or proceeding in any other forum, then this Section shall have no effect upon and shall not control, prohibit or limit the exercise of jurisdiction by any other court, public authority or commission having competent jurisdiction over such matters.

D. Procedures for Resolving Contested Claims. Objections to Claims and interests, except for those Claims more specifically deemed Allowed in the Plan, may be filed by the reorganized debtor or any party in interest up to and including sixty (60) days following the entry of the Confirmation Order. With respect to disputed Claims or interests, the Disbursing Agent will hold in a separate interest bearing reserve account such funds as would be necessary in order to make the required distribution on the Claim or interest, as listed either in the Debtor's schedules or the filed proof(s) of claim.

E. Notices under the Plan. All notices, requests or demands with respect to this Plan shall be in writing and shall be deemed to have been received within five (5) days of the date of mailing, provided they are sent by registered mail or certified mail, postage prepaid, return receipt requested, and if sent to the Proponent, addressed to: _____[23]

IV. EFFECT OF CONFIRMATION OF PLAN

A. Discharge. This Plan provides that upon confirmation of the Plan, Debtor shall be discharged of liability for payment of debts incurred before Confirmation, to the extent specified in 11 U.S.C.§ 1141. However, any liability imposed by the Plan will not be discharged. If Confirmation of this Plan does not occur, the Plan shall be deemed null and void. In such event, nothing contained in this Plan shall be deemed to constitute a waiver or release of any claims against the Debtor or its estate or any other persons, or to prejudice in any manner the rights of the Debtor or its estate or any person in any further proceeding involving the Debtor or its estate. The provisions of this Plan shall be binding upon Debtor, all Creditors and all Equity Interest Holders, regardless of whether such Claims or Equity Interest Holders are impaired or whether such parties accept this Plan, upon Confirmation thereof.

B. Revesting of Property in the Debtor. Except as provided in Section IV.D. hereinafter, and except as provided elsewhere in the Plan, the Confirmation revests all of the property of the estate in the Debtor.

C. Modification of Plan. The Proponent of the Plan may modify the Plan at any time before Confirmation. However, the Court may require a new disclosure statement or revoting on the Plan if Proponent modifies the Plan before Confirmation.

The Proponent may also seek to modify the Plan at any time after Confirmation so long as (1) the Plan has not been substantially consummated and (2) the Court authorizes the proposed modification after notice and a hearing.

D. Post–Confirmation Conversion/Dismissal. A creditor or party in interest may bring a motion to convert or dismiss the case under § 1112(b), after the Plan is confirmed, if there is a default in performing under the Plan. If the Court orders the case converted to Chapter 7 after the Plan is confirmed, then all property that had been property of the Chapter 11 estate, and that has not been disbursed pursuant to the Plan, will revest in the Chapter 7 estate, and the automatic stay will be reimposed upon the revested property only to the extent that relief from stay was not previously granted by the Court during this case.

E. Post–Confirmation Quarterly Fees. Quarterly fees pursuant to 28 U.S.C. § 1930(a)(6) continue to be payable to the office of the United States trustee post-confirmation until such time as the case is converted, dismissed, or closed pursuant to a final decree.

Date: _______

Name of Plan Proponent

By: ____________________

[Effective January 2001.]

1 Vicinage in which case is pending (i.e., Newark, Trenton or Camden).

2 Case No. (lead case number in substantively or administratively consolidated cases).

3 Put which version of the Plan this is (i.e., Original, First Modified, Second Modified, etc.). Also note whether it is a plan of reorganization or orderly liquidation.

4 Debtor's name.

5 Petition date.

6 Insert the applicable information, depending on who filed the petition:

A. Debtor's name

B. Names of the petitioning creditors

7 Insert one of the following:

A. a involuntary

B. a voluntary

8 Plan proponent's name.

9 Insert the applicable phrases:

A. liquidating

B. reorganizing

C. combined liquidating and reorganizing

10 Provide a brief summary of how Proponent proposes to fund the Plan.

11 Effective date of the Plan.

12 Name of Debtor.

13 Name of Debtor.

14 Name of Disbursing Agent under the Plan.

15 Name of Plan Proponent.

16 Describe the source of funding for this Plan. Be specific.

17 For each entity who will be involved in post-confirmation management, state or explain he following:

A. Identity

B. Post-confirmation managerial duties

C. Amount of compensation paid pre-petition and to be paid postconfirmation

D. Description of expertise

18 Name and identity of disbursing agent.

19 Select one:

A. with

B. without

20 Explain whether Disbursing Agent will be compensated or reimbursed for services and expenses rendered and incurred in connection with making distributions under the Plan. If Disbursing Agent will compensated or reimbursed, specify the exact amount and the interval of payment.

21 Deadline for filing proof of claim based on claim arising from rejection of contract or lease is fixed by D.N.J. LBR 3003–1(b).

22 Select one:

A. is

B. is not

23 Address and telephone number of attorneys for Plan Proponent.

D.N.J. LOCAL FORM 20. INTERIM ORDER AUTHORIZING USE OF CASH COLLATERAL

UNITED STATES BANKRUPTCY COURT
DISTRICT OF NEW JERSEY
Caption in Compliance with D.N.J. LBR 9004–2(c)

In Re:	Case No.: ______
	Hearing Date: ______
	Judge: ______

INTERIM ORDER AUTHORIZING USE OF CASH COLLATERAL

The relief set forth on the following pages, numbered two (2) through nine (9) is hereby ORDERED.

This matter is before the Court on the motion of ______ (the "Debtor") for authority to use cash collateral on an interim basis pursuant to Bankruptcy Rule 4001(b) and 11 U.S.C. Section 363(c)(2)(B). Notice of the motion together with notice of the preliminary hearing thereon has been given and served by the Debtor to the (1) the United States Trustee, (2) the Debtor's secured creditors, (3) any committee appointed under Section 1102 if one has been appointed, and if not, to the twenty (20) largest unsecured creditors on the Rule 1007(d) list. The Court considered the motion, and after due deliberation and good and sufficient cause appearing for the entry of the within order, it is hereby found:

A. Notice and Hearing. Notice of the motion and order shortening time pursuant to D.N.J. LBR 9013–1(e) and Federal Rule of Bankruptcy Procedure 9006(c) for the preliminary hearing on the Debtor's use of cash collateral has been served in accordance with Section 102(1) of the Bankruptcy Code and Federal Rule of Bankruptcy Procedure 4001(b), [or if by Consent, under Federal Rule of Bankruptcy Procedure 4001(d)] which notice is appropriate in the particular circumstances and is sufficient for all purposes under the Bankruptcy Code and the applicable Bankruptcy Rules in respect to the relief requested.

B. Chapter 11 Filed. Debtor filed its petition under Chapter 11 of the Bankruptcy Code on ______ (the "Petition Date") and is presently operating as a debtor-in-possession in accordance with sections 1107 and 1108 of the Bankruptcy Code.

C. Pre–Petition Debt. ______. [The Secured Creditor] has asserted a secured claim against the Debtor in the approximate principal amount of $______ (the "Pre–Petition Debt") as of the Petition Date.

If consensual: ______ [The Secured Creditor] has, and the Debtor has acknowledged and agreed that [the Secured Creditor] has, as of the Petition Date, a valid and subsisting first lien and security interest in ______, ______, ______, and______ (the "Collateral") securing the Debtor's indebtedness, in the principal amount of $______, together with accrued interest, fees and costs, which indebtedness is not subject to defense, offset or counterclaim of any kind or nature and that said debt is an allowed, fully secured claim under Sections 506(a) and 502 of the Bankruptcy Code. Said determination shall be binding upon the Debtor-in-Possession, but shall not bind any Creditors' Committee or successor-in-interest to the Debtor-in-Possession, who shall have sixty (60) days after appointment to contest the scope, validity, perfection and/or amount of ______ [the Secured Creditor's] claim.

D. Pre–Petition Collateral. The Secured Creditor has made a prima facie showing that it has a properly perfected lien on the Debtor's property (including proceeds) at the commencement of the case, including the Debtor's accounts, inventory and other collateral which is or may result in cash collateral.

[For Revolving Loans:

Further, the Debtor acknowledges that its Pre–Petition loan agreement with ______ [the Secured Creditor] provided for a revolving line of credit subject to the following borrowing formula: ______% of Eligible Accounts Receivable [up to a maximum of $______] plus ______% of Eligible Inventory [up to a maximum of $______] (Eligible Accounts Receivable and Eligible Inventory shall have their respective meanings as defined in the loan documents between ______ [the Secured Creditor] and the Debtor.)]

E. Cash Collateral. "Cash Collateral" as defined by Section 363(a) of the Bankruptcy Code includes post-petition proceeds, products, offspring, rents, or profits of property and the fees, charges, accounts or other payments for the use or occupancy of rooms and other public facilities in hotels, motels, or other lodging properties subject to a security interest as provided in Section 552(b) and as the term "proceeds" is described in UCC Section 9–306.

F. Necessity and Best Interest. The Debtor does not have sufficient unencumbered cash or other assets with which to continue to operate its business in Chapter 11. The Debtor requires immediate authority to use cash collateral as defined herein in order to continue its business operations without interruption toward the objective of formulating an effective plan of reorganization. Debtor's use of cash collateral to the extent and on the terms and conditions set forth herein is necessary to avoid immediate and irreparable harm to the estate pending a final hearing. The amount of cash collateral authorized to be used pending a final hearing or entry of a final order is not to exceed the amounts reflected in the Debtor's budget, annexed hereto as Exhibit A, for the time period from ______ (the Petition Date) through ______ (the "Cash Collateral Budget").

G. Purposes. The Debtor is authorized to use cash collateral to meet the ordinary cash needs of the Debtor (and for such other purposes as may be approved in writing by the Secured Creditor) for the payment of actual expenses of the Debtor necessary to (a) maintain and preserve its assets, and (b) continue operation of its business, including payroll and payroll taxes, and insurance expenses as reflected in the cash collateral budget.

The Court having determined there is a reasonable likelihood that the Debtor will prevail upon the merits at the final hearing of the Motion as required by Section 363(c)(3) of the Bankruptcy Code, and for good cause shown, it is

ORDERED as follows:

1. Use of Cash Collateral. [If applicable: The Secured Creditor consents and] the Debtor is authorized, for the periods and in accordance with the cash collateral budget attached hereto as Exhibit A, to use cash collateral up to the aggregate amount of $______ for the following purposes:

a. maintenance and preservation of its assets:

b. the continued operation of its business, including but not limited to payroll, payroll taxes, employee expenses, and insurance costs:

c. the completion of work-in-process: and

d. the purchase of replacement inventory:

Provided, however, in the event of a Revolving Loan, the Debtor's authorization to use cash collateral shall remain subject to the borrowing ratios set forth in the pre-petition loan agreement between the Debtor and the Secured Creditor, unless otherwise agreed in writing by the Secured Creditor or until further Order of the Court.

2. Adequate Protection. As adequate protection for use of cash collateral, the Secured Creditor is GRANTED:

a. Replacement Lien. A replacement perfected security interest under Section 361(2) of the Bankruptcy Code to the extent the Secured Creditor's cash collateral is used by the Debtor, to the extent and with the same priority in the Debtor's post-petition collateral, and proceeds thereof, that the Secured Creditor held in the Debtor's pre-petition collateral.

b. Statutory Rights Under Section 507(b). To the extent the adequate protection provided for hereby proves insufficient to protect the Secured Creditor's interest in and to the cash collateral, the Secured Creditor shall have a superpriority administrative expense claim, pursuant to Section 507(b) of the Bankruptcy Code, senior to any and all claims against the Debtor under Section 507(a) of the Bankruptcy Code, whether in this proceeding or in any superseding proceeding.

c. Deemed Perfected. The replacement lien and security interest granted herein is automatically deemed perfected upon entry of this Order without the necessity of the Secured Creditor taking possession, filing financing statements, mortgages or other documents. Although not required, upon request by the Secured Creditor, Debtor shall execute and deliver to the Secured Creditor any and all UCC Financing Statements, UCC Continuation Statements, Certificates of Title or other instruments or documents considered by the Secured Creditor to be necessary in order to perfect the security interests and liens in the Debtor's post-petition collateral and proceeds granted by this Order, and the Secured Creditor is authorized to receive, file and record the foregoing at the Secured Creditor's own expense, which actions shall not be deemed a violation of the automatic stay.

d. Periodic Accountings. Within fifteen (15) days of the entry of this Order, the Debtor shall provide______ (weekly) (monthly) periodic accountings to the Secured Creditor setting forth the cash receipts and disbursements made by the Debtor under this Order. In addition, the Debtor shall provide the Secured Creditor all other reports required by the prepetition loan documents and any other reports reasonably required by the Secured Creditor, as well as copies of the Debtor's monthly United States Trustee operating reports. Upon appointment of a Creditor's Committee, the Debtor shall submit a copy of the monthly U.S. Trustee operating reports to counsel to said Committee if counsel has been appointed, and until counsel is retained, to the Chairman of said Committee.

e. Default Hearing. In the event Debtor defaults or violates this Order, the Secured Creditor is entitled to request a hearing within ten (10) days (or if immediate and irreparable injury, loss or damage may occur, an emergency hearing within 48 hours).

3. **Creditor's Rights of Inspection and Audit.** Upon reasonable notice by the Secured Creditor, Debtor shall permit such creditor and any of its agents reasonable and free access to the Debtor's records and place of business during normal business hours to verify the existence, condition and location of collateral in which said creditor holds a security interest and to audit Debtor's cash receipts and disbursements.

4. **Interlocutory Order and No Modification of Creditor's Adequate Protection.** This is an interlocutory order. Nothing contained herein shall be deemed or construed to (a) limit the Secured Creditor to the relief granted herein: (b) bar the Secured Creditor from seeking other and further relief (including without limitation relief from the terms of this Order) for cause shown on appropriate notice to the Debtor and other parties-in-interest entitled to notice of same: or (c) require the Secured Creditor to make any further loans or advances to the Debtor. The Order may be modified for cause shown by the Debtor, the Secured Creditor or any other party-in-interest on due notice. No such modification, however, shall deprive the Secured Creditor of its interest in Debtor's property (pre-petition and post-petition).

FINAL HEARING ORDER

IT IS FURTHER ORDERED, AND NOTICE IS HEREBY GIVEN

That any creditor or other interested party having any objection to this Interim Order shall file with the Clerk of this Court and serve upon counsel for the Debtor on or before the ______ day of ______ of ______ [year], at ______, a written objection and shall appear to advocate said objection at a Final Hearing to be held at ______. m. on the ______ day of ______ [year] in Courtroom ______ of the United States Bankruptcy Court, ______, New Jersey. In the event no objections are filed or not advocated at such hearing, then this Order shall continue in full force and effect and shall be deemed a Final Order without further notice or hearing in accordance with Federal Rules of Bankruptcy Procedure 4001(d)(3).

NOTICE ORDER

IT IS FURTHER ORDERED that the Debtor serve a copy of this Order and Notice by first class mail within one (1) business day from the date hereof, on (1) the

United States Trustee, (2) the District Director of the Internal Revenue Service, (3) the New Jersey Division of Taxation, (4) all known secured creditors and (5) counsel to any committee appointed under Section 1102 of the Bankruptcy Code, if one has been appointed and if not, to Debtor's twenty (20) largest Rule 1007(d) unsecured creditors. Debtor shall immediately file with the Clerk a Certificate of Service of said mailing.

Approved in Advance:

____

Debtor:______

____

Secured Creditor:_______

____

[Revised May 23, 2002.]

D.N.J. LOCAL FORM 21. REAFFIRMATION AGREEMENT

UNITED STATES BANKRUPTCY COURT
FOR THE DISTRICT OF NEW JERSEY

____

Debtor's Name Bankruptcy Case No.

____

Chapter 7

Creditor's Name and Address

____

____

Instructions: 1) Attach a copy of all court judgments, security agreements, and evidence of their perfection.
2) File all the documents by mailing them or delivering them to the Clerk of the Bankruptcy Court.

NOTICE TO DEBTOR:

Under this agreement, you will remain liable to pay this debt. This debt will no longer be included in the debts discharged by your bankruptcy filing.

As a result of this agreement, the creditor may be able to take your property or wages if you do not pay the agreed amounts. The creditor may also act to collect the debt in other ways.

***You may rescind (cancel) this agreement at any time before the bankruptcy court enters a discharge order or within 60 days after this agreement is filed with the court, whichever is later,* by notifying the creditor IN WRITING that the agreement is canceled.**

You are not required to enter into this agreement by any law. It is not required by the Bankruptcy Code, by any other law, or by any contract (except another reaffirmation agreement made in accordance with Bankruptcy Code § 524(c)).

You do not have to sign this agreement in order to voluntarily repay this debt. If you choose to voluntarily repay this debt without signing this agreement, and you are later unwilling or unable to pay the full amount of the debt, the creditor will not be able to collect the debt from you. The creditor also will not be allowed to take your property to pay the debt unless the creditor has a valid lien on that property.

If the creditor has a lien on your personal property, you may have a right to redeem the property and eliminate the lien by making a single payment to the creditor equal to the current value of the property, as agreed by the parties or determined by the court.

This agreement is not valid or binding unless it is filed with clerk of the bankruptcy court. If you were not represented by an attorney during the negotiation of this reaffirmation agreement, the agreement cannot be enforced by the creditor unless 1) you have attended a reaffirmation hearing in the bankruptcy court, and 2) the agreement has been approved by the bankruptcy court. (Court approval is not required if this is a consumer debt secured by a mortgage or other lien on your real estate.)

REAFFIRMATION AGREEMENT

The debtor and creditor named above agree to reaffirm the debt described in this agreement as follows.

THE DEBT

Total Amount of Debt When Case was Filed	$________
Total Amount of Debt Reaffirmed	$________
Above total includes the following:	
Interest Accrued to Date: ________	$________
Attorney Fees	$________
Late Fees	$________
Other Expenses or Costs Relating to the Collection of this Debt: ________________	$________
Credit for payment(s) made	$________ cr
Annual Percentage Rate (APR)	________ %
Amount of Monthly Payment	$________
Date Payments Start	________
Total Number of Payments to be made (Estimated)	________
Total of Payments if paid according to schedule (Estimated)	$________
Date Any Lien is to be Released if paid according to schedule	________

The debtor agrees that any and all remedies available to the creditor under the security agreement remain available.

All additional Terms Agreed to by the Parties (if any):

____

____

Payments on this debt [were] [were not] in default on the date on which this bankruptcy case was filed.

This agreement differs from the original agreement with the creditor as follows:

____

____

CREDITOR'S STATEMENT CONCERNING AGREEMENT AND SECURITY/ COLLATERAL (IF ANY)

Description of Collateral. If applicable, list manufacturer, year and model.

____

____

Value $________

Basis or Source for Valuation ______________________

If a mortgage, designate position of mortgage (i.e., first, second, etc.) and estimated amount of any other liens ______________________

Check Applicable Boxes:

[ ] Any lien described herein is valid and perfected.

[ ] This agreement is part of a settlement of a dispute regarding the dischargeability of this debt under section 523 of the Bankruptcy Code (11 U.S.C. § 523) or any other dispute. The nature of this dispute is ______________________

DEBTOR'S STATEMENT OF EFFECT OF AGREEMENT ON DEBTOR'S FINANCES

My Monthly Income (take home pay plus any other income received) is $______.

My current monthly expenses total $______, not including any payment due under this agreement or any debt to be discharged in this bankruptcy case.

I believe this agreement [will] [will not] impose an undue hardship on me or my dependents.

Current Location and Use of Collateral ______________________

Estimated Amount Due on Any Prior Liens ______________________

Expected Future Use of Collateral ______________________

DEBTOR'S STATEMENT CONCERNING DECISION TO REAFFIRM

I agreed to reaffirm this debt because

____

____

I believe this agreement is in my best interest because

____

____

I [considered] [did not consider] redeeming the collateral under section 722 of the Bankruptcy Code (11 U.S.C. § 722). I chose not to redeem because

____

____

I [was] [was not] represented by an attorney during negotiations on this agreement.

CERTIFICATION OF ATTACHMENTS

Any documents which created and perfected the security interest or lien [are] [are not] attached. [*If documents are not attached:* The documents which created and perfected the security interest or lien are not attached because

____

____

SIGNATURES

_______________________ (Signature of Debtor)	_______________________ (Name of Creditor)
Date ________	_______________________ (Signature of Creditor Representative)
_______________________ (Signature of Joint Debtor)	Date ________
Date ________	

CERTIFICATION BY DEBTOR'S ATTORNEY (IF ANY)

I hereby certify that 1) this agreement represents a fully informed and voluntary agreement by the debtor(s); 2) this agreement does not impose a hardship on the debtor or any dependent of the debtor; and 3) I have fully advised the debtor of the legal effect and consequences of this agreement and any default under this agreement.

____
(Signature of Debtor's Attorney, if any) Date

D.N.J. LOCAL FORM 22. CHAPTER 13 PLAN TRANSMITTAL LETTER

CHAPTER 13 PLAN TRANSMITTAL LETTER

Second Notice to Creditors affected by Motions in Chapter 13 Plans:

You should have previously received from the court a copy of the plan proposed by the Debtor and a Notice of the Hearing on Confirmation.

The enclosed plan is a copy of the one sent to you by the court. It has been served upon you again because **the plan contains motions that may affect your interest adversely.** All forms of relief sought by motion appear in Article 6 of the plan.

The Confirmation Hearing has been scheduled for ____________. **Objections** to any relief sought in the plan, including relief sought by motion, **must be filed seven days prior to the Confirmation Hearing.**

YOU SHOULD CONSULT WITH YOUR ATTORNEY PROMPTLY, SINCE ENTRY OF AN ORDER OF CONFIRMATION WILL BIND YOU TO ALL OF THE TERMS OF THE CONFIRMED PLAN

February 14, 2003.

D.N.J. LOCAL FORM 23. CHAPTER 13 DEBTOR'S CERTIFICATION IN OPPOSITION TO CREDITOR'S MOTION OR CERTIFICATION OF DEFAULT

UNITED STATES BANKRUPTCY COURT
DISTRICT OF NEW JERSEY

Caption in Compliance with D.N.J. LBR 9004–2(c)

In Re:	Case No.: ________
	Judge: ________
	Chapter: 13

CHAPTER 13 DEBTOR'S CERTIFICATION IN OPPOSITION TO
☐ CREDITOR'S MOTION or CERTIFICATION OF DEFAULT
☐ TRUSTEE'S MOTION or CERTIFICATION OF DEFAULT

The debtor in the above-captioned chapter 13 proceeding hereby objects to the following **(choose one)**:

1. ☐ Motion for Relief from the Automatic Stay filed by ________, creditor. A hearing has been scheduled for ________, at ________ __ m.

OR

☐ Motion to Dismiss filed by the Standing Chapter 13 Trustee. A hearing has been scheduled for ________, at ________ __ m.

☐ Certification of Default filed by ________, creditor. I am requesting a hearing be scheduled on this matter.

OR

☐ Certification of Default filed by Standing Chapter 13 Trustee. I am requesting a hearing be scheduled on this matter.

2. I am objecting to the above for the following reasons **(choose one)**:

☐ Payments have been made in the amount of $ _____, but have not been accounted for. Documentation in support is attached hereto.

☐ Payments have not been made for the following reasons and debtor proposes repayment as follows **(explain your answer)**: ____________________

____

____

☐ Other **(explain your answer)**: ____________________

____

____

3. This certification is being made in an effort to resolve the issues raised by the creditor in its motion.

4. I certify under penalty of perjury that the foregoing is true and correct.

Date: ________________ ________________
Debtor's Signature

Date: ________________ ________________
Debtor's Signature

NOTE:

1. This form must be filed with the court and served upon the Standing Chapter 13 Trustee and creditor at least seven (7) days before the return date pursuant to DNJ LBR 9013–1(d), if filed in opposition to a *Motion for Relief from the Automatic Stay or Trustee's Motion to Dismiss.*

2. This form must be filed with the court and served upon the Standing Chapter 13 Trustee and creditor within ten (10) days of the filing of a *Creditor's Certification of Default* (under an *Order Resolving Motion to Vacate Stay and/or Dismiss with Conditions) or a Trustee's Certification of Default.*

If this form is not filed the Motion or Certification of Default will be deemed uncontested and no hearing will be scheduled.

[January 1, 2005; Revised effective June 1, 2006; June 20, 2006.]

D.N.J. LOCAL FORM 24. REQUEST FOR PAYMENT OF ADMINISTRATIVE EXPENSE

D.N.J. LOCAL FORM 24

UNITED STATES BANKRUPTCY COURT
DISTRICT OF NEW JERSEY

REQUEST FOR PAYMENT OF ADMINISTRATIVE EXPENSE

In re

Chapter 11

Case Number

NOTE: This form should not be used for an unsecured claim arising prior to the commencement of the case. In such cases, a proof of claim should be filed in accordance with Official Form 10.

Name of Creditor
(The person or other entity to whom the debtor owed money or property.)

☐ Check box if you are aware that anyone else has filed a proof of claim relating to your claim. Attach copy of statement giving particulars.

Name and Address Where Notices Should Be Sent:

☐ Check box if you have never received any notices from the bankruptcy court in this case.

☐ Check box if the address differs from the address on the envelope sent to you by the court.

THIS SPACE IS FOR COURT USE ONLY

ACCOUNT OR OTHER NUMBER BY WHICH CREDITOR IDENTIFIES DEBTOR:

Check here is this request:
☐ replaces a previously filed request, dated:
☐ amends a previously filed request, dated:

1. BASIS FOR CLAIM
☐ Goods Sold
☐ Services performed
☐ Money loaned
☐ Personal injury/wrongful death
☐ Taxes
☐ Other (Describe briefly)

☐ Retiree benefits as defined in 11 U.S.C. § 114(a)
☐ Wages, salaries and compensations (Fill out below)

Provide last four digits of your social security number ______

2. DATE DEBT WAS INCURRED:

3. TOTAL AMOUNT OF REQUEST AS OF ABOVE DATE:

______

☐ Check this box if the request includes interest or other charges in addition to the principal amount of the request. Attach itemized statement of all interest or additional charges.

4. Secured Claim
☐ Check this box if your claim is secured by collateral (including a right of setoff).
Brief Descriptions of Collateral:

☐ Real Estate ☐ Motor Vehicle
☐ Other (Describe briefly) ______
Value of Collateral: $______

☐ Check this box if there is no collateral or lien securing your claim.

5. **Credits:** The amount of all payments have been credited and deducted for the purposes of making this request for payment of administrative expenses.

THIS SPACE IS FOR COURT USE ONLY

6. **Supporting Documents:** *Attach copies of supporting documents*, such as purchase orders, invoices, itemized statements of running accounts, contracts as well as any evidence of perfection of a lien.

DO NOT SEND ORIGINAL DOCUMENTS. If the documents are not available, explain. If the documents are voluminous, attach a summary.

7. **Date-Stamped Copy:** To receive an acknowledgment of the filing of your request, enclose a self-addressed envelope and copy of this request.

Date: **Sign and print below the name and title, if any, of the creditor or other person authorized to file this request (attach copy of power of attorney, if any).**

____

Penalty for presenting fraudulent claim: Fine of up to $500,000 or imprisonment for up to 5 years, or both. 18 U.S.C. § 152 and 3571.

NOTE: The filing of this request will not result in the scheduling of a hearing to consider payment of your administrative claim but will result in the registry of your administrative claim with the Bankruptcy Court. If you wish to have a hearing scheduled on your claim, you must file a motion in accordance with Bankruptcy Rule 9013.

Local Form 24, new. 8/1/06.jml

Effective September 16, 2006.

CHAPTER 11 CASES

GENERAL ORDER ADOPTING GUIDELINES FOR FINANCING REQUESTS

UPON CONSIDERATION of the recommendations of the Chapter 11 Subcommittee of the Lawyers' Advisory Committee of the Bankruptcy Court for the District of New Jersey, the Court finds a need to implement policies and procedures to better serve the bench, bar and public in Chapter 11 cases. Accordingly, by resolution of the Board of Judges of the United States Bankruptcy Court for the District of New Jersey,

IT IS ORDERED that the Guidelines For Financing Requests attached hereto as Exhibit A are hereby ADOPTED; and

IT IS FURTHER ORDERED that

1. The Court reserves the right to modify the provisions of this General Order to accommodate the needs of a Chapter 11 case before it; and

2. The Exhibits/Standard Forms and Orders referenced in this General Order may be revised by the Court at any time on an individual basis without the need to further amend this General Order; and

IT IS FURTHER ORDERED that this Order shall apply to Chapter 11 cases pending on the date of this Order.

[Dated: March 31, 2003.]

EXHIBIT A. GUIDELINES FOR FINANCING REQUESTS

The purpose of this document is to establish guidelines for cash collateral and financing requests under §§ 363 and 364 of the Bankruptcy Code in the United States Bankruptcy Court for the District of New Jersey (the "Court"). Although it is recognized that each case is different, the following guidelines are designed to help practitioners identify common material issues that typically are of concern to the Court (at least on the first day of a case and/or where there is limited notice), and to highlight such matters so that, among other things, determinations can be made, if necessary, on an expedited basis.

Substantively, these guidelines do not purport to establish rules that cannot be varied, but they do require disclosure of the "Extraordinary Provisions," discussed below, that ordinarily will not be approved in interim orders without substantial cause shown, compelling circumstances and reasonable notice.

It will be evident that many of the following guidelines are designed to deal with debtor in possession financing requests documented with a loan agreement and (for want of a better term) a long-form financing order. However, the Court would welcome the use of simplified orders, whenever possible, particularly in smaller cases and in connection with the debtor's use of cash collateral not involving the extension of new funds.

These guidelines are intended to supplement the requirements of §§ 363 and 364 of the Bankruptcy Code and Fed. R. Bankr. P. 4001(b) and (c).

I. MOTIONS.

A. MOTION CONTENT.

1. *Single Motion.*

(a) A single motion may be filed seeking entry of an interim order and a final order, which orders would be normally entered at the conclusion of the preliminary hearing and the final hearing, respectively, as those terms are used in Fed. R. Bankr. P. 4001(b)(2) and (c)(2). In addition, where circumstances warrant, the debtor may seek emergency relief for financing limited to the amount necessary to avoid immediate and irreparable harm to the estate pending the preliminary hearing, but in the usual case, only a preliminary and a final hearing will be required.

(b) If the financing is to be extended pursuant to a loan agreement or similar agreement ("Agreement"), the Agreement should be attached to the motion.

(c) The motion should also include a copy of any proposed order for which entry is sought.

(d) Motions must be double-spaced and in form that complies with all applicable rules of the Court.

(e) All such motions must be supported by an affidavit.

2. *Description of Use of Cash Collateral or the Material Provisions of DIP Financing.* The motion should ordinarily contain the following disclosure relative to the use of cash collateral or the financing, either in the text of the motion or in an attached term sheet:

(a) Amount of cash to be used or borrowed, including (if applicable) committed amount, maximum borrowings (if less), any borrowing base formula, availability under the formula, and the purpose of the borrowing;

(b) Material conditions to closing and borrowing, including any budget provisions;

(c) Pricing and economic terms, including interest rates, letter of credit fees, commitment fees, any other fees, and the treatment of costs and expenses of the lender (and its professionals);

(d) Collateral or adequate protection provided to the lender and any priority or superpriority provisions, including the effect thereof on existing liens, and any carve-outs from liens or super-priorities;

(e) Maturity, termination and default provisions, including events of default, effect on the automatic stay and any cross-default provisions; and

(f) Any other material provisions, including any Extraordinary Provisions, as defined in Section II(A), any provisions relating to change of control, and key covenants.

3. *Adequacy of Budget.* Any motion for new financing or use of cash collateral must also include disclosure by the debtor as to whether it has reason to believe that, after diligent consideration of all known circumstances, in its reasonable business judgment, that the budget is achievable and will allow the debtor to operate in Chapter 11 without the accrual of unpaid liabilities.

4. *Extraordinary Provisions.* The motion must disclose prominently whether the financing includes any of the Extraordinary Provisions set forth in Section II(A) of these guidelines, and any accompanying order must also set forth these provisions prominently and conspicuously.

5. *Efforts to Obtain Financing.* The motion should describe in general terms the debtor's efforts to obtain financing, the basis on which the debtor determined that the proposed financing was on the best terms available, and material facts bearing on the issue of whether the extension of credit is being extended in good faith.

6. *Emergency Applications.* A motion that seeks entry of an Emergency Order or Interim Order should also describe the amount and purpose of funds sought to be borrowed on an emergency or interim basis and set forth facts to support a finding that immediate or irreparable harm will be caused to the estate if immediate financing is not obtained at a preliminary hearing or on an emergency basis.

B. NOTICE.

7. Notice of the hearing on (i) the Interim and (ii) the Final Order shall be given to the persons required by Fed. R. Bankr. P. 4001(b)(3) and 4001(c)(3), as the case

may be, the United States Trustee and any other persons whose interests may be directly affected by the outcome of the motion or any provision of the proposed order. Notwithstanding the foregoing, emergency and interim relief may be entered after the best notice available under the circumstances; however, emergency and interim relief will not be considered unless the United States Trustee and the Court have had a reasonable opportunity to review the motion, the financing agreement, and the proposed interim order, and the Court normally will not approve provisions that directly affect the interests of landlords, taxing and environmental authorities and other third-parties without notice to them.

8. Prospective debtors may provide substantially complete drafts of the motion, interim order, and related financing documents to the Office of the United States Trustee in advance of a filing, and the United States Trustee will hold such documents in confidence and without prejudice to the prospective debtor, and attempt to comment on such documents on or shortly after the filing. Debtors are strongly encouraged to provide drafts of financing requests, including proposed orders, to the United States Trustee as early as possible in advance of filing and preferably 24 hours in advance of the hearing.

9. The hearing on a Final Order will not commence earlier than fifteen (15) days after service of the motion, in accordance with Fed. R. Bankr. P. 4001(b)(2) and 4001(c)(2), and ordinarily will not commence until there has been a reasonable opportunity for the formation of a creditors committee under § 1102 of the Bankruptcy Code and either the creditors committee's appointment of counsel or reasonable opportunity to do so.

C. PRESENCE AT HEARING. Except as otherwise ordered by the Court:

10. Counsel for the postpetition lender (or the entity whose cash collateral is to be consensually used) must be present at any hearing with respect to its financing or its collateral; and

11. A business representative of the debtor and lender and any party objecting to the financing, each with appropriate authority, must be reasonably available by telephone or present at the hearing for the purpose of making necessary decisions.

II. ORDERS

A. EXTRAORDINARY PROVISIONS. The following provisions in a cash collateral or DIP financing order, or in a financing agreement to be approved under such an order, called "Extraordinary Provisions," must be disclosed conspicuously in the motion and order and justification therefor separately set forth:

1. *Cross-Collateralization.* Extraordinary Provisions include all provisions that elevate prepetition debt to administrative expense (or higher) status or secure prepetition debt with liens on postpetition assets that such debt would not have by virtue of the prepetition security agreement or applicable law (for the purposes of these Guidelines, "Cross–Collateralization"), unless such status and liens are limited in extent to that necessary to accord the prepetition lender in a reorganization case adequate protection against a decline in the value of its collateral during the postpetition period. In connection with a request for Cross–Collateralization, the Court will consider, among other factors:

(a) The extent of the notice provided;

(b) The terms of the DIP financing and a comparison to the terms that would be available absent the Cross–Collateralization;

(c) The degree of consensus among parties in interest supportive of Cross–Collateralization;

(d) The extent and value of the prepetition liens held by the prepetition lender (and in particular the amount of any "equity cushion" that the prepetition lender may have); and

(e) Whether Cross–Collateralization will give an undue advantage to prepetition lenders without a countervailing benefit to the estate.

An order approving Cross–Collateralization must ordinarily reserve the right of the Court to unwind the postpetition protection provided to the prepetition lender in the event that there is a timely and successful challenge to the validity, enforceability, extent, perfection, and (where appropriate) priority of the prepetition lender's claims or liens, or a determination that the prepetition debt was undersecured as of the petition date, and the Cross–Collateralization unduly advantaged the lender.

2. *"Rollups"*. Rollups include the application of proceeds of postpetition financing to pay, in whole or in part, prepetition debt. Determination of the propriety of a rollup will normally take into account, to the extent applicable, the factors mentioned above in connection with Cross-Collateralization, and, in addition, the following:

(a) The nature and amount of new credit to be extended, beyond the application of proceeds of postpetition financing used to pay in whole or in part the prepetition debt;

(b) Whether the advantages of the postpetition financing justify the loss to the estate of the opportunity to satisfy the prepetition secured debt otherwise in accordance with applicable provisions of the Bankruptcy Code, and the burdens on the estate of incurring an administrative claim;

(c) Whether the rollup can be unwound (see below);

(d) Availability under the terms of the DIP financing and a comparison to the terms that would be available in the absence of the rollup;

(e) The extent to which prepetition and postpetition collateral can, as a practical matter, be identified and/or segregated;

(f) The extent to which difficult "priming" issues would have to be addressed in the absence of a rollup; and

(g) Whether the postpetition advances are used to repay a prebankruptcy, "emergency" liquidity facility secured by first priority liens on the same collateral as the postpetition financing, where the prepetition facility was provided in anticipation of, or in an effort to avoid, a bankruptcy filing.

An order approving a rollup must ordinarily reserve the right of the Court to unwind the paydown of the prepetition debt in the event that there is a timely and successful challenge to the validity, enforceability, extent, perfection, and (where appropriate) priority of the prepetition lender's claims or liens, or a determination that the prepetition debt was undersecured as of the petition date.

3. *Waivers and Concessions as to Validity of Prepetition Debt.* The Court will not consider as extraordinary the debtor's stipulation as to validity, perfection, enforceability, priority and non-avoidability of a prepetition lender's claim and liens, and the lack of any defense thereto, provided that:

(a) The Official Committee of Unsecured Creditors (the "Committee"), appointed under § 1102 of the Bankruptcy Code, has a minimum of 60 days (or such longer period as the Committee may obtain for cause shown before the expiration of such period) from the date of the order approving the appointment of counsel to the Committee to investigate the facts and bring any appropriate proceedings as representative of the estate; or

(b) If no Committee is appointed, any party in interest has a minimum of 75 days (or a longer period for cause shown before the expiration of such period) from the entry of the final financing order to investigate the facts and file a motion seeking authority to bring any appropriate proceedings as representative of the estate; provided that

(c) The foregoing periods may be shortened in prepackaged or prearranged cases for cause shown.

4. *Waivers.* Extraordinary Provisions include those that divest the Court of its power or discretion in a material way, or interfere with the exercise of the fiduciary duties of the debtor or Creditors Committee in connection with the operation of the

business, administration of the estate, or the formulation of a reorganization plan, such as provisions that deprive the debtor or the Creditors Committee of the ability to file a request for relief with the Court, to grant a junior postpetition lien, or to obtain future use of cash collateral. Notwithstanding the foregoing, and where duly disclosed, it will not be considered "extraordinary" for the debtor to agree to repay the postpetition financing in connection with any plan; for the debtor to waive any right to incur liens that prime or are *pari passu* with liens granted under § 364 of the Bankruptcy Code; and for a financing order to contain reasonable limitations and conditions regarding future borrowings under § 364 of the Bankruptcy Code or cash collateral usage under § 363 of the Bankruptcy Code (including consent of the lender, subordination of future borrowings to the priorities and liens given to the initial lender, and repayment of the initial loan with the proceeds of a subsequent borrowing).

5. *Section 506(c) Waivers.* Extraordinary Provisions include any waiver of the debtor's right to a surcharge against collateral under § 506(c) of the Bankruptcy Code; factors to be considered in connection with any order seeking such a waiver include whether the debtor's rights are (to the extent permitted by law) delegated to the Committee and whether the carve-out includes expenses under § 726(b) of the Bankruptcy Code (see below).

6. *Liens on Avoidance Actions.* Extraordinary Provisions include the granting of liens on the debtor's claims and causes of action arising under §§ 544, 545, 547, 548 and 549 of the Bankruptcy Code (but not liens on recoveries under § 549 on account of collateral as to which the lender has a postpetition lien), and the proceeds thereof, or a superpriority administrative claim payable from the proceeds of such claims and causes of action.

7. *Carve-outs.* Provisions relating to a carve-out that will be considered "extraordinary" include those that provide disparate treatment for the professionals retained by the Committee compared to professionals retained by the debtor or that do not include the fees of the U.S. Trustee, the reasonable expenses of Committee members, and reasonable fees and expenses of a trustee under § 726(b) of the Bankruptcy Code; however, reasonable allocations among such expenses can be proposed, and the lender may refuse to include in a carve-out the costs of litigation against it (but not the costs of investigating whether any claims or causes of action exist). Provisions relating to carve-outs should make clear when the carve-out takes effect (and, in this connection, whether it remains unaltered after payment of interim fees made before an event of default under the facility), and any effect of the carve-out on availability under the postpetition loan.

8. *Termination: Default; Remedies.* Extraordinary Provisions include terms that provide that the use of cash collateral will cease, or the financing agreement will default, on (i) the filing of a challenge to the lender's prepetition lien or to the lender's prepetition conduct; (ii) entry of an order granting relief from the automatic stay (except as to material assets); (iii) the grant of a change of venue with respect to the case or any adversary proceeding; (iv) the making of a motion by a party in interest seeking any relief (as distinct from an order granting such relief); (v) management changes or the departure, from the debtor, of any identified employees; (vi) filing of a plan of reorganization not supported by lender; and (vii) appointment of a trustee or an examiner. Clauses providing a reasonable maturity date for the postpetition debt and for termination of the loan or default of the postpetition debt (if not repaid) on dismissal of the case or on confirmation of a plan of reorganization or on conversion to Chapter 7 will not be considered to be extraordinary. Termination of the postpetition lender's commitment to continue to advance funds after an event of default will not be considered extraordinary, but the following provisions will:

(a) Failure to provide at least five business days' notice to the debtor and the Committee before the automatic stay terminates and the lender's remedies can be enforced; and

(b) Failure to provide at least three business days' notice before use of cash collateral ceases, provided that the use of cash collateral conforms to any budget in effect.

B. INTERIM ORDERS.

9. An Interim Order will not ordinarily bind the Court with respect to the provisions of the Final Order provided that (i) the lender will be afforded all the benefits and protections of the Interim Order, including a DIP lender's §§ 364(e) and 363(m) protection with respect to obligations during the interim period, and (ii) the Interim Order will not bind the lender to advance funds pursuant to a Final Order that contains provisions contrary to or inconsistent with the Interim Order.

C. FORMAL PROVISIONS OF ORDERS.

10. *Findings of Fact.* The Order should limit recitation of findings to essential facts, including the facts required under § 364 of the Bankruptcy Code regarding efforts to obtain financing on a less onerous basis and (where required) facts sufficient to support a finding of good faith under § 364(e) of the Bankruptcy Code. Non-essential facts regarding prepetition dealings and agreements may be included under the rubric of "stipulations" between the debtor and the lender or "background." Any emergency or interim order should include a finding that immediate and irreparable loss or damage will be caused to the estate if immediate DIP financing is not obtained and should state with respect to notice only that the hearing was held pursuant to Fed. R. Bankr. P. 4001(b)(2) or (c)(2), that notice was given to certain parties in the manner described, and that the notice was, in the debtor's belief, the best available under the circumstances. The Final Order may include factual findings as to notice. The Order should not incorporate by reference or refer to specific sections of a pre- or post-petition loan agreement or other document without a statement of the section's import. The Order should not contain any findings or provisions extraneous to the use of cash collateral or to the DIP financing.

11. *Decretal Provisions.* The Order should specify, in particular: any Extraordinary Provisions; any priorities or collateral granted; any effect of the borrowing on pre-existing liens; bankruptcy-specific events of default and the consequences thereof; any provisions relating to adequate protection; any acknowledgments or stipulations by the debtor as to the prepetition debt; the purpose for which the loan is being made, and any restrictions on use of borrowings. The Order may permit the parties to enter into waivers or consents to the DIP loan agreement or amendments thereof provided that (i) the agreement as so modified is not materially different from that approved, (ii) notice of all amendments is filed with the Court, and (iii) notice of all amendments (other than those that are ministerial or technical and do not adversely affect the debtor) are provided in advance to counsel for any Committee, all parties requesting notice, and the U.S. Trustee.

12. *Conclusions of Law.* The Interim Order should not state that the Court has examined and approved the loan or other agreement; it may say, however, that the debtor is authorized to enter into it. Normally, the Interim and Final Orders are sufficient if they state that the debtor is authorized to borrow on the terms and conditions of the loan or other agreement.

13. *Order to Control.* The Order should ordinarily state that to the extent the loan or other agreement differs from the Order, the Order will control.

14. *Statutory Provisions Affected.* The Order should specify those sections of the Bankruptcy Code that are being relied on, and identify those sections that are, to the extent permitted by law, being limited or abridged.

15. *Conclusions Of Law As It Relates To Notice.* The Final Order may contain conclusions of law with respect to the adequacy of notice under § 364 of the Bankruptcy Code and Fed. R. Bankr. P. 4001.

GENERAL ORDER ADOPTING GUIDELINES GOVERNING FIRST DAY MATTERS

UPON CONSIDERATION of the recommendations of the Chapter 11 Subcommittee of the Lawyers' Advisory Committee to the United States Bankruptcy Court For the District of New Jersey, the Court finds a need to implement policies and procedures to better serve the bench, bar and public in Chapter 11 cases. Accordingly, by resolution of the Board of Judges of the United States Bankruptcy Court for the District of New Jersey

IT IS ORDERED that the Guidelines Governing First Day Matters attached hereto as Exhibit A are hereby ADOPTED; and

IT IS FURTHER ORDERED that

1. The Court reserves the right to modify the provisions of this General Order to accommodate the needs of a Chapter 11 case before it; and

2. The Exhibits/Standard Forms and Orders referenced in this General Order may be revised by the Court at any time on an individual basis without the need to further amend this General Order; and

IT IS FURTHER ORDERED that this Order shall apply to Chapter 11 cases pending on the date of this Order.

[Dated: March 31, 2003.]

EXHIBIT A. GUIDELINES GOVERNING FIRST DAY MATTERS

The procedures set forth below concern the submission and entry of first day motions to guide the orderly administration of newly filed Chapter 11 cases throughout the District of New Jersey. This will enable both the Court and practitioners to understand the procedures in advance and ensure that motions and corresponding relief they seek conform to procedures that have been generally approved by the Court. Accordingly, the following guidelines governing first day matters have been approved by the Court.

A. DEFINITION.

1. A "First Day Matter" is defined as a motion filed simultaneously with the Chapter 11 petition which, in the opinion of counsel, requires expedited consideration by the Court within two business days of the filing.

2. *While the relief requested by counsel will be considered by the Court, those First Day Matters which seek extraordinary relief will be granted in the Court's discretion only upon good cause shown.*

B. FILING THE REQUEST.

3. If a debtor in a Chapter 11 case has matters requiring expedited consideration by the Court, it should submit an Application For Expedited Consideration of First Day Matters in the standard form attached hereto as Schedule "1", together with a proposed form of Order Regarding Application For Expedited Consideration Of First Day Matters in the standard form attached hereto as Schedule "2". Counsel shall file their respective pleadings with the Court leaving a blank for the return date.

4. First Day Matters shall be supported by certification(s).

5. The Court shall issue its Order Regarding Application For Expedited Consideration Of First Day Matters and immediately advise Debtor's counsel of same.

C. SERVICE.

6. Counsel for the Debtor shall:

(a) notify by telecopy and serve electronically, if the e-mail address is available, (or by overnight delivery or immediate hand delivery) a copy of the Application For Expedited Consideration and supporting documents, upon all affected parties, including the United States Trustee, simultaneously with filing same with the Court; and

(b) notify by telecopy and serve electronically, if the e-mail address is available (or by overnight delivery or hand delivery) a copy of the Court's Order Regarding Application For Expedited Consideration, upon all affected parties, including the United States Trustee, within one (1) business day, after receipt of said Order.

D. OBJECTIONS/RESPONSES TO FIRST DAY MATTERS.

7. Objection(s) and/or response(s) to First Day Matter(s) may be filed with the Court anytime prior to the hearing(s) on the First Day Matter(s). The Court will also entertain any oral objection(s) and/or response(s) to a First Day Matter(s) at the time of hearing(s).

8. Should a matter for which expedited consideration is requested in the Application For Expedited Consideration Of A First Day Matter(s) is sought and is **not** set down for hearing as a First Day Matter, but yet scheduled for hearing on an expedited basis, it is incumbent upon movant's counsel to inquire from the Court the deadline(s) for filing and serving objection(s) upon all parties in interest of the objection deadline and method by which the Court will entertain objection(s) and/or response(s) in writing to all parties in interest within one (1) business day of the Court's decision as to the objection/response deadline, service of objection/response and the acceptable method of objecting and/or responding to a matter.

E. OTHER ADMINISTRATIVE MATTERS.

9. Should counsel for the Debtor have requested and received an Order Granting Complex Chapter 11 Case Treatment, the provisions of the Court's *General Order Governing Procedures for Complex Chapter 11* cases shall also apply.

SCHEDULE "1"

UNITED STATES BANKRUPTCY COURT
DISTRICT OF NEW JERSEY

IN RE:	:	
	:	CHAPTER 11
	:	
	:	CASE NO. ______
	:	
DEBTOR.	:	JUDGE: ______

APPLICATION FOR EXPEDITED CONSIDERATION OF FIRST DAY MATTERS

On ______, ______ filed a petition for relief under Chapter 11 of the Bankruptcy Code.

Counsel for the Debtor requests that the following relief be provided on a first day basis (check those that apply):

1. ___ MOTION SEEKING THE JOINT ADMINISTRATION OF MULTIPLE DEBTOR BANKRUPTCY CASES.

Requested hearing date and time: ______________________

Brief recitation of the reason why expedited consideration is necessary as set forth in supporting certification: ______________________

____

____

2. ___ MOTION FOR AN ORDER AUTHORIZING THE DEBTOR AN EXTENSION OF TIME WITHIN WHICH TO FILE STATEMENTS AND SCHEDULES.

Requested hearing date and time: ______________________

Brief recitation of the reason why expedited consideration is necessary as set forth in supporting certification: ______________________

____

____

3. ___ MOTION FOR AN ORDER AUTHORIZING THE EMERGENCY OR INTERIM USE OF CASH COLLATERAL OR DEBTOR–IN–POSSESSION FINANCING PENDING THE NOTICING AND SCHEDULING OF AN INTERIM OR FINAL HEARING FOR FINANCING PURSUANT TO BANKRUPTCY CODE §§ 363 AND 364 AND FED. R. BANKR. P. 4001.

Requested hearing date and time: ______________________

Brief recitation of the reason why expedited consideration is necessary as set forth in supporting certification: ______________________

____

____

4. ___ MOTION FOR AN ORDER AUTHORIZING THE DEBTOR TO MAINTAIN EXISTING BANK ACCOUNTS AND BUSINESS FORMS AND CASH MANAGEMENT PROCEDURES PROVIDING THE UNITED STATES TRUSTEE'S OFFICE WITH A 60 DAY PERIOD TO OBJECT TO SAID ORDER BEFORE IT BECOMES A FINAL ORDER.

Requested hearing date and time: ______________________

Brief recitation of the reason why expedited consideration is necessary as set forth in supporting certification: ______________________

____

____

5. ___ MOTION FOR AN ORDER AUTHORIZING A DEBTOR TO MODIFY THE INVESTMENT GUIDELINES SET FORTH IN BANKRUPTCY CODE § 345 ON AN INTERIM BASIS, PROVIDING THE UNITED STATES TRUSTEE'S OFFICE AND ANY OTHER PARTIES–IN–INTEREST A 60–DAY PERIOD TO OBJECT TO SAID ORDER BEFORE IT BECOME A FINAL ORDER.

Requested hearing date and time: ______________________

Brief recitation of the reason why expedited consideration is necessary as set forth in supporting certification: ______________________

____

____

6. ___ MOTION FOR AN ORDER AUTHORIZING THE DEBTOR TO PAY PREPETITION WAGES, SALARIES, COMPENSATION, EMPLOYEE BENEFITS AND REIMBURSABLE BUSINESS EXPENSES UP TO THE LIMITS SET FORTH IN BANKRUPTCY CODE § 507(a).

Requested hearing date and time: ______________________

Brief recitation of the reason why expedited consideration is necessary as set forth in supporting certification: ______________________

____

____

7. ___ MOTION FOR AN ORDER AUTHORIZING THE DEBTOR TO PAY PREPETITION SALES, USE, PAYROLL AND OTHER TAXES THAT ARE OTHERWISE PRIORITY CLAIMS UNDER BANKRUPTCY CODE § 507.

Requested hearing date and time: ______________________

Brief recitation of the reason why expedited consideration is necessary as set forth in supporting certification: ______________________________

8. ___ MOTION FOR AN ORDER AUTHORIZING THE DEBTOR TO CONTINUE CREDIT CARD FACILITIES.

Requested hearing date and time: ______________________________

Brief recitation of the reason why expedited consideration is necessary as set forth in supporting certification: ______________________________

9. ___ MOTION FOR AN ORDER AUTHORIZING THE DEBTOR TO HONOR CERTAIN PRE–PETITION CUSTOMER OBLIGATIONS, DEPOSITS, REBATES, ETC.

Requested hearing date and time: ______________________________

Brief recitation of the reason why expedited consideration is necessary as set forth in supporting certification: ______________________________

10. ___ MOTION FOR AN ORDER AUTHORIZING THE DEBTOR TO CONTINUE WITH AND PAY PRE–PETITION OUTSTANDING AMOUNTS DUE ON VARIOUS INSURANCE POLICIES.

Requested hearing date and time: ______________________________

Brief recitation of the reason why expedited consideration is necessary as set forth in supporting certification: ______________________________

11. ___ MOTION FOR AN ORDER AUTHORIZING PAYMENT OF OUTSTANDING AND UNPAID PRE–PETITION DEBT TO CERTAIN VENDORS WHO PROVIDE CRITICAL AND NECESSARY SERVICES AND/OR PRODUCTS TO THE DEBTOR.

Requested hearing date and time: ______________________________

Brief recitation of the reason why expedited consideration is necessary as set forth in supporting certification: ______________________________

12. ___ MOTION FOR AN ORDER PURSUANT TO BANKRUPTCY CODE § 366 REGARDING ADEQUATE ASSURANCE FOR THE FUTURE PERFORMANCE FOR UTILITIES AND ESTABLISHING PROCEDURES FOR DETERMINING REQUESTS FOR ADDITIONAL ADEQUATE ASSURANCE.

Requested hearing date and time: ______________________________

Brief recitation of the reason why expedited consideration is necessary as set forth in supporting certification: ______________________________

13. ___ MOTION FOR AN ORDER AUTHORIZING THE DEBTOR TO RETAIN A CLAIMS AND NOTICING AGENT.

Requested hearing date and time: ______________________________

Brief recitation of the reason why expedited consideration is necessary as set forth in supporting certification: ______________________________

14. ____ MOTION FOR AN ORDER ESTABLISHING NOTICING PROCEDURES.

Requested hearing date and time: ______________________

Brief recitation of the reason why expedited consideration is necessary as set forth in supporting certification: ______________________

____

____

15. ____ OTHERS [COUNSEL SHOULD ADD ALL OTHER MOTIONS FOR WHICH IT SEEKS CONSIDERATION AS A FIRST DAY MATTER.]

Requested hearing date and time: ______________________

Brief recitation of the reason why expedited consideration is necessary as set forth in supporting certification: ______________________

____

____

__________, 200__

____

Name

____

Address

____

Telephone and Fax numbers

____

E-mail Address

NOTE: Each motion or application for which expedited consideration is requested shall be filed with the Clerk of the U.S. Bankruptcy Court For The District Of New Jersey and served upon the United States Trustee and all affected parties.

SCHEDULE "2"

UNITED STATES BANKRUPTCY COURT
DISTRICT OF NEW JERSEY

IN RE:	:	CHAPTER 11
	:	CASE NO.
DEBTOR.	:	

ORDER REGARDING APPLICATION FOR EXPEDITED CONSIDERATION OF FIRST DAY MATTERS

This bankruptcy case was filed on ______, 200__. An Application For Expedited Consideration Of First Day Matters was filed. After review of the initial pleadings filed in this case which have been designated by counsel as requiring expedited consideration, and for good cause shown;

IT IS HEREBY ORDERED that the following motions are set down for hearing before The Honorable ______ in Courtroom #______ located at ______ at the date and time as set forth below:

	Hearing Date and Time
1. MOTION SEEKING THE JOINT ADMINISTRATION OF MULTIPLE DEBTOR BANKRUPTCY CASES.	______ at ______.M.
2. MOTION FOR AN ORDER AUTHORIZING THE DEBTOR AN EXTENSION OF TIME WITHIN WHICH TO FILE STATEMENTS AND SCHEDULES.	______ at ______.M.
3. MOTION FOR AN ORDER AUTHORIZING THE EMERGENCY USE OF CASH COLLATERAL OR DEBTOR–IN–POSSESSION FINANCING PENDING THE NOTICING AND SCHEDULING OF AN INTERIM HEARING FOR FINANCING PURSUANT TO BANKRUPTCY CODE §§ 363 AND 364 AND FED. R.BANKR.P. 4001.	______ at ______.M.
4. MOTION FOR AN ORDER AUTHORIZING THE DEBTOR TO MAINTAIN EXISTING BANK ACCOUNTS AND BUSINESS FORMS AND CASH MANAGEMENT PROCEDURES PROVIDING THE UNITED STATES TRUSTEE'S OFFICE WITH A 60 DAY PERIOD TO OBJECT TO SAID ORDER BEFORE IT BECOMES A FINAL ORDER.	______ at ______.M.
5. MOTION FOR AN ORDER AUTHORIZING A DEBTOR TO MODIFY THE INVESTMENT GUIDELINES SET FORTH IN BANKRUPTCY CODE § 345 ON AN INTERIM BASIS, PROVIDING THE UNITED STATES TRUSTEE'S OFFICE AND ANY OTHER PARTIES–IN–INTEREST A 60–DAY PERIOD TO OBJECT TO SAID ORDER BEFORE IT BECOMES A FINAL ORDER.	______ at ______.M.
6. MOTION FOR AN ORDER AUTHORIZING THE DEBTOR TO PAY PRE–PETITION WAGES, SALARIES, COMPENSATION, EMPLOYEE BENEFITS AND REIMBURSABLE BUSINESS EXPENSES UP TO THE LIMITS SET FORTH IN BANKRUPTCY CODE § 507(a).	______ at ______.M.
7. MOTION FOR AN ORDER AUTHORIZING THE DEBTOR TO PAY PRE–PETITION SALES, USE PAYROLL AND OTHER TAXES THAT ARE OTHERWISE PRIORITY CLAIMS UNDER BANKRUPTCY CODE § 507.	______ at ______.M.

8. MOTION FOR AN ORDER AUTHORIZING THE DEBTOR TO CONTINUE CREDIT CARD FACILITIES. ______ at ______.M.

9. MOTION FOR AN ORDER AUTHORIZING THE DEBTOR TO HONOR CERTAIN PRE–PETITION CUSTOMER OBLIGATIONS, DEPOSITS, REBATES, ETC. ______ at ______.M.

10. MOTION FOR AN ORDER AUTHORIZING THE DEBTOR TO CONTINUE WITH AND PAY PRE–PETITION OUTSTANDING AMOUNTS DUE ON VARIOUS INSURANCE POLICIES. ______ at ______.M.

11. MOTION FOR AN ORDER AUTHORIZING PAYMENT OF OUTSTANDING AND UNPAID PRE–PETITION DEBT TO CERTAIN VENDORS WHO PROVIDE CRITICAL AND NECESSARY SERVICES AND/OR PRODUCTS TO THE DEBTOR. ______ at ______.M.

12. MOTION FOR AN ORDER PURSUANT TO BANKRUPTCY CODE § 366 REGARDING ADEQUATE ASSURANCE FOR THE FUTURE PERFORMANCE FOR UTILITIES AND ESTABLISHING PROCEDURES FOR DETERMINING REQUESTS FOR ADDITIONAL ADEQUATE ASSURANCE. ______ at ______.M.

13. MOTION FOR AN ORDER AUTHORIZING THE DEBTOR TO RETAIN A CLAIMS AND NOTICING AGENT. ______ at ______.M.

14. MOTION FOR AN ORDER ESTABLISHING NOTICING PROCEDURES. ______ at ______.M.

15. ***OTHERS [COUNSEL SHOULD ADD ALL OTHER MOTIONS FOR WHICH IT SEEKS CONSIDERATION AS FIRST DAY MATTERS AS SET FORTH IN THE UNDERLYING REQUEST.]*** ______ at ______.M.

IT IS FURTHER ORDERED, that Service of the within Order shall be made in accordance with the Court's *General Order Adopting Guidelines Governing First Day Matters*; and

IT IS FURTHER ORDERED, that objections and/or responses to First Day Matters, if any, shall be made in accordance with the Court's *General Order Adopting Guidelines Governing First Day Matters.*

Dated:________

____
United States Bankruptcy Judge
District of New Jersey

GENERAL ORDER GOVERNING PROCEDURES FOR COMPLEX CHAPTER 11 CASES

UPON CONSIDERATION of the recommendations of the Chapter 11 Subcommittee of the Lawyers' Advisory Committee to the United States Bankruptcy Court for the District of New Jersey, the Court finds a need to implement policies and procedures to better serve the bench, bar and public in complex Chapter 11 cases, as hereinafter defined. Accordingly, by resolution of the Board of Judges of the United States Bankruptcy Court for the District of New Jersey

IT IS ORDERED that the following procedures shall be implemented in Complex Chapter 11 cases.

1. A "Complex Chapter 11 Case" is defined as a case pending in the District of New Jersey under Chapter 11 of the Bankruptcy Code that requires special scheduling and other procedures because of the existence of one or more of the following factors:

a. The size of the case in terms of assets, liabilities or number of creditors and/or parties in interest;

b. The fact that claims against the debtor and/or equity interests in the debtor are publicly traded; or

c. The case, for reasons satisfactory to the Court, would be more efficiently administered as a Complex Chapter 11 Case.

2. If a party filing a Chapter 11 bankruptcy petition believes that the case should be classified as a Complex Chapter 11 Case, the party shall file with the Chapter 11 petition, an Application For Designation As Complex Chapter 11 Case in the standard form attached hereto as Exhibit A.

3. If a party submitting an Application For Designation As Complex Chapter 11 Case has matters requiring expedited consideration by the Court, it should simultaneously submit an Application For Expedited Consideration Of First Day Matters in the standard form attached hereto as Exhibit B in accordance with the General Order Adopting Guidelines Governing First Day Matters.

4. The Court shall proceed as follows:

a. If the Court determines that the case does not qualify as a Complex Chapter 11 Case, issue an Order Denying Complex Chapter 11 Case Treatment in the standard order form attached hereto as Exhibit C; or

b. If the Court determines that the case appears to be a Complex Chapter 11 Case, issue an Order Granting Complex Chapter 11 Case Treatment in the standard order form attached hereto as Exhibit D; and

c. Issue an Order Regarding Application For Expedited Consideration Of The First Day Matters in the standard order form attached hereto as Exhibit E; and

d. Immediately notify and serve counsel for the Debtor with the Order entered by the Court relating to the complex case treatment; and

e. Immediately notify and serve counsel for the Debtor with the Order Regarding Application For Expedited Consideration Of First Day Matters.

5. Counsel for the debtor, upon receipt of the above-referenced orders, shall serve by telecopy, electronic transmission, hand delivery or overnight mail a copy of the Order Granting or Denying Complex Chapter 11 Case Treatment and/or Order Regarding Application For Expedited Consideration Of First Day Matters on all affected parties and the United States Trustee within one (1) business day.

6. In a Complex Chapter 11 Case, counsel for the debtor, at the hearing on First Day Matters, shall:

a. Discuss with the Court, provisions regarding the entry of a proposed case management order in accordance with the instructions set forth in the Guidelines Establishing Case Management and Administrative Procedures For Cases Designated As Complex Chapter 11 Cases, a copy of which is attached hereto as Exhibit F;

b. Submit within the time prescribed by the Court, a proposed case management order in accordance with said Guidelines; and

c. Show cause, if necessary, as set forth in the Guidelines as to why all motions, pleadings, memoranda of law or other documents to be filed with the Court in a Complex Chapter 11 Case, should not be filed electronically on the Courts' Case Management/Electronic Filing System ("CM/ECF").

7. The Court reserves the right to modify the provisions of this General Order to accommodate the needs of the Complex Chapter 11 Case before it.

8. The above referenced Exhibit/Standard Forms and Orders, may be revised by the Court at any time on an individual basis, without the need to further amend this General Order.

9. To the extent that the complex Chapter 11 procedures referenced herein conflict with the Court's Local Rules, these Procedures shall control for purposes of Complex Chapter 11 Cases.

IT IS FURTHER ORDERED that the, procedures set forth herein for Complex Chapter 11 Cases shall apply to cases pending on the date of this Order.

[March 31, 2003.]

EXHIBIT A

UNITED STATES BANKRUPTCY COURT
DISTRICT OF NEW JERSEY

IN RE:) CHAPTER 11
) CASE NO.
DEBTOR.)

APPLICATION FOR DESIGNATION AS COMPLEX CHAPTER 11 CASE

This bankruptcy case was filed on ______, 200__. The undersigned party in interest believes that this case qualifies under the Court's General Order Authorizing Procedures For Complex Chapter 11 cases, dated, ____, as a complex Chapter It case because: **(check those items that are applicable)**

___ The Debtor has total liabilities of more than $______ million;
___ The Debtor has total assets of more than $______ million;
___ There are more than ______ creditors in this case;
___ Claims against the Debtor are publicly traded;
___ Other: Substantial explanation is required. (Attach additional sheets if necessary.)

____
____
____
____

______________, 200__

____
Name

____
Address

____
Telephone and Fax numbers

____
E-mail Address

EXHIBIT B

UNITED STATES BANKRUPTCY COURT
DISTRICT OF NEW JERSEY

IN RE:) CHAPTER 11
) CASE NO.
DEBTOR.)

APPLICATION FOR EXPEDITED CONSIDERATION OF FIRST DAY MATTERS

On _____, _________ filed a petition for relief under Chapter 11 of the Bankruptcy Code.

Counsel for the Debtor requests that the following relief be provided on a first day basis **(check those that apply)**:

1. __MOTION SEEKING THE JOINT ADMINISTRATION OF MULTIPLE DEBTOR BANKRUPTCY CASES.

2. __MOTION FOR AN ORDER AUTHORIZING THE DEBTOR AN EXTENSION OF TIME WITHIN WHICH TO FILE STATEMENTS AND SCHEDULES.

3. __MOTION FOR AN ORDER AUTHORIZING THE EMERGENCY OR INTERIM USE OF CASH COLLATERAL OR DEBTOR–IN–POSSESSION FINANCING PENDING THE NOTICING AND SCHEDULING OF AN INTERIM OR FINAL HEARING FOR FINANCING PURSUANT TO BANKRUPTCY CODE §§ 363 AND 364 AND FED. R. BANKR. P. 4001.

4. __MOTION FOR AN ORDER AUTHORIZING THE DEBTOR TO MAINTAIN EXISTING BANK ACCOUNTS AND BUSINESS FORMS AND CASH MANAGEMENT PROCEDURES PROVIDING THE UNITED STATES TRUSTEE'S OFFICE WITH A 60 DAY PERIOD TO OBJECT TO SAID ORDER BEFORE IT BECOMES A FINAL ORDER.

5. __MOTION FOR AN ORDER AUTHORIZING A DEBTOR TO MODIFY THE INVESTMENT GUIDELINES SET FORTH IN BANKRUPTCY CODE § 345 ON AN INTERIM BASIS, PROVIDING THE UNITED STATES TRUSTEE'S OFFICE AND ANY OTHER PARTES–IN–INTEREST A 60–DAY PERIOD TO OBJECT TO SAID ORDER BEFORE IT BECOME A FINAL ORDER.

6. __MOTION FOR AN ORDER AUTHORIZING THE DEBTOR TO PAY PRE-PETITION WAGES, SALARIES, COMPENSATION, EMPLOYEE BENEFITS AND REIMBURSABLE BUSINESS EXPENSES UP TO THE LIMITS SET FORTH IN BANKRUPTCY CODE § 507(a).

7. __MOTION FOR AN ORDER AUTHORIZING THE DEBTOR TO PAY PRE-PETITION SALES, USE, PAYROLL AND OTHER TAXES THAT ARE OTHERWISE PRIORITY CLAIMS UNDER BANKRUPTCY CODE § 507.

8. __MOTION FOR AN ORDER AUTHORIZING THE DEBTOR TO CONTINUE CREDIT CARD FACILITIES.

9. __MOTION FOR AN ORDER AUTHORIZING THE DEBTOR TO HONOR CERTAIN PRE–PETITION CUSTOMER OBLIGATIONS, DEPOSITS, REBATES, ETC.

10. __MOTION FOR AN ORDER AUTHORIZING THE DEBTOR TO CONTINUE WITH AND PAY PRE–PETITION OUTSTANDING AMOUNTS DUE ON VARIOUS INSURANCE POLICIES.

11. __MOTION FOR AN ORDER AUTHORIZING PAYMENT OF OUTSTANDING AND UNPAID PRE–PETITION DEBT TO CERTAIN VENDORS WHO PROVIDE CRITICAL AND NECESSARY SERVICES AND/OR PRODUCTS TO THE DEBTOR.

12. __MOTION FOR AN ORDER PURSUANT TO BANKRUPTCY CODE § 366 REGARDING ADEQUATE ASSURANCE FOR THE FUTURE PERFORMANCE FOR UTILITIES AND ESTABLISHING PROCEDURES FOR DETERMINING REQUESTS FOR ADDITIONAL ADEQUATE ASSURANCE.

13. __MOTION FOR AN ORDER AUTHORIZING THE DEBTOR TO RETAIN A CLAIMS AND NOTICING AGENT.

14. ___MOTION FOR AN ORDER ESTABLISHING NOTICING PROCEDURES.

15. ___OTHERS [COUNSEL SHOULD ADD ALL OTHER MOTIONS FOR WHICH IT SEEKS CONSIDERATION AS A FIRST DAY MATTER.]

________, 200__

____

Name

____

Address

____

Telephone and Fax numbers

____

E-mail Address

NOTE: Each motion or application for which expedited consideration is requested shall be filed with the Clerk of the U.S. Bankruptcy Court For The District Of New Jersey and served upon the United States Trustee and all affected parties.

EXHIBIT C

UNITED STATES BANKRUPTCY COURT
DISTRICT OF NEW JERSEY

IN RE:	)	
	)	
	)	CHAPTER 11
	)	
	)	CASE NO.
	)	
	)	
	)	
DEBTOR.	)	

ORDER DENYING COMPLEX CHAPTER 11 CASE TREATMENT

This bankruptcy case was filed on ______, 200_. An Application For Designation as Complex Chapter 11 Case was filed. After review of the initial pleadings filed in this case, the Court concludes that this case does not constitute a Complex Chapter 11 case. Therefore, the case will proceed under the local bankruptcy rules and procedures generally applicable to bankruptcy cases without entry of the designation as a complex chapter 11 case pursuant to the *General Order Governing Procedures For Complex Chapter 11 Cases.*

IT IS ORDERED that the Application For Designation As Complex Chapter 11 Case is **HEREBY DENIED**, without prejudice.

Dated: ______

____

United States Bankruptcy Judge
District of New Jersey

EXHIBIT D

UNITED STATES BANKRUPTCY COURT
DISTRICT OF NEW JERSEY

IN RE:)
)
) CHAPTER 11
)
) CASE NO.
)
)
)
DEBTOR.)

ORDER GRANTING COMPLEX CHAPTER 11 CASE TREATMENT

This bankruptcy case was filed on ______, 200_. An Application For Designation as Complex Chapter 11 Case was filed. After review of the initial pleadings filed in this case, the Court concludes that this case constitutes a Complex Chapter 11 case.

IT IS ORDERED that the request set forth in the Application For Designation As Complex Chapter 11 Case pursuant to the Court's *General Order Governing Procedures For Complex Chapter 11 Cases* is **HEREBY GRANTED**; and

IT IS FURTHERED ORDERED that the *Guidelines Establishing Case Management And Administrative Procedures For Cases Designated As Complex Chapter 11 Cases* as set forth at Exhibit F to the Court's *General Order Governing Procedures For Complex Chapter 11 Cases* shall apply.

Dated: ______

____
United States Bankruptcy Judge
District of New Jersey

EXHIBIT E

UNITED STATES BANKRUPTCY COURT
DISTRICT OF NEW JERSEY

IN RE:)
)
) CHAPTER 11
)
) CASE NO.
)
DEBTOR.)

ORDER REGARDING APPLICATION FOR EXPEDITED CONSIDERATION OF FIRST DAY MATTERS

This bankruptcy case was filed on ______, 200_. An Application For Expedited Consideration Of First Day Matters was filed. After review of the initial pleadings filed in this case which has been designated by counsel as requiring consideration, and for good cause shown;

IT IS HEREBY ORDERED that the following motions are set down for hearing before The Honorable ______________________________
in Courtroom # ______ located at ______________________________
at the date and time as set forth below:

	Hearing Date and Time
1. MOTION SEEKING THE JOINT ADMINISTRATION OF MULTIPLE-DEBTOR BANKRUPTCY CASES.	________ at ________ .M.
2. MOTION FOR AN ORDER AUTHORIZING THE DEBTOR AN EXTENSION OF TIME WITHIN WHICH TO FILE STATEMENTS AND SCHEDULES.	________ at ________ .M.
3. MOTION FOR AN ORDER AUTHORIZING THE EMERGENCY USE OF CASH COLLATERAL OR DEBTOR–IN–POSSESSION FINANCING PENDING THE NOTICING AND SCHEDULING OF AN INTERIM HEARING FOR FINANCING PURSUANT TO BANKRUPTCY CODE §§ 363 AND 364 AND FED. R. BANKR. P. 4001.	________ at ________ .M.
4. MOTION FOR AN ORDER AUTHORIZING THE DEBTOR TO MAINTAIN EXISTING BANK ACCOUNTS AND BUSINESS FORMS AND CASH MANAGEMENT PROCEDURES PROVIDING THE UNITED STATES TRUSTEE'S OFFICE WITH A 60 DAY PERIOD TO OBJECT TO SAID ORDER BEFORE IT BECOMES A FINAL ORDER.	________ at ________ .M.
5. MOTION FOR AN ORDER AUTHORIZING A DEBTOR TO MODIFY THE INVESTMENT GUIDELINES SET FORTH IN BANKRUPTCY CODE § 345 ON AN INTERIM BASIS, PROVIDING THE UNITED STATES TRUSTEE'S OFFICE AND ANY OTHER PARTIES–IN–INTEREST A 60–DAY PERIOD TO OBJECT TO SAID ORDER BEFORE IT BECOME A FINAL ORDER.	________ at ________ .M.
6. MOTION FOR AN ORDER AUTHORIZING THE DEBTOR TO PAY PRE–PETITION WAGES, SALARIES, COMPENSATION, EMPLOYEE BENEFITS AND REIMBURSABLE BUSINESS EXPENSES UP TO THE LIMITS SET FORTH IN BANKRUPTCY CODE § 507(a).	________ at ________ .M.
7. MOTION FOR AN ORDER AUTHORIZING THE DEBTOR TO PAY PRE–PETITION SALES, USE, PAYROLL AND OTHER TAXES THAT ARE OTHERWISE PRIORITY CLAIMS UNDER BANKRUPTCY CODE § 507.	________ at ________ .M.
8. MOTION FOR AN ORDER AUTHORIZING THE DEBTOR TO CONTINUE CREDIT CARD FACILITIES.	________ at ________ .M.

	Hearing Date and Time
9. MOTION FOR AN ORDER AUTHORIZING THE DEBTOR TO HONOR CERTAIN PRE–PETITION CUSTOMER OBLIGATIONS, DEPOSITS, REBATES, ETC.	______ at ______ .M.
10. MOTION FOR AN ORDER AUTHORIZING THE DEBTOR TO CONTINUE WITH AND PAY PRE–PETITION OUTSTANDING AMOUNTS DUE ON VARIOUS INSURANCE POLICIES.	______ at ______ .M.
11. MOTION FOR AN ORDER AUTHORIZING PAYMENT OF OUTSTANDING AND UNPAID PRE–PETITION DEBT TO CERTAIN VENDORS WHO PROVIDE CRITICAL AND NECESSARY SERVICES AND/OR PRODUCTS TO THE DEBTOR.	______ at ______ .M.
12. MOTION FOR AN ORDER PURSUANT TO BANKRUPTCY CODE § 366 REGARDING ADEQUATE ASSURANCE FOR THE FUTURE PERFORMANCE FOR UTILITIES AND ESTABLISHING PROCEDURES FOR DETERMINING REQUESTS FOR ADDITIONAL ADEQUATE ASSURANCE.	______ at ______ .M.
13. MOTION FOR AN ORDER AUTHORIZING THE DEBTOR TO RETAIN A CLAIMS AND NOTICING AGENT.	______ at ______ .M.
14. MOTION FOR AN ORDER ESTABLISHING NOTICING PROCEDURES.	______ at ______ .M.
15. **OTHERS [COUNSEL SHOULD ADD ALL OTHER MOTIONS FOR WHICH IT SEEKS CONSIDERATION AS FIRST DAY MATTERS AS SET FORTH IN THE UNDERLYING REQUEST].**	______ at ______ .M.

IT IS FURTHER ORDERED, that Service of the within Order shall be made in accordance with the Court's *General Order Adopting Guidelines Governing First Day Matters*; and

IT IS FURTHER ORDERED, that objections and/or responses to First Day Matters, if any, shall be made in accordance with the Court's *General Order Adopting Guidelines Governing First Day Matters*.

Dated: __________

____
United States Bankruptcy Judge
District of New Jersey

EXHIBIT F

GUIDELINES ESTABLISHING CASE MANAGEMENT AND ADMINISTRATIVE PROCEDURES FOR CASES DESIGNATED AS COMPLEX CHAPTER 11 CASES

After review of the initial pleadings filed in a case designated and approved as "complex" and the Court conducting its initial status conference at the hearing on

First Day Matters, and for which the court concludes that the case is appropriate for the entry of a case management and administrative procedures order, the following guidelines as they relate to case management and administrative procedures may be requested by Debtor's counsel upon the submission of an "Order Establishing Case Management And Administrative Procedures For Cases Designated As Complex Chapter 11 Cases."

A. OMNIBUS HEARING DATES

1. The Court may conduct omnibus hearings on a weekly/bi-monthly/monthly basis as dictated by the circumstances of the case (the "Omnibus Hearing Dates").

2. Omnibus Hearing Dates will occur thereafter as may be scheduled by the Court. To the extent possible, all matters requiring a hearing in this case shall be set for and be heard on Omnibus Hearing Dates unless alternative hearing dates are approved by the Court for good cause shown.

B. EXPEDITED HEARINGS

3. If a party in interest has an emergency or other situation that it believes requires consideration on less than the 20–days notice as required by D.N.J.LBR 9013–1(c), the moving party should file and serve, a separate written application requesting shortened time and expedited hearing in respect of the underlying motion in the form provided at D.N.J.LBR 9013–1(e).

4. The Court will rule on the request for shortened time within twenty-four (24) hours of the time it is presented. If the court grants the motion for expedited hearing, the underlying motion will be set at the next available omnibus hearing date or at some other appropriate shortened date approved by the Court.

5. Requests for expedited hearings will only be granted under emergency or exigent circumstances.

6. This section does not apply to matters filed under an Application For Expedited Consideration Of First Day Matters and all parties are directed to consult the *General Order Adopting Guidelines Governing First Day Matters.*

C. COMPLIANCE WITH TERMS OF ORDER ESTABLISHING CASE MANAGEMENT AND ADMINISTRATIVE PROCEDURES

7. If any person makes any filing in contravention of the omnibus dates process established pursuant to a particular chapter 11 case Order Establishing Case Management and Administrative Procedures entered by the Court by, among other things, setting a hearing on such filing for a date and time other than an omnibus hearing date without an order from this Court authorizing such hearing for cause, the Debtor's counsel shall forward a copy of the Order Establishing Case Management And Administrative Procedures to such person within three (3) business days of the receipt of such filing. If such filing is filed at least twenty (20) days from the next Omnibus Hearing Date, then the hearing with respect to such filing shall be deemed to be on such omnibus hearing date. If such filing is less than twenty (20) days prior to the next omnibus hearing date then the hearing with respect to such filing shall be the next omnibus hearing date thereafter. The movant must provide notice of the corrected hearing date to all affected parties and thereafter file a certificate of service regarding the notice.

D. NOTICING PROCEDURES

8. All filings in this case, unless otherwise ordered by the Court, shall be served upon the following entities constituting the "Core Service List"—

(a) The Debtor(s);

(b) The Debtor's counsel;

(c) The Newark office of the United States Trustee for Region III;

(d) The chairperson of any official committees established pursuant to section 1102 of the Bankruptcy Code;

(e) Counsel retained by any official committees established pursuant to Section 1102 of the Bankruptcy Code, or twenty (20) largest creditors if an official committee has not been appointed;

(f) Counsel to secured creditors; and

(g) Any other person, entity as authorized by the Court.

9. Debtor's counsel or counsel to the trustee, if one is appointed, must maintain and update the Core Service List at least every fifteen (15) days during the first sixty (60) days of the case and at least every thirty (30) days thereafter. Further, Debtor's counsel must file a Core Service List with the Court every time it is updated.

10. Debtor's counsel or counsel to the trustee shall also maintain and update a master service list (the "Master Service List") which shall be comprised of the Core Service List and the parties that have filed a notice of appearance and request for notices in the Debtor's case. Service on the persons/entities listed on the Master Service List shall be made only with respect to those matters enumerated in the Order Establishing Case Management And Administrative Procedures. Debtor's counsel must update the Master Service List at least every fifteen (15) days during the first sixty (60) days of the case and at least every thirty (30) days thereafter. Further, Debtor's counsel must file the Master Service List with the Court each time it is updated.

11. The certificate of service for each filing must be filed with the Court together, with the complete service list that was utilized and served for a particular filing but said certificate of service is not to be served via hard copy on the recipients of the filing.

12. Whether filed conventionally or electronically, summons and complaints or the initiating motion in a contested matter shall be served in hard copy format pursuant to Fed. R.Bankr.P. 7004, upon all parties having a particularized interest in the subject of the filings or motions and parties listed on the Core Service List.

13. All notices required by subdivisions (a)(2), (3) and (6) of Fed. R.Bankr.P. 2002 and by Fed. R.Bankr.P. 4001 shall be served upon:

(a) Each entity designated on the Core Service List; and

(b) When the notice is of a proposed use, sale, lease or abandonment of property or of a hearing thereon, each entity designated on the most recent Master Service List and each entity having an interest in the property; and

(c) When the notice relates to relief from the stay in order to take action against property of the Debtor's Estate, each entity having a lien, encumbrance or interest in the subject property; and

(d) When the notice relates to use of cash collateral or obtaining credit, each entity who has an interest in the cash collateral or each entity who has a lien or other interest in property on which a lien is proposed to be granted; and

(e) When the notice is of a proposed compromise or settlement or of a hearing thereon, each entity designated on the most recent Master Service List and each entity who is a party to the compromise or settlement; and

(f) When the notice is of an application for compensation or reimbursement of expenses or of a hearing thereon, each entity designated on the most recent Master Service List and each professional person who is seeking compensation or reimbursement whose retention in these cases is authorized by the Court.

E. NEGATIVE NOTICING PROCEDURES

14. Subject to the Court's discretion, the Court may approve notice procedures which provide that if no objections are timely filed and served by a deadline set in accordance with the Federal Rules of Bankruptcy Procedure and/or the Order Establishing Case Management And Administrative Procedures and/or the District of New Jersey Local Bankruptcy Rules, the Court may enter an order granting the

relief requested without further notice or a hearing ("Negative Notice"). The notice of motion accompanying such motion must specifically advise parties of the objection deadline, and must also inform the recipient that if no objections are filed and served, the Court may enter an order granting the motion without further notice or hearing.

15. "Negative Notice" may be used in connection with motions including, but not limited to, matters requesting the following relief:

(a) Rejection of a non-residential real property lease or executory contract pursuant to 11 U.S.C. § 365;

(b) Retention and employment of professional pursuant to 11 U.S.C. §§ 327, 328 and 330 and 28 U.S.C. § 156(*o*);

(c) Extension of deadline to seek removal action pursuant to Federal Rule of Bankruptcy Procedure 9027;

(d) Sales of assets outside the ordinary course of business pursuant to 11 U.S.C. § 363 with a purchase price set on a case by case basis;

(e) Approval of settlements and compromises pursuant to Federal Rules of Bankruptcy Procedures 9019 of claims where the settled amount of the claim does not exceed an amount set on a case by case basis; and

(f) Nothing contained herein shall be construed to limit a party in interest's ability to request that the court approve the use of Negative Notice procedures in connection with motions not specifically identified above.

16. If an objection is timely filed and served, a hearing will be scheduled for the next omnibus hearing date unless otherwise ordered by the Court.

F. CERTIFICATION OF NO OBJECTION

17. After the objection date has passed with no objection having been filed or served, counsel for the movant may file a Certification of No Objection substantially in the form as it appears on the annexed Schedule "1" stating that no objection has been filed or served on the movant.

18. By filing such certifications, counsel for the movant is representing to the Court that the movant is unaware of any objection to the motion or application and that counsel has reviewed the Court's docket and no objection appears thereon.

19. Upon receipt of the Certification Of No Objection, the Court may enter the Order accompanying the motion or application without further pleading or hearing and, once the Order is entered, the hearing scheduled on the motion or application shall be cancelled without further notice.

G. NOTICE OF AGENDA

20. Subject to the Court's discretion, in a case that has been designated as complex and if the Court has authorized a Notice of Agenda to be utilized, debtor's counsel or counsel to the trustee, if one is appointed shall maintain file and serve a Notice of Agenda for each hearing held in the case in conformity with the proposed form annexed hereto as Schedule "2" and the guidelines set forth below (G 21-G 28) unless modified or otherwise directed by the Court to the contrary.

21. Counsel (as described above in section "G 20") shall file a proposed Notice of Agenda before 12:00 Noon on the day that is two (2) business days before the date of the omnibus hearing.

22. Resolved or continued matters shall be listed ahead of unresolved matters on the Notice of Agenda. Contested matters shall be listed in the order of docketing with corresponding docket number.

23. All amended Notices of Agenda shall list matters as listed in the original Notice of Agenda with all edits and additional information being listed in **boldface type.**

24. Copies of the Notice of Agenda shall be served upon local counsel who have entered an appearance in the case, as well as all other counsel with a direct interest in any matter on the Notice of Agenda and the United States Trustee simultaneously with the filing of the Notice of Agenda with the Court.

25. For each motion and/or application the Notice of Agenda shall indicate the movant and/or the applicant, the nature of the motion and the docket number. Supporting papers of the movant/applicant shall be similarly denoted.

26. For each motion and/or application the Notice of Agenda shall indicate the objection deadline and any objection filed and its docket number, if available.

27. For each motion/application the Notice of Agenda shall indicate whether the matter is going forward, whether a continuance is requested (and any opposition to the continuance if known), whether any or all of the objections have been resolved and any other pertinent status information.

28. When an adversary proceeding is scheduled the Notice of Agenda shall indicate the adversary proceeding number and the corresponding docket number for pleadings filed in the adversary proceeding on the Notice of Agenda, in addition to the information regularly required in a Notice of Agenda.

H. PRO HAC VICE APPLICATIONS

29. Application by non-resident attorneys for permission to practice before the Court in this case, *pro hac vice*, may not be set for hearing unless the Court requires otherwise. These applications may be GRANTED by the Court unless objections are promptly filed thereto. *Pro hac vice* applications must be served upon each entity designated on the Core Service List.

30. The Court will require parties to obtain local counsel in accordance with the District of New Jersey Local District Court Rules and Local Bankruptcy Rules.

I. ELECTRONIC FILING PROCEDURES

31. Pursuant to this Court's *General Order Authorizing Administrative Procedures for the Electronic Filing, Signing And Verification of Documents*, dated March 27, 2002, except with regard to documents which may be filed under seal, unless good cause can be demonstrated and established to the contrary at the return date on the hearing(s) of the First Day Matters, all motions, pleadings, memoranda of law or other documents to be filed with the Court in a Complex Chapter 11 Case shall be electronically filed on the Court's Electronic, Filing System.

32. Notwithstanding the above, the Office of the United States Trustee for Region III–New Jersey Office requires service upon it of the following documents in hard copy format regardless of whether the United States Trustee's Office receives same electronically:

a. Petition;

b. Schedules and Statement of Financial Affairs;

c. Chapter 11 plan and Disclosure Statement;

d. Fee applications;

e. All First Day Matters and supporting pleadings and documents thereto; and

f. Monthly Operating Reports.

J. MAILING MATRIX

33. A mailing matrix submitted electronically shall be prepared in accordance with D.N.J. LBR 1007–2.

K. OTHER ADMINISTRATIVE ISSUES

34. Any party may at anytime apply for reconsideration or modification of the Order Establishing Case Management And Administrative Procedures. Service of said motion shall be made to all persons/entities on the Master Service List. The court may amend the Order Establishing Case Management And Administrative Procedure from time to time as is necessary.

____

SCHEDULE "1"

PROPOSED FORM OF CERTIFICATION OF NO OBJECTION

UNITED STATES BANKRUPTCY COURT
FOR THE DISTRICT OF NEW JERSEY

In Re	)	
,	)	
	)	Chapter 11
Debtor.	)	
	)	Bankruptcy Case No. ( )
	)	

CERTIFICATION OF NO OBJECTION REGARDING [*INSERT TITLE OF MOTION*] DOCKET NO. ____

The undersigned hereby certifies that, as of [insert date[, [insert attorney's name] has received no answer, objection or other responsive pleading to [insert name of motion/application]] [Docket No. ______] filed on [insert date of filing]. The undersigned further certifies that I have reviewed the Court's docket in this case and no answer, objection or other responsive pleading to the [insert title of motion/application] appears thereon. Pursuant to Notice of [insert title of motion/application], objections to the [insert title of motion/application] were to be filed and served no later than [insert objection date].

It is hereby respectfully requested that the Order attached to the [insert title of motion/application] be entered at the earliest convenience of the Court.

Dated: Law Firm
Counsel to [ ]

By: ____________________
Name of Attorney

SCHEDULE "2"

"PROPOSED FORM OF NOTICE OF AGENDA"

UNITED STATES BANKRUPTCY COURT
FOR THE DISTRICT OF NEW JERSEY

In Re	)	
,	)	
	)	Chapter 11
Debtor.	)	
	)	Bankruptcy Case No. ( )
	)	

NOTICE OF AGENDA OF MATTERS
SCHEDULED ON ________, 200__@__.M.

CONTINUED MATTERS

1. Title of Motion [Docket #]

- Response Deadline:
- Response (s) Received:
- Related Documents-
- Status: (Practice Note For Bar—state the continued hearing date, if known or date needs to be determined)

UNCONTESTED MATTERS

2. Title of Motion [Docket #]

- Response Deadline:
- Response(s) Received:
- Related Documents:
- Status: (Practice Note For Bar—state no objections leave been received and a Certification Of No Objection has or will be filled.)

PRETRIAL CONFERENCES

3. Pretrial Conference on Complaint re: [Caption of Adversary] Adversary Pro. No. ( )

- Related Documents:
- Adversary Complaint of _____ [Docket No. _____]
- Response/Answer Deadline:
- Response(s) Received:
- Scheduling Order:
- Status: (Practice Note For Bar - state whether first pre-trial conference; whether parties are discussing settlement; discovery ongoing; need for mediation; need for settlement conference, etc.)

CONTESTED MATTERS

4. Title of Motion [Docket #]

- Response Deadline:
- Response(s) Received:
- Related Documents:
- Status: (The matter is going forward, Practice Note for Bar: If the parties are still negotiating please also state this development to the court)

CONTESTED MATTER—EVIDENTIARY HEARING REQUIRED

5. Title of Motion [Docket #]

- Response Deadline:
- Response(s) Received:
- Related Documents:
- Status: (Practice Note For Bar — state number witnesses to testify and estimated time needed.)

FEE APPLICATIONS

- Title of Fee Application [Docket #]
- Response Deadline:

- Response(s) Received:
- Related Documents:
- Status

Date:

____

Signature

[Dated: March 31, 2003.]

IMPORTANT NOTES TO NOTICE OF AGENDA

*Number agenda matters consecutively. Therefore, do not start with number 1 at each new section.

*Include docket numbers for any pleadings referenced on Notice of Agenda.

*List response(s)/objection(s) in order they appear on the docket.

*Amended Notices of Agenda should have new material in **bold** only. There is no need to italicize, underline, or blackline. DO NOT REARRANGE the numbering of the Notice of Agenda when and if submitting an amended Notice of Agenda.

*Double check the updated docket before filing a Notice of Agenda to be sure you have included all docket numbers on pleadings listed. If for some reason a pleading in not docketed please note TBD and state date when pleading filed with the court.

GENERAL ORDER ADOPTING GUIDELINES GOVERNING PROCEDURES FOR PAYMENT OF INTERIM COMPENSATION AND REIMBURSEMENT OF EXPENSES TO PROFESSIONALS

UPON CONSIDERATION of the recommendations of the Chapter 11 Subcommittee of the Lawyer's Advisory Committee of the Bankruptcy Court for the District of New Jersey, the Court finds a need to implement policies and procedures to better serve the bench, bar and public in chapter 11 cases. Accordingly, by resolution of the Board of Judges of the United States Bankruptcy Court for the District of New Jersey,

IT IS ORDERED pursuant to 11 U.S.C. §§105(a) and 331 that the Guidelines Governing Procedures For Payment Of Interim Compensation And Reimbursement Of Expenses To Professionals attached hereto as Exhibit A are hereby **ADOPTED**; and

IT IS FURTHER ORDERED that

1. The Court reserves the right to modify the provisions of this General Order to accommodate the needs of a chapter 11 case before it; and

2. The Exhibits/Standard Forms And Orders referenced in this General Order may be revised by the Court at any time on an individual basis without the need to further amend this General Order; and

IT IS FURTHER ORDER that this Order shall apply to chapter 11 cases pending on the date of this order.

[Dated: March 31, 2003.]

GUIDELINES GOVERNING PROCEDURES FOR PAYMENT OF INTERIM COMPENSATION AND REIMBURSEMENT OF EXPENSES TO PROFESSIONALS PURSUANT TO 11 U.S.C. §§ 105(a) AND 331

The procedures set forth below concern the submission of motions seeking the entry of an administrative order establishing procedures for payment of interim compensation and reimbursement of expenses to professionals pursuant to 11 U.S.C. §§ 105(a) and 331 for services rendered and expenses incurred during a Chapter 11 case. This will enable both the Court and practitioners to understand the procedures in advance and ensure that motions and corresponding relief they seek conform to procedures that are accepted by the Court when it is appropriate to enter such types of orders. Accordingly, the following guidelines governing procedures for payment of interim compensation and reimbursement of expenses to professionals pursuant to 11 U.S.C. §§ 105(a) and 331 have been approved by the Court.

A. SCOPE, OF APPLICABILITY

1. All professionals retained in a Chapter 11 case pursuant to Bankruptcy Code §§ 327 and 1103 (the "Professional") may seek post-petition interim compensation pursuant to the within guidelines by filing the appropriate motion seeking the entry of an administrative fee order ("Administrative Fee Order").

B. SUBMISSION AND MONTHLY STATEMENTS

2. On or before the twenty-fifth (25th) day of each month following the month for which compensation is sought, each Professional seeking compensation pursuant to an Administrative Fee Order shall file with the Court and serve a monthly fee and expense statement (the "Monthly Fee Statement"), by hand or overnight delivery or by any means directed by the Court upon the following persons (the "Notice Parties"):

(a) the officer designated by the Debtor to be responsible for such matters;

(b) counsel to the Debtor;

(c) counsel to all official committees;

(d) United States Trustees Office for Region III—Newark, NJ office;

(e) counsel to all post-petition lenders or their agents; and

(f) any other party the Court may so designate.

C. CONTENT OF MONTHLY STATEMENT

3. Each Monthly Fee Statement shall comply with the Bankruptcy Code, the Federal Rules of Bankruptcy Procedure and the Local Rules for the United States Bankruptcy Court for the District of New Jersey with the exception that provisions of D.N.J. LBR 2016–1 (a)(8) [cover sheet] and (a)(9) [narrative explanation] are not required.

4. All timekeepers must maintain contemporaneously time entries for each individual in increments of tenths (1/10th) of an hour.

D. REVIEW PERIOD

5. Each person receiving a Monthly Fee Statement shall have twenty (20) days after service of the Monthly Fee Statement to review it (the "Objection Deadline").

E. PAYMENT

6. Upon the expiration of the Objection Deadline, each Professional may file and serve upon each of the parties set forth in Section B2 herein, including, but not limited to, the Debtor a certificate of no objection or a certificate of partial objection, whichever is applicable, after which the Debtor is authorized to pay each Professional an amount (the "Actual Interim Payment") equal to the lesser of (i) eighty percent (80%) of the fees and 100 percent (100%) of the expenses requested in the Monthly Fee Statement or (ii) eighty percent (80%) of the fees and 100 percent (100%) of the expenses not subject to any objection.

F. OBJECTIONS

7. If any party objects to a Monthly Fee Statement, it must file a written objection (the "Notice Of Objection To Monthly Fee Statement") and serve it upon the Professional and each of the Notice Parties including, but not limited to, the Debtor so that the Notice Of Objection To Monthly Fee Statement is received on or before the Objection Deadline.

8. The Notice Of Objection To Monthly Fee Statement must set forth the nature of the objection and the amount of fees and/or expenses at issue.

9. If the Debtor received an objection to a particular Monthly Fee Statement, the Debtor shall withhold payment of that portion of the Monthly Fee Statement to which the objection is directed and promptly pay the remainder of the fees and disbursements in the percentages set forth in Section E6 herein.

10. If the parties to an objection are able to resolve their respective dispute(s) following the service of a Notice Of Objection To Monthly Fee Statement and if the party whose Monthly Fee Statement was objected to serves upon all the Notice Parties a statement indicating that the objection is withdrawn and describing in detail the terms of the resolution, then the Debtor shall promptly pay in accordance with Section E6 herein that portion of the Monthly Fee Statement which is no longer subject to an objection.

11. If the parties are unable to reach a resolution of the objection within twenty (20) days after service of the objection, then the affected Professional may either (a) file a response to the objection with the Court together with a request for payment of the difference, if any, between the Actual Interim Payment and the non-objected to portion of the Actual Interim Payment made to the affected Professional (the "Incremental Amount"); or (b) forego payment of the Incremental Amount until the next interim or final fee application or any other date and time so directed by the Court at which time it will consider and dispose of the objection, if so requested.

12. The service of an objection to a Monthly Fee Statement shall not prejudice the objecting party's right to object to any fee application made to the Court in accordance with the Bankruptcy Code on any ground whether raised in the objection or not.

13. Furthermore, the decision by any party not to object to a Monthly Fee Statement shall not be a waiver of any kind or prejudice that party's right to object to any fee application subsequently made to the Court in accordance with the Bankruptcy Code and applicable rules.

G. FEE APPLICATIONS

14. Parties can file at three (3) month intervals or such other intervals directed by the Court ("Interim Period") an interim fee application. Each Professional seeking approval of its interim fee application shall file with the Court and serve upon the Notice Parties an interim application for allowance of compensation and reimbursement of expenses, pursuant to Bankruptcy Code § 331, of the amounts sought in the Monthly Fee Statements issued during such period (the "Interim Fee Application").

15. The Interim Fee Application must include a summary of the Monthly Fee Statements that are the subject of the request and any other information requested by the Court and shall comply with the mandates of the Bankruptcy Code, the Federal Rules of Bankruptcy Procedures, the Local Rules for the United States Bankruptcy Court for the District of New Jersey and the applicable Third Circuit law.

16. An Interim Fee Application must be filed and served within forty-five (45) days of the conclusion of the Interim Period.

17. Any Professional who fails to file an Interim Fee Application when due will be ineligible to receive further interim payments of fees or expenses under the Administrative Fee Order until such time as the Interim Fee Application is submitted.

18. Notice of the Interim Fee Application shall be served on (a) the Notice Parties and (b) all parties that filed a notice of appearance with the Clerk of this Court pursuant to Bankruptcy Rule 2002 and requested such notice. The Notice Parties shall be entitled to receive both the Monthly Fee Statements and Interim Fee Applications as indicated above and the notice of hearing thereon (the "Hearing Notice") and all other parties entitled to notice shall be entitled to receive only the Hearing Notice. Notice given in accordance with this paragraph is deemed sufficient and adequate and in full compliance with the applicable provisions of the Bankruptcy Code, the Bankruptcy Rules and the Local Rules of this Court.

19. The pendency of a fee application or a Court order that payment of compensation or reimbursement of expenses was improper as to a particular Monthly Fee Statement shall not disqualify a Professional from the further payment of compensation or reimbursement of expenses as set forth above, unless otherwise ordered by the Court. Additionally, the pendency of the an objection to payment of compensation or reimbursement of expenses will not disqualify a Professional from future payment of compensation or reimbursement of expenses, unless the Court orders otherwise.

20. Neither the payment of, nor the failure to pay, in whole or in part, monthly compensation and reimbursement as provided herein shall have any effect on this Court's interim or final allowance of compensation and reimbursement of expenses of any Professionals.

21. Counsel for each official committee may, in accordance with the foregoing procedure for monthly compensation and reimbursement to professionals, collect and submit statements of expenses, with supporting vouchers, from members of the committee he or she represents; provided, however, that such committee counsel ensures that these reimbursement requests comply with the applicable rules and these guidelines.

22. Each Professional may seek, in its first request for compensation and reimbursement of expenses pursuant to these guidelines, compensation for work performed and reimbursement for expenses incurred during the period of time between the commencement of the case through and including a specific date.

H. ADMINISTRATIVE ISSUES

23. Any party may object to requests for payments made pursuant to the Administrative Fee Order on the grounds that the Debtors have not timely filed monthly operation reports, remained current with their administrative expenses and 28 U.S.C. § 1930 fees, or a manifest exigency exists. by seeking a further order of this Court.

24. Otherwise, the Administrative Fee Order shall continue and shall remain in effect during the pendency of the case.

25. Debtor shall include all payments to Professionals on their monthly operating reports, detailed so as to state the amount paid to the Professionals.

26. All time periods set forth in this Order shall be calculated in accordance with Federal Rule of Bankruptcy Procedure 9006(a).

27. All fees and expenses paid to Professionals are subject to disgorgement until final allowance by the Court.

I. SERVICE OF THE ADMINISTRATIVE FEE ORDER

28. Debtors must serve a copy of the Administrative Fee Order upon all parties served with the underlying motion seeking an Administrative Fee Order; all affected Professionals; all Notice Parties and any other party the Court shall designate.

[Dated: March 31, 2003; revised December 1, 2003.]

CHAPTER 13 CASES

CASES UNDER CHAPTER 13 OF THE BANKRUPTCY CODE. ORDER RELATING TO MOTIONS FOR RELIEF FROM THE AUTOMATIC STAY; AND REQUIRING THE FILING OF CHAPTER 13 DEBTOR'S CERTIFICATION IN OPPOSITION TO CREDITOR'S MOTION OR CERTIFICATION OF DEFAULT AND RELATED FORMS

(AS AMENDED 04–15–05)

A proposal for an Order of the Court resolving certain payment dispute issues commonly arising in cases under Chapter 13 of the Bankruptcy Code having been reviewed by the Court, and the Court having considered the benefit to the bench, bar, and parties in interest, and good cause having been shown;

IT IS ORDERED that:

1. No appearances will be required for *uncontested* Chapter 13 Motions relating to the automatic stay. This procedural transition contemplates amendment to *D.N.J. LBR 4001–1, Automatic Stay-Relief From,* pending approval of Local Bankruptcy Rule Amendments by the United States District Court for the District of New Jersey pursuant to the Court's Annual Rule Making Cycle for the year 2005.

2. A new form entitled *Chapter 13 Debtor's Certification in Opposition to Creditor's Motion or Certification of Default* (attached as *Exhibit A*) must be filed with the Court and served upon the creditor and the Standing Chapter 13 Trustee, at least seven (7) days before the return date, pursuant to *DNJ LBR 9013–1(d), Motion Practice,* if filed in opposition to a *Motion for Relief from the Automatic Stay*; and within 10 days of the filing of a *Creditor's Certification of Default* under an *Order Resolving Motion to Vacate Stay and/or Dismiss with Conditions.* Absent the filing of this mandatory new form, the creditor's stay relief motion will be deemed uncontested, and the creditor's appearance at the hearing will *not* be required.

3. Local Forms 16 (Post Petition Payment History On Note and Mortgage) or 16A (Post Petition Payment History on Vehicle Loan/Lease) must be filed by secured creditors in conjunction with the filing of a *Creditor's Certification of Default.*

4. Secured creditors shall be required to accept debtors' post petition payments, and to apply those payments to debtors' accounts; any such acceptance shall be without any prejudice to, waiver of, or estoppel as to the position of secured creditors in disputes with debtors, including payment and accounting disputes.

5. A new form entitled *Joint Scheduling Order Regarding Dispute On Motion for Relief From the Automatic Stay,* may be entered upon consent of the parties requiring the exchange of payment records before the hearing, on the terms and conditions set forth therein.

6. The establishment on the Court's website www.njb.uscourts.gov, of a new Creditor Address Database for purposes of forwarding post petition payments is approved, subject to timely implementation of this Database subsequent to the effective date of this General Order.

7. This General Order as amended becomes effective April 15, 2005, upon which date, the above referenced procedural transitions are to be implemented; use of Local Forms 16, or 16A in conjunction with a *Creditor's Certification of Default* is to become mandatory; as is use of the new mandatory form *Chapter 13 Debtor's Certification In Opposition to Creditor's Motion.*

8. Notice to the Bar of this Order as amended April 15, 2005, shall be provided on the Court's website: www.njb.uscourts.gov.

[Dated: April 15, 2005.]

Exhibit A

UNITED STATES BANKRUPTCY COURT
DISTRICT OF NEW JERSEY

Caption in Compliance with D.N.J. LBR 9004-2(c)
In Re:

Case No.: ____________________
Judge: ______
Chapter: 13

CHAPTER 13 DEBTOR'S CERTIFICATION IN OPPOSITION TO CREDITOR'S MOTION OR CERTIFICATION OF DEFAULT

The debtor in the above-captioned chapter 13 proceeding hereby objects to the following **(choose one)**:

1. ☐ Motion for Relief from the Automatic Stay filed by creditor ______. A hearing has been scheduled for ______, at _____m.

OR

2. ☐ Certification of Default filed by creditor, ______. I am requesting a hearing be scheduled on this matter.

I am objecting to the above for the following reasons **(choose one)**:

☐ Payments have been made in the amount of $______, but have not been accounted for. Documentation in support is attached hereto.

☐ Payments have not been made for the following reasons and debtor proposes repayment as follows **(explain your answer)**:______________________________
____
____

☐ Other **(explain your answer)**: ______________________________
____
____

3. This certification is being made in an effort to resolve the issues raised by the creditor in its motion.

4. I certify the above facts to be true. I am aware that if the above facts are willfully false, I am subject to punishment.

Date: ________ ________________________
Debtor's Signature

Date: ________ ________________________
Debtor's Signature

NOTE: Pursuant to the Court's General Orders entered on January 4th, 2005, this form must be filed with the Court and served upon the creditor and the Standing Chapter 13 Trustee, **at least seven (7) days before the return date, pursuant to *D.N.J. LBR 9013-1(d), Motion Practice*,** if filed in opposition to a *Motion for Relief from the Automatic Stay*; **and within 10 days of the filing of a *Creditor's Certification of Default* under an *Order Resolving Motion to Vacate Stay and/or Dismiss with Conditions*. Absent the filing of this mandatory new form, the creditor's stay relief motion will be deemed uncontested, and the creditor's appearance at the hearing will *not* be required.**

GENERAL ORDER PENDING AMENDMENT OF 3015–6, OBJECTION TO CONFIRMATION OF CHAPTER 13 PLAN

A proposal for an Order of the Court resolving certain payment dispute issues commonly arising in cases under Chapter 13 of the Bankruptcy Code having been reviewed by the Court, and the Court having considered the benefit to the bench, bar, and parties in interest, and good cause having been shown;

IT IS ORDERED that:

1.(a) An objection to confirmation of the plan shall be filed with the court and served upon the debtor, debtor's attorney, the chapter 13 trustee and any other party in interest at least seven (7) days prior to the confirmation hearing date set in the *Notice of Hearing on Confirmation of Plan or Notice of Modification of Chapter 13 Plan,* whichever occurs first.

(b) A proof of claim filed in an amount greater than that set forth in the plan, shall constitute an objection to confirmation as to the amount of the claim, and shall be served in accordance with subsection (a) of this rule. The party in interest filing the proof of claim shall file a Proof of Service of compliant with this section at least seven (7) days prior to the scheduled confirmation hearing.

(c) If the plan contains a motion to avoid liens or partially avoid liens pursuant to D.N.J. LBR 3015–1(b), a proof of claim filed and served in conformance with subsections (a) and (b) will be considered opposition to the motion. The Debtor shall request a hearing to resolve the motion no later than 60 days after entry of the order of confirmation.

2. This procedural transition contemplates a proposed amendment to D.N.J. LBR 3015–6, *Objections To Confirmation of Chapter 13 Plan* which is pending approval of Local Bankruptcy Rule Amendments by the United States District Court for the District of New Jersey pursuant to the Court's Annual Rule Making Cycle for the year 2006.

3. This General Order becomes effective December 12, 2005 upon which date, the above referenced procedural transitions are to be implemented.

4. Notice to the Bar of this General Order shall be provided on the Court's Web site: www.njb.uscourts.gov.

[Dated: December 5, 2005.]

GENERAL ORDER DIRECTING DISPOSITION OF CHAPTER 13 CASES IN WHICH 11 U.S.C. SECTION 1328(f) IS INVOKED

A proposal for a *sua sponte* order of the Court resolving certain issues relating to the debtor's ineligibility to receive a discharge in cases under Chapter 13 in which 11 U.S.C. Section 1328(f)(1) or 1328(f)(2) is invoked, having been reviewed by the Court, and the Court having recognized the statutory bar to its issuance of a discharge in such cases, and good cause having been shown,

IT IS ORDERED that:

1. After providing the debtor with notice and an opportunity to be heard, as defined in paragraph 2 below, at the conclusion of the Chapter 13 case, the Clerk shall close the case without issuance of a discharge, if the debtor has received a discharge-

a) in a case filed under Chapter 7, 11 or 12 during the 4-year period preceding the date of the order for relief under Chapter 13, or

b) in a case filed under Chapter 13, during the 2-year period preceding the date of the order for relief under Chapter 13.

2. Upon the Clerk's evidence of the issuance of a discharge in a previous case commenced within the times frames set forth in paragraph 1 above, the docket entry in the case will reflect the Clerk's evidence of repeat filing and the debtor's ineligibility to receive a discharge pursuant to 11 U.S.C. Section 1328(f)(1) or 1328(f)(2). The debtor will receive notice of the Clerk's evidence of repeat filing and statutory inability to receive a discharge. The notice will offer the debtor the opportunity to file an objection. If an objection is filed, a hearing in the matter will be scheduled.

3. Pursuant to Interim Rule 4006, upon the closing of a case without the entry of an order of discharge, the Clerk shall promptly give notice thereof to all parties in interest in the manner provided in Rule 2002.

4. This General Order does not modify or supercede the independent opportunity of the Office of the United States Trustee, the Chapter 13 Standing Trustee, or a creditor to act pursuant to 11 U.S.C. 1328(f)(1) or (f)(2).

5. This General Order becomes effective on December 14, 2006, upon which date this procedure will be implemented with respect to all Chapter 13 cases filed under the Bankruptcy Abuse Prevention and Consumer Protection Act of 2005 ("BAPCPA").

6. Notice to the Bar of this Order shall be provided on the Court's Website: www.njb.uscourts.gov.

[Date: December 14, 2006.]

GENERAL ORDERS

IN RE: AMENDMENT OF D.N.J. L. CIV. R. 101.1(c)(3)

GENERAL ORDER RESPECTING AMENDMENT OF D.N.J. L. CIV. R. 101.1(c)(3) REQUIRING PAYMENT ON EACH PRO HAC VICE ADMISSION TO THE CLERK OF THE DISTRICT COURT

The United States Bankruptcy Court for the District of New Jersey having required pursuant to D.N.J. LBR 101–1 that the Local Rules of the Bankruptcy Court (hereinafter "Bankruptcy Court Local Rules") as well as the Local Civil Rules of the United States District Court for the District of New Jersey (hereinafter "District Court Local Rules") shall be followed insofar as they are not inconsistent with the Bankruptcy Code and the Federal Rules of Bankruptcy Procedure; and further that from time to time, the Court may issue General Orders to supplement the Bankruptcy Court Local Rules; and the District Court having amended District Court Local Rule 101.1(c)(3) on March 22, 2005 to require that an order of the Court granting a motion to appear pro hac vice shall require the out of state attorney to make a payment of $150.00 on each admission payable to the Clerk of the United States District Court; and the Board of Judges of the Bankruptcy Court having specifically approved the application of this amendment to the admission of attorneys pro hac vice in the Bankruptcy Court for the District of New Jersey.

It is on this 14th day of December 2005, **ORDERED that:**

1. The order of the Bankruptcy Court granting a motion to appear pro hac vice shall require the out-of-state attorney to make a payment of $150.00 on each admission payable to the Clerk of the United States District Court.

2. The United States Bankruptcy Court for the District of New Jersey's recommended form order for admission pro hac vice as found on the Court's web site www.njb.uscourts.gov shall be followed.

3. This procedural transition contemplates a proposed amendment to D.N.J. LBR 2090–1 *Attorneys—Admission to Practice*, which is pending approval of Local Bankruptcy Rule Amendments by the United States District Court for the District of New Jersey pursuant to the Court's Annual Rule Making Cycle for the year 2006.

4. This General Order becomes effective on January 1, 2006 upon which date, the above referenced procedural transitions are to be implemented.

5. Notice to the Bar of this General Order shall be provided on the Court's Web site: www.njb.uscourts.gov.

[Dated: December 14, 2005.]

IN RE: THE BANKRUPTCY ABUSE PREVENTION AND CONSUMER PROTECTION ACT OF 2005

GENERAL ORDER ADOPTING INTERIM BANKRUPTCY RULES

Whereas, on April 20, 2005, the Bankruptcy Abuse Prevention and Consumer Protection Act of 2005 (the Act) was enacted into law; and

Whereas, most provisions of the Act are to become effective on October 17, 2005; and

Whereas, the Advisory Committee on Bankruptcy Rules has prepared Interim Rules designed to implement the substantive and procedural changes mandated by the Act; and

Whereas, the Committee on Rules of Practice and Procedure of the Judicial Conference of the United States has also approved these Interim Rules and recommends the adoption of the Interim Rules to provide uniform procedures for implementing the Act; and

Whereas, the general effective date of the Act has not provided sufficient time to promulgate rules after appropriate public notice and an opportunity for comment;

NOW THEREFORE, pursuant to 28 U.S.C. section 2071, Rule 83 of the Federal Rules of Civil Procedure and Rule 9029 of the Federal Rules of Bankruptcy Procedure, the attached Interim Rules* are adopted in their entirety without change by the Board of Judge of this Court to be effective October 17, 2005, to conform with the Act. For cases and proceedings not governed by the Act, the Federal Rules of Bankruptcy Procedure and the Local Rules of this Court, other than the Interim Rules, shall apply.

The Interim Rules shall remain in effect until further order of the Court.

[Dated: September 22, 2005.]

* Publisher's Note: The Interim Bankruptcy Rules (IBRs) are set forth following the "General Orders" of this court *post.*

IN RE: AMENDMENT OF D.N.J. LBR 1073-1, ASSIGNMENT OF CASES

GENERAL ORDER PENDING AMENDMENT OF D.N.J. LBR 1073–1, ASSIGNMENT OF CASES

For purposes of the division of business, the Court is divided into three units known as the Newark,

Trenton and Camden "vicinages," which consist of the counties served by such units in the three federal Courthouses in this District. A proposal for an Order realigning the Trenton Vicinage to include the County of Middlesex having been reviewed by the Court, and the Court having considered its benefits to the bench, bar, and parties in interest, and good cause having been shown;

IT IS ORDERED that:

1. The Trenton Vicinage is realigned to include the County of Middlesex.

2. This procedural transition contemplates a proposed amendment to *D.N.J. LBR 1073–1, Assignment of Cases*, which is pending approval of the Local Bankruptcy Rule Amendments by the United States Bankruptcy Court for the District of New Jersey, pursuant to the Court's Annual Rule Making Cycle.

3. This General Order becomes effective on October 1, 2006.

4. Notice to the Bar of this General Order shall be provided on the Court's Website: www.njb.uscourts.gov.

[Dated: September 25, 2006.]

GENERAL ORDER ESTABLISHING CRIMINAL REFERRAL AND REPORTING PROCEDURES MANDATED BY 18 U.S.C. SECTIONS 158(d) AND 3057

WHEREAS section 203(b) of the Bankruptcy Abuse Prevention and Consumer Protection Act of 2005 (BAPCPA) enacted section 158 of Title 18 of the United States Code to require the Attorney General of the United States to designate United States attorneys and agents of the Federal Bureau of Investigation as referred to in 18 U.S.C. section 158(b) to have primary responsibility in carrying out enforcement activities in addressing violations of 18 U.S.C. section 152 or 157 relating to abusive reaffirmations of debt and materially fraudulent statements in bankruptcy schedules that are intentionally fraudulent or misleading; and

WHEREAS 18 U.S.C. 158(d) requires that bankruptcy courts establish procedures for referring any case that may contain a materially fraudulent statement in a bankruptcy schedule to the individuals designated under 18 U.S.C. 158(b); and

WHEREAS 18 U.S.C. section 3057 requires any judge, or trustee having reasonable grounds for believing that any violation of the criminal bankruptcy statutes under Chapter 9 of Title 18 has been committed, to report violations to the appropriate United States attorney;

IT IS ORDERED that the following criminal referral and reporting procedures shall be adopted by the Bankruptcy Court for the District of New Jersey:

1. The procedures for referral of materially fraudulent statements in bankruptcy schedules to the United States Attorney and Federal Bureau of Investigation pursuant to 18 U.S.C. Section 158 are attached hereto as Exhibit A.

2. The Notification Statement for potential use by the Court in referring materially fraudulent statements in a bankruptcy schedule is attached hereto as Exhibit B.

3. The Notification Statement attached hereto as Exhibit B may also be used by the Court in carrying out its reporting obligations to the United States attorney pursuant to 18 U.S.C. section 3057.

4. The Clerk shall maintain and update, as required, the Addendum Attached as Exhibit C, which sets forth the designations required under 18 U.S.C. section 158.

IT IS FURTHER ORDERED that this General Order shall become effective as of March 22, 2007, and that notice to the bar and public shall be given by posting of this General Order on the Court's Website: www.njb.uscourts.gov.

/s/ HON. JUDITH H. WIZMUR

HON. JUDITH H. WIZMUR
CHIEF JUDGE
UNITED STATES BANKRUPTCY COURT
DISTRICT OF NEW JERSEY

Exhibit A

Referral Procedures—Materially Fraudulent Statements—18 U.S.C. section 158, *Designation of United States attorneys and agents of the Federal Bureau of Investigation to materially fraudulent statements in bankruptcy schedules;* 18 U.S.C. section 152, *Concealment of assets; false oaths and claims; bribery*; 18 USC section 157, *Bankruptcy Fraud*

If a bankruptcy judge determines that a case may contain a materially fraudulent statement in a bankruptcy schedule, the judge shall refer the case to the designated United States attorney and the designated agent of the Federal Bureau of Investigation noted on **Exhibit C** attached. The referral may be made by completing the referral form attached as **Exhibit B,** or by otherwise providing the same information in writing.

Exhibit B

United States Bankruptcy Court for the District of New Jersey

NOTIFICATION STATEMENT

REGARDING POTENTIAL

VIOLATION OF 18 U.S.C. § 152 OR 157

TO: ____________ POSITION: ____________

FROM: ____________ TITLE (if applicable): ____________

DATE: ____________ SIGNATURE ____________

1. **Background Information**
   a. Name of Debtor ____________
      i. Case number ____________
      ii. Debtor's Address ____________
      iii. Debtor's Telephone no. ____________
   b. Debtor's Attorney ____________
      i. Address ____________
      ii. Telephone no. ____________
   c. Name of Trustee (if applicable) ____________
      i. Address ____________
      ii. Telephone no. ____________
2. **Case Chapter**
   a. Under what chapter was the case originally filed: 7 ( ); 11 ( ); 12 ( ); 13 ( )
   b. Under what chapter is the case now pending: 7 ( ); 11 ( ); 12 ( ); 13 ( )
   c. Type of Case: Voluntary ( ) *or* Involuntary ( )
3. Report all facts and circumstances of the offense believed to have been committed (provide as much information as possible), including the following:
   a. Identify the schedule that contains the materially fraudulent statement.

____

____

____

____

   b. Explain why the statement is materially fraudulent.

____

____

____

____

   c. Provide the names, addresses, and telephone numbers of persons with knowledge of an information relating to the suspected offense.

____

____

____

____

   d. Disclose any other pertinent information regarding the suspected offense.

____

____

____

____

Exhibit C

INDIVIDUALS DESIGNATED BY THE ATTORNEY GENERAL OF THE UNITED STATES PURSUANT TO 18 U.S.C.158(d) TO HAVE PRIMARY RESPONSIBILITY IN CARRYING OUT ENFORCEMENT ACTIVITIES IN ADDRESSING VIOLATIONS OF 18 U.S.C. SECTION 152 OR 157

OFFICE OF THE UNITED STATES ATTORNEY:

Donna Gallucio
Assistant United States Attorney
970 Broad Street, Suite 700
Newark, New Jersey 07102

FEDERAL BUREAU OF INVESTIGATION:

Special Agent Andrew Rosenbaum
Federal Bureau of Investigation
11 Center Place
Newark, NJ 07102

[Dated: March 22, 2007.]

IN RE: ELECTRONIC TRANSCRIPT POLICY

GENERAL ORDER GOVERNING TRANSCRIPT REDACTION PROCEDURES UNDER THE JUDICIAL CONFERENCE PRIVACY POLICY

WHEREAS *The Judicial Conference Privacy Policy for Public Access to Electronic Case Files (The Judicial Conference Privacy Policy)* contains procedures for redacting certain protected personal information from court filings that are electronically available to the public, including transcripts of court proceedings available to the public in electronic format; and

WHEREAS the protected personal information under *The Judicial Conference Privacy Policy* includes social security numbers, birth dates, the names of individuals known to be minors, and financial account numbers ("*Personal Data Identifiers*"); and

WHEREAS this Court seeks to adopt the transcript redaction procedures required by *The Judicial Conference Privacy Policy;*

IT IS ORDERED that the following transcript redaction procedures shall be implemented by the Bankruptcy Court for the District of New Jersey:

1. A party to a case or adversary proceeding may order transcripts of Court proceedings from the transcriber.

2. The transcriber shall electronically file the transcript to the Court's CM/ECF system and simultaneously provide a copy to the ordering party. Other parties may order a copy of the transcript from the Court or directly from the transcriber.

3. Access to transcripts filed with the Court initially will be restricted in order to allow parties the opportunity to review the transcript for *Personal Data Identifiers* prior to the transcript being made available to the public.

4. It is the responsibility of each party to monitor the Court's docket for the filing of an official transcript and to review the transcript for *Personal Data Identifiers.*

5. Within five (5) business days of the filing of the transcript by the transcriber, a party shall inform the Court by filing a *Notice of Intent to Request Redaction* of the party's intent to redact *Personal Data Identifiers.* (The form *Notice of Intent to Request Redaction* may be found on the Court's Website: www.njb.uscourts.gov under "Forms."). A party is responsible for reviewing the opening and closing statements made on behalf of the party, any statements made by the party, and the testimony of any witnesses called by the party.

6. If a timely *Notice of Intent to Request Redaction* is filed, the transcript shall not be made electronically available to the public until the redaction occurs.

7. Within twenty-one (21) calendar days of the filing of the transcript, or longer if the Court so orders, the party having filed the *Notice of Intent to Request Redaction* shall file with the Court and serve on the transcriber a *List of Items to be Redacted* indicating the transcript page, paragraph and line in which the *Personal Data Identifiers* appear and the manner in which they are to be redacted. (The form *List of Items to Be Redacted may be found on the Court's Website*: www.njb.uscourts.gov under "Forms.").

8. Upon receipt of the *List of Items to be Redacted*, the transcriber shall redact the *Personal Data Identifiers* from the transcript as follows:

Social security numbers to the last four digits;
Financial account numbers to the last four digits;
Names of minor children to the initials;
Dates of birth to the year.

9. During the twenty-one (21) day period, or longer if the Court so orders, a party may file a motion for additional requested redactions to a transcript. The transcript shall not be available electronically until the Court has ruled upon any such motion.

10. If a *Notice of Intent to Request Redaction* is *not* filed within five (5) business days of the filing of the transcript by the transcriber, the Court and parties will assume redaction of *Personal Data Identifiers* is not required and the transcript will be made available electronically on the sixth business day of the filing of the transcript by the transcriber, unless the Court, for good cause finds that a transcript should not be made available electronically for a period of up to 60 days.

IT IS FURTHER ORDERED that this General Order shall become effective as of August 31, 2007 and that notice to the bar and public shall be given by posting of this General Order on the Court's Website:

www.njb.uscourts.gov. *The Judicial Conference Privacy Policy* is available at: www.privacy.uscourts.gov

[Dated: August 24, 2007.]

INTERIM BANKRUPTCY RULES

INTERIM RULE 1006. FILING FEE

(a) General Requirement. *Every petition shall be accompanied by the filing fee except as provided in subdivisions (b) and (c) of this rule. For the purpose of this rule, "filing fee" means the filing fee prescribed by 28 U.S.C. § 1930(a)(1)–(a)(5) and any other fee prescribed by the Judicial Conference of the United States under 28 U.S.C. § 1930(b) that is payable to the clerk upon the commencement of a case under the Code.*

(b) Payment of Filing Fee in Installments.

(1) Application to Pay Filing Fee in Installments. *A voluntary petition by an individual shall be accepted for filing if accompanied by the debtor's signed application, prepared as prescribed by the appropriate Official Form, stating that the debtor is unable to pay the filing fee except in installments.*

* * * * *

(3) Postponement of Attorney's Fees. *All installments of the filing fee must be paid in full before the debtor or chapter 13 trustee may make further payments to an attorney or any other person who renders services to the debtor in connection with the case.*

(c) Waiver of Filing Fee. *A voluntary chapter 7 petition filed by an individual shall be accepted for filing if accompanied by the debtor's application requesting a waiver under 28 U.S.C. § 1930(f), prepared as prescribed by the appropriate Official Form.*

Amended, on an interim basis, effective October 17, 2005.

INTERIM RULE 1007. LISTS, SCHEDULES, STATEMENTS, AND OTHER DOCUMENTS; TIME LIMITS

(a) List of Creditors and Equity Security Holders, and Corporate Ownership Statement.

* * * * *

(4) Chapter 15 Case. *Unless the court orders otherwise, a foreign representative filing a petition for recognition under chapter 15 shall file with the petition a list containing the name and address of all administrators in foreign proceedings of the debtor, all parties to any litigation in which the debtor is a party and that is pending in the United States at the time of the filing of the petition, and all entities against whom provisional relief is being sought under § 1519 of the Code.*

(5) Extension of Time. *Any extension of time for the filing of lists required by this subdivision may be granted only on motion for cause shown and on notice to the United States trustee and to any trustee, committee elected under § 705 or appointed under § 1102 of the Code, or other party as the court may direct.*

(b) Schedules, Statements, and Other Documents Required.

(1) Except in a chapter 9 municipality case, the debtor, unless the court orders otherwise, shall file the following schedules, statements, and other documents, prepared as prescribed by the appropriate Official Forms, if any:

(A) schedules of assets and liabilities;

(B) a schedule of current income and expenditures;

(C) a schedule of executory contracts and unexpired leases;

(D) a statement of financial affairs;

(E) copies of all payment advices or other evidence of payment, if any, with all but the last four digits of the debtor's social security number redacted, received by the debtor from an employer within 60 days before the filing of the petition; and

(F) a record of any interest that the debtor has in an account or program of the type specified in § 521(c) of the Code.

(2) An individual debtor in a chapter 7 case shall file a statement of intention as required by § 521(a) of the Code, prepared as prescribed by the appropriate Official Form. A copy of the statement of intention shall be served on the trustee and the creditors named in the statement on or before the filing of the statement.

(3) Unless the United States trustee has determined that the credit counseling requirement of § 109 does not apply in the district, an individual debtor must file the certificate and debt repayment plan, if any, required by § 521(b), a certification under § 109(h)(3), or a request for a determination by the court under § 109(h)(4).

(4) Unless § 707(b)(2)(D) applies, an individual debtor in a chapter 7 case with primarily consumer debts shall file a statement of current monthly income prepared as prescribed by the appropriate Official Form, and, if the debtor has current monthly income greater than the applicable median family income for the applicable state and household size, the calculations in accordance with § 707(b), prepared as prescribed by the appropriate Official Form.

(5) An individual debtor in a chapter 11 case shall file a statement of current monthly income, prepared as prescribed by the appropriate Official Form.

(6) A debtor in a chapter 13 case shall file a statement of current monthly income, prepared as

prescribed by the appropriate Official Form, and, if the debtor has current monthly income greater than the median family income for the applicable state and family size, a calculation of disposable income in accordance with § 1325(b)(3), prepared as prescribed by the appropriate Official Form.

(7) An individual debtor in a chapter 7 or chapter 13 case shall file a statement regarding completion of a course in personal financial management, prepared as prescribed by the appropriate Official Form.

(c) Time Limits. *In a voluntary case, the schedules, statements, and other documents required by subdivision (b)(1), (4), (5), and (6) shall be filed with the petition within 15 days thereafter, except as otherwise provided in subdivisions (d), (e), (f), and (h) of this rule. In an involuntary case, the list in subdivision (a)(2), and the schedules, statements, and other documents required by subdivision (b)(1) shall be filed by the debtor within 15 days of the entry of the order for relief. The documents required by subdivision (b)(3) shall be filed with the petition in a voluntary case. The statement required by subdivision (b)(7) shall be filed by the debtor within 45 days after the first date set for the meeting of creditors under § 341 of the Code in a chapter 7 case, and no later than the last payment made by the debtor as required by the plan or the filing of a motion for entry of a discharge under § 1328(b) in a chapter 13 case. Lists, schedules, statements, and other documents filed prior to the conversion of a case to another chapter shall be deemed filed in the converted case unless the court directs otherwise. Except as provided in § 1116(3) of the Code, any extension of time for the filing of the schedules, statements, and other documents may be granted only on motion for cause shown and on notice to the United States trustee and to any committee elected under § 705 or appointed under § 1102 of the Code, trustee, examiner, or other party as the court may direct. Notice of an extension shall be given to the United States trustee and to any committee, trustee, or other party as the court may direct.*

* * * * *

Amended, on an interim basis, effective October 17, 2005; amended effective October 1, 2006.

INTERIM RULE 1009. AMENDMENTS OF VOLUNTARY PETITIONS, LISTS, SCHEDULES AND STATEMENTS

* * * * *

(b) Statement of Intention. *The statement of intention may be amended by the debtor at any time before the expiration of the period provided in § 521(a) of the Code. The debtor shall give notice of the amendment to the trustee and to any entity affected thereby.*

* * * * *

Amended, on an interim basis, effective October 17, 2005.

INTERIM RULE 1010. SERVICE OF INVOLUNTARY PETITION AND SUMMONS; PETITION FOR RECOGNITION OF A FOREIGN NONMAIN PROCEEDING

On the filing of an involuntary petition or a petition for recognition of a foreign nonmain proceeding the clerk shall forthwith issue a summons for service. When an involuntary petition is filed, service shall be made on the debtor. When a petition for recognition of a foreign nonmain proceeding is filed, service shall be made on the debtor, any entity against whom provisional relief is sought under § 1519 of the Code, and on any other parties as the court may direct. The summons shall be served with a copy of the petition in the manner provided for service of a summons and complaint by Rule 7004(a) or (b). If service cannot be so made, the court may order that the summons and petition be served by mailing copies to the party's last known address, and by at least one publication in a manner and form directed by the court. The summons and petition may be served on the party anywhere. Rule 7004(e) and Rule 4(l) F.R.Civ.P. apply when service is made or attempted under this rule.

Amended, on an interim basis, effective October 17, 2005.

INTERIM RULE 1011. RESPONSIVE PLEADING OR MOTION IN INVOLUNTARY AND CROSS-BORDER CASES

(a) Who May Contest Petition. *The debtor named in an involuntary petition or a party in interest to a petition for recognition of a foreign proceeding may contest the petition. In the case of a petition against a partnership under Rule 1004, a nonpetitioning general partner, or a person who is alleged to be a general partner but denies the allegation, may contest the petition.*

* * * * *

Amended, on an interim basis, effective October 17, 2005.

INTERIM RULE 1017. DISMISSAL OR CONVERSION OF CASE; SUSPENSION

* * * * *

(e) Dismissal of an Individual Debtor's Chapter 7 Case or Conversion to a Case Under Chapter 11 or 13 for Abuse. *The court may dismiss or, with the debtor's consent, convert an individual debtor's case for abuse under § 707(b) only on motion and after a* *hearing on notice to the debtor, the trustee, the United States trustee, and any other entities as the court directs.*

(1) Except as otherwise provided in § 704(b)(2), a motion to dismiss a case for abuse under § 707(b) or (c) may be filed only within 60 days after the first date set for the meeting of creditors under § 341(a), unless, on request filed before the time has expired, the court for cause extends the time for filing the motion to dismiss. The party filing the motion shall set forth in the motion all matters to be considered at the hearing. A motion to dismiss under § 707(b)(1) and (3) shall state with particularity the circumstances alleged to constitute abuse.

* * * * *

Amended, on an interim basis, effective October 17, 2005.

INTERIM RULE 1019. CONVERSION OF CHAPTER 11 REORGANIZATION CASE, CHAPTER 12 FAMILY FARMER'S DEBT ADJUSTMENT CASE, OR CHAPTER 13 INDIVIDUAL'S DEBT ADJUSTMENT CASE TO A CHAPTER 7 LIQUIDATION CASE

* * * * *

(2) New Filing Periods. *A new time period for filing a motion under § 707(b) or (c), a claim, a complaint objecting to discharge, or a complaint to obtain a determination of dischargeability of any debt shall commence under Rules 1017, 3002, 4004, or 4007, provided that a new time period shall not commence if a chapter 7 case had been converted to a chapter 11, 12, or 13 case and thereafter reconverted to a chapter 7 case and the time for filing a motion under § 707(b) or (c), a claim, a complaint objecting to discharge, or a complaint to obtain a determination of the dischargeability of any debt, or any extension thereof, expired in the original chapter 7 case.*

* * * * *

Amended, on an interim basis, effective October 17, 2005.

INTERIM RULE 1020. SMALL BUSINESS CHAPTER 11 REORGANIZATION CASE

(a) Small Business Debtor Designation. *In a voluntary chapter 11 case, the debtor shall state in the petition whether the debtor is a small business debtor. In an involuntary chapter 11 case, the debtor shall file within 15 days after entry of the order for relief a statement as to whether the debtor is a small business debtor. Except as provided in subdivision (c), the status of the case with respect to whether it is a small business case shall be in accordance with the debtor's statement under this subdivision, unless and until the court enters an order finding that the debtor's statement is incorrect.*

(b) Objecting to Designation. *Except as provided in subdivision (c), the United States trustee or a party in interest may file an objection to the debtor's statement under subdivision (a) not later than 30 days after the conclusion of the meeting of creditors held under § 341(a) of the Code, or within 30 days after any amendment to the statement, whichever is later.*

(c) Appointment of Committee of Unsecured Creditors. *If the United States trustee has appointed a committee of unsecured creditors under § 1102(a)(1), the case shall proceed as a small business case only if, and from the time when, the court enters an order determining that the committee has not been sufficiently active and representative to provide effective oversight of the debtor and that the debtor satisfies all the other requirements for being a small business. A request for a determination under this subdivision may be filed by the United States trustee or a party in interest only within a reasonable time after the failure of the committee to be sufficiently active and representative. The debtor may file a request for a determination at any time as to whether the committee has been sufficiently active and representative.*

(d) Procedure for Objection or Determination. *Any objection or request for a determination under this rule shall be governed by Rule 9014 and served on the debtor, the debtor's attorney, the United States trustee, the trustee, any committee appointed under § 1102 or its authorized agent, or, if no committee of unsecured creditors has been appointed under § 1102, on the creditors included on the list filed under Rule 1007(d), and on such other entities as the court may direct.*

Amended, on an interim basis, effective October 17, 2005.

INTERIM RULE 1021. HEALTH CARE BUSINESS CASE

(a) Health Care Business Designation. *Unless the court orders otherwise, if a petition in a case under chapter 7, chapter 9, or chapter 11 states that the debtor is a health care business, the case shall proceed as a case in which the debtor is a health care business.*

(b) Motion. *The United States trustee or a party in interest may file a motion for a determination as to whether the debtor is a health care business. The motion shall be transmitted to the United States trustee and served on the debtor, the trustee, any committee elected under § 705 or appointed under § 1102 of the Code or its authorized agent, or, if the case is a chapter 9 municipality case or a chapter 11* *reorganization case and no committee of unsecured creditors has been appointed under § 1102, on the creditors included on the list filed under Rule 1007(d), and such other entities as the court may direct. The motion shall be governed by Rule 9014.*

Amended, on an interim basis, effective October 17, 2005.

INTERIM RULE 2002. NOTICES TO CREDITORS, EQUITY SECURITY HOLDERS, ADMINISTRATORS IN FOREIGN PROCEEDINGS, PERSONS AGAINST WHOM PROVISIONAL RELIEF IS SOUGHT IN FOREIGN PROCEEDINGS, PERSONS AGAINST WHOM PROVISIONAL RELIEF IS SOUGHT IN ANCILLARY AND OTHER CROSS–BORDER CASES, UNITED STATES, AND UNITED STATES TRUSTEE

(a) Twenty-Day Notices to Parties in Interest. *Except as provided in subdivisions (h), (i), (l), (p), and (q) of this rule, the clerk, or some other person as the court may direct, shall give the debtor, the trustee, all creditors and indenture trustees at least 20 days' notice by mail of:*

* * * * *

(b) Twenty-Five-Day Notices to Parties in Interest. *Except as provided in subdivision (l) of this rule, the clerk, or some other person as the court may direct, shall give the debtor, the trustee, all creditors and indenture trustees not less than 25 days notice by mail of (1) the time fixed for filing objections and the hearing to consider approval of a disclosure statement or, under § 1125(f), to make a final determination whether the plan provides adequate information so that a separate disclosure statement is not necessary; and (2) the time fixed for filing objections and the hearing to consider confirmation of a chapter 9, chapter 11, or chapter 13 plan.*

(c) Content of Notice.

(1) Proposed Use, Sale, or Lease of Property. *Subject to Rule 6004 the notice of a proposed use, sale, or lease of property required by subdivision (a)(2) of this rule shall include the time and place of any public sale, the terms and conditions of any private sale and the time fixed for filing objections. The notice of a proposed use, sale, or lease of property, including real estate, is sufficient if it generally describes the property. The notice of a proposed sale or lease of personally identifiable information under § 363(b)(1)(A) or (B) of the Code shall state whether the sale is consistent with a policy prohibiting the transfer of the information.*

* * * * *

(f) Other Notices. *Except as provided in subdivision (l) of this rule, the clerk, or some other person as the court may direct, shall give the debtor, all creditors, and indenture trustees notice by mail of: (1) the order for relief; (2) the dismissal or the conversion of the case to another chapter, or the suspension of proceedings under § 305; (3) the time allowed for filing claims pursuant to Rule 3002; (4) the time fixed for filing a complaint objecting to the debtor's discharge pursuant to § 727 of the Code as provided in Rule 4004; (5) the time fixed for filing a complaint to determine the dischargeability of a debt pursuant to § 523 of the Code as provided in Rule 4007; (6) the waiver, denial, or revocation of a discharge as provided in Rule 4006; (7) entry of an order confirming a chapter 9, 11, or 12 plan; (8) a summary of the trustee's final report in a chapter 7 case if the net proceeds realized exceed $1,500; (9) a notice under Rule 5008 regarding the presumption of abuse; and (10) a statement under § 704(b)(1) as to whether the debtor's case would be presumed to be an abuse under § 707(b). Notice of the time fixed for accepting or rejecting a plan pursuant to Rule 3017(c) shall be given in accordance with Rule 3017(d).*

* * * * *

(p) Notice to a Foreign Creditor.

(1) If, at the request of a party in interest or the United States trustee, or on its own initiative, the court finds that a notice mailed within the time prescribed by these rules would not be sufficient to give a creditor with a foreign address to which notices under these rules are mailed reasonable notice under the circumstances, the court may order that the notice be supplemented with notice by other means or that the time prescribed for the notice by mail be enlarged.

(2) Unless the court for cause orders otherwise, a creditor with a foreign address to which notices under this rule are mailed shall be given at least 30 days' notice of the time fixed for filing a proof of claim under Rule 3002(c) or Rule 3003(c).

(q) Notice of Petition for Recognition of Foreign Proceeding and of Court's Intention to Communicate With Foreign Courts and Foreign Representatives.

(1) Notice of Petition for Recognition. *The clerk, or some other person as the court may direct, shall forthwith give the debtor, all administrators in foreign proceedings of the debtor, all entities against whom provisional relief is being sought under § 1519 of the Code, all parties to any litigation in which the debtor is a party and that is pending in the United States at the time of the filing of the petition, and such other entities as the court may direct, at least 20 days' notice by mail of the hearing on the petition for recognition of a foreign proceeding. The notice shall state whether the petition seeks recognition as a foreign main proceeding or foreign nonmain proceeding.*

(2) Notice of Court's Intention to Communicate with Foreign Courts and Foreign Representatives. *The clerk, or some other person as the court may direct, shall give the debtor, all administrators in foreign proceedings of the debtor, all entities against whom provisional relief is being sought under § 1519 of the Code, all parties to any litigation in which the debtor is a party and that is pending in the United States at the time of the filing of the petition, and such other entities as the court may direct, notice by mail of the court's intention to communicate with a foreign court or foreign representative as prescribed by Rule 5012.*

Amended, on an interim basis, effective October 17, 2005.

INTERIM RULE 2003. MEETING OF CREDITORS OR EQUITY SECURITY HOLDERS

(a) Date and Place. *Except as provided in § 341(e) of the Code, in a chapter 7 liquidation or a chapter 11 reorganization case, the United States trustee shall call a meeting of creditors to be held no fewer than 20 and no more than 40 days after the order for relief. In a chapter 12 family farmer debt adjustment case, the United States trustee shall call a meeting of creditors to be held no fewer than 20 and no more than 35 days after the order for relief. In a chapter 13 individual's debt adjustment case, the United States trustee shall call a meeting of creditors to be held no fewer than 20 and no more than 50 days after the order for relief. If there is an appeal from or a motion to vacate the order for relief, or if there is a motion to dismiss the case, the United States trustee may set a later date for the meeting. The meeting may be held at a regular place for holding court or at any other place designated by the United States trustee within the district convenient for the parties in interest. If the United States trustee designates a place for the meeting which is not regularly staffed by the United States trustee or an assistant who may preside at the meeting, the meeting may be held not more than 60 days after the order for relief.*

* * * * *

Amended, on an interim basis, effective October 17, 2005.

INTERIM RULE 2007.1 APPOINTMENT OF TRUSTEE OR EXAMINER IN A CHAPTER 11 REORGANIZATION CASE

* * * * *

(b) Election of Trustee.

* * * * *

(3) Report of Election and Resolution of Disputes.

(A) Report of Undisputed Election. If no dispute arises out of the election, the United States trustee shall promptly file a report certifying the election, including the name and address of the person elected and a statement that the election is undisputed. The report shall be accompanied by a verified statement of the person elected setting forth the person's connections with the debtor, creditors, any other party in interest, their respective attorneys and accountants, the United States trustee, or any person employed in the office of the United States trustee.

(B) Dispute Arising Out of an Election. If a dispute arises out of an election, the United States trustee shall promptly file a report stating that the election is disputed, informing the court of the nature of the dispute, and listing the name and address of any candidate elected under any alternative presented by the dispute. The report shall be accompanied by a verified statement by each candidate elected under each alternative presented by the dispute, setting forth the person's connections with the debtor, creditors, any other party in interest, their respective attorneys and accountants, the United States trustee, or any person employed in the office of the United States trustee. Not later than the date on which the report of the disputed election is filed, the United States trustee shall mail a copy of the report and each verified statement to any party in interest that has made a request to convene a meeting under § 1104(b) or to receive a copy of the report, and to any committee appointed under § 1102 of the Code.

(c) Approval of Appointment. *An order approving the appointment of a trustee or an examiner under § 1104(d) of the Code, shall be made on application of the United States trustee. The application shall state the name of the person appointed and, to the best of the applicant's knowledge, all the person's connections with the debtor, creditors, any other parties in interest, their respective attorneys and accountants, the United States trustee, or persons employed in the office of the United States trustee. The application shall state the names of the parties in interest with whom the United States trustee consulted regarding the appointment. The application shall be accompanied by a verified statement of the person appointed setting forth the person's connections with the debtor, creditors, any other party in interest, their respective attorneys and accountants, the United States trustee, or any person employed in the office of the United States trustee.*

Amended, on an interim basis, effective October 17, 2005.

INTERIM RULE 2007.2 APPOINTMENT OF PATIENT CARE OMBUDSMAN IN A HEALTH CARE BUSINESS CASE

(a) Order to Appoint Patient Care Ombudsman. *In a chapter 7, chapter 9, or chapter 11 case in which* *the debtor is a health care business, the court shall order the appointment of a patient care ombudsman under § 333 of the Code, unless the court, on motion of the United States trustee or a party in interest filed not later than 20 days after the commencement of the case or within another time fixed by the court, finds that the appointment of a patient care ombudsman is not necessary for the protection of patients under the specific circumstances of the case.*

(b) Motion for Order to Appoint Ombudsman. *If the court has ordered that the appointment of an ombudsman is not necessary, or has ordered the termination of the appointment of an ombudsman, the court, on motion of the United States trustee or a party in interest, may order the appointment at any time during the case if the court finds that the appointment of an ombudsman has become necessary to protect patients.*

(c) Appointment of Ombudsman. *If a patient care ombudsman is appointed under § 333, the United States trustee shall promptly file a notice of the appointment, including the name and address of the person appointed. Unless the person appointed is a State Long–Term Care Ombudsman, the notice shall be accompanied by a verified statement of the person appointed setting forth the person's connections with the debtor, creditors, patients, any other party in interest, their respective attorneys and accountants, the United States trustee, and any person employed in the office of the United States trustee.*

(d) Termination of Appointment. *On motion of the United States trustee or a party in interest, the court may terminate the appointment of a patient care ombudsman if the court finds that the appointment is not necessary for the protection of patients.*

(e) Motion. *A motion under this rule shall be governed by Rule 9014. The motion shall be transmitted to the United States trustee and served on the debtor, the trustee, any committee elected under § 705 or appointed under § 1102 of the Code or its authorized agent, or, if the case is a chapter 9 municipality case or a chapter 11 reorganization case and no committee of unsecured creditors has been appointed under § 1102, on the creditors included on the list filed under Rule 1007(d), and such other entities as the court may direct.*

Amended, on an interim basis, effective October 17, 2005.

INTERIM RULE 2015. DUTY TO KEEP RECORDS, MAKE REPORTS, AND GIVE NOTICE OF CASE OR CHANGE OF STATUS

* * * * *

(d) Foreign Representative. *In a case in which the court has granted recognition of a foreign proceeding under chapter 15, the foreign representative shall file any notice required under § 1518 of the Code within 15 days after the date when the representative becomes aware of the subsequent information.*

(e) Transmission of Reports. *In a chapter 11 case the court may direct that copies or summaries of annual reports and copies or summaries of other reports shall be mailed to the creditors, equity security holders, and indenture trustees. The court may also direct the publication of summaries of any such reports. A copy of every report or summary mailed or published pursuant to this subdivision shall be transmitted to the United States trustee.*

Amended, on an interim basis, effective October 17, 2005.

INTERIM RULE 2015.1 PATIENT CARE OMBUDSMAN

(a) Reports. *Unless the court orders otherwise, a patient care ombudsman, at least 10 days before making a report under § 333(b)(2) of the Code, shall give notice that the report will be made to the court. The notice shall be transmitted to the United States trustee, posted conspicuously at the health care facility that is the subject of the report, and served on the debtor, the trustee, all patients, and any committee elected under § 705 or appointed under § 1102 of the Code or its authorized agent, or, if the case is a chapter 9 municipality case or a chapter 11 reorganization case and no committee of unsecured creditors has been appointed under § 1102, on the creditors included on the list filed under Rule 1007(d), and such other entities as the court may direct. The notice shall state the date and time when the report will be made, the manner in which the report will be made, and, if the report is in writing, the name, address, telephone number, e-mail address, and website, if any, of the person from whom a copy of the report may be obtained at the debtor's expense.*

(b) Authorization to Review Confidential Patient Records. *A motion by a health care ombudsman under § 333(c) to review confidential patient records shall be governed by Rule 9014, served on the patient and any family member or other contact person whose name and address has been given to the trustee or the debtor for the purpose of providing information regarding the patient's health care, and transmitted to the United States trustee subject to applicable nonbankruptcy law relating to patient privacy. Unless the court orders otherwise, a hearing on the motion may be commenced no earlier than 15 days after service of the motion.*

Amended, on an interim basis, effective October 17, 2005.

INTERIM RULE 2015.2 TRANSFER OF PATIENT IN HEALTH CARE BUSINESS CASE

Unless the court orders otherwise, if the debtor is a health care business, the trustee may not transfer a patient to another health care business under § 704(a)(12) of the Code unless the trustee gives at least 10 days' notice of the transfer to the patient care ombudsman, if any, and to the patient and any family member or other contact person whose name and address has been given to the trustee or the debtor for the purpose of providing information regarding the patient's health care subject to applicable nonbankruptcy law relating to patient privacy.

Amended, on an interim basis, effective October 17, 2005.

INTERIM RULE 3002. FILING PROOF OF CLAIMS OR INTEREST

* * * * *

(c) Time for Filing. *In a chapter 7 liquidation, chapter 12 family farmer's debt adjustment, or chapter 13 individual's debt adjustment case, a proof of claim is timely filed if it is filed not later than 90 days after the first date set for the meeting of creditors called under § 341(a) of the Code, except as follows:*

(1) A proof of claim filed by a governmental unit, other than for a claim resulting from a tax return filed under § 1308, is timely filed if it is filed not later than 180 days after the date of the order for relief. On motion of a governmental unit before the expiration of such period and for cause shown, the court may extend the time for filing of a claim by the governmental unit. A proof of claim filed by a governmental unit for a claim resulting from a tax return filed under § 1308 is timely filed if it is filed not later than 180 days after the date of the order for relief or 60 days after the date of the filing of the tax return, whichever is later.

* * * * *

(6) If notice of the time for filing a proof of claim has been mailed to a creditor at a foreign address, on motion filed by the creditor before or after the expiration of the time, the court may extend the time by not more than 60 days if the court finds that the notice was not sufficient under the circumstances to give the creditor a reasonable time to file a proof of claim.

Amended, on an interim basis, effective October 17, 2005.

INTERIM RULE 3003. FILING PROOF OF CLAIM OR EQUITY SECURITY INTEREST IN CHAPTER 9 MUNICIPALITY OR CHAPTER 11 REORGANIZATION CASES

* * * * *

(c) Filing Proof of Claim.

(1) Who May File. *Any creditor or indenture trustee may file a proof of claim within the time prescribed by subdivision (c)(3) of this rule.*

(2) Who Must File. *Any creditor or equity security holder whose claim or interest is not scheduled or scheduled as disputed, contingent, or unliquidated shall file a proof of claim or interest within the time prescribed by subdivision (c)(3) of this rule; any creditor who fails to do so shall not be treated as a creditor with respect to such claim for the purposes of voting and distribution.*

(3) Time for Filing. *The court shall fix and for cause shown may extend the time within which proofs of claim or interest may be filed. Notwithstanding the expiration of such time, a proof of claim may be filed to the extent and under the conditions stated in Rule 3002(c)(2), (c)(3), (c)(4), and (c)(6).*

(4) Effect of Filing Claim or Interest. *A proof of claim or interest executed and filed in accordance with this subdivision shall supersede any scheduling of that claim or interest pursuant to § 521(a)(1) of the Code.*

(5) Filing by Indenture Trustee. *An indenture trustee may file a claim on behalf of all known or unknown holders of securities issued pursuant to the trust instrument under which it is trustee.*

* * * * *

Amended, on an interim basis, effective October 17, 2005.

INTERIM RULE 3016. FILING OF PLAN AND DISCLOSURE STATEMENT IN A CHAPTER 9 MUNICIPALITY OR CHAPTER 11 REORGANIZATION CASE

* * * * *

(b) Disclosure Statement. *In a chapter 9 or 11 case, a disclosure statement under § 1125 or evidence showing compliance with § 1126(b) of the Code shall be filed with the plan or within a time fixed by the court, unless the plan is intended to provide adequate information under § 1125(f)(1). If the plan is intended to provide adequate information under § 1125(f)(1), it shall be so designated and Rule 3017.1 shall apply as if the plan is a disclosure statement.*

* * * * *

Amended, on an interim basis, effective October 17, 2005.

INTERIM RULE 3017.1 COURT CONSIDERATION OF DISCLOSURE STATEMENT IN A SMALL BUSINESS CASE

(a) Conditional Approval of Disclosure Statement. *In a small business case, the court may, on application of the plan proponent or on its own initiative, conditionally approve a disclosure state-*

ment filed in accordance with Rule 3016. On or before conditional approval of the disclosure statement, the court shall:

(1) fix a time within which the holders of claims and interests may accept or reject the plan;

(2) fix a time for filing objections to the disclosure statement;

(3) fix a date for the hearing on final approval of the disclosure statement to be held if a timely objection is filed; and

(4) fix a date for the hearing on confirmation.

(b) Application of Rule 3017. *Rule 3017(a), (b), (c), and (e) do not apply to a conditionally approved disclosure statement. Rule 3017(d) applies to a conditionally approved disclosure statement, except that conditional approval is considered approval of the disclosure statement for the purpose of applying Rule 3017(d).*

(c) Final Approval.

(1) Notice. *Notice of the time fixed for filing objections and the hearing to consider final approval of the disclosure statement shall be given in accordance with Rule 2002 and may be combined with notice of the hearing on confirmation of the plan.*

(2) Objections. *Objections to the disclosure statement shall be filed, transmitted to the United States trustee, and served on the debtor, the trustee, any committee appointed under the Code and any other entity designated by the court at any time before final approval of the disclosure statement or by an earlier date as the court may fix.*

(3) Hearing. *If a timely objection to the disclosure statement is filed, the court shall hold a hearing to consider final approval before or combined with the hearing on confirmation of the plan.*

Amended, on an interim basis, effective October 17, 2005.

INTERIM RULE 3019. MODIFICATION OF ACCEPTED PLAN BEFORE OR AFTER CONFIRMATION IN A CHAPTER 9 MUNICIPALITY OR CHAPTER 11 REORGANIZATION CASE

(a) *In a chapter 9 or chapter 11 case, after a plan has been accepted and before its confirmation, the proponent may file a modification of the plan. If the court finds after hearing on notice to the trustee, any committee appointed under the Code, and any other entity designated by the court that the proposed modification does not adversely change the treatment of the claim of any creditor or the interest of any equity security holder who has not accepted in writing the modification, it shall be deemed accepted by all creditors and equity security holders who have previously accepted the plan.*

(b) *If the debtor is an individual, a request to modify the plan under § 1127(e) of the Code shall identify the proponent and shall be filed together with the proposed modification. The clerk, or some other person as the court may direct, shall give the debtor, the trustee, and all creditors not less than 20 days' notice by mail of the time fixed for filing objections and, if an objection is filed, the hearing to consider the proposed modification, unless the court orders otherwise with respect to creditors who are not affected by the proposed modification. A copy of the notice shall be transmitted to the United States trustee. A copy of the proposed modification shall be included with the notice. Any objection to the proposed modification shall be filed and served on the debtor, the proponent of the modification, the trustee, and any other entity designated by the court, and shall be transmitted to the United States trustee. An objection to a proposed modification is governed by Rule 9014.*

Amended, on an interim basis, effective October 17, 2005.

INTERIM RULE 4002. DUTIES OF DEBTOR

(a) In General. *In addition to performing other duties prescribed by the Code and rules, the debtor shall:*

(1) attend and submit to an examination at the times ordered by the court;

(2) attend the hearing on a complaint objecting to discharge and testify, if called as a witness;

(3) inform the trustee immediately in writing as to the location of real property in which the debtor has an interest and the name and address of every person holding money or property subject to the debtor's withdrawal or order if a schedule of property has not yet been filed pursuant to Rule 1007;

(4) cooperate with the trustee in the preparation of an inventory, the examination of proofs of claim, and the administration of the estate; and

(5) file a statement of any change of the debtor's address.

(b) Individual Debtor's Duty to Provide Documentation.

(1) Personal Identification. *Every individual debtor shall bring to the meeting of creditors under § 341:*

(A) a picture identification issued by a governmental unit, or other personal identifying information that establishes the debtor's identity; and

(B) evidence of social security number(s), or a written statement that such documentation does not exist.

(2) Financial Information. *Every individual debtor shall bring to the meeting of creditors under § 341 and make available to the trustee the following documents or copies of them, or provide a written statement that the documentation does not exist or is not in the debtor's possession:*

(A) evidence of current income such as the most recent payment advice;

(B) unless the trustee or the United States trustee instructs otherwise, statements for each of the debtor's depository and investment accounts, including checking, savings, and money market accounts, mutual funds and brokerage accounts for the time period that includes the date of the filing of the petition; and

(C) documentation of monthly expenses claimed by the debtor when required by § 707(b)(2)(A) or (B).

(3) Tax Return. *At least 7 days before the first date set for the meeting of creditors under § 341, the debtor shall provide to the trustee a copy of the debtor's Federal income tax return for the most recent tax year ending immediately before the commencement of the case and for which a return was filed, including any attachments, or a transcript of the tax return, or provide a written statement that the documentation does not exist.*

(4) Tax Returns Provided to Creditors. *If a creditor, at least 15 days before the first date set for the meeting of creditors under § 341, requests a copy of the debtor's tax return that is to be provided to the trustee under subdivision (b)(3), the debtor shall provide to the requesting creditor a copy of the return, including any attachments, or a transcript of the tax return, or provide a written statement that the documentation does not exist at least 7 days before the first date set for the meeting of creditors under § 341.*

(5) The debtor's obligation to provide tax returns under Rule 4002(b)(3) and (b)(4) is subject to procedures for safeguarding the confidentiality of tax information established by the Director of the Administrative Office of the United States Courts.

Amended, on an interim basis, effective October 17, 2005.

INTERIM RULE 4003. EXEMPTIONS

* * * * *

(b) Objecting to a Claim of Exemptions.

(1) Except as provided in paragraph (2), a party in interest may file an objection to the list of property claimed as exempt within 30 days after the meeting of creditors held under § 341(a) is concluded or within 30 days after any amendment to the list or supplemental schedules is filed, whichever is later. The court may, for cause, extend the time for filing objections if, before the time to object expires, a party in interest files a request for an extension.

(2) An objection to a claim of exemption based on § 522(q) shall be filed before the closing of the case. If an exemption is first claimed after a case is reopened, an objection shall be filed before the reopened case is closed.

(3) Copies of the objections shall be delivered or mailed to the trustee, the person filing the list, and the attorney for that person.

* * * * *

Amended, on an interim basis, effective October 17, 2005.

INTERIM RULE 4004. GRANT OR DENIAL OF DISCHARGE

* * * * *

(c) Grant of Discharge.

(1)

* * * * *

(F) a motion to extend the time for filing a motion to dismiss the case under Rule 1017(e) is pending,

(G) the debtor has not paid in full the filing fee prescribed by 28 U.S.C. § 1930(a) and any other fee prescribed by the Judicial Conference of the United States under 28 U.S.C. § 1930(b) that is payable to the clerk upon the commencement of a case under the Code, unless the court has waived the fees under 28 U.S.C. § 1930(f);

(H) the debtor has not filed with the court a statement regarding completion of a course in personal financial management as required by Rule 1007(b)(7);

(I) a motion to delay or postpone discharge under § 727(a)(12) is pending; or

(J) a presumption that a reaffirmation agreement is an undue hardship has arisen under § 524(m).

Amended, on an interim basis, effective October 17, 2005.

INTERIM RULE 4006. NOTICE OF NO DISCHARGE

If an order is entered denying or revoking a discharge or if a waiver of discharge is filed, the clerk, after the order becomes final or the waiver is filed, or, in the case of an individual, if the case is closed without the entry of an order of discharge, shall promptly give notice thereof to all parties in interest in the manner provided in Rule 2002.

Amended, on an interim basis, effective October 17, 2005.

INTERIM RULE 4007. DETERMINATION OF DISCHARGEABILITY OF A DEBT

* * * * *

(c) Time for Filing Complaint Under § 523(c) in a Chapter 7 Liquidation, Chapter 11 Reorganization, Chapter 12 Family Farmer's Debt Adjustment Case, or Chapter 13 Individual's Debt Adjustment Case; Notice of Time Fixed. *Except as provided in subdivision (d), a complaint to determine the dischargeability of a debt under § 523(c) shall be filed no later than 60 days after the first date set for the meeting of creditors under § 341(a). The court shall give all creditors no less than 30 days' notice of the time so fixed in the manner provided in Rule 2002. On motion of a party in interest, after hearing on notice, the court may for cause extend the time fixed under this subdivision. The motion shall be filed before the time has expired.*

(d) Time for Filing Complaint Under § 523(a)(6) in Chapter 13 Individual's Debt Adjustment Case; Notice of Time Fixed. *On motion by a debtor for a discharge under § 1328(b), the court shall enter an order fixing the time to file a complaint to determine the dischargeability of any debt under § 523(a)(6) and shall give no less than 30 days' notice of the time fixed to all creditors in the manner provided in Rule 2002. On motion of any party in interest after hearing on notice the court may for cause extend the time fixed under this subdivision. The motion shall be filed before the time has expired.*

* * * * *

Amended, on an interim basis, effective October 17, 2005.

INTERIM RULE 4008. DISCHARGE AND REAFFIRMATION HEARING

Not more than 30 days following the entry of an order granting or denying a discharge, or confirming a plan in a chapter 11 reorganization case concerning an individual debtor and on not less than 10 days notice to the debtor and the trustee, the court may hold a hearing as provided in § 524(d) of the Code. A motion by the debtor for approval of a reaffirmation agreement shall be filed before or at the hearing. The debtor's statement required under § 524(k) shall be accompanied by a statement of the total income and total expense amounts stated on schedules I and J. If there is a difference between the income and expense amounts stated on schedules I and J and the statement required under § 524(k), the accompanying statement shall include an explanation of any difference.

Amended, on an interim basis, effective October 17, 2005.

INTERIM RULE 5003. RECORDS KEPT BY THE CLERK

* * * * *

(e) Register of Mailing Addresses of Federal and State Governmental Units and Certain Taxing Authorities. *The United States or the state or territory in which the court is located may file a statement designating its mailing address. The United States, state, territory, or local governmental unit responsible for the collection of taxes within the district in which the case is pending may file a statement designating an address for service of requests under § 505(b) of the Code, and the designation shall describe where further information concerning additional requirements for filing such requests may be found. The clerk shall keep, in the form and manner as the Director of the Administrative Office of the United States Courts may prescribe, a register that includes the mailing addresses designated under this subdivision, but the clerk is not required to include in the register more than one mailing address for each department, agency, or instrumentality of the United States or the state or territory. If more than one address for a department, agency, or instrumentality is included in the register, the clerk shall also include information that would enable a user of the register to determine the circumstances when each address is applicable, and mailing notice to only one applicable address is sufficient to provide effective notice. The clerk shall update the register annually, effective January 2 of each year. The mailing address in the register is conclusively presumed to be a proper address for the governmental unit, but the failure to use that mailing address does not invalidate any notice that is otherwise effective under applicable law.*

* * * * *

Amended, on an interim basis, effective October 17, 2005.

INTERIM RULE 5008. NOTICE REGARDING PRESUMPTION OF ABUSE IN CHAPTER 7 CASES OF INDIVIDUAL DEBTORS

In a chapter 7 case of an individual with primarily consumer debts in which a presumption of abuse has arisen under § 707(b), the clerk shall give to creditors notice of the presumption of abuse in accordance with Rule 2002 within 10 days after the date of the filing of the petition. If the debtor has not filed a statement indicating whether a presumption of abuse has arisen, the clerk shall give notice to creditors within 10 days after the date of the filing of the petition that the debtor has not filed the statement and that further notice will be given if a later filed statement indicates that a presumption of abuse has arisen. If a debtor later files a statement indicating that a presumption of abuse has arisen, the clerk shall give notice to creditors of the presumption of abuse as promptly as practicable.

Amended, on an interim basis, effective October 17, 2005.

INTERIM RULE 5012. COMMUNICATION AND COOPERATION WITH FOREIGN COURTS AND FOREIGN REPRESENTATIVES

Except for communications for scheduling and administrative purposes, the court in any case commenced by a foreign representative shall give at least 20 days' notice of its intent to communicate with a foreign court or a foreign representative. The notice shall identify the subject of the anticipated communication and shall be given in the manner provided by Rule 2002(q). Any entity that wishes to participate in the communication shall notify the court of its intention not later than 5 days before the scheduled communication.

Amended, on an interim basis, effective October 17, 2005.

INTERIM RULE 6004. USE, SALE, OR LEASE OF PROPERTY

* * * * *

(g) Sale of Personally Identifiable Information.

(1) Motion. *A motion for authority to sell or lease personally identifiable information under § 363(b)(1)(B) shall include a request for an order directing the United States trustee to appoint a consumer privacy ombudsman under § 332. The motion shall be governed by Rule 9014 and shall be served on any committee elected under § 705 or appointed under § 1102 of the Code, or if the case is a chapter 11 reorganization case and no committee of unsecured creditors has been appointed under § 1102, on the creditors included on the list of creditors filed under Rule 1007(d), and on such other entities as the court may direct. The motion shall be transmitted to the United States trustee.*

(2) Appointment. *If a consumer privacy ombudsman is appointed under § 332, no later than 5 days before the hearing on the motion under § 363(b)(1)(B), the United States trustee shall file a notice of the appointment, including the name and address of the person appointed. The United States trustee's notice shall be accompanied by a verified statement of the person appointed setting forth the person's connections with the debtor, creditors, any other party in interest, their respective attorneys and accountants, the United States trustee, or any person employed in the office of the United States trustee.*

(h) STAY OF ORDER AUTHORIZING USE, SALE, OR LEASE OF PROPERTY. *An order authorizing the use, sale, or lease of property other than cash collateral is stayed until the expiration of 10 days after entry of the order, unless the court orders otherwise.*

Amended, on an interim basis, effective October 17, 2005.

INTERIM RULE 6011. DISPOSAL OF PATIENT RECORDS IN HEALTH CARE BUSINESS CASE

(a) Notice by Publication Under § 351(1)(A). *A notice regarding the claiming or disposing of patient records under § 351(1)(A) shall not identify patients by name or other identifying information, but shall:*

(1) identify with particularity the health care facility whose patient records the trustee proposes to destroy;

(2) state the name, address, telephone number, e-mail address, and website, if any, of a person from whom information about the patient records may be obtained and how those records may be claimed; and

(3) state the date by which patient records must be claimed, and that if they are not so claimed the records will be destroyed.

(b) Notice by Mail Under § 351(1)(B). *Subject to applicable nonbankruptcy law relating to patient privacy, a notice regarding the claiming or disposing of patient records under § 351(1)(B) shall, in addition to including the information in subdivision (a), direct that a patient's family member or other representative who receives the notice inform the patient of the notice, and be mailed to the patient and any family member or other contact person whose name and address have been given to the trustee or the debtor for the purpose of providing information regarding the patient's health care, and to insurance companies known to have provided health care insurance to the patient.*

(c) Proof of Compliance with Notice Requirement. *Unless the court orders the trustee to file proof of compliance with § 351(1)(B) under seal, the trustee shall not file, but shall maintain, the proof of compliance for a reasonable time.*

(d) Report of Destruction of Records. *The trustee shall file, not later than 30 days after the destruction of patient records under § 351(3), a report certifying that the unclaimed records have been destroyed and explaining the method used to effect the destruction. The report shall not identify patients by name or other identifying information.*

Amended, on an interim basis, effective October 17, 2005.

INTERIM RULE 8001. MANNER OF TAKING APPEAL; VOLUNTARY DISMISSAL; CERTIFICATION TO COURT OF APPEALS

* * * * *

(f) Certification for Direct Appeal to Court of Appeals.

(1) Timely Appeal Required. *A certification of a judgment, order, or decree of a bankruptcy court to a court of appeals under 28 U.S.C. § 158(d)(2) shall not be treated as a certification entered on the docket within the meaning of § 1233(b)(4)(A) of Public Law No. 109–8 until a timely appeal has been taken in the manner required by subdivisions (a) or (b) of this rule and the notice of appeal has become effective under Rule 8002.*

(2) Court Where Made. *A certification that a circumstance specified in 28 U.S.C. § 158(d)(2)(A)(i)–(iii) exists shall be filed in the court in which a matter is pending for purposes of 28 U.S.C. § 158(d)(2) and this rule. A matter is pending in a bankruptcy court until the docketing of the appeal of a final judgment, order, or decree in accordance with Rule 8007(b) or the grant of leave to appeal an interlocutory judgment, order, or decree under 28 U.S.C. § 158(a). A matter is pending in a district court or bankruptcy appellate panel after an appeal of an interlocutory judgment, order, or decree has been docketed in accordance with Rule 8007(b) or leave to appeal has been granted under 28 U.S.C. § 158(a).*

(A) Certification by Court on Request or Court's Own Initiative.

(i) Before Docketing or Grant of Leave to Appeal. Only a bankruptcy court may make a certification on request or on its own initiative while the matter is pending in the bankruptcy court.

(ii) After Docketing or Grant of Leave to Appeal. Only the district court or bankruptcy appellate panel involved may make a certification on request of the parties or on its own initiative while the matter is pending in the district court or bankruptcy appellate panel.

(B) Certification by All Appellants and Appellees Acting Jointly. A certification by all the appellants and appellees, if any, acting jointly may be made by filing the appropriate Official Form with the clerk of the court in which the matter is pending. The certification may be accompanied by a short statement of the basis for the certification, which may include the information listed in subdivision (f)(3)(C) of this rule.

(3) Request for Certification; Filing; Service; Contents.

(A) A request for certification shall be filed, within the time specified by 28 U.S.C. § 158(d)(2), with the clerk of the court in which the matter is pending.

(B) Notice of the filing of a request for certification shall be served in the manner required for service of a notice of appeal under Rule 8004.

(C) A request for certification shall include the following:

(i) the facts necessary to understand the question presented;

(ii) the question itself;

(iii) the relief sought;

(iv) the reasons why the appeal should be allowed and is authorized by statute or rule, including why a circumstance specified in 28 U.S.C. § 158(d)(2)(A)(i)–(iii) exists; and

(v) an attached copy of the judgment, order, or decree complained of and any related opinion or memorandum.

(D) A party may file a response to a request for certification or a cross-request within 10 days after the notice of the request is served, or another time fixed by the court.

(E) The request, cross request, and any response shall not be governed by Rule 9014 and shall be submitted without oral argument unless the court otherwise directs.

(F) A certification of an appeal under 28 U.S.C. § 158(d)(2) shall be made in a separate document served on the parties.

(4) Certification on Court's Own Initiative.

(A) A certification of an appeal on the court's own initiative under 28 U.S.C. § 158(d)(2) shall be made in a separate document served on the parties in the manner required for service of a notice of appeal under Rule 8004. The certification shall be accompanied by an opinion or memorandum that contains the information required by subdivision (f)(3)(C)(i)–(iv) of this rule.

(B) A party may file a supplementary short statement of the basis for certification within 10 days after the certification.

Amended, on an interim basis, effective October 17, 2005.

INTERIM RULE 8003. LEAVE TO APPEAL

* * * * *

(d) *If leave to appeal is required by 28 U.S.C. § 158(a) and has not earlier been granted, the author-*

ization of a direct appeal by a court of appeals under 28 U.S.C. § 158(d)(2) shall be deemed to satisfy the requirement for leave to appeal.

Amended, on an interim basis, effective October 17, 2005.

INTERIM RULE 9006. TIME

* * * * *

(b) Enlargement.

(1) In General. *Except as provided in paragraphs (2) and (3) of this subdivision, when an act is required or allowed to be done at or within a specified period by these rules or by a notice given thereunder or by order of court, the court for cause shown may at any time in its discretion (1) with or without motion or notice order the period enlarged if the request therefor is made before the expiration of the period originally prescribed or as extended by a previous order or (2) on motion made after the expiration of the specified period permit the act to be done where the failure to act was the result of excusable neglect.*

(2) Enlargement Not Permitted. *The court may not enlarge the time for taking action under Rules 1007(d), 2003(a) and (d), 7052, 9023, and 9024.*

(3) Enlargement Limited. *The court may enlarge the time for taking action under Rules 1006(b)(2), 1007(c) with respect to the time to file schedules and statements in a small business case, 1017(e), 3002(c), 4003(b), 4004(a), 4007(c), 8002 and 9033, only to the extent and under the conditions stated in those rules.*

* * * * *

Amended, on an interim basis, effective October 17, 2005.

INTERIM RULE 9009. FORMS

The Official Forms prescribed by the Judicial Conference of the United States shall be observed and used with alterations as may be appropriate. Forms may be combined and their contents rearranged to permit economies in their use. The Director of the Administrative Office of the United States Courts may issue additional forms for use under the Code. The forms shall be construed to be consistent with these rules and the Code. References in the Official Forms to these rules shall include the Interim Rules approved by the Committee on Rules of Practice and Procedure to implement Public Law No. 109–8.

Amended, on an interim basis, effective October 17, 2005.

ELECTRONIC FILING PROCEDURES

ELECTRONIC MEANS FOR FILING, SIGNING, AND VERIFICATION OF DOCUMENTS

GENERAL ORDER

(Electronic Filing Procedures)

In Re:

ELECTRONIC MEANS FOR FILING, SIGNING, AND VERIFICATION OF DOCUMENTS

Federal Rule of Civil Procedure 83 and Federal Rules of Bankruptcy Procedure 5005(a)(2), 9011, 9029, and District of New Jersey Local Bankruptcy Rules 5005–1 and 1001–1, authorize this Court to establish practices and procedures for the filing, signing and verification of documents by electronic means; and

A proposal for *Administrative Procedures for Filing, Signing, and Verifying Documents by Electronic Means* (collectively the "*Administrative Procedures*"), has been reviewed by the Court;

IT IS ORDERED that:

1. The *Administrative Procedures* (attached as *Exhibit A* to this Order), including the procedure for registration of approved participants ("Participants") and for distribution of passwords to permit electronic filing and notice of pleadings and other papers are hereby approved by the Court.

2. As set forth in the *Administrative Procedures*, the electronic filing of any document using a login and password issued by the Court shall constitute the Participant's signature for purposes of signing the document under Fed. R. Bankr. P. 9011.

3. No Participant shall knowingly permit or cause to permit his/her password to be utilized by anyone other than an authorized employee of his/her law firm.

4. No person shall knowingly utilize or cause another person to utilize the password of a Participant unless such a person is an authorized employee of the law firm.

5. Electronic transmission of a document to the Electronic Case Filing System ("ECFS") consistent with the Local Rules and Administrative Procedures of this Court, together with the transmission of a Notice of Electronic Filing ("Notice of Electronic Filing") from the Court, constitutes filing of the document for all purposes of the Federal Rules of Bankruptcy Procedure and the Local Rules of this Court, and constitutes entry of the document on the docket kept by the Clerk under Fed. R. Bankr.P. 5003.

6. When a document has been filed electronically, the official record is the electronic recording of the document as stored by the court, and the filing party is bound by the document as filed.

7. Filing a document electronically does not alter the filing deadline for that document. Filing must be completed before midnight in order to be considered timely filed that day.

8. All orders, decrees, judgments, and proceedings of the Court will be filed in accordance with the *Administrative Procedures*, which shall constitute entry of the order, decree, judgment, or proceeding on the docket kept by the Clerk under Fed. R. Bank. P. 5003 and 9021.

9. All signed orders will be filed electronically by the Court or Court personnel. Any order filed electronically without the original signature of a judge has the same force and effect as if the judge had affixed the judge's signature to a paper copy of the order and it had been entered on the docket in a conventional manner. A Participant submitting a document electronically that requires a judge's signature, must deliver the document in accordance with the *Administrative Procedures*.

10. Immediately upon the entry of an order or judgment in the ECFS, the Clerk will transmit to Participants in the case, in electronic form, the Notice of Electronic Filing. Electronic transmission of the Notice of Electronic Filing constitutes the notice required by Fed.R.Bankr.P. 9022. The Clerk must give notice in paper form, in accordance with the Federal Rules of Bankruptcy Procedure, to a person who has not agreed pursuant to paragraph I.B.6 of the Court's Administrative Procedures, to receive electronic notice and service.

11. A Participant whose filing is made untimely as the result of a technical failure may seek appropriate relief from the Court.

12. In connection with the filing of any material in the ECFS, any person may apply by motion for an order limiting electronic access to or prohibiting the electronic filing of certain specifically identified materials on the grounds that such material is subject to privacy interests and that electronic access or electronic filing in the action is likely to prejudice those privacy interests.

13. This Order shall become effective April 1, 2002 or as soon thereafter, as the ECFS is activated by the Court for live use by Participants.

14. Amendments to this Order or the *Administrative Procedures* may be entered from time to time in keeping with the needs of the Court.

15. The original of this Order shall be filed with the Clerk of the Court both conventionally and in accordance with the *Administrative Procedures.*

March 27, 2002, effective April 1, 2002.

EXHIBIT A

UNITED STATES BANKRUPTCY COURT

DISTRICT OF NEW JERSEY

ADMINISTRATIVE PROCEDURES FOR FILING, SIGNING, AND VERIFYING DOCUMENTS BY ELECTRONIC MEANS

I. REGISTRATION FOR THE ELECTRONIC CASE FILING SYSTEM

A. Designation of Cases.

1. All pending and newly filed cases and adversary proceedings shall be assigned to the Electronic Case Filing System ("ECFS") as of the effective date of the March 26, 2002 General Order. The Clerk will continue to accept paper filings although all parties are encouraged to use ECFS whenever possible.

B. Registration.

1. Each approved participant ("Participant") will be assigned one or more login and password combinations to permit electronic filing and retrieval of pleadings and other documents in the ECFS. The Court reserves the right to change the assigned ECFS login from time to time as may become necessary.

2. A registration form, will be available electronically, and shall be submitted for each Participant.

3. All registration forms shall be electronically mailed to the Office of the Clerk, at the following e-mail address: *cmecf_helpdesk@njb.uscourts.gov.*

4. Each Participant registering for the ECFS will receive notice by electronic mail from the Office of the Clerk indicating the Participant's assigned ECFS login and password combination. This login and password combination, as initially assigned, will be used for training purposes only, and will not be activated for use on the ECFS until the Participant is approved for use on the ECFS by the Court in accordance with the training as set forth in the ECFS User's Guide. Only the Participant, or an authorized representative, may receive the electronic notice of the assigned login and password combination.

5. Participants may find it desirable to change their passwords periodically. This ran be done as set forth in the ECFS User's Guide. In the event a Participant believes that the security of an existing password has been compromised, the Participant shall give immediate notice to the Clerk of the Court in order to prevent access to the ECFS by use of that password. Such notice may be given to the Clerk of the Court either by telephone to the telephone number(s) set forth in the User's Guide for such purpose; or by electronic mail to *cmecf_helpdesk@njb.uscourts.gov.*

6. Participants in the ECFS, by accepting a login and password from the Court, waive the right to receive notice by first class mail, including notice pursuant to Fed.R.Bank.P. 2002(a), and agree to receive notice electronically. Participants in the ECFS, by accepting a login and password from the Court, also waive their right to service by personal service or first class mail and agree to electronic service, except with regard to service of process of a summons and complaint in an adversary proceeding under Fed. R.Bank.P. 7004 and the initiating motion in a contested matter under Fed.R.Bank.P. 9014. The waiver of service and notice by first class mail includes notice of the entry of an order or judgment under Fed. R.Bank.P. 9022.

II. ELECTRONIC FILING AND SERVICE OF DOCUMENTS

A. Filing.

1. Except as expressly provided for in paragraph III.A. below, *Conventional Filings*, any Participant who is registered with ECFS may electronically file all petitions, motions, pleadings, memoranda of law, or other documents in the ECFS. Emergency motions, supporting pleadings and objections may also be filed electronically as provided in these Administrative Procedures.

2. All documents that form part of a pleading and which are being filed at the same time and by the same party shall be electronically filed as individual documents, as attachments to the initiating pleading, under one docket entry, e.g. the motion, supporting affidavit, memorandum of law, and proposed form of order.

B. Service.

1. General Rule: Except as otherwise provided in paragraph 2 below, *Consent to Electronic Service*, all documents required to be served shall be served in paper (i.e. "hard copy") form in the manner mandated by the applicable law and rules.

2. Consent to Electronic Service: Whenever service is required to be made on a person who has agreed to electronic service as defined at paragraph I.B.6 above, the Court's automatically generated "Notice of Electronic Filing" constitutes service. If ECFS service is impracticable, service may be made by hand or by any other means authorized by Fed. R. Bank.P. 7005.

3. In addition to electronic service by the ECFS as identified in paragraph 2, service of documents in hard copy, shall be required in the following circumstances:

(a) Service is required to be made in accordance with Fed. R. Bankr.P. 7004, 9014 and 9016.

(b) The Federal Rules of Bankruptcy Procedure, District of New Jersey Local Bankruptcy Rules, or an order of the Court requires delivery or service upon a state or federal government entity, including, the United States Attorney.

C. Signatures

1. Filing any document using a login and password issued by the Court shall constitute the Participant's signature for purposes of signing the document under Fed.R.Bankr.P. 9011. The name of the Participant under whose log-in and password the document is submitted must be displayed by an "/s/" and typed in the space where the signature would otherwise appear, e.g., "/s/Jane Doc." No person shall knowingly utilize or cause another person to utilize the password of a Participant unless such a person is an authorized employee of the law firm

2. Documents that are electronically filed and require original signatures, other than that of the Participant ("third party signatures"), must be maintained in paper form by the Participant for a period not less than seven years from the date of closure of the case or proceeding in which the document is filed. Upon request, the original document must be provided to other parties or the court for review. The document requiring third party signatures must be electronically filed either by (1) submitting a scanned document containing the third party signature; or (2) by submitting a document displaying the name of the person signing the document, preceded by an "/s/" and typed in the space where the signature would otherwise appear, e.g., "/s/Jane Doe."

D. Fees Payable to the Clerk

For filings that require a fee, application for authorization of credit card payment must be completed through the registration process.

E. Orders

All proposed forms of orders may be submitted electronically as outlined below.

1. Electronically submitted orders must comply with all Local Bankruptcy Rules. Subject to the requirements of paragraph 3 below, Orders Shortening Time must be electronically filed with the moving papers in a form substantially the same as Local Forms 1 and 2 as required by D.N.J LBR 9013–1(e). Orders to Show Cause shall be limited to adversary proceedings in accordance with D.N.J LBR 9013–1(e) and D.N.J. LBR 9075–1.

2. With the exception of Consent Orders, and Orders submitted under D.N.J LBA 9072–2, electronically filed proposed forms of orders, shall be combined with the application or motion into one docket entry in accordance with Paragraph II.A.2 of these Administrative Procedures.

3. Electronically submitted orders shall he formatted in accordance with template instructions provided by the Clerk.

4. All orders, including consent orders, must be in PDF text format at the time of submission.

5. The Court will make an electronic copy of the proposed form of order as submitted by the Participant, and sign same electronically by affixing the signature of the presiding judge. Once signed, the Office of the Clerk or the Judge will make the appropriate entry on the ECFS to docket the order.

6. Where a Participant seeks the entry of an emergent order, such as an order shortening time or order to show cause through the ECFS, the Participant shall simultaneously bring such filing, once submitted, to the attention of the Judge's Courtroom Deputy at the e mail addresses set forth in the User's Guide.

7. Notification of defects in an order may be provided by e-mail.

8. Service of signed orders is to be effectuated by the Clerk electronically to Participants.

F. Consent Orders

Consent orders shall be circulated and signed conventionally. The Participant shall submit a copy of the consent order, in the manner set forth in the User's Guide, to the presiding judge's electronic mail box designated for such purpose. The original consent order, bearing original signatures of the consenting parties, shall be maintained by the Participant for a period of time prescribed in subparagraph 11.C.2 of these *Administrative Procedures.* The Participant must also simultaneously file with the Court, a Certificate of Consent, which certifies that the signatories have affixed their consent, and that the Participant will retain the original consent order as executed by the parties for the period of time required under subparagraph 11.C.2 of these *Administrative Procedures.* For the court's ease of reference, in addition to the electronic filing of the Certificate of Consent, a chambers' copy of the Certificate of Consent must be annexed by the Participant to the copy of the consent order sent to the presiding judge's electronic mailbox.

G. Exhibits

Documents, including proofs of claim, should be filed electronically in PDF text format on the ECFS. Exhibits should be submitted electronically as attachments to the document or proof of claim, and if originally produced in hard copy (paper) format exceeding 20 pages in length, shall include only those excerpts of each exhibit that are directly germane to the matter under consideration by the Court. Such exhibits must be clearly and prominently identified as excerpts, and, with the exception of attachments to proofs of claim, the complete exhibit must be made available as a chambers' copy provided to the Court. All exhibits to documents, including proofs of claim, must be made available forthwith to counsel upon request and at any hearing pertaining to the matter. Persons filing excerpts of exhibits do so without prejudice to their right to file additional excerpts or the complete exhibit with the Court at any time. Opposing parties may file additional excerpts if they believe that they are germane.

If the entire exhibit is deemed germane to the document being submitted and the exhibit is in a format that must be electronically imaged, the attorney shall make every effort to electronically image the document(s), including utilization of the Court's facilities.

H. Title of Docket Entries

The person electronically filing a pleading or other document will be responsible for designating a title for the document by using one of the main categories and specific events provided in the ECFS, as e.g. motion for relief from stay, application for retention of counsel, etc.

III. CONVENTIONAL FILING OF DOCUMENTS

A. Conventional Filings

The following documents shall be filed conventionally and not electronically unless specifically authorized by the Court:

1. Document(s) to be filed under seal. However, a motion to file documents under seal may be filed electronically. The order of the Court authorizing the filing of such document(s) under seal may be filed electronically by the presiding judge. A paper copy of the order shall be attached to the document(s) under seal and be delivered to the Clerk of Court.

IV. PUBLIC ACCESS TO THE DOCKET

A. Internet Access. Any person or organization, may access the Court's Internet site at: *www.njb.uscourts.gov.* Access to the docket through the Internet site will require registration with the Pacer Billing Center (1–800–676–6856).

B. Public Access at the Court. Access by the public to the documents filed in the ECFS and to the ECFS docket is available in the Office of the Clerk for viewing during regular business hours, Monday through Friday.

C. Conventional Copies and Certified Copies. Conventional copies and certified copies of the electronically filed documents may be purchased during business hours, Monday through Friday, at the Office of the Clerk at any one of the following locations: Martin Luther King, Jr. Federal Building, 50 Walnut Street, Newark, New Jersey 07102; 402 East State Street, Trenton, New Jersey 08608; or Federal Building 401 Market Street, Camden, New Jersey, 08101–2067. The fee for copying and certification is in accordance with 28 U.S.C. section 1930.

RULES OF PROCEDURE OF THE JUDICIAL PANEL ON MULTIDISTRICT LITIGATION

Renumbered and Amended Effective November 2, 1998

Including Amendments Effective July 30, 2007

I. GENERAL RULES/RULES FOR MULTIDISTRICT LITIGATION UNDER 28 U.S.C. § 1407

RULE 1.1. DEFINITIONS

As used in these Rules "Panel" means the members of the Judicial Panel on Multidistrict Litigation appointed by the Chief Justice of the United States pursuant to Section 1407, Title 28, United States Code.

"Clerk of the Panel" means the official appointed by the Panel to act as Clerk of the Panel and shall include those deputized by the Clerk of the Panel to perform or assist in the performance of the duties of the Clerk of the Panel.

"Chairman" means the Chairman of the Judicial Panel on Multidistrict Litigation appointed by the Chief Justice of the United States pursuant to Section 1407, or the member of the Panel designated by the Panel to act as Chairman in the absence or inability of the appointed Chairman.

A "tag-along action" refers to a civil action pending in a district court and involving common questions of fact with actions previously transferred under Section 1407.

(Former Rule 1 adopted May 3, 1993, eff. July 1, 1993; renumbered Rule 1.1 Sept. 1, 1998, eff. Nov. 2, 1998.)

RULE 1.2. PRACTICE

Where not fixed by statute or rule, the practice shall be that heretofore customarily followed by the Panel.

(Former Rule 5 adopted May 3, 1993, eff. July 1, 1993; renumbered Rule 1.2 Sept. 1, 1998, eff. Nov. 2, 1998.)

RULE 1.3. FAILURE TO COMPLY WITH RULES

The Clerk of the Panel may, when a paper submitted for filing is not in compliance with the provisions of these Rules, advise counsel of the deficiencies and a date for full compliance. If full compliance is not accomplished within the established time, the non-complying paper shall nonetheless be filed by the Clerk of the Panel but it may be stricken by order of the Chairman of the Panel.

(Former Rule 4 adopted May 3, 1993, eff. July 1, 1993; renumbered Rule 1.3 and amended Sept. 1, 1998, eff. Nov. 2, 1998.)

RULE 1.4. ADMISSION TO PRACTICE BEFORE THE PANEL AND REPRESENTATION IN TRANSFERRED ACTIONS

Every member in good standing of the Bar of any district court of the United States is entitled without condition to practice before the Judicial Panel on Multidistrict Litigation. Any attorney of record in any action transferred under Section 1407 may continue to represent his or her client in any district court of the United States to which such action is transferred. Parties to any action transferred under Section 1407 are not required to obtain local counsel in the district to which such action is transferred.

(Former Rule 6 adopted May 3, 1993, eff. July 1, 1993; renumbered Rule 1.4 Sept. 1, 1998, eff. Nov. 2, 1998.)

RULE 1.5. EFFECT OF THE PENDENCY OF AN ACTION BEFORE THE PANEL

The pendency of a motion, order to show cause, conditional transfer order or conditional remand order before the Panel concerning transfer or remand of an action pursuant to 28 U.S.C. § 1407 does not affect or suspend orders and pretrial proceedings in the district court in which the action is pending and does not in any way limit the pretrial jurisdiction of that court. A transfer or remand pursuant to 28 U.S.C. § 1407 shall be effective when the transfer or remand order is filed in the office of the clerk of the district court of the transferee district.

(Former Rule 18 adopted May 3, 1993, eff. July 1, 1993; renumbered Rule 1.5 Sept. 1, 1998, eff. Nov. 2, 1998.)

RULE 1.6. TRANSFER OF FILES

(a) Upon receipt of a certified copy of a transfer order from the clerk of the transferee district court, the clerk of the transferor district court shall forward to the clerk of the transferee district court the complete original file and a certified copy of the docket sheet for each transferred action.

(b) If an appeal is pending, or a notice of appeal has been filed, or leave to appeal has been sought under 28 U.S.C. § 1292(b) or a petition for an extraordinary writ is pending, in any action included in an order of transfer under 28 U.S.C. § 1407, and the original file or parts thereof have been forwarded to the court of appeals, the clerk of the transferor district court shall notify the clerk of the court of appeals of the order of transfer and secure the original file long enough to prepare and transmit to the clerk of the transferee district court a certified copy of all papers contained in the original file and a certified copy of the docket sheet.

(c) If the transfer order provides for the separation and simultaneous remand of any claim, cross-claim, counterclaim, or third-party claim, the clerk of the transferor district court shall retain the original file and shall prepare and transmit to the clerk of the transferee district court a certified copy of the docket sheet and copies of all papers except those relating exclusively to separated and remanded claims.

(d) Upon receipt of an order to remand from the Clerk of the Panel, the transferee district court shall prepare and send to the clerk of the transferor district court the following:

(i) a certified copy of the individual docket sheet for each action being remanded;

(ii) a certified copy of the master docket sheet, if applicable;

(iii) the entire file for each action being remanded, as originally received from the transferor district court and augmented as set out in this rule;

(iv) a certified copy of the final pretrial order, if applicable; and

(v) a "record on remand" to be composed of those parts of the files and records produced during coordinated or consolidated pretrial proceedings which have been stipulated to or designated by counsel as being necessary for any or all proceedings to be conducted following remand. It shall be the responsibility of counsel originally preparing or filing any document to be included in the "record on remand" to furnish on request sufficient copies to the clerk of the transferee district court.

(e) The Clerk of the Panel shall be notified when any files have been transmitted pursuant to this Rule.

(Former Rule 19 adopted May 3, 1993, eff. July 1, 1993; renumbered Rule 1.6 and amended Sept. 1, 1998, eff. Nov. 2, 1998.)

RULE 5.1. KEEPING RECORDS AND FILES

(a) The records and files of the Panel shall be kept by the Clerk of the Panel at the offices of the Panel. Records and files may be temporarily or permanently removed to such places at such times as the Panel or the Chairman of the Panel shall direct. The Clerk of the Panel may charge fees, as prescribed by the Judicial Conference of the United States, for duplicating records and files. Records and files may be transferred whenever appropriate to the Federal Records Center.

(b) In order to assist the Panel in carrying out its functions, the Clerk of the Panel shall obtain the complaints and docket sheets in all actions under consideration for transfer under 28 U.S.C. § 1407 from the clerk of each district court wherein such actions are pending. The Clerk of the Panel shall similarly obtain any other pleadings and orders that could affect the Panel's decision under 28 U.S.C. § 1407.

(Former Rule 2 adopted May 3, 1993, eff. July 1, 1993; renumbered Rule 5.1 and amended Sept. 1, 1998, eff. Nov. 2, 1998.)

RULE 5.11. PLACE OF FILING OF PAPERS

All papers for consideration by the Panel shall be submitted for filing to the Clerk of the Panel by mailing or delivering to:

Clerk of the Panel
Judicial Panel on Multidistrict Litigation
Thurgood Marshall Federal Judiciary Building
One Columbus Circle, N.E., Room G–255, North Lobby
Washington, D.C. 20002–8004

No papers shall be left with or mailed to a Judge of the Panel.

(Former Rule 3 adopted May 3, 1993, eff. July 1, 1993; renumbered Rule 5.11 and amended Sept. 1, 1998, eff. Nov. 2, 1998.)

RULE 5.12. MANNER OF FILING OF PAPERS

(a) An original of the following papers shall be submitted for filing to the Clerk of the Panel: a proof of service pursuant to Rule 5.2(a) and (b) of these Rules, a notice of appearance pursuant to Rule 5.2(c) and (d) of these Rules, a corporate disclosure statement pursuant to Rule 5.3 of these Rules, a status notice pursuant to Rules 7.2(f), 7.3(e) and 7.4(b) of these Rules, a notice of opposition pursuant to Rules 7.4(c) and 7.6(f)(ii) of these Rules, a notice of related action pursuant to Rules 7.2(i), 7.3(a) and 7.5(e) of these Rules, an application for extension of time pursuant to Rule 6.2 of these Rules, or a notice of presentation or waiver of oral argument pursuant to Rule 16.1(d) of these Rules. An original and ~~eleven~~ four* copies of all other papers shall be submitted for filing to the Clerk of the Panel. The Clerk of the Panel may require that additional copies also be submitted for filing.

(b) When papers are submitted for filing, the Clerk of the Panel shall endorse thereon the date for filing.

(c) Copies of motions for transfer of an action or actions pursuant to 28 U.S.C. § 1407 shall be filed in each district court in which an action is pending that will be affected by the motion. Copies of a motion for remand pursuant to 28 U.S.C. § 1407 shall be filed in the Section 1407 transferee district court in which any action affected by the motion is pending.

(d) Papers requiring only an original may be faxed to the Panel office with prior approval of the Clerk of the Panel. No papers requiring multiple copies shall be accepted via fax.

(Former Rule 7 adopted May 3, 1993, eff. July 1, 1993; renumbered Rule 5.12 and amended Sept. 1, 1998, eff. Nov. 2, 1998; amended Apr. 2, 2001, eff. Apr. 2, 2001; paragraph (a) suspended in part by Order filed April 19, 2005.)

* Publisher's Note: April 19, 2005, the Judicial Panel on Multidistrict Litigation issued an Order reducing the number of copies from eleven to four. The Order reads as follows:

IT IS HEREBY ORDERED that, because the Panel is utilizing papers and electronic distribution of those papers, Panel Rule 5.12(a), Manner of Filing Papers, R.P.J.P.M.L., 199 F.R.D. 425, 429 (2001), is partially suspended insofar as papers submitted for filing requiring an original and eleven copies shall be reduced to four copies along with an original.

RULE 5.13. FILING OF PAPERS: COMPUTER GENERATED DISK REQUIRED

(a) Whenever an original paper and eleven copies is required to be submitted for filing to the Clerk of the Panel pursuant to Rule 5.12(a) of these Rules, and where a party is represented by counsel, one copy of that paper must also be submitted on a computer readable disk and shall be filed at the time the party's paper is filed. The disk shall contain the entire paper exclusive of computer non-generated exhibits. The label of the disk shall include i) "MDL #___," ii) an abbreviated version of the MDL descriptive title, or other appropriate descriptive title, if not yet designated by the Panel, iii) the identity of the type of paper being filed (i.e. motion, response, reply, etc.), iv) the name of the counsel who signed the paper, and v) the first named represented party on the paper.

(b) The paper must be on a disk in Adobe Acrobat (PDF) format.

(c) One copy of the disk may be served on each party separately represented by counsel. If a party chooses to serve a copy of the disk, the proof of service, as required by Rule 5.2 of these Rules, must indicate service of the paper in both paper and electronic format.

(d) A party may be relieved from the requirements of this Rule by submitting a written application for a waiver, in a timely manner in advance of submission of the paper, certifying that compliance with the Rule would impose undue hardship, that the text of the paper is not available on disk, or that other unusual circumstances preclude compliance with this Rule. The requirements of this Rule shall not apply to parties appearing pro se. Papers embraced by this Rule and submitted by counsel after June 1, 2000 without a computer disk copy or Panel-approved waiver of the requirements of this Rule shall be governed by Rule 1.3 of these Rules.

(Added May 22, 2000, eff. June 1, 2000; and amended July 30, 2007, eff. July 30, 2007.)

RULE 5.2. SERVICE OF PAPERS FILED

(a) All papers filed with the Clerk of the Panel shall be accompanied by proof of previous or simultaneous service on all other parties in all actions involved in the litigation. Service and proof of service shall be made as provided in Rules 5 and 6 of the Federal Rules of Civil Procedure. The proof of service shall indicate the name and complete address of each person served and shall indicate the party represented by each. If a party is not represented by counsel, the proof of service shall indicate the name of the party and the party's last known address. The proof of service shall indicate why any person named as a party in a constituent complaint was not served with the Section 1407 pleading. The original proof of service shall be filed with the Clerk of the Panel and copies thereof shall be sent to each person included within the proof of service. After the "Panel Service List" described in subsection (d) of this Rule has been received from the Clerk of the Panel, the "Panel Service List" shall be utilized for service of responses to motions and all other filings. In such instances, the "Panel Service List" shall be attached to the proof of service and shall be supplemented in the proof of service in the event of the presence of additional parties or subsequent corrections relating to any party, counsel or address already on the "Panel Service List."

(b) The proof of service pertaining to motions for transfer of actions pursuant to 28 U.S.C. § 1407 shall certify that copies of the motions have been mailed or otherwise delivered for filing to the clerk of each district court in which an action is pending that will be affected by the motion. The proof of service pertaining to a motion for remand pursuant to 28 U.S.C. § 1407 shall certify that a copy of the motion has been mailed or otherwise delivered for filing to the clerk of the Section 1407 transferee district court in which any action affected by the motion is pending.

(c) Within eleven days of filing of a motion to transfer, an order to show cause or a conditional transfer order, each party or designated attorney shall notify the Clerk of the Panel, in writing, of the name and address of the attorney designated to receive service of all pleadings, notices, orders and other papers relating to practice before the Judicial Panel on Multidistrict Litigation. Only one attorney shall be designated for each party. Any party not represented by counsel shall be served by mailing such pleadings to the party's last known address. Requests for an extension of time to file the designation of attorney shall not be granted except in extraordinary circumstances.

(d) In order to facilitate compliance with subsection (a) of this Rule, the Clerk of the Panel shall prepare and serve on all counsel and parties not represented by counsel, a "Panel Service List" containing the names and addresses of the designated attorneys and the party or parties they represent in the actions under consideration by the Panel and the names and addresses of the parties not represented by counsel in the actions under consideration by the Panel. After the "Panel Service List" has been received from the Clerk of the Panel, notice of subsequent corrections relating to any party, counsel or address on the "Panel Service List" shall be served on all other parties in all actions involved in the litigation.

(e) If following transfer of any group of multidistrict litigation, the transferee district court appoints liaison counsel, this Rule shall be satisfied by serving each party in each affected action and all liaison counsel. Liaison counsel designated by the transferee district court shall receive copies of all Panel orders concerning their particular litigation and shall be responsible for distribution to the parties for whom he or she serves as liaison counsel.

(Former Rule 8 adopted May 3, 1993, eff. July 1, 1993; renumbered Rule 5.2 and amended Sept. 1, 1998, eff. Nov. 2, 1998.)

RULE 5.3. CORPORATE DISCLOSURE STATEMENT

(a) Any nongovernmental corporate party to a matter before the Panel shall file a statement identifying all its parent corporations and listing any publicly held company that owns 10% or more of the party's stock.

(b) A party shall file the corporate disclosure statement within eleven days of the filing of a motion to transfer or remand, an order to show cause, or a motion to vacate a conditional transfer order or a conditional remand order.

(c) Once a corporate disclosure statement by a party has been filed in an MDL docket pursuant to subsection (b) of this Rule, such a party is required to update the statement to reflect any change in the information therein i) until the matter before the Panel is decided, and ii) within eleven days of the filing of any subsequent motion to transfer or remand, order to show cause, or motion to vacate a conditional transfer order or a conditional remand order in that docket.

(Added Apr. 2, 2001, eff. Apr. 2, 2001.)

RULE 6.2. APPLICATIONS FOR EXTENSIONS OF TIME

Any application for an extension of time to file a pleading or perform an act required by these Rules must be in writing, must request a specific number of additional days and may be acted upon by the Clerk of the Panel. Such an application will be evaluated in relation to the impact on the Panel's calendar as well as on the basis of the reasons set forth in support of the application. Any party aggrieved by the Clerk of the Panel's action on such application may submit its objections to the Panel for consideration. Absent exceptional circumstances, no extensions of time shall be granted to file a notice of opposition to either a conditional transfer order or a conditional remand order. All applications for extensions of time shall be filed and served in conformity with Rules 5.12, 5.2 and 7.1 of these Rules.

(Former Rule 15 adopted May 3, 1993, eff. July 1, 1993; renumbered Rule 6.2 and amended Sept. 1, 1998, eff. Nov. 2, 1998.)

RULE 7.1. FORM OF PAPERS FILED

(a) Averments in any motion seeking action by the Panel shall be made in numbered paragraphs, each of which shall be limited, as far as practicable, to a statement of a single factual averment.

(b) Responses to averments in motions shall be made in numbered paragraphs, each of which shall correspond to the number of the paragraph of the motion to which the responsive paragraph is directed. Each responsive paragraph shall admit or deny wholly or in part the averment of the motion, and shall contain the respondent's version of the subject matter when the averment or the motion is not wholly admitted.

(c) Each pleading filed shall be:

(i) flat and unfolded;

(ii) plainly written, typed in double space, printed or prepared by means of a duplicating process, without erasures or interlineations which materially deface it;

(iii) on opaque, unglazed, white paper (not onionskin);

(iv) approximately 8–1/2 x 11 inches in size; and

(v) fastened at the top-left corner without side binding or front or back covers.

(d) The heading on the first page of each pleading shall commence not less than three inches from the top of the page. Each pleading shall bear the heading "Before the Judicial Panel on Multidistrict Litigation," the identification "MDL Docket No.___" and the descriptive title designated by the Panel for the litigation involved. If the Panel has not yet designated a title, an appropriate descriptive title shall be used.

(e) The final page of each pleading shall contain the name, address and telephone number of the attorney or party in active charge of the case. Each attorney shall also include the name of each party represented.

(f) Except with the approval of the Panel, each brief submitted for filing with the Panel shall be limited to twenty pages, exclusive of exhibits. Absent exceptional circumstances, motions to exceed page limits shall not be granted.

(g) Exhibits exceeding a cumulative total of 50 pages shall be fastened separately from the accompanying pleading.

(h) Proposed Panel orders shall not be submitted with papers for filing.

(Former Rule 9 adopted May 3, 1993, eff. July 1, 1993; renumbered Rule 7.1 and amended Sept. 1, 1998, eff. Nov. 2, 1998; amended Apr. 2, 2001, eff. Apr. 2, 2001.)

RULE 7.2. MOTION PRACTICE

(a) All requests for action by the Panel under 28 U.S.C. § 1407 shall be made by written motion. Every motion shall be accompanied by:

(i) a brief in support thereof in which the background of the litigation and factual and legal contentions of the movant shall be concisely stated in separate portions of the brief with citation of applicable authorities; and

(ii) a schedule giving

(A) the complete name of each action involved, listing the full name of each party included as such on the district court's docket sheet, not shortened by the use of references such as "et al." or "etc.";

(B) the district court and division in which each action is pending;

(C) the civil action number of each action; and

(D) the name of the judge assigned each action, if known.

(b) The Clerk of the Panel shall notify recipients of a motion of the filing date, caption, MDL docket number, briefing schedule and pertinent Panel policies.

(c) Within twenty days after filing of a motion, all other parties shall file a response thereto. Failure of a party to respond to a motion shall be treated as that party's acquiescence to the action requested in the motion.

(d) The movant may, within five days after the lapse of the time period for filing responsive briefs, file a single brief in reply to any opposition.

(e) Motions, their accompaniments, responses, and replies shall also be governed by Rules 5.12, 5.2 and 7.1 of these Rules.

(f) With respect to any action that is the subject of Panel consideration, counsel shall promptly notify the Clerk of the Panel of any development that would partially or completely moot the matter before the Panel.

(g) A joinder in a motion shall not add any action to the previous motion.

(h) Once a motion is filed, any other pleading that purports to be a "motion" in the docket shall be filed by the Clerk of the Panel as a response unless the "motion" adds an action. The Clerk of the Panel, upon designating such a pleading as a motion, shall acknowledge that designation by the distribution of a briefing schedule to all parties in the docket. Response time resulting from an additional motion shall ordinarily be extended only to those parties directly affected by the additional motion. An accelerated briefing schedule for the additional motion may be set by the Clerk of the Panel to conform with the hearing session schedule established by the Chairman.

(i) Any party or counsel in a new group of actions under consideration by the Panel for transfer under Section 1407 shall promptly notify the Clerk of the Panel of any potential tag-along action in which that party is also named or in which that counsel appears.

(Former Rule 10 adopted May 3, 1993, eff. July 1, 1993; renumbered Rule 7.2 and amended Sept. 1, 1998, eff. Nov. 2, 1998; amended Apr. 2, 2001, eff. Apr. 2, 2001.)

RULE 7.3. SHOW CAUSE ORDERS

(a) When transfer of multidistrict litigation is being considered on the initiative of the Panel pursuant to 28 U.S.C. § 1407(c)(i), an order shall be filed by the Clerk of the Panel directing the parties to show cause why the action or actions should not be transferred for coordinated or consolidated pretrial proceedings. Any party or counsel in such actions shall promptly notify the Clerk of the Panel of any other federal district court actions related to the litigation encompassed by the show cause order. Such notification shall be made for additional actions pending at the time of the issuance of the show cause order and whenever new actions are filed.

(b) Any party may file a response to the show cause order within twenty days of the filing of said order unless otherwise provided for in the order. Failure of a party to respond to a show cause order shall be treated as that party's acquiescence to the Panel action contemplated in the order.

(c) Within five days after the lapse of the time period for filing a response, any party may file a reply limited to new matters.

(d) Responses and replies shall be filed and served in conformity with Rules 5.12, 5.2 and 7.1 of these Rules.

(e) With respect to any action that is the subject of Panel consideration, counsel shall promptly notify the Clerk of the Panel of any development that would partially or completely moot the matter before the Panel.

(Former Rule 7.3 adopted May 3, 1993, eff. July 1, 1993; renumbered Rule 7.3 and amended Sept. 1, 1998, eff. Nov. 2, 1998.)

RULE 7.4. CONDITIONAL TRANSFER ORDERS FOR "TAG-ALONG ACTIONS"

(a) Upon learning of the pendency of a potential "tag-along action," as defined in Rule 1.1 of these Rules, an order may be entered by the Clerk of the Panel transferring that action to the previously designated transferee district court on the basis of the prior hearing session(s) and for the reasons expressed in previous opinions and orders of the Panel in the litigation. The Clerk of the Panel shall serve this order on each party to the litigation but, in order to afford all parties the opportunity to oppose transfer, shall not send the order to the clerk of the transferee district court for fifteen days from the entry thereof.

(b) Parties to an action subject to a conditional transfer order shall notify the Clerk of the Panel within the fifteen-day period if that action is no longer pending in its transferor district court.

(c) Any party opposing the transfer shall file a notice of opposition with the Clerk of the Panel within the fifteen-day period. If a notice of opposition is received by the Clerk of the Panel within this fifteen-day period, the Clerk of the Panel shall not transmit said order to the clerk of the transferee district court until further order of the Panel. The Clerk of the Panel shall notify the parties of the briefing schedule.

(d) Within fifteen days of the filing of its notice of opposition, the party opposing transfer shall file a motion to vacate the conditional transfer order and brief in support thereof. The Chairman of the Panel shall set the motion for the next appropriate hearing session of the Panel. Failure to file and serve a motion and brief shall be treated as withdrawal of the opposition and the Clerk of the Panel shall forthwith transmit the order to the clerk of the transferee district court.

(e) Conditional transfer orders do not become effective unless and until they are filed with the clerk of the transferee district court.

(f) Notices of opposition and motions to vacate such orders of the Panel and responses thereto shall be governed by Rules 5.12, 5.2, 7.1 and 7.2 of these Rules.

(Former Rule 12 adopted May 3, 1993, eff. July 1, 1993; renumbered Rule 7.4 and amended Sept. 1, 1998, eff. Nov. 2, 1998; amended Apr. 2, 2001, eff. Apr. 2, 2001.)

RULE 7.5. MISCELLANEOUS PROVISIONS CONCERNING "TAG–ALONG ACTIONS"

(a) Potential "tag-along actions" filed in the transferee district require no action on the part of the Panel and requests for assignment of such actions to the Section 1407 transferee judge should be made in accordance with local rules for the assignment of related actions.

(b) Upon learning of the pendency of a potential "tag-along action" and having reasonable anticipation of opposition to transfer of that action, the Panel may direct the Clerk of the Panel to file a show cause order, in accordance with Rule 7.3 of these Rules, instead of a conditional transfer order.

(c) Failure to serve one or more of the defendants in a potential "tag-along action" with the complaint and summons as required by Rule 4 of the Federal Rules of Civil Procedure does not preclude transfer of such action under Section 1407. Such failure, however, may be submitted by such a defendant as a basis for opposing the proposed transfer if prejudice can be shown. The inability of the Clerk of the Panel to serve a conditional transfer order on all plaintiffs or defendants or their counsel shall not render the transfer of the action void but can be submitted by such a party as a basis for moving to remand as to such party if prejudice can be shown.

(d) A civil action apparently involving common questions of fact with actions under consideration by the Panel for transfer under Section 1407, which was either not included in a motion under Rule 7.2 of these Rules, or was included in such a motion that was filed too late to be included in the initial hearing session, will ordinarily be treated by the Panel as a potential "tag-along action."

(e) Any party or counsel in actions previously transferred under Section 1407 or under consideration by the Panel for transfer under Section 1407 shall promptly notify the Clerk of the Panel of any potential "tag-along actions" in which that party is also named or in which that counsel appears.

(Former Rule 13 adopted May 3, 1993, eff. July 1, 1993; renumbered Rule 7.5 and amended Sept. 1, 1998, eff. Nov. 2, 1998; amended Apr. 2, 2001, eff. Apr. 2, 2001.)

RULE 7.6. TERMINATION AND REMAND

In the absence of unusual circumstances—

(a) Actions terminated in the transferee district court by valid judgment, including but not limited to summary judgment, judgment of dismissal and judgment upon stipulation, shall not be remanded by the Panel and shall be dismissed by the transferee district court. The clerk of the transferee district court shall send a copy of the order terminating the action to the Clerk of the Panel but shall retain the original files and records unless otherwise directed by the transferee judge or by the Panel.

(b) Each action transferred only for coordinated or consolidated pretrial proceedings that has not been terminated in the transferee district court shall be remanded by the Panel to the transferor district for trial. Actions that were originally filed in the transferee district require no action by the Panel to be reassigned to another judge in the transferee district at the conclusion of the coordinated or consolidated pretrial proceedings affecting those actions.

(c) The Panel shall consider remand of each transferred action or any separable claim, cross-claim, counterclaim or third-party claim at or before the conclusion of coordinated or consolidated pretrial proceedings on

(i) motion of any party,

(ii) suggestion of the transferee district court, or

(iii) the Panel's own initiative, by entry of an order to show cause, a conditional remand order or other appropriate order.

(d) The Panel is reluctant to order remand absent a suggestion of remand from the transferee district court. If remand is sought by motion of a party, the motion shall be accompanied by:

(i) an affidavit reciting

(A) whether the movant has requested a suggestion of remand from the transferee district court, how the court responded to any request, and, if no such request was made, why;

(B) whether all common discovery and other pretrial proceedings have been completed in the action sought to be remanded, and if not, what remains to be done; and

(C) whether all orders of the transferee district court have been satisfactorily complied with, and if not, what remains to be done; and

(ii) a copy of the transferee district court's final pretrial order, where such order has been entered.

Motions to remand and responses thereto shall be governed by Rules 5.12, 5.2, 7.1 and 7.2 of these Rules.

(e) When an order to show cause why an action or actions should not be remanded is entered pursuant to subsection (c), paragraph (iii) of this Rule, any party may file a response within twenty days of the filing of said order unless otherwise provided for in the order. Within five days of filing of a party's response, any party may file a reply brief limited to new matters. Failure of a party to respond to a show cause order regarding remand shall be treated as that party's acquiescence to the remand. Responses and replies shall be filed and served in conformity with Rules 5.12, 5.2 and 7.1 of these Rules.

(f) Conditional Remand Orders.

(i) When the Panel has been advised by the transferee district judge, or otherwise has reason to believe, that pretrial proceedings in the litigation assigned to the transferee district judge are concluded or that remand of an action or actions is otherwise appropriate, an order may be entered by the Clerk of the Panel remanding the action or actions to the transferor district court. The Clerk of the Panel shall serve this order on each party to the litigation but, in order to afford all parties the opportunity to oppose remand, shall not send the order to the clerk of the transferee district court for fifteen days from the entry thereof.

(ii) Any party opposing the remand shall file a notice of opposition with the Clerk of the Panel within the fifteen-day period. If a notice of opposition is received by the Clerk of the Panel within this fifteen-day period, the Clerk of the Panel shall not transmit said order to the clerk of the transferee district court until further order of the Panel. The Clerk of the Panel shall notify the parties of the briefing schedule.

(iii) Within fifteen days of the filing of its notice of opposition, the party opposing remand shall file a motion to vacate the conditional remand order and brief in support thereof. The Chairman of the Panel shall set the motion for the next appropriate hearing session of the Panel. Failure to file and serve a motion and brief shall be treated as a withdrawal of the opposition and the Clerk of the Panel shall forthwith transmit the order to the clerk of the transferee district court.

(iv) Conditional remand orders do not become effective unless and until they are filed with the clerk of the transferee district court.

(v) Notices of opposition and motions to vacate such orders of the Panel and responses thereto shall be governed by Rules 5.12, 5.2, 7.1 and 7.2 of these Rules.

(g) Upon receipt of an order to remand from the Clerk of the Panel, the parties shall furnish forthwith to the transferee district clerk a stipulation or designation of the contents of the record or part thereof to be remanded and furnish the transferee district clerk all necessary copies of any pleading or other matter filed so as to enable the transferee district clerk to comply with the order of remand.

(Former Rule 14 adopted May 3, 1993, eff. July 1, 1993; renumbered Rule 7.6 and amended Sept. 1, 1998, eff. Nov. 2, 1998; amended Apr. 2, 2001, eff. Apr. 2, 2001.)

RULE 16.1. HEARING SESSIONS AND ORAL ARGUMENT

(a) Hearing sessions of the Panel for the presentation of oral argument and consideration of matters taken under submission without oral argument shall be held as ordered by the Panel. The Panel shall convene whenever and wherever desirable or necessary in the judgment of the Chairman. The Chairman shall determine which matters shall be considered at each hearing session and the Clerk of the Panel shall give notice to counsel for all parties involved in the litigation to be so considered of the time, place and subject matter of such hearing session.

(b) Each party filing a motion or a response to a motion or order of the Panel under Rules 7.2, 7.3, 7.4 or 7.6 of these Rules may file simultaneously therewith a separate statement limited to one page setting forth reasons why oral argument should, or need not, be heard. Such statements shall be captioned "Reasons Why Oral Argument Should [Need Not] Be Heard," and shall be filed and served in conformity with Rules 5.12 and 5.2 of these Rules.

(c) No transfer or remand determination regarding any action pending in the district court shall be made by the Panel when any party timely opposes such transfer or remand unless a hearing session has been held for the presentation of oral argument except that the Panel may dispense with oral argument if it determines that:

(i) the dispositive issue(s) have been authoritatively decided; or

(ii) the facts and legal arguments are adequately presented in the briefs and record, and the decisional process would not be significantly aided by oral argument.

Unless otherwise ordered by the Panel, all other matters before the Panel, such as a motion for reconsideration, shall be considered and determined upon the basis of the papers filed.

(d) In those matters in which oral argument is not scheduled by the Panel, counsel shall be promptly advised. If oral argument is scheduled in a matter the Clerk of the Panel may require counsel for all parties who wish to make or to waive oral argument to file and serve notice to that effect within a stated time in conformity with Rules 5.12 and 5.2 of these Rules. Failure to do so shall be deemed a waiver of oral argument by that party. If oral argument is scheduled but not attended by a party, the matter shall not be rescheduled and that party's position shall be treated as submitted for decision by the Panel on the basis of the papers filed.

(e) Except for leave of the Panel on a showing of good cause, only those parties to actions scheduled for oral argument who have filed a motion or written response to a motion or order shall be permitted to appear before the Panel and present oral argument.

(f) Counsel for those supporting transfer or remand under Section 1407 and counsel for those opposing such transfer or remand are to confer separately prior to the oral argument for the purpose of organizing their arguments and selecting representatives to present all views without duplication.

(g) Unless otherwise ordered by the Panel, a maximum of twenty minutes shall be allotted for oral argument in each matter. The time shall be divided equally among those with varying viewpoints. Counsel for the moving party or parties shall generally be heard first.

(h) So far as practicable and consistent with the purposes of Section 1407, the offering of oral testimony before the Panel shall be avoided. Accordingly, oral testimony shall not be received except upon notice, motion and order of the Panel expressly providing for it.

(i) After an action or group of actions has been set for a hearing session, consideration of such action(s) may be continued only by order of the Panel on good cause shown.

(Former Rule 16 adopted May 3, 1998, eff. July 1, 1993; renumbered Rule 16.1 and amended Sept. 1, 1998, eff. Nov. 2, 1998; amended Apr. 2, 2001, eff. Apr. 2, 2001.)

RULE 16.2 NOTICE OF PRESENTATION OR WAIVER OF ORAL ARGUMENT, AND MATTERS SUBMITTED ON THE BRIEFS [REPEALED]

(Former Rule 17 adopted May 3, 1993, eff. July 1, 1993; renumbered Rule 16.2 and amended Sept. 1, 1998, eff. Nov. 2, 1998; repealed eff. Apr. 2, 2001.)

II. RULES FOR MULTICIRCUIT PETITIONS FOR REVIEW UNDER 28 U.S.C. § 2112(a)(3)

RULE 17.1. RANDOM SELECTION

(a) Upon filing a notice of multicircuit petitions for review, the Clerk of the Panel or designated deputy shall randomly select a circuit court of appeals from a drum containing an entry for each circuit wherein a constituent petition for review is pending. Multiple petitions for review pending in a single circuit shall be allotted only a single entry in the drum. This random selection shall be witnessed by the Clerk of the Panel or a designated deputy other than the random selector. Thereafter, an order on behalf of the Panel shall be issued, signed by the random selector and the witness,

(i) consolidating the petitions for review in the court of appeals for the circuit that was randomly selected; and

(ii) designating that circuit as the one in which the record is to be filed pursuant to Rules 16 and 17 of the Federal Rules of Appellate Procedure.

(b) A consolidation of petitions for review shall be effective when the Panel's consolidation order is filed at the offices of the Panel by the Clerk of the Panel.

(Former Rule 24 adopted May 3, 1993, eff. July 1, 1993; renumbered Rule 17.1 Sept. 1, 1998, eff. Nov. 2, 1998.)

RULE 25.1. FILING OF NOTICES

(a) An original of a notice of multicircuit petitions for review pursuant to 28 U.S.C. § 2112(a)(3) shall be submitted for filing to the Clerk of the Panel by the affected agency, board, commission or officer. The term "agency" as used in Section II of these Rules shall include agency, board, commission or officer.

(b) All notices of multicircuit petitions for review submitted by the affected agency for filing with the Clerk of the Panel shall embrace exclusively petitions for review filed in the courts of appeals within ten days after issuance of an agency order and received by the affected agency from the petitioners within that ten-day period.

(c) When a notice of multicircuit petitions for review is submitted for filing to the Clerk of the Panel, the Clerk of the Panel shall file the notice and endorse thereon the date of filing.

(d) Copies of notices of multicircuit petitions for review shall be filed by the affected agency with the clerk of each circuit court of appeals in which a petition for review is pending that is included in the notice.

(Former Rule 20 adopted May 3, 1993, eff. July 1, 1993; renumbered Rule 25.1 and amended Sept. 1, 1998, eff. Nov. 2, 1998.)

RULE 25.2. ACCOMPANIMENTS TO NOTICES

(a) All notices of multicircuit petitions for review shall be accompanied by:

(i) a copy of each involved petition for review as the petition for review is defined in 28 U.S.C. § 2112(a)(2); and

(ii) a schedule giving

(A) the date of the relevant agency order;

(B) the case name of each petition for review involved;

(C) the circuit court of appeals in which each petition for review is pending;

(D) the appellate docket number of each petition for review;

(E) the date of filing by the court of appeals of each petition for review; and

(F) the date of receipt by the agency of each petition for review.

(b) The schedule in Subsection (a)(ii) of this Rule shall also be governed by Rules 25.1, 25.3 and 25.4(a) of these Rules.

(Former Rule 21 adopted May 3, 1993, eff. July 1, 1993; renumbered Rule 25.2 and amended Sept. 1, 1998, eff. Nov. 2, 1998.)

RULE 25.3. SERVICE OF NOTICES

(a) All notices of multicircuit petitions for review shall be accompanied by proof of service by the affected agency on all other parties in all petitions for review included in the notice. Service and proof of service shall be made as provided in Rule 25 of the Federal Rules of Appellate Procedure. The proof of service shall state the name and address of each person served and shall indicate the party represented by each. If a party is not represented by counsel, the proof of service shall indicate the name of the party and his or her last known address. The original proof of service shall be submitted by the affected agency for filing with the Clerk of the Panel and copies thereof shall be sent by the affected agency to each person included within the proof of service.

(b) The proof of service pertaining to notices of multicircuit petitions for review shall certify that copies of the notices have been mailed or otherwise delivered by the affected agency for filing to the clerk of each circuit court of appeals in which a petition for review is pending that is included in the notice.

(Former Rule 22 adopted May 3, 1993, eff. July 1, 1993; renumbered Rule 25.3 Sept. 1, 1998, eff. Nov. 2, 1998.)

RULE 25.4. FORM OF NOTICES

(a) Each notice of multicircuit petitions for review shall be

(i) flat and unfolded;

(ii) plainly written, typed in double space, printed or prepared by means of a duplicating process, without erasures or interlineations which materially deface it;

(iii) on opaque, unglazed white paper (not onionskin);

(iv) approximately 8–1/2 x 11 inches in size; and

(v) fastened at the top-left corner without side binding or front or back covers.

(b) The heading on the first page of each notice of multicircuit petitions for review shall commence not less that three inches from the top of the page. Each notice shall bear the heading "Notice to the Judicial Panel on Multidistrict Litigation of Multicircuit Petitions for Review," followed by a brief caption identifying the involved agency, the relevant agency order, and the date of the order.

(c) The final page of each notice of multicircuit petitions for review shall contain the name, address and telephone number of the individual or individuals who submitted the notice on behalf of the agency.

(Former Rule 23 adopted May 3, 1993, eff. July 1, 1993; renumbered Rule 25.4 and amended Sept. 1, 1998, eff. Nov. 2, 1998.)

RULE 25.5. SERVICE OF PANEL CONSOLIDATION ORDER

(a) The Clerk of the Panel shall serve the Panel's consolidation order on the affected agency through the individual or individuals, as identified in Rule 25.4(c) of these Rules, who submitted the notice of multicircuit petitions for review on behalf of the agency.

(b) That individual or individuals, or anyone else designated by the agency, shall promptly serve the Panel's consolidation order on all other parties in all petitions for review included in the Panel's consolidation order, and shall promptly submit a proof of that service to the Clerk of the Panel. Service and proof of that service shall also be governed by Rule 25.3 of these Rules.

(c) The Clerk of the Panel shall serve the Panel's consolidation order on the clerks of all circuit courts of appeals that were among the candidates for the Panel's random selection.

(Former Rule 25 adopted May 3, 1993, eff. July 1, 1993; renumbered Rule 25.5 and amended Sept. 1, 1998, eff. Nov. 2, 1998.)

CONVERSION TABLE

Renumbered Rule	Previous Rule
1.1	1
1.2	5
1.3	4
1.4	6
1.5	18
1.6	19
5.1	2
5.11	3
5.12	7
5.13	—
5.2	8
5.3	—
6.2	15
7.1	9
7.2	10
7.3	11
7.4	12
7.5	13

Renumbered Rule	Previous Rule
7.6	14
16.1	16, 16.2 & 17
17.1	24
25.1	20
25.2	21
25.3	22
25.4	23
25.5	25

*

FEDERAL COURTS MISCELLANEOUS FEE SCHEDULES

COURT OF APPEALS FEE SCHEDULE

(Issued in accordance with 28 U.S.C. § 1913)

(Eff. 01/01/2007)

The following are fees to be charged for services provided by the courts of appeals. No fees are to be charged for services rendered on behalf of the United States, with the exception of those specifically prescribed in items 2, 4 and 5. No fees under this schedule shall be charged to federal agencies or programs which are funded from judiciary appropriations, including, but not limited to, agencies, organizations, and individuals providing services authorized by the Criminal Justice Act, 18 U.S.C. § 3006A, and Bankruptcy Administrator programs.

(1) For docketing a case on appeal or review, or docketing any other proceeding, $450. A separate fee shall be paid by each party filing a notice of appeal in the district court, but parties filing a joint notice of appeal in the district court are required to pay only one fee. A docketing fee shall not be charged for the docketing of an application for the allowance of an interlocutory appeal under 28 U.S.C. § 1292(b), unless the appeal is allowed. A docketing fee shall not be charged for the docketing of a direct bankruptcy appeal or a direct bankruptcy cross appeal when the fee has been collected by the bankruptcy court in accordance with Item 15 or Item 21 of the Bankruptcy Court Miscellaneous Fee Schedule.

(2) For every search of the records of the court and certifying the results thereof, $26. This fee shall apply to services rendered on behalf of the United States if the information requested is available through electronic access.

(3) For certifying any document or paper, whether the certification is made directly on the document, or by separate instrument, $9.

(4) For reproducing any record or paper, 50 cents per page. This fee shall apply to paper copies made from either: (1) original documents; or (2) microfiche or microfilm reproductions of the original records. This fee shall apply to services rendered on behalf of the United States if the record or paper requested is available through electronic access.

(5) For reproduction of recordings of proceedings, regardless of the medium, $26, including the cost of materials. This fee shall apply to services rendered on behalf of the United States if the reproduction of the recording is available electronically.

(6) For reproduction of the record in any appeal in which the requirement of an appendix is dispensed with by any court of appeals pursuant to Rule 30(f), F.R.A.P., a flat fee of $71.

(7) For each microfiche or microfilm copy of any court record, where available, $5.

(8) For retrieval of a record from a Federal Records Center, National Archives, or other storage location removed from the place of business of the court, $45.

(9) For a check paid into the court which is returned for lack of funds, $45.

(10) Fees to be charged and collected for copies of opinions shall be fixed, from time to time, by each court, commensurate with the cost of printing.

(11) The court may charge and collect fees commensurate with the cost of providing copies of the local rules of court. The court may also distribute copies of the local rules without charge.

(12) The clerk shall assess a charge for the handling of registry funds deposited with the court, to be assessed from interest earnings and in accordance with the detailed fee schedule issued by the Director of the Administrative Office of the United States Courts.

(13) Upon the filing of any separate or joint notice of appeal or application for appeal from the Bankruptcy Appellate Panel, or notice of the allowance of an appeal from the Bankruptcy Appellate Panel, or of a writ of certiorari, $5 shall be paid by the appellant or petitioner.

(14) The court may charge and collect a fee of $200 per remote location for counsel's requested use of videoconferencing equipment in connection with each oral argument.

(15) For original admission of attorneys to practice, $150 each, including a certificate of admission. For a duplicate certificate of admission or certificate of good standing, $15.

DISTRICT COURT FEE SCHEDULE

(Issued in accordance with 28 U.S.C. 1914)

(Eff. 06/01/2004)

Following are fees to be charged for services provided by the district courts. No fees are to be charged for services rendered on behalf of the United States, with the exception of those specifically prescribed in items 2, 4 and 5. No fees under this schedule shall be charged to federal agencies or programs which are funded from judiciary appropriations, including, but not limited to, agencies, organizations, and individuals providing services authorized by the Criminal Justice Act, 18 U.S.C. § 3006A, and Bankruptcy Administrator programs.

(1) For filing or indexing any document not in a case or proceeding for which a filing fee has been paid, $39.

(2) For every search of the records of the district court conducted by the clerk of the district court or a deputy clerk, $26 per name or item searched. This fee shall apply to services rendered on behalf of the United States if the information requested is available through electronic access.

(3) For certification of any document or paper, whether the certification is made directly on the document or by separate instrument, $9. For exemplification of any document or paper, twice the amount of the fee for certification.

(4) For reproducing any record or paper, $.50 per page. This fee shall apply to paper copies made from either: (1) original documents; or (2) microfiche or microfilm reproductions of the original records. This fee shall apply to services rendered on behalf of the United States if the record or paper requested is available through electronic access.

(5) For reproduction of recordings of proceedings, regardless of the medium, $26, including the cost of materials. This fee shall apply to services rendered on behalf of the United States, if the reproduction of the recording is available electronically.

(6) For each microfiche sheet of film or microfilm jacket copy of any court record, where available, $5.

(7) For retrieval of a record from a Federal Records Center, National Archives, or other storage location removed from the place of business of the court, $45.

(8) For a check paid into the court which is returned for lack of funds, $45.

(9) For an appeal to a district judge from a judgment of conviction by a magistrate in a misdemeanor case, $32.

(10) For original admission of attorneys to practice, $50 each, including a certificate of admission. For a duplicate certificate of admission or certificate of good standing, $15.

(11) The court may charge and collect fees commensurate with the cost of providing copies of the local rules of court. The court may also distribute copies of the local rules without charge.

(12) The clerk shall assess a charge for the handling of registry funds deposited with the court, to be assessed from interest earnings and in accordance with the detailed fee schedule issued by the Director of the Administrative Office of the United States Courts.

(13) For filing an action brought under Title III of the Cuban Liberty and Democratic Solidarity (LIBERTAD) Act of 1996, P.L. 104–114, 110 Stat. 785 (1996), $5,431. (This fee is in addition to the filing fee prescribed in 28 U.S.C. § 1914(a) for instituting any civil action other than a writ of habeas corpus.)

BANKRUPTCY COURT FEE SCHEDULE

(Issued in accordance with 28 U.S.C. 1930(b))

(Eff. 1/1/2007)

Following are fees to be charged for services provided by the bankruptcy courts. No fees are to be charged for services rendered on behalf of the United States, with the exception of those specifically prescribed in items 1, 3, and 5, or to bankruptcy administrators appointed under Public Law No. 99–554, § 302(d)(3)(I). No fees under this schedule shall be charged to federal agencies or programs which are funded from judiciary appropriations, including, but not limited to, agencies, organizations, and individuals providing services authorized by the Criminal Justice Act, 18 U.S.C. § 3006A.

(1) For reproducing any record or paper, $.50 per page. This fee shall apply to paper copies made from either: (1) original documents; or (2) microfiche or microfilm reproductions of the original records. This fee shall apply to services rendered on behalf of the United States if the record or paper requested is available through electronic access.

(2) For certification of any document or paper, whether the certification is made directly on the document or by separate instrument, $9. For exemplification of any document or paper, twice the amount of the charge for certification.

(3) For reproduction of recordings of proceedings, regardless of the medium, $26, including the cost of materials. This fee shall apply to services rendered on behalf of the United States, if the reproduction of the recording is available electronically.

(4) For amendments to a debtor's schedules of creditors, lists of creditors, matrix, or mailing lists, $26 for each amendment, provided the bankruptcy judge may, for good cause, waive the charge in any case. No fee is required when the nature of the amendment is to change the address of a creditor or an attorney for a creditor listed on the schedules or to add the name and address of an attorney for a listed creditor.

(5) For every search of the records of the bankruptcy court conducted by the clerk of the bankruptcy court or a deputy clerk, $26 per name or item searched. This fee shall apply to services rendered on behalf of the United States if the information requested is available through electronic access.

(6) For filing a complaint, $250. If the United States, other than a United States trustee acting as a trustee in a case under Title 11, or a debtor is the plaintiff, no fee is required. If a trustee or debtor in possession is the plaintiff, the fee should be payable only from the estate and to the extent there is any estate realized. If a child support creditor or its representative is the plaintiff, and if such plaintiff files the form required by § 304(g) of the Bankruptcy Reform Act of 1994, no fee is required.

(7) For filing or indexing any document not in a case or proceeding for which a filing fee has been paid, $39.

(8) In all cases filed under title 11, the clerk shall collect from the debtor or the petitioner a miscellaneous administrative fee of $39. This fee may be paid in installments in the same manner that the filing fee may be paid in installments, consistent with the procedure set forth in Federal Rule of Bankruptcy Procedure 1006.

(9) Upon the filing of a petition under Chapter 7 of the Bankruptcy Code, the petitioner shall pay $15 to the clerk of the court for payment to trustees serving in cases as provided in 11 U.S.C. § 330(b)(2). An application to pay the fee in installments may be filed in the manner set forth in Federal Rule of Bankruptcy Procedure 1006(b).

(10) Upon the filing of a motion to convert a case to Chapter 7 of the Bankruptcy Code, the movant shall pay $15 to the clerk of court for payment to trustees serving in cases as provided in 11 U.S.C. § 330(b)(2). Upon the filing of a notice of conversion pursuant to Section 1208(a) or Section 1307(a) of the Code, $15 shall be paid to the clerk of the court for payment to trustees serving in cases as provided in 11 U.S.C. § 330(b)(2). If the trustee serving in the case before the conversion is the movant, the fee shall be payable only from the estate that exists prior to conversion. For filing a motion to convert or a notice of conversion, a fee shall be charged in the amount of the difference between the current filing fee for the chapter under which the case was originally commenced and the current filing fee for the chapter to which the case is requested to be converted. If the filing fee for the chapter to which the case is requested to be converted is less than the fee paid at the commencement of the case, no refund shall be provided. A fee shall not be assessed under this item for converting a Chapter 7 or 13 case to a Chapter 11 case as the fee for these actions is collected pursuant to statute under 28 U.S.C. 1930(a).

(11) For filing a motion to reopen a Bankruptcy Code case, a fee shall be collected in the same amount as the filing fee prescribed by 28 U.S.C. 1930(a) for commencing a new case on the date of reopening. The reopening fee should be charged when a case is closed

without a discharge being entered. If the motion to reopen is made for a Chapter 7 case, an additional fee of $15 shall be paid to the clerk of the court for payment to trustees serving in cases as provided in 11 U.S.C. 330(b)(2). For filing a motion to reopen a Chapter 15 case, a fee shall be charged in the same amount as the filing fee required under Item 16 of this schedule for commencing a new case on the date of reopening. The reopening fee will not be charged if the reopening is necessary: (1) to permit a party to file a complaint to obtain a determination under Rule 4007(b), or, (2) when a creditor is violating the terms of the discharge under 11 U.S.C. 524. The court may waive this fee under appropriate circumstances or may defer payment of the fee from trustees pending discovery of additional assets. If payment is deferred, the fee shall be waived if no additional assets are discovered.

(12) For each microfiche sheet of film or microfilm jacket copy of any court record, where available, $5.

(13) For retrieval of a record from a Federal Records Center, National Archives, or other storage location removed from the place of business of the court, $45.

(14) For a check paid into the court which is returned for lack of funds, $45.

(15) For docketing a proceeding on appeal or review from a final judgment of a bankruptcy judge pursuant to 28 U.S.C. § 158(a) and (b), $250. A separate fee shall be paid by each party filing a notice of appeal in the bankruptcy court, but parties filing a joint notice of appeal in the bankruptcy court are required to pay only one fee. If a trustee or debtor in possession is the appellant, the fee should be payable only from the estate and to the extent there is any estate realized. Upon notice from the court of appeals that a direct appeal from the bankruptcy court has been authorized, the appellant shall pay an additional $200.

(16) For filing a Chapter 15 proceeding, the fee shall be the same amount as the fee for a case commenced under Chapter 11 of Title 11 as required by 28 U.S.C. § 1930(a)(3).

(17) The court may charge and collect fees commensurate with the cost of providing copies of the local rules of court. The court may also distribute copies of the local rules without charge.

(18) The clerk shall assess a charge for the handling of registry funds deposited with the court, to be assessed from interest earnings and in accordance with the detailed fee schedule issued by the Director of the Administrative Office of the United States Courts.

(19) When a joint case filed under § 302 of Title 11 is divided into two separate cases at the request of the debtor(s), a fee shall be charged equal to the current filing fee for the chapter under which the joint case was commenced. If the motion to divide the case is made for a Chapter 7 case, an additional fee of $15 shall be paid to the clerk of the court for payment to trustees serving in cases as provided in 11 U.S.C. § 330(b)(2).

(20) For filing a motion to terminate, annul, modify, or condition the automatic stay provided under § 362(a) of Title 11, a motion to compel abandonment of property of the estate pursuant to Rule 6007(b) of the Federal Rules of Bankruptcy Procedure, or a motion to withdraw the reference of a case or proceeding under 28 U.S.C. § 157(d), $150. No fee is required for a motion for relief from the co-debtor stay or for a stipulation for court approval of an agreement for relief from a stay. If a child support creditor or its representative is the movant, and if such movant files the form required by § 304(g) of the Bankruptcy Reform Act of 1994, no fee is required.

(21) For docketing a cross appeal from a bankruptcy court determination, $250. If a trustee or debtor in possession is the appellant, the fee should be payable only from the estate and to the extent there is any estate realized. Upon notice from the court of appeals that a direct cross from the bankruptcy court has been authorized, the cross appellant shall pay an additional $200.

JUDICIAL PANEL ON MULTIDISTRICT LITIGATION FEE SCHEDULE

Following are fees to be charged for services provided by the Judicial Panel on Multidistrict Litigation. No fees are to be charged for services rendered on behalf of the United States, with the exception of those specifically prescribed in items 1 and 3. No fees under this schedule shall be charged to federal agencies or programs which are funded from judiciary appropriations, including, but not limited to, agencies, organizations, and individuals providing services authorized by the Criminal Justice Act, 18 U.S.C. § 3006A.

(1) For every search of the records of the court conducted by the clerk of the court or a deputy clerk, $26 per name or item searched. This fee shall apply to services rendered on behalf of the United States if the information requested is available through electronic access.

(2) For certification of any document or paper, whether the certification is made directly on the document or by separate instrument, $9.

(3) For reproducing any record or paper, $.50 per page. This fee shall apply to paper copies made from either: (1) original documents; or (2) microfiche or microfilm reproductions of the original records. This fee shall apply to services rendered on behalf of the United States if the record or paper requested is available through electronic access.

(4) For retrieval of a record from a Federal Records Center, National Archives, or other storage location removed from the place of business of the court, $45.

(5) For a check paid into the Panel which is returned for lack of funds, $45.

ELECTRONIC PUBLIC ACCESS FEE SCHEDULE

(Issued in accordance with 28 U.S.C. 1913, 1914, 1926, 1930, 1932)

(Eff. 3/11/2008)

As directed by Congress, the Judicial Conference has determined that the following fees are necessary to reimburse expenses incurred by the judiciary in providing electronic public access to court records. These fees shall apply to the United States unless otherwise stated. No fees under this schedule shall be charged to federal agencies or programs which are funded from judiciary appropriations, including, but not limited to, agencies, organizations, and individuals providing services authorized by the Criminal Justice Act, 18 U.S.C. 3006A, and bankruptcy administrator programs.

I. For electronic access to court data via a federal judiciary Internet site: eight cents per page, with the total for any document, docket sheet, or case-specific report not to exceed the fee for thirty pages- provided however that transcripts of federal court proceedings shall not be subject to the thirty-page fee limit. Attorneys of record and parties in a case (including pro se litigants) receive one free electronic copy of all documents filed electronically, if receipt is required by law or directed by the filer. No fee is owed under this provision until an account holder accrues charges of more than $10 in a calendar year. Consistent with Judicial Conference policy, courts may, upon a showing of cause, exempt indigents, bankruptcy case trustees, individual researchers associated with educational institutions, courts, section 501(c)(3) not-for-profit organizations, court appointed pro bono attorneys, and pro bono ADR neutrals from payment of these fees. Courts must find that parties from the classes of persons or entities listed above seeking exemption have demonstrated that an exemption is necessary in order to avoid unreasonable burdens and to promote public access to information. Any user granted an exemption agrees not to sell for profit the data obtained as a result. Any transfer of data obtained as the result of a fee exemption is prohibited unless expressly authorized by the court. Exemptions may be granted for a definite period of time and may be revoked at the discretion of the court granting the exemption.

II. For printing copies of any record or document accessed electronically at a public terminal in the courthouse: ten cents per page. This fee shall apply to services rendered on behalf of the United States if the record requested is remotely available through electronic access.

III. For every search of court records conducted by the PACER Service Center, $26 per name or item searched.

IV. For the PACER Service Center to reproduce on paper any record pertaining to a PACER account, if this information is remotely available through electronic access, 50 cents per page.

V. For a check paid to the PACER Service Center which is returned for lack of funds, $45.

JUDICIAL CONFERENCE POLICY NOTES

Courts should not exempt local, state or federal government agencies, members of the media, attorneys or others not members of one of the groups listed above. Exemptions should be granted as the exception, not the rule. A court may not use this exemption language to exempt all users. An exemption applies only to access related to the case or purpose for which it was given. The prohibition on transfer of information received without fee is not intended to bar a quote or reference to information received as a result of a fee exemption in a scholarly or other similar work.

The electronic public access fee applies to electronic court data viewed remotely from the public records of individual cases in the court, including filed documents and the docket sheet. Electronic court data may be viewed free at public terminals at the courthouse and courts may provide other local court information at no cost. Examples of information that can be provided at no cost include: local rules, court forms, news items, court calendars, opinions, and other information—such as court hours, court location, telephone listings—determined locally to benefit the public and the court.

†